D1327254

The Nature of Reasoning

We are bombarded with information – press releases, television news, internet websites, and office memos, just to name a few – on a daily basis. However, the important conclusions that may, or need, to be inferred from such information are typically not provided. We must draw the conclusions by ourselves. How do we draw these conclusions? This book addresses how we reason to reach sensible conclusions.

The purpose of this book is to organize in one volume what is known about reasoning, such as its structural prerequisites, its mechanisms, its susceptibility to pragmatic influences, its pitfalls, and the bases for its development. Given that reasoning underlies so many of our intellectual activities – when we learn, criticize, analyze, judge, infer, evaluate, optimize, apply, discover, imagine, devise, and create – we stand to gain a great deal if we can learn to define, operate, apply, and nurture our reasoning.

Jacqueline P. Leighton is Assistant Professor in the Center for Research in Applied Measurement and Evaluation (CRAME) in the Department of Educational Psychology at the University of Alberta, Canada. She has held a Social Sciences and Humanities Research Council of Canada (SSHRC) Postdoctoral Fellowship and Doctoral Fellowship, as well as a Postgraduate Fellowship from the Natural Sciences and Engineering Research Council of Canada (NSERC). Professor Leighton's research is on the assessment of reasoning and problem solving and is currently funded by SSHRC.

Robert J. Sternberg is IBM Professor of Psychology and Education and Director of the Center for the Psychology of Abilities, Competencies, and Expertise at Yale University. He is also currently President-Elect of the American Psychological Association and Editor of the *APA Review of Books: Contemporary Psychology*. Professor Sternberg is the author of roughly 900 books, book chapters, and articles in the field of psychology.

The Nature
of Reasoning

Edited by
JACQUELINE P. LEIGHTON
University of Alberta

ROBERT J. STERNBERG
Yale University

CAMBRIDGE
UNIVERSITY PRESS

PUBLISHED BY THE PRESS SYNDICATE OF THE UNIVERSITY OF CAMBRIDGE
The Pitt Building, Trumpington Street, Cambridge, United Kingdom

CAMBRIDGE UNIVERSITY PRESS
The Edinburgh Building, Cambridge CB2 2RU, UK
40 West 20th Street, New York, NY 10011-4211, USA
477 Williamstown Road, Port Melbourne, VIC 3207, Australia
Ruiz de Alarcón 13, 28014 Madrid, Spain
Dock House, The Waterfront, Cape Town 8001, South Africa

http://www.cambridge.org

© Cambridge University Press 2004

First published 2004

Printed in the United States of America

Typeface Palatino 10/12 pt.   System LATEX 2$_\varepsilon$ [TB]

A catalog record for this book is available from the British Library.

Library of Congress Cataloging in Publication Data
The nature of reasoning / edited by Jacqueline P. Leighton, Robert J. Sternberg.
    p.   cm.
Includes bibliographical references and index.
ISBN 0-521-81090-6 – ISBN 0-521-00928-6 (pbk.)
1. Reasoning (Psychology).   I. Leighton, Jacqueline P.   II. Sternberg, Robert J.
BF442.N38   2003
153.4'3 – dc21   2003041966

ISBN 0 521 81090 6 hardback
ISBN 0 521 00928 6 paperback

Contents

List of Contributors

Denise D. Cummins
Department of Philosophy
University of California–Davis
Davis, CA 95616, USA
    Email: dcummins@ucdavis.edu

Jonathan St. B. T. Evans
Centre for Thinking and Language
Department of Psychology
University of Plymouth
Plymouth, PL4 8AA, UK
    Email: jevans@plym.ac.uk

Aidan Feeney
Department of Psychology
University of Durham
Science Site, South Road
Durham, DH1 3LE, UK.
    Email: Aidan.Feeney@durham.ac.uk

Gerd Gigerenzer
Center for Adaptive Behavior and Cognition
Max Planck Institute for Human Development
Lentzeallee 94, 14195 Berlin, Germany
    Email: gigerenzer@mpib-berlin.mpg.de

Kenneth J. Gilhooly
Psychology Group, Human Sciences Dept.
Brunel University, West London
Uxbridge UB8 3PH, UK
    Email: ken.gilhooly@brunel.ac.uk

Vittorio Girotto
Laboratoire de Psychologie Cognitive
Université de Provence/CNRS
29 Avenue Robert Schuman
13621 Aix-en-Provence, France
Email: girotto@up.univ-mrs.fr; girotto@univ.trieste.it

Philip N. Johnson-Laird
Department of Psychology
Princeton University, Green Hall
Princeton, NJ 08544, USA
Email: phil@princeton.edu

Anton E. Lawson
Department of Biology
Arizona State University
Tempe, AZ 85287-1501, USA
Email: anton.lawson@asu.edu

Jacqueline P. Leighton
Centre for Research in Applied Measurement and Evaluation (CRAME)
Department of Educational Psychology
6-110 Education North
University of Alberta
Edmonton, Alberta T6G 2G5, Canada
Email: Jacqueline.Leighton@ualberta.ca

Henry Markovits
Département de psychologie
Université du Québec à Montréal
C.P. 8888, Succ. "A"
Montréal, Québec H3C 3P8, Canada
Email: markovits.henry@uqam.ca

Barnaby Marsh
New College
Oxford University
Oxford OX1 3BN, UK
Email: barnaby.marsh@new.oxford.ac.uk

Padraic Monaghan
Department of Psychology
University of Warwick
Coventry CV4 7AL, UK
Email: Padraic.Monaghan@warwick.ac.uk

Raymond S. Nickerson
Tufts University
The Psychology Building
490 Boston Ave.
Medford, MA 02155, USA
Email: r.nickerson@tufts.edu

David P. O'Brien
Department of Psychology
Baruch College
Graduate Center of the City University of New York
Box B8/215,
17 Lexington Avenue
New York, NY 10010, USA
Email: david_obrien@baruch.cuny.edu

Maxwell J. Roberts
Department of Psychology
University of Essex
Wivenhoe Park
Colchester, Essex CO4 3SQ, UK
Email: mjr@essex.ac.uk

Walter C. Sá
Department of Psychology
2126 Au Sable Hall
Grand Valley State University
Allendale, MI 49401-9403, USA
Email: SaW@gvsu.edu

Keith E. Stanovich
OISE, University of Toronto
252 Bloor Street West
Toronto, ON, M5S 1V6, Canada
Email: kstanovich@oise.utoronto.ca

Keith Stenning
Human Communication Research Centre
Edinburgh University
2, Buccleuch Place
Edinburgh EH8 9LW, Scotland
Email: keith@cogsci.ed.ac.uk

Robert J. Sternberg
Center for the Psychology of Abilities, Competencies, and Expertise
   (PACE Center)
340 Edwards Street
Yale University
New Haven, CT 06520-8358, USA
   Email: robert.sternberg@yale.edu

Peter M. Todd
Center for Adaptive Behavior and Cognition
Max Planck Institute for Human Development
Lentzeallee 94, 14195 Berlin, Germany
   Email: ptodd@mpib-berlin.mpg.de

Richard F. West
MSC 7401, Department of Psychology
James Madison University
Harrisonburg, VA 22807, USA
   Email: WestRF@jmu.edu

PART ONE

THE BASICS OF REASONING

1

Defining and Describing Reason

Jacqueline P. Leighton

Approximately a year ago I began to believe that reasoning was problem solving's poor cousin. In comparison to problem solving, which involves strategically overcoming obstacles in pursuit of a solution, reasoning seemed vague in function. In fact, reasoning has undergone a variety of definitions. As Raymond Nickerson indicates in this volume, reasoning has, on the one hand, been defined narrowly as the process of drawing deductive inferences and, on the other hand, as an aspect of thinking that is involved not only in drawing inferences but in making decisions and solving problems as well. Has reasoning been defined so broadly and redefined so frequently that it has lost its significance? Put another way, could reasoning be legitimately subsumed under problem solving or decision making without any loss? I no longer think so.

The purpose of the present book, *The Nature of Reasoning*, is to provide a comprehensive examination of the significance and distinctiveness of reasoning and, of course, at the same time, to indicate how it mediates other cognitive operations, such as problem solving and decision making. The book organizes in one volume what is known about reasoning, including its structural prerequisites, mechanisms, susceptibility to pragmatic influences and pitfalls, and bases for development. By focusing on factors that are pertinent to reasoning across domains, we present a united and comprehensive analysis of reasoning – an analysis that will inform anyone who is interested in learning about the fundamental factors and critical issues in reasoning research today.

DEFINING AND DESCRIBING REASONING: REASONING AS MEDIATOR

Defining Reasoning. In the present book, reasoning is broadly defined as the process of drawing conclusions. Moreover, these conclusions inform problem-solving and decision-making endeavors because human beings are goal driven, and the conclusions they draw are ultimately drawn to help them serve and meet their goals.

Describing Reasoning. A prominent theme in the book is that of reasoning as mediator. If we wanted to personify reasoning, it would take on the character of a middleman or middlewoman in a company or enterprise. As a middleman, reasoning works behind the scenes, coordinating ideas, premises, or beliefs in the pursuit of conclusions. These conclusions may sometimes find their way to the surface in the form of observable behavior as when someone exclaims "I have an idea!" or argues "I think your idea is not going to work because. . . ." Other times, the conclusions do not find their way to the surface but, rather, stay beneath the surface and function internally as antecedent conditions that feed into chains of productions for problem solving (Simon, 1999). For example, when a conclusion (e.g., I know that some plants flourish in the presence of sunlight) functions as an antecedent condition to initiate an action (e.g., moving the plant to a sunny spot in the house) that is key to solving a problem (e.g., the plant is dying). In either case, whether conclusions become externally observable or stay beneath the surface to help to initiate problem-solving endeavors, reasoning processes are at work. Unfortunately, these processes may not often be acclaimed because they work behind the scenes and in the shadow of more observable functions such as problem solving and decision making. Despite their covert nature, however, understanding how reasoning processes function is imperative to maximizing our efforts at solving problems and making decisions.

DRAWING CONCLUSIONS: EVALUATING OUR CLAIMS TO TRUTH

In Cervantes' (1605, 1615/1998) *Don Quijote de la Mancha*, some of the disastrous adventures of the self-proclaimed knight and his sidekick Sancho do not result from slips in problem solving. Quijote and Sancho's misfortunes arise from faulty reasoning. For example, upon seeing the huge windmills, Quijote concludes the windmills to be giants and immediately thinks to charge at them with a lowered lance. Despite Sancho's protests, Quijote leads the charge against "the giants" without stopping to evaluate how he concluded *giants* from *windmills*. After the charge, the wounded Quijote blames the disaster on the work of a magician but, in fact, the reader knows this to be untrue.

It could be argued that Quijote's disaster came about from faulty reasoning. Quijote drew a false conclusion from observable evidence – he inferred giants from the windmills at the distance – and this led him to initiate an inappropriate action that was doomed for failure. What we can learn from Don Quijote's adventures is that the conclusions we draw can either steer us to problem-solving disasters or problem-solving successes.

Drawing true conclusions facilitates problem solving. True conclusions facilitate problem solving because they are reliable representations of the external environment. Therefore, true conclusions increase the likelihood that a problem's features are being depicted faithfully so that the best strategy for solving the problem can be selected.

The conclusions we draw underlie the problem-solving initiatives we undertake. Therefore, we want to draw true conclusions so that we can get the most out of our problem-solving efforts. However, verifying the truth of a conclusion is not always easily accomplished. The truth of a conclusion is ultimately decided by its correspondence with reality (e.g., physically checking whether the windmills are indeed large human beings), which can be a little difficult to negotiate in some circumstances. If one draws a conclusion in the middle of an island without any means of verifying its truth, what does one do?

The difficulty of verifying a conclusion's truth does not mean that we are doomed to a life of false conclusions. In the absence of being able to verify a conclusion directly, we can evaluate how our premises (or beliefs) entail the conclusion of interest. In other words, we can learn to scrutinize our claims to truth. Our claims to truth are the processes by which we generate conclusions. Do we generate conclusions that follow necessarily from a given set of premises? Or only very likely from a given set of premises? In the end, we may not be able to control our ability to directly verify a conclusion's truth, but we may be able to control the cohesion or soundness of the reasoning that lead up to it.

Conclusions are commonly described as being generated either deductively or inductively. For example, a conclusion that is derived deductively from a set of premises follows necessarily from its premises; that is, the premises provide conclusive grounds for the conclusion. Moreover, if the conclusion is derived deductively from true premises, then the conclusion is necessarily true (see Copi & Cohen, 1990, for a review of validity and deduction). This is one way to yield true conclusions without checking them against reality: If the premises are true, then the conclusion drawn must be true. Conclusions derived deductively are considered necessary because they contain the same amount of information as that found in the premises leading up to it; necessary conclusions represent information that is already implicitly contained in the premises.

In contrast, a conclusion that is derived inductively from a set of premises does not follow necessarily from its premises, although it might be strongly supported by them. A conclusion that is derived inductively from true premises is likely to be true but it is still not necessarily true (see Copi & Cohen, 1990, for a review of strength and induction). Conclusions derived inductively are considered unnecessary because they contain more information than that found in the premises leading up to it. Unnecessary conclusions represent information that goes beyond the information already contained in the premises. Although the truth of necessary or unnecessary conclusions must be checked against reality (except when reasoning deductively from true premises), knowing a conclusion's necessity is still informative because it indicates the cohesion of the reasoning that underlies it.

Understanding the difference in the necessity among conclusions can be informative. For example, imagine someone tells you that looking at a computer monitor for too long brings about nearsightedness. How should you evaluate this conclusion? Is it helpful to know that this person derived the conclusion deductively or inductively? Knowing that he or she arrived at the conclusion deductively suggests that the premises, if true, guarantee the truth of the conclusion. It is difficult to deny a necessary conclusion unless its premises are also denied. In contrast, if the conclusion was derived inductively then the conclusion is possible but unnecessary. You might be more critical of the conclusion once you discover that is only a possible conclusion, and you might therefore not change your behavior drastically in light of it. Or you may want to inspect the evidence yourself to determine the strength that it lends to the conclusion. In the end, we want to judge conclusions suitably so that we can capitalize on their information and act accordingly.

The advantage of problem solving is that its outcome can be judged right or wrong, unequivocally, by determining how well it resolves the problem in the first place. In contrast, the outcome of reasoning is not so unequivocally judged because reasoning does not yield a solution but, rather, a conclusion; a conclusion whose origin is not from a problem but from a set of beliefs. To judge a conclusion, then, one must know how it was generated and the truth of the beliefs leading up to it. The standard for judging a conclusion depends on different principles (for a review of these principles see Copi & Cohen, 1990; also Creighton & Smart, 1932). As mentioned previously, a conclusion can be judged according to its necessity and according to its truth. If a conclusion is drawn deductively from true premises, it is a necessary and true conclusion that must be accepted unless its premises are denied. By evaluating our claims to truth – how we generate conclusions – we can be confident about the cohesion of the reasoning that produced the conclusions even when we cannot directly verify these conclusions against reality.

ORGANIZATION OF THE NATURE OF REASONING: AN OVERVIEW

Although we do not normally think about how fundamental reasoning is to our well-being, reasoning is like breathing to the mind. We are constantly doing it but we rarely take notice of it. If it fails, however, we are paralyzed. Imagine being unable to infer conclusions from a conversation? Or being unable to reach a solution to an important life problem? We reason when we learn, criticize, analyze, judge, infer, evaluate, optimize, apply, discover, imagine, devise, and create – and the list goes on because we draw conclusions during so many of our daily activities. Given that reasoning underlies so many of our intellectual activities, how do we operate, apply, and nurture our reasoning? These questions are addressed in the following chapters.

In Part One, "*The Basics of Reasoning*", Chapter 1, "Defining and Describing Reasoning," examines briefly the importance of reasoning in our daily life, the mediating role reasoning plays in problem solving, and the methods used to evaluate our claims to truth.

The second chapter, "Reasoning and Brain Function" by Anton E. Lawson, identifies the brain structures involved in reasoning. Lawson explores the brain functions that accompany the reasoning processes used when people solve problems in personal settings and during scientific discovery. By examining the reasoning processes in these different circumstances, a model of brain function during reasoning is created. This is a chapter that anchors every other chapter in the book because it identifies the physical nature of reasoning; that is, it reveals the material side of the mental phenomenon we call reasoning.

The third chapter, "Working Memory and Reasoning" by K. J. Gilhooly, discusses the role of working memory in reasoning. This chapter defines working memory and reasoning and then surveys empirical investigations of their interrelations and complementary functions. Gilhooly explains how explicit reasoning processes manifest themselves in working memory by manipulating the temporary contents of working memory. This chapter reminds us that reasoning does not occur in a vacuum but, rather, its function necessitates other processes.

The fourth chapter, "The Role of Prior Belief in Reasoning" by Jonathan St. B. T. Evans and Aidan Feeney, examines the traditional views that psychologists have had about the influence of prior beliefs on deductive reasoning. Evans and Feeney explain that although prior beliefs have traditionally been regarded as a negative influence on deductive reasoning, researchers are now reexamining this view. From this chapter, we learn that the effects of beliefs on reasoning are so pervasive that most researchers have abandoned deductive logic as a descriptive and normative theory of human reasoning. Evans and Feeney highlight the powerful role of knowledge and beliefs in reasoning.

The fifth chapter, "Task Understanding" by Vittorio Girotto, examines the ways in which participants of reasoning experiments might interpret the tasks they are asked to solve. This chapter is significant because it helps us to understand that participants' solutions to reasoning tasks originate from their interpretations. When their solutions do not conform to expected solutions, their interpretations must be considered. Girotto discusses the emergence of linguistic-pragmatics, a recent experimental development that has made investigators aware of how interpretative processes can influence inferential processes. Moreover, Girotto compares how representational complexity and pragmatic irregularities in reasoning tasks can lead participants to erroneous inferences.

These five chapters present the basics of reasoning and build on each other: Reasoning is a mental phenomenon that is driven by specific sections of the brain. Explicit reasoning processes manipulate information in working memory in order to generate conclusions. The information that is manipulated in working memory often involves prior beliefs along with situation or task variables. Prior beliefs are invoked because participants impose their own interpretation on tasks. In Part Two, the mechanics of reasoning are presented.

The second part of the book, *"The Workings of Reasoning,"* focuses on the "mechanics" of reasoning, for example, how reasoning takes form through strategies and knowledge representation, and whether the conclusions drawn from reasoning processes are better described through the lens of mental model theory, mental logic theory, or simple heuristics.

In the sixth chapter, "Strategies and Knowledge Representation," Keith Stenning and Padraic Monaghan, discuss the difference between how knowledge is manipulated (i.e., strategies) and how knowledge is formalized or represented. This is a fascinating chapter because it clarifies the subtle distinction between strategies and knowledge representation. In so doing, the clarification informs the debate about the nature of reasoning processes – whether these processes are better viewed under the lens of mental models or mental rules.

In the seventh chapter, "Mental Models and Reasoning," Philip N. Johnson-Laird presents the theory of mental models, one of the two most prominent theories of reasoning processes today. The chapter begins with an introduction to the theory, and then follows with a review of the empirical evidence that supports Johnson-Laird's theory as an account not only of deduction but also of induction. Johnson-Laird's empirical and theoretical contribution as presented in this chapter is essential to understanding the current debate about the nature of reasoning processes.

The eighth chapter, "Mental-Logic Theory: What it Proposes, and Reasons to Take This Proposal Seriously," by David P. O'Brien, presents the theory of mental logic, the other most prominent theory of reasoning processes today. The chapter begins with a discussion of why mental rules characterize reasoning processes and why mental rules "make sense" as a description of reasoning. O'Brien then addresses one of the major criticisms that has been levied against mental rules and presents arguments showing that this criticism is unfounded when the facts of the theory are considered. The chapter then describes the particulars of the mental logic theory as developed by Martin Braine and David O'Brien and presents empirical evidence that supports the predictions derived from the theory. O'Brien's presentation of mental logic theory is fundamental to appreciating the debate between the mental models camp and mental rules camp.

Maxwell J. Roberts, in Chapter 9, "Heuristics and Reasoning: Making Deduction Simple," presents a new theoretical twist in the debate between mental model theory and mental logic theory. Roberts discusses the idea that heuristics characterize most of the reasoning that people do on a daily basis. He argues that heuristics or simple rules of thumb characterize reasoning because other processes such as models or rules would take too long and would be too costly to apply. This chapter presents a new, and increasingly strong, third voice in the debate over whether mental models or mental rules characterize reasoning processes.

Chapter 10, "Cognitive Heuristics: Reasoning the Fast and Frugal Way," by Barnaby Marsh, Peter M. Todd, and Gerd Gigerenzer, presents the operations of a specific set of heuristics – fast and frugal heuristics. These heuristics, such as the recognition heuristic, are shown to provide good solutions for many kinds of problems without the need to expend too much time or effort or even too much knowledge of what is being reasoned about. Marsh, Todd, and Gigerenzer underscore the third voice in the debate over whether mental models or mental rules characterize reasoning. These investigators present the possibility of accounting for reasoning without using elaborate models of behavior.

These five chapters present the mechanics of reasoning – the difference between strategies and knowledge representation, and the different theories that have been proposed to account for the reasoning processes that generate our conclusions. These chapters describe what is currently known about reasoning as it occurs on a daily basis. Finally, Part Three of the book focuses on the improvement and development of reasoning.

Part Three, *"The Bases of Reasoning,"* focuses on reasoning from an ontological perspective, exploring how reasoning can be assessed, how it develops, how it has evolved, how it manifests itself uniquely in human beings, and how we can nurture it through instruction.

The eleventh chapter, "The Assessment of Logical Reasoning, which I wrote, explores the fairness of evaluating or assessing reasoning without first measuring how well participants understand the domain of the task. In this chapter, I argue that making judgments and building theories about human reasoning using logical tasks that require at least some knowledge about formal logic – even if only to interpret the logical terms in the task in a specified and formal manner – may result in biased theories about how people actually reason.

In Chapter 12, "The Development of Deductive Reasoning," Henry Markovits discusses the pervasiveness of deductive reasoning in daily life and the importance of understanding how this form of reasoning manifests itself and develops in children and adults. In his review of empirical studies, Markovits demonstrates that there is disagreement about the deductive reasoning skills children and adults are believed to possess. The chapter ends with an examination of how Johnson-Laird's theory of mental models may be adapted within a developmental framework and used to explain some of the contradictory results in the literature. This chapter helps us to understand the early stages of what it means to reason well and why it is a challenging pursuit.

The thirteenth chapter, "The Evolution of Reasoning," by Denise D. Cummins, traces our reasoning pedigree. Cummins examines the evolutionary forces that have shaped the processes through which we reason and the environmental variables that invoke those processes. The chapter explores the adaptive value of deontic reasoning and its legacy to understanding higher cognition in general, including the errors that participants make on abstract reasoning tasks. It is clear in this chapter that human reasoning cannot be understood fully by ignoring the ecological variables of our past.

Chapter 14, "Individual Differences in Thinking, Reasoning, and Decision Making," by Keith E. Stanovich, Walter C. Sá, and Richard F. West, explores the variables that distinguish reasoning performance among individuals, and provides a basis for using these variables as keys to understanding the nature of reasoning. For instance, Stanovich, Sá, and West offer a fascinating analysis of how cognitive ability and thinking dispositions are associated to performance on standard reasoning tasks. In addition, the chapter presents the implications of individual differences for generating normative standards of reasoning and evaluating the rationality of human performance.

The fifteenth chapter, "Teaching Reasoning," by Raymon S. Nickerson, presents a discussion of what good reasoning entails and the variables that facilitate it. For example, Nickerson surveys the cognitive qualities that encourage good reasoning and how instruction can nurture these qualities. In addition, the chapter addresses the issue of whether good reasoning is situation-specific or whether it can be transferred across domains. This chapter is vital to anyone who is interested in improving his or her reasoning and fostering sound reasoning in others.

Finally, in Chapter 16, "What Do We Know about the Nature of Reasoning," Robert J. Sternberg, concludes the book and, in so doing, presents a unified look at the nature of reasoning, including what we know, how we know it, and what is still left to investigate and learn.

These final six chapters explore some of the major issues that border our understanding of reasoning, such as how we can assess it, how it develops, how it evolved, how it is manifested in different people, how we can teach it, and finally how we can put it all together to understand its nature.

CONCLUSION

Reasoning, the mediator leaves its mark on almost everything we do and think. This is because almost everything we do and think involves drawing conclusions. When we learn, criticize, analyze, judge, infer, evaluate, optimize, apply, discover, imagine, devise, and create, we draw conclusions from information and from our beliefs.

References

Cervantes, Miguel de. (1998). Don Quijote de la Mancha (B. Raffel, Trans.). New York: W. W. Norton. (Original work published 1605, 1615).

Copi, I. M., & Cohen, C. (1990). *Introduction to logic* (8th ed.). NY: Macmillan.

Creighton, J. E., & Smart, H. R. (1932). *An introductory logic* (5th ed.). NY: Macmillan.

Simon, H. A. (1999). Production systems. In R. A. Wilson & F. C. Keil (Eds.), *The MIT encyclopedia of the cognitive sciences* (pp. 676–677). Cambridge, MA: MIT Press.

2

Reasoning and Brain Function

Anton E. Lawson

The primary objective of this chapter is to identify the brain structures involved in reasoning. We will begin with a brief exploration into brain function and then look at how the brain processes visual input. We will then consider the reasoning children use when attempting to characterize imaginary creatures and acquire descriptive concepts. Next we will explore the reasoning used when trying to solve a problem in a personal setting. Lastly, we will consider how reasoning and brain function guide scientific discovery. These examples should reveal how people reason and learn and should help us understand how the brain functions, at least in a general sense, during such reasoning and learning. In short, the goal is to construct a model of brain function during reasoning general enough to encompass sensory-motor information processing, concept acquisition, problem solving and scientific discovery.

AN EXPLORATION INTO BRAIN FUNCTION

Let us start with a little exploration. Take a few minutes to try the task presented in Figure 2.1. You will need a mirror. Once you have a mirror, place the figure down in front of it so that you can look into the mirror at the reflected figure. Read and follow the figure's reflected directions. Look only in the mirror – no fair peeking directly at your hand. When finished, read on.

How did you do? If you are like most people, the task proved rather difficult and frustrating. Of course, this should come as no surprise. After all, you have spent a lifetime writing and drawing without a mirror. So

This material is based in part upon research supported by the National Science Foundation under grant No. DUE 0084434. Any opinions, findings, and conclusions or recommendations expressed in this publication are those of the author and do not necessarily reflect the views of the National Science Foundation.

Please copy each figure one or more times in the rectangle below
the pattern.

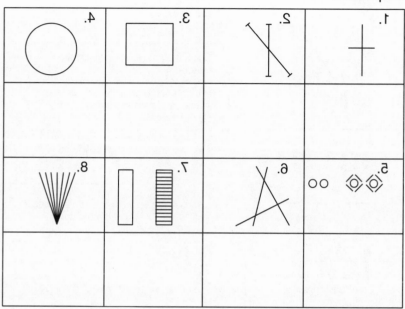

FIGURE 2.1. Place this figure in front of a mirror. Read and follow its reflected directions. No fair looking directly at your hand.

what does this mirror-drawing task tell us about how people learn and about how the brain functions?

I think it reveals the basic learning pattern depicted in Figure 2.2 and described as follows: First, the reflected images of the figure, your pencil, and your hand are assimilated by specific "mental structures" that are currently part of your brain's long-term memory. These mental structures then guide behavior that, in the past, has been linked to consequences (i.e., actual outcomes). Thus, when the structures are used to guide behavior in the present context, the behavior is linked to an expected outcome. All is well if the behavior is successful – that is the actual outcome matches the expected outcome. However, if unsuccessful, that is, if its actual outcome does not match the expected (e.g., you move your hand down and to the left and expect to see a line drawn up and to the right, but instead you see one drawn up and to the *left*), contradiction results. This contradiction then provokes a search for another behavior and perhaps a closer inspection of the figure until either another behavior is found that works (in the sense that it produces a successful, noncontradicted outcome), or you become so frustrated that you quit. In which case, your mental structures and behaviors will not undergo the necessary accommodation (cf. Lawson, 1994;

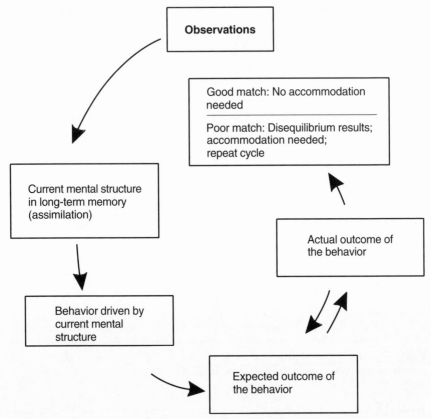

FIGURE 2.2. The basic learning pattern begins with spontaneous assimilation. Disequilibrium and the need for accommodation result when expected and observed outcomes do not match.

Piaget, 1985). In other words, you will not learn to draw successfully in a mirror.

Clearly this learning, or lack thereof, is conducted largely on the sensory motor level. Nevertheless, if we attempt to capture its pattern in words, it might go something like this:

> *If*...I have assimilated this visual input correctly (initial mental structure),
>
> *and*...I move my hand down and to the left (behavior driven by that structure),
>
> *then*...the line should move up and to the right (expected outcome).
>
> *But*...the line goes up and to the *left* (actual outcome).
>
> *Therefore*...I have the wrong mental structure and/or wrong behavior and need to try something new (conclusion).

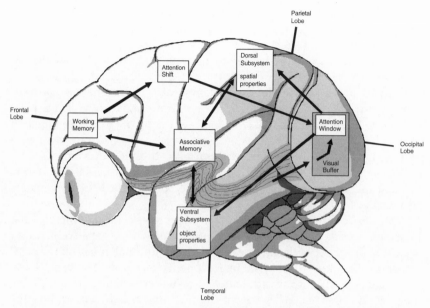

FIGURE 2.3. Brain areas involved in visual object recognition. Kosslyn and Koenig's model of the visual system consists of six major subsystems. The order in which information passes from one subsystem to the next is shown. The subsystems generate and test hypotheses about what is seen in the visual field.

HOW DOES THE BRAIN PROCESS VISUAL INPUT?

Let us now consider in some detail how the brain spontaneously processes visual input as vision is the most thoroughly researched and understood area of information processing. Kosslyn and Koenig (1995) review research that develops and tests neural network models, also known as parallel distributed processing or connectionist models. These models indicate that the ability to visually recognize objects requires participation of the six major brain areas shown in Figure 2.3.

How do these six areas identify objects? First, sensory input from the eyes produces a pattern of electrical activity in an area referred to as the visual buffer, located in the occipital lobe at the back of the brain. This activity produces a spatially organized image within the visual buffer (Daniel & Whitteridge, 1961; Tootell, Silverman, Switkes, & De Valois, 1982). Next, a smaller region within the occipital lobe, called the attention window, performs detailed processing (Posner, 1988; Treisman & Gelade, 1980; Treisman & Gormican, 1988). The activity pattern in the attention window is then simultaneously sent along two pathways on each side of the brain, one that runs down to the lower temporal lobe, and one that runs up to the parietal lobe. The lower temporal lobe, or ventral subsystem, analyses object properties, such as shape, color and texture, while the upper parietal lobe, or dorsal subsystem, analyses spatial properties, such as size and location (Desimone & Ungerleider, 1989; Farah, 1990; Haxby, Grady, Horowitz, Ungerleider, Mishkin, Carson, Herscovitch, Schapiro, & Rapoport 1991; Maunsell & Newsome, 1987; Ungerleider & Mishkin, 1982). Activity patterns within the lower temporal lobe are matched to patterns stored in visual memory (Desimone, Albright, Gross, & Bruce 1984; Desimone & Ungerleider, 1989; Miyashita & Chang, 1988). If a good match is found, the object is recognized. Otherwise, it is not. The dorsal subsystem of the parietal lobes encodes input used to guide movements such as those of the eyes or limbs/hands/arms. The neurons in that region fire just before movement, or register the consequences of movements (Andersen, 1987).

Outputs from the ventral and dorsal subsystems come together in what Kosslyn and Koenig (1995) call associative memory. Associative memory is located primarily in the hippocampus, the limbic thalamus and the basal forebrain (Mishkin, 1978; Mishkin & Appenzeller, 1987). The ventral and dorsal subsystem outputs are matched to patterns stored in associative memory. If a good match between output from visual memory and the pattern in associative memory is obtained, then the observer knows the object's name, categories to which it belongs, sounds it makes, and so on. But if a good match is not obtained, the object remains unrecognized and additional sensory input must be obtained.

Importantly, the search for additional sensory input is far from random. Rather, stored patterns are used to make a second hypothesis about what is being observed, and this hypothesis leads to new observations and to further encoding. In the words of Kosslyn and Koenig (1995), when additional input is sought, "One actively seeks new information that will bear on the hypothesis. . . . The first step in this process is to look up relevant information in associative memory" (p. 57). This information search involves activity in the prefrontal lobes in an area referred to as working memory. However, current research suggests that working memory cannot be pinned down to a single prefrontal region. Rather its location depends in part on the type of information being processed. With its many projections to other brain areas, working memory plays a crucial role in keeping representations active while it coordinates mental activity (Friedman & Goldman-Rakic, 1994; Fuster, 1989). Details of the working memory system will be discussed later. For now it suffices to say that activating working memory causes an attention shift of the eyes to a location where an informative component *should be* located. Once attention is shifted, the new visual input is processed in turn. The new input is then matched to shape and spatial patterns stored in the ventral and dorsal subsystems and kept active in working memory. Again in Kosslyn and Koenig's words, "The matching shape and spatial properties may in fact correspond to the hypothesized part. If so, enough information may have accumulated in associative memory to identify the object. If not, this cycle is repeated until enough information has been gathered to identify the object or to reject the first hypothesis, formulate a new one, and test it" (p. 58).

In summary, visual information processing consists of the following steps:

1. Looking at an object allows a pattern of visual input to pass into the brain.
2. This input is matched against (assimilated by) a stored pattern. The stored pattern is the brain's initial hypothesis of the object's identity.
3. If the input pattern and the stored pattern match well, the object is recognized. If not, a nonrandom search mediated by working memory begins. The search involves selection of a new pattern from associative memory (an alternative hypothesis), which thanks to its connections in associative memory carries with it a number of implied consequences.
4. Excitation of the alternative hypothesis and its implied consequences in working memory then drive a shift of attention to a new part of the object where informative details (implied consequences) *should be* found.
5. New input resulting from the shift of attention is then fed back to working memory where it is compared with the expected input.
6. This comparison then allows one to draw a conclusion about the relative "correctness" of the alternative hypothesis.

For example, suppose Joe, who is extremely myopic, is rooting around the bathroom and spots one end of an object that appears to be a shampoo tube. In other words, the nature of the object and its location prompt the spontaneous generation of a shampoo-tube hypothesis. Based on this initial hypothesis, as well as knowledge of shampoo tubes stored in associative memory, when Joe looks at the other end of the object, he expects to find a cap. Thus he shifts his gaze to the other end. Upon seeing the expected cap, he concludes that the object is in fact a shampoo tube. The pattern of information processing can be summarized as follows:

If... the object is a shampoo tube (hypothesis),
and... Joe looks at the other end of the object (imagined test),
then... he should find a cap (predicted result).
And... upon looking at the other end (actual test), he does find a cap (observed result).
Therefore... the hypothesis is supported; the object is most likely a shampoo-tube (conclusion).

In other words, as one seeks to identify objects, the brain generates and tests stored patterns selected from memory. Kosslyn and Koenig even speak of these stored patterns as hypotheses (although we should note that the term "hypothesis" is being used its broadest sense and not as generally used in the sciences – to refer to a possible *cause* of some puzzling observation). Thus, brain activity during visual processing utilizes an *If/Then/Therefore* pattern that can be characterized as hypothetico-predictive. One looks at part of an unknown object and by subconsciously searching associative memory the brain spontaneously generates an idea of what it is – a hypothesis. Thanks to links in associative memory, the hypothesis carries implied consequences (expectations/predictions). Consequently, to test the validity of the hypothesis, one can carry out a simple behavior to see if the prediction does in fact follow. If it does, one has support for the hypothesis. If it does not, then the hypothesis is not supported and the cycle repeats. Of course, we saw this pattern previously in the mirror drawing.

Is Auditory Input also Processed in a Hypothetico-Predictive Manner?

The visual system is only one of several of the brain's information processing systems. Is information processed in a similar hypothetico-predictive manner in other brain systems? Unfortunately, less is known about other systems, but the answer appears to be "yes." For example, with respect to understanding the meaning of individual spoken words, Kosslyn and Koenig (1995) state: "Similar computational analyses can be performed for visual object identification and spoken word identification, which will lead us to infer analogous sets of processing subsystems" (p. 213).

After providing details of their hypothesized word identification subsystem, Kosslyn and Koenig offer the following summary of what presumably happens when verbal input is inadequate to provide an initial match with verbal representations in associative memory:

If the input is so degraded that there is no good match in the pattern activation subsystem, or there are several potential matches, the best-matching word will be sent to associative memory and treated as a hypothesis. The categorical look-up subsystem then accesses a description of distinctive properties of the sound of the word, which is used to prime the auditory pattern activation subsystem and to guide the auditory window to select additional properties represented in the auditory buffer. These properties are then encoded into the preprocessing subsystem and then the pattern activation subsystem, where they are included in the match process; this information is integrated with that extracted from the whole word, and serves to implicate a specific representation. This top-down search process is repeated until a single representation is matched, just as in vision. (1995, pp. 237–238)

For our purposes, the details of this hypothesized word recognition subsystem are not important. Rather, what is important is that word recognition, like visual recognition, presumably involves brain activity in which hypotheses come spontaneously, immediately, and before any other activity. In other words, the brain does not make several observations before it generates a hypothesis of what it thinks is out there. The brain does not operate in some sort of enumerative inductivist manner in which several observations are needed prior to hypothesis generation. Instead, while processing sensory information, the brain functions in a way that can be characterized as hypothetico-predictive.

DO CHILDREN ACQUIRE CONCEPTS IN A HYPOTHETICO-PREDICTIVE FASHION?

Do children use this *If/Then/Therefore* hypothetico-predictive pattern of information processing to acquire descriptive concepts? Lawson (1993) used several tasks involving descriptive concept acquisition that attempted to find out. One of the tasks appears in Figure 2.4. As shown, the top row contains several Mellinarks (Elementary Science Study, 1974). None of the creatures in the second row are Mellinarks. The task is to figure out which creatures in the third row are Mellinarks.

Previously, Lawson, McElrath, Burton, James, Doyle, Woodward, Kellerman, and Snyder (1991) found that many students failed Mellinark-type tasks when administered without instruction. To discover if these failures were due to developmental deficiencies or due to easily resolved confusion about task objectives, Lawson (1993) employed brief one-on-one training showing children a similar task and describing how the *If/Then/Therefore* pattern could be used to solve it. For example, training on the Mellinark task went like this:

Suppose we look closely at the Mellinarks in the first row and see that they all contain one large dot. Could one large dot be the key feature of Mellinarks? We could test this idea like this:

If . . . Mellinarks are creatures with one large dot
and . . . we look at the non-Mellinarks in row two,
then . . . none of them should contain a large dot.
But . . . when we look at row two, we see that creatures one, three, and five do contain a large dot.
Therefore . . . Mellinarks cannot be creatures defined solely by the presence of one large dot. We need to generate and test another idea.

If children actually reason in this *If/Then/Therefore* way, then this brief verbal training should enable them to successfully employ the pattern to solve the tasks. However, if they do not normally reason this way, then the training should be confusing and they should not be successful.

Mellinarks

All of these are Mellinarks.

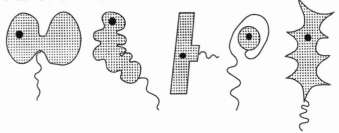

None of these is a Mellinark.

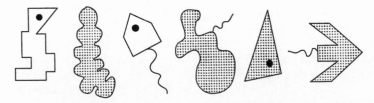

Which of these is a Mellinark?

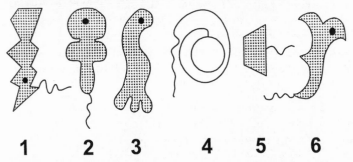

1   2   3   4   5   6

FIGURE 2.4. The Mellinark Task (Elementary Science Study, 1974).

Interestingly none of the six-year-olds (0 of 30) were successful in solving the Mellinark task (i.e., identifying that creatures 1, 2, and 6 in row three are Mellinarks). However, half of the seven-year-olds (15 of 30) solved the task, as did virtually all of the eight-year-olds (29 of 30), and all of the nine through sixteen-year-olds. This result provides experimental evidence that the *If/Then/Therefore* pattern can easily be assimilated and used by children ages eight and older to learn in this context. Therefore, we have evidence that supports the hypothesis that the brain employs active use of hypothetico-predictive reasoning, at least among children eight years and older.

But why did younger children fail to use the necessary reasoning to solve the Mellinark task? In a very real sense, their brains simply did not function properly when confronted with the need to use *If/Then/Therefore* reasoning. Finding out the cause of the reasoning failure may shed additional light on the relationship between reasoning and brain function.

Perhaps the younger children simply failed to recognize contradictory evidence when it appeared. To test this hypothesis another sample of 25 six-year-olds were individually administered a series of eight evidence evaluation tasks in which each child was shown eight cards with either a triangle or a square on one side and either green dots or blue dots on the other side. They were then verbally given the following rule: If a card has a triangle on one side (*p*), then it has green dots on the other side (*q*). The child was then told to state whether or not the cards, once turned over to reveal the other sides, broke the rule (*p* ? *q*). The cards, in order of presentation showed:

a. triangle then green dots (*p* then *q*)
b. green dots then triangle (*q* then *p*)
c. square then green dots (not *p* then *q*)
d. green dots then square (*q* then not *p*)
e. triangle then blue dots (*p* then not *q*)
f. blue dots then triangle (not *q* then *p*)
g. square then blue dots (not *p* then not *q*)
h. blue dots then square (not *q* then not *p*)

The percentages of children who thought that the respective cards broke the rule were: a. 16%, b. 12%, c. 44%, d. 56%, e. 88%, f. 73%, g. 48%, and h. 44%. None responded correctly to all the cards (only cards e and f break the rule), but most of them did state that cards e and f broke the rule; 88% and 73% respectively. In other words, 88% and 73% of the children in the two instances in which it was presented correctly identified contradictory evidence. Therefore the hypothesis was not supported.

The fact that many children thought that cards other than e and f broke the rule indicates some confusion on their part. But this confusion does not appear to be the cause of their failure on the Mellinark-type tasks. This can be stated with considerable confidence because similar confusion has been found on Mellinark-type tasks even among many high school and college students who have no trouble responding successfully to the minimal instruction on the tasks (Lawson, 1990). Again, this indicates that the failure of the younger children is not due to their inability to recognize

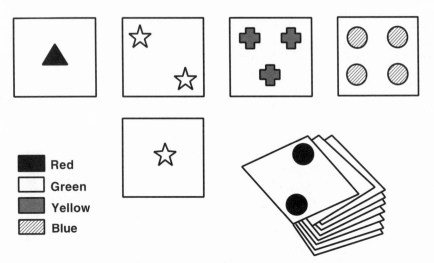

FIGURE 2.5. The Wisconsin Card Sorting Test (Heaton et al., 1993).

contradictory evidence. Rather the failure appears to be caused by a lack in appropriate *use* of that evidence, which is to say, the failure is a performance failure, not a competence failure. If this is the case, then the performance failure needs to be explained.

Importantly, the performance failure amounts to not rejecting ideas when confronted with contradictory evidence. In the psychological literature, this sort of failure has been referred to as a "perseveration" error (the child perseveres with previous ideas in spite of the presentation of contradictory evidence). Perseveration errors are also exhibited by children below seven years in age and by adults with frontal lobe damage when administered the Wisconsin Card Sorting Test (Heaton, Chelune, Tally, Kay & Curtiss, 1993). The Wisconsin Card Sorting Test (WCST) consists of four stimulus cards and 128 response cards (see Figure 2.5). The first stimulus card shows one red triangle. The second shows two green stars. The third shows three yellow crosses. And the fourth shows four blue circles. The 128 response cards have different shapes (crosses, circles, triangles, or stars), colors (red, yellow, blue, or green) and numbers of figures (one, two, three, or four). During the test, the subject is given the 128 response cards and asked to match each card to one of the 4 stimulus cards. After each attempted match, the subject is told whether the match is correct or incorrect, but not told the matching principle (match by color, match by shape, match by number). Suppose the first matching principle is match by color. All other attempted matches would be called incorrect. Once the subject makes 10 consecutive correct color matches, the sorting principle is secretly shifted to another feature, shape for example. If the subject continues to incorrectly match by color, in spite of negative feedback from the interviewer, he or she is said to have committed a perseveration error (an incorrect response in card sorting in the face of negative feedback). After 10 consecutive correct responses to shape, the principle is shifted (number and then back to color). This procedure continues until the subject successfully completes 6 matching categories or until all 128 cards have been used.

Thus, perseveration errors occur when subjects fail to shift from, say, a previously successful sorting based on color, to another feature (e.g., shape) even when the experimenter repeatedly tells the subject that the selection is in error. In a sense, contradictory evidence has no impact on the subject's thinking; consequently they do not generate and test other ideas. Dempster (1992) reviewed research that implicates children's failure to suppress misleading or irrelevant information as a major impediment in performance on a variety of interference-sensitive tasks such as the WCST, measures of field independence, conservation tasks, selective attention tasks, and the Brown-Peterson task. Dempster's review provides considerable support for two points that suggest a possible explanation for the very young children's failure to respond positively to the brief training. First, research by Luria (1973) and several associates is cited in which Luria concludes:

It must also be noted that the prefrontal regions of the cortex do not mature until very late in ontogeny, and not until the child has reached the age of four to seven years do they become prepared for action.... the rate of increase in area of the frontal regions of the brain rises sharply by the age of three-and-a-half to four years, and this is followed by a second jump towards the age of seven to eight. (pp. 87–88)

Second, adult patients with frontal lobe damage make significantly more errors and significantly fewer shifts (greater numbers of perserveration errors) on the WCST than do adult patients with damage to other parts of the brain. As Dempster (1992) points out, a comparison of the mean number of perserveration errors of adult patients with frontal lesions (Heaton, 1981) with normal six-year-old children reveals that they perform in a similar manner (Chelune & Baer, 1986).

Hence a possible explanation for the failure of the six-year-olds on the present concept acquisition tasks is that the prefrontal lobes play a key role in successful task performance and that the prefrontal lobes are not sufficiently operational until seven to eight years of age. It is well known that the prefrontal lobes are the seat of several of the brain's "higher" executive functions associated with working memory such as extracting information from other brain systems and anticipating, selecting goals, experimenting and monitoring information to produce novel responses (Gazzanaga, Ivry & Mangun, 1998; Stuss & Benson, 1986). If it can be demonstrated that the concept acquisition tasks place, general cognitive demands such as these on children and, more specifically, have cognitive demands similar to those of the WCST, then this prefrontal lobe hypothesis will gain support.

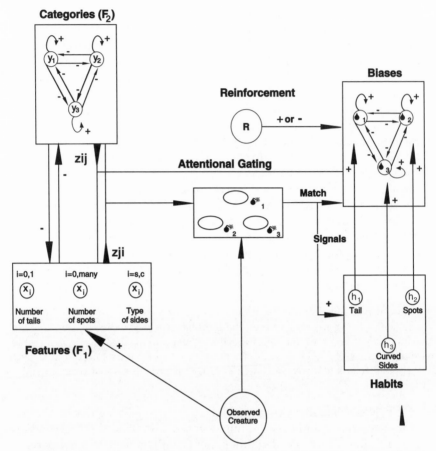

FIGURE 2.6. The neural network patterned after that of Levine and Prueitt (1989) that presumably depicts the neural processes involved in the Bloops task.

Levine and Prueitt (1989) provide a detailed neural network and computer simulation of the role of the prefrontal lobes on the WCST. Can this network also be applied to the present tasks?

The Levine-Prueitt Neural Network

Figure 2.6 depicts the neural network isomorphic to the Levine and Prueitt prefrontal lobe network that may be operative in the present concept acquisition tasks. The Bloops Task (see Figure 2.7), has been selected as the sample task. The network includes populations of cells called nodes. A field of nodes referred to as F_1 code input features. The input features in the WCST are color (red, yellow, blue, green), shape (circle, square, triangle, cross) and number of figures (1, 2, 3, 4). In the Bloops Task, the features

All of these are Bloops.

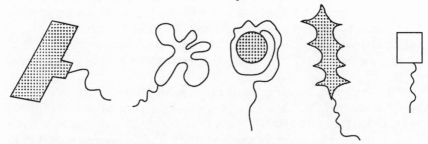

None of these is a Bloop.

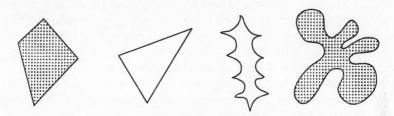

Which of these are Bloops?

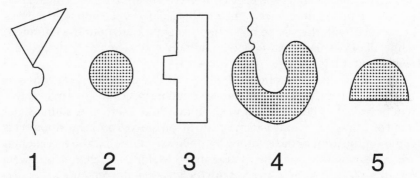

| 1 | 2 | 3 | 4 | 5 |

FIGURE 2.7. The Bloops task (Lawson, 1993).

are number of tails (0 or 1), number of spots (0 or many), and type of side (straight or curvy). Nodes in field F_2(Categories nodes) code the template cards in the Levine and Prueitt network. The template cards in the WCST show one red triangle, two green stars, three yellow crosses, and four blue circles. The template cards serve as sources of ideas about what the relevant feature upon which to base the sorting of the response cards (e.g., sort by the color red, sort by the shape circle) might be. The figures in row one of the Bloops Task serve the same role in that they contain the relevant features that can be induced as the basis for sorting the creatures in row three into categories of Bloops and non-Bloops (e.g., Y_1 = It's a Bloop if it has one tail; Y_2 = It's a Bloop if it has spots; Y_3 = It's a Bloop if it has straight sides). Thus, possible categories at F_2 on the Bloops Task are groups of, say, all creatures with a tail, all creatures with spots, all creatures with straight sides.

The Levine and Prueitt network also includes Habits nodes and Biases nodes as shown in the figure. These nodes correspond to each of the sub-fields in F_1. The Habits nodes detect how often prior classifications have been correctly and incorrectly made. On the WCST this means, for instance, how many times a sorting based on color has been reinforced by a correct or incorrect response from the examiner. In the present series of concept acquisition tasks this detects how many times a prior classification has been made based upon say, type of side or presence of spots. In other words, if, for example, the presence of spots has been the relevant feature on previous tasks, then the "habit" of classifying based upon this feature is strengthened. Here the word "strengthened" refers to an increase in the rate of neuro-transmitter release at synapses within the node's cell population. A greater release rate increases the probability that a signal will pass across a synapse from one neuron to another.

It should be noted that most of the subjects in the Lawson (1993) study began by using the matching strategy based on overall shape presumably because shape matching had been reinforced numerous times in their pasts. Of considerable importance is the fact that many of the younger subjects persevered with this shape matching strategy throughout the interview, while all of the eight-year-olds who initially considered only shape were able to shift their strategy.

The Biases nodes are affected both by activity in the Habits nodes and by reinforcement. In the WCST the experimenter gives positive or negative reinforcement as he or she responds to the child's sorting with the statement of "right" or "wrong." Reinforcement on the concept acquisition tasks comes in the form of the creatures in row two and from the experimenter when he or she suggests alternative strategies for task solution. Suppose, for example, that a child, armed with the idea that the presence of spots is a relevant feature based upon his or her experience with a previous task, inspects the creatures in row one and notes that the first, third, and fourth Bloops have spots. The presence of these three spotted Bloops then reinforces the idea that the presence of spots is the relevant feature. Of course, the first row also contains negative reinforcement in the form of creatures two and five that do not have spots. Nevertheless, if the positive reinforcement signal is too great, or if the negative signal is too weak, the habit will prevail (i.e., the child exhibits perserveration errors as he or she fails to switch from previous ways of classifying the creatures). Note also that row two contains creatures that may serve as positive (unspotted creatures two and three) or negative (spotted creatures one and four) reinforcement. The Z_{ij} and Z_{ji} between F_1 and F_2 represent synaptic strengths of the neuron connections between the two nodes. These are large when node X_i (e.g., the creatures that one is attending to, such as creature one of row one in the Bloops Task with spots) contains a feature that is active at F_2 (e.g., the presence of spots is the key feature). Attentional gating from the Biases nodes increases some F_1 to F_2 signals. If, for instance, the "It's a Bloop if it has spots" bias is high and the "It's a Bloop if it has a tail" bias is low, then attending to creature one of row one that contains spots and one tail will excite the "It's a Bloop if it has spots" node at F_2 more than it will excite the "It's a Bloop if it has a tail" node. When a creature is attended to, the proposal category whose activity (y_i) is largest in response to the input creature is chosen as the match. A match signal corresponding to the shared feature(s) is sent to the Habits and Biases nodes. These signals either increase or decrease the activity of the Biases nodes depending upon whether the creature is in row one (is a Bloop) or in row two (not a Bloop). In other words, if one initiates the idea that the presence of spots is the relevant feature and attends to creature one of row one that has many spots and is a Bloop, then signals to the Habits and Biases nodes increase. Conversely, if one attends to creature one of row two that has many spots but is not a Bloop, then the signals decrease.

Additional details of the network, including equations that the various signals obey, can be found in Levine and Prueitt (1989). For our purposes the one remaining key variable is reinforcement R that activates the Biases nodes. As shown in Figure 2.6, this reinforcement can take on the value $+\alpha$ or $-\alpha$, where α is parameter assumed to be relatively high in normal adults and relatively low in adults with prefrontal lobe damage. This is to say that the reinforcement arrow (either + or −) from the reinforcement locus to the Biases nodes corresponds to the role of the prefrontal lobes in task performance. Thus in the present study the α value for our six-year-olds is assumed to be relatively low because their prefrontal lobes are not yet sufficiently operational, whereas the α value for the eight-year-olds is relatively high because their prefrontal lobes are assumed to be operational. In brief, the failure of adults with prefrontal lobe damage to shift sorting strategy is explained by the failure of the reinforcement locus in the prefrontal lobes to send sufficiently strong signals (either + or −) to the Biases nodes to alter their activity. Without sufficiently strong signals the currently active bias will continue to control behavior. It is possible that the six-year-olds in the present study failed to shift their classification criteria for the same reason.

Levine and Prueitt (1989) cite a number of experimental and anatomical findings (Mishkin & Appenzeller, 1987; Mishkin, Malamut, & Bachevalier, 1984; Nauta, 1971; Ulinski, 1980) in support of the distinctions made in their neural network. They also report results of a simulation of normal and frontally damaged persons on the WCST in which α was the only parameter altered. To simulate prefrontal damage α was set at 1.5 while controls α was set at 4. Results of the simulations were nearly identical to previously reported results with actual normal and frontally damaged persons. The results, therefore, provide support for the accuracy of their network and, by inference, for the network presented in Figure 2.6.

IS HYPOTHETICO-PREDICTIVE REASONING USED TO SOLVE "EVERYDAY" PROBLEMS?

Apparently the brain processes sensory-motor information and acquires relatively simple concepts in a hypothetico-predictive fashion. Is a similar hypothetico-predictive pattern also at work in "everyday" contexts? Let us consider an example of problem solving in a personal setting in which the reasoning pattern was identified by introspection. Of course introspection is difficult because reasoning takes place very rapidly and at least partially on a subconscious level. In addition, prior conceptions about how reasoning and learning take place may distort the introspective process. Nevertheless, one might correctly identify steps in reasoning if consciously trying to do so when memory is not clouded by intervening experiences. Further, independent methods that do not suffer from these potential pitfalls exist to test the validity of introspectively constructed reasoning patterns. Consequently, the following example is offered for your consideration.

Before I arrived home one evening, my wife had lit the gas barbecue and put some meat on for dinner. Upon arriving, she asked me to check the meat. While doing so, I noticed that the barbecue was no longer lit. So I had a problem. I had to relight the barbeque so I could finish cooking the meat. It was windy, so I suspected that the wind had blown out the flames as it had a few times before. So I tried to relight the barbecue by striking a match and inserting its flame into a small "lighting" hole just above one of the unlit burners, but the barbecue did not relight. I tried a second, and then a third match, but it still did not relight. At this point, I suspected that the tank might be out of gas. So I lifted the tank and sure enough it lifted easily as though it were empty. I then checked the gas gauge and saw that it was pointed at empty. Therefore, it seemed that the barbecue was no longer lit, not because the wind had blown out its flames, but because its tank was out of gas. So to solve my problem, I had to refill the tank.

What reasoning pattern was guiding this simple problem solving? Retrospectively, it would seem that reasoning was initiated by a causal question: Why was the barbecue no longer lit? In response to this causal question, the reconstructed pattern goes like this:

If... the wind had blown out the flames,
and... a match is used to relight the barbecue
then... the barbecue should relight.
But... when the first match was tried the barbecue did not relight.
Therefore... either the wind hypothesis is wrong or something is wrong with the test. Perhaps the match flame went out before it could ignite the escaping gas. This seems plausible as the wind had blown out several matches in the past. So retain the wind hypothesis and try again.

Thus,

If... the wind had blown out the flames,
and... a second match is used to relight the barbecue
then... the barbecue should relight.
But... when the second match was used the barbecue still did not relight.
Therefore... once again, either the wind hypothesis is wrong or something is wrong with the test. Although it appeared as though the inserted match flame reached the unlit burner, perhaps it nevertheless did get blown out. So again retain the wind hypothesis and repeat the experiment. But this time closely watch the match flame to see if it does in fact reach its destination.

Thus,

If... the wind had blown out the flames,
and... a third match is used to relight the barbecue while closely watching the flame
then... the flame should reach its destination and the barbecue should relight.
But... when the third match was used while closely watching the flame, the flame appeared to reach its destination, but the barbecue still did not relight.
Therefore... apparently there was nothing wrong with the test. Instead the wind hypothesis is probably wrong. Perhaps the tank is out of gas, and so on.

If this reconstruction is accurate, then it seems that hypothetico-predictive reasoning is also used to solve problems in "everyday" contexts. Presumably this is because the brain is "hard-wired" to process information and to learn in a hypothetico-predictive fashion, whether at the sensory-motor level, at the level of descriptive concept acquisition, or at the level of everyday problem solving.

IS HYPOTHETICO-PREDICTIVE REASONING ALSO USED DURING
SCIENTIFIC DISCOVERY?

Does the hypothetico-predictive pattern of reasoning and brain function
also apply to scientific reasoning and discovery? To find out, let us consider
a classic case of scientific discovery, namely Galileo Galilei's discovery of
Jupiter's moons. In 1610 in his *Sidereal Messenger*, Galileo Galilei reported
some observations of heavenly bodies made by a new, more powerful
telescope of his invention. In that report Galileo claims to have discovered
four never before seen "planets" circling Jupiter (Galilei, 1610, as translated
and reprinted in Shapley, Rapport & Wright, 1954, p. 59).

Unlike many modern scientific papers, Galileo's report is striking in the
way it chronologically reveals many of the steps in his discovery process.
Thus, it provides an extraordinary opportunity to gain insight into the
reasoning involved in an important scientific discovery. Galileo's key observations were made during the nights of January 7th, 8th, 10th, and 11th
in 1610. What follows is a recapitulation of part of that report followed by
an attempt to fill in gaps with how Galileo may have been reasoning as he
interpreted his observations. Galileo's reasoning will then be modeled in
terms of Piaget's general theory of equilibration as well as three prominent
theories of brain function.

Galileo's Observations and Conclusions

January 7th. Galileo made a new observation on January 7th that he
deemed worthy of mention. In his words:

On the 7th day of January in the present year, 1610, in the first hour of the following night, when I was viewing the constellations of the heavens through a
telescope, the planet Jupiter presented itself to my view, and as I had prepared
for myself a very excellent instrument, I noticed a circumstance which I had
never been able to notice before, owing to want of power in my other telescope,
namely that three little stars, small but very bright, were near the planet; and
although I believed them to belong to the number of the fixed stars, yet they
made me somewhat wonder, because they seemed to be arranged exactly in a
straight line, parallel to the ecliptic, and to be brighter than the rest of the stars.
The position of them with reference to one another and to Jupiter was as follows:
(p. 59)

(east)   *   *   O   *   (west)

January 8th. The next night Galileo made a second observation:

On January 8th . . . I found a very different state of things, for there were three little
stars all west of Jupiter, and nearer together than on the previous night, and they

were separated from one another by equal intervals, as the accompanying figure shows.

(east)   O   *   *   *   (west)

At this point, although I had not turned my thoughts at all upon the approximation of the stars to one another, yet my surprise began to be excited, how Jupiter could one day be found to the east of all the aforementioned stars when the day before it had been west of two of them; forthwith I became afraid lest the planet might have moved differently from the calculation of astronomers, and so had passed those stars by its own proper motion. (pp. 59–60)

January 9 th

I, therefore waited for the next night with the most intense longing, but I was disappointed of my hope, for the sky was covered with clouds in every direction. (p. 60)

January 10 th

But on January 10th the stars appeared in the following position with regard to Jupiter, the third, as I thought, being hidden by the planet.

(east)   *   *   O   (west)

When I had seen these phenomena, as I knew that corresponding changes of position could not by any means belong to Jupiter, and as, moreover, I perceived that the stars which I saw had always been the same, for there were no others either in front or behind, within the great distance, along the Zodiac – at length, changing from doubt into surprise, I discovered that the interchange of position which I saw belonged not to Jupiter, but to the stars to which my attention had been drawn and I thought therefore that they ought to be observed henceforward with more attention and precision. (p. 60)

January 11 th

Accordingly, on January 11th I saw an arrangement of the following kind:

(east)   *   *   O   (west)

namely, only two stars to the east of Jupiter, the nearer of which was distant from Jupiter three times as far as from the star to the east; and the star furthest to the east was nearly twice as large as the other one; whereas on the previous night they had appeared nearly of equal magnitude. I, therefore, concluded, and decided unhesitatingly, that there are three stars in the heavens moving about Jupiter, as Venus and Mercury round the sun. (p. 60)

January 12 th and Later

Which at length was established as clear as daylight by numerous other subsequent observations. These observations also established that there are not only three, but four, erratic sidereal bodies performing their revolutions round Jupiter. . . . These are my observations upon the four Medicean planets, recently discovered for the first time by me. (pp. 60–61)

What Was the Nature of Galileo's Reasoning?

Background Knowledge as a Source of Hypotheses. To analyze Galileo's reasoning, let us start with what he initially "brought to the table." In other words, what was Galileo's background knowledge? Presumably this knowledge, which is stored in associative memory, will serve as a source of hypotheses when the need arises. It is safe to assume that Galileo's knowledge about heavenly objects included at least the following three categories:

1. Fixed stars that are immovable because they are embedded in an external celestial sphere.
2. Planets within the celestial sphere that orbit the sun (e.g., Earth, Venus, and Jupiter).
3. Moons that orbit the planets that orbit the sun (e.g., our moon).

Presumably these categories of heavenly objects function as "mental models" by which observations can be "assimilated" (Grossberg, 1982; Johnson-Laird, 1983; Piaget, 1985). Also, if the category into which the new objects should be assimilated is unclear, the categories will function as hypothesized categories into which they might be placed (Gregory, 1970). The process of using these categories as alternative hypotheses has been referred to as analogical reasoning or analogical transfer (Biela, 1993; Boden, 1994; Bruner, 1962; Dreistadt, 1968; Finke, Ward, & Smith, 1992; Gentner, 1989; Hestenes, 1992; Hoffman, 1980; Hofstadter, 1981; Holland, Holyoak, Nisbett, & Thagard, 1986; Johnson, 1987; Koestler, 1964; Sternberg & Davidson, 1995; and Wong, 1993). It should be pointed out that the processes of assimilation and hypothesis formation take place largely at the subconscious level. Also in many cases, the analogical transfer requires more insight than shown in Galileo's case because the "distance" between the analogous category and the target phenomenon is greater, as with Darwin's use of artificial selection as an analogue for natural selection or Kekule's use of snakes eating their tails as an analogue for the benzene ring.

Galileo's Reasoning on January 7th. Recall that concerning his January 7th observations, Galileo stated: "I noticed a circumstance which I had never been able to notice before, owing to want of power in my other telescope, namely that three little stars, small but very bright, were near the planet." This statement is important because it suggests that Galileo's new observations have been immediately assimilated by his fixed star category (listed as 1 above). But Galileo's continued thinking led to some initial doubt that he was really observing fixed stars as this following remark reveals that: "although I believed them to belong to the number of the fixed stars, yet they made me somewhat wonder, because they seemed to be arranged exactly in a straight line, parallel to the ecliptic, and to be brighter than the rest of the stars, equal to them in magnitude."

Why would this observation lead Galileo to "somewhat wonder?" Of course, we can never really know what was on Galileo's mind (in his working memory). But perhaps he was reasoning along these lines:

If... the three objects are fixed stars
and... their sizes, brightness and positions are compared to each other and to other nearby stars,
then... variations in size, brightness and position should be random, as is the case for other fixed stars.
But... upon closer inspection, "they seem to be arranged exactly in a straight line, parallel to the ecliptic, and to be brighter than the rest of the stars."
Therefore... the fixed-star hypothesis is not supported. Or as Galileo put it, "yet they made me somewhat wonder."

Galileo's Reasoning on January 8th. The next night Galileo made a second observation. Again in his words: "On January 8th, I found a very different state of things, for there were three little stars all west of Jupiter, and nearer together than on the previous night, and they were separated from one another by equal intervals, as the accompanying figure shows."

(east)   O   *   *   *   (west)

The new observation puzzled Galileo and raised another question. Once again in Galileo's words: "At this point, although I had not turned my thoughts at all upon the approximation of the stars to one another, yet my surprise began to be excited, how Jupiter could one day be found to the east of all the aforementioned stars when the day before it had been west of two of them." Why did this observation puzzle Galileo? Basically the puzzling observation was that the stars were now closer together than before and all were west of Jupiter, but still along a straight line. I believe that this observation was puzzling because it was not the predicted one based on the fixed-star hypothesis, that is: Prediction – the stars' positions relative to each other should be the same and they should not pass Jupiter; observation – the stars are closer together than on the previous night and they are now all west of Jupiter. In other words, connections in associative memory indicated that fixed stars should not change relative positions and should not pass Jupiter. But new information processed in working memory showed that they did indeed precisely that. Consequently, when this mismatch of predictions with observations was noted in working memory, Galileo began to doubt the fixed-star hypothesis.

Galileo continues: "Forthwith I became afraid lest the planet might have moved differently from the calculation of astronomers, and so had passed those stars by its own proper motion." This statement suggests that Galileo has not yet rejected the fixed-star hypothesis. Instead he has generated an *ad hoc* hypothesis to possibly keep the hypothesis alive. In other words, Galileo guessed that perhaps the astronomers made a mistake. He guessed that perhaps their records were wrong about how Jupiter is supposed to move relative to the stars in the area. Let us call this the astronomers-made-a-mistake hypothesis. How could Galileo test the astronomers-made-a-mistake hypothesis? Consider the following:

If... the astronomers made a mistake,
and... I observe the next night
then... Jupiter should continue to move east relative to the stars, and
the objects should look like this:

(east)   O   * * *   (west)

Of course we cannot know if this is how Galileo was really reasoning, but if he were reasoning along these lines, he would have had a very clear prediction to compare with the observations he hoped to make the following night.

Galileo's Reasoning on January 9 th and 10 th. Galileo continues: "I, therefore waited for the next night with the most intense longing, but I was disappointed of my hope, for the sky was covered with clouds in every direction. But on January 10th the stars appeared in the following position with regard to Jupiter, the third, as I thought, being hidden by the planet."

(east)   * * O   (west)

What conclusion can be drawn from this observation in terms of the astronomers-made-a-mistake hypothesis? Consider the following argument:

If... the astronomers made a mistake,
and... I observe the next night
then... Jupiter should continue to move east relative to the "stars," and
the objects should look like this:

(east)   O   * * * (west)

But... upon observation, the objects did not look like that. Instead they looked like this:

(east)   * * O   (west)

Therefore... the astronomers-made-a-mistake hypothesis is not supported.

Let us return to the report to see what conclusion Galileo drew. Galileo states:

When I had seen these phenomena, as I knew that corresponding changes of position could not by any means belong to Jupiter, and as, moreover, I perceived that the stars which I saw had always been the same, for there were no others either in front or behind, within the great distance, along the Zodiac – at length, changing from doubt into surprise, I discovered that the interchange of position which I saw belonged not to Jupiter, but to the stars to which my attention had been drawn. (p. 60)

So Galileo concluded that the astronomers had not made a mistake (i.e., the astronomers-made-a-mistake hypothesis should be rejected). In other words, the changes of position were not the result of Jupiter's motion. Instead they were due to motions of the "stars."

Galileo's Reasoning on January 11ᵗʰ and Later. Having rejected the astronomers-made-a-mistake hypothesis, Galileo is left with the task of formulating and testing another explanation for his puzzling observations. It is not clear exactly when he formulated a viable explanation, but his remarks concerning his January 11th and later observations cited previously make it clear that he did not take long. Indeed, it is clear that he has "conceptualized" a situation in which these objects are orbiting Jupiter in a way analogous to the way Venus and Mercury orbit the sun and in the way our moon orbits Earth. Thus, he has rejected the fixed-star hypothesis and accepted an alternative in which the objects are orbiting Jupiter. I will leave it up to you to construct the *If/Then/Therefore* argument that Galileo may have used to arrive at this conclusion.

HOW CAN GALILEO'S REASONING BE MODELED?

Galileo's Reasoning within Piaget's Theory

According to Piaget (1985), cognition involves equilibration with its dual processes of assimilation and accommodation. Galileo's hypothetico-predictive reasoning fits nicely within Piaget's theory. Within that theory we can say that Galileo immediately assimilated his observations by his fixed-star schema ("I noticed . . . that three little stars . . . were near the planet."). This assimilation soon led to a small amount of disequilibrium when his fixed-star hypothesis was initially tested ("Yet they made me somewhat wonder."). This initial disequilibrium resulted because certain characteristics of the new "stars" differed from typical stars (they were in a straight line and equidistant from one another). Disequilibrium then grew when subsequent observations also did not match predictions drawn from the fixed-star schema (How could Jupiter be found to the east of all the aforementioned stars when the day before it had been west of two of them?). But Galileo's disequilibrium did not last long. After rejecting the *ad hoc* astronomers-made-a-mistake hypothesis, Galileo rejected the fixed-star hypothesis. This rejection then led to an accommodation as Galileo generated a new hypothesis – the moons hypothesis, which the evidence supported. Generating and testing the moons hypothesis enabled Galileo to assimilate all of his observations without disequilibrium. Thus, equilibrium was restored.

Galileo's Reasoning within Grossberg's Theory of Adaptive Resonance

We can go further than Piaget's general concepts of equilibration, assimilation, and accommodation to think about Galileo's reasoning. Grossberg (1982) introduced an adaptive resonance theory of information processing complete with an account of activity within successive slabs of neurons within the brain. It should be pointed out that Grossberg's theory does not contradict Piaget's theory. Rather it adds to it. Grossberg's theory (part of which is represented in Figure 2.8) can be used to understand some of what might have been going on in Galileo's mind in terms of neurological events.

Figure 2.8 depicts two successive slabs of neurons in the brain, $F^{(1)}$ and $F^{(2)}$. According to Grossberg, sensory input at a specific point in time $X_{(1)}$ (e.g., light coming from the three objects near Jupiter on the night of January 7th) excites an electrical pattern of activity at slab $F^{(1)}$ and sends a signal to inhibit orienting arousal. Orienting arousal (OA) is a neural pathway that when activated unleashes a pulse on $F^{(2)}$, which in turn initiates a search through associative memory for a new pattern. The electrical pattern X_1 at $F^{(1)}$ then excites another electrical pattern X_2 at the next slab of neurons at $F^{(2)}$, which feeds signals back to $F^{(1)}$. In the case of Galileo's initial observations, the pattern at $F^{(2)}$ corresponds to his star category and initially matches the pattern at $F^{(1)}$. So all is well both neurologically (a resonant state is achieved) and conceptually.

But as reported, Galileo's continued thinking led to a partial mismatch (his star category implied that stars should *not* be lined up along a straight line and should not be equidistant from each other). This partial mismatch led Galileo to "somewhat wonder." Neurologically speaking, a mismatch

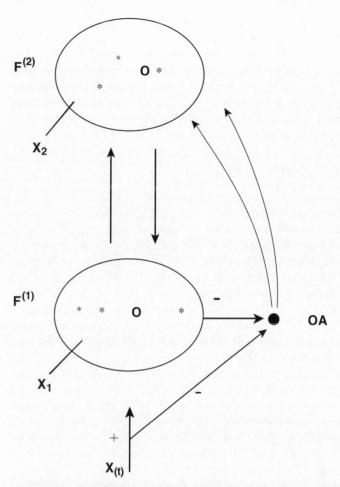

FIGURE 2.8. Grossberg's model of the match and mismatch of activity patterns on successive slabs of neurons in the brain. Input $X_{(t)}$ (e.g., three spots of light near Jupiter) excites an activity pattern at slab $F^{(1)}$ and inhibits orienting arousal (OA). The pattern at slab $F^{(1)}$ excites a pattern at slab $F^{(2)}$, which feeds back to $F^{(1)}$. A mismatch (a new observation that does not match an expectation), causes quenching of activity at $F^{(1)}$ and shuts off inhibition of OA. OA is then free to search for another pattern (another hypothesis) to match the input.

(a new observation that does not match a prediction), causes quenching of activity at $F^{(1)}$ and shuts off inhibition of OA. OA is then free to search associative memory for another pattern (another hypothesis) to match the input. In other words, with Galileo's continued observations and reasoning, the mismatch (the lack of a resonant state) between the patterns at $F^{(1)}$ and $F^{(2)}$ presumably became so great that activity at $F^{(1)}$ was quenched. Thus, inhibition of orienting arousal was shut down. Orienting arousal was then free to excite $F^{(2)}$ leading to a search for another pattern of activity to hopefully match the input pattern at $F^{(1)}$. On the conceptual level, Galileo's mind was now free to search for alternative hypotheses (e.g., the planet hypothesis, the moon hypothesis) to replace the rejected fixed-star hypothesis. Once an activity pattern at $F^{(2)}$ was found that matched the input pattern at $F^{(1)}$, the resonant state was again achieved and orienting arousal was shut down and Galileo's search was complete. He had "discovered" four new moons orbiting Jupiter.

Galileo's Reasoning within the Kosslyn/Koenig and Levine/Prueitt Models

As previously discussed, Kosslyn and Koenig's (1995) model of brain function indicates that the ability to visually recognize objects requires participation of the six major brain areas. Kosslyn and Koenig's description of system functioning is about recognizing relatively complex objects present in the visual field during a very brief time period – not distant spots of light seen through a telescope. Nevertheless, the hypothetico-predictive nature of this system's functioning is clear. All one needs to apply the same principles to Galileo's case, is to extend the time frame over which observations are made – observations that will either match or not match predictions, thus allow hypotheses to be tested.

Levine and Prueitt's model also seems to account for the processes involved in hypothesis testing. Figure 2.9 suggests how it can be used in the present context. As you recall, the model includes Features nodes referred to as F_1. In Galileo's case, these nodes code input features (number of spots of light, the sizes of those spots, their positions). Categories into which the input can be placed (e.g., fixed stars, planets, moons) are categorized into Categories nodes (F_2). Once again, these categories serve as alternative hypotheses. The model also includes Habits and Biases nodes. The Habits nodes detect how often prior classifications have correctly and incorrectly been made. The Biases nodes are affected by activity in the Habits nodes and by reinforcement. Details of network function can be found in Levine and Prueitt (1989). The important point in terms of the present argument is that information processing, whether it involves basic descriptive concept formation, simple hypothesis testing, or the "discovery" of Jupiter's moons, is basically a hypothetico-predictive process driven by working memory in which new input is gathered and matched against prior categories stored in associative memory.

Using Working Memory to Activate and Inhibit Input

As mentioned, working memory is seated in the lateral prefrontal cortex. Following Baddeley (1995), working memory, at least in adults, is seen

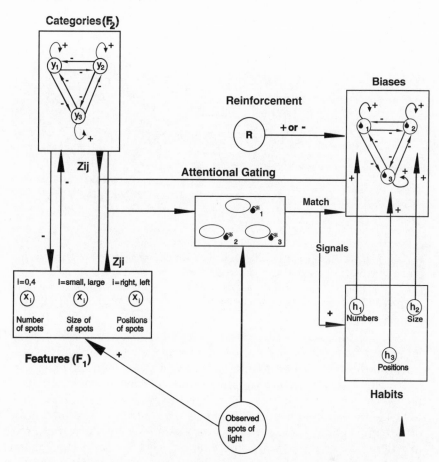

FIGURE 2.9. Levine and Prueitt's model of neural activity including feature, cate-gory, Biases and Habits nodes. The Features nodes code observable input features (numbers, sizes, positions). The Categories nodes represent prior knowledge cate-gories into which the input may fit (star category, planet category, moon category). The Habits and Biases nodes keep track of past decisions and influence subsequent decisions.

as consisting of at least three components – a visuo-spatial scratch pad, a central executive, and a phonological loop. In Baddeley's model, the visuo-spatial scratch pad activates representations of objects and their properties, while the phonological loop does the same for linguistic representations. Research by Smith and Jonides (1994) and Paulesu, Frith, and Frackowiak (1993) suggest respective right and left hemisphere specialization for the scratch pad and loop. Working memory can be thought of as a tempo-rary network to sustain information while it is processed. However, as we have seen, during reasoning, one must pay attention to task-relevant

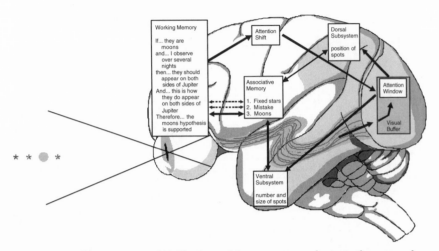

FIGURE 2.10. The contents of Galileo's working memory as he tests the moons hypothesis. Note how previously generated hypotheses stored in associative memory need to be inhibited (the dashed arrows) during the time the moons hypothesis, it predicted consequences, and the relevant evidence are highlighted (the bold arrow).

information and inhibit task-irrelevant information. Consequently, working memory involves more than simply allocating attention and temporarily keeping track of it. Rather, working memory actively selects information relevant to one's goals and actively inhibits irrelevant information. In terms of Galileo's reasoning, Figure 2.10 shows the contents of working memory in terms of one cycle of *If/Then/Therefore* reasoning. As you can see, in order to use *If/Then/Therefore* reasoning to generate and test his moon hypothesis, Galileo has to not only allocate attention to it and its predicted consequences, he also has to inhibit his previously generated fixed-star and astronomers-made-a-mistake hypotheses.

THE ELEMENTS OF HYPOTHETICO-PREDICTIVE REASONING

Because the hypothetico-predictive reasoning pattern appears to capture the way the brain functions in a wide variety of contexts, this and the next section will provide additional details as to its basic elements and to its relationship to three well-known rules of logic. The previous analyses suggest that the brain processes information during concept acquisition, during simple problem solving, and during scientific discovery in a way similar to the way it processes sensory-motor information, that is in terms of cycles of *If/Then/Therefore* reasoning. In the unlit barbecue scenario, the hypothetico-predictive reasoning seems to involve the following seven elements, which are presumably coordinated in working memory in the prefrontal lobes:

1. Making an initial puzzling observation.
2. Raising a causal question.
3. Generating one or more possible hypotheses (e.g., the barbecue is no longer lit because the wind blew out its flames. The spots of light are fixed stars. Previous astronomers made a mistake.). As mentioned, the process of hypothesis generation is seen as one involving analogies, analogical transfer, or analogical reasoning, that is borrowing ideas that have been found to "work" in one or more past related contexts and using them as possible solutions/hypotheses in the present context.
4. Assuming that the hypothesis under consideration is correct. This assumption is necessary so that the hypothesis can be tested. A test requires imagining relevant condition(s) that along with the assumed hypothesis allow the generation of an expectation, a prediction.
5. Carrying out the imagined test.
6. Comparing predicted and observed results. This comparison allows one to draw a conclusion. A good match means that the hypothesis is supported, but not proven, while a poor match means that something is wrong with the hypothesis, the test, or both. Finding a good match between predicted and observed results means that the hypothesis in question is supported, but not proven because one or more unstated and perhaps unimagined alternative hypotheses may give rise to the same prediction under the test condition (Hempel, 1966; Salmon, 1995). Similarly, a poor match cannot disprove or falsify a hypothesis in any ultimate sense. Recall that in the present example, finding evidence that contradicted the initial wind hypothesis did not immediately lead to its rejection. This is because the failure of predicted results to match observed results can arise from one of two sources, a faulty hypothesis or a faulty test. Consequently, before a plausible hypothesis is rejected, one has to be reasonably sure that its test is not faulty. And because one can never be certain the test is perfect, one cannot reject a hypothesis with certainty.
7. Recycling the procedure. The procedure must be recycled until a hypothesis is generated, which when tested, is supported on one or more occasions.

This summary paints a fairly clear view of reasoning as a hypothetico-predictive enterprise, a view that compares favorably with that advanced by some biologists about the nature of biological research (Baker & Allen, 1977; Lewis, 1988; Medawar, 1969; Moore, 1993; Platt, 1964) and by some philosophers about the nature of scientific research in general (Carey, 1998; Chamberlain, 1965; Giere, 1997; Hempel, 1966; Popper, 1965). However, these authors typically refer to scientific discovery as hypothetico-deductive, not as hypothetico-predictive. I have chosen the phrase hypothetico-predictive because the word deduction often connotes a rather rote application of deductive logic, that is: If A > B, and B > C, then it deductively follows that A > C. However, in my view, seldom if ever, do predictions follow so "automatically" from premises. Instead the process of generating reasonable predictions involves elements of insight and creativity (Lawson, 1999). Therefore, the phrase hypothetico-predictive may be more descriptive of what actually occurs during the reasoning process.

THE "LOGIC" OF HYPOTHETICO-PREDICTIVE REASONING

As mentioned, hypothetico-predictive reasoning cannot lead to proof or disproof in any ultimate sense. Thus, one might wonder how it relates to standard rules of conditional logic such as modus tollens and modus ponens. The standard conditional logic of modus tollens reads as follows: p implies q; not-q; therefore, not-p. In the unlit barbecue context we get the following:

> *If*... the wind blew out the flames (p),
> *and*... I stick a lighted match in the lighting hole,
> *then*... the barbecue should relight (q).
> *But*... the barbecue did not relight (not q).
> *Therefore*... the wind did not blow out its flames (not p).

However, as previously pointed out, the failure of an actual result to match a predicted result may not stem from a faulty hypothesis. Rather the failure may stem from a faulty test. Consequently, a more "reasonable" application of modus tollens might read as follows:

> *If*... the wind blew out the flames (p),
> *and*... I stick a lighted match in the lighting hole,
> *then*... the barbecue should relight (q) – assuming nothing goes wrong
>   with the test.
> *But*... the barbecue did not relight (not q).
> *Therefore*... most likely the wind did not blow out its flames (not p) –
>   unless, of course, something did go wrong with the test.

Next consider the conditional logic of modus ponens, that is, p implies q; p; therefore q. Interestingly, this logic does not appear to apply to the barbecue situation as the following illustrates:

> *If*... the wind blew out the flames (p),
> *and*... I stick a lighted match in the lighting hole,
> *then*... the barbecue should relight (q).
> *And*... the wind did blow out the flames (p).
> *Therefore*... the barbecue should relight (q).

Clearly, this argument makes no sense. The point of hypothetico-predictive reasoning is to test an idea. In contrast, the point of modus ponens seems to be to generate a "logical" prediction. So once again, a standard logical rule seems to fail to capture the essence of reasoning. Interestingly, the logical fallacy known as affirming the consequent seems to do a better job of capturing the essence of hypothetico-predictive reasoning than modus ponens (cf., Hempel, 1966, pp. 6–7). Affirming the consequent reads as follows: p implies q; q; therefore p. In the context of the unlit barbecue we get the following:

If ... the tank is out of gas (p),
and ... the tank is lifted,
then ... it should feel light (q).
And ... it does feel light (q).
Therefore ... the tank is out of gas (p).

But as previously noted, drawing this conclusion represents a logical fallacy. The conclusion is also "unreasonable" because the tank could feel light for other reasons (i.e., alternative hypotheses exist that have not been tested and eliminated). For example, perhaps the tank feels light but still contains a small amount of gas. Perhaps this is why I checked the gas gauge and found it pointed at empty before I was satisfied that the cause of the unlit barbecue was indeed an empty gas tank. Consequently, the more reasonable conclusion that one draws from these kinds of data is that the initial hypothesis has been supported, but one cannot be certain that it is correct.

The following summarizes the necessary modifications.
For modus tollens:

If ... p
and ... the planned test,
then ... *probably* q (assuming that nothing goes wrong with the test).
But ... not q.
Therefore ... *probably* not p (meaning that the hypothesis p is not supported, but not disproved).

And for affirming the consequent:

If ... p
and ... the planned test,
then ... *probably* q (assuming that nothing goes wrong with the test).
And ... q.
Therefore ... *possibly* p (meaning that the hypothesis is supported, but not proven as other hypotheses could lead to the same prediction).

Consequently, the rules of modus tollens and modus ponens do not fully capture the essence of hypothetico-predictive reasoning. But this does not mean that humans are unreasonable. Said another way, it would appear that our brains do not necessarily reason with these rules of conditional logic. But this is not a bad thing because these rules are not necessarily reasonable!

CONCLUSION

In conclusion, the present chapter paints human reasoning in terms of cycles of *If/Then/Therefore* hypothetico-predictive reasoning – reasoning in which working memory accesses and sustains hypotheses from associative memory to be tested and then actively seeks predictions and evidence that follow. In most instances, for most people, these reasoning cycles occur without conscious awareness on the part of the reasoner. And most certainly, unlike the streamlined *If/Then/Therefore* arguments presented in this chapter, the cycles most often occur with many fits and starts. Nevertheless, successful hypothetico-predictive reasoning, while not necessarily logical, is reasonable, and follows the *If/Then/Therefore* pattern presumably because the brain is "hard-wired" to process information in this way.

Successful reasoning also involves the inhibition of previously rejected hypotheses and/or irrelevant information. But due to a variety of conditions, including lack of maturation of the prefrontal lobes, prefrontal lobe damage, and lack of relevant physical and social experience, human reasoning is not always successful. At higher levels, failure may result from a lack of any fruitful hypotheses to test, or more often, a premature acceptance of a pet hypothesis, often with little or no evidence in its favor. This leads to a failure to consider alternatives and potentially relevant evidence, or in terms of problem solving, a failure to consider and test alternative solution strategies – a condition of perseveration often referred to as fixation or functional fixedness in the problem-solving literature (Dominowski & Dallob, 1995).

A classic example of a collective reasoning failure has been reported by Angell (1996) in which juries have awarded plaintiffs huge sums of money based on the claim (the hypothesis) that breast implants cause connective tissue disease. Amazingly, these awards were made prior to the collection of any real scientific evidence to test the hypothesis. Indeed, when that evidence was finally collected, it turned out not to match predictions from the hypothesis. For example, in one study, the hypothesis led to the prediction of a higher incidence of disease in women with implants than in a comparable group of women without implants. But the evidence revealed exactly the same disease incidence in both groups (Gabriel, O'Fallon, Kurland, Beard, Woods, & Melton 1994).

Examples such as this indicate that many adults do not understand the power and importance of hypothetico-predictive reasoning. The example also indicates the importance of emotion in the deployment, or lack of deployment, of such reasoning. This is an issue not dealt with in the present chapter, but one of considerable importance nonetheless (Damasio, 1994; LeDoux, 1996). Clearly, an unmet educational challenge is the design and implementation of instructional programs that enable all students to develop and successfully employ hypothetico-predictive reasoning at the highest levels.

References

Andersen, R. A. (1987). Inferior parietal lobule function in spatial perception and visuomotor integration. In F. Plum (Vol. Ed.), & V. B. Mountcastle (Sec. Ed.), *Handbook of physiology, section 1: The nervous system, volume 5: Higher functions of the brain*. Bethesda, MD: American Physiological Society.

Angell, M. (1996). Evaluating the health risks of breast implants: The interplay of medical science, the law, and public opinion. *The New England Journal of Medicine, 334*(23), 1513–1518.

Baddeley, A. (1995). Working memory. In M. S. Gazzaniga (Ed.), *The cognitive neurosciences* (pp. 755–764). Cambridge, MA: MIT Press.

Baker, J. J. W. & Allen, G. E. (1977). *The study of biology* (3rd ed.). Reading, MA: Addison-Wesley.

Biela, A. (1993). *Psychology of analogical inference*. Stuttgart: S. Hirzel Verlag.

Boden, M. A. (1994). What is creativity? In M. A. Boden (Ed.), *Dimensions of creativity*. Cambridge, MA: MIT Press.

Bruner, J. (1962). *On knowing: Essays for the left hand*. Cambridge, MA: Harvard University Press.

Carey, S. S. (1998). *A beginner's guide to scientific method* (2nd ed.). Belmont, CA: Wadsworth.

Chamberlain, T. C. (1965). The method of multiple working hypotheses. *Science, 148*, 754–759. (Originally published in 1898).

Chelune, G. J., & Baer, R. A. (1986). Developmental norms for the Wisconsin Card Sorting Test. *Journal of Clinical and Experimental Neuropsychology, 8*, 219–228.

Damasio, A. R. (1994). *Descartes' error: Emotion, reasoning, and the human brain*. New York: G. P. Putnam.

Daniel, P. M., & Whitteridge, D. (1961). The representation of the visual field on the cerebral cortex in monkeys. *Journal of Physiology, 159*, 203–221.

Dempster, F. N. (1992). Resistance to interference: Developmental changes in a basic processing mechanism. *Developmental Review, 12*, 45–57.

Desimone, R., Albright, T. D., Gross, C. G., & Bruce, C. J. (1984). Simultaneous selective properties of inferior temporal neurons in the macaque. *Journal of Neuroscience, 4*, 2051–2062.

Desimone, R., & Ungerleider, L. G. (1989). Neural mechanisms of visual processing in monkeys. In H. Goodglass, & A. R. Damasio (Eds.), *Handbook of neuropsychology*. New York: Elsevier.

Dominowski, R. L., & Dallob, P. (1995). Insight and problem solving. In R. J. Sternberg & J. E. Davidson (Eds.), *The nature of insight*. Cambridge, MA: MIT Press.

Dreistadt, R. (1968). An analysis of the use of analogies and metaphors in science. *Journal of Psychology, 68*, 97–116.

Elementary Science Study. (1974). *Teachers' guide for attribute games and problems.* New York: McGraw-Hill.

Farah, M. J. (1990). *Visual agnosia: Disorders of object recognition and what they tell us about normal vision.* Cambridge, MA: MIT Press.

Finke, R. A., Ward, T. B., & Smith, S. M. (1992). *Creative cognition: Theory research and practice.* Cambridge, MA: The MIT Press.

Friedman, H. R., & Goldman-Rakic, P. S. (1994). Coactivation of prefrontal cortex and inferior parietal cortex in working memory tasks revealed by 2DG functional mapping in the rhesus monkey. *Journal of Neuroscience, 14*, 2775–2788.

Fuster, J. M. (1989). *The prefrontal cortex: anatomy, physiology, and neuropsychology of the frontal lobe* (2nd ed.). New York: Raven Press.

Gabriel, S. E., O'Fallon, W. M., Kurland, L. T., Beard, C. M., Woods, J. E., & Melton, I. I. (1994). Risk of connective-tissue disease and other disorders after breast implantation. *New England Journal of Medicine, 330*, 1697–1702.

Galilei, G. (1610). The sidereal messenger. In H. Shapley, S. Rapport, & H. Wright, (Eds.), (1954). *A treasury of science.* New York: Harper & Brothers.

Gazzaniga, M. G., Ivry, R. B., & Mangun, G. R. (1998). *Cognitive neuroscience: The biology of the mind.* New York: Norton.

Gentner, D. (1989). The mechanisms of analogical learning. In S. Vosniadou & A. Ortony (Eds.), *Similarity and analogical reasoning.* Cambridge: Cambridge University Press.

Giere, R. N. (1997). *Understanding scientific reasoning.* (4th ed.). New York: Harcourt Brace.

Gregory, R. L. (1970). *The intelligent eye.* New York: McGraw-Hill.

Grossberg, S. (1982). *Studies of mind and brain.* Dordrecht, Holland: D. Reidel.

Haxby, J. V., Grady, C. L., Horowitz, B., Ungerleider, L. G., Mishkin, M., Carson, R. E., Herscovitch, P., Schapiro, M. B., & Rapoport, S. I. (1991). Dissociation of object and spatial visual processing pathways in human extrastriate cortex. *Proceedings of the National Academy of Sciences of the United States of America, 88*, 1621–1625.

Heaton, R. K. (1981). *Wisconsin card sorting test manual.* Odessa, FL: Psychological Assessment Resources.

Heaton, R. K., Chelune, G. J., Tally, J. L., Kay, G. G., & Curtiss, G. (1993). *Wisconsin card sorting test manual: Revised and expanded.* Odessa, FL: Psychological Assessment Resources, Inc.

Hempel, C. (1966). *Philosophy of natural science.* Upper Saddle River, NJ: Prentice-Hall.

Hestenes, D. (1992). Modeling Games in a Newtonian World. *American Journal of Physics, 55*, 440–454.

Hoffman, R. R. (1980). Metaphor in Science. In P. R. Honeck & R. R. Hoffman (Eds.), *The Psycholinguistics of figurative language.* Hillsdale, NJ: Erlbaum.

Hofstadter, D. R. (1981). Metamagical themas: How might analogy, the core of human thinking, be understood by computers? *Scientific American, 249*, 18–29.

Holland, J. H., Holyoak, K. J., Nisbett, R. E., & Thagard, P. R. (1986). *Induction: Processes of Inference, Learning, and Discovery.* Cambridge, MA: The MIT Press.

Johnson, M. (1987). *The body in the mind.* Chicago, IL: University of Chicago Press.

Johnson-Laird, P. N. (1983). *Mental models*. Cambridge, MA: Harvard University Press.

Koestler, A. (1964). *The act of creation*. London: Hutchinson.

Kosslyn, S. M., & Koenig, O. (1995). *Wet mind: The new cognitive neuroscience*. New York: The Free Press.

Lawson, A. E. (1990). The use of reasoning to a contradiction in grades three to college. *Journal of Research in Science Teaching, 27*(6), 541–552.

Lawson, A. E. (1993). Deductive reasoning, brain maturation, and science concept acquisition: Are they linked? *Journal of Research in Science Teaching, 30*(9), 1029–1051.

Lawson, A. E. (1994). Research on the acquisition of science knowledge: Epistemological foundations of cognition. In D. L. Gabel (Ed). *Handbook of research on science teaching and learning*. New York: MacMillan.

Lawson, A. E. (1999). What should students learn about the nature of science and how should we teach it? *Journal of College Science Teaching, 28*(6), 401–411.

Lawson, A. E., McElrath, C. B., Burton, M. S., James, B. D., Doyle, R. P., Woodward, S. L., Kellerman, L., & Snyder, J. D. (1991). Hypothetico-deductive reasoning and concept acquisition: Testing a constructivist hypothesis. *Journal of Research in Science Teaching, 28*(10), 953–970.

LeDoux, J. (1996). *The emotional brain*. New York: Touchstone.

Levine, D. S., & Prueitt, P. S. (1989). Modeling some effects of frontal lobe damage: Novelty and perseveration. *Neural Networks, 2*, 103–116.

Lewis, R. W. (1988). Biology: A hypothetico-deductive science. *The American Biology Teacher, 54*(3), 137–152.

Luria, A. R. (1973). *The working brain: An introduction to neuropsychology*. New York: Basic Books.

Maunsell, J. H. R., & Newsome, W. T. (1987). Visual processing in monkey extrastriate cortex. *Annual Review of Neuroscience, 10*, 363–401.

Medawar, P. B. (1969). *Induction and intuition in scientific thought*. Philadelphia: American Philosophical Society.

Mishkin, M. (1978). Memory in monkeys severely impaired by combined but not separate removal of amygdala and hippocampus. *Nature, 273*, 297–298.

Mishkin, M., & Appenzeller, T. (1987). The anatomy of memory. *Scientific American, 256*, 80–89.

Mishkin, M., Malamut, B., & Bachevalier, J. (1984). Memories and habits: Two neural systems. In G. Lynch, J. McGaugh, & N. Weinberger (Eds.), *Neurobiology of learning and memory* (pp. 65–77). New York: Guilford.

Miyashita, Y., & Chang, H. S. (1988). Neuronal correlate of pictorial short-term memory in the primate cortex. *Nature, 331*, 68–70.

Moore, J. A. (1993). *Science as a way of knowing*. Cambridge, MA: Harvard University Press.

Nauta, W. J. H. (1971). The problem of the frontal lobe: A reinterpretation. *Journal of Psychiatric Research, 8*, 167–187.

Paulesu, E., Frith, D. D., & Frackowiak, R. S. J. (1993). The neural correlates of the verbal component of working memory. *Nature, 362*, 342–345.

Piaget, J. (1985). *The equilibration of cognitive structures: The central problem of intellectual development*. Chicago and London: The University of Chicago Press.

Popper, K. (1965). *Conjectures and refutations. The growth of scientific knowledge.* New York: Basic Books.

Platt, J. R. (1964). Strong inference. *Science, 146,* 347–353.

Posner, M. I. (1988). Structures and functions of selective attention. In T. Boll & B. K. Bryant (Eds.), *Clinical neuropsychology and brain function: Research, measurement and practice.* Washington, D.C: American Psychological Association.

Salmon, M. H. (1995). *Introduction to logic and critical thinking* (3rd ed.). Harcourt Brace: Fort Worth, Texas.

Smith, E. E., & Jonides, J. (1994). Working memory in humans: Neuropsychological evidence. In M. S. Gazzaniga (Ed.), *The Cognitive Neurosciences* (pp. 1009–1020). Cambridge, MA: MIT Press.

Sternberg, R. J., & Davidson, J. E. (Eds.) (1995). *The nature of insight.* Cambridge, MA: The MIT Press.

Stuss, D. T., & Benson, D. F. (1986). *The Frontal Lobes.* New York: Raven Press.

Tootell, R. B. H., Silverman, M. S., Switkes, E., & De Valois, R. L. (1982). Deoxyglucose analysis of retinotopic organization in primate striate cortex. *Science, 218,* 902–904.

Treisman, A. M., & Gelade, G. (1980). A feature of integration theory of attention. *Cognitive Psychology, 12,* 97–136.

Treisman, A. M., & Gormican, S. (1988). Feature analysis in early vision: Evidence from search asymmetries. *Psychological Review, 95,* 15–48.

Ulinski, P. S. (1980). Functional morphology of the vertebrate visual system: An essay on the evolution of complex systems. *American Zoologist, 20,* 229–246.

Ungerleider, L. G., & Mishkin, M. (1982). Two cortical visual systems. In D. J. Ingle, M. A. Goodale, & R. J. W. Mansfield (Eds.), *Analysis of visual behavior.* Cambridge, MA: MIT Press.

Wong, E. D. (1993). Self-generated analogies as a tool for constructing and evaluating explanations of scientific phenomena. *Journal of Research in Science Teaching, 30*(4), 367–380.

3

Working Memory and Reasoning

Kenneth J. Gilhooly

Memory and reasoning serve complementary functions. Memory serves to maintain access to previously acquired information (including information recently generated in the course of a task) while reasoning seeks to derive new information from old. The present chapter will be focusing particularly on the interrelations between *working memory* and reasoning. The role of working memory in reasoning was a key concern of the first papers setting out the highly influential Baddeley-Hitch working memory model (Baddeley & Hitch, 1974; Hitch & Baddeley, 1976) and this concern continues. Clearly, reasoning processes must draw on concepts and rules retrieved from long-term memory, but it would seem to be generally agreed that explicit reasoning acts on the transient contents of working memory. Such a view has been common to otherwise opposed perspectives on reasoning, such as mental model and mental rule approaches. First, I will outline initial definitions of working memory and of reasoning and then review the main empirical studies. Finally, I will draw some interim conclusions and indicate directions for future research in this area.

WORKING MEMORY

A recent definition of working memory is as follows: "Working memory is those mechanisms or processes that are involved in the control, regulation, and active maintenance of task-relevant information in the service of complex cognition" (Miyake & Shah, 1999, p. 450). Although there would be general agreement that the human information processing system does indeed control, regulate, and actively maintain task-relevant information, the nature of the underlying mechanisms is subject to considerable debate (Andrade, 2001; Miyake & Shah, 1999). Two main approaches to specifying the mechanisms or processes of working memory can be distinguished. One approach suggests that working memory involves a single pool of resources ("activation"), which varies from individual to individual in average levels and also can vary within the individual over time. The single pool of resources can be flexibly allocated between storage and processing within a single task (Daneman & Carpenter, 1980; Just & Carpenter, 1992). The second approach invokes the idea of multiple components of working memory (Baddeley & Logie, 1999) which have specialized storage and processing roles for dealing with attentional control, visuo-spatial, and verbal information.

The "single pool of resources" approach has led to a focus on the consequences of individual differences in working memory capacity over a range of tasks. Working memory capacity has been measured by a variety of working memory span tasks that involve both storage and processing. The sentence span task of Daneman and Carpenter (1980) is a prototypical example and involves presenting participants with a series of sentences to read. At the end of a sequence of sentences, participants are asked to recall the last words of each sentence in the correct sequence. The longest sequence of sentences for which all the final words could be recalled correctly in order is taken to be the participant's sentence span. Sentence span has been found to be correlated with reading comprehension (Daneman & Carpenter, 1980, 1983) and with other span measures using different materials such as digit strings (Yuill, Oakhill, & Parkin, 1988), simple equations (Turner & Engle, 1989), and a counting span task (Baddeley, Logie, Nimmo-Smith, & Brereton, 1985). It would appear then that such span tasks that involve "storage + processing" are tapping a general working memory capacity which underlies a wide range of cognitive tasks.

In the influential model developed by Baddeley and colleagues (Baddeley, 1992; Baddeley & Hitch, 1974; Baddeley & Logie, 1999), performance in many complex tasks is seen as requiring a multicomponent working memory system. Originally, a three-part system was proposed that was divided into a *central executive*, which coordinates the activities of two "slave" storage systems, namely, the *visuo-spatial sketch pad* and the *phonological loop*. The phonological loop was seen as holding a limited amount of phonological or speech-based information. The visuo-spatial sketch pad was thought to hold a limited amount of visual or spatially coded information. Supporting evidence for this fractionation comes from (a) dual task studies, which show selective interference by visuo-spatial and verbal secondary tasks on memory for visuo-spatial and verbal information respectively, and (b) differential patterns of impairment observed in individuals with focal brain damage (for reviews see Baddeley & Logie, 1999; Della Sala & Logie, 1993). The central executive component is seen as having no storage functions but rather operates as an attentional controller. The model is subject to continuous refinement and its components are themselves open to fractionation into subcomponents as evidence accumulates. Since the original model, the phonological loop has been fractionated into a passive *phonological store* and an active *rehearsal process*.

Logie (1995) has proposed that the visuo-spatial sketch pad might better be considered more broadly as visuo-spatial working memory. Visuo-spatial tasks would draw on the central executive and two temporary memory systems: a passive *visual cache* that stores static visual patterns and an active spatially based system that stores dynamic information, namely an *inner scribe*. The inner scribe has been particularly linked to temporary memory for movements and movement sequences (Logie, Englekamp, Dehn & Rudkin, 2001). The central executive is also considered open to fractionation into a number of functions (focusing attention, switching attention, activating representations in long-term memory, coordinating multiple task performance). Whether a central, general purpose controlling function is ultimately required is left as a current question for research. Baddeley (2000) has recently proposed a new component labeled the *episodic buffer* for temporarily holding multimodal information. So far, this component has not been sufficiently specified to lead to experimental manipulations. It may also be noted at this point that the "single pool of resources" view has been taken to map onto the concept of central executive capacity of the multicomponent approach (Andrade, 2001).

Secondary task methods have been the main means of investigating the contribution of working memory components to various tasks. Concurrent articulation and concurrent spatial actions are taken to load the phonological loop and the visuo-spatial sketch pad respectively. If a primary task is disrupted by articulatory suppression (such as, repeating aloud "the, the, the" continuously) but not by concurrent spatial activity (such as moving one hand in a simple pattern), then it may be inferred that the primary task involves the phonological loop but not the visuo-spatial sketch pad. Central executive involvement is typically tested by concurrent random generation of items from a well-defined set (e.g., digits from 1 to 9) and may be verbal (speaking numbers) or spatial (tapping a keypad at random). A large number of studies have found these and similar methods to be useful ways of assessing the involvement of working memory components in a wide range of tasks (Andrade, 2001; Baddeley & Logie, 1999).

Reasoning

A recent definition of reasoning is as follows: "When most psychologists talk about 'reasoning' they mean an explicit sequential thought process of some kind, consisting of propositional representations" (Evans & Over, 1996, p. 15). This definition stresses that reasoning is an *explicit* rather than an implicit process and is *sequential* rather than parallel. However, this definition could apply to most cases of problem-directed thinking, such as planning, and not just to reasoning. For present purposes, I suggest that "reasoning" involves explicit sequential thought processes that are effectively equivalent to the application of a sequence of rules of some formal system. Formal systems provide sets of general rules for reaching correct conclusions from given statements. The principal formal systems are those of deductive logic, mathematics, statistics, probability, decision theory and, although less fully formalized, inductive and deontic logics. Such theories are couched in abstract, de-contextualised terms and can apply to any contents for which the appropriate relationships (such as, set inclusion, exclusion, overlap, implication, negation, and so on) hold. Thus, reasoning involves the application of very general, abstract rules to specific contents. My focus will be on deductive reasoning that has the special property that if the inputs to the reasoning process (the premises) are true, then the outputs (conclusions) are necessarily true also. In this way, new information can be derived with certainty from old information. Deductive reasoning *tasks* then, can be defined as tasks that can be successfully tackled by the application of a formal deductive theory. Such tasks require no real-world knowledge of the objects being reasoned about. Approaches to how people respond to reasoning tasks may be divided into three broad types at present. Two approaches propose what might be called "unified theories" of reasoning (Roberts, 1993), and these are the *mental models* approach associated with Johnson-Laird (Johnson-Laird, 1983; Johnson-Laird & Byrne, 1991) and the *mental rules* approach associated with Braine, O'Brien, and Rips (Braine & O'Brien, 1998; Rips, 1994). The third approach stresses the role of *strategies* that vary depending on task demands, training and individual differences (Gilhooly, Logie, & Wynn, 1999; Roberts, 2000).

Theoretical Approaches. "Unified theories" propose that there is a *fundamental reasoning mechanism* that underlies all deductive reasoning and constrains individual differences quite narrowly (Roberts, 1993). The *mental models* approach of Johnson-Laird (1983) proposes a particular fundamental reasoning mechanism and has been applied to many reasoning tasks subsequent to its initial strong association with syllogistic reasoning. The main assumptions of this approach are that people form representations of the premises consisting of tokens linked together to exemplify the stated relationships and then seek to combine the premise representations into integrated representations from which possible conclusions can be read off directly. The main stages proposed are as follows (Evans, Newstead, & Byrne, 1993). Initially, a single model is formed to represent a possible state of the world in which the premises would be true. Next, the reasoner forms a putative conclusion by discovering a proposition that is true in the model and is informative (not a repetition of a premise or a trivial inference). If there are a number of possible ways of combining premise models then all combinations should be generated and checked against the putative conclusion until either a counter example to the putative conclusion is found or all possibilities have been exhausted without the discovery of a counterexample. Only conclusions that hold for all ways of combining premise models are valid deductions. If the putative conclusion is falsified by a counter-example, then the reasoner should attempt to identify a new conclusion compatible with all model combinations. If no such conclusion is found then there is no valid conclusion. Suboptimal performance is explained by failures to consider all ways of combining premise information, perhaps because of working memory limitations. It may be noted that Johnson-Laird (1983) specifically proposed a role for working memory in reasoning. In discussing figural effects in syllogistic reasoning (which are effects due to different ways of arranging the subject, predicate, and middle terms in syllogistic arguments), Johnson-Laird wrote:

> The effects of both number of models and figure arise from an inevitable bottleneck in the inferential machinery: the processing capacity of working memory, which must hold one representation in a store, while at the same time the relevant information from the current premise is substituted in it. This problem is not obviated by allowing the subjects to have the written premises in front of them throughout the task: the integration of premises has to occur in working memory, unless the subjects are allowed to use pencil and paper so as to externalise the process. (p. 115)

The mental models theory proposes that all participants follow the basic mental models approach and the only allowance for individual differences lies in completeness of generating different integrated models from the premise models.

The *mental rules* approach is similarly insistent that all participants follow the same general approach with a few quantitative differences due to working memory limitations. On the mental rules approach (Braine, 1978; Rips, 1994) reasoning involves the application of a sequence of inference rules drawn from a set available to all normal adults and that are a subset of those available in formal logic. For example, the modus ponens rule ("if p then q, and p, therefore, q") is almost always followed and would be regarded as part of normal adult competence. The more inference steps that must be executed the more difficult the inference problem should be and Braine, Reiser, and Rumain (1984) report latency results which bear out this expectation. Again working memory limitations are invoked, in that the more steps required to reach a conclusion, the larger the load on working memory and the more errors should occur.

The third broad approach does not propose any universal mechanisms, but rather advocates the view that participants adopt a wide range of different *strategies* which vary both across participants and within participants with experience and training (Roberts, 2000). A useful definition of "strategy" has been offered by Siegler and Jenkins (1989) as "any procedure that is nonobligatory and goal directed." On the strategy approach, use of mental models and/or mental rules can be regarded as optional strategies which can be adopted depending on circumstances rather than invariable approaches followed by all participants in all reasoning tasks.

A wide variety of heuristic strategies have been postulated as underlying performance in reasoning tasks (Roberts, 2000) and such strategies, while generally superior in results to guessing, are typically not equivalent to logical rule application. The use of heuristic strategies is consistent with the general observation that participants are quite prone to error in abstract reasoning tasks; for example, the modal answer to most syllogisms is an error of some sort (Erickson, 1978).

Since reasoning, in the sense defined above, is not modal even in response to reasoning tasks, this chapter would be rather brief if it was limited to thinking which was equivalent to logical rule application. Instead, this chapter will address the role of working memory in reasoning *tasks* and consider how that role may vary with different strategies and different tasks. The following sections of this chapter focus on empirical studies of the possible role of working memory and its components in tasks designed to evoke reasoning, with special reference to differences among strategies. The sections will consider studies that manipulate loads (through dual tasking), manipulate strategies (through training or selection of participants), or take an individual differences approach.

WORKING MEMORY IN REASONING TASKS: EMPIRICAL RESULTS

The AB task

Baddeley and Hitch (1974) and Hitch and Baddeley (1976), in the papers that first set out the multicomponent model reported studies of the role of working memory in reasoning using the AB reasoning task (Baddeley, 1968). In the AB task, participants are presented with sentences that may or may not correctly describe the order of two letters at the end of each sentence. Participants must indicate as quickly as possible whether each sentence is true or false. For example, given "A does not precede B -AB," the correct response is "False." The sentences varied in terms of being positive or negative, active or passive, true or false, in letter order (AB, BA) and whether the term "follows" or "precedes" was used.

The following results emerged. Memory preloads of up to six digits could be successfully maintained with no effects on reasoning speed or accuracy. However, when six-item preloads had to be articulated concurrently with the reasoning task, there was slowing of reasoning, which was most marked for the more difficult items. Hammerton (1969) had also found a similar effect of concurrent articulation (of the sentence "Mary had a little lamb") on the AB task. These dual task data support an involvement of the phonological loop in the AB task. Further support for this conclusion came from Baddeley and Hitch (1974), which varied the phonemic and visual similarity of the letters in the task. Phonemic similarity reduced the number of items correctly solved but there was no effect of visual similarity, which indicates that the visuo-spatial sketch pad was not implicated in the AB task. Farmer, Berman, and Fletcher (1986) reported that articulatory suppression (repeating "1234" as fast as possible) impaired AB task performance but that a spatial suppression task (repeatedly tapping four keys in order) had no effect. These data are consistent with those of Baddeley and Hitch (1974) and Hammerton (1969) in suggesting that the AB task involves the phonological loop but not the visuo-spatial sketch pad.

While the AB reasoning task discussed above has received little attention in the main reasoning literature, the next two task areas to be discussed, propositional and syllogistic reasoning, have received considerable attention and in recent times there has been growing interest in the detailed role of working memory in these key domains of reasoning.

Propositional Reasoning

Given as premises, "if p then q" and "p," what follows? The valid (modus ponens) inference is "q." Given, "if p then q" and "not-q," "not-p" follows validly (modus tollens). Given, "if p then q" and "$not\ p$" (denial of the antecedent), or "q" (affirmation of the consequent), nothing validly follows. These problems are examples of conditional reasoning and represent basic problems in propositional logic.

Two broad theoretical approaches that indicate rather different strategies for tackling such problems are the mental models (Johnson-Laird & Byrne, 1991) and the mental rules approaches (Braine, 1978; Rips, 1994). The mental models approach explains task difficulty in terms of the number of mental models that must be generated and evaluated to test possible conclusions, while the rules approaches offer explanations in terms of the number of steps in a mental logic that must be applied to move from premises to conclusion. Both approaches propose that working memory can be overloaded, by models or by rules, and that working memory loading is a major cause of error. A number of studies have used dual tasks with conditional reasoning in order to explore this hypothesis and the salient results will now be outlined (Evans & Brooks, 1981; Klauer, Stegmaier, & Meiser, 1997; Meiser, Klauer, & Naumer, 2001; Toms, Morris, & Ward, 1993).

Experimental Manipulations: Dual tasks, Training, and Mood. Evans and Brooks (1981), in a dual task study, found no evidence of central executive or phonological loop involvement in conditional reasoning. It has been suggested (Halford, Bain, & Maybery, 1984) that the dual tasks in Evans and Brooks (1981) may have imposed too low a concurrent load to produce any interference. Furthermore, there was no check for trading off between primary and secondary tasks, so the null results might reflect priority being given to the reasoning task at the expense of the secondary tasks. Toms et al. (1993) investigated conditional inference tasks with and without dual tasks of tapping, tracking, articulation, and memory loads. Neither tracking nor tapping affected conditional inference performance, suggesting no role for the visuo-spatial sketch pad in this task. Although articulatory suppression did not affect conditional inferences, memory load did have a detrimental effect particularly on modus tollens problems. The memory load and artic- ulation conditions were similar in that articulation involved repeating the digits 1–6 over and over at a rate of 2 digits per sec while the memory load condition involved a different random order of digits 1–6 per trial which were to be repeated aloud at a rate of 2 digits per sec. The additional load of recalling random sequences rather than the overlearned sequence appears to have been critical in bringing about an interfering effect on the main task. Further, the concurrent memory load task was also shown to interfere with a spatial memory task (which was also disrupted by concurrent tapping but not by articulatory suppression). Overall, Toms et al. concluded that conditional reasoning did not involve the visuo-spatial sketch pad or the articulatory loop but required some abstract representation in working memory, which could be provided by the central executive. A cautionary note that may be made here, regarding the null results, is that Toms et al. did not check for possible trade-offs. Participants may have maintained inference performance at the cost of concurrent articulation and tapping performance thus giving the impression that the visuo-spatial sketch pad and phonological loop were not involved if only inference performance is examined. A further reservation is that the conclusion regarding the cen- tral executive is somewhat indirect, since secondary tasks that clearly load the central executive, such as random generation, were not used to test directly for central executive involvement.

Klauer et al. (1997) overcame many of the limitations of the earlier stud- ies. They ran studies on a number of propositional reasoning tasks in- cluding conditionals, biconditionals, exclusive and inclusive disjunctions with a range of secondary tasks, and they examined possible trade-offs. Their results revealed small interfering effects of articulatory suppression, marked interference of verbal random generation and no interference from a visual tracking task on propositional reasoning. Looking at effects of propositional reasoning on the dual tasks, propositional reasoning had marked effects on random generation, did not disrupt articulatory sup- pression, but did have a mildly impairing effect on visual tracking. Overall it seems that propositional reasoning strongly involves the central execu- tive, with lesser roles for the articulatory loop and visuo-spatial sketch pad. However, this conclusion may be limited to untrained participants. Klauer et al. suggested that untrained participants may tend to apply heuristics that impose only a relatively low load on working memory and that train- ing in considering the possible truth values of the terms in the premises would lead to an analytic approach similar to that proposed by mental models theory (Johnson-Laird & Byrne, 1991).

A training method was piloted and then used as pretraining in a study that used tapping as a secondary task. The propositional reasoning of participants with pretraining was more disrupted by tapping than that of untrained participants, as expected. Neither trained nor untrained group showed any trade-offs between primary and secondary tasks. The conclusion was that use of a mental model like strategy leads to loading of the visuo-spatial sketch pad. It can also be concluded that the pattern of loading of working memory in a task depends on the strategy applied to the task.

The role of working memory components in executing different strategies was examined further by Meiser et al. (2001). This study involved the training of participants in three strategies (1) a truth table strategy (as in Klauer et al., 1997), which was intended to induce a mental models approach, (2) a mental logic strategy and (3) a pragmatic reasoning schema strategy. The training methods had been explored previously by Klauer, Meiser, and Naumer (2000) and been found to have differential benefits in a pre- versus post-test study, such that the truth table and pragmatic reasoning training produced more benefit than mental logic training, which was no more effective than a neutral "pseudo-training" condition. In their first experiment, Meiser et al. (2001) found that propositional reasoning was disrupted by concurrent spatial tapping as in Klauer et al. (1997). However, the degree of spatial interference was equal for all training methods against the often made assumption that mental models strategies should be especially susceptible to spatial interference since mental models seem to lend themselves to a spatial representation. Subsequent experiments in this paper found that random number generation and concurrent articulation were more disruptive after truth table training than after the other training methods. A possible conclusion is that the mental model strategy is relatively demanding of working memory resources in propositional reasoning with abstract materials. However, the presumed particular importance of the visuo-spatial sketch pad for execution of a mental models strategy does not seem to have been clearly established, given that the effects of visuo-spatial loading by tapping were not different between the different strategies.

The effect of spatial versus nonspatial content was investigated by Duyk, Vandierendonck, and De Vooght (2001). It was hypothesised that conditional reasoning problems that used spatial materials would show a greater involvement of the visuo-spatial sketch pad than problems involving nonspatial items. Spatial tasks were of the following type:

1. If Pete lives next to Paul then Sue does not live next door to Kurt.
2. Pete lives next to Paul.

Therefore, Sue does not live next to Kurt. (Valid).
Nonspatial problems were as follows:

1. If Pete plays tennis with Paul then Sue does not play tennis with Kurt.
2. Pete plays tennis with Paul

Therefore, Sue does not play tennis with Kurt. (Valid)
Participants carried out conditional reasoning tasks with such spatial and nonspatial contents, with and without a concurrent visuo-spatial sketch pad loading task. Each premise was exposed for a self–set period and so premise reading times were recorded in addition to response accuracy. The main result was that times to read the first premise were markedly affected by visuo-spatial loading when the contents were spatial but not when they were nonspatial. The finding was interpreted as consistent with the mental models framework and as suggesting that the first phase of the mental model inference process makes use of visuo-spatial working memory resources when the content is spatial.

Mood states, such as happiness and sadness, have been found to affect a range of cognitive tasks. Watts, MacLeod, and Morris (1988) found that depression impaired planning in the Tower of London Task (Shallice, 1982). Further, Seibert, and Ellis (1991) reported that recall was impaired in a memory task for both happy and sad mood states relative to neutral mood controls. A working memory interpretation is that mood states that depart from neutral bring about task-irrelevant processing of mood-related materials and so deplete central executive resources. Oaksford, Morris, Grainger, and Williams (1996) used suitable film clips to induce positive, negative, and neutral moods in participants who tackled conditional reasoning tasks. Both positive and negative induced moods suppressed performance on "deontic" versions of Wason's (1966, 1968) four-card selection task. In the standard abstract version of the selection task, participants are presented with four cards each of which has a number on one side and a letter on the other side. A rule is presented such as "If there is a vowel on one side, there is an even number on the other side" and four cards showing "A," "K," "4," and "7." The task is to select only those cards that need be turned over to determine whether the rule is true or false. Very few participants select the correct cards "A" and "7"; most select "A" and "4." Deontic versions of the task involve a rule about what ought to be done, for example, "If a person drinks beer, then that person should be 18 or older" (Griggs & Cox, 1982). Presented with cards representing drinkers with age on one side and type of drink on the other side, participants are asked which cards should be turned over to check if the rule is being broken. With this deontic form of the task, performance is generally high and so Oaksford et al. used a deontic task to avoid floor effects. Under induced positive and negative moods they found that participants tended to select confirming cards rather than disconfirming cards. Oaksford et al. suggest that the result is consistent with the use of a default hypothesis testing strategy that is normally inhibited in deontic tasks. Mood induced depletion of central executive resources results in lowered inhibition of the habitual strategy and insufficient facilitation of the deontic procedure. Support for this interpretation came from further studies in the same paper, which found (a) that random generation (a standard executive-loading task) had a similar effect on deontic reasoning to that of mood and (b) that mood impaired performance on the Tower of London task (Shallice, 1982), which is often taken as a good marker of central executive functioning.

Individual Difference Studies. Most approaches to explaining reasoning would expect that larger working memory spans should facilitate better performance. Two studies of this issue with regard to propositional reasoning have been reported recently by Barrouillet and Lecas (1999) and Markovits, Doyon, and Simoneau (in press).

Barrouillet and Lecas (1999) point out that according to mental models theory the construction and manipulation of mental models are carried out in a limited capacity working memory (Johnson-Laird & Byrne, 1991). Participants, it is argued, would tend to reduce the load on working memory by making implicit some of the information to be represented by constructing *simplified* "initial models." These models can then be *fleshed out* as need be. As an example, the initial model for the conditional *if p then q* would correspond to:

$$[p] \qquad q$$
$$....$$

The first row is a model that represents the co-occurrence of antecedent (p) and consequent (q). The second line (the three dots) is an implicit model. The brackets, [p], indicate an exhaustive representation so that p cannot occur in any other model without q. Fleshing out the model could produce the biconditional –

$$p \qquad q$$
$$\neg p \qquad \neg q$$

or the conditional –

$$p \qquad q$$
$$\neg p \qquad \neg q$$
$$\neg p \qquad q$$

Barruillet and Lecas (1999) argue that more working memory capacity is required to construct the three model representation of the conditional than the two model biconditional or one model conjunction representation.

Since working memory span increases as children develop, it would be expected that with age the interpretation of conditional statements would move from the one model conjunction to the two model biconditional to the three model conditional. A study in which participants had to identify cases that violated *if p then q* (Barrouillet & Lecas, 1998) found that as participants increased in age from third grade to ninth grade, the dominant interpretation changed as expected.

Barrouillet and Lecas (1999) used a different method of identifying how participants interpreted the rule. They asked participants to generate from suitable cards as many examples as they could that matched the rule. For example, one rule was "If you wear a white shirt, you wear green trousers"; participants had available a number of cards reading "white shirt," "blue shirt," "green trousers," and "red trousers" and were asked to produce as many combinations as they could of trouser and shirt cards that fitted the rule. As expected, the older the children, the more their combinations indicated representations based on a larger number of models. Furthermore, the children were tested on a counting span task as a measure of working memory span and, at all ages, counting span strongly predicted the number of models in the child's representation of the conditional. Overall, these results are consistent with the view that reasoning involves constructing and manipulating mental models in working memory. The multicomponent theory of working memory would interpret counting span as involving the central executive and the phonological loop and so, these results suggest a role for those components in forming complex mental models. A span test involving the visuo-spatial component would be worth exploring here as mental models theorists tend to emphasise spatial representation.

Markovits et al. (in press) examined relationships between accuracy of conditional inferences for concrete and abstract conditionals as a function of working memory measures. Participants were assessed for verbal (sentence) and for visual working memory spans. The verbal span task was taken from Baddeley et al. (1985), which itself was derived from Daneman and Carpenter's (1980) procedure. Participants had to judge whether sentences were sensible or not, then were cued to recall either the subject or the object of each sentence in order of hearing. The visual span task involved recalling the positions of five small black circles that appeared randomly within a square shape for 1 second each. This visual span task was repeated over five trials. The results indicated that there was a positive correlation between verbal working memory span and reasoning with both concrete and abstract premises. A positive correlation was also obtained between visual span scores and accuracy of reasoning with concrete premises but not with abstract premises. Since the verbal span test required both storage and processing it would load more on the central executive than the more passive visual span test which required storage only. Thus, the results may be taken to indicate a role for the central executive in both abstract and concrete conditional reasoning while the visuo-spatial sketch pad is only involved in conditional reasoning with concrete materials.

Further evidence on the interplay between patterns of working memory loads, individual differences, and strategies comes from studies on syllogistic reasoning and these studies will be described and discussed in the following sections.

Categorical and Linear Syllogistic Reasoning Tasks

The area of *syllogistic reasoning*, which includes both categorical and linear syllogisms (see Evans et al., 1993, for a review), has attracted considerable research interest over many years. It is notable that many theorists have specifically proposed an involvement of working memory in syllogistic task performance (Fisher, 1981; Johnson-Laird, 1983; Johnson-Laird & Byrne, 1991; Sternberg & Turner, 1981).

Linear syllogisms involve relational terms such as "taller than," "shorter than." For example, "John is taller than Tom and Tom is taller than Fred. Is John taller than Fred?" Relational inferences, especially transitive inferences as in the preceding example, have attracted considerable attention (Evans et al., 1993); our focus will be on the role of working memory in such tasks.

Categorical syllogistic arguments invite reasoning about category relationships and involve two statements (premises) assumed true; for example, "all dogs are mammals" and "all corgis are dogs." One premise relates the subject of the argument (corgis) to the middle term (dogs) and the other premise relates the middle term to the predicate (mammals). The types of relationships between subject, middle, and predicate terms used in categorical syllogistic arguments are those of set inclusion, overlap, and exclusion, namely, all, some, none, some not. The task is to indicate what conclusion, if any, can be validly drawn relating the subject and predicate terms. In the example above, it can be validly inferred that "all corgis are mammals." Despite over seventy years of experimental and theoretical study (e.g., Begg & Denny, 1969; Ford, 1995; Johnson-Laird & Bara, 1984; Polk & Newell, 1995; Stenning & Oberlander, 1995; Wetherick & Gilhooly, 1995; Wilkins, 1928; Woodworth & Sells, 1935) there is still no generally agreed account of how people process such arguments. Many accounts agree that working memory load is a major factor in causing difficulty (e.g., Fisher, 1981; Johnson-Laird, 1983; Sternberg & Turner, 1981) but until recently few studies addressed the detailed involvement of working memory in syllogistic reasoning.

Experimental Manipulations, Dual Tasks, and Training. Gilhooly, Logie, Wetherick, and Wynn (1993) reported two experiments on the role of working memory in syllogistic reasoning using abstract materials. In the first,

working memory load was varied by presenting syllogisms either verbally (causing a high memory load) or visually (so that the premises were
continuously available for inspection and memory load was low). Memory load significantly impaired accuracy of categorical syllogistic performance. In the second experiment, both premises were simultaneously presented visually for a participant determined time. Dual task methods were
used to assess the role of working memory components. Syllogistic performance was disrupted by concurrent random number generation but
not by concurrent articulatory suppression or by concurrent tapping in a
preset pattern. The syllogism task interfered with random generation and
with articulatory suppression but not with tapping. Overall, the results
indicated that the central executive played a major role in syllogistic task
performance, the phonological loop had a lesser role and the visuo-spatial
sketch pad was not involved.

Gilhooly et al. (1993) identified alternative strategies employed in the
categorical syllogism task. These were:

1. The atmosphere strategy (Woodworth & Sells, 1935) according to
   which if one or both premises are negative a negative conclusion is
   given (else a positive conclusion); and if one or both premises are
   particular, a particular conclusion is given, otherwise a universal
   conclusion.
2. The matching strategy (Wetherick & Gilhooly, 1995) according to
   which the conclusion is a proposition of the same logical form as
   the more conservative of the premises, where the logical forms are
   ordered for conservatism, from most to least, "no," "some not,"
   "some," and "all."
3. Logic equivalent strategies – these were not specified in detail but
   lead to logically correct answers to most categorical syllogisms.
4. Guessing – in which participants simply guess among the five alternatives presented on each trial.

The categorical syllogisms used allowed the identification of atmosphere, matching, and logic equivalent strategies from the patterns of responses. Participants were classified on the basis of which strategy best
fitted their response patterns. Response patterns that did not fit the main
strategies and led to low correct rates were classed as guessing patterns.
In control, articulatory suppression and tapping conditions the matching
strategy predominated. No significant shifting of strategy frequency occurred with tapping or articulatory suppression. With random generation
there was a marked increase in the incidence of guessing. However, even
in the high-load situation of the random generation dual task average accuracy (8.56) was significantly above chance levels (4.00). Thus, it would
appear that high secondary loads can bring about changes in strategy,

typically from matching or atmosphere to guessing, to avoid overloading working memory. These results complement those of Klauer et al. (1997) who found that changing strategy (increasing strategy load) affected the impact of a fixed secondary load (tapping).

Gilhooly, Logie, and Wynn (in press) used sequential premise presentation as against the simultaneous premise presentation of our previous study (Gilhooly et al., 1993). Sequential presentation would involve a greater memory load, and so it was expected that the slave systems would show a greater involvement in these circumstances as those systems would be recruited to maintain relevant information not available from external displays. We found no effect from concurrent tapping on accuracy or latencies in the reasoning task with sequential presentation, but there were impairments of average tapping speed and of consistency of tapping rate in the dual condition. These results suggest a difficulty in performing both syllogistic reasoning and tapping simultaneously with sequential premise presentation and therefore some involvement of the visuo-spatial sketch pad in the categorical syllogism task even with abstract materials. The articulatory suppression conditions showed impairment of both syllogistic accuracy and speed of conclusion reporting and also slowing down and greater variation in articulation rates in the dual condition. These results support the conclusion that the phonological loop is heavily involved in categorical syllogistic reasoning in this study. Random generation rate was significantly slower and more variable in the dual condition, and there was also a highly significant impairment of reasoning task performance and a deterioration in randomness of generation as measured by the Evans (1978) RNG (random number generation) index.

A plausible explanation for the mutual interference between syllogisms and random generation is the high loading that the dual condition places on the central executive because of the requirement to continuously generate and select responses at the same time as processing the different elements of the syllogistic problem. The load on memory is heavy with participants having to maintain randomness of numbers by remembering those already generated and at the same time having to keep the syllogistic statements and the subject of the argument in memory, in order to reach a conclusion. In terms of strategies, the atmosphere strategy was most prevalent in control and dual tasks, which loaded the slave memory systems. However, random generation, as in our earlier simultaneous premise presentation study, produced a significant increase in the percentage of participants classed as guessing to 56% versus 15% in control conditions. It may be noted, however, that average accuracy, even in random generation (7.44), was significantly above chance levels (4.00). As in the simultaneous premise presentation study, varying load produced a shift in preferred strategy. Let us now discuss the effect of sequential as against simultaneous presentation of the premises in terms of working memory loading.

With simultaneous display of the syllogistic argument premises throughout the premise processing period, as in Gilhooly et al. (1993), there is a relatively light load on working memory components with participants able to use the display to *refresh* their memory of the different elements of the problem while attempting to draw a conclusion. *Sequential* premise presentation ensures a heavier load on the slave memories, and this leads to mutual interference between reasoning and articulatory suppression and interference from reasoning to tapping. However, a major portion of central executive capacity would be taken up by the random generation task, and the mutual impairment of syllogistic reasoning and random generation in the sequential presentation study corresponds to the finding in our previous simultaneous presentation study. The results of these experiments (Gilhooly et al., 1993, in press) support the view that there is a major involvement of the central executive in syllogistic reasoning tasks, whether presentation of the premises is simultaneous or sequential. When sequential presentations are used, dual task methods indicate a clear involvement of the phonological loop and some involvement of the visuo-spatial sketch pad. The slave components of working memory, especially the visuo-spatial sketch pad, are less involved, if at all, when simultaneous premise presentation is used.

Part of the motivation for our syllogism studies was to help elucidate the exact roles played by working memory subsystems in syllogistic reasoning. It may be argued that these roles will depend (a) on the task environment (e.g., sequential vs. simultaneous premise presentation) and (b) on the strategies adopted by participants (e.g., guessing, matching, atmosphere, or a more logical strategy). If the task environment only provides limited external memory support (as with sequential premise presentation) then there would tend to be greater use of the slave memories.

The studies of categorical syllogistic reasoning outlined so far used unselected, untrained participants who varied widely in the strategies they adopted. Gilhooly et al. (1999) reported two experiments aimed at investigating groups that were relatively homogeneous in strategy use. In one of the studies participants were preselected as low or high skill and in the other initially low skill participants were trained to follow a systematic procedure for solving categorical syllogisms. In both cases, patterns of interference from secondary tasks were obtained.

In the first study, participants were preselected into groups of high and low skill at categorical syllogisms on the basis of a paper and pencil pretest. The high and low skill participants did not overlap in their scores on the pretest. Six separate high and low skill groups were formed and completed syllogistic tasks in control conditions and under one of the following six dual task conditions: articulatory suppression, unattended speech (to load the phonological store but not the loop), verbal random generation, spatial random generation, simple pattern tapping and unattended pictures (to load the passive visual store or visual cache but not the inner scribe). The results indicated that the more skilled participants were generally following a relatively high demand strategy (modally, atmosphere strategy) that loaded the central executive, phonological loop, and passive visual store sub systems, but that lower skill participants were generally following a less demanding strategy (modally, matching) that did not load working memory so heavily.

In the second study by Gilhooly et al. (1999), participants were selected on the basis of a screening test as being of low skill at categorical syllogisms but performing above guessing level. These participants underwent a training program that stressed use of set relationships and reordering of premises to ease inference. This training scheme had been validated by pilot studies as transferring to new problems and having lasting effects. Following such training, separate groups of trained participants carried out syllogistic tasks with and without one of the following four secondary tasks (which had shown interference with the skilled group in the first study): articulatory suppression, unattended pictures, spatial random generation, and verbal random generation. The results indicated that training had induced high-demand strategies (modally, logic-equivalent) that loaded the central executive and to a lesser extent the phonological loop and visuo-spatial sketch pad.

Overall, it seems clear that the three groups of participants in the present studies (trained, high skill and low skill) typically followed rather different strategies and that these strategy differences were associated with different patterns of working memory loading. The low-skill participants' modal matching strategy mainly loaded the central executive, with little load on the slave subsystems; the high skill participants' modal atmosphere strategy loaded the central executive, phonological loop, and passive visual store or cache and the trained participants' modal logic-equivalent strategy loaded the central executive, phonological loop, and spatial subsystems.

Turning to linear syllogisms, Vandierendonck and DeVooght (1997) investigated the role of working memory components in linear series problems with spatial and temporal materials. An example spatial problem would be:

The umbrella is left of the hat; the hat is left of the jacket; is the umbrella left of the jacket?

An example temporal problem would be:

Stan went to Paris before he went to London; Alfred went to Brussels before Stan went to Paris; did Alfred go to Brussels before Stan went to London?

In the first experiment, four groups of participants attempted four-term linear series problems with temporal and with spatial contents, either with or without a secondary task (viz., articulatory suppression, visuo-spatial suppression, or central executive suppression). The second experiment varied whether participants self-paced presentation of premises or not and also examined the impact of dual tasks as in the first study. Both studies found effects of all secondary tasks on accuracy of linear syllogistic reasoning with both spatial and temporal contents. A similar result was also reported by Klauer et al. (1997), using spatial linear syllogisms but with somewhat different secondary tasks. This suggests that spatial representations are used in both spatial and temporal series problems as was advocated by the spatial array model of linear reasoning (Huttenlocher, 1968) and by more recent mental model approaches. The articulatory suppression condition did not affect time to process the premises but did affect accuracy in the second study. Visuo-spatial and central executive suppression both affected premise processing time as well as accuracy. It is argued that the premise representation processes in particular involve the visuo-spatial sketch pad and the central executive while the phonological loop is probably involved at the stage of generating and reporting the conclusion.

Knauff, Jola, and Strube (2001) sought to distinguish between the possible involvement of the visual and the spatial subcomponents of the visuo-spatial sketch pad in spatial three-term series problems. Participants tackled such problems with and without secondary tasks which were either spatial or nonspatial and either visual or nonvisual (auditory). The spatial visual task required participants to report the direction of movement of a square shape across a screen; the spatial auditory task required a report of whether a tone heard over headphones was moving to the left or right. The nonspatial visual task required a report of whether a square on a screen became darker or lighter; the nonspatial auditory task required a report of whether a tone had become louder or softer. The reasoning tasks were presented visually. It was found that the spatial secondary tasks interfered more with the spatial reasoning task than did the nonspatial secondary tasks; that is, reasoning was disrupted by the spatial auditory task (and the spatial visual task) but not by the nonspatial visual task (or by the nonspatial auditory task). The authors conclude that these results support a mental models interpretation of spatial linear syllogisms since mental models are assumed to be spatial in character.

Knauff and Johnson-Laird (in press) point out that there have been somewhat mixed results from studies of the role of imagery in reasoning in general. Clement and Falmagne (1986) and Shaver, Pierson, and Lang (1974) found facilitating effects of imagery in reasoning tasks. However, Johnson-Laird, Byrne, and Tabossi (1989), Richardson (1987), and Sternberg (1980) found no benefit of imagability of materials on reasoning. Knauff and Johnson–Laird suggested that there may have been a confounding of ease of spatial representation with ease of visual imagery representation. According to the mental models approach, ease of spatial representation should be the effective factor. Rating studies showed that relations used in linear series reasoning problems could be separated into four types: *visuo-spatial*, which are easy to represent both visually and spatially ("above-below"), *visual*, which are easy to represent visually but not spatially ("cleaner-dirtier"), *spatial*, which are easy to represent spatially but not visually ("ancestor of–descendant of"), and *control*, which were hard to represent both visually and spatially ("better-worse"). Over a series of experiments it was found that visual relations slowed down reasoning whereas visuo-spatial and spatial relations were generally facilitating. The results support the authors' *visual–imagery impedance hypothesis*, which states that relations that evoke visual images including details irrelevant to the inference will impede effective reasoning. The results are also taken as being in support of the mental models approach, which emphasizes the role of spatial representations as against imagery. It is noteworthy that the results can also be related to recent views (Andrade, 2001; Logie, 1995; Pearson, De Beni, & Cornoldi, 2001) concerning imagery within the framework of the Baddeley and Hitch (1974) multicomponent model of working memory. Logie (1995) and Pearson et al. (2001) have pointed to an important role of central executive processes in image generation, maintenance, and manipulation as indicated by patterns of interference from various dual tasks on imagery. Also, Andrade (2001, pp. 68–69.) reports some as yet unpublished work, which indicates that carrying out AB reasoning as a secondary task impairs vividness of imagery when imaging is the primary task. So, if imagery and reasoning both load the central executive, as seems to be the case, invoking visual imagery as part of the reasoning process is likely to be counter-productive. On this point, the multicomponent working memory approach and the mental models approach have an interesting convergence.

The role of spatial processing in reasoning was also supported by a brain imaging study of spatial-relational reasoning and of conditional reasoning with nonspatial contents by Knauff, Mulack, Kassubek, Salih, and Greenlee (in press). They found that both types of reasoning activated areas of the brain associated with spatial perception as against parts of the brain associated with visual imagery. The results regarding the conditional reasoning tasks are particularly interesting in that the materials were not spatial in nature. Areas of the brain associated with executive functioning were also activated by both tasks but areas associated with verbal processing were not. The results are again taken to support the mental models approach.

Individual Difference Studies. Aging has been found to differentially affect measures of central executive functioning, such as sentence span and random generation, as against measures of slave system capacities (digit span, visual pattern span, e.g., Fisk & Warr, 1996; Van der Linden, Bregart, & Beerton, 1994.) Given the strong evidence from dual task studies for central executive involvement in syllogistic reasoning, it would be expected that aging would lead to poorer syllogistic reasoning performance and that a significant part of that deficit could be attributed to declines in central executive capacity. Gilinsky and Judd (1994) assessed 278 adults ranging in age from 19 to 96 years on three verbal measures of working memory span, namely, Baddeley and Hitch's (1974) Auditory Digit Span, Daneman and Carpenter's (1980) Reading Span and Salthouse's (1991) Computation Span. The separate measures were combined into a composite score of working memory capacity. The participants were also tested on a range of syllogistic reasoning tasks and showed a fairly steady decline in accuracy of syllogistic reasoning after about 40 years of age. Hierarchical regression analyses indicated that variance in the composite working memory measure, presumed to tap central executive capacity, explained a significant portion of the age differences in syllogistic reasoning. This is consistent with findings from the dual task studies reviewed previously, which have consistently implicated central executive functioning in syllogistic reasoning.

Quayle and Ball (2000) examined the role of working memory in the *belief bias* effect in categorical syllogisms. Belief bias occurs when responses are given on the basis of a conclusion's believability rather than its validity. The effects of believability are stronger on invalid than on valid syllogisms. Quayle and Ball proposed that people fall back on a "belief heuristic" when the processing demands of syllogisms exceed working memory capacities. So, low working memory capacity individuals should show more belief bias than high working memory capacity individuals as their limits will be more often exceeded. Participants were assessed on a spatial span recall test based on the Corsi block test (De Renzi & Nichelli, 1975; Smyth & Scholey, 1996) to give a measure of visuo-spatial sketch pad capacity. They were also tested on an articulatory span recall test based on the memory span test of Halford et al. (1984) to provide a measure of phonological loop capacity. The categorical syllogistic reasoning task involved valid and invalid syllogisms, which were in turn split into those with believable and unbelievable conclusions. Lower visuo-spatial working memory scores were associated with more belief bias; the relationship between verbal span scores and belief bias was similar in direction to that of the spatial span scores, but not significant. These results do suggest a role for the visuo-spatial sketch pad in categorical syllogistic tasks with unselected participants and concrete materials. However, the results are somewhat ambiguous in that the Corsi test is not a pure measure of visuo-spatial storage capacity in that it also appears to draw on central executive resources (Phillips & Hamilton, 2001). Capon, Handley, and Dennis (2000) reported studies of individual differences in categorical syllogisms as a function of short term-span and working memory span tests of a visuo-spatial and a verbal character. Performance on categorical syllogisms, presented both verbally and in written form, using concrete materials was correlated with all the span measures, both the simple measures reflecting passive memory and the more complex working memory span measures. This suggests that the participants were using strategies that drew on both verbal and visuo-spatial resources for both modes of presentation of categorical syllogisms. In contrast, performance on five-term series spatial reasoning tasks was better predicted by visual span measures when presentation was written, but was equally predicted by all span measures when presentation was verbal, that is, sequential.

WORKING MEMORY AND STRATEGIES IN REASONING: OVERVIEW AND FUTURE DIRECTIONS

Overview

The early dual task studies of propositional reasoning (Evans & Brooks, 1981; Toms et al., 1993) had certain methodological limitations and their "null" results for involvement of all components (Evans & Brooks, 1981) and of the phonological loop and visuo-spatial sketch pad (Toms et al., 1993) cannot be taken at face value. Later studies overcame the problems in interpretation caused by having dual tasks of insufficient difficulty and not taking account of possible trade-offs. All approaches would agree that central executive involvement is to be expected in reasoning tasks (with the possible exception of highly practiced tasks which may become automated or tasks which invoke implicit processes for other reasons). However, of the five experiments reviewed above that have examined the role of the central executive in propositional reasoning (Klauer, et al., 1997; Meiser et al., 2001; Toms et al., 1993) all report positive findings. This is what would be expected given that the tasks are unpracticed and quite complex.

The considerable interest in the mental models approach led to most studies addressing the possible role of the visuo-spatial sketch pad since mental models are generally assumed to be spatially represented and so would suggest a strong role for the visuo-spatial sketch pad. Of the seven experiments (from Duyck et al., 2001; Klauer et al., 1997; Meiser et al., 2001) reviewed earlier in this chapter that addressed the possible role of the visuo-spatial sketch pad in propositional reasoning through dual task methods, six report positive findings. These include tasks with abstract materials as well as concrete, and with participants trained in strategies and untrained. Although involvement of the visuo-spatial sketch pad has been taken as a critical indicator of a mental models approach being followed, it should be noted that Meiser et al. (2001) did not find that participants trained in a mental models approach were affected any more severely by spatial suppression than others trained in a mental rules or pragmatic schema approach. So, the inference from visuo-spatial sketch pad involvement to mental models approach is not a certain one.

Four of the experiments addressed the role of the phonological loop in conditional reasoning using dual tasks (Klauer et al., 1997; Meiser et al., 2001). Of these, two positive results were reported for untrained participants and for participants trained in a mental models approach (Klauer, et al., 1997; Meiser et al., 2001). The negative results arose from participants trained in mental logic and pragmatic reasoning schemas (Meiser et al., 2001). It appears that training in mental models produces a high load strategy that draws on all components of working memory.

The Barrouillet and Lecas (1999) study of individual differences found a relationship between the complexity of representation of conditionals and counting span, suggesting an involvement of the central executive and perhaps the phonological loop. Further studies to clarify whether one or both components are involved and whether the visuo-spatial sketch pad is involved would be of interest. Markovits et al. (in press) found correlations with verbal working memory span scores and propositional reasoning with both concrete and abstract items, suggesting use of verbal strategies drawing on the central executive and phonological loop. Concrete items showed correlations also with a visual span measure which could be interpreted as tapping the passive visual cache. This suggests that concrete materials elicit a strategy that draws on the visuo-spatial sketch pad in at least some participants.

In the area of categorical syllogisms, of the five experiments reviewed above, which addressed the role of the central executive through dual tasks (Gilhooly et al., 1993, 1999, in press), all reported positive findings as expected. Of the five experiments (all using abstract terms) that addressed the role of the visuo-spatial sketch pad (Gilhooly et al., 1993, 1999, in press), three reported positive results, which is perhaps not a completely comfortable result for the mental models approach. The two cases with negative results involved participants classified as following the relatively undemanding "matching" strategy (Gilhooly et al., 1993, 1999). In two experiments, the dual tasks were such that more specifically, the visual cache subcomponent was implicated in participants following an atmosphere strategy, while the inner scribe was implicated for participants following a logic-equivalent strategy after training. The phonological loop was implicated in four out of the five studies reviewed that addressed the issue through dual task methods (Gilhooly et al., 1993, 1999, in press).

In the case of linear syllogisms, of the three dual task studies that have addressed the question of central executive involvement using dual task methods (Klauer et al., 1997; Vandierendonck & De Vooght, 1997) all report positive results. It seems that over all areas of reasoning, central executive involvement is invariable. Of the five studies that have addressed the role of the visuo-spatial sketch pad using dual tasks (Klauer et al., 1997; Meiser et al., 2001), again all report positively and this was found with temporal as well as spatial relations. Knauff et al. (2001) found specific evidence for the involvement of the spatial subcomponent of the visuo-spatial sketch pad in spatial three-term series problems. These results are encouraging for the mental models and other spatial array approaches to linear syllogisms. Brain activation studies (Knauff et al., in press) also support the role of visuo-spatial and central executive processes in linear syllogisms (and in conditional reasoning with nonspatial materials). Of the three studies that have addressed the role of the phonological loop in linear syllogisms through dual tasks (Klauer et al., 1997; Vandierendonck & De Vooght, 1997), all report positive results. (However, the brain activation study by Knauff et al., in press, did not find activation in verbal areas.) Knauff and Johnson-Laird (in press) indicate that spatial relations are particularly helpful for linear reasoning as mental model theory would suggest. The interfering effects of imagery in reasoning can be linked also to the working memory model theory (Logie, 1995), which suggests that imagery requires central executive involvement and so could compete with the central executive requirements of reasoning if one tries to reason with images.

In an individual differences study, Gilinsky and Judd (1994) found that aging impaired categorical syllogistic reasoning. This result could be attributed to a decline in central executive functioning, which is consistent with the invariable finding in dual task studies of central executive involvement in reasoning. Quayle and Ball (2000) found a positive correlation between a measure of visuo-spatial span (Corsi) and resistance to belief bias, but since the Corsi is generally seen as also drawing on the central executive the result is ambiguous. Capon et al. (2000) found that performance on categorical syllogisms, presented both verbally and in written form, using concrete materials was positively correlated with visual and verbal working memory span measures. This suggests that strategies drawing on verbal and visuo-spatial resources were used for both modes of presentation of categorical syllogisms. Performance on five-term series spatial reasoning tasks was only predicted by visual span measures when presentation was written, suggesting use of a visuo-spatial approach. (Which is consistent with the general finding from dual task studies of visuo-spatial sketch pad involvement in such series tasks). However, performance on the same task was equally predicted by all span measures when presentation was verbal, that is, sequential. It may be that sequential presentation posed sufficient memory load to engage all the slave systems.

To sum up research to date, the studies reviewed here are consistent with a general interpretation of reasoning tasks as involving a range of strategies, which cause a variety of loading patterns on working memory. Central executive loading seems to be invariable in the strategies induced by reasoning tasks. The types of strategies induced (i.e., drawing on verbal or visuo-spatial resources) are affected by the task material (abstract or spatial). The way in which the premises are presented (in sequence or simultaneously) affects the degree of use of the "slave" or "cache" memories.

Future Directions

Research so far on the role of working memory in reasoning tasks might be characterized as "first generation" research that has established the broad picture that the central executive and, to varying degrees, the phonological loop and visuo-spatial sketch pad are involved in reasoning. Degree of involvement of the "slave" systems depends on the kind of reasoning task, how information is made available, and individual difference factors. This research is undoubtedly informative but inevitably there are limitations that will stimulate further waves of research.

One limitation is that current methods indicate only that certain working-memory components were involved at some point during the task concerned. It would be useful if ways could be devised to identify when different components are loaded as the task is worked through.

A further limitation is that, at present, there is no agreed way of assessing the degree of loading of the different components. Reports of significant disruption by a dual task of the primary task or vice versa, could reflect small effects with a large sample. Possibly, effect sizes could be obtained and reported routinely. A related difficulty is that multiple measures of primary and secondary task performance are often available (e.g., for random generation we can have mean latencies, variability of latencies, and a range of possible measures of randomness) and it is unclear how they might be best combined into an overall measure of performance. In practice, the various measures are often reported separately and not combined.

More precisely targeted dual tasks would be useful, for example, to enable researchers to go beyond simply finding that the central executive is involved, to identify which particular executive functions, such as "task-switching," "updating," and "inhibition," (Miyake, Friedman, Emerson, Witzki, & Howerter, 2000) are involved.

The strategies that draw on working memory resources have often been specified in a very general way, for example, as "verbal" or "spatial." More complete specifications of the information processing steps would help tie in the execution of strategies to moment by moment loadings of the working memory components. Even when a proposed strategy is well specified in terms of what outputs would arise from the possible inputs, questions of implementation remain. For example, the "atmosphere" strategy is stated in a way that makes clear what is computed in response to each input. However, a person could reproduce the predicted atmosphere pattern of responses through different implementations of the atmosphere strategy, for example, by direct retrieval of stored responses to each combination of quantifiers or by sequentially determining whether the answer is affirmative or negative and whether particular or universal. Different implementations would have different implications for working memory loading. Finally, a fuller specification of strategies and their proposed implementations would be a useful goal for future research in this area.

References

Andrade, J. (2001). The contribution of working memory to conscious experience. In J.Andrade (Ed.), *Working memory in perspective*. Hove, UK: Psychology Press.

Baddeley, A. D. (1968). A three-minute reasoning test based on grammatical transformation. *Psychonomic Science, 10*, 341–342.

Baddeley, A. D. (1992) Is working memory working? *Quarterly Journal of Experimental Psychology, 44A*, 1–32.

Baddeley, A. D. (2000). The episodic buffer: a new component of working memory? *Trends in Cognitive Sciences, 4*, 417–423.

Baddeley, A. D., & Hitch, G. J. (1974) Working memory. In G. Bower (Ed.), *Recent advances in learning and motivation: Vol. VIII*. New York: Academic Press.

Baddeley, A. D., & Logie, R. H. (1999). Working memory: the multiple component model. In A. Miyake & P. Shah (Eds.), *Models of working memory: mechanisms of active maintenance and executive control*. Cambridge: Cambridge University Press.

Baddeley, A. D., Logie, R. H., Nimmo-Smith, I., & Brereton, N. (1985). Components of fluent reading. *Journal of Memory and Language, 24*, 119–131.

Barrouillet, P., & Lecas, J-F. (1998). How can mental models account for content effects in conditional reasoning: A developmental perspective. *Cognition, 67*, 209–253.

Barrouillet, P., & Lecas, J-F. (1999). Mental models in conditional reasoning and working memory. *Thinking and Reasoning, 5*, 289–302

Begg, I., & Denny, J. P. (1969). Empirical reconciliation of atmosphere and conversion interpretations of syllogistic reasoning errors. *Journal of Experimental Psychology, 81*, 351–354.

Braine, M. D. S. (1978). On the relation between the natural logic of reasoning and standard logic. *Psychological Review, 85*, 1–21.

Braine, M. D. S., & O'Brien, D. P. (1998). *Mental logic*. Mahwah, NJ: Erlbaum.

Braine, M. D. S., Reiser, B. J., & Rumain, B. (1984). Some empirical justification for a theory of natural propositional logic. In G. Bower (Ed.), *The psychology of learning and motivation: Advances in theory and research: Vol 18*. NY: Academic Press.

Capon, A., Handley, S., & Dennis, I. (2000, September). *Working memory and individual differences in reasoning*. Paper presented at 4th International Conference on Thinking, Durham, NC.

Clement, C. A., & Falmagne, R. J. (1986). Logical reasoning, world knowledge, and mental imagery: Interconnections in cognitive processes. *Memory and Cognition, 4*, 299–307.

Daneman, M., & Carpenter, P. A. (1980). Individual differences in working memory and reading. *Journal of Verbal Learning and Verbal Behavior, 19*, 450–466.

Daneman, M., & Carpenter, P. A. (1983). Individual differences in integrating information between and within sentences. *Journal of Experimental Psychology: Learning, Memory and Cognition, 9*, 561–584.

Della Sala, S., & Logie, R. H. (1993). When working memory does not work: The role of working memory in neuropsychology. In F. Boller & H. Spinnler (Eds.), *Handbook of neuropsychology: Vol. 8*. Amsterdam: Elsevier.

De Renzi, E., & Nichelli, P. (1975). Verbal and non-verbal short-term memory impairment following hemispheric damage. *Cortex, 11*, 341–354.

Duyck, W., Vandierendonck, A., & De Vooght, G. (2001, September). *Conditional rea-soning with a spatial content requires visuo-spatial working memory.* Paper presented at European Society for Cognitive Psychology Conference, Edinburgh.

Erickson, J. R. (1978). Research in syllogistic reasoning. In R. Revlin & R. E. Meyer (Eds.), *Human reasoning.* Washington, DC: Winston.

Evans, F. J. (1978). Monitoring attention deployment by random number gener-ation: An index to measure subjective randomness. *Bulletin of the Psychonomic Society, 12,* 35–38.

Evans, J. St. B. T., & Brooks, P. G. (1981). Competing with reasoning: A test of the working memory hypothesis. *Current Psychological Research, 1,* 139–147.

Evans, J. St. B. T., Newstead, S. E., & Byrne, R. (1993). *Human reasoning: The psychology of deduction.* Hove, UK: Erlbaum.

Evans, J. St. B. T., & Over, D. (1996). *Rationality and reasoning.* Hove, UK: Psychology Press.

Farmer, E. W., Berman, J. V. F., & Fletcher, Y. L. (1986). Evidence for a visuo-spatial scratch-pad in working memory. *Quarterly Journal of Experimental Psychology, 38A,* 675–688.

Fisher, D. L. (1981). A three-factor model of syllogistic reasoning: The study of isolable stages. *Memory and Cognition, 9,* 496–514.

Fisk, J. E., & Warr, P. (1996). Age and working memory: The role of perceptual speed, the central executive, and the phonological loop. *Psychology and Aging, 11,* 316–323.

Ford, M. (1995). Two modes of mental representation and problem solution in syllogistic reasoning. *Cognition, 54,* 1–71

Gilhooly, K. J., Logie, R. H., Wetherick, N. E., & Wynn, V. (1993). Working mem-ory and strategies in syllogistic reasoning tasks. *Memory and Cognition, 21,* 115–124.

Gilhooly, K. J., Logie, R. H., & Wynn, V. (1999). Syllogistic reasoning tasks, working memory and skill. *European Journal of Cognitive Psychology, 11,* 473–498.

Gilhooly, K. J., Logie, R. H., & Wynn, V. (in press). Syllogistic reasoning tasks and working memory: evidence from sequential presentation of premises. *Current Psychological Research.*

Gilinsky, A. S., & Judd, B. B. (1994). Working memory and bias in reasoning across the life span. *Psychology and Aging, 9,* 356–371.

Griggs, R. A., & Cox, J. R. (1982). The elusive thematic-materials effect in Wason's selection task. *British Journal of Psychology, 73,* 407–420.

Halford, G. S., Bain, J. D., & Maybery, M. T. (1984). Does a concurrent memory load interfere with reasoning? *Current Psychological Research and Reviews, 3,* 14–23.

Hammerton, M. (1969). Interference between low information verbal output and a cognitive task. *Nature, 222,* 196.

Hitch, G. J., and Baddeley, A. D. (1976). Verbal reasoning and working memory. *Quarterly Journal of Experimental Psychology, 28,* 603–621.

Huttenlocher, J. (1968). Constructing spatial images: a strategy in reasoning. *Psychological Review, 75,* 550–560.

Johnson-Laird, P. N. (1983). *Mental models.* Cambridge: Cambridge University Press.

Johnson-Laird, P. N., & Bara, B. (1984). Syllogistic inference. *Cognition, 16,* 1–62.

Johnson-Laird, P. N., & Byrne, R. (1991). *Deduction.* Hove, UK: Erlbaum.

Johnson-Laird, P. N., Byrne, R., & Tabossi, P. (1989). Reasoning by model: The case of multiple quantifiers. *Psychological Review, 96*, 658–673.

Just, M. A., & Carpenter, P. A. (1992). A capacity theory of comprehension: Individual differences in working memory. *Psychological Review, 99*, 122–149.

Klauer, K. C., Meiser, T., & Naumer, B. (2000). Training propositional reasoning. *Quarterly Journal of Experimental Psychology, 53A*, 868–895.

Klauer, K. C., Stegmaier, R., & Meiser, T. (1997) Working memory involvement in propositional and spatial reasoning. *Thinking and Reasoning, 3*, 9–48.

Knauff, M., & Johnson-Laird, P. N. (in press) Visual imagery can impair reasoning. *Memory and Cognition.*

Knauff, M., Jola, C., & Strube, G. (2001). Spatial reasoning: No need for visual information. In D. R. Montello (Ed.), *Spatial information theory*. New York: Springer.

Knauff, M., Mulack, T., Kassubek, J., Salih, H. R., & Greenlee, M. W. (in press). Spatial imagery in deductive reasoning: A functional MRI study. *Cognitive Brain Research.*

Logie, R. H. (1995) *Visuo-spatial working memory*. Hove, UK: Erlbaum.

Logie, R. H., Englekamp, J., Dehn, D., & Rudkin, S. (2001). Actions, mental actions, and working memory. In M. Denis, R. H. Logie, C. Cornoldi, M. De Vega, & J. Engelkamp (Eds.), *Imagery, language and visuo-spatial thinking*. Hove, UK: Psychology Press.

Markovits, H., Doyon, C., & Simoneau, M. (in press). Individual differences in working memory and conditional reasoning with concrete and abstract content. *Thinking and Reasoning.*

Meiser, T., Klauer, K. C., & Naumer, B. (2001). Propositional reasoning and working memory: The role of prior training and pragmatic content. *Acta Psychologica, 106*, 303–327.

Miyake, A., Friedman, N. P., Emerson, M. J., Witzki, A. H., & Howerter, A. (2000). The unity and diversity of executive functions and their contributions to complex "frontal lobe" tasks: A latent variable analysis. *Cognitive Psychology, 41*, 49–100.

Miyake, A., & Shah, P. (1999). Toward unified theories of working memory. In A. Miyake & P. Shah (Eds.), *Models of working memory: Mechanisms of active maintenance and executive control*. Cambridge: Cambridge University Press.

Oaksford, M., Morris, F., Grainger, B., & Williams, J. G. (1996). Mood, reasoning and central executive process. *Journal of Experimental Psychology: Learning, Memory and Cognition, 22*, 477–493.

Pearson, D., De Beni, R., & Cornoldi, C. (2001). The generation, maintenance, and transformation of visuo-spatial mental images. In M. Denis, R. H. Logie., C. Cornoldi, M. De Vega, & J. Engelkamp (Eds). *Imagery, language and visuo-spatial thinking*. Hove, UK: Psychology Press.

Phillips, L. H., & Hamilton, C. (2001). The working memory model in adult aging research. In J. Andrade (Ed.), *Working memory in perspective*. Hove, UK: Psychology Press.

Polk, T. A., & Newell, A. (1995). Deduction as verbal reasoning. *Psychological Review, 102*, 533–566.

Quayle, J. D., & Ball, L. J. (2000). Working memory, metacognitive uncertainty, and belief bias in syllogistic reasoning. *Quarterly Journal of Experimental Psychology, 53A*, 1202–1223.

Richardson, J. T. E. (1987). The role of mental imagery in in models of transitive inference. *British Journal of Psychology, 78*, 189–203.

Roberts, M. J. (2000). Individual differences in reasoning strategies: a problem to solve or an opportunity to seize? In, W. Schaeken, G. De Vooght, A. Vandierendonck, & G. D'Ydewalle (Eds.), *Deductive reasoning and strategies*. Mahwah, NJ: Erlbaum.

Roberts, M. J. (1993). Human reasoning: deduction rules or mental models, or both? *Quarterly Journal of Experimental Psychology, 46A*, 569–589.

Rips, L. J. (1994). *The psychology of proof: Deductive reasoning in human thinking.* Cambridge, MA: MIT Press.

Salthouse, T. A. (1991). *Status of working memory as a mediator of adult age differences in cognition.* Paper presented at the 99th Annual Convention of the American Psychological Association, San Francisco.

Seibert, P. S., & Ellis, H. C. (1991). Irrelevant thoughts, emotional mood states, and cognitive task performance. *Memory and Cognition, 19*, 507–513.

Shallice, T. (1982). Specific impairments of planning. *Philosophical Transactions of the Royal Society of London B, 298*, 199–209.

Shaver, P., Pierson, L., & Lang, S. (1974). Converging evidence for the functional significance of imagery in problem solving. *Cognition, 3*, 359–375.

Siegler, R. S., & Jenkins, E. A. (1989). *How children discover new strategies.* Hillsdale, NJ: Erlbaum.

Smyth, M. M., & Scholey, K. A. (1996). The relationship between articulation time and memory performance in verbal and visuo-spatial tasks. *British Journal of Psychology, 87*, 179–191.

Stenning, K., & Oberlander, J. (1995). A cognitive theory of graphical and linguistic reasoning: Logic and implementation. *Cognitive Science, 19*, 97–140.

Sternberg, R. J. (1980). Representation and process in linear syllogistic reasoning. *Journal of Experimental Psychology: General, 109*, 119–159.

Sternberg, R. J., & Turner, M. E. (1981). Components of syllogistic reasoning. *Acta Psychologica, 47*, 245–265.

Toms, M., Morris, N., & Ward, D. (1993). Working memory and conditional reasoning. *Quarterly Journal of Experimental Psychology, 46A*, 679–699.

Turner, M. L., & Engle, R. (1989). Is working memory capacity task dependent? *Journal of Memory and Language, 28*, 127–154.

Van der Linden, M., Bregart, S., & Beerton, A. (1994). Age related differences in updating working memory. *British Journal of Psychology, 84*, 145–152.

Vandierendonck, A., & De Vooght, G. (1997). Working memory constraints on linear reasoning with spatial and temporal contents. *Quarterly Journal of Experimental Psychology, 50A*, 803–820.

Watts, F. N., MacLeod, A. K., & Morris, L. (1988). Associations between phenomenal and objective aspects of concentration problems in depressed patients. *British Journal of Psychology, 79*, 241–250.

Wason, P. C. (1966). Reasoning. In B. M. Foss (Ed.), *New horizons in psychology*. Harmondsworth, UK: Penguin.

Wason, P. C. (1968). Reasoning about a rule. *Quarterly Journal of Experimental Psychology, 20*, 273–281.

Wetherick, N. E., & Gilhooly, K. J. (1995). "Atmosphere," matching and logic in syllogistic reasoning. *Current Psychology, 14,* 169–178.

Wilkins, M. C. (1928). The effect of changed material on the ability to do formal syllogistic reasoning. *Archives of Psychology,* No. 102, 83.

Woodworth, R. J., & Sells, S. B. (1935). An atmosphere effect in formal syllogistic reasoning. *Journal of Experimental Psychology, 18,* 451–460.

Yuill, N., Oakhill, J., & Parkin, A. J. (1988). Working memory, comprehension ability and the resolution of text anomaly. *British Journal of Psychology, 80,* 351–361.

4

The Role of Prior Belief in Reasoning

Jonathan St. B. T. Evans and Aidan Feeney

In this chapter we examine research that uses well-defined laboratory problems requiring hypothetical thinking and reasoning for their solution. By "well-defined" we mean that all information required to solve the problem according to the instructions is explicitly presented. For this reason, psychologists have traditionally regarded any influence of prior knowledge or belief about the problem content or context to be normatively irrelevant to the definition of a correct answer. Consequently, where such beliefs exert an influence this has often been termed a "bias" by the investigators concerned. The effects of prior belief, however, turn out to be so pervasive in these studies that reasoning researchers in the past decade or so have begun radically to reexamine their assumptions about the nature of rational reasoning.

This reassessment has been no where more visible than in the study of deductive reasoning, one of the major paradigms in this field. Typical experiments involve presenting participants with the premises of logical arguments and asking them to evaluate a conclusion presented, or draw one of their own (for reviews, see Evans, Newstead, & Byrne, 1993; Manktelow, 1999). The deduction paradigm has its origins in logicism – the belief that logic provides the rational basis for human reasoning (Evans, 2000a). The modern study of deductive reasoning dates from the 1960s, where it was motivated by the writings of psychologists such as Henle (1962) and especially Jean Piaget (Inhelder & Piaget, 1958), who proposed that adult human reasoning was inherently logical. It was therefore natural to test this idea by presenting people with problems of well-defined logical structure and comparing their answers to a formal solution. The paradigm was also motivated by those who disagreed with Piaget and wished to show that people were illogical and irrational in their reasoning, a school of thinking led by Peter Wason (see Wason, 1977; Wason & Johnson-Laird, 1972). At this time, there was little dispute that logic provided the appropriate *normative* framework for assessing the accuracy of human reasoning.

If human reasoning were based on logic, then it would be an entirely domain independent process. However, that is not to say that we would expect no influence of problem content or context. Logicist authors have argued (Henle, 1962; Smedslund, 1970) that there is an interpretative process in which the particular problem content must be translated into an underlying abstract form before logical processes can be applied. If participants in the experiment represent the premises of an argument in a different manner to that expected by the experimenter, then they may be classified as making errors even though the process of reasoning was logical. For example, someone given the statement "Some widget makers belong to a trade union" might draw the conclusion that "Some widget makers do not belong to a trade union." This could be classified as a logical fallacy because "some" does not exclude "all." However, pragmatically it is a violation of relevance in communication (Grice, 1975; Sperber & Wilson, 1995) to say less than you mean. Hence, it is perfectly reasonable for people to represent "some" as meaning "some but not all," as indeed they do (Newstead & Griggs, 1983). Given this personalized representation, the conclusion drawn is in fact logically sound.

Over the years, however, the role of knowledge and belief in deductive reasoning tasks has proved so influential that many researchers have abandoned logic as both a descriptive and a normative theory of human reasoning. The modern debate about normative rationality dates from the critical discussion of the philosopher Cohen (1982), who argued that participants may adopt alternative logics or normative frameworks to the standard normative systems rather naively applied by psychologists. Since then some psychologists in the field have attacked logic as a normative system for human reasoning (Evans & Over, 1996a; Oaksford & Chater, 1998) and have proposed alternative bases for personal rationality. There have been several proposals of nonlogical mechanisms of reasoning, especially in pragmatically rich contexts. For example, it has been suggested that people may reason using heuristics that help to maximize information gain (Chater & Oaksford, 1999; Oaksford & Chater, 1994), that people treat reasoning problems as decision-making tasks in which personal goals and utilities come into play (Evans & Over, 1996a; Kirby, 1994; Manktelow & Over, 1991; Over & Manktelow, 1993), that reasoning is governed by principles of pragmatic relevance (Sperber, Cara, & Girotto, 1995) and that people reason using domain-specific processes resulting from innate reasoning modules (Cosmides, 1989; Fiddick, Cosmides, & Tooby, 2000).

In the sections that follow, we examine the research on the influence of prior knowledge on deductive reasoning in which we consider some of the detailed arguments of the authors cited above. In particular, we will look at the influence of pragmatic factors in conditional reasoning and the Wason selection task, and at the so-called belief bias effect in syllogistic reasoning. We then examine the role of prior belief in other cognitive tasks, especially those involving the testing of hypotheses, the evaluation of evidence, and the revision of belief. In these literatures, we find widespread claims of a general "confirmation bias" in human reasoning, which leads people to seek evidence that will confirm rather than contradict their prior beliefs. We find arguments about the role of background beliefs and rationality that stand in parallel to the debate in the deduction literature. For example, the generally accepted normative solution to the pseudo-diagnosticity task (Doherty, Mynatt, Tweney, & Schiavo, 1979) has been questioned, with evidence that people introduce background beliefs in a rational and appropriate manner.

PRAGMATIC FACTORS IN CONDITIONAL REASONING

Conditional statements of the form "if p then q" have received very substantial attention from psychologists and philosophers alike. Psychologists have tended to assess the accuracy of conditional inference by the norms of material implication, treating "if p then q" as equivalent to "$p \supset q$," following the example of authors of basic logic textbooks. The material conditional interpretation of "if p then q" means that the statement is true in all situations except where we have p and *not-q*, making it equivalent to the statement "either *not p* or q." This leads to a variety of technical problems and paradoxes that has led the majority of contemporary philosophical logicians to abandon the material conditional as an account of the ordinary conditional of everyday discourse (Edgington, 1995). Both philosophical and psychological investigations into conditionals have revealed a very wide and rich range of usage of "if" in different contexts and for differing purposes.

The arguments surrounding the logic of ordinary conditionals particularly concern the problem of how to interpret such statements when p is not the case, or in logical jargon when the antecedent is false. However, all are agreed that the statement "if p then q" precludes the possibility of "p and *not q*." This is a sufficient basis to show that two inferences known as modus ponens (MP) and modus tollens (MT) are logically valid. We will illustrate these by use of an arbitrary conditional statement:

If there is a D on the left, then there is a 4 on the right.
Given that there is a D on the left, it follows that here is a 4 on the right (MP).
Given that there is not a 4 on the right, it follows that there is not a D on the left (MT).

These inferences follow because we cannot have a D with a number other than 4. The description of two inferences known as denial of the antecedent (DA) and affirmation of the consequent (AC) as fallacies, is a little more controversial. These are the following arguments:

Given that there is not a D on the left, it follows that there is not a 4 on the right (DA).
Given that there is a 4 on the right, it follows that there is a D on the left (AC).

A fallacy is an argument whose conclusion may be true, but does not have to be true given the premises. The standard argument is that DA and AC are fallacies because the rule only specifies that a D must have a 4 and not vice versa. The difficulty is that the ordinary conditional may take this biconditional meaning in many everyday contexts and so people may also adopt it as a reading of "if" in an arbitrary context. The distinction between the valid and fallacious conditional inferences is, however, sharply drawn in the theoretical tradition that attributes a rule-based mental logic to ordinary people (Braine & O'Brien, 1998). These theorists account for the valid inferences by the mechanism of their mental logic and the fallacies as "invited inferences" reflecting a separate pragmatic process. By contrast, the rival mental model theory of conditional reasoning (Johnson-Laird & Byrne, 1991; Johnson-Laird & Byrne, in press) accounts for all the conditional inferences by the same reasoning mechanism. A person with a biconditional reading would simply represent the possibilities of the conditional by a different set of mental models, resulting in different inferences.

Experimental studies of abstract conditional reasoning usually show very high rates (near 100%) endorsement of MP, but substantially lower rates of MT (typically 60%–70%). Studies of this kind commonly find quite high rates of DA and AC inference as well, although this is fairly variable across studies (see Evans et al., 1993, chap. 2; Evans, Clibbens, & Rood, 1995). Once thematic content and context is introduced, however, these inference rates can change dramatically. For example, the normally universal modus ponens can be suppressed in certain contexts, as first shown by Byrne (1989, 1991). Given the statements:

If Ruth has an essay deadline to meet, she will work late in the library.
Ruth has an essay deadline to meet.

people will make the obvious MP inference that Ruth works late in the library. However, adding an additional premise reduces significantly the frequency with which this inference is drawn:

If Ruth has an essay deadline to meet, she will work late in the library.
If the library stays open, Ruth will work late in the library.
Ruth has an essay deadline to meet.

The extra premise suggests a disabling condition that may prevent p leading to q in the original conditional. Subsequent research has shown that people appear to reason probabilistically, reducing their rating of the likelihood of the conclusion when such a second premise is introduced (Stevenson & Over, 1995). It also shows that ordinary reasoning is *defeasible* (see Oaksford & Chater, 1991), meaning that an inference may be withdrawn in the light of new information. Neither probabilistic nor defeasible reasoning is permitted in the textbook standard propositional logic that psychologists have tended to adopt as their normative reference. One interpretation of the phenomenon is that the additional premise undermines belief in the original conditional (Politzer & Braine, 1991) and there is independent evidence that people are reluctant to draw conclusions from premises that they do not believe (Thompson, 2001). People are also adept at adjusting their probability estimate of a conclusion in the light of explicit information about the likelihood of the premises (George, 1997, 1999).

There are studies showing a range of content and context effects that can both suppress or facilitate the four kinds of conditional inference. These influences can arise from additional premises, from contextual information or from inherent beliefs about the terms in the conditional premises present, such as the sufficiency and necessity relationships between the events described as p and q (Cummins, Lubart, Alksnis, & Rist, 1991; Markovits, 1986; Thompson, 1994; Thompson, 2000; Thompson & Mann, 1995). People seem to respond to all manner of pragmatic factors, including their beliefs about the intentions and capabilities of the speaker of the conditional statement. For example, Newstead, Ellis, Evans, and Dennis (1997) investigated conditional reasoning in a variety of contexts where the conditional premises were provided as quoted speech attributed to an individual in a small scenario. One of the findings in this study was that all four conditional inferences were endorsed more frequently for promises and threats than for tips and warnings. To illustrate these types of conditionals, consider the following examples:

PROMISE (Father to son). If you pass the exam, I will buy you a new bicycle.
TIP (Friend to friend). If you pass the exam, your father will buy you a new bicycle.
THREAT (Boss to employee). If you are late for work again, I will fire you.
WARNING (Colleague to colleague). If you are late for work again, the boss will fire you.

Newstead et al. (1997) speculated that promises are stronger than tips, and threats are stronger than warnings because the speaker is perceived to have control over the consequent event, an hypothesis confirmed in a subsequent study where the two factors were separated (Evans & Twyman-Musgrove, 1998). These types of conditional are particularly interesting since they are uttered not so much to convey information, but more as an attempt to control the behavior of the listener. It can be argued that to talk of logical errors or fallacies in the case of such conditionals is inappropriate.

On this view, what is personally rational is to be responsive to all the subtle pragmatics conveyed by "if" in the wide range of applications that it has in everyday language.

This brief survey of research on conditional inference well illustrates the role of belief in human reasoning. Whatever the instructions, participants in reasoning experiments do not seem to accept the task as one of deductive reasoning, but rather to reason probabilistically, taking into account all relevant and present pragmatic cues. The main division of opinion among authors seems to lie in the assessment of the rationality of such reasoning. One view is that it is rational and appropriate for people to be influenced by their beliefs in this way, as it would help them to achieve their ordinary personal goals (e.g., Evans & Over, 1996a, 1996b). On the other hand, the pervasive tendency to contextualize all problems has been described as a "fundamental computational bias" by Stanovich (1999), which may interfere with the need for more abstract reasoning in a modern technological society. Stanovich has shown in a variety of studies that the ability to decontextualize and find normative solutions is associated with individuals of high general intelligence.

THE WASON SELECTION TASK

Wason (1966) reported a problem that was to become a major paradigm in the psychology of reasoning. Participants were told that a set of cards each had a capital letter on one side and a single digit number on the other side. They were told that the following rule applied to the cards:

If there is a vowel on one side of the card, then there is an even number on the other side of the card.

They were then shown four cards whose upper faces exposed the characters:

A   D   2   7

The task was to choose those cards and only those cards that needed to be turned over in order to decide whether the rule was true or false.

Wason argued that the logically correct choice was the A and 7. This was based on the argument that people should seek to falsify the rule, and this could only be achieved by finding a card that had a vowel on one side and did *not* have an even number on the other. In general terms for a rule of the form "if p then q," the correct choice is the p card and the *not-q* card. However, most participants did not make this choice (typically around 10% in studies of the abstract selection task). The most common responses were A and 2 (p and q) or just A (p). Wason concluded that participants had a verification bias, although he later withdrew this when evidence was produced that people were choosing cards that matched the items explicitly referenced in the rule (see Evans & Lynch, 1973; Wason & Evans, 1975; and for a recent review of "matching bias," Evans, 1998).

After a number of experiments with variations of this abstract task, all of which confirmed the robustness of the phenomenon, Wason discovered that people performed much better on a structurally isomorphic version of the task using a thematic rule set in context (Wason & Shapiro, 1971); an early demonstration of the content dependency of reasoning. This led to the proposal of a *thematic facilitation effect* in which it was proposed that realistic material facilitated logical reasoning (Wason & Johnson-Laird, 1972). In the event, the materials of Wason and Shapiro (1971) did not prove robust nor did the original explanation hold up for very long. What was established, however, was the facilitation of *p* and *not-q* choices could be reliably achieved in versions that were both realistic and deontic in nature. Deontic logic concerns permissions and obligations and the first experiments on the deontic selection task were published by Griggs and Cox (1982). In their Drinking Age problem, for example, people were asked to imagine that they were police officers observing people drinking in a bar, in order to check whether the following rule was being obeyed:

If a person is drinking beer, then that person must be over 19 years of age.

The four cards represented drinkers, with the beverage written on one side and the age on the other. The four exposed sides were:

| Drinking | Drinking | 20 years | 16 years |
| beer | coke | of age | of age |

corresponding to the *p*, *not-p*, *q* and *not-q* cards of the original problem. While concerned with the breaking of rules, rather than the truth or falsity of an indicative conditional, the correct answer was asserted to be *p* and *not-q*. This is because potential violators are people drinking beer and people under 19 years of age. A huge facilitation was reported, with around 75% of participants responding correctly to this task.

Subsequent research on this task (see Evans et al., 1993) quickly established a number of pertinent facts. First, although the rule used by Griggs and Cox (1982) corresponded to the actual drinking law in the state of Florida where student participants were run, the facilitation could be demonstrated on permission and obligation rules in contexts of which participants had no direct experience or knowledge. Second, the facilitation was dependent upon several of the components of the Drinking Age problem being in place. Framing an abstract problem with violation, as opposed to truth and falsity instructions, would not produce facilitation. Presenting the Drinking Age rule without the introductory police officer scenario also produced performance no better than on the abstract task (Pollard & Evans, 1987). However, framing an abstract problem of the form "if you take action A then you need permission P" was shown to facilitate (Cheng &

Holyoak, 1985), in support of the theory of pragmatic reasoning schemas. This theory proposed that abstract schemas for reasoning, restricted to the scope of a domain such as permission or obligation, could be retrieved and applied to achieve success on the task.

Wason's original proposal that a process of logical reasoning was being facilitated by the pragmatically rich versions quickly came under scrutiny. For example, Griggs (1983) argued that this could not be the case as solving thematic versions provided no insight into abstract versions of the task presented immediately afterward. There was no transfer of performance at all. The logical facilitation argument was further damaged by the later discovery of what are now known as perspective shift effects on the task, demonstrated by several authors at much the same time (Gigerenzer & Hug, 1992; Manktelow & Over, 1991; Politzer & Nguyen-Xuan, 1992). It was found in these experiments that under some circumstances a thematic selection task would produce the illogical choice pattern of *not-p* and *q*. For example, Manktelow and Over (1991) used a scenario in which a mother says to her son,

If you tidy up your room, then you may go out to play.

The cards recorded the relevant actions on different occasions, showing on one side whether the room was tidied and the other side whether the child went out to play. The four cards were then showing "room tidied" (*p*), "room not tidied" (*not-p*), "went out to play" (*q*), "did not go out to play" (*not-q*). The task was given to participants from one of two perspectives – the mother or the child. In each case, the instruction was to discover whether the other party was breaking the rule. Given the son's perspective, participants chose the logically correct *p* and *not-q* cards. That is, they checked occasions on which the room was tidied up and those on which the child was not allowed to go out to play. This, of course, would detect a violation of the mother's rule, that is, the child tidying up and not being allowed out. However, when given the mother's perspective, people selected the *not-p* and *q* cards. This makes sense if you think that the child would be cheating if he did not tidy his room, but went out to play anyway. It confirms people's responsiveness to subtle pragmatic factors in the scenario, discussed in the previous section. However, it presents an apparent problem for the theory of pragmatic reasoning schemas, which would seem to map a permission rule in only one way (but see Holyoak & Cheng, 1995).

Gigerenzer and Hug (1992) interpret the perspective-shift effect within the proposals of social contract theory, initially proposed by Cosmides (1989). This is a domain-specific reasoning process that is presented in the context of evolutionary-psychology theory and variously described as a Darwinian algorithm or an innate reasoning module. The idea is that fairness in social exchange would have been so critical in the early development of mankind that a specialized module would have evolved, enabling people to detect cheaters or violators. According to this view, both a social-contract rule and a contextual cue toward cheater detection are needed to invoke the algorithm. More recently, Fiddick et al. (2000) have acknowledged that there are contexts other than social contracts that facilitate performance on the selection task, but deny that this could be a criticism of a domain-specific mechanism. Instead, they have identified a separate reasoning module that is specialized for hazard detection.

Social contract theory has proved somewhat controversial (see Cheng & Holyoak, 1989), not least because it proposes an evolutionary basis for reasoning processes that are adaptive in current society and that therefore might have been acquired by social learning. We leave aside this issue here but address another: To what extent are pragmatic influences on the selection task attributable to domain-specific as opposed to domain-general processes? A recent attempt to provide a domain-general account of pragmatic influences has been proposed by Sperber et al. (1995), building upon the general relevance theory of discourse put forward by Sperber and Wilson (1995). They propose that cognitive relevance is directly related to the cognitive effects of some information and inversely related to the processing effort required to obtain it. Their theory of the selection task is domain general in that they propose that contexts may cue one of three levels of logical representation of the conditional statement.

The minimum that is conveyed by the claim "if p then q" is that (a) occurrences of p will be accompanied by occurrences of q. The next level is that the claim implies (b) the existence of cases of p and q. This does not follow logically, but in most contexts we would not assert "if p then q" otherwise. The final level (c) is where the conditional is seen to preclude cases of p and *not-q*. This usually only occurs when there is some presupposition that such cases might exist, as for example, would occur in a social contract problem with an orientation toward detection of cheaters. Sperber et al. propose that on the selection task, these representations would lead to the card choices: (a) p, (b) p and q, (c) p and *not-q*, and present a number of experiments in support of their argument. Fiddick et al. (2000) have challenged this account, claiming that specialized reasoning mechanisms, where available, will always take priority over domain-general processes such as relevance.

As an example of the experiments reported by Fiddick et al. consider their Experiment 3. The rule used was, "if you make poison darts then you may use rubber gloves." The context was varied slightly to facilitate either a social contract or precaution interpretation. In the social contract version the rule was portrayed as a privilege that might be abused. Accordingly, participants chose cards that could detect a cheater: those not making darts and those wearing gloves. In the precaution version, participants are asked to detect people putting themselves at risk, and here chose to examine those making darts and not wearing gloves. Fiddick et al. argue that as the logical form is the same, a domain-general mechanism, such as relevance theory, would not be able to predict this difference.

The selection task continues to be a major vehicle for the exploration of theories about content and context effects in reasoning. We would express the cautionary view that perhaps too much reliance is being placed upon this single reasoning task by some of the theorists concerned. For example, there is no reason why the debate between domain-specific modules and relevance theory could not be explored with regard to a wider range of tasks, including the conditional inference problems described earlier.

THE BELIEF-BIAS EFFECT

The belief-bias effect in deductive reasoning has been most commonly investigated using classical syllogisms and is traditionally (but we think incorrectly) defined as a tendency for people to endorse as valid arguments those conclusions they believe. The phenomenon was first reported by Wilkins (1928) and subjected to sporadic investigation of questionable methodology (see Evans, 1982, pp. 107–111, for a critical review of early studies). Modern interest in the phenomenon dates from the paper of Revlin, Leirer, Yopp, and Yopp (1980), who claimed that the effect was artifactual and unreliable. In response, Evans, Barston, and Pollard (1983) introduced all relevant controls and showed the belief-bias effect to be both reliable and robust, using a syllogistic conclusion-evaluation task. The paradigm involves presenting four types of argument that are either valid or invalid, and whose conclusions are either unbelievable or believable.

As an example of the materials used by Evans et al. (1983), the following syllogism is of the type Invalid-Unbelievable:

No police dogs are vicious.
Some highly trained dogs are vicious.
Therefore, some police dogs are not highly trained.

This argument is not logically valid nor does its conclusion concord with belief. Accordingly, very few participants endorsed it. The following problem is Invalid-Believable:

No addictive things are inexpensive.
Some cigarettes are inexpensive.
Therefore, some addictive things are not cigarettes.

Careful comparison of the two syllogisms will reveal that they have an identical logical form. However, in this case the majority of participants declare the (believable and fallacious) conclusion to be valid. Across the four categories endorsement rates were as follows:

Valid-Believable: 89%
Valid-Unbelievable: 56%
Invalid-Believable: 71%
Invalid-Unbelievable: 10%

These data reflect two main effects: People endorse more valid than invalid conclusions and more believable than unbelievable conclusions. There is also a significant interaction: The belief bias effect is greater for invalid than valid arguments. Evans et al. (1983) discussed two alternative explanations of these findings that have become known as the Selective Scrutiny Model and the Misinterpreted Necessity Model. According to Selective Scrutiny, people tend to accept believable conclusions uncritically but to examine the argument much more carefully when they disagree with the conclusion. This leads them more often to reject invalid conclusions when they have unbelievable arguments. The Misinterpreted Necessity explanation of the interaction is different. On this account, people tend to accept valid arguments, regardless of beliefs, but fall back on belief when the conclusions are not determined by the premises. Subsequent research produced equivocal evidence not clearly favoring either model (see Evans et al., 1993, chap. 8).

A mental model theory of the belief-bias effect was put forward by Oakhill and Johnson-Laird (1985; see also Oakhill, Johnson-Laird, & Garnham, 1989) and investigated further by Newstead, Pollard, and Allen (1992), Santamaria, Garcia-Madruga, and Carretero (1996) and Torrens, Thompson, and Cramer (1998). The model theory of syllogistic reasoning proposed originally by Johnson-Laird and Bara (1984) stated that people form a mental model of the premises, derive a provisional conclusion, and then attempt to validate that conclusion by searching for counterexamples – that is, models of the premises that did not support the conclusion. In the absence of counterexamples the conclusion is accepted as valid. Hence, it was suggested that people tend to accept believable conclusions without searching for counterexamples, but are motivated to disprove unbelievable conclusions. However, in the light of subsequent research, this mental models account would have to be revised. Recent work suggests that people do not normally search for counterexamples in syllogistic reasoning, but tend to base conclusions on the first model that comes to mind (Evans, Handley, Harper, & Johnson-Laird, 1999; Newstead, Handley, & Buck, 1999). Also, when abstract or belief neutral conclusions are introduced, these tend to be accepted as readily as believable conclusions (Evans, Handley, & Harper, 2001; Krauth, 1982; Newstead et al., 1992).

This last finding is the reason why we believe that the belief-bias effect is normally misrepresented. Early research did not use belief-neutral conclusions, and led to the assumption that people were accepting believable fallacies. Actually, people have a strong tendency to accept fallacies in syllogistic reasoning, unless they have unbelievable conclusions. Hence, we might see the phenomenon as a *debiasing* effect of unbelievable conclusions, rather than a biasing effect of believable conclusions. Two recent studies, conducted independently, reached very similar conclusions about the basic phenomena. Both Evans, Handley, and Harper (2001) and Klauer, Musch, and Naumer (2000) proposed two aspects to the belief-bias effect. First, there is a general response bias leading to suppression of acceptance of unbelievable conclusions, regardless of the logic of the arguments. This is what produces the main effect of belief. Second, there is a component of belief that interferes with the reasoning process that must also be present to account for the higher acceptance of invalid arguments. This produces the interaction, enabling people to reject more fallacies that are unbelievable. Evans, Handley, and Harper (2001) have also shown that this process can lead to endorsement of fallacies, which are normally resisted, when the conclusion given accords with belief.

Research on the belief-bias effect confirms the highly pervasive influence of prior knowledge on reasoning that we saw in studies of conditional inference and the selection task. The ability to reason in a content independent manner has been shown, with the belief-bias paradigm, to relate to general intelligence and working memory capacity. For example, Stanovich and West (1997) have shown that people good at resisting beliefs have high SAT scores while Gilinsky and Judd (1994) have shown the same ability declines sharply in aging adults. In contrast with the claims of some authors in the selection task literature, these studies support the view that the influence of belief concerns a domain-general reasoning system. Accumulating evidence across the three deductive reasoning literatures reviewed in this chapter suggests that the original conception of reasoning as a logical process with which beliefs might interfere is dubious. The evidence might be seen as more consistent with the view that ordinary reasoning is inherently pragmatic and that logical reasoning is a specialized strategy (Evans, 2000b) that may be induced when high IQ participants are exposed to specific experimental instructions.

BACKGROUND BELIEF AND HYPOTHESIS TESTING

In this section, we will review work demonstrating that belief structures often have profound effects on the way people test hypotheses. A common claim is that there is a pervasive *confirmation bias* consisting of a tendency to seek evidence that confirms rather than contradicts one's prior beliefs. Wason (1960) presented evidence for such an effect when he first published details of his now famous 2 4 6 task. In the 2 4 6 task people are told that the experimenter has in mind a rule that generates sets of three numbers. The triple 2 4 6 is an example of such a set. Participants have to guess what the rule is and test their hypotheses by generating triples of their own. As they produce each triple the experimenter tells each participant whether it conforms to his or her rule. Wason's participants predominantly generated triples that were positive instances of the hypothesis they were currently considering. For example, if they held the hypothesis "ascending at equal intervals" they might offer such triples as "10 20 30," "12 14 16," "7 8 9," and so on. In all such cases the experimenter gave them positive feedback, since the actual rule was "any ascending sequence." The fact that participants became convinced that they had the correct rule by this positive testing method was interpreted by Wason as evidence for a confirmation bias. This is because disconfirmatory cases such as "9 8 7" were rarely offered.

Although there is widespread evidence of confirmation bias in a range of cognitive and social psychological literatures (for an excellent overview see Klayman, 1995), Wason's interpretation of the "2 4 6" problem has been open to dispute as to whether it shows simply a positive testing bias that is not necessarily linked to any motivation to confirm the hypothesis (Evans, 1989; Klayman & Ha, 1987; Wetherick, 1962). Klayman and Ha (1987), in a landmark paper, argued that both positive and negative tests may provide either confirmation or disconfirmation of an hypothesis, depending on the scope of that hypothesis. For example, imagine you are a geneticist trying to determine how widespread a particular gene is among animals. Suppose you hypothesize that all mice, but only mice, possess the gene. Positive tests of this hypothesis would involve testing the genes of some mice. Your hypothesis is confirmed if the mice you test turn out to possess the gene while it is disconfirmed if they do not. A negative test of your hypothesis would be to test some animal other than mice to see whether they possess the gene. Confirmation in this case would result from a negative result whereas disconfirmation would result from a positive result. Klayman and Ha go on to show that in general the optimal strategy is to test a positive rather than a negative instance of the hypothesis currently under scrutiny. As this is what people tend to do, Klayman and Ha are able to recast human hypothesis testing as broadly rational.

More recent work on belief structures and hypothesis testing has focused on the role of beliefs about the evidence. Specifically, researchers have been interested in whether people use information about the probability of a particular outcome when selecting tests of an hypothesis. For example, Kirby (1994) reported a series of experiments with Wason's selection task where he used the scenario to manipulate the probability of there being a p on the back of the *not-q* card. He found that as the probability of p increased (and the probability of *not-p* decreased) so too did the rate at which people chose the *not-q* card. Although there are problems with Kirby's methodology (see Over & Evans, 1994), similar results have been reported by Pollard and Evans (1981, 1983). For example, if people believe the rule likely to be false, and therefore that *p* and *not-q* counterexamples are probable, they much more often choose the correct cards.

Recent researchers have suggested other ways in which the prior expectations of the participant will influence choices on the selection task. For example, Oaksford and Chater (1994; see also, Nickerson, 1996) proposed that expected information gain for each card, defined in information theory terms, will determine selections that normatively are correct from this viewpoint. For discussions and experimental investigations of this approach see Evans and Over (1996b); Feeney and Handley (2000); Handley, Feeney, and Harper (2002); Laming (1996); Oaksford, Chater, and Grainger (1999); Oaksford, Chater, Grainger, and Larkin (1997); Oberauer, Wilhelm, and Diaz (1999). Oaksford and Chater (1994) claim that the likely information to be gained from any card is related to the relative probabilities of *p* and *q*. They assume that people, lacking any information to the contrary, treat *p* and *q* as rare. This approach also assumes the role of a disinterested observer, while others have emphasized the role of personal utilities, taking into account the goals of the reasoner (Evans & Over, 1996a, 1996b; Manktelow & Over, 1991).

The rarity assumption has been one of the most contentious aspects of Oaksford and Chater's (1994) reanalysis of the selection task. They argue that, for reasons of informativeness, people are likely to phrase conditional statements in terms of rare events. This claim is supported by recent evidence from McKenzie, Ferreira, Mikkelsen, McDermott, and Skrable (2001), who asked participants to use conditional statements in order to describe trends present in sets of data. For example, in one experiment participants were shown information about five students, only one of whom had been accepted into a prestigious college and had high, rather than average, SAT scores. Participants tended to phrase their conditional statements in terms of the rare (if applicants obtain high SAT scores then they are accepted) rather than the common events (If applicants obtain average SAT scores then they are rejected). As well as supporting Oaksford and Chater's assumption of rarity, the data of McKenzie et al. (2001) provide evidence that people use their beliefs about the probabilities of events when formulating as well as testing hypotheses.

BACKGROUND BELIEFS AND PSEUDODIAGNOSTICITY

The tasks that we have described thus far ask people to decide how to test or to formulate conditional hypotheses. Accordingly, they can be conceived of in logical terms (even if logic is now often regarded as an inappropriate normative account of the task (see Evans & Over, 1996a; Oaksford & Chater, 1994). The pseudodiagnosticity (PD) paradigm (Doherty et al., 1979) has also been used to examine confirmation bias, as well as the role of beliefs about the evidence and people's understanding of evidential diagnosticity.

There are several variants of the PD paradigm but in the variant to be discussed here (see Mynatt, Doherty, & Dragan, 1993) participants are presented with a scenario such as the following:

Your sister has a car she bought a couple of years ago. It's either a car X or a car Y but you can't remember which. You do remember that her car does over 25 miles per gallon and has not had any major mechanical problems in the two years she's owned it. You have the following information:

A. 65% of car Xs do over 25 miles per gallon.
   Three additional pieces of information are also available:
B. The percentage of car Ys that do over 25 miles per gallon.
C. The percentage of car Xs that have had no major mechanical problems for the first two years of ownership.
D. The percentage of car Ys that have had no major mechanical problems for the first two years of ownership.

Assuming you could find out only one of these three pieces of information (B, C or D) which would you want in order to help you to decide which car your sister owns? Please circle your answer.

In this scenario, participants are presented with a scenario describing two hypotheses (X and Y) and two evidential features (fuel economy and mechanical reliability). The evidence presented (A) concerns the probability with which instances governed by one of the hypotheses possess one of the evidential features, $P(D_1/Hx)$, while B concerns the probability that instances governed by the alternative hypotheses possess that evidential feature, $P(D_1/Hy)$. C and D refer to the equivalent information for the second evidential feature, $P(D_2/Hx)$ and $P(D_2/Hy)$, respectively.

The appropriate normative analysis for this task is provided by Bayes's theorem, which in odds form is as follows:

$$\frac{P(Hx/D_1)}{P(Hy/D_1)} = \frac{P(Hx)}{P(Hy)} \cdot \frac{P(D_1/Hx)}{P(D_1/Hy)}$$

From left to right, this equation claims that the posterior odds (the odds after the evidence is received) are equal to the prior odds (the odds in the absence of the evidence) multiplied by the likelihood ratio: In this instance the ratio of how likely it is that Xs do over 25 mpg to how likely it is that Ys do. The only way to apply Bayes's theorem in the PD task above is to select option B, which will provide information about how diagnostic the fuel consumption feature is when attempting to tell model Xs from model Ys. However, with the materials presented above, Mynatt et al. (1993) found that only 28% of people chose B while 59% chose C. The tendency to select further information about the hypothesis mentioned in the initial evidence is termed *pseudodiagnosticity* and the finding has been replicated several times (e.g., Covey & Lovey, 1998; Doherty, Chadwick, Garavan, Barr, & Mynatt, 1996; Evans, Feeney, & Venn, 2001). Mynatt et al.

explained participants' modal choice in terms of a confirmation bias: They suggested that people consider only the hypotheses that they currently believe most likely to be true, and they select evidence relevant to that hypothesis. However, as with the Wason's 2 4 6 problem, we could argue that this was evidence only of a positive testing bias.

The task has more recently been used to examine how background beliefs about the evidence affect hypothesis testing. Evans, Feeney, and Venn (2001) told half of their participants that the character in the scenario was interested in fuel economy and mechanical reliability and manipulated whether the initial piece of evidence was that model X cars did 20, 35, or 50 miles per gallon. While the manipulation of the initial piece of evidence did not influence information selections in the standard version of the task, decreasing fuel consumption in the version with the altered preamble produced an increasing tendency to select the hypothesis-matching option. Participants' background beliefs about fuel consumption in cars lead to assumptions about whether the character in the scenario is likely to be interested in a particular car. As fuel consumption increases, participants consider it to be more likely that the character has bought a model Y and, hence, they become more likely to select information concerning the Y hypothesis.

The PD paradigm has also been used to demonstrate that people consider the probability of the evidence when selecting and evaluating statistical evidence. For example, Feeney, Evans, and Venn (2001) have demonstrated that when the initial piece of evidence concerns a rare feature (e.g., a top speed of 165 mph in cars) and the second feature is common (e.g., having a radio), then people will seek to discover a second piece of evidence about the rare feature. This leads to a significant drop in the usual pseudodiagnostic choice rate. Also investigated has been a variant of the paradigm in which participants rate their degree of belief in the hypotheses after receiving one or two pieces of "pseudodiagnostic" information chosen by the experimenter. Here, it was found that people are much more confident in a hypothesis supported by rare rather than common evidence (Feeney, Evans, & Clibbens, 2000).

In this section and the one preceding, we hope we have demonstrated that although people have a tendency to propose tests of hypotheses that are positive instances of the hypothesis under consideration, the effects of belief in hypothesis testing extend beyond simple beliefs about whether the hypothesis being tested is true or false. People often have beliefs about the likely outcome of various tests of an hypothesis which are based upon how probable they consider the events governed by the hypothesis to be. Such beliefs have been clearly shown to inform their selection and interpretation of information as well as their formulation of conditional hypotheses. In particular, people are able to use their probabilistic beliefs about the evidence in a broadly rational manner.

FROM REASONING TO BELIEF CHANGE

Up to now we have considered various ways in which prior beliefs influence reasoning. However, we do not go through life with fixed and unchanging beliefs. Hence our examination of evidence and the reasoning we do about it can also change our beliefs. Belief revision can be studied in a number of paradigms, but surprisingly has only recently been examined with regard to deductive reasoning (Elio & Pelletier, 1997; Politzer & Carles, 2001). Much relevant work is, however, found in the domain of statistical reasoning. Bayes's theorem provides a strong normative framework for belief revision. In Bayesian reasoning, prior belief is revised by multiplying the prior odds by the likelihood ratio (diagnosticity) arising from new evidence. The resulting posterior odds represent the revised belief in an hypothesis resulting from the evidence. There has hence been considerable interest in the statistical reasoning literature in the extent to which people follow Bayesian principles when judging posterior probabilities.

At first sight, the findings of the Bayesian reasoning literature may seem surprising. We have shown the pervasive influence of prior belief on reasoning in this chapter and yet the major claim in this literature is that people ignore or at least relatively neglect Bayesian prior probabilities in the light of diagnostic evidence (for a review see Koehler, 1996). This stands in apparent stark contrast to the social psychological literature on stereotypes in which people are strongly biased by prior beliefs about social groups (Funder, 1996). We believe that the reason for this is that typical research on the "base rate fallacy" uses statistically defined base rates that have no connection with people's belief system. A recent study by Evans, Handley, Over, and Perham (2002) showed that Bayesian prior probabilities can have substantially more influence when supplied by actual prior beliefs of the participants. In a similar vein, Feeney (2001) has shown that evidential rarity effects on the pseudodiagnosticity task are not obtained when the problem concerns arbitrary content with the rarity information supplied explicitly. The effects are only obtained when people are reasoning about features of objects for which they already possess beliefs.

There are, however, other kinds of evidence suggesting that people regularly violate the prescriptions of Bayesian norms. For example, if a number of pieces of information are fed into the Bayesian revision process, the final posterior odds will be the same, regardless of the order in which the information is processed. By contrast, there are numerous experimental demonstrations that people's belief revision following exposure to sequential pieces of evidence is strongly sensitive to order, producing primacy or recency effects. Such effects have been found in domains as varied as impression formation (Asch, 1946), mock trials and simulated legal evidence (Tetlock, 1983; Walker, Thibaut, & Andreoli, 1972) and auditor's judgments about whether a company is a growing concern (Ashton & Ashton, 1988).

A number of psychologists have hence rejected the Bayesian model and proposed descriptive (Anderson, 1981) or procedural (e.g., Hogarth & Einhorn, 1992; Lopes, 1987) models of belief revision. These alternative approaches attempt to describe or predict human judgments and have been successful in accounting for order effects (see Ashton & Ashton, 1988; Hogarth & Einhorn, 1992). Another, particularly productive response has been to suggest that people use heuristics, such as representativeness or availability, when they make judgments or revise their beliefs (for a review of the variety of work inspired by this approach see Kahneman, Slovic, and Tversky [1982] and for some recent proposals see Kahneman and Frederick [in press]). The emphasis on bias resulting from such heuristics has, however, been disputed together with the framework of normative rationality underlying it (see Gigerenzer, 1996; Kahneman & Tversky, 1996; Vranas, 2000). Gigerenzer and colleagues have recently advocated the use of simple, computationally well-specified heuristics for the explanation of judgment and decision making, emphasizing their adaptive and effective nature (see Gigerenzer, Todd, and the ABC Research Group, 1999).

As mentioned earlier, belief revision following deduction has received comparatively little attention in the psychological literature. However, in the literature on artificial intelligence there has been quite a lot of work on how beliefs might change following deduction (e.g., Gardenfors, 1988). The problem is that real life reasoning is defeasible or nonmonotonic, meaning that inferences may be withdrawn in the light of new evidence (Oaksford & Chater, 1991). Why might humans have to update their beliefs following a deductive inference? The answer is well demonstrated by Elio and Pelletier (1997), who consider the class of situations where a reasoner has inferred a conclusion from some premises and that conclusion is contradicted by some subsequent observation. For example, given the premises:

a. If John is in New York then he stays in the Hilton.
b. John is in New York.

we infer by modus ponens that John is staying in the Hilton. However, suppose we ring the Hilton and find out that John is not staying there. This contradiction gives us a belief revision problem where we have to decide whether premise (a), premise (b), or both are most likely to be false. Elio and Pelletier's work suggests that, overall, people are more likely to reject the conditional hypothesis than the minor premise, although this is also affected by whether the contradiction follows a modus ponens or a modus tollens inference. Politzer and Carles (2001) in a similar task show that people prefer to express uncertainty about the premises rather than to express absolute disbelief. This finding supports earlier work demonstrating that belief in a premise is a matter of degree and that this determines the believability of the conclusion (see George, 1995, 1997; Stevenson &

Over, 1995). Politzer and Carles's (2001) results also suggest that the conditional hypothesis is more likely to be disbelieved because it is a compound premise (i.e., made up of two propositions) and therefore more likely to be false than is the simpler minor premise. There are also clear links with our earlier discussion of pragmatic factors in conditional reasoning, in which we provided evidence that inferences are made with a degree of confidence or probability that can easily be affected by subtle changes in content or context.

CONCLUSIONS

This brief review has illustrated the highly pervasive influence of prior knowledge and belief on human reasoning. In the case of deductive reasoning, for example, it seems to us difficult to maintain the central role for logic that inspired this paradigm in the first place. Indeed the continued use of the standard paradigm that effectively defines any use of prior knowledge as a bias is open to question (Evans, 2000a). What has emerged recently is the idea that these phenomena are best understood by the proposal of dual process theories of reasoning variously described as implicit and explicit (Evans & Over, 1996a), associative or rule-based (Sloman, 1996), or by the generic labels, System 1 and System 2 (Stanovich, 1999). System 1 processes are automatic, associative, and pragmatic in nature. System 2 processes are slow and sequential, loaded on working memory, and potentially enable people to reason in an abstract logical manner.

One application of this framework is to suggest that System 1 and System 2 processes effectively compete for the control of behavior. Thus in their belief bias work, Evans et al. (1983) talked of the competing influences of logic and belief, showing by protocol analysis that when people attended to the premises, their conclusion tended to be more influenced by logic and when focusing on conclusions they showed more belief bias. It has also been argued that preconscious pragmatic processes may disguise the potential logical competence of participants by diverting attention away from logical relevant information or toward irrelevant information (Evans, 1989). Stanovich (1999) has shown that the ability of people to find normatively correct solutions to a wide range of reasoning and decision tasks (and hence to engage effective System 2 thinking) is strongly linked with general intelligence. The ability to suppress the influence of prior belief and reason with the abstract structure of tasks is particularly linked to high intelligence, but also to measures of cognitive style, or thinking dispositions, as well (Stanovich & West, 1998).

Other authors, while not describing themselves as dual process theorists, have also posited separate mechanisms underlying deductive and pragmatic influences. For example, proponents of mental logic (see Braine & O'Brien, 1998) maintain that there is an abstract rule-based system for deduction, supplemented by a wide range of pragmatic mechanisms, including invited inferences and pragmatic reasoning schemas. The authors who are holding most strongly to a singular mechanism for reasoning are those in the mental model tradition who maintain that the manipulation of mental models representing logical possibilities provides both the potential for deductive competence and also the scope for influence of problem content and context. The idea is that the possibilities actually represented and considered in a particular context are influenced by prior beliefs. For the latest proposals about conditional reasoning see Johnson-Laird and Byrne (in press) and for a critique, Evans, Over, and Handley (in press).

In conclusion, while the extensive role of prior belief in reasoning is established beyond argument, the theoretical debate regarding the mechanisms underlying these influences is far from decided.

References

Anderson, N. H. (1981). *Foundations of information integration theory.* London: Academic Press.

Asch, S. E. (1946). Forming impressions of personality. *Journal of Abnormal and Social Psychology, 41,* 258–290.

Ashton, A. H., & Ashton, R. H. (1988). Sequential belief in auditing. *The Accounting Review, 63,* 623–641.

Braine, M. D. S., & O'Brien, D. P. (Eds.) (1998). *Mental logic.* Mahwah, NJ: Erlbaum.

Byrne, R. M. J. (1989). Suppressing valid inferences with conditionals. *Cognition, 31,* 61–83.

Byrne, R. M. J. (1991). Can valid inferences be suppressed? *Cognition, 39,* 71–78.

Chater, N., & Oaksford, M. (1999). The probability heuristics model of syllogistic reasoning. *Cognitive Psychology, 38,* 191–258.

Cheng, P. W., & Holyoak, K. J. (1985). Pragmatic reasoning schemas. *Cognitive Psychology, 17,* 391–416.

Cheng, P. W., & Holyoak, K. J. (1989). On the natural selection of reasoning theories. *Cognition, 33,* 285–314.

Cohen, L. J. (1982). Are people programmed to commit fallacies? Further thought about the interpretation of data on judgement. *Journal for the Theory of Social Behaviour, 12,* 251–274.

Cosmides, L. (1989). The logic of social exchange: Has natural selection shaped how humans reason? *Cognition, 31,* 187–276.

Covey, J. A., & Lovie, A. D. (1998). Information selection and utilization in hypothesis testing: A comparison of process-tracing and structural analysis techniques. *Organizational Behaviour and Human Decision Processes, 75,* 56–74.

Cummins, D. D., Lubart, T., Alksnis, O., & Rist, R. (1991). Conditional reasoning and causation. *Memory and Cognition, 19,* 274–282.

Doherty, M. E., Chadwick, R., Garavan, H., Barr, D., & Mynatt, C. R. (1996). On people's understanding of the diagnostic implications of probabilistic data. *Memory and Cognition, 24,* 644–654.

Doherty, M. E., Mynatt, C. R., Tweney, R. D., & Schiavo, M. D. (1979). Pseudodiagnosticity. *Acta Psychologica, 43,* 11–21.

Edgington, D. (1995). On conditionals. *Mind, 104*, 235–329.

Elio, R., & Pelletier, F. J. (1997). Belief change as propositional update. *Cognitive Science, 21*, 419–460.

Evans, J. St. B. T. (1982). *The psychology of deductive reasoning.* London: Routledge.

Evans, J. St. B. T. (1989). *Bias in human reasoning: Causes and consequences.* Hove: Erlbaum.

Evans, J. St. B. T. (1998). Matching bias in conditional reasoning: Do we understand it after 25 years? *Thinking and Reasoning, 4*, 45–82.

Evans, J. St. B. T. (2000a). *Why study deduction? History and future of the paradigm.* Paper presented at the BPS 4th International Conference on Thinking, Durham University, UK.

Evans, J. St. B. T. (2000b). What could and could not be a strategy in reasoning. In W. Schaeken, G. DeVooght, & A. d. G. Vandierendonck (Eds.), *Deductive reasoning and strategies* (pp. 1–22). Mahwah, NJ.: Erlbaum.

Evans, J. St. B. T., Barston, J. L., & Pollard, P. (1983). On the conflict between logic and belief in syllogistic reasoning. *Memory and Cognition, 11*, 295–306.

Evans, J. St. B. T., Clibbens, J., & Rood, B. (1995). Bias in conditional inference: Implications for mental models and mental logic. *Quarterly Journal of Experrimental Psychology, 48A*, 644–670.

Evans, J. St. B. T., Feeney, A., & Venn, S. (2001). Explicit and implicit processes in an hypothesis evaluation task. *British Journal of Psychology, 93*, 31–46.

Evans, J. St. B. T., Handley, S. H., & Harper, C. (2001). Necessity, possibility and belief: A study of syllogistic reasoning. *Quarterly Journal of Experimental Psychology, 54A*, 935–958.

Evans, J. St. B. T., Handley, S. J., Harper, C., & Johnson-Laird, P. N. (1999). Reasoning about necessity and possibility: A test of the mental model theory of deduction. *Journal of Experimental Psychology: Learning, Memory and Cognition, 25*, 1495–1513.

Evans, J. St. B. T., Handley, S. H., Over, D. E., & Perham, N. (2002). Background beliefs in Bayesian inference. *Memory and Cognition, 30*, 179–190.

Evans, J. St. B. T., & Lynch, J. S. (1973). Matching bias in the selection task. *British Journal of Psychology, 64*, 391–397.

Evans, J. St. B. T., Newstead, S. E., & Byrne, R. M. J. (1993). *Human reasoning: The psychology of deduction.* Hove & London: Erlbaum.

Evans, J. St. B. T., & Over, D. E. (1996a). *Rationality and reasoning.* Hove, East Sussex: Psychology Press.

Evans, J. St. B. T., & Over, D. E. (1996b). Rationality in the selection task: Epistemic utility versus uncertainty reduction. *Psychological Review, 103*, 356–363.

Evans, J. St. B. T., Over, D. E., & Handley, S. H. (in press). Rethinking the model theory of conditionals. In W. Schaeken, A. Vandierendonck, W. Schroyens, & G. d'Ydewalle (Eds.), *The mental model theory of reasoning: Refinements and extensions.* Hove, UK: Erlbaum.

Evans, J. St. B. T., & Twyman-Musgrove, J. (1998). Conditional reasoning with inducements and advice. *Cognition, 69*, B11–B16.

Feeney, A. (2001). *On knowing versus being told: The effects of belief and statistics about rarity on hypothesis testing.* Unpublished manuscript, University of Durham, UK.

Feeney, A., Evans, J. St. B. T., & Clibbens, J. (2000). Background beliefs and evidence interpretation. *Thinking and Reasoning, 6*, 193–272.

Feeney, A., Evans, J. St. B. T., & Venn, S. (2001). *Rarity and hypothesis testing*. Unpublished manuscript.

Feeney, A., & Handley, S. H. (2000). The suppression of q card selections: Evidence for deductive inference in Wason's selection task. *Quarterly Journal of Experimental Psychology, 53A*, 1224–1243.

Fiddick, L., Cosmides, L., & Tooby, J. (2000). No interpretation without representation: The role of domain-specific representations and inferences in the Wason selection task. *Cognition, 77*, 1–79.

Funder, D. C. (1996). Base rates, stereotypes, and judgmental accuracy. *Behavioral and Brain Sciences, 19*, 22–23.

Gardenfors, P. (1988). *Knowledge in flux: Modeling the dynamics of epistemic states*. Cambridge, MA: MIT Press.

George, C. (1995). The endorsement of the premises: Assumption based or belief-based reasoning. *British Journal of Psychology, 86*, 93–111.

George, C. (1997). Reasoning from uncertain premises. *Thinking and Reasoning, 3*, 161–190.

George, C. (1999). Evaluation of the plausibility of a conclusion derivable from several arguments with uncertain premises. *Thinking and Reasoning, 5*, 245–281.

Gigerenzer, G. (1996). On narrow norms and vague heuristics: A reply to Kahneman and Tversky (1996). *Psychological Review, 103*, 592–596.

Gigerenzer, G., & Hug, K. (1992). Domain-specific reasoning: Social contracts, cheating and perspective change. *Cognition, 43*, 127–171.

Gigerenzer, G., Todd, P. M., & the ABC Research Group (1999). *Simple heuristics that make us smart*. New York & Oxford: Oxford University Press.

Gilinsky, A. S., & Judd, B. B. (1994). Working memory and bias in reasoning across the life-span. *Psychology and Aging, 9*, 356–371.

Grice, P., (1975). Logic and conversation. In P. Cole & J. L. Morgan (Eds.), *Studies in syntax* (vol. 3, pp. 41–58). *Speech Acts*. New York: Academic Press.

Griggs, R. A. (1983). The role of problem content in the selection task and in the THOG problem. In J. St. B. T. Evans (Ed.), *Thinking and reasoning: Psychological approaches* (pp. 16–43). London: Routledge.

Griggs, R. A., & Cox, J. R. (1982). The elusive thematic materials effect in the Wason selection task. *British Journal of Psychology, 73*, 407–420.

Handley, S. J., Feeney, A., & Harper, C. (2002). Alternative antecedents, probabilities and the suppression of fallacies on Wason's selection task. *Quarterly Journal Experimental Psychology, 55A*, 799–818.

Henle, M. (1962). On the relation between logic and thinking. *Psychological Review, 69*, 366–378.

Hogarth, R. M., & Einhorn, H. J. (1992). Order effects in belief updating: The belief adjustment model. *Cognitive Psychology, 24*, 1–55.

Holyoak, K., & Cheng, P. (1995). Pragmatic reasoning with a point of view. *Thinking and Reasoning, 1*, 289–314.

Inhelder, B., & Piaget, J. (1958). *The growth of logical thinking*. New York: Basic Books.

Johnson-Laird, P. N., & Bara, B. G. (1984). Syllogistic inference. *Cognition, 16*, 1–61.

Johnson-Laird, P. N., & Byrne, R. (1991). *Deduction*. Hove & London: Erlbaum.

Johnson-Laird, P. N., & Byrne, R. (in press). Conditionals: A theory of meaning, pragmatics and inference. *Psychological Review*.

Kahneman, D., & Frederick, S. (in press). Representativeness revisited: Attribute substitution in intuitive judgement. In T. Gilovich, D. Griffin, & D. Kahneman (Eds.), *Heuristics and biases*. New York: Cambridge University Press.

Kahneman, D., Slovic, P., & Tversky, A. (1982). *Judgment under uncertainty: Heuristics and biases*. Cambridge: Cambridge University Press.

Kahneman, A., & Tversky, A. (1996). On the reality of cognitive illusions: A reply to Gigerenzer's critique. *Psychological Review, 103,* 582–591.

Kirby, K. N. (1994). Probabilities and utilities of fictional outcomes in Wason's four card selection task. *Cognition, 51,* 1–28.

Klauer, K. C., Musch, J., & Naumer, B. (2000). On belief bias in syllogistic reasoning. *Psychological Review, 107,* 852–884.

Klayman, J. (1995). Varieties of confirmation bias. *The psychology of learning and motivation, 32,* 385–417.

Klayman, J., & Ha, Y. W. (1987). Confirmation, disconfirmation and information in hypothesis testing. *Psychological Review, 94,* 211–228.

Koehler, J. J. (1996). The base rate fallacy reconsidered: Descriptive, normative and methodological challenges. *Behavioral and Brain Sciences, 19,* 1–53.

Krauth, J. (1982). Formulation and experimental verification of models in propositional reasoning. *Quarterly Journal of Experimental Psychology, 34A,* 285–298.

Laming, D. (1996). On the analysis of irrational data selection: A critique of Oaksford & Chater (1994). *Psychological Review, 103,* 364–373.

Lopes, L. L. (1987). Procedural debiasing. *Acta Psychologica, 64,* 167–185.

Manktelow, K. I. (1999). *Reasoning and Thinking*. Hove, UK: Psychology Press.

Manktelow, K. I., & Over, D. E. (1991). Social roles and utilities in reasoning with deontic conditionals. *Cognition, 39,* 85–105.

Markovits, H. (1986). Familiarity effects in conditional reasoning. *Journal of Educational Psychology, 78,* 492–494.

McKenzie, C. R. M., Ferreira, V. S., Mikkelsen, L. A., McDermott, K. J., & Skrable, R. P. (2001). Do conditional hypotheses target rare events? *Organizational Behaviour and Human Decision Processes, 85,* 56–74.

Mynatt, C. R., Doherty, M. E., & Dragan, W. (1993). Information relevance, working memory, and the consideration of alternatives. *The Quarterly Journal of Experimental Psychology, 46A,* 759–778.

Newstead, S. E., Ellis, C., Evans, J. St. B. T., & Dennis, I. (1997). Conditional reasoning with realistic material. *Thinking and Reasoning, 3,* 49–76.

Newstead, S. E., & Griggs, R. A. (1983). Drawing inferences from quantified statements: A study of the square of opposition. *Journal of Verbal Learning and Verbal Behavior, 22,* 535–546.

Newstead, S. E., Handley, S. H., & Buck, E. (1999). Falsifying mental models: Testing the predictions of theories of syllogistic reasoning. *Journal of Memory and Language, 27,* 344–354.

Newstead, S. E., Pollard, P. E., & Allen, J. L. (1992). The source of belief bias effects in syllogistic reasoning. *Cognition, 45,* 257–284.

Nickerson, R. S. (1996). Hempel's paradox and the Wason selection task: Logical and psychological puzzles of confirmation. *Thinking and Reasoning, 2,* 1–32.

Oakhill, J., & Johnson-Laird, P. N. (1985). The effects of belief on the spontaneous production of syllogistic conclusions. *Quarterly Journal of Experimental Psychology, 37A,* 553–569.

Oakhill, J., Johnson-Laird, P. N., & Garnham, A. (1989). Believability and syllogistic reasoning. *Cognition, 31*, 117–140.

Oaksford, M., & Chater, N. (1991). Against logicist cognitive science. *Mind & Language, 6*, 1–38.

Oaksford, M., & Chater, N. (1994). A rational analysis of the selection task as optimal data selection. *Psychological Review, 101*, 608–631.

Oaksford, M., & Chater, N. (1998). *Rationality in an uncertain world.* Hove, Sussex: Psychology Press.

Oaksford, M., Chater, N., & Grainger, B. (1999). Probabilistic effects in data selection. *Thinking and Reasoning, 5*, 193–244.

Oaksford, M., Chater, N., Grainger, B., & Larkin, J. (1997). Optimal data selection in the reduced array selection task (RAST). *Journal of Experimental Psychology: Learning, Memory and Cognition, 23*, 441–458.

Oberauer, K., Wilhelm, O., & Diaz, R. R. (1999). Bayesian rationality for the Wason selection task? A test of optimal data selection theory. *Thinking and Reasoning, 5*, 115–144.

Over, D. E., & Evans, J. St. B. T. (1994). Hits and misses: Kirby on the selection task. *Cognition, 52*, 235–243.

Over, D. E., & Manktelow, K. I. (1993). Rationality, utility and deontic reasoning. In K. I. Manktelow & D. E. Over (Eds.), *Rationality* (pp. 231–259). London: Routledge.

Politzer, G., & Braine, M. D. S. (1991). Responses to inconsistent premises cannot count as suppression of valid inferences. *Cognition, 38*, 103–108.

Politzer, G., & Carles, L. (2001). Belief revision and uncertain reasoning. *Thinking and Reasoning, 7*, 217–234.

Politzer, G., & Nguyen-Xuan, A. (1992). Reasoning about conditional promises and warnings: Darwinian algorithms, mental models, relevance judgements or pragmatic schemas? *Quarterly Journal of Experimental Psychology, 44*, 401–412.

Pollard, P., & Evans, J. St. B. T. (1981). The effect of prior beliefs in reasoning: An associational interpretation. *British Journal of Psychology, 72*, 73–82.

Pollard, P., & Evans, J. St. B. T. (1983). The effect of experimentally contrived experience on reasoning performance. *Psychological Research, 45*, 287–301.

Pollard, P., & Evans, J. St. B. T. (1987). On the relationship between content and context effects in reasoning. *American Journal of Psychology, 100*, 41–60.

Revlin, R., Leirer, V., Yopp, H., & Yopp, R. (1980). The belief bias effect in formal reasoning: The influence of knowledge on logic. *Memory and Cognition, 8*, 584–592.

Santamaria, C., Garcia-Madruga, J. A., & Carretero, M. (1996). Beyond belief bias: Reasoning from conceptual structures by mental models manipulation. *Memory and Cognition, 24*, 250–261.

Sloman, S. A. (1996). The empirical case for two systems of reasoning. *Psychological Bulletin, 119*, 3–22.

Smedslund, J. (1970). Circular relation between understanding and logic. *Scandinavian Journal of Psychology, 11*, 217–219.

Sperber, D., Cara, F., & Girotto, V. (1995). Relevance theory explains the selection task. *Cognition, 57*, 31–95.

Sperber, D., & Wilson, D. (1995). *Relevance (2nd ed.).* Oxford: Basil Blackwell.

Stanovich, K. E. (1999). *Who is rational? Studies of individual differences in reasoning.* Mahwah, NJ: Erlbaum.

Stanovich, K. E., & West, R. F. (1997). Reasoning independently or prior belief and individual differences in actively open-minded thinking. *Journal of Educational Psychology, 89*, 342–357.

Stanovich, K. E., & West, R. F. (1998). Cognitive ability and variation in selection task performance. *Thinking and Reasoning, 4*, 193–230.

Stevenson, R. J., & Over, D. E. (1995). Deduction from uncertain premises. *The Quarterly Journal of Experimental Psychology, 48A*, 613–643.

Tetlock, P. E. (1983). Accountability and perseverance of first impressions. *Social Psychology Quarterly, 46*, 285–292.

Thompson, V. A. (1994). Interpretational factors in conditional reasoning. *Memory and Cognition, 22*, 742–758.

Thompson, V. A. (2000). The task-specific nature of domain-general reasoning. *Cognition, 76*, 209–268.

Thompson, V. A. (2001). Reasoning from false premises: The role of soundness in making logical deductions. *Canadian Journal of Experimental Psychology, 50*, 315–319.

Thompson, V. A., & Mann, J. (1995). Perceived necessity explains the dissociation between logic and meaning: The case of "only if." *Journal of Experimental Psychology: Learning, Memory and Cognition, 21*, 1554–1567.

Torrens, D., Thompson, V. A., & Cramer, K. M. (1998). Individual differences and the belief bias effect: Mental models, logical necessity, and abstract reasoning. *Thinking and Reasoning, 5*, 1–28.

Vranas, P. B. M. (2000). Gigerenzer's normative critique of Kahneman and Tversky. *Cognition, 76*, 179–793.

Walker, L., Thibaut, J., & Andreoli, V. (1972). Order of presentation at trial. *Yale Law Review, 82*, 216–226.

Wason, P. C. (1960). On the failure to eliminate hypotheses in a conceptual task. *Quarterly Journal of Experimental Psychology, 12*, 129–140.

Wason, P. C. (1966). Reasoning. In B. M. Foss (Ed.), *New Horizons in Psychology I* (pp. 106–137). Harmandsworth: Penguin.

Wason, P. C. (1977). The theory of formal operations: A critique. In B. Gerber (Ed.), *Piaget and knowing* (pp. 119–135). London: Routledge and Kegan Paul.

Wason, P. C., & Evans, J. St. B. T. (1975). Dual processes in reasoning? *Cognition, 3*, 141–154.

Wason, P. C., & Johnson-Laird, P. N. (1972). *Psychology of reasoning: Structure and content.* London: Batsford.

Wason, P. C., & Shapiro, D. (1971). Natural and contrived experience in a reasoning problem. *Quarterly Journal of Experimental Psychology, 23*, 63–71.

Wetherick, N. E. (1962). Eliminative and enumerative behaviour in a conceptual task. *Quarterly Journal of Experimental Psychology, 14*, 246–249.

Wilkins, M. C. (1928). The effect of changed material on the ability to do formal syllogistic reasoning. *Archives of Psychology, New York*, No. 636.

5

Task Understanding

Vittorio Girotto

How should experimenters interpret participants' solutions of reasoning tasks, in particular, solutions that appear to diverge from normative models? This question has produced a vast theoretical debate (e.g., Stein, 1996; Stich, 1990), a large part of which concerns the issue that will be addressed in the present chapter: How do *participants* interpret reasoning tasks? The fact that participants may interpret and represent the premises or the instructions of an experimental problem in a way that differs from the experimenter's interpretation has been recognized for some time (e.g., Henle, 1962; Orne, 1962). In the last couple of decades, several studies have been designed to investigate how verbal comprehension factors may affect inferential processes. The emergence of linguistic-pragmatics, including its recent experimental developments, has made researchers aware of the role of these factors in inferential processes (see Noveck & Sperber, 2002). The reasoning literature, however, has produced evidence that comprehension and representation mechanisms other than pragmatic factors determine performance in reasoning problems.

A necessarily reduced selection of this literature will be presented in this chapter, whose structure follows the conventional distinction between deductive and probabilistic reasoning. The chapter begins with a review of some of the evidence that shows how linguistic-pragmatic factors determine simple deductive inferences, and preempt domain-specific reasoning processes in the most famous problem in the psychology of reasoning. It then compares pragmatic anomalies and representational difficulties as potential sources of erroneous relational and probabilistic inferences. Finally, it considers some implications of these results for evolutionary theories of reasoning.

The author is grateful to Luca Bonatti, Simonetta Fabrizio, Michel Gonzalez, Jacqueline Leighton, Guy Politzer, and Robert Sternberg for their comments on a previous version of this chapter.

DEDUCTIVE REASONING

Linguistic-Pragmatic Effects in Verbal Reasoning

Most reasoning researchers, regardless of their theoretical position about reasoning mechanisms, share the idea that the laws of language use (or linguistic-pragmatic factors) can affect deductive inferences (Braine & O'Brien, 1991; Johnson-Laird & Byrne, 2002). Typically, deductive reasoning problems present participants with verbal premises and require them to draw or evaluate a verbal conclusion. It is not surprising then that studying the way participants interpret the premises or the instructions has been considered a fundamental step in the investigation of deductive inferences (for reviews, see Hilton, 1995; Politzer, 1986, 2002). Consider the following problem:

All Anne's children are blond. Does it follow that some of Anne's children are blond?

This problem asks for an *immediate deduction*, that is, an inference from one explicit premise containing a quantifier (*all, some, no, some...not*) to another sentence containing a quantifier. The inference from *all A are B* to *some A are B* is logically valid (if all A are in fact B the conclusion is necessarily true, given that there are no cases of A that are not B), and it is called subalternation in Aristotle's logic. Most participants, however, do not endorse this inference. In particular, Politzer (1990) found that 70% of them consider it as false. This result is robust: It has been obtained with speakers of English and various non-Indo–European languages and with problems asking for an inference or for an interpretation of a premise or conclusion by means of Euler diagrams (Begg & Harris, 1982; Newstead, 1989; Politzer, 1991). Do failures to solve such a simple reasoning problem indicate that normal adults are not able to reason deductively? The answer would be affirmative, if the ordinary interpretation of quantified sentences were the same as the logical one.

Terms expressing quantifiers (*all, some*) form what in linguistic pragmatics is known as a *Horn scale*, that is, a set of verbal items ordered along a common dimension (for a review, see Levinson, 2000). Horn scales range various sets of terms like numerals < ... 6, 5, ... 2,1>, modals <*must, might*>, and connectives <*and, or*>, from most to less informative. How are these terms used outside reasoning experiments? In ordinary conversations, a speaker is supposed to observe what linguistic-pragmaticists call maxims of conversation, one of which is "make your contribution as informative as is required (for the current purposes of the exchange)" (Grice, 1989). Now, in the exchange:

PAUL: Are all Anne's children blond?
MARY: Some are.

Mary has apparently violated such a maxim, given that she has not confirmed Paul's question with a "Yes" or with "All are blond." In order to reconcile what she has said with the observance of the maxim, Paul has to draw an inference (a *conversational implicature*, in pragmatics terms) attributing to Mary an implicit meaning that goes beyond the explicit meaning of her utterance. He has to reason that, if she has used the term *some*, which is not the most informative term of the scale *<all, some>*, it means that she does not know whether the term *all* is applicable or knows that it is not. Otherwise, she would have used it. In other words, if Mary utters *some*, she implicates that *not all* is the case. This conversational meaning of *some* is at odds with its logical meaning, which could be spelled out as *some and perhaps all*. Now, if sentences in verbal reasoning problems are interpreted as sentences in ordinary conversation, participants are likely to prefer the restricted meaning of *some* dictated by the implicature *not all*, over its logical meaning. Therefore, if required to evaluate whether *some A are B* follows from *all A are B*, participants are likely to consider the conclusion as contradictory with the premise and to reject it as false.

Erroneous inferences of this sort, however, do not imply that naive participants fail to reason correctly in very elementary problems. These erroneous inferences only demonstrate the role of conversational implicatures in deductive reasoning. This conclusion is supported by two sets of empirical results. On the one hand, almost all participants solve the following problem:

All Anne's children are blond. Does it follows that none of Anne's children is not blond?

Like the previous one, this immediate inference problem asks for a logically valid deduction (in Aristotle's logic, inferring *no A are not-B* from *all A are B* is called obversion). Unlike the previous one, however, in this problem the quantifiers do not lead to scalar implicatures conflicting with their logical meaning. Thus, most participants answer "yes," showing that they are able to draw correct immediate inferences (Politzer, 1990). On the other hand, in some reasoning problems young children produce correct inferences more often than adults do. For instance, consider the following problem (adapted from Noveck, 2001):

You see here three boxes. Two of them are open. The first one contains a parrot and a bear, the second one only a parrot. The third box stays covered. It has the same content of either the first box (a parrot and a bear) or the second box (a parrot). This puppet says that *there might be a parrot in the closed box*. Is the puppet right or not?

Following a logical interpretation, the modal *might* has a meaning compatible with *must*. From a pragmatic point of view, however, the two modals form a Horn scale *<must, might>*, in which *must* is the more informative term. If a speaker uses the weaker term *might* (as in *there might be a parrot*), it implies that she had reason not to use the stronger term *must* (as in *there must be a parrot*). Thus, following a pragmatic interpretation, *might* is not compatible with *must*. Now, given that the context indicates that there must be a parrot, participants who adopt a pragmatic interpretation of *might* will conclude that the puppet's claim is wrong. Indeed, Noveck (2001) has demonstrated that only a third of adult participants conclude that the puppet's claim is right. By contrast, most seven-year-olds give such a logically correct answer, showing that they adopt a logical interpretation of *might*. Similar results have been obtained with the connective *or*. The logical interpretation of *or* is inclusive (i.e., from *A or B* one infers validly *A and B*). Pragmatically, however, *or* is exclusive. It is the lower term of the scale <*and, or*>, because it is less informative than *and*. Hence, if a speaker utters *A or B*, it implies that she had reason not to utter *and*. This generates the exclusive interpretation, which is the normal one for adult participants, by conveying the implicature *not(A and B)*. Children, however, tend to interpret *or* in an inclusive way (Braine & Rumain, 1981; Paris, 1973; Sternberg, 1979). These findings do not show that children are better reasoners than adults, but only that in some problems they may draw more logical inferences, being pragmatically less sophisticated than the latter. In sum, children's correct inferences indicate the source of apparently erroneous inferences in adult reasoning (i.e., conversational implicatures).

There is an open debate about whether implicatures determine inferences in more complex reasoning problems, such as categorical syllogisms (e.g., Newstead, 1995; Noveck, 2001). In any case, the reviewed results demonstrate that, in order to appropriately assess naive deduction, experimenters should analyze the way in which participants interpret verbal premises.

Understanding the Selection Task

In the previous section, we considered the role of comprehension factors in standard reasoning problems in which participants are required to reason from premises to conclusions. In the present section, we will consider a more complex problem in which the process of understanding the text and the instruction seems to provide individuals with an intuitive solution to the problem itself, so that they do not seem to engage in a proper reasoning effort. Not surprisingly, a pragmatic account of this problem does exist. Surprisingly, perhaps, this happens to be the most famous problem in the psychology of reasoning, namely, Wason's selection task (1966). In its standard version, it reads as follow:

Here are four cards. Each has a letter on one side and a number on the other side. Two of these cards are here with the letter side up and two with the number side up. [Four cards are represented with, on the visible side, A, C, 2, and 7]. Indicate which of these cards you need to turn over in order to judge whether the following rule is true: "If a card has a vowel on one side, then it has an even number on the other side."

With such a version of the task, typically only about 10% of participants make the correct selection of the A and 7 cards, that is, those that could present the falsifying combination "vowel and odd number." In other words, most participants fail to select the potential counterexamples (*p* and *not-q*) of a *descriptive* conditional statement with the linguistic form "If an item has the property P, then it has the property Q."

Since the early seventies, it has been shown that participants, including children, can solve versions of the selection task in which they have to test a *deontic* conditional with the linguistic form; "If an item has the property P, then it should have the property Q." In these cases, participants select the proper cards indicating the potential violations of conditionals expressing duties or rights resulting from contractual, social, or prudential arrangements (Cheng & Holyoak, 1985; Girotto, Gilly, Blaye, & Light, 1989; Griggs & Cox, 1982; Johnson-Laird, Legrenzi, & Legrenzi, 1972). For example, given the task of checking whether the rule "If one is drinking beer, then that person must be over 19 years of age" has been followed or not, most participants select the correct card combination ("This person drinks beer" and "This person is under 19 years of age").

Why do participants behave differently in these two versions of the selection task? There is a large literature trying to answer this question (for a recent review, see Manktelow, 1999). Some explanations are based on the assumption that deontic selections are not comparable with descriptive selections, because the two versions ask for a different task (Evans & Over, 1996; Manktelow & Over, 1991; Noveck & O'Brien, 1996). By contrast, Sperber, Cara, and Girotto (1995) have put forward a common explanation of descriptive and deontic selections based on a general theory of linguistic comprehension. According to Sperber et al. (1995), participants interpret the text of the selection problem, and in particular the conditional rule, by using the standard comprehension abilities they use in interpreting utterances in conversation or in reading. The very fact that an utterance is presented to a hearer raises expectations of relevance, and he or she searches for an interpretation that satisfies these expectations. The relevance of an utterance is a positive function of the inferences that can be derived from it in the context where it is processed and a negative function of the amount of effort it takes to derive these inferences (Sperber & Wilson, 1995). This justifies drawing inferences in their order of accessibility and stopping when the resulting interpretation meets one's expectations of relevance. For instance, from the conditional "If a card has a vowel on one side, then it has an even number on the other side," participants may infer that there are cards with a vowel and an even number. This implication is much more accessible than the more effort-demanding implication that there are no cards presenting a vowel and lacking an even number (on the difficulty of processing negations, see Horn, 1989). If participants solve the task by selecting the cards that are apt to test what they have inferred from the rule, those who make the existential interpretation of the conditional will select the logically incorrect cases. Given the inference that "there are vowel-even number cards," they will select the card with a vowel in order to see if it has an even number on the other side and the card with the even number to see if it has a vowel on the other side. Conditional statements, however, may achieve relevance in other ways. Consider the exchange:

PAUL: Let's buy some cheap champagne!
MARY: If it is real champagne, then it is expensive.

In this case, Mary's utterance achieves relevance by contradicting Paul's positive existential presupposition that there is cheap champagne. Now, suppose that the conditional rule of a selection task is interpreted in this way; that is, as the denial of the occurrence of (p and not-q) cases. If participants test the rule on the basis of this interpretation, they will select the cards corresponding to the cases that may test the truth or falsity of the proposition denied. These cards, of course, are p and not-q. In sum, in contexts in which the conditional rule is interpreted as a denial, and the denied (p and not-q) cases are as easy to represent as (p and q) cases, participants should select the logically correct cards in response to the selection task. This is what Sperber et al. (1995) found. They succeeded in eliciting good and bad performance with nearly identical descriptive versions of the task by rendering the negative inference more or less relevant. For example, they used a version of the task in which the free-market-oriented prince of Bargustan described his country in a way that could suggest that it suffers from many social or economic ills ("In my country people have no social security, no right to work. . . ."). Yet, the prince argued that Bargustan had no serious economic or social problems, asserting, "For instance, if a person is of working age, then this person has a job." In this case, the conditional statement is uttered in a context in which it is likely to be understood as a denial of the existence of working age people without a job. Moreover, this denied combination is a highly salient and lexicalized concept (*unemployed*). By contrast, in a control condition, the prince's assertion was "Of course, if a person is older than sixty-five, then this person is without a job." In this case, the context is unlikely to favor a negative interpretation of the conditional, the counterexample of which is a nonlexicalized concept of no particular salience for the participants of the study (person older than 65 and with a job). As predicted by the pragmatic account, in the former condition, most participants checked whether the prince's claim was true by selecting the correct cards ("person of working age" and "person with no job"). By contrast, only a few participants made the right selection in the control condition. These results contravened previous standard explanations, according to which descriptive problems were irredeemably difficult. They showed that, given appropriate context-rule pairs that make a *negative* interpretation of the conditional relevant, individuals do solve descriptive selection problems (for converging evidence, see e.g., Almor & Sloman, 2000; Green & Larking, 1995; Hardman, 1998; Liberman & Klar, 1996; Love & Kessler, 1995).

The same pragmatic account can be applied to deontic versions. Deontic conditionals typically achieve relevance through implicitly forbidding the occurrence of (*p* and *not-q*) cases (for a similar view, see Johnson-Laird & Byrne, 1991). These cases are instances of at least one lexicalized concept (e.g., *violation*), and are not more difficult to represent than the rule-abiding (*p* and *q*) cases. Therefore, when asked to check a deontic conditional, participants will select the cards corresponding to potential violations (i.e., *p* and *not-q*). For instance, from the drinking-age conditional rule, participants might infer that there should be no beer drinker of less than 19 years of age. They would then select the card representing a beer drinker and the card representing a person less than 19, thus, providing the correct selection. In sum, deontic selection performances can be attributed to the same comprehension mechanisms that determine intuitions of relevance in the descriptive tasks. If this explanation is correct, one should obtain deontic selections other than *p* and *not-q*, by manipulating relevance factors. Consider the deontic conditional: "If a person travels to any East African country, then that person must be immunized against cholera."

In standard problems, in which they are asked to test whether such a rule has been followed, participants are likely to interpret it as forbidding the occurrence of the violating cases (i.e., "people who went to an East African country without immunization against cholera"). Hence, they will tend to select the corresponding cards *p* and *not-q*. Suppose that the same conditional is uttered in a context in which the speaker knows that such a rule is no longer in force, and wants to know whether people have nevertheless followed it. In this context, the most relevant cases are not the potential violators, but the rule-abiding people who may have been immunized unnecessarily. Participants would then select the *p* ("this person went to an East African country") and *q* ("this person has been immunized against cholera") cards. This prediction has been corroborated in a study with a within-participants design (Girotto, Kemmelmeir, Sperber, & van der Henst, 2001). Given the same deontic rule presented in different contexts, participants selected either violating or rule-abiding cases (i.e., the cards that, regardless of their logical values, were apt to test their intuitions of relevance). Thus, by devising appropriate rule-context pairs, it is possible to elicit various patterns of deontic selection, without modifying participants' point of view (Gigerenzer & Hug, 1992; Light, Girotto, &

Legrenzi, 1990), or the plausibility of the potential violation (Girotto et al. 1989; Liberman & Klar, 1996).

In sum, comprehension mechanisms appear to be the main determinant of inferences in the most famous reasoning problem, such that it does not seem to be a reasoning problem in the strict sense (see also Evans, 1989).

Pragmatic Anomalies and Deductive Errors

Recognizing the roles of pragmatic factors in experimental reasoning problems does not imply that all erroneous inferences should be attributed to these factors. In particular, it does not imply that removing any pragmatic anomalies from reasoning problems will necessarily eliminate errors. To illustrate this point, we will examine a set of relational reasoning problems used by Byrne and Johnson-Laird (1989) to compare the model theory and the mental logic theory of reasoning (see below). Consider the following problems, where A, B, C, etc. refer to common objects:

Problem 1:   Problem 2:
A is on the right of B   B is on the right of A
B is on the right of C   C is on the left of B
D is in front of C   D is in front of C
E is in front of A   E is in front of B

In both problems, the question is "What is the relation between D and E?" The correct answer is "D is on the left of E." According to Byrne and Johnson-Laird, problem 1 is a one-model problem, that is, its premises are consistent with the mental representation of a single possibility:

C   B   A
D   E

Problem 2, instead, is a multiple-model problem, given that its premises are consistent with two distinct models, each representing a true possibility:

A   C   B   C   A   B
      D   E   D   E

The model theory predicts that problems are more difficult if they require reasoners to construct more mental models, because of the limited processing capacity of working memory. The results obtained by Byrne and Johnson-Laird corroborated this prediction. Although the two problems were similar, problem 1 turned out to be reliably easier than problem 2. In addition, Schaeken, Johnson-Laird and d'Ydewalle (1996) showed that, with premises referring to both spatial and temporal relations, participants need more time to solve a multiple-model problem such as problem 2, than to solve a one-model problem such as problem 1.

These results are theoretically important, given that the model theory and alternative theories based on rules of inferences make different predictions about the two problems. According to standard rules theories, individuals apply inference rules to the logical form of the premises and the difficulty of a reasoning problem depends on the number of inferential steps required to draw a conclusion (Braine & O'Brien, 1991; Hagert, 1984). Now, in problem 1 the premises do not explicitly assert the relation between A and C (which is the basis for inferring the relation between D and E). Individuals have to infer the relation between A and C by applying a transitivity rule to the first two premises. In problem 2, however, they do not need to perform an inferential step to obtain the corresponding, crucial relation between B and C, given that it is expressed by the second premise. Given the additional inferential step required by problem 1, individuals should solve problem 2 more easily than problem 1. In fact, the opposite is true. The advocates of the inference rules theories conceded that spatial inferences may be based on mental models, rather than on rules (Bonatti, 1994; for the possibility that different individuals rely on different reasoning processes, see Sternberg, 1980). Others have questioned the conclusiveness of Byrne and Johnson-Laird's (1989) results, by noticing that in problem 2 there is a premise (the first one) that is not relevant to reach the conclusion and that could impede reasoning. In particular, according to Rips (1994), "There is no reason to suppose that the final length of a derivation is the only pertinent factor . . . searching for a correct deduction can be sidetracked by the presence of irrelevant information, such as the first premise of these problems" (p. 415). Indeed, the following problem demonstrated the hindering role of the irrelevant premise (Van der Henst, 1999):

Problem 3:
C is on the left of B.
D is in front of C.
E is in front of B.
B is on the right of A.
What is the relation between D and E?

The premises of problem 3 are the same as the premises of problem 2. They are presented in a different order, however. Unlike problem 2, in which the irrelevant premise is presented first, in problem 3 the irrelevant premise is presented last. Following the model theory, problem 3 should be as difficult as problem 2, given that it should activate the representation of two distinct models. In fact, problem 3 turned out to be easier than problem 2. According to Van der Henst (1999), the model theory could explain this result by positing that in problem 3 reasoners draw the correct conclusion without integrating the model consistent with the final premise (i.e., without processing it). By contrast, Rips's (1994) interpretation cannot easily explain the correct inferences that participants draw in problem 3, given that it contains an irrelevant premise that should hinder the reasoning process, although presented last. In any case, in order to determine whether the complexity of representation is a source of difficulty in relational problems, one has to use problems that do not contain irrelevant premises.

Consider the following problems, whose premises describe cards with two cells (each of which contains a number) or cards with one cell (containing a letter). In addition to the number or the letter, each cell can also contain a symbol: * or $:

Problem 4:
7 is on the left of 3.
3 is on the left of C.
* is in the same cell as the 7.
$ is in the same cell as C.
What is the relation between * and $?
Problem 5:
7 is on the same card as 3.
3 is on the left of C.
* is in the same cell as 7.
$ is in the same cell as C.
What is the relation between * and $?

Both problems contain only relevant premises and require reasoners to infer the relationship between the number 7 and the letter C in order to draw the correct conclusion (i.e., "* is on the left of $"). In problem 4, however, the premises are consistent with only one model:

$$7^*3 \quad C\$$$

By contrast, problem 5 can be represented by two distinct models:

$$7^*3 \quad C\$$$

and

$$3\,7^* \quad C\$$$

Indeed, the former problem turned out to be reliably easier than the latter (Schaeken, Girotto, & Johnson-Laird, 1998). In sum, contrary to Rips's (1994) interpretation, the difficulty of relational problems appears to be caused by the degree of complexity of the activated representation, rather than by the mere presence of some irrelevant premises. These results suggest that removing pragmatic anomalies does not always guarantee correct reasoning. In more general terms, they suggest that linguistic-pragmatic factors are not the only determinants of deductive inferences.

PROBABILISTIC REASONING

The interpretation of premises and instructions seem to affect inferences also in probabilistic reasoning problems (for reviews, see Hilton, 1995; Nickerson, 1996). We will consider first linguistic-pragmatic factors and then more general comprehension factors.

The Role of Linguistic-Pragmatic Factors

Consider the well-known Linda problem (Tversky & Kahneman, 1983):

Linda is 31 years old, single, outspoken and very bright. She majored in philosophy. As a student, she was deeply concerned with issues of discrimination and social justice, and also participated in anti-nuclear demonstrations. Indicate which of the following alternatives is more probable:
Linda is a bank teller.
Linda is a bank teller and is active in the feminist movement.

According to the additivity rule of probabilities, the second outcome cannot be more likely than the first one. If Linda is a bank teller, she can be either feminist or not. The probability that she is a bank teller (T), therefore, is the sum of the probability that she is a feminist bank teller (T&F) and that she is a nonfeminist bank teller (T&not-F). Thus, the probability of T&F cannot be greater than the probability of T. Contrary to this fundamental rule of probability, a large majority of participants evaluate the outcome T&F as more likely than the outcome T. This error, called the *conjunction fallacy*, has been attributed to an intuitive procedure (a heuristic) that leads participants to evaluate the probability of an event on the basis of its representativeness. Given that the conjunction T&F represents Linda's description better than its constituent T, it is considered as more probable than T. Several researchers have questioned this explanation (Dulany & Hilton, 1991; Politzer & Noveck, 1991). A common criticism is that the presence of pragmatic anomalies in the problem, rather than the influence of an intuitive heuristic, could be the source of the apparently erroneous answers. In particular, the request to compare T versus T&F involves comparing a class and one of its subclasses, something that individuals do correctly at least since the age of seven. Given that in ordinary conversations adults are not usually asked questions whose answers are obvious to both speaker and hearer, the required comparison is pragmatically anomalous. In order to make it plausible or reconcile the comparison with the observance of conversational maxims (see section "Linguistic-Pragmatic Effects in Verbal Reasoning"), participants are induced to consider the statement T, "Linda is a bank teller," in an exclusive way; that is, participants are induced to generate the implicature T&not-F, interpreting the statement T as "Linda is a bank teller and NOT active in the feminist movement." If this explanation is correct, participants should solve problems that are less likely to induce such an implicature. Consider the problem (adapted from Politzer & Noveck, 1991):

> Daniel was a brilliant high school student. He is altruistic and deter-
> mined. Which of the following possibilities is more probable?
> Daniel entered medical school.
> Daniel graduated from medical school.

In this case, the inclusion of the events is based on the presupposition that in order to graduate one must enter medical school. Moreover, the statement expressing the conjunctive event "graduated" (G) does not contain the term *and*. Thus, the constituent event "entered" (E) is unlikely to be interpreted as "entered and not graduated" (E&not-G). As predicted by the pragmatic interpretation, most participants correctly evaluated E as more probable than G.

Not all difficulties in probabilistic reasoning, however, can be easily interpreted on the basis of a pragmatic analysis. For instance, consider the problem (adapted from Tversky & Kahneman, 1983):

Consider a regular six-sided die with four green faces and two red faces. The die will be rolled 20 times and the sequence of greens (G) and reds (R) will be recorded. You are asked to select one sequence, from a set of two, and you will win $25, if the sequence you chose appears on successive rolls of the die. Please check the sequence of greens and reds on which you prefer to bet:

1. RGRRR
2. RGRRRG

Sequence 2 is sequence 1 with an added G. Therefore, if sequence 2 occurs, sequence 1 necessarily occurs for it is contained in sequence 2. Hence, sequence 1 cannot be less probable than sequence 2. Sequence 2, however, is more representative of the die, given that it contains four Rs and two Gs (i.e., it contains a higher proportion of the more likely color). Being favored by representativeness, therefore, sequence 2 is likely to be considered as more probable than sequence 1. Indeed, most participants prefer to bet on sequence 2; they prefer to give up the chances of gain offered by sequence 1. Notice that the die problem is more similar to the Daniel problem than to the Linda problem. In the latter the conjunction is explicit and expressed by means of the word *and* (i.e., T&F). In both the die and Daniel problems, the two compared options are clearly nested (i.e., the occurrence of sequence 2 presupposes the occurrence of sequence 1; "graduated" presupposes "en-tered"), and there is no explicit conjunction. For this reason, participants should be less likely to interpret sequence 1 in an exclusive way (i.e., to generate the implicature "sequence 1 is sequence 2 with a final R instead of a final G or RGRRRR"). Yet, most participants fail the die problem. In sum, as in the case of relational reasoning (see section "Pragmatic Anomalies and Deductive Errors"), pragmatic factors do not seem to be the only source of error in probabilistic reasoning.

The Role of Question Form and Information Structure

Suppose one presents participants with various versions of a probability problem in which the *same* probability question is posed but formulated in different ways. If participants' interpretation of the question statement does not affect their reasoning, then they should draw the same inferences in response to the various versions. In fact, however, interpretations of the question statement do appear to affect inferences. Recent studies on naive probability reasoning have demonstrated that the form of a question, along with the structure of the information provided, does affect probability evaluations. This has been shown, in particular, in conditional probability problems. The most famous of them is the test-disease problem (see Hammerton, 1973), which, in its standard version, reads as follows:

A screening test of an infection is being studied. Here is the information about the infection and the test results.
There is a 4% chance that a person who is tested has the infection.
If the person is infected, there is a 75% chance that he/she will have a positive reaction to the test.
If the person is not infected, there is still a 12.5% chance that he/she will have a positive reaction to the test.
Imagine that Pierre is tested now. If Pierre has a positive reaction, what is the probability that he actually is infected?____%

In this problem, participants are required to evaluate the conditional probability that Pierre is infected, given that he is positive [i.e., p(infected| positive)]. In order to do so, they should apply the conditional probability rule:

p(infected|positive) =
p(infected & positive)/p(positive).

The standard test-disease problem, however, does not provide them with the values of the two terms of the ratio in the equation. In particular, in order to obtain the denominator [p(positive)], reasoners have to compute the probabilities of the two conjunctive events (i.e., "infected&positive" and "uninfected&positive"), both of which can be inferred by applying the conditional rule:

p(infected & positive) =
p(positive|infected) $\times$ p(infected) = 75% $\times$ 4% = 3%

and

p(uninfected & positive) =
p(positive|uninfected) × p(uninfected) = 12.5% × 96% = 12%

On the basis of these values, participants can compute the two terms of the required probability ratio:

p(infected|positive) = 3%/(3% + 12%) = 20%

Most participants fail this problem. A typical, erroneous conclusion is that Pierre has a 75% chance of being infected, if he is positive. In fact, these are his chances of being positive, if he is infected.

Failures to solve problems of this sort have been attributed to an incorrect application of heuristics (Kahneman, Slovic, & Tversky, 1982), or, even more pessimistically, to an innate limitation of the human mind. According to the "frequentist" view, natural selection has shaped a module in the mind to deal with frequencies, but not with probabilities of single events, as those expressed in the test-disease problem (Cosmides & Tooby, 1996; Gigerenzer & Hoffrage, 1995). These negative conclusions about naive probabilistic reasoning have been highly influential. Are they also well founded? If applying the rules of probability calculus were the only way to evaluate a conditional probability, the answer would be affirmative. However, when evaluating uncertain events, naive individuals may use much simpler procedures. Consider the following problem (Girotto & Gonzalez, 2002a):

You cast two dice simultaneously. You do not see how they land. If your friend tells you that the number of points is 7, what is the probability that one of the two dice landed 5?

Unless individuals are expert in probability calculus, they are likely to solve this problem in a very simple way. If they consider and enumerate the various possibilities in which the indicated events can occur, they may easily infer the required probability. Given that there are three pairs of points summing up to 7 (i.e., {1, 6}, {2, 5}, {3, 4}), and that in only one of them a die lands 5, individuals may conclude that the probability of the latter event is 1/3. In other words, they may reason *extensionally*, inferring the probability of an event from the different ways in which it can occur (Johnson-Laird, Legrenzi, Girotto, Sonino-Legrenzi, & Caverni, 1999). There is evidence that naive individuals (including children and people who lived before the advent of modern probability theory) make correct probability evaluations by enumerating the favorable possibilities in the finite set of all possibilities, that is, by means of extensional reasoning (Girotto & Gonzalez, 2002a). Consequently, one has to consider whether standard probability problems present adequate information and pose appropriate questions to assess naive probabilistic reasoning.

In problems like the test-disease one, participants have to calculate a conditional probability by means of a percentage, on the basis of other probability values expressed as percentages. The point is that if they are provided with percentages, individuals are unlikely to reason about possibilities. In particular, from percentage information, they cannot enumerate the subset of possibilities corresponding to the conjunctive events (i.e., "infected&positive" and "noninfected&positive"). For instance, given the information "a person has a 4% chance of being infected and a 75% chance of being positive, if she is infected," participants cannot easily enumerate the chances of being infected and positive. Asking participants to compute the chances favoring a single hypothesis, on the basis of percentages, however, is not the only way to phrase this probability question. Instead, individuals can be required to evaluate the chances favoring a given hypothesis *and* those favoring its alternative, on the basis of probabilities expressed in terms of *chances*, rather than in terms of percentages. Comparing the number of chances favoring each of two alternative hypotheses seems to be a spontaneous way of evaluating uncertain events. The earliest treatments of probability did not use percentages (or fractions), and expressed probabilities as comparisons of number of chances. For example, in 1776 William Emerson wrote, "The probability or improbability of an event is the judgment we form of it by comparing the number of chances there are for its happening, with the number of chances for its failing" (quoted by Hacking, 1975, p. 129). In everyday life, statements expressing probability in terms of number of chances are common. We may say, for instance, that a die has 1 chance in 6 (rather than a 16% chance) of landing on a given point. Moreover, comparing the chances of a hypothesis and those of its alternative is the natural way of assessing uncertain events in betting contexts, and it seems to predate the advent of probability theory. For instance, a character of Shakespeare says: "Twenty to one then he is shipped already." (Shakespeare, *The Two Gentlemen of Verona*, 1.1).

If probabilities are spontaneously expressed as chances and evaluated in a comparative way, individuals should easily solve the following version of the test-disease problem:

A person who was tested had 4 chances out of 100 of having the infection.
Three of the 4 chances of having the infection were associated with a positive reaction to the test.
Twelve of the remaining 96 chances of not having the infection were also associated with a positive reaction to the test.
If Pierre has a positive reaction, there will be____chance(s) that the infection is associated with his positive reaction, vs.____chance(s) that no infection is associated with his positive reaction.

In this version, the percentages of the original problem are expressed as numbers of chances (e.g., "4% chances of being infected" corresponds to

"4 chances out of 100 of having the infection"). In the resulting set of 100 chances, the values of the conjunctive events are available and can easily be used to answer the *comparative* question about *both* hypotheses (i.e., "3 vs. 12"). Indeed, most participants (85%) generate these correct answers, despite the fact that this is a proper probability problem (i.e., it concerns probabilities and asks for the evaluation of a single-event probability). Presenting the problem information in terms of chances, however, is not sufficient to improve reasoning, if the question asks the standard probability evaluation: "If Pierre has a positive reaction, there will be____chance(s) out of____that the infection is associated with his positive reaction." Indeed, only a few participants (8%) solve the chance problem posing such a question, which requires them to evaluate the *absolute* probability of *one* hypothesis (i.e., "3/15"), by combining the information from both hypotheses (Girotto & Gonzalez, 2001). In sum, contrary to current pessimistic views of probabilistic reasoning, naive individuals correctly estimate conditional probabilities in problems in which they can apply their intuitive extensional procedures. The major determinants of success appear to be the way probability information is presented and the evaluation question is posed.

TASK UNDERSTANDING AND EVOLUTIONARY EXPLANATIONS OF REASONING

In the recent years, several evolutionary explanations of reasoning have been put forward. They share the assumption that natural selection has endowed the human mind with adaptive mechanisms (modules) to reason about specific domains. What are the relations between the comprehension mechanisms we considered in the previous sections and these modules? According to the advocates of one of the most controversial evolutionary explanations of reasoning, the specialized reasoning modules preempt the more general comprehension mechanisms.

According to Cosmides (1989), the stabilization of cooperation among humans in evolutionary time implies that our mind is equipped with an adaptive mechanism to deal with social contracts, in particular to detect potential cheaters. A social contract is a situation in which an individual has to meet a requirement in order to be entitled to receive a benefit from another individual (or group), and cheaters are the individuals who take the benefit without satisfying the requirement. A social contract can be presented in a selection task in which cards represent on one side whether the benefit has been taken or not, and on the other side whether the requirement has been satisfied or not. If a specialized module to reason about social contracts does exist, participants should select the cards corresponding to the potential cheaters. Indeed, this is what participants seem to do in deontic selection tasks. For instance, when they have to test a social contract such as the drinking-age rule (see section "Understanding the Selection Task"), most participants select the cards that may represent beer drinkers of less than 19 years of age (i.e., the potential cheaters). Given that content-specialized mechanisms preempt the more general ones, Fiddick, Cosmides, and Tooby (2000) have concluded that the more specialized cheater detection device preempts comprehension mechanisms. In support of this claim, they showed that participants look for potential cheaters, regardless of whether the social contract is expressed by a conditional (i.e., "If you give me some potatoes, then I will give you some corn"), or not (i.e., one party says, "I want some potatoes." The other party replies "I want some corn"). According to Fiddick and colleagues, the finding that individuals look for instances of cheating regardless of the verbal form of the social contract corroborates the evolutionary explanation and falsifies relevance theory, according to which individuals look for cheaters because they interpret a social contract conditional as an implicit denial. A problem with this explanation is that general cognitive mechanisms may preempt more specialized ones, if the former provides the inputs for the latter. Suppose that there is an evolved mechanism specialized to reason about social contracts. Still, participants who receive a selection task must first comprehend it and, for this, must use their pragmatic comprehension mechanisms. As we have seen (see section "Understanding the Selection Task"), these mechanisms provide participants with intuitive solutions (Sperber et al., 1995). Why then do participants perform as well with or without an explicit social contract conditional? Does this mean that they simply look for cheaters ignoring the verbal form of the contract, as suggested by the evolutionary theory? In fact, verbal exchanges do not need an explicit conditional form in order to be interpreted conditionally (consider, for instance, the exchange: Child: "I want to go out." Mother: "You must put on your raincoat!"). More important, the evidence provided by Fiddick et al. (2000) is based on versions of the selection task in which participants (who played the role of a farmer interested in obtaining corn from other farmers, by giving them potatoes) were required to check whether they had been cheated. In order to identify cheaters, however, participants do not need to reason about the respect for or violation of a conditional statement. What they have to do is simply look for cards that exhibit one of the two features that jointly define the concept of cheating (i.e., "taking a benefit" and "failing to fulfill a requirement"). Unlike the selection task, this categorization task is trivially simple, regardless of whether the social contract is presented in conditional terms or not. Now, suppose that participants are not required to look for instances of *cheating* (i.e., "check whether they have cheated you"), but for instances of *exchange* (i.e., "check whether they have made an exchange with you"). If the evolutionary explanation is correct, this modification should have no effect, given that the social contract situation triggers the selection of possible instances of cheating (i.e., "you gave this person potatoes" and "this person gave you nothing"). By contrast, if the pragmatic explanation is correct, participants should select the cards representing possible instances of exchange (i.e., "you gave this person potatoes" and "this person gave you corn"), given that they are required to do so. Contrary to the evolutionary explanation, participants appear to select possible instances of either cheating or exchange, as a function of the task they are required to solve (Sperber & Girotto, 2002). In sum, participants do not automatically look for cheaters, even if they have to reason about situations that are supposed to activate the specialized cheating-detection mechanism. This demonstrates that such a mechanism does not preempt more general comprehension mechanisms.

Analogous conclusions can be drawn about probabilistic reasoning. According to the evolutionary explanation presented above (see section "The Role of Question Form and Information Structure"), probability information is unobservable, so that no specialized mechanism to deal with probabilities has been shaped by natural selection. By contrast, the human mind contains an evolved mechanism specialized to treat "natural frequencies" (Cosmides & Tooby, 1996; Gigerenzer & Hoffrage, 1995). Following this explanation, individuals are predicted to fail problems that convey probability information and ask for a probability evaluation and solve the same problems when they present observation frequencies and ask for a frequency prediction. Indeed, participants solve versions of the test-disease problem like the following one:

Four of the 100 people tested were infected.
Three of the 4 infected people had a positive reaction to the test.
Twelve of the 96 uninfected people also had a positive reaction to the test.
Imagine that this test is given to a new group of people. Among those who have a positive reaction, how many will actually have the infection?

In this case, the problem conveys information about absolute frequencies in a sample of observations, and the question requires participant to predict a frequency. Thus, the finding that participants solve it has been considered as evidence for the evolutionary frequentist hypothesis. As we have seen, however, evidence exists that participants do solve single event probability problems, when the structure of information and the question form allow them to reason extensionally, in particular when they are required to compare the number of chances of two competing hypotheses (see section "The Role of Question Form and Information Structure"). The advocates of the frequentist hypothesis have criticized these findings, claiming that individuals who solve chance problems do not solve genuine probability problems, because the number of chances are natural frequencies disguised as probabilities, though lacking the properties of proper probabilities (Hoffrage, Gigerenzer, Krauss, & Martignon, 2002). In fact, as indicated above, using number of chances is a common way to communicate probabilities. Suppose you toss a die 10 times, obtain a "4" twice, and say "I obtained '4' twice in 10 tosses, but I know that my chances were 1 out of 6." In this case, "1 out of 6" does not express a frequency, that is, you do not mean that you tossed a coin 6 times and you obtained a "4" once, but that you had 1 possibility of obtaining that outcome out of a total set of 6 possibilities. In other words, the number of chances conveys information about probabilities. Indeed, naive individuals do not confuse number of chance statements with natural frequency ones (Girotto & Gonzalez, 2002b). Moreover, evidence exists that participants fail frequency problems, when it is difficult for them to treat frequencies extensionally. For instance, most participants fail frequency versions of the test-disease problem in which they are asked to predict the frequency of the disease in a new sample of 100 people who had a positive reaction (e.g., "Among 100 positive people, there will be___out of___infected people"). In principle, this version is much simpler than the standard probability version (see section "The Role of Question Form and Information Structure"), given that it does not present information in terms of percentages. The question, however, mentions the frequency of positive people in the sample under consideration (i.e., 100). This leads participants to use such a frequency as the denominator of the required frequency ratio, generating the typical, erroneous answer "3/100." In contrast, virtually all participants solve frequency versions that ask for a *comparative* prediction about *both* hypotheses (Girotto & Gonzalez, 2001). That is, they solve frequency questions similarly to the comparative probability questions we discussed above (i.e., "Among the people who will have a positive reaction to the test, there will be___people whose positive reaction is associated with the infection, vs.___people whose positive reaction is associated with no infection"). Interestingly, the question form seems to affect frequency predictions not only in the more artificial verbal problems, but also in problems in which participants have to extract frequencies from actual observations in natural-like settings (e.g., Shanks, 1990). In sum, even probabilistic and statistical inferences seem to depend on general factors related to problem representation and question interpretation, rather than on some innate and specialized mechanisms.

CONCLUSIONS

The first part of the chapter presented examples of the role of linguistic-pragmatic factors in deductive reasoning, both in simple inferential problems and in the more complex selection task. It then presented evidence that errors in both deductive and probabilistic reasoning may depend on factors related to the complexity of problem representation and the structure of the question, rather than on the hindering presence of pragmatic anomalies in the text problem. The chapter ended with a caveat about the use of verbal problems as tools to test hypotheses about the existence and character of evolved reasoning mechanisms.

Taken together, the evidence reviewed in this chapter indicates a possible answer to the initial question. In several cases, the inferences drawn by participants differ from the inferences that the experimenters want to investigate, because the former apply their reasoning abilities on a problem representation that does not coincide with the experimenters' one. This does not mean that all reasoning errors depend on similar discrepancies, and that naive reasoning is potentially error-free. It suggests, however, that, in order to interpret participants' solutions to verbal reasoning problems, experimenters should carefully consider the way participants interpret and represent premises and instructions.

References

Almor A., & Sloman, S. A. (2000). Reasoning versus text processing in the Wason selection task: A nondeontic perspective on perspective effects. _Memory and Cognition, 28,_ 1060–1070.

Begg, I., & Harris, G. (1982). On the interpretation of syllogisms. _Journal of Verbal Learning and Verbal Behavior, 21,_ 595–620.

Bonatti, L. (1994). Propositional reasoning by model? _Psychological Review, 101,_ 725–733.

Braine, M. D. S., & Rumain, B. (1981). Children's comprehension of "or": Evidence for a sequence of competencies. _Journal of Experimental Child Psychology, 31,_ 46–70.

Braine, M. D. S., & O'Brien, D. P. O. (1991). A theory of if: A lexical entry, reasoning program, and pragmatic principles. _Psychological Review, 98,_ 182–203.

Byrne, R. M. J., & Johnson-Laird, P. N. (1989). Spatial reasoning. _Journal of Memory and Language, 28,_ 564–575.

Cheng, P. N., & Holyoak, K. J. (1985). Pragmatic reasoning schemas. _Cognitive Psychology, 17,_ 391–416.

Cosmides, L. (1989). The logic of social exchange: Has natural selection shaped how humans reason? Studies with the Wason selection task. _Cognition, 31,_ 187–276.

Cosmides, L., & Tooby, J. (1996). Are humans good intuitive statisticians after all? Rethinking some conclusions from the literature on judgment under uncertainty. _Cognition, 58,_ 1–73.

Dulany, D. E., & Hilton, D. J. (1991). Conversational implicature, conscious representation, and the conjunction fallacy. _Social Cognition, 9,_ 85–110.

Evans, J. St. B. T. (1989). _Bias in human reasoning: Causes and consequences._ Hillsdale, NJ: Erlbaum.

Evans, J. St. B. T., & Over, D. E. (1996). _Rationality and reasoning._ Hove, UK: Psychology Press.

Fiddick, L., Cosmides, L., & Tooby, J. (2000). No interpretation without representation: The role of domain-specific representations in the Wason selection task. _Cognition, 77,_ 1–79.

Gigerenzer, G., & Hoffrage, U. (1995). How to improve Bayesian reasoning without instruction: Frequency format. _Psychological Review, 102,_ 684–704.

Gigerenzer, G., & Hug, K. (1992). Domain specific reasoning: Social contracts, cheating, and perspective change. *Cognition, 43,* 127–71

Girotto, V., Gilly, M., Blaye, A., & Light, P. H. (1989). Children's performance in the selection task: Plausibility and familiarity. *British Journal of Psychology, 80,* 79–95.

Girotto, V., & Gonzalez, M. (2001). Solving probabilistic and statistical problems: A matter of question form and information structure. *Cognition, 78,* 247–276.

Girotto, V., & Gonzalez, M. (2002a). Extensional reasoning about chances. In W. Schaeken, G. De Vooght, A. Vandierendonck, & G. d'Ydewalle. (Eds.). *Mental model theory: Extensions and Refinements.* Mahwah, N.J.: Erlbaum.

Girotto, V., & Gonzalez, M. (2002b). Chances and frequencies in probabilistic reasoning: Rejoinder to Hoffrage, Gigerenzer, Krauss, and Martignon. *Cognition, 84,* 353–359.

Girotto, V., Kemmelmeir, M., Sperber, D., & van der Henst, J. B. (2001). Inept reasoners or pragmatic virtuosos? Relevance and the deontic selection task. *Cognition, 81,* 69–76.

Green, D. W., & Larking, R. (1995). The locus of facilitation in the abstract selection task. *Thinking and Reasoning, 1,* 183–199.

Grice, P. (1989). *Studies in the way of words.* Cambridge, MA.: Harvard University Press.

Griggs, R. A., & Cox, J. R. (1982). The elusive thematic-materials effect in Wason's selection task. *British Journal of Psychology, 73,* 407–420.

Hacking, I. (1975). *The emergence of probability.* Cambridge: Cambridge University Press.

Hagert, G. (1984). Modeling mental models: Experiments in cognitive modeling of spatial reasoning. In T. O'Shea (Ed.), *Advances in artificial intelligence.* Amsterdam: North-Holland.

Hammerton, M. (1973). A case of radical probability estimation. *Journal of Experimental Psychology, 101,* 252–254.

Hardman, D. (1998). Does reasoning occur in the selection task? A comparison of relevance-based theories. *Thinking and Reasoning, 4,* 353–376.

Henle, M. (1962). On the relation between logic and thinking. *Psychological Review, 69,* 366–378.

Hilton, D. (1995). The social context of reasoning: Conversational inference and rational judgement. *Psychological Bulletin, 118,* 248–271.

Hoffrage, U., Gigerenzer, G., Krauss, S., & Martignon, L. (2002). Representation facilitates reasoning: What natural frequencies are and what they are not. *Cognition, 84,* 343–352.

Horn, L. (1989). *A natural history of negation.* Chicago: Chicago University Press.

Johnson-Laird, P. N., & Byrne, R. M. J. (1991). *Deduction.* Hillsdale, N.J.: Erlbaum.

Johnson-Laird, P. N., & Byrne, R. M. J. (2002) Conditionals: a theory of meaning, pragmatics, and inference. *Psychological Review, 109,* 646–678.

Johnson-Laird, P. N., Legrenzi, V., Girotto, V., Sonino-Legrenzi, M., & Caverni, J. P. (1999). Naive probability: A mental model theory of extentional reasoning. *Psychological Review, 106,* 62–88.

Johnson-Laird, P. N., Legrenzi, P., & Legrenzi, M. S. (1972). Reasoning and a sense of reality. *British Journal of Psychology, 63,* 395–400.

Kahneman, D., Slovic, P., & Tversky, A. (Eds.). (1982). *Judgment under uncertainty: Heuristics and biases.* Cambridge: Cambridge University Press.

Levison, S. (2000). *Presumptive meaning: The theory of generalized conversational implicature.* Cambridge, MA.: MIT Press.

Liberman, N., & Klar, Y. (1996). Hypothesis testing in Wason's selection task: Social exchange, cheating detection or task understanding. *Cognition, 58,* 127–56.

Light, P. H., Girotto, V., & Legrenzi, P. (1990). Children's reasoning on conditional promises and permissions. *Cognitive Development, 5,* 369–83.

Love, R., & Kessler, C. (1995). Focussing in Wason's selection task: Content and instruction effects. *Thinking and Reasoning, 1,* 153–82.

Manktelow, K. I. (1999). *Reasoning and thinking.* Hove, UK: Psychology Press.

Manktelow, K. I., & Over, D. E. (1991). Social rules and utilities in reasoning with deontic conditionals. *Cognition, 39,* 85–105.

Newstead, S. E. (1989). Interpretational errors in syllogistic reasoning. *Journal of Memory and Language, 28,* 78–91.

Newstead, S. (1995). Griceian implicatures and syllogistic reasoning. *Journal of Memory and Language, 34,* 644–664.

Nickerson, S. (1996). Ambiguities and unstated assumptions in probabilistic reasoning. *Psychological Bulletin, 120,* 410–433.

Noveck, I. A., (2001). When children are more logical than adults: Experimental investigations of scalar implicature. *Cognition, 78,* 165–188.

Noveck, I. A., & O'Brien, D. P. (1996). To what extent do pragmatic reasoning schemas affect performance on Wason's selection task? *Quarterly Journal of Experimental Psychology, 49A,* 463–489.

Noveck, I. A., & Sperber, D. (2002). *Experimental pragmatics.* London: Palgrave.

Orne, M. T. (1962). On the social psychology of the psychological experiment: With particular reference to demand characteristics and their implications. *American Psychologist, 17,* 776–783.

Paris, S. (1973). Comprehension of language connectives and propositional logical relationships. *Journal of Experimental Child Psychology, 16,* 278–291.

Politzer, G. (1986). Laws of language use and formal logic. *Journal of Psycholinguistic Research, 15,* 47–92.

Politzer, G. (1990). Immediate deduction between quantified sentences. In K. J. Gilhooly, M. T. Keane, R. H. Logie, & G. Erdos (Eds.) *Lines of thinking: Reflections on the psychology of reasoning.* Chichester: Wiley.

Politzer, G., (1991). Comparison of deductive abilities across language. *Journal of Cross-Cultural Psychology, 22,* 389–402.

Politzer, G., (2002). Reasoning, judgement and pragmatics. In I. Noveck & D. Sperber (Eds.), *Experimental pragmatics.* London: Palgrave.

Politzer, G., & Noveck, I. A. (1991). Are conjunction rule violations the results of conversational rule violations? *Journal of Psycholinguistic Research, 20,* 83–103.

Rips, L. J. (1994). *The psychology of proof.* Cambridge, MA: Bradford, MIT Press.

Shanks, D. R. (1990). Connectionism and the learning of probabilistic concepts. *Quarterly Journal of Experimental Psychology, 42A,* 209–237.

Schaeken, W., Girotto, V., & Johnson-Laird, P. N. (1998) The effect of an irrelevant premise on temporal and spatial reasoning. *Kognitionswisschenschaft, 7,* 27–32.

Schaeken, W., Johnson-Laird, P. N., & d'Ydewalle (1996). Mental models and temporal reasoning. *Cognition, 60,* 205–234.

Sperber, D., Cara, F., & Girotto, V. (1995). Relevance theory explains the selection task. *Cognition, 52,* 3–39.

Sperber, D., & Girotto, V. (2002). *Does the selection task detect cheater-detection?* Manuscript submitted for publication.

Sperber, D., & Wilson, D. (1995). *Relevance: Communication and Cognition (2nd ed.).* Oxford: Blackwell.

Stein, E. (1996). *Without good reason. The rationality debate in philosophy and cognitive science.* Oxford: Clarendon Press.

Sternberg, R. (1979). Developmental patterns in the encoding and comprehension of logical connectives. *Journal of Experimental Child Psychology, 28,* 469–498.

Sternberg, R. (1980). Representation and process in linear syllogistic reasoning. *Journal of Experimental Psychology: General, 109,* 119–159.

Stich, D. (1990).*The Fragmentation of reason.* Cambridge, MA: Bradford, MIT Press.

Tversky, A., & Kahneman, D. (1983). Extensional versus intuitive reasoning: The conjunction fallacy in probability judgment. *Psychological Review, 90,* 293–315.

Van der Henst, J. B. (1999). The mental model theory and spatial reasoning re-examined: The role of relevance in premise order. *British Journal of Psychology, 90,* 73–84.

Wason, P. C. (1966). Reasoning. In B. M. Foss. (Ed.) *New horizons in psychology.* Harmondsworth: Penguin.

PART TWO

THE WORKINGS OF REASONING

6

Strategies and Knowledge Representation

Keith Stenning and Padraic Monaghan

Logic, computer science, artificial intelligence, psychology, and linguistics all study human reasoning. Unfortunately, much of the insight into reasoning gained by these methods has not spread beyond the rather stringent bounds of each discipline. As a result, the study of human reasoning has suffered from balkanization. This chapter rethinks the relationship between theory, formalization, and empirical investigations to bring a more interdisciplinary approach to human reasoning. We will show that combining these fields of study clarifies the nature and status of knowledge representation in reasoning, and highlights the strategies underpinning variations in performance, raising new empirical questions, and backgrounding others.

So, why include logical studies in human reasoning? Logic had its origins in attempting to provide agreement about which arguments are acceptable. Aristotle was concerned that those who were good at arguing could convince an audience of the truth of an argument, irrespective of how valid the argument itself was. Rhetoric would get the upper hand over truth. He specified a formal system of reasoning – the syllogistic form – to reflect which patterns of argument ought to be accepted, and which ought not. Logic, then, developed in classical Greece, as an educational technology for teaching people to learn and to communicate, chiefly in the professional practices of law and politics.

More recently, however, logical theory has taken a more mathematical turn, but it has not discarded its origins nor its relevance to human reasoning. Roughly speaking, logic and computational theory are the mathematics of reasoning (whether reasoning occurs in people or machines), and their relation to psychology is analogous to the relation between geometry and the study of visual perception. No psychologist of vision would dream of discarding geometry, or inventing new ad hoc geometries, in going about their business, nor would they worry that geometry is in competition with perceptual theories. Theories of visual perception without geometrical foundation are just confused. As in all sciences, mathematics and its attendant conceptualizations are a foundation for empirical investigation. Far from competing, the formal and empirical partners need to interact in driving forward programs of research. We need to be very clear at any given point what are conceptual issues and what are empirical ones.

Of course, mathematics can be a misleading guide if turned directly into cognitive theory. As Gibson (1979) showed us, depth perception is not based directly on perceivers solving theorems of projective geometry with binocular disparities as their inputs. But Gibson's solution was not to discard geometry, but to exploit it in a much more abstract way. His analyses in terms of "optic flow" showed that there are abstract invariants in the environment that perceivers can be sensitive to, and that allow much more direct perceptual inferences to be drawn. Similarly, we will argue that an abstract understanding of logical foundations of reasoning is a necessary basis for an insightful psychology of reasoning.

We begin by discussing some varieties of reasoning, but we do so only very briefly in order to focus on deductive reasoning. We then look at some empirical evidence about how subjects (and experimenters) construe the tasks that experimenters describe as deductive reasoning. The question of how subjects understand reasoning tasks is one example of the need for *meta reasoning* – reasoning about how to reason. In this case, the subject has to reason about how to construe the experimenter's intentions about the task that has been set. This is indicated in the rightmost part of Figure 6.1. The experimenter and the participant might have different initial ideas about the task, and much of the participant's hard work is in seeing what the experimenter is trying to get at (not just the experimenter trying to understand the participant's perspective). This shift from reasoning within a system to reasoning about systems alters the focus of empirical research from *reasoning* to *learning*, and learning to reason. If subjects do not understand what they are being asked to do when given reasoning tasks, then an alternative empirical approach is to study what happens when they are

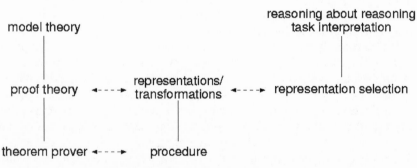

FIGURE 6.1. Levels of theory and empirical reasoning.

taught to understand deduction. We propose that many laboratory reasoning tasks are more productively thought of as learning tasks – learning what it is the experimenter might have in mind – and the empirical exploration of the mental processes involved can be enriched by studying learning overtly. We return to review some work that takes this approach in the final section.

Starting with questions about how subjects construe these tasks reveals that even experimenters have not always been clear themselves about how they interpret the tasks they set. This is empirically a serious situation, and we must turn to logical concepts of deduction to clarify what deduction is.

Logic employs several levels of abstraction to understand representational systems and their use in reasoning. Figure 6.1 shows these levels on the left, and relates them to aspects of psychological practice and theory on the right. Our first goal is to explain what is meant by the logical distinctions.

Our second goal is to show how they get mismapped onto psychological distinctions in discussions of systems of representation in reasoning. One of the most prominent conceptual confusions in deductive reasoning is the issue about whether human reasoning is based on systems of rules which rewrite sentences in the mind – "mental logic" (e.g., Rips, 1994) – or whether human reasoning is based on rules that manipulate representations of individuals in the mind – mental models (e.g., Johnson-Laird & Byrne, 1991). This debate has been extremely influential in the psychology of human reasoning. It supposes that people have some sort of "fundamental reasoning mechanism" and that the goal of investigations is to figure out what sort of representations it employs – sentences or models.

We will argue that this debate fundamentally confuses levels of logical analysis. On the one hand, mental models theory is presented as a theory of a particular mental representation system together with the rules that manipulate its representations and guide proof (a system on a par with particular "mental logics"). At the same time mental models theory is presented as parallel to logical model theory in which reasoning about representation systems is carried out in some meta-language. Either view maintained consistently might be useful. Mixed together they lead to at least two confusions.

First, there is no way to discriminate the representations people are using in the reasoning experiments as presented. The insightful level of description of these experiments is more abstract than mental models or mental rules, or whatever. Second, describing mental models as analogous to logical model theory would mean that mental models could not specify *processes* of reasoning because logical model theory is abstract with regard to processing.

In Figure 6.1 the confusion can be illustrated as trying to interpret mental models at both model theory and theorem prover levels in the diagram.

In fact, we will argue that switching between these levels is an important part of human processing, but then that requires us to distinguish the levels carefully. Clearly, understanding the levels of logical characterization of systems (model theory, proof theory, and theorem prover) is of some importance to the psychology of reasoning, and we spend some time on this further on in this chapter. The details of these confusions will follow from clarifying the logical concepts.

In summary, our goal is to realign the relationship between formal and empirical studies of reasoning and to show that this is not some philosophical exercise but makes blunt differences to our empirical understandings. Psychologists sometimes find this insistence on the mathematical and conceptual underpinnings of their subject threatening. Mathematical logic is a daunting undertaking. But just as with geometry's involvement in visual perception research, the real importance of logic is not the advanced mathematical niceties but the fundamental concepts. The concepts are abstract and easily misunderstood, but the grasp required is not highly technical. We will assume no background in computation or logic, and wherever possible we will illustrate how conceptual distinctions make real differences to the gathering and interpretation of empirical data – the best reassurance that the effort is both worthwhile and necessary for psychology.

THE MANY KINDS OF REASONING

Reasoning happens when we have representations of information about some situation, and we transform those representations in ways that lead them to re represent information about the same situation. That is a very general definition, and here are some examples: (1) We may see the sun rise each morning for a number of mornings and conclude that the sun will rise every morning; (2) we may assume that the earth is a planet and that planets orbit stars, and we may conclude that the earth orbits a star; (3) we may observe that there is a general tendency for the sun to rise later when the air temperature is cooler and that it is cool this morning, so we may reason that the sun will tend to rise later than some norm this morning; (4) alternatively, we may observe the sun rise late and reason that the temperature was probably colder this morning; (5) we may hypothesize that the electrons spinning around a nucleus are like planets orbiting around the sun and conclude that atoms are larger than their nuclei; (6) we may have the problem of finding out when the earth, mars, and the sun will next be in syzygy and conclude that it will be the 29th of February, 3000.

All of these are instances of reasoning according to our definition. Each involves some representations of information about some situation and each involves transforming the given pieces of information, possibly along with other information, to yield different representations of information about the same situation. In the cases given above, the information is presented in sentences, but the representations could also be diagrams or some other representational system: (1) is a case of inductive reasoning which goes from information about specific instances to a generalization about an open-ended set of possible instances. Bertrand Russell has a famous description of this sort of reasoning at play. Every day a turkey is fed by the farmer, until it comes to know that it is going to be fed, so it runs to meet the farmer each morning. The turkey's generalization stands well for several weeks, until Christmas Eve.... (2) in contrast is deductive reasoning, which merely draws out information that is already contained in the meaning of the first two statements (the earth is a planet, planets orbit stars) and expresses some of it in new form (the earth orbits a star). (3) is probabilistic reasoning about whether things are more or less probable in the future in a situation given certain other things. (4) is also probabilistic reasoning but concerned with what caused present symptoms, rather than predicting their occurrence-diagnostic reasoning. (5) is reasoning by analogy from one domain (the solar system) to another (atomic structure). (6) is usually thought of as problem solving, which may involve all of these other sorts of reasoning in combination.

These kinds of reasoning are not exhaustive, nor are they always easy to discriminate or neatly separated in real world human reasoning processes. Indeed, as we shall see, even experts may disagree about which kind or kinds of reasoning a given task elicits from reasoners. However, they do represent theoretically important classes of reasoning. Understanding the dimensions on which they differ, and the relations they bear to each other, is critical to making sense of human reasoning.

DEDUCTIVE REASONING

We defined deductive reasoning above as reformulating information taken to be true and expressing it, or part of it, in a conclusion. Each piece of information that is taken to be true is called a *premise* (sometimes an *assumption*). Deductive reasoning works on the relations between the meanings of representations in systems of representation (such as languages – either artificial or natural, diagrammatic systems, mathematical systems, and so on).

Deductive reasoning is theoretically basic to understanding the other types of reasoning discussed above. For example, inductive reasoning has to be understood as introducing new assumptions (that the sun rises every morning) on the basis of evidence (I have seen that the sun has risen for the last few days). Introducing assumptions is a fundamental operation in deductive reasoning. But deduction draws out what is contained in assumptions. It does not tell us what assumptions to make. So induction and deduction are pretty much complementary. They are very different processes. Deduction is about the relationship between form and meaning of representations. Induction is about the relationship between evidence and generalization.

Similarly, probabilistic reasoning, at a deeper level, can be cast as deductive reasoning about probabilities – drawing out the information contained in representations of probability. But the reasoning still has to be founded on a language whose statements are what have probabilities of truth and falsity and whose logical relations are still essential. Reasoning by analogy, or analogical reasoning, is about constructing new representation systems (ones that use relations between planets to represent the structure of atoms, for example) and reasoning deductively within those new systems. These other kinds of reasoning involve more than deduction, but they cannot be understood except in relation to the concepts of deductive reasoning.

We begin by looking at some empirical evidence about how participants (and experimenters) see the tasks that are described as deductive reasoning tasks in the literature. This evidence strongly suggests that subjects (and some experimenters) have a variety of interpretations, not all of which treat the tasks as deductive tasks, and that this strongly influences their observed behavior.

Having looked at how laboratory tasks are interpreted, we give an introduction to the logical concept of deduction. There are three levels of abstraction in logic that must be understood to clarify how logicians conceptualize deduction: model theory, proof theory, and theorem provers. All are germane to studies of human reasoning. We then take this conceptualization of deduction and look afresh at the debate between "mental models" and "mental logics" as accounts of human deductive reasoning, indicating the dispute is not as fundamental as it appears.

HOW DO SUBJECTS (AND EXPERIMENTERS) INTERPRET DEDUCTIVE TASKS?

Here is a common kind of logical question:

Assume that *all A are B* is true. Does it follow logically that *all B are A* must be true?

After thinking for a moment about this, it becomes clear that there are several points where misunderstandings might arise between the experimenter's expectations and the participant's understanding. Participants, when told to make assumptions and instructed to "say what follows logically," generally do not understand these instructions.

This question and others like it are designed to assess naive logical intuitions about the quantifiers "all," "some," "no," and "some.... not" (Newstead, 1989, 1995; Stenning & Cox, 1995; Stenning, Yule, & Cox, 1996). Sometimes the material contains abstract variables such as these As and

Bs and sometimes it is contentful words such as "artists" and "botanists." In this task these differences do not make a great deal of difference.

These questions are repeated for all four quantifiers, and for subjects/ predicates in the question "in place" relative to their positions in the assumption (i.e., AB) or, as in the example, "reversed" (i.e., BA). This task is designed to elicit how subjects interpret quantifiers (*all, some, some . . . not, none*), but they are also about how subjects construe the task of "deciding what follows," and about the influence of subject/predicate structure on logical intuitions.

It is testimony to the likelihood that participants may not know what "logically follows" means that experimenters have had their problems in this respect, too. They have sometimes only allowed the responses "yes this sentence must be true" or "no, this sentence must be false" to these questions. But if subjects are to assess what logically follows, they would have to answer that "the conclusion could be true or could be false" to our example question above. If *all A are B* is true, *all B are A* may be true or it may be false. In logical terms, the two sentences are *logically independent* – there are some interpretations where the conclusion is true and some where it is false. Without being given the third response option to say that the conclusion is logically independent, subjects cannot begin to reflect their intuitions about deductive validity, as opposed to intuitions about what is *likely* true or *likely* false.

In fact, asking the question with only two options strongly suggests that the experimenter has an inductive or probabilistic understanding of the task. "If the assumption is true, does that make it more or less likely that the conclusion is true, relative to some baseline expectation?" This is a perfectly sensible interpretation of how arguments are often intended, but it is not a deductive interpretation.

Needless to say, when participants are given the third response option and, therefore, are able to reflect deductive validity, many still do not perform according to the logical concept of deduction. Why should they without being taught the technical sense of *follows logically*? But their responses do come in coherent patterns which reflect different misunderstandings of the task and can be used to predict, for example, their syllogistic reasoning.

Several other chapters in this book provide detailed discussion of syllogisms, so we define them only briefly here. The word syllogism comes from the Greek *syl-* meaning "with" and *logizomai* meaning "to reason," so a syllogism is a problem to be solved "with reason." In the literature we discuss here, it has come to be used to refer to problems comprised of two quantified premises with a shared (or "middle") term, for example: "all B are A, some B are C." The shared term is "B." The task is to provide a deductively valid conclusion linking A and C, if there is any such connection, and express it in terms of one of the four quantifiers "all," "no," "some," or "some not. . . . "

Newstead's (1989, 1995) interest in interpretation was to see if Grice's (1975) theory of conversational pragmatics could explain problems that participants have with syllogistic reasoning. Grice argued that "ordinary conversation" is a cooperative activity and that we frequently reason from our interlocutor's cooperativeness in interpreting what they mean. So if someone who knows everything about As and Bs tells us that some As are Bs we may conclude that some As are not Bs, on the grounds that if all As were Bs she would, being a cooperative communicator, have told us so. You (and we) do this kind of reasoning all the time in order to understand each other. Notice that *if* this is what participants are doing in experiments, they are not even *trying* to do the deductive task the experimenter intends. This drawing of what Grice called *implicatures* on a cooperative model of communication is distinct both from deduction and from the probabilistic interpretation just mentioned.

Newstead interpreted his results as showing that although Grice's theory of conversational pragmatics gains considerable support from the interpretation data (subjects frequently drew implicatures like the example), he could not predict their subsequent reasoning about syllogisms from these Gricean interpretations. Stenning et al. (1996) and Stenning and Cox (2003) found that people responded with coherent patterns of responses across sets of the interpretation questions, and these patterns could predict performance on subsequent syllogistic reasoning.

Stenning and Cox (1995) identify two groups of participants who respond in consistent ways. A substantial group of the participants, "hesitants," almost always answer questions of the form *XA is B* does it follow that *YB is A* by saying "perhaps and perhaps not" regardless of whether the quantifiers X and Y are all, no, some or some . . . not. So, when the problem is *all A are B* does it follow that *all B are A*, "hesitants" answer legitimately. But when the question is *some A are B* does it follow that *some B are A*, their answer is illegitimate. A second group, "rash" responders, shows the opposite tendency, illegitimately responding "true" to the first question but legitimately responding "true" to the second, again largely independently of quantifier. The rash group's problem is one of understanding validity, but the hesitant group's problem is not so much with understanding validity as understanding when transformations change meaning and when they just change "information packaging." *Some A are B* is undoubtedly differently packaged to *some B are A*, but in deduction, we have to recognize the invariant proposition underneath the different ways of expressing the same proposition.

Responding that "all A are B" means that "all B are A" must be true is an instance of the much discussed fallacy of "illicit conversion" (e.g., Chapman & Chapman, 1959). A substantial number of the participants making such responses do not understand validity (i.e., what they are being asked). The hesitant group gets the conversion of the "all" correct (i.e., they refuse to convert *all A are B* to *all B are A*), but only because they believe conversion is always illicit, and therefore at the expense of failing to conclude that "some" propositions are reversible. In short, there are systematic differences in participants' understandings of the task. Furthermore, these differences can be systematically related to participants' reasoning about syllogisms. For example, hesitant participants show much stronger tendencies to preserve the order of the terms in the premises when making a conclusion (i.e., for a syllogism, they respond to *all A are B, some B are C* with *some A are C* rather than *some C are A*) and they often fail to find conclusions when the only valid ones have the reversed grammatical structure that changes the grammatical category of both end terms (e.g. *all A are B, no C are B*, therefore *some A are not C*). A logically careful description of naive intuitions can yield an *explanation* for fallacies like illicit conversion, and also point to incompleteness in Grice's theory of informativeness, as well as restoring a principled connection between interpretation and reasoning.

Details aside, the relevant observation here is that the vast majority of the deductive reasoning literature studies did not identify mixtures of participants with different interpretations of the task. Some take it as an inductive task, some as a cooperative communication task, and some as a deductive task. Some may vacillate between interpretations during the task. We do not mean to claim that participants have neatly compartmentalized and explicitly understood interpretations. They, like the experimenters, have only implicitly distinguished interpretations, and which interpretation becomes uppermost may be controlled by all sorts of unidentified factors.

These observations tell us something important about how the participants construe the task, why they find it difficult, and how they assimilate it in different ways to more familiar tasks. Gricean implicature arises in cooperative communication in that speaker and hearer cooperate to construct a single common model of mutual knowledge using whatever background knowledge and guesswork they can muster. Deduction is adversarial communication, in that it tests to make sure that conclusions follow in all possible interpretations of the explicit assumptions, excluding all background knowledge, belief, and guesswork.

In real communication both of these activities are interwoven and deduction particularly becomes foregrounded when there is a problem of repairing misaligned interpretations. Although participants can do both of these things in familiar communicative contexts, they do not have an explicit grasp of what they do, and they cannot separate the explicitly stated information from implicitly imported general knowledge. To do that, they have to unlearn many of their communicative habits. *Some A are B* is tailored for use in different cooperative communicative circumstances than *some B are A* but the student has to learn a deductive invariance – they have the same truth conditions. So it comes as no surprise that when participants are merely instructed in two words to say what "logically follows," they do not suddenly behave according to a logical model of deduction. But it should also be remembered that there is a substantial minority who do respond to Newstead's (1989, 1995) task with a classical logical understanding of validity.

Interpreting Tasks Statistically

If participants in fact adopt a common vernacular interpretation of what "validity" means, they might well apply probabilistic reasoning to these tasks. Roughly, validity of a conclusion on this reading means that the truth of the premises of the argument, together with whatever else is known about the situation, make it more likely that the conclusion is true. This makes the task into something much closer to what is conventionally thought of as decision making. For example, if a town has a premiere soccer team, it is likely to be a larger town than if it does not. If a town is a provincial capital, it is likely to be larger than if it is not. If a town (but not its size) is known to the subject before the experiment, it is likely to be larger than if the subject has never heard of it. So if we are asked whether town A, which is a provincial capital, has a premiere team and is known to the participant to be bigger than town B, which the participant knows has none of these properties, then A is likely to be larger than B. Participants are very adept at this kind of decision making (see Gigerenzer, Todd, & the ABC Research Group, 1999) but it is not deductive reasoning. Nor is it deductive reasoning achieved by some other computational means.

So there is an active possibility that participants (quite reasonably) construe tasks that the experimenter intends to be taken as deductive as being meant to be about probabilities of the truth of the conclusion. Chater and Oaksford (1999) have developed this possibility into a theory about what participants are actually doing in "deductive" tasks. Their theory, applied to syllogisms, is based on some simple heuristics for responding: (1) Participants respond with the least informative quantifier from the premises ("some" premises are less informative than "all" or "no" premises. So, if there is a "some" premise, then the conclusion will be a "some"); (2) the next most preferred conclusion will be the one entailed by probability from the premise statement (i.e., all A are B entails probabilistically that some A are B); and (3) if one of the premises begins with a term that is not the middle term (i.e., not a B) then that will be the subject of the conclusion. So, subjects faced with the syllogism all B are A, all B are C, discussed above, would select the conclusions all A are C or all C are A, or, with less frequency some A are C, or some C are A.

If Chater and Oaksford are right, then participants are representing the task as well as the materials in a quite different way than a deductive theory of this reasoning requires, and they are using different reasoning rules and different strategies for solving the problem. As a theory of what all participants are doing in these tasks, their claims have certain draw-backs. One is the implicit claim that all subjects are doing the same thing. The evidence of studying immediate inferences just cited is strong evidence that there are several systematic patterns of interpretation and some participants do construe the task deductively.

Nevertheless, their theory brings to light some deep relations between deduction and induction. It points to the critical nature of participants' assumptions about interpretations and presents a salutary reminder that we should not too quickly assume that participants share the experimenters' conceptualization of the task.

LOGICAL CONCEPTS AND DEDUCTION

So there is a real conceptual problem about what reasoning is called for in what tasks. We now turn to look at the logician's conception of deduction. Some psychologists might challenge the resort to logician's concepts. "Why can't we have our own psychological concept of deduction?" This is analogous to the visual psychologists wanting their own psychological conception of geometry. All the logician supplies is a conceptual framework for understanding what deduction is. It is up to the psychologist to find out how people achieve deductive reasoning in the variety of circumstances they encounter. They might conclude that people *never* reason deductively – that the mathematics fits nothing people ever do. We think there is strong evidence this would be wrong, but it is a logical possibility. However, careful observation of the psychologists who believe they want to get away from logical conceptions invariably sees them smuggle versions of those concepts in through the back door – to abolish logic is to be forced to reinvent it. Better to learn to love it for what it is (and is not).

In compressing a logic course into one section, we will have to proceed mostly by way of example, and only hint at the apparatus that lies behind those examples.

Model Theory

In deduction we are concerned with relations between some premises and a conclusion.[1] Specifically, we are concerned with whether the conclusion is a *deductively valid* conclusion to draw from those premises, and from those premises alone, without recourse to other information. Considering again the earth example, we want to be able to say whether or not the conclusion *the earth orbits a star* follows (only) from *the earth is a planet* and *planets orbit stars*. For example, we may know in addition that the earth orbits the sun, but this is irrelevant with regard to the deductive argument, so we must disregard this extra information. A valid argument is one that produces a conclusion that *has to be true* if the premises are true. So, we want to know if the truth of the premises has as a consequence that the conclusion is true. This looks like a deceptively simple problem, and deceptively easy to study psychologically. It looks as if all that is involved is the sentences or diagrams that appear as premises and conclusions in the statement of the problem, which can be achieved by entirely formal, or mathematical, means.

What is deceptive is that there is an iceberg of submerged interpretation that lies behind the representations, be they diagrams or sentences. This is a problem because we are supposed to reason *only* from the representations, and not all the extra subliminal information behind the premises. The problem becomes more convoluted as we must reason from the premises in respect of what they mean. Returning to the earth example, there is a problem because we know the earth orbits the sun, and this is very difficult, if not impossible, to disentangle from our representation of the sentence *the earth is a planet*. Furthermore, we must reason with what we believe about the kind of reasoning we are intended to do, and it becomes a rather bizarre exercise to ask a participant in a reasoning experiment to forget everything they ever knew before. Yet, all the information that we use in deductive reasoning has to be explicitly assumed, or to be derived by the transformations from what is explicitly assumed. We must not surreptitiously introduce (knowingly or not) extraneous knowledge, belief, or conjecture into our reasoning. It is this explicit demarcation of reasoning from background information that is one of the hallmarks of pure deduction, and one of the greatest sources of problems participants have in deductive reasoning tasks, and as we have seen, experimenters too.

We have quickly defined a deductively valid argument above. Here it is restated: A deductively valid argument is one whose conclusion is true if its premises are true, under *all* interpretations of premises and conclusions. Put the other way around, if we can find a single interpretation of premises and conclusion under which the premises are true and the conclusion false, then the argument pattern is invalid. So, however you interpret *the earth is a planet* and *planets orbit stars*, can you think of an interpretation where they are true and *the earth orbits a star* is not true? Set as an exercise for the reader, this may take quite a long time before you are convinced one way or the other about the validity of the argument. We suggest that, for this argument, under all interpretations the conclusion is true if the premises are also true. To make this point clearer, consider the following invalid argument: *planets orbit stars; rocks orbit stars*; therefore, we conclude that *rocks are planets*. Now, there are several interpretations where the premises are true, and also the conclusion true (if we restrict the rocks we think of only to the planets, for instance; or if we interpret the conclusion as *some* rocks, the planety ones, are planets). But there is also an interpretation where the premises are true and the conclusion false (if we interpret the conclusion to mean that *all* rocks are planets, then my quartz paperweight does not confound the truth of the premises; it is still hurtling around a star), but the fact that it does not make the grade as a planet, means the conclusion is false. This means that the argument is not deductively valid.

Clearly this study of deduction is in need of some way of defining what are the range of possible interpretations of a representation system so that it can treat *all* interpretations – the whole iceberg. If we do not have such a definition, then it will be very difficult to be sure we have searched through all the possibilities. Logic accomplishes this by invoking a distinction between *form* and *content*. The formal part of a representation system has a fixed interpretation, and the contentful part has a variable interpretation. So we can define all possible contents for a given form, as we will illustrate shortly. In the earth example, we can substitute "earth" for another term without changing the form of the argument. In fact we can change all the contentful words without changing the argument. Replace "earth" with E, "planet" with P and "star" with S and you get something like: *E is a P, P orbits S, therefore E orbits S*. We do not then need to consider what is meant by "earth," but just concentrate on the argument form. But changing a term like "is" in the earth argument is going to radically change things; "earth *has* a planet," for example, means something rather different.

This treatment of deduction seems to reduce it to something very formal and irrelevant to everyday life. However, people face deductive tasks all the time. As we said above, they face them most commonly when they are trying to communicate and cannot be certain that they and their interlocutor are using words the same way (and that is much of the time). When we encounter a communication and we are not sure what interpretation was intended, or doubt that it is coherent, then we need to start reasoning about the range of possible intended interpretations. We rarely need to reason about all possible ones, because we generally have a lot of information to narrow them down, but we still need the same general apparatus for the task of interpretation. In this situation, what we observe are the inferences the originator makes (and therefore presumably believes valid) and our inferences are from them, back to interpretations that are likely. So, we ask, "What did she mean by that in order to get to that conclusion?" But people are not used to the problem of drawing an explicit line between what is involved in interpreting the language and all other information they may have about the conclusion. Learning logic is about getting an explicit theoretical grasp of that demarcation. The evidence is that learning logic can help people improve their skills of interpreting communications (e.g., Stenning, 2002; Stenning, Cox, & Oberlander 1995), at which point we have come a full circle back to Aristotle who intended logic to do just that.

Dealing with all possible interpretations specified in a precise way means that truth is backgrounded. Replacing earth, planet, star with letters shows that we can limit our interpretations to relations between these terms, without being sidetracked by questions about whether it is relevant whether the earth's surface is 70% covered in water for this argument or whether it really is the case that the earth is a planet. The truth of the premises or the conclusions in and of itself is *never* relevant to an argument's deductive validity. All that matters is the relation between the premises and conclusion under an interpretation. We are beginning to use "interpretation" now in a rather specialized way, in terms of whether the premises and conclusion are true or false. This abstraction away from background information means that deduction is particularly indispensible for reasoning about fictions, suppositions, fantasies, and hypotheses, even more indispensable than for reasoning about beliefs and knowledge. This abstraction means that deduction is especially indispensable for reasoning about uncertain interpretations, either others' or our own.

We have so far used reasoning in simple languages to illustrate the concepts that constitute deductive reasoning, but it is important to remember that deduction can just as well go on with diagrams and other representations – we provide some examples later which will show the connections between representations and strategies in reasoning. We now discuss in detail an example of a syllogistic argument, highlighting the distinction between its form and its content, and show how the notion of *all possible interpretations* applies.

Take the familiar old chestnut of an argument (slightly tweaked): All men are mortal. Some man (Socrates) is a philosopher. Therefore, some philosopher is mortal. In this argument, some of the words are formal, whereas others are contentful. *All, some, are, is, therefore* are form words. *Men, mortal, Socrates, philosopher* are content words. Some aspects of the order of words are also part of the formal structure of the argument – what is subject and what predicate in the sentences, and which sentences occur before the "therefore" and which after it. Crucially, we can pick entirely different content words and the argument will remain valid. For example, we can change "mortal" for "female" and the argument remains valid. It might turn out that our interlocutor actually has a different dialect of English in which mortal means female, but we would never know it from this argument since systematically changing content preserves validity.

Notice that the changes in content have to be made systematically. We have to exchange mortal for female every time mortal occurs. The only part played by "mortal" in the formal part of the argument is the arrangement of its occurrences in the argument. We have to be consistent in applying meanings to the terms – we had better not mean mortal by "mortal" first time, and female by "mortal" second time. Equally, words in the premises have to be interpreted the same way as the same words in the conclusion.

Of course one's first response to such an argument is likely to be that the premise *all men are female* is false. The technical response to this objection is "Yes, but truth is irrelevant, this is about validity." But the substantive answer is that the premise is only false under the interpretation that is likely to jump first into the mind of English speakers. There are contexts in which it is true even with our usual meanings of the words (perhaps one morning in some sex-change clinic) and when we rummage a little harder even in our commonly accepted lexicon of English words, we find that the first meaning listed for "man" in the Oxford English Dictionary is "a human being irrespective of gender."[2] We can then think up an interpretation such that "all men are female" is true – an interpretation where the statement is made about a world populated only by female human beings (perhaps some convent). We call this "world" a domain. We can use other domains of interpretation for the statements – ones where we extend meanings further, or look at special uses in which "female" is a property of electrical connectors, or in new coinages – all of these throw up novel interpretations for the same sentences.

Arguments are never coherently interpreted as being about literally everything. They are always interpreted on what is technically known as the *domain of interpretation* – the set of things or people or entities that matter. When I come into the apparently empty office and say to the sole secretary that "everyone's gone to the beach," I do not mean all past, present, and future human beings. The domain of interpretation of my utterance is local to a few staff and students of this department now. If someone counters by pointing out the pope is not at the beach, I rightly refuse to accept this as a counterexample to my intended interpretation – the pope is not in the domain. Only if Sam, one of our graduate students, is found hiding behind his computer monitor is it a counterexample. Notice that I am also unlikely to accept that I myself (or the secretary) should be included in the domain of interpretation, since it is clear we are not at the beach (unless the beach is actually a part of the office, of course). Domains can also be domains of "nonexistent" entities. When a character on *Neighbours* says that "everyone's gone to the beach," they generally mean a set of fictional characters has gone to a fictional beach. There are deep philosophical problems about what kinds of thing characters are, but logic is not bothered. Only if it is unclear what is in the domain and what is not does it present a *logical* problem.

It is easy to miss this fact that we literally have to agree what we are talking about (and what we are not including) because these matters are normally signaled by all sorts of subtle cues. We are perhaps accustomed to the illusion that we speak natural languages that have mutually agreed fixed meanings, but this illusion is not shared by logicians who note that when we actually look at the precise cataloging of objects implicated in actual word occurrences in fully specified contexts, it is unusual to find two interpretations of the same word, which are exactly the same across two arguments. This is why such a lot of effort goes into understanding each other, and why we need deductive reasoning to help keep our interpretations aligned. With a little thought, it becomes clear that natural languages could not be any other way granted the range of contexts they are used in. In fact, artificial languages, such as logical or computer programming languages, are exactly similar in this respect – they get reinterpreted in each context of application, each time with a particular domain of interpretation.

Returning to the Socrates argument, out of context we know little about what the truth value of *all men are female* is, but we can still know that the argument cited above remains valid if "female" is substituted for "mortal" in a systematic way. Validity, in deduction, is the property that arguments have if their conclusions are true *whenever* their premises are true. As we have now seen, this central idea of fixed meanings for formal words and variable meanings for content words is what is meant by the notion of a conclusion's being true *under all interpretations* (including all possible choices of domain of interpretation).

In order to study more than just examples of deductive arguments, we need a general apparatus. The central part of that apparatus is a representation system (including its range of interpretations). In the case of arguments presented in words, a representation system is a language. A language is a set of sentences, usually infinite, generated from a vocabulary (usually finite) according to syntactic rules, and interpreted by semantic rules. The interpretation of a sentence in the language is the assignment of what things in the world the terms in the sentence apply to in the current context. An example of an assignment of things in the larger world to the term "Socrates" in several possible domains of interpretation for the above argument is shown in the first column of Table 6.1.

Once we have specified a representation system in this way, we have specified for all the possible interpretations which sentences are true in that interpretation, and which false. So, in Table 6.1, interpreting "Socrates" as referring to a goldfish, for example, means that the sentence "Socrates is a man" is false in this interpretation. Interpreting "Socrates" as referring to an ancient Greek philosopher means that the sentence "Socrates is a man" is true. So, we could, theoretically, line up all the premises and the conclusion

TABLE 6.1. *Some Interpretations for the Socrates Argument*

Interpretation	All men are mortal	Socrates is a man	Socrates is mortal
An ancient Greek philosopher Socrates who died from hemlock.	TRUE	TRUE	TRUE
My goldfish is called Socrates.	TRUE	FALSE	TRUE
My computer is called Socrates.	TRUE	FALSE	FALSE
The Socrates who lives forever in Plato's writing.	FALSE?	TRUE?	FALSE?

sentences as column headings and write for each interpretation a row of Ts and Fs that indicate whether the sentence is true or false in that interpretation (so table 6.1 is just a fragment of the full table of interpretations). Then if we find all the rows in which all the premises are true, we simply check to make sure that the conclusion is true in that row. We do this for every row, and if it holds, then the argument pattern is valid, according to this definition of validity. This is essentially what is known as the method of truth tables. Table 6.1 gives an example truth table for the Socrates argument, with the intended interpretation for each row hinted at in the left hand column. The last row illustrates the point that it can be hard to know what words mean in some interpretations and so it is hard to decide whether Socrates, in this sense, is a man (perhaps he is a legendary figure), and whether he is mortal (he is immortal, but he did die from hemlock). Nevertheless, it is still true that if we decide our meanings make both the first two columns true, then they will make the third column true, and that is all that matters for this argument pattern.

An initial reaction to these comments about interpretations might be that the validity of the argument tells us nothing about what any of the content words mean – it is a purely *formal* affair to do with the arrangements of a few fixed words. At one level this is true. Logic has nothing to tell us about philosophers or goldfish or immortality (they are the business of philosophy, zoology, and theology departments, respectively). But at a deeper level it is a big mistake to suppose that this apparatus is "purely formal." Consider the bottom row of the table where we have to deal with tricky meanings of words. In this sort of situation it is all too easy to let our meanings shift in equivocation from occurrence to occurrence. Observing that certain formal patterns of arguments have to be valid regardless of which meaning we assign is often the only way we have to keep a grip on what we or others mean. In science, for example, words are continually undergoing changes of meaning and we have to keep track of the "technical sense" and the previous sense. Just think of some of the new uses of words in this paper. Logic will not tell us about what contents we should give words, but it gives us tools for ensuring that we (and others) are assigning content coherently. The only alternative is to adopt Humpty Dumpty's stance in *Alice Through the Looking Glass* that our words mean what we mean them to mean, which would be a rather frustrating way to communicate:

"There's glory for you!"
"I don't know what you mean by 'glory,' " Alice said.
Humpty Dumpty smiled contemptuously. "Of course you don't – till I tell you. I meant 'there's a nice knock-down argument for you!' "
"But 'glory' doesn't mean 'a nice knock-down argument,' " Alice objected.
"When *I* use a word," Humpty Dumpty said in rather a scornful tone, "it means just what I choose it to mean – neither more nor less."

What we have just described, somewhat breathlessly, is model theory. Model theory is the study of what argument patterns are valid in an interpreted representation system. It is the most fundamental and most abstract level of logical study. But, crucially, model theory says nothing about how any conclusions might be derived, or computed – in short, it says nothing about *how* people may reason, but merely defines what constitutes valid reasoning in some system of representations. The attentive reader might object that the method of truth tables outlined above is a mechanism for computing conclusions, but it is only specifiable for very simple systems where the infinities of interpretations are not a problem. For these simple systems the distinction between model theory and the computation of proofs collapses, but for larger, more interesting systems, model theory does not supply any ways of getting from premises to conclusions.[3]

This observation that logic is abstract with regard to mechanisms of computation is the crucial point in our discussion of model theory. In the psychological literature, logic is widely thought of as a *mechanism* for producing, or assessing, conclusions. A logic is first and foremost a set of abstract mappings of sets of premises onto valid conclusions. The candidates proposed as fundamental reasoning mechanisms (mental models or mental logics) are not akin to model theory, as they also incorporate mechanisms for producing conclusions from premises. Mental models cannot be construed as logical model theory, as then it would tell us nothing about the processes of reasoning (which would be a big disappointment). We will return to discussing these systems later when we connect strategies to mechanisms in reasoning.

In summary, our discussion of model theory has shown that deductive reasoning is as commonplace as language itself, and that we are constantly, almost effortlessly, forging mappings between terms within a representational system and people/places/things in a domain of interpretation. Studying deductive reasoning requires us to make explicit this structure and cast it in a suitably abstract manner. This abstract characterization demonstrates that logic is not about mechanisms, but that studying human reasoning very much is about getting from premises to conclusions. We now move on to discuss the next level of logical concepts from Figure 6.1: proof theory.

What is Proof Theory?

Truth tables grow like Topsy, but rather faster. The combination of all the different interpretations for each of the premises very quickly becomes very large even in the simple language we have considered. For many logical languages the tables become infinite as soon as we talk of infinitely many things, even without using infinitely many words. We need ways of generating arguments that can validate conclusions more efficiently.

In order to generate valid arguments from premises to conclusions we need to add to our representation system some apparatus for transforming representations into other representations in a manner that preserves truth. If we start with true premises, we want to know that our conclusions will be true, in line with our notion of validity. Such transformations are commonly known as *rules of inference*. An example rule might be one that transforms the two sentences *If Socrates is a man, then Socrates is female* and *Socrates is a man* into *Socrates is female*. To see the abstract version of the rule, replace "Socrates is a man" with "p," and "Socrates is female" with "q." (Remember, we can replace the content parts of the sentence with anything we like, but of course we cannot alter the form words.) Then the rule transforms the form *if p then q*, and p and produces the conclusion q. It is called "if-elimination" (because we get rid of the "if" from the first sentence in the conclusion) or if we were speaking Latin, modus ponens. In all interpretations, if the first two sentences are true then the third sentence produced by applying the rule is true. The rule works because it instantiates the model theory of sentences of the form "if ... then...." If the proof theory included the rule that from p conclude $\neg p$ (i.e., *not p*), then it would be unsound because this does not accord with the model theoretic characterisation of $\neg$.

Suitable rules of inference can be specified for diagrammatic systems, or for mental model systems, or any other kind of representation system. They constitute the proof-theory of a system.

Proof theory is an important logical level of abstraction because it is relations between proof theories and model theories that constitute the metalogical properties of systems. We can ask, "Does this proof theory produce all and only the model-theoretic consequences of that system of representations?" If it produces only semantically valid conclusions then it is *sound* and if it produces all of them it is *complete*. These relations between levels only became clear in twentieth-century logic. They are important in justifying *why* the rules of inference are as they are. Until metalogical properties were understood, it was difficult to say what justified rules of inference – who says so? Now the justification can be seen as simply the need for soundness (i.e., not wanting to arrive at falsehoods from truths). Perhaps the most important foundation for our modern understanding of representation and computation is the proof (due to Gödel in 1931) that an important range of representation systems are fundamentally incomplete and incompletable. This finding more than any other is what tells us about possible relations between computation and cognition. What might be algorithmic and what cannot. In a word, it tells us that even some simple formal systems cannot be completely mechanized.

So proof theory studies arguments, which are conceived of as sequences of sentences related by rule applications. Proof theory provides ways of generating arguments and assessing their validity. An argument, as we have seen, consists of one or more premises and a conclusion. Then, if we take any set of premises and any candidate conclusion, we can try to find whether there is a sequence of applications of the rules of inference to the premises which will yield the conclusion. This sequence may be a very long and winding route, with lots of intermediate stages between the initial premises and the conclusion. The indirectness of proof is exemplified *in extremis* by the proof of Fermat's last theorem by Wiles and Taylor, which runs to over 100 pages of the *Annals of Mathematics* (1995, vol. 141, pp. 443–572). But mathematicians work in a kind of shorthand. This proof fully formalized in a logical language would be tens or hundreds of times longer. A sound proof theory ensures that no matter how long the sequence, we can be sure that, provided the premises are true, and the rules applied correctly, the conclusion is guaranteed to be true as well.

However, proof theory is still not a mechanism for *finding* particular conclusions, all it does is provide means for assessing the transformations between premises and conclusions. Finding Wiles's proof was a feat of mathematical genius over several years by Wiles, and several centuries before him by a sequence of talented mathematicians. The exploding number of possibilities for which rule to apply when, quickly gets out of hand: At each stage we face more branching choices. Finding a proof is like walking through a garden of forking paths, where at each point we can apply any of the rules of inference to any of the subsets of premises or intermediate stages. Even if we can make zillions of rule applications per second, we are likely to die before we reach an answer of any use to us. So again there is a rather lethal *lack* of mechanism at the relevant level. There are interesting psychological questions about the level such formal structures are accessed by human mathematicians and the answer must be not just the microlevel.

Theorem Provers

To reason purposefully we need to add to our proof theory a mechanism for finding proofs of targeted conclusions from specified premises. This is what is called a theorem prover. If the representation system provides a garden of forking paths, then the theorem prover makes the choices at the forks in the path. In complex proofs, it will also have more synoptic views of the developing proof. If we can specify a theorem prover that has a determinate recipe for making its decisions that guarantees getting to a conclusion, then this is called an *algorithmic* theorem prover. In a maze, an example of an algorithmic theorem prover would be "always turn left," which might guarantee that you get to the center of some class of mazes ("perfect," or "simply-connected" mazes), even if only after rather a long walk. Any clearly specified recipe that always yields a course of action and is guaranteed eventual success on some class of problems is an algorithm.

The alternative is a heuristic theorem prover that has some policy for deciding which way to proceed in the garden of forking paths but which does not guarantee reaching the goal. In the maze example, it might involve, say, using a compass, and turning north if possible. Such a simple policy would fail if there was not always a northward turning, so it might be necessary to guess.

Theorem provers can have all sorts of mechanisms within them that contribute to choosing a proof's path. We have mentioned a compass in a maze. Other theorem provers might toss coins. Some collect elaborate statistics about past experience. Yet others could consult the entrails. Any mechanism known to man[4] could be applied. Whether or not any of these mechanisms are thought of as rules, many of them are certainly not rules that transform sentences into sentences. Here at the heart of processes of deduction we find nonlogical mechanisms and these mechanisms are the most natural focus of psychology.

It is an important result of logic that most logics of much interest, such as those used to analyze whole natural languages, do not have general algorithmic theorem provers guaranteed to find any specified conclusion (or its negation) and thereby decide whether a conclusion is valid, so heuristics are as necessary for machines reasoning with these logics as for folk reasoning with them.

The theorem-prover level is the third and final level of analysis of logical theory pertinent to psychological studies of human reasoning, completing the description of the first column of Figure 6.1. So, how do these levels relate to the psychology of reasoning? We have seen that deduction underlies many of our reasoning and metareasoning processes, so this is the right place to start in studies of human reasoning. The first two levels of logical analysis of deduction – model theory and proof theory – do not provide any mechanisms for reasoning, as we have seen. The image that logic is about sentential rule-mechanisms is a highly misleading one. Logic is not especially about sentential systems: it is just as much about transforming diagrams, or "mental models" or any other kind of representation. Logic (model and proof theory) is not about mechanisms. Even when theorem-prover mechanisms are devised to work over logical languages, those mechanisms are additions of all sorts of nonlogical nonsentence stuff (tossing coins perhaps) to the logical apparatus. Theorem provers describe such additions of mechanisms to the logic.

This distinction between theorem-prover mechanisms and representation systems is critical. There are sheds full of different possible mechanisms for each representational system and sheds full of systems. It is not at all clear what in all this profusion is supposed to be fundamental about any fundamental reasoning mechanism. In performing an experiment, we may be able to tell something about which theorem prover is being used, but not which representation system it is operating on.

Fortunately, this is an area where remarkable progress has been achieved in the psychology of deductive reasoning. All that is needed is for it to be reconceived as experiments about theorem provers and not about representations. We provide this reconception in the next part of the chapter, indicating how studies of syllogistic reasoning have highlighted the different mechanisms attached to the logic.

STRATEGIES AND THEOREM PROVERS

In psychological experiments on syllogisms, the participant is given two premises to be taken as true, and the task is to say what, if anything, follows from these premises (and only from the information contained in these premises). The Socrates argument was one example, as another, consider the following premises:

All beekeepers are artists.
All beekeepers are communists.

Assuming there is at least one person who is a beekeeper, one person who is an artist, and one who is a communist, can any connection be made between artists and communists? One valid answer is that some artists are communists. Another that some communists are artists. These are logically equivalent answers though not necessarily psychologically equivalent as we shall see.

But how does the naive participant go about thinking of these problems? There have been several theories about what is happening in the mind when one is solving these problems, and proponents of different views have suggested that they are describing alternative theories of the "fundamental reasoning mechanism." Accounts of representations in terms of mental models or mental rules have been propounded. We will go through three different ways of solving this syllogism. The important point to bear in mind as we present these theories is the level at which they differ. Though the methods rely on different representations, the observable differences (what you can see outside the head) are in the theorem prover that works on the representations, and this is not tied to the representation itself.

Figure 6.2 shows the above syllogism solved in three different representation systems. The system on the left is mental models, as described in Johnson-Laird and Byrne (1991).[5] The mental models theory is discussed in another chapter of this book, so here we offer only a schematic description of the process. The first premise "all Bs are As" is represented as two individuals with the properties of B and A. The brackets around the Bs indicate that all the individuals that are Bs are captured within the model.[6] The dots indicate that there might be other individuals that have not yet been specified: There will not be any more Bs, but there might be other As. The second premise is translated similarly. In the next stage, the second

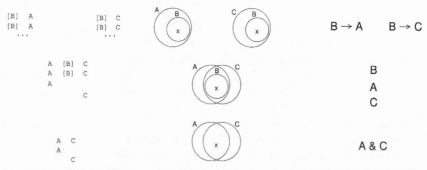

FIGURE 6.2. Solving all Bs are As, all Bs are Cs using mental models, Euler's circles, and a natural deduction method.

premise is attached to the first, showing there are As that are Bs that are Cs, but there are also As that may or may not be Bs or Cs, and Cs that may or may not be As or Bs. The final stage involves removing the Bs from the reckoning and concluding that "some As are Cs."

The second method is a version of Euler's circles developed by Stenning and Oberlander (1995). In Euler's circles the relationships between individuals is represented in terms of overlapping circles defining areas where individuals may be found. So, an area of the diagram where A and B circles overlap indicates that there may be an individual who is both an A and a B. In order to solve syllogisms we need to find kinds of individuals that must exist (like those enclosed in square brackets in mental models in Figure 6.2, for example). To indicate this, we mark the area in the diagram where there has to be an individual with a cross. In Figure 6.2, "all Bs are As" is represented in terms of circles one inside the other. There is a cross inside the smaller B circle, which shows that there has to be at least one individual who is a B and an A. The other areas of the diagram (inside the A circle but outside the B circle; outside the A and the B circle) show areas where there might be individuals – there might be an individual who is an A but not a B. There might be an individual who is neither an A or a B – but we do not know for sure. It depends on the interpretation as to whether there are individuals in these other areas. For example, if we are thinking about the whole animal kingdom, then in the case of "all bandicoots are animals," there would be something in the "animal" circle, outside the bandicoot circle, because there are animals that are not bandicoots (such as tapirs). But if we are thinking only of pointy-nosed marsupial animals with backward-facing pouches (so that they do not get filled with dirt while burrowing), then there are no such animals that are not bandicoots, so the A and non-B area of the graph would be empty. The Euler's circles diagram represents all these possible interpretations simultaneously.

Similarly, the second premise is represented as a small B circle inside a larger C circle. In the second stage, the two premise diagrams are put together in such a way that there are areas of the diagram representing all the resulting possibilities of A, B, and C individuals that are consistent with the premise diagrams. This works by superimposing the B circles and then keeping the same relationship between the B circle and the A and C circles. Then, the A and C circles are arranged so that they overlap, provided this does not affect their relationship with the B circle. In Figure 6.2 there are areas in the diagram that represent the following possible individuals: ABC, A¬BC, A¬B¬C, ¬A¬BC,¬A¬B¬C. However, as with the mental models method, there is only one type of individual that we know *has* to exist – and that is the area of the diagram marked with a cross – the ABC individual. To make the conclusion, the final stage involves removing the B circle, and concluding that "some As are Cs."

The third method is a simplified version of natural deduction (so corresponding to a sentential mental system [e.g., Rips, 1994]), derived from Stenning and Yule (1997). "All Bs are As" is represented as $B{\rightarrow}A$, which can be read as "if an individual is a B then the individual is an A."[7] As with the Euler's circles method, this rule-like representation holds open all the possibilities from different interpretations of the premise "all Bs are As" – it is consistent with there being Bs that are As, As that are non-Bs, and non-Bs that are non-As. But it entails that there has to be at least one B that is also an A.

Then, in the second stage of the method, we focus on one of the individuals – in this case the individual who is a B – and then use rules to transform the description of the individual in terms of A and C. We use B and $B{\rightarrow}A$ to show that the individual is also an A. Then, from B and $B{\rightarrow}C$, we show the individual is a C as well. So, there is an ABC individual. Removing the B, we derive the conclusion $A \,\&\, C$ – "some As are Cs."

As might be apparent from this rather vague description of the methods, the really tricky part is in putting together the representations of the premises. This is difficult because there are so many different ways of doing it – there are many different ways of applying the transformations to the representations. In fact, the method of putting the representations together in each method is rather tangential to the representations themselves. We have seen that the mechanism of the theorem prover is outside the model theory or proof theory of the logic. Similarly, the method for each version is outside the system of representation used. Crucially, there are many different mechanisms *for each representational system.*

To make this more concrete, consider the natural deduction method for solving the syllogism in Figure 6.2 again. We have seen one rule being used in the method: modus ponens or *if-elimination*: P and $P{\rightarrow}Q$ gives Q (where P and Q can be any of A, B, or C). The other type of rule we can use is called modus tollens: $\neg Q$ and $P{\rightarrow}Q$ gives $\neg P$. Now, to begin

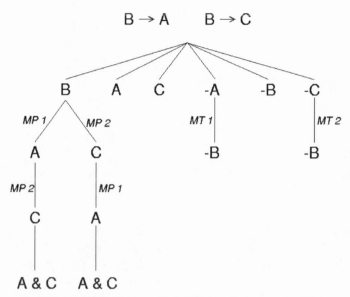

FIGURE 6.3. Solving all Bs are As, all Bs are Cs using an exhaustive strategy in the natural deduction method.

the method, we need to make an assumption about which individual to begin to describe? Do we begin by describing an A, a B, a C, or a non-A, a non-B, or a non-C? This gives us six initial options. Then, for each of these individuals, we can try and apply either rule. Figure 6.3 shows all the possible branches for applying the rules to the individuals. Down the left side is the initial method from Figure 6.2. The labels on the branches indicate whether modus ponens (MP) or modus tollens (MT) is being used, and the numbers indicate whether it is the first premise or the second premise that the rule is applying to.

So, the task of solving syllogisms using this method is to be able to find a way that finds the right path through these possible branches, to get to the answer "some As are Cs." There are several heuristics we could use to do this. One possibility is to go through each individual – A, B, C, non-A, non-B, non-C – one at a time and see if the rules lead us anywhere. Another possibility is to have some decision about which individual to begin with (once we start with the B then most of our problems are solved). This latter possibility is what each of the methods indicated in Figure 6.2 is doing. We call this heuristic the "identify critical individuals" method, and it is independent of whether our representational system is mental models, Euler's circles, or natural deduction. It is about selecting the right individual and then describing it in terms of the other properties.

In fact, for these three methods, Stenning and Oberlander (1995) and Stenning and Yule (1997) have shown that for every stage in using the

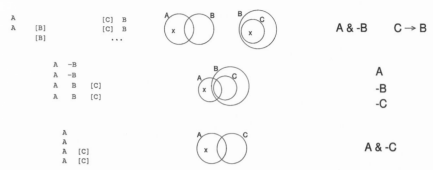

FIGURE 6.4. Solving some As are not Bs, all Cs are Bs using mental models, Euler's circles, and a sentential method.

representations in one method there is a comparable stage in each of the other methods. This means that, in terms of the externally observable behavior of people mentally solving syllogisms, it is impossible to say which method they are using.[8] The relevant descriptions of the processes of deductive reasoning are more abstract than the theorists realize.

For each of these systems, for this problem, what is actually going on is the use of the rule *modus ponens*, but in different guises (or disguises). This is abundantly clear in the natural deduction method shown in Figure 6.2, but it is also taking place in the mental models and Euler's circles systems. In mental models, it is about attaching the "C" property to the individual already described as a B and an A. In the Euler's circles method the rule is accomplished by positioning the C circle around the B circle containing the cross in the first diagram.

The comparability between these three methods is clarified by another example where the abstract characterization of the solution to the syllogism implements the other type of rule – modus tollens. This rule has to be used to solve the syllogism "some As are not Bs, all Cs are Bs," and is shown in the three representational systems in Figure 6.4.

In the Mental Models system, modus tollens consists of adding the Cs to descriptions of Bs, when the critical individuals are the As that are non-Bs. In the Euler's Circles method, modus tollens is adding the C circle to the diagram so that it falls outside the A and non-B area containing the cross. In the sentential method, the rule application is explicit – we derive the ¬C from ¬B and C→B.

Equivalences and Empirical Methods

These equivalences between mental models, Euler's circles, and some natural deduction systems require two responses from empirical psychological investigators. First, existing results need to be redescribed in theory-neutral terms, and the real psychological work of investigating the memory structures that implement these systems should begin. Second, we need to seek richer kinds of evidence about the representations employed.

Under the first heading, much of the empirical work in all frameworks can be redescribed in terms of the sequence of cases that participants' theorem provers choose to explore, and where they terminate their explorations in this sequence. Given a syllogism such as *all A are B, some B are C*, participants may consider the case of an A that is B and ask whether it is a B that is C, rather than proceeding in any of the other possible orders. Indeed, many participants stop prematurely, not considering any case other than this one, possibly because they have a different task in mind, as discussed earlier.

Under the second heading, there is already work on the memory implementation of syllogistic reasoning, for example in Baddeley's working memory framework (Gilhooly, Logie, Wetherick, & Wynn, 1993). Their investigations indicate that the articulatory loop ("voice-in-the-head" memory) is used in syllogistic reasoning, and there is weaker evidence that the visuo-spatial scratch pad is also used under some circumstances. Stenning and Oberlander (1995) reviewed the reasoning and text comprehension literatures from the perspective of explaining performance limitations on the basis of working-memory architecture.

At a greater level of detail, the mental models framework generally claims that participants reorder the terms A, B, and C into a canonical order in their mental representations employing a first-in-first-out working memory (Johnson-Laird, 1983). They make this (unnecessary) claim because they think in terms of a particular kind of rule for "reading off" conclusions. Stenning and Yule (1997) showed that, rather, the commonest order in working memory is middle-term-first, and that a variety of other orders are common, being determined by choice of the premise on which the conclusion is founded. A more abstract approach again enriches empirical observation.

So investigating the empirical details of how syllogistic reasoning is implemented in human memory is the kind of study we might expect from the psychology of reasoning. These studies will not resolve whether the representations held in memory are mental models or sets of mental sentences because of the equivalences described above, but they do contribute to a psychological understanding of the strategies of reasoning common to both methods.

Suppose we still want to find out something more about the nature of the representations used in reasoning – whether they are sentence-like or model-like? How could this problem be approached? Or is it fundamentally unresolvable? We would argue that it is potentially resolvable but only when an adequate logical understanding of the different levels of study of reasoning systems can be used as a basis for broadening empirical investigations beyond the experimental situations the field has fixed on. Our answer would be in terms of a semantic theory that distinguishes *direct* from *indirect* representation systems (see Stenning, 2002). Direct representation systems such as Euler's circles (and probably mental models when their logical level is clarified), because they only express limited abstractions, make certain reasoning easy. Indirect systems, because they can generally express lots of abstraction, can make reasoning much less tractable – the search space is much larger. This semantic basis for exploring representation systems is beyond the scope of this paper. Suffice to say that it has consequences for reasoning and especially for learning to reason with systems of representations, and we turn to the topic of learning in the last section. But first, as an introduction to the problem, we consider the meaning of failure.

Concluding There Is No Conclusion

In deductive reasoning experiments participants are routinely asked to draw valid conclusions and to say if there are none. Just as with drawing valid conclusions, some of the problems to which the correct answer is "no valid conclusion" are very easy – almost everyone gets them right. Others are very hard – almost everyone get them wrong.

So far we have considered systems of representation and associated theorem provers that take some premises and set about attempting to derive targeted conclusions. These systems are proposed as models of participants' mental processes after being presented with premises and asked whether a particular conclusion follows. The participant is often given premises from which the target conclusion does not validly follow, or where none of the range of targets validly follows. Then they are requested to say that there is no valid conclusion. What mechanisms working over a representational system are required to cover this latter kind of decision? How can we prove *nonconsequence* – that something does not follow? Or even that some set of premises are inconsistent with each other – that they are unsatisfiable, and therefore, logically, *everything* follows? After all, if the premises can never all be true, then no conclusion drawn from them will ever be a false conclusion from true premises – it will never be invalid.

Mental models theory has attempted to make much of this issue in distinguishing mental models from mental logics (Johnson-Laird, Legrenzi, Girotto, & Legrenzi, 2000). They claim that proofs of nonconsequence or satisfiability present a problem for sentential systems. In fact, a sentential system known as "tableau" due to Beth (see Hodges, 1977, for its use in introductory logic teaching) achieves exactly this purpose. Certainly for the very simple logical systems that mental models theory encompasses, it *is* possible to conclude from the *failure* of a theorem prover to prove a theorem, after a specified amount of search, that there is no valid conclusion among a range of possible ones. In these systems it is also possible to conclude from the nonrepresentability of sets of premises that they are unsatisfiable (or inconsistent with each other).

Nevertheless, relatively little attention has been paid by psychologists to the question how "no valid conclusion" judgments are made. Generally it is assumed that participants simply run their procedures, which enable them to draw conclusions until those procedures are exhausted (or until they think they are) and then respond "no valid conclusion" if no conclusion has been drawn. But it is hard to explain how it could be, on this account, that some "no valid conclusion" judgments are made just as fast and accurately as the easiest valid conclusions are drawn. This problem is useful to us here because it provokes us to think about quite different ways of solving syllogisms – different from all the previously discussed example systems. This, in turn is important because one might come to think that *all* methods of solving syllogisms are equivalent at this abstract-theorem-prover level.

A useful antidote to this idea that the three individual identification methods described above embody the only way of solving syllogisms is the "Sieve," a method invented in medieval times. This works by successively filtering out syllogisms that have no valid conclusion until only valid ones are left.

Suppose an experimenter set you to draw valid conclusions from the premises *some A are B, some B are C*. Granted that you understood what it means to draw a deductively valid conclusion, you might have the intuition that it is *obvious* that there is no conclusion without exploring any candidate conclusions. Pressed to explain your intuition you might say something like "Well, it's obvious that some As that are Bs might not be the same as any of the Bs that are Cs, so nothing follows about any relation between As and Cs." This sounds like metalogical reasoning.

Just to see that not all "no valid conclusion" problems are easy, consider instead the problem *all B are A, some C are not B*. Whereas perhaps 70% or more will get our first example right, only about 20% or less will correctly see that there is no valid conclusion from this second pair of premises. Most will conclude either that *some C are not A* or that *no C are A*.

The Sieve consists of an ordered set of rules that begin by identifying classes of syllogisms that have no valid conclusions. We start with a syllogism and see whether the rules apply to it one by one. Our examples "fall down" through the rules until it gets stuck – hence "Sieve." Try taking the *some A are B, some B are C* example first. Here are the rules:

1. Two existential (*some* or *some...not*) premises have no valid conclusion.
2. Two negative premises have no valid conclusion.
3. If there is a negative premise then any valid conclusion is negative.

4. The middle term must be distributed in at least one premise.
5. For a term to be distributed in the conclusion, it must be distributed in its premises.

The easy example fails at the very first rule. An example like *no B are A, some C are not B* passes the first rule but fails the second – it has two negative quantifiers. Participants generally also find this an easy problem.

After the first two rules, the Sieve starts to rule out only specific kinds of conclusions and life becomes much more complex. Indeed, in general, the more of these rules a problem without valid conclusions passes, the harder participants find it. Our hard problem (*all B are A, some C are not B*) gets deep into issues of which terms are "distributed" in its premises and possible conclusions. You do not need to know what distributed means.[9] The Sieve introduces this concept because it allows an elegant statement of the rules for using the Sieve to draw conclusions. The method is of importance here because of its general structure rather than its later rules. Without introducing distribution one might, for example, use Rules 1–3 to immediately identify most NVC (no valid conclusion) problems prior to drawing any object-level inferences by some other mechanism.

The Sieve is the complement of the other methods we have seen. It is good at rapidly detecting a wide range of NVC problems, which the other methods can only discover by running their conclusion drawing mechanisms to exhaustion. Conversely, using the Sieve to draw valid conclusions requires a potentially exhaustive search. It is bad at what the other methods are good at.

The Sieve focuses our attention on what metalogical principles participants know, implicitly or explicitly. Of course, there is no reason why participants should not combine the Sieve with other methods, and there is evidence that something like this is exactly what they do. Galotti, Baron, and Sabini (1986) and Ford (1995) both provided direct evidence that participants abstract some of these principles. Stenning and Yule (1997) showed that the generalizations in Rules 1 and 2 pick out the NVC problems that are particularly easy, and that participants can adapt their metalogical principles to a closely related syllogistic task where the second generalization has to be modified.

ENRICHING THE EMPIRICAL BASE: EXTERNAL REPRESENTATIONS, LEARNING, AND SEMANTICS

Individual Differences in Syllogistic Reasoning

If diagrammatic and sentential mental representations are so hard to discriminate why not study them out in the open on paper or computer screen? If we have reason to doubt whether participants fully understand the concepts of deduction, then why not study the processes by which they learn those concepts under suitable instruction? We cannot expect to make immediate inferences from behavior with external representations to what mental representations are used, but we can get at least some indirect evidence – and at the moment it is more or less the only discriminating evidence we have. We cannot make direct inferences about how participants reason before they explicitly understand the concepts of deduction, from observations of the learning of those concepts, but if participants do not understand *what* they are supposed to be doing let alone *how* to do it, then it is not clear what we are studying. If participants have varying interpretations of the task, then we will merely be studying an unknown mixture of things without knowing what.

There is abundant evidence that participants differ in the external representations they use to solve syllogisms (given the chance). Ford (1995) investigated the representations and theorem provers used by participants in solving syllogisms using think-aloud protocols. Participants were required to externalize their reasoning and were free to use pencil and paper to assist them. Some participants used diagrams akin to Euler's circles, whereas other participants made transformations of the sentential form of the premises. Ford classified participants according to whether they used these "graphical" or "verbal" representations, and showed that the think-aloud data did predict reasoning. The two groups found different problems difficult and easy. For example the problem (*all Bs are As, all Bs are Cs*), was found to be difficult for the people reporting using a verbal strategy, and much easier for those using diagrammatic strategies.

Should we make the inference that the external representations used were just externalizations of the internal representations? And, if so, at what level is the correspondence? One should be very wary of direct identification. For one thing, having pencil and paper almost certainly changes the memory demands of the task, and one might expect this to change representational strategy (Roberts, Gilmore, & Wood, 1997). So we should be careful. The data argues for some correspondence, though this might not be at the level of the representation itself, but rather at the level of abstract theorem provers used by these groups of students. Monaghan (2000) argues that the difference between Ford's groups of participants is due to variations in the order of applying rules – it is really just differences in the theorem provers – and this is an independent issue from the question of which representations are used.

Bucciarelli and Johnson-Laird (1999) also discussed strategies in syllogistic reasoning, and showed that their mental-models-based computer model of syllogistic reasoning is not sufficient for describing the variation found both within and between participants as they solved syllogisms. This is precisely because proof theories provide indefinitely many routes to conclusions. Stenning and Yule's (1997) correspondences mean that there are the same range of alternatives in the two types of representation. The empirical meat is all in the theorem provers.

Learning to Reason

If there is evidence of spontaneous individual differences in approach to the standard laboratory task of syllogism solution, there is still stronger evidence of individual differences in learning what the experimenter intends the task to be, and how to do it. We have been particularly interested in how participants respond to diagrammatic and sentential presentations of reasoning.

The semantic distinction between direct and indirect representations mentioned above has its cognitive impact through the different ways these two kinds of representation express abstraction. In general, direct systems are concrete – they naturally represent single situations – think of a map, for example. When direct systems have to express abstractions (over more than one situation) they do so through annotational "tricks" that permit a single diagram to represent several situations. The crosses in the Euler diagrams are an example. For example, there are four arrangements of two circles that make *some A are B* true, but the single diagram with a cross in the intersection between two circles is sufficient to represent all four (because of the way the cross is interpreted). Mental models use the square parentheses as abstraction tricks in this sense.

Sentential languages, because they are indirectly interpreted through an abstract syntax, have no need of abstraction tricks. They can express open-ended abstractions. We hypothesized that these differences in ways of expressing abstraction would be what determined participants' learning from different presentations using diagrams or not.

This prediction was supported in two studies of real undergraduate logic courses that either did or did not use diagrammatic presentations (with abstraction tricks) (Monaghan, Stenning, Oberlander, & Sönströd, 1999; Stenning et al., 1995). Detailed analysis of the strategies of proof adopted showed that students who developed good strategies for using abstraction tricks learned well from diagrams; students who did not develop good strategies for using the diagrammatic abstractions learned relatively poorly from diagrams. A simple pretest predicts how students will learn from the two presentations.

This finding is made more interesting by the fact that it is accompanied by the reverse finding that students who do learn well from diagrams learn relatively less well from sentential presentations. It is not just that there are smart and less smart students. There are contrasting learning styles. These two studies showed that a GRE Analytical Scale pretest reliably distinguished these two subgroups of student. Analyzing the semantic properties of these problems, which required different levels of abstraction for solution, explained why (Monaghan et al., 1999).

Monaghan and Stenning (1998) extended these results to syllogisms taught either with Euler's circles diagrams or with Stenning and Yule's (1997) exactly equivalent sentential method for teaching. The same GRE pretest predicted how many tutor interventions and student errors would occur with the two different teaching methods. This is a replication in a very different domain with different measures, in a 40-minute laboratory task as compared to a 12-week logic course.

Both these sets of results show that students who learn well from diagrams are ones that know when *not* to use them: Those who learn poorly from diagrams are generally trying to overuse diagrammatic methods when they are inappropriate – a far cry from simple distinctions in terms of "visual" and "verbal" thinking. This finding accords well with the view that many spatial ability measures are really measures of whether the participant is flexible in using diagrams or other methods of solving problems to support their problem solving (Roberts, Wood, & Gilmore, 1994).

When we study learning to reason with external diagrams or language, there is good evidence that students respond quite differently to teaching with and without diagrams, but the best explanation of that response is in terms of the details of the different theorem provers that the representations encourage. Our distinction between direct and indirectly interpreted systems is shown to have real purchase in understanding students' responses to different modes of expressing abstraction, a great improvement on theorizing simply in terms of visual and verbal thinking.

REASONING, MODULARITY AND EVOLUTION

We began this chapter with evidence that participants (and experimenters) have many different construals of reasoning tasks. We have argued that a more careful use of logical concepts can change the empirical landscape of the study of reasoning. We should not end without considering the most spectacular case for this approach applied to an argument that is supposed to take us from the reasoning laboratory to the very origins of humanity. Some startling claims have been made about cognitive architecture and human evolution based on particular construals of logical conceptions of reasoning. Again we will argue that a modicum of logical care exposes the empirical as well as the theoretical inadequacies of these conclusions. It can also, at least tentatively, suggest almost opposite evolutionary conclusions.

The reasoning task at the base of these evolutionary claims is Wason's (1968) selection task. From observations that one version of this task is difficult and a supposedly logically equivalent task is easy, we are supposed to follow sweeping conclusions about our ancestors' and our own mental equipment.

Wason's task presents a conditional rule (e.g., "If there is a vowel on one side of a card, there is an even number on the other") and some views of single sides of cards. The participant is told that the cards have letters on one side and numbers on the other and is asked to select the cards that must be turned in order to check the truth of the rule. This task has probably attracted more attention than any other in the literature on deductive reasoning because participants systematically flout one theory of what they *ought* to do. Wason assumed a particular logical interpretation of the conditional (technically known as a "material conditional") and on that basis defined "correct performance" as choice of "A" and "7." The modal response is to choose "A" and "4" (about 40%) and only about 5%–10% of first year undergraduates do what Wason designated as correct.

However, participants are much more likely to perform in accordance with Wason's chosen competence model with different material (e.g., with the rule "If a customer drinks alcohol, they must be over 18," where the cards have drinks on one side and ages of drinkers on the other, and the task is to select which cards must be turned to check if people are complying with a law, for example, Cosmides, 1989; Wason & Johnson-Laird, 1972). In the first kind of material (the rule about letters and numbers) the rule has *descriptive* force: It says how the cards are. In the second (drinking age) material, the rule has *deontic* force: It says how the people referred to on the cards *should* be.

On the divergence of performance with these two kinds of conditionals, Cosmides and Tooby (1992) argue that our reasoning with deontics, such as the drinking age law, is based on the operation of "cheating detectors": innate modular mechanisms that evolved to underwrite the development of "social contractual" exchanges in human evolution. Our ability to reason with descriptive conditionals is poor (they argue) because we did not evolve a module for the general capacity for judging the truth values of descriptive expressions in our natural languages. Logic, in particular, is claimed to be a theory that predicts that reasoning is domain independent and purely formal and so can be rejected as a basis for a theory of human reasoning.

We believe that this argument is wrong on just about every count. Logic, as we have tried to illustrate here, is precisely a theory of how domain general reasoning (in virtue of logical form) interacts with domain dependent knowledge encoded in domain specific premises through the apparatus of interpretation. Any logic-based theory should expect participants' ascription of form to be crucially guided by content, and subsequent reasoning to be thereby fundamentally affected.

But it is not just the general interpretation of logic that is at fault here. The two kinds of rules are logically very different as is easy to see by considering the semantic (model theoretic) relations between cards and rule with the two kinds of material. This difference is already explicit in the instructions in that the descriptive material is accompanied by the goal of testing *truth* of rule, whereas the legal example is accompanied by the goal of testing *compliance* of cases.

In the descriptive task, the semantic relations are complex and asymmetrical. The rule applies, or not, to the cards; single cards may (or may not) make the rule false; but single cards cannot make the rule true. Only sets of cards can make the rule true, and even then it is debatable whether sets of cards are sufficient (because it is debatable whether the material interpretation of the implication is the only reasonable one in this circumstance). After all, all rules have exceptions. Furthermore, because sets of cards are at issue, there is a problem about whether decisions to turn cards are to be taken in the light of what is found on earlier turns. Yet another source of discomfort is the fact that the source of all the information (both what one is instructed to take on trust, and what one is instructed to test) comes from the same source (the experimenter). It is strange to question some but not all of the information equally, and it is perhaps also a source of discomfort to essentially call the experimenter a liar.

In contrast, with the drinking ages and drinks, the semantic relations are simple. Laws make drinkers' behavior compliant or noncompliant. Viewed from the other end of the relation, drinkers either comply or break the law. No relations between the behavior of one drinker and another affect these relations. So sets of drinkers do not enter into it, so there is no dependency between what we might learn from one card turn and what we might learn from another. Nor is there any problem about whether the law admits of exceptions as there is in the descriptive case about whether the generalization admits exceptions. Legal laws may be in force even if everyone breaks them: Generalizations do not remain true if all examples are counterexamples. Finally, the participant is asked to judge whether some miscreant is guilty, not whether the experimenter is honest.

Stenning and van Lambalgen (2002) present argument and evidence that it is the complexity of the semantic relations of the descriptive cases that leads to participants' problems. They show participants have trouble with understanding whether their choice of cards should be influenced by the information they may or may not get from earlier chosen turns. They show many more participants performing correctly on a variant of the task that makes the semantic complexities clearer, and they show social psychological effects of whether doubting the truth of the experimenter's rule casts doubt on the truthfulness of the experimenter. Again a more adequate analysis of the semantics of the material leads to quite different expectations (and empirical observations) of behavior.

The ancient logical distinction between deontic and descriptive conditionals (and the differences in their semantics) goes a remarkably long way toward explaining the available data on the selection task. In other words, participants have a highly general grasp of whether representations are being used to represent how things *are* as opposed to how things *ought to be*. They have highly sophisticated grasps of the great subtlety of descriptive conditional semantics, but what they are not used to are tasks that force them to assign truth values to statements and to evaluate hypothetical evidence without the rich contextual cues that indicate what interpretation is intended. These problems do not arise in the deontic tasks.

One may or may not worry about Wason's task, but these arguments about deontic reasoning and its relation to logic and to the "theory of mind" ramify right across developmental psychology and theories of human evolution. Cosmides and Tooby (1992) are essentially trying to found the evolution of human communication on the basis of contractual exchange. A more adequate reading of the logical situation seems to justify (if tentatively) exactly the opposite conclusion – that contractual exchange is founded on human communication. For a fuller discussion of the evolutionary arguments see Stenning (2002).

This reanalysis of the work on deontic conditionals provides an illustration of the methodological importance of the logical level of model theory for psychological methodology. The reader will have noticed that the differences between descriptive and deontic conditionals were described purely at the level of the semantic relations between cards and the two types of rules – a model theoretic description. This allows us to remain completely neutral about what processes (proof theory plus theorem prover) operate on what mental representations. This neutrality of model theory is crucial for the theorist who needs to seek empirical evidence about reasoning without access to the processes participants use. This methodological importance is reflected in the top-right entry in Figure 6.5.

CONCLUSIONS

We have argued that taking logical conceptions of deduction seriously and linking empirical investigation to conceptual and theoretical understanding can lead to more productive empirical science. The scientific product is rather different. We have not produced a proprietary system claiming to be the "fundamental reasoning mechanism" or posited widgets in the brain for implementing reasoning. Instead we have made claims about what deduction is; where deduction is most significantly engaged in everyday life; how to compare different representation systems, and to assess available behavioral evidence about which system underlies behavior at an appropriate level of abstraction; how to gain a better understanding of how participants understand the tasks we set them; how to enrich our empirical base for theorizing about human reasoning; how our understanding of deduction touches our understandings of induction, decision, communication, analogical reasoning, and conceptual learning; how the interpretation of representation systems is local and so reasoning in them is domain specific; but also what aspects of deduction are general; how meta-level reasoning about which reasoning systems to adopt is a critical part of understanding reasoning; and how representation systems with different kinds of semantic interpretation have different cognitive consequences for their users.

Some colleagues react with disappointment to the suggestion that the main goal of the psychology of representation and reasoning is not the specification of one fundamental reasoning mechanism. Once these laboratory tasks (the syllogism, collection of logical intuitions, the selection task, etc.) are shown to be ill-understood by participants, and amenable to explanation in terms of participants' attempts to interpret them, these colleagues' reaction is that the field is then of little interest. In contrast, we would claim the opposite. This reconceptualization gives a much better account of how deduction relates to the everyday activity of interpreting others' representations and our own. It thereby relates deduction to major educational goals such as learning the discourse of proof; learning how to interpret arguments; learning techniques for interpretations of representations (learning to learn); and learning to reason about the balance of cooperative and adversarial processes in communication. If it is thought that these processes are less interesting because they apply most directly in education, then we would reason this is an odd position for professors to take. We would also argue that comparable processes can be found much earlier in development and more universal representational learning, like learning to speak and learning to write. But that is another argument entirely.

The substance of this chapter can be summarized in Figure 6.5. Metareasoning, and learning to reason concerns choice, development, and

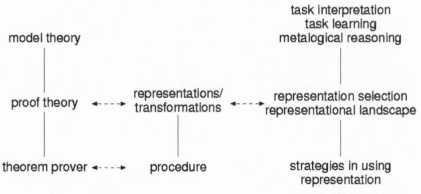

FIGURE 6.5. Levels of theory, empirical reasoning, and knowledge representation and strategies.

application of the representations and transformations that can implement a system of logic. Looking around a logic class at university or a mathematics class at high school, it is immediately apparent that students have very different understandings of the task, and consequently bring to bear very different representational systems to the problem. At the lower levels, participants differ in the way they use given systems of representations – the theorem provers define performance over the representations used.

Notes

1. Again, note that the premises and conclusions can be specified in a variety of systems – languages, diagrams, etc.
2. "Oh *man*! These guys' language is archaic!" addressed to a female human is an example of the Oxford English Dictionary's archaic usage hidden in modern oral vernacular English.
3. In fact, for many logical systems it is provable from rather plausible assumptions that the full range of valid conclusions cannot be computed by *any* device whatsoever.
4. In the archaic sense of man.
5. We report here the representations used in Johnson-Laird's computer program illustrating the method. Available from http: //www.cogsci. princeton.edu/phil
6. In this respect the enclosure of Bs in square brackets is like the Euler enclosure of all points corresponding to Bs in a circle; and the fact these square bracketed Bs definitely exist corresponds to the subregions marked by Xs in Euler's circles.
7. The logically sophisticated reader will be puzzled that quantified statements are treated here in propositional logic. It is a crucial property of the syllogism that this is possible, as explained in Stenning and Yule (1997), and this form of representation makes it easier to see the equivalences.
8. Of course, one can nowadays look inside the head using imaging techniques, but even then one still needs to know how to interpret what one sees, and we do not yet know how to interpret these representational differences.
9. For the curious: In each premises-type, subject and predicate terms are either distributed or not, according to whether the proposition asserts something of all of the term's extension set. So in *all A are B*, the subject term is distributed but the predicate term is not. The proposition asserts something about all As but not about all Bs. In *some A are B*, neither term is distributed. In *no A are B*, both terms are distributed (something is asserted of all As [i.e., that they are not Bs] and all Bs [i.e., that they are not As]).

References

Bucciarelli, M., & Johnson-Laird, P. N. (1999). Strategies in syllogistic reasoning. *Cognitive Science*, *23*, 247–303.

Chapman, I. J., & Chapman, J. P. (1959). Atmosphere effect re-examined. *Journal of Experimental Psychology*, *58*, 220–226.

Chater, N., & Oaksford, M. (1999). The probability heuristics model of syllogistic reasoning. *Cognitive Psychology, 38,* 191–258.

Cosmides, L. (1989). The logic of social exchange: Has natural selection shaped how humans reason? Studies with the Wason selection task. *Cognition, 31,* 187–276.

Cosmides, L., & Tooby, J. (1992). Cognitive adaptations for social exchange. In J. Barkow, L. Cosmides, & Tooby (Eds). *The adapted mind: Evolutionary psychology and the generation of culture* (pp.163–228). New York: Oxford University Press.

Ford, M. (1995). Two modes of mental representation and problem solution in syllogistic reasoning. *Cognition, 54,* 1–71.

Galotti, K. M., Baron, J., & Sabini, J. P. (1986). Individual differences in syllogistic reasoning: deduction rules or mental models? *Journal of Experimental Psychology: General, 115*(1), 16–25.

Gibson, J. J. (1979). *The ecological approach to visual perception.* Boston: Houghton Mifflin.

Gigerenzer, G., Todd, P., & ABC Research Group (1999). *Simple heuristics that make us smart.* Oxford: Oxford University Press.

Gilhooly, K. J., Logie, R. H., Wetherick, N. E., & Wynn, V. (1993). Working memory and strategies in syllogistic-reasoning tasks. *Memory and Cognition, 21*(1), 115–124.

Grice, P. (1975). Logic and conversation. In P. Cole & J. L. Morgan (Eds.), *Studies in syntax: Vol. 3. Speech acts.* New York: Academic Press.

Hodges, W. (1977) *Logic.* Harmondsworth: Penguin.

Johnson-Laird, P. N. (1983). *Mental models.* Cambridge: Cambridge University Press.

Johnson-Laird, P. N., & Byrne, R. M. J. (1991). *Deduction.* Hillsdale, NJ: Erlbaum.

Johnson-Laird, P. N., Legrenzi, P., Girotto, V., & Legrenzi, M. (2000). Illusions in reasoning about consistency. *Science, 288,* 531–532.

Monaghan, P. (2000). *Representation and strategy in reasoning, an individual differences approach.* Unpublished doctoral dissertation, Division of Informatics, University of Edinburgh, Edinburgh.

Monaghan, P., & Stenning, K. (1998). Effects of representational modality and thinking style on learning to solve reasoning problems. In M. Gernsbacher (Ed.), *Proceedings 20th Annual Meeting of the Cognitive Science Society* (pp. 716–721). Madison, Wisconsin.

Monaghan, P., Stenning, K., Oberlander, J., & Sönströd, C. (1999). Integrating psychometric and computational approaches to individual differences in multimodal reasoning. *21st Annual Conference of the Cognitive Science Society* (pp. 405–410). Vancouver: Erlbaum.

Newstead, S. E. (1989). Interpretation errors in syllogistic reasoning. *Journal of Memory and Language, 28,* 78–91.

Newstead, S. E. (1995). Gricean implicatures and syllogistic reasoning. *Journal of Memory and Language, 34,* 644–664.

Rips, L. J. (1994). *The psychology of proof: Deductive reasoning in human thinking.* Cambridge, MA: MIT Press.

Roberts, M. J., Gilmore, D. J., & Wood, D. J. (1997). Individual differences and strategy selection in reasoning. *British Journal of Psychology, 88,* 473–492.

Roberts, M. J., Wood, D. J., & Gilmore, D. J. (1994). The sentence-picture verification task: Methodological and theoretical difficulties. *British Journal of Psychology, 85,* 413–432.

Stenning, K. E. (2002). *Seeing reason: Language and image in learning to think.* Oxford University Press.

Stenning, K., & Cox, R. (1995) Attitudes to logical independence: Traits in quantifier interpretation. *Proceedings of the 17th Annual Conference of the Cognitive Science Society* (pp. 742–747). Pittsburgh: Erlbaum.

Stenning, K., & Cox, R. (2003). *Rethinking deductive tasks: Relating interpretation and reasoning processes through individual differences.* Manuscript submitted for publication.

Stenning, K., Cox, R., & Oberlander, J. (1995). Contrasting the cognitive effects of graphical and sentential logic teaching: reasoning, representation and individual differences. *Language and Cognitive Processes, 10,* 333–354.

Stenning, K., & Oberlander, J. (1995). A cognitive theory of graphical and linguistic reasoning: Logic and implementation. *Cognitive Science, 19,* 97–140.

Stenning, K., & van Lambalgen, M. (2001). Semantics as a foundation for psychology: A case study of Wason's selection task. *Journal of Logic, Language and Information, 10,* 273–317.

Stenning, K., & van Lambalgen, M. (2002). *A little logic goes a long way: Basing experiment on semantic theory in the cognitive science of conditional reasoning.* Manuscript submitted for publication.

Stenning, K., & Yule, P. (1997). Image and language in human reasoning: A syllogistic illustration. *Cognitive Psychology, 34,* 109–159.

Stenning, K., Yule, P., & Cox, R. (1996) Quantifier interpretation and syllogistic reasoning. *Proceedings of the 18th Annual Conference of the Cognitive Science Society* (pp. 678–683). CA: Erlbaum.

Wason, P. (1968). Reasoning about a rule. *Quarterly Journal of Experimental Psychology, 20,* 273–281.

Wason, P. C., & Johnson-Laird, P. N. (1972). *Psychology of reasoning.* London: Batsford.

7

Mental Models and Reasoning

Philip N. Johnson-Laird

Let us begin with three problems that call for you to reason:

1. Suppose that you are on the jury of a murder trial, and that two propositions are established beyond a reasonable doubt: The stabbing occurred on an Amtrak train to Washington, and the suspect was in a cinema at the time of the stabbing. What conclusion would you draw? You may want to take a pencil and paper, and record your answer to this problem and the two that follow.
2. Suppose that you have the following information: Either Omar is in Kandahar or at least he is in Afghanistan. In fact, he is not in Afghanistan. Is he in Kandahar: "yes," "no," or "don't know"?
3. You park your car in London on a double yellow line drawn at the side of the road. When you return, you car has been wheel-clamped, and a note on the windshield tells you where to pay the fine to get the wheel released. What offense have you committed?

Nearly everyone responds to problem (1): the suspect is innocent. They respond to problem (2): no, he is not in Kandahar. And they respond to problem (3): the offense was to park in a "no parking" zone. Our ability to reason is perhaps our preeminent cognitive skill. Without it, as these examples show, daily life would be impoverished, and there would be no science or mathematics, no legal systems or social conventions.

The three examples illustrate different sorts of reasoning, but, as this chapter argues, they have something in common. People are likely to use the same sort of mental representation in tackling these problems, and indeed for reasoning in general. They use their understanding of the

Preparation of this article was supported by a grant from the National Science Foundation (Grant 0076287) to study strategies in reasoning. It was made possible by the community of reasoning researchers. There are too many individuals to name, but the author thanks them all.

description of a problem, and their knowledge, to construct a mental representation of the relevant situation. Cognitive scientists refer to these representations as *mental models*, and the idea goes back to a remarkable Scottish psychologist, Kenneth Craik. He wrote:

If the organism carries a "small-scale model" of external reality and of its own possible actions within its head, it is able to try out various alternatives, conclude which is the best of them, react to future situations before they arise, utilize the knowledge of past events in dealing with the present and the future, and in every way to react in a much fuller, safer, and more competent manner to the emergencies which face it. (Craik, 1943)

Craik's idea was farsighted, but sketchy. Cognitive scientists took many years to develop mental models as an account of visual perception (see Marr, 1982). Likewise, the theory that reasoning depends on mental models did not develop until some forty years after Craik's book. It was originally proposed by the present author and his colleagues (Johnson-Laird, 1983, 1999; Johnson-Laird & Byrne, 1991), but others have contributed to the theory too (Evans, 1993; Garnham & Oakhill, 1994; Polk & Newell, 1995; Richardson & Ormerod, 1997).

The aim of this chapter is to explain the role of mental models in reasoning. It begins with an account of mental models (part 1). It then presents the model theory of logical reasoning or *deduction* (part 2). It shows how recent discoveries corroborate the use of mental models (part 3). It extends the theory to deductions depending on knowledge of the meanings of words and knowledge of the world (part 4). The second half of the chapter deals with *induction*, that is, reasoning yielding conclusions that are plausible, but, unlike deduction, not necessarily guaranteed to be true if their premises are true. It describes the role of mental models in simple inductions (part 5). It considers the role of models in reasoning to consistency, that is, in the detection of inconsistency, the revision of beliefs, and the resolution of inconsistency (part 6). Finally, the chapter draws some general conclusion about human reasoning (part 7).

THE THEORY OF MENTAL MODELS

The theory postulates that individuals use the meaning of assertions and general knowledge to construct *mental models* of the possibilities under description. It makes three main assumptions. The first assumption is that each mental model represents a possibility, capturing what is common to the different ways in which the possibility could occur. For example, if you spin a coin, then it comes down heads or tails. The coin could spin in infinitely many different trajectories. Mental models reduce all these different ways to two possibilities:

Heads
Tails

If the description of the coin toss calls for a more refined analysis, then individuals can represent more possibilities. These diagrams use words, but it is important not to think of mental models as words. Models are structures in the mind that represent states of affairs, real or imaginary. Mental models should not be confused with the words or diagrams that are used throughout this chapter to refer to them.

The second assumption is that mental models are *iconic*, that is, the parts of a mental model correspond to the parts of what it represents, and so its structure corresponds to the structure of what it represents. Visual images are iconic, and mental models may be experienced as visual images. But, you can have a mental model of abstract assertions, such as: "The author is not allowed to own a house." You may form an image of the author, and an image of a house, but no mere image can capture the meaning of negation, permission, or ownership (Barsalou, 1999; Markman & Dietrich, 2000).

One advantage of the iconic nature of mental models is that you can use some assertions to build a model and then use the model to draw a conclusion that does not correspond to any of these assertions. Here is an example (from Schaeken, Johnson-Laird, & d'Ydewalle, 1996). Someone tells you:

Pete listens to the radio before he reads the newspaper.
He reads the newspaper before he does his washing.
He eats his breakfast while he listens to the radio.
He plans his day while he does his washing.

You can envisage a mental model with the following iconic structure:

Radio   Newspaper   Washing
Breakfast   Plans

where "radio" denotes a model of Pete listening to the radio, and so on, time is the left-to-right axis, and the vertical axis allows for different events to be contemporaneous. Granted that each event takes roughly the same amount of time, you can draw the conclusion:

Pete eats his breakfast before he plans his day.

The conclusion emerges from the model. It is tricky to use formal logic to draw the same conclusion. One difficulty is that logic does not tell you *which* conclusion to draw from a set of premises, and an infinite number of different conclusions follow logically from any set of premises.

From the premises above, for instance, the following conclusion is a valid deduction:

Pete listens to the radio before he reads the newspaper.
and
Pete listens to the radio before he reads the newspaper.

Only lunatics and logicians are likely to draw such a conclusion. It does not tell you anything new. Yet, it must be true if the premises are true.

The third assumption of the theory is that mental models represent what is true, but do not represent what is false. This principle is so important that it is dignified with a name: the principle of *truth*. As an example of the principle, consider an assertion in the form of an "exclusive" disjunction – exclusive because both possibilities cannot be true:

Either Phil is in Philadelphia or otherwise Mo is in Mobile, but not both.

It is compatible with two possibilities, and so it has two mental models, as laid out here in separate rows:

(Phil Philadelphia)
                    (Mo Mobile)

where the parentheses demarcate a place named by the last word, and any other word inside them denotes a person in the place, that is, Phil is in Philadelphia in the first model, and Mo is in Mobile in the second model. These models represent what is possible given the truth of the assertion; they do not represent what is possible given its falsity. The principle of truth also applies to the individual clauses in assertions. A mental model represents a clause, affirmative or negative, only when the clause is true in the possibility. Hence, the first model of the disjunction above represents that Phil is in Philadelphia, but it does not represent explicitly that in this possibility it is *false* that Mo is in Mobile. Similarly, the second model represents that Mo is in Mobile, but it does not represent explicitly that in this possibility it is *false* that Phil is in Philadelphia. It is important not to confuse falsity with a negation. Negation is a syntactic property of sentences, for example, a negative sentence contains "not." But falsity is a semantic property of sentences: whether affirmative or negative, false sentences do not correspond to the facts of the matter. Mental models represent what is true, but not what is false.

Individuals can overrule the principle of truth in simple tasks with simple assertions. They make "mental footnotes" about what is false, and if they retain the footnotes they can flesh out mental models into *fully explicit* models, which represent clauses even when they are false in possibilities. The following fully explicit models represent the disjunction above:

(Phil Philadelphia)   Mo (Mobile)
Phil (Philadelphia)   (Mo Mobile)

so in the first model, Mo is not in Mobile, and in the second model Phil is not in Philadelphia.

Although individuals can represent fully explicit models, the principle of truth is the norm. It yields parsimonious representations, because reasoners do not have to bother with what is false, and so they reduce the amount of information that they have to hold in mind. One consequence is illustrated in the preceding models. They correspond to the fully explicit possibilities for a so-called "biconditional" assertion:

If, and only if, Phil is in Philadelphia then Mo is not in Mobile.

Because individuals normally rely on mental models, they do not grasp at once the equivalence between the exclusive disjunction and this biconditional.

The principle of truth governs the models based on other connectives, such as "and" and "if." A conjunction of two clauses: *Phil is in Philadelphia and Mo is in Mobile*, calls for a single mental model of the only true possibility:

(Phil Philadelphia)   (Mo Mobile)

An "inclusive" disjunction of the form: *Phil is in Philadelphia or Mo is in Mobile, or both*, has three mental models:

(Phil Philadelphia)
                       (Mo Mobile)
(Phil Philadelphia)   (Mo Mobile)

A conditional of the form: *If Phil is in Philadelphia then Mo is in Mobile*, has one explicit mental model that represents the possibility in which both clauses are true. Individuals do not immediately think about cases in which the "if" clause is false. They defer a detailed representation of these possibilities, which they represent in a wholly implicit model denoted here by an ellipsis:

(Phil Philadelphia)   (Mo Mobile)
          . . .

Reasoners need to make a mental footnote about what is false in the wholly implicit model, namely, that it represents the possibilities in which it is false that *Phil is in Philadelphia*. The fully explicit models of the conditional are accordingly:

(Phil Philadelphia)   (Mo Mobile)
Phil (Philadelphia)   (Mo Mobile)
Phil (Philadelphia)   Mo (Mobile)

Adults indeed do list these three possibilities (Barrouillet & Lecas, 1999). A biconditional such as: *If, and only if, Phil in Philadelphia then Mo is in Mobile*, has exactly the same initial mental model, but reasoners need to make a footnote that both its clauses are false in the implicit model. Reasoners soon lose access to mental footnotes, especially in the case of more complex assertions. If they retain them, then they can flesh out their mental models into fully explicit models. But, as we will see, knowledge of various sorts can block the construction of models. It is incompatible with the possibilities that they would represent.

MENTAL MODELS AND DEDUCTION

Logical reasoning, or deduction, aims to yield *valid* inferences, that is, those for which the conclusion must be true given that the premises are true. As an example, consider the following inference:

Phil is in Philadelphia or Mo is in Mobile.
But, Phil is *not* in Philadelphia.
So, Mo is in Mobile.

Granted that the premises are true, the conclusion must be true too, and so the inference is valid. Validity preserves truth. Of course, if the premises are false, all bets are off. Mo could still be in Mobile, but there is no guarantee. Naive individuals, that is, people who have had no training in logic, can make this inference. It is tempting to suppose, as I did at one time and as others still do, that individuals have an unconscious logic in their heads and it enables them to make valid deductions. We return to this idea later, but right now let us consider the model theory of deduction.

The theory provides a simple account of deduction. For the previous inference, reasoners envisage the possibilities compatible with the first premise:

(Phil Philadelphia)
                                  (Mo Mobile)
(Phil Philadelphia)   (Mo Mobile)

The second premise eliminates the first and third of these models, and so only the second model remains. This model yields the conclusion that Mo is in Mobile, which is valid because it holds in all the models – in this case, the single model – of the possibilities compatible with the premises.

Now, consider the following inference:

Phil is in Philadelphia or Mo is in Mobile.
Phil is in Philadelphia.
So, Mo is not in Mobile.

One way in which reasoners can convince themselves that the conclusion is invalid is by envisaging a *counterexample*, that is, a model in which the premises are true but the conclusion is false. The third model of the disjunction (see above):

(Phil Philadelphia)   (Mo Mobile)

is a counterexample. It is compatible with both premises, but incompatible with the putative conclusion. We will see later that naive individuals do indeed construct counterexamples to refute inferences (see "Strategies and Reasoning"), later in this chapter.

The model theory makes several predictions about deductive inference. Inferences of the previous sort, for instance, can be made easier if the premises refer to just a single individual:

Phil is in Philadelphia or he is in Mobile.
Phil is not in Philadelphia.
So, he is in Mobile.

In such cases, individuals know that one person cannot be in two places at the same time, and so there are only two simple possibilities, which are likely to be represented in a fully explicit way:

(Phil Philadelphia) (Mobile)
(Philadelphia) (Phil Mobile)

Here, the first model represent that Phil is in Philadelphia and not in Mobile, and the second model represents that Phil is in Mobile and not in Philadelphia. Such inferences are made more accurately and more rapidly (Bouquet & Warglien, 1999; Ormerod & Johnson-Laird, 2002).

The model theory also makes an obvious prediction about how to increase the difficulty of deductions: increase the number of models that inferences require. The more models that you have to hold in mind – more precisely, in your working memory – the longer it is going to take you to draw a conclusion, and the more likely you are to err by overlooking a model. The prediction has been corroborated for many different sorts of reasoning, including spatial and temporal reasoning based on relations such as, "in front of" and "afterward," reasoning based on "if" and "or," and reasoning based on "all" and "some" (see Bucciarelli & Johnson-Laird, 1999; Byrne & Johnson-Laird, 1989; Johnson-Laird, Byrne, & Schaeken, 1992; Vandierendonck & de Vooght; 1997). A straightforward example comes from a study of "double disjunctions" (Bauer & Johnson-Laird, 1993). Deductions from a pair of exclusive disjunctions are relatively easy, for example:

Raphael is in Tacoma or Julia is in Atlanta, but not both.
Julia is in Atlanta or Paul is in Philadelphia, but not both.
What follows?

Reasoners can envisage the two possibilities compatible with the first assertion:

(Raphael Tacoma)

(Julia Atlanta)

But, it is a little difficult to incorporate the possibilities from the second assertion. In fact, the solution is as follows:

(Raphael Tacoma)   (Paul Philadelphia)

(Julia Atlanta)

Hence, there are only two models of possibilities, and an emergent conclusion is: Either Raphael is in Tacoma and Paul is in Philadelphia or else Julia is in Atlanta. The analogous inference based on inclusive disjunctions is much harder:

Raphael is in Tacoma or Julia is in Atlanta, or both.
Julia is in Atlanta or Paul is in Philadelphia, or both.
What follows?

The first assertion is consistent with three models:

(Raphael Tacoma)

(Julia Atlanta)

(Raphael Tacoma)   (Julia Atlanta)

The task of adding the three possibilities compatible with the second assertion is very difficult. The correct answer is:

(Raphael Tacoma)   (Paul Philadelphia)

(Julia Atlanta)

(Julia Atlanta)   (Paul Philadelphia)

(Raphael Tacoma)   (Julia Atlanta)

(Raphael Tacoma)   (Julia Atlanta)   (Paul Philadelphia)

An emergent conclusion from these five possibilities is: Raphael is in Tacoma and Paul is in Philadelphia, or Julia is in Atlanta. The experiment showed that reasoners tend to overlook models of the premises, and so they draw conclusions consistent with only some of the models of the premises. In fact, the most frequent error was to draw a conclusion consistent with only *one* of the models of a double disjunction. Some researchers have indeed proposed that naive reasoners typically consider only one model at a time.

A super-human reasoner would grasp at once that the two preceding assertions yield five possibilities. Such a reasoner is embodied in the computer program implementing the theory so that it can check the correct conclusions. Yet, any finite organism including a computer will ultimately be defeated by an increase in the number of possibilities. Technically speaking, reasoning based on disjunctions and other connectives, such as conditionals, is "computationally intractable." As the number of possibilities goes up, eventually any computer – even one as big as the universe running at the speed of light – will be unable to cope. But, it is striking that human reasoners cannot cope with more than a handful of possibilities. The task can be made easier if, instead of verbal premises, diagrams make the possibilities explicit (Bauer & Johnson-Laird, 1993). Even diagrams, as they increase in complexity, will ultimately overwhelm finite reasoners.

The failure to consider all models often leads to difficulty with certain sorts of inference. A robust finding, for example, concerns conditional reasoning (Evans, Newstead, & Byrne, 1993). An easy inference with a conditional is one of the form known as modus ponens, such as:

If Raphael is in Tacoma then Julia is in Atlanta.　(If A then B)
Raphael is in Tacoma.　(A)
Therefore, Julia is in Atlanta.　(Therefore, B)

The inference follows at once from the mental models of the conditional:

(Raphael Tacoma)　　(Julia Atlanta)

．．．

The *categorical* premise that Raphael is in Tacoma rules out all but the first model. (A categorical asserts definite information corresponding to a single model.) In contrast, reasoners often say that nothing follows when they are given only the premises for the following sort of inference known as modus tollens:

If Raphael is in Tacoma then Julia is in Atlanta.　(If A then B)
Julia is not in Atlanta.　(Not-B)
Therefore, Raphael is not in Tacoma.　(Therefore, not-A)

According to the model theory, the difficulty arises because the mental models of conditionals need to be fleshed out to be fully explicit in order to make the inference:

(Raphael Tacoma)　　(Julia Atlanta)
Raphael (Tacoma)　　(Julia Atlanta)
Raphael (Tacoma)　　Julia (Atlanta)

At the very least, reasoners need to envisage the last of these models, because the categorical premise that Julia is not in Atlanta rules out the other two. This remaining model yields the valid conclusion: Raphael is not in Tacoma. Hence, the theory predicts that reasoning should be improved by any manipulation that helps individuals to envisage this model (or the possibility in which both clauses of the conditional are false). Girotto, Mazzocco, and Tasso (1997) have corroborated this prediction. They manipulated the order of the two premises. When the conditional occurs first, it preoccupies working memory during the interpretation of the categorical premise, and so reasoners are unlikely to construct the additional fully explicit models of the conditional. But, when the categorical premise occurs first, it blocks the explicit mental model of the conditional:

(Raphael Tacoma)   (Julia Atlanta)

because it asserts that Julia is not in Atlanta. The lack of this model frees up working memory, and allows reasoners to use the categorical premise to construct the fully explicit model required for modus tollens:

Raphael (Tacoma)   Julia (Atlanta)

As the theory also predicts, modus tollens is easier with a biconditional, which has just two fully explicit models, than with a conditional, which has three fully explicit models (Johnson-Laird, et al., 1992; see also Evans, 1977; Evans & Beck, 1981). Another way to enhance modus tollens, as Byrne and her colleagues have shown, is to use conditionals in the subjunctive mood, such as:

If Linda were in Galway then Cathy would be in Dublin.

They have an interpretation conveying that, in fact, Linda is not in Galway and Cathy is not in Dublin, but in the "counterfactual" possibility in which Linda had been in Galway then Cathy would have been in Dublin. This interpretation calls for two models, one of the facts and the other of the counterfactual possibility, which makes explicit what is needed for modus tollens:

Facts: Linda (Galway)   Cathy (Dublin)
Counterfactual possibility: (Linda Galway)   (Cathy Dublin)

As predicted, reasoners made more modus tollens inferences from these "counterfactual" conditionals than from ordinary conditionals (Byrne & Tasso, 1999). Some reasoners, as Thompson and Byrne (2000) have shown, focus on only one of the two models above, and this focus predicts whether or not they are likely to draw the modus tollens inference.

   One study failed to find an effect of number of models. The model theory predicts that inferences based on a conjunction (one model) should be easier than those based on a disjunction (multiple models). Yet, Rips (1994) reported that an inference of the following form:

A and B. If A then C. If B then C. Therefore, C.

was no easier to evaluate than one in which the first premise was a disjunction: *A or B*. García-Madruga and his colleagues, however, have corroborated the model theory's prediction when reasoners drew their own conclusion from these premises, as opposed to evaluating a given conclusion. And when the premises were presented one at a time on a computer screen, the results corroborated the model theory even in the evaluation task (García-Madruga, Moreno, Carriedo, Gutiérrez, & Johnson-Laird, 2001). Reasoners' strategies (see "Strategies and Reasoning") are likely to differ from one task to another.

The principle of truth postulates that mental models represent only what is true (see part 1 – "The Theory of Mental Models"). This constraint may be a sensible adaptation to the limited processing capacity of working memory, that is, reasoners can hold in mind only a limited amount of information at any one time. But, they pay a price for their inability to think about both what is true and what is false. Consider the following problem:

Only one of the following assertions is true about a particular hand of cards:
There is a king in the hand or there is an ace, or both.
There is a queen in the hand or there is an ace, or both.
There is a jack in the hand or there is a ten, or both.

Is it possible that there is an ace in the hand?

Ninety- nine percent of responses in an experiment were: "yes" (Goldvarg & Johnson-Laird, 2000). The participants appeared to think in the following way: "The first assertion allows three possibilities, an ace occurs in two of them, and so an ace is possible." The inference is tempting, but it is an illusion. If there were an ace in the hand, both the first and the second assertion would be true. And that would be contrary to the problem's rubric, which states that only *one* of the three assertions is true. To reach the correct answer, reasoners need to think about both the truth of an assertion and the concurrent falsity of the other two assertions. They may then realize that it is impossible for an ace to be in the hand. In fact, there are five possibilities compatible with the information in the problem, and an ace does not occur in any of them. It is also easy to construct illusions of impossibility. That is, problems to which nearly everyone responds, "No, that's impossible," and where the response is again an illusion.

When the preceding premises were given with the following question:

Is it possible that there is a jack?

the participants nearly all responded, "yes." They considered the third of the assertions in the problem, and its mental models showed that there was a jack. But, this time they were correct: A jack is possible. Hence, the focus on truth does not invariably lead to error. In fact, as the computer program implementing the theory shows, the inferences that give rise to illusions are fairly rare in the set of possible inferences.

The previous problems are artificial, though participants do respond correctly to the control problems, which are equally artificial. As a step toward more realistic problems, consider a highly potent illusion:

If there is a king in the hand then there is an ace or else if there isn't a king in the hand then there is an ace. There is a king in the hand. What follows?

Over two thousand individuals have tackled this problem (Johnson-Laird & Savary, 1999). Nearly all of them have responded: There is an ace. When the author's computer program told him that the response was wrong, he spent half a day looking for a bug in the program. There was none. The program was right; the author was wrong; and this experience led to the discovery of the illusions.

With the preceding problem, most people think that if the first conditional is true then one possibility is that there is a king and an ace, and that if the second conditional is true then another possibility is that there is not a king but there is an ace. There are accordingly two possibilities:

King   Ace
¬ King   Ace

where "¬" denotes a mental symbol for negation. So, either way there is an ace. The premise that there is a king eliminates the second of the two possibilities. Hence, there is bound to be an ace. The trouble with this line of thinking is that it neglects what is false. In particular, the force of "or else" conveys that one of the conditionals may be false. With an exclusive interpretation, one of them *must* be false. So, suppose that the first conditional is false. That means that there could be a king in the hand without an ace. Hence, even though the second premise asserts that there *is* a king in the hand, the potential falsity of the conditional shows that an ace may not be in the hand. The inference that there is an ace in the hand is illusory.

Assertions akin to those in this second illusion occur in daily life. Unfortunately, our evidence suggests that the illusions are not easy to eliminate. In one study, the experimenter, Bonnie Meyer, warned some participants that the problems were very difficult, and that they needed to think carefully to reach the right answer. She also asked these participants to think aloud as they were working on the problems. Here is what a participant said as she tackled the preceding illusion:

If there is a king there is an ace or else if there is not a king there is an ace. So there's always an ace. There is a king. . . . If there is a king then there is an ace or if there is not a king then there is an ace. So, either way you have an ace, and you have a king. So, you have a king and an ace – I guess. If there is a king there is an ace . . . or if there is not a king then there is an ace. Yes. So regardless you have an ace. I think. . . . So there has to be something else because that just seems way too easy. And something is wrong somewhere – I don't know what it is.

The protocol is typical. The participant falls straight into the trap, and never succeeds in climbing out of it.

The author and his colleagues treat illusory inferences as a litmus test for the use of mental models. They occur in all sorts of reasoning, including reasoning based on probabilities, causal relations, and what is permissible (see Bucciarelli & Johnson-Laird, 2001; Goldvarg & Johnson-Laird, 2001; Johnson-Laird, Legrenzi, Girotto, Legrenzi, & Caverni, 1999). In many studies, we have tried various ways to eliminate them. We have been able to reduce the difference in accuracy between the illusions and the matching control problems. But, it is not easy. My former colleague Yingrui Yang carried out a study in which he taught the participants to think explicitly about what is true and what is false. Such thinking is time consuming. It eliminated the difference between illusions and control problems. But, performance on the control problems fell from almost a 100% correct to around 75% correct (Yang & Johnson-Laird, 2000). So far, we have been unable to discover any simple antidote to the illusions. They corroborate the use of mental models in reasoning.

STRATEGIES OF REASONING

Psychologists sometimes suppose that reasoning depends on a single fixed sequence of elementary mental operations depending on the particular problem (e.g., Rips, 1994). Such a *deterministic* strategy unwinds like clockwork: Each step depends solely on the current state of the process and whatever input it may have (see Hopcroft & Ullman, 1979). In contrast, the model theory postulates that reasoning is *not* deterministic. Just as variation among individuals is necessary for evolution, variation in reasoning is valuable. It yields novel thoughts, which are necessary for learning and creativity. It also yields different inferential strategies. The model theory makes the following assumption (Van der Henst, Yang, & Johnson-Laird, 2002): *Reasoners develop different strategies using inferential operations based on mental models* (see assumptions 1 through 3 in "The Theory of Mental Models"). Naive individuals tackling problems spontaneously try out different sequences of model-based tactics. In this way, they develop different strategies. Once they have developed a strategy, the strategy itself can control inferential performance. A corollary of the assumption is that if psychologists can list all the possible model-based tactics, they will have specified the basis for all humanly feasible strategies.

The pioneering studies of inferential strategies investigated "series" problems, such as:

John is taller than Pete.   Pete is smaller than Bob.   Who is the tallest?

These studies showed that individuals develop strategies (see e.g., Ormrod, 1979; Quinton & Fellows, 1975; Wood, Shotter, & Godden, 1974).

But, few studies examined strategies in reasoning with connectives, such as "if," and investigators used inferences that were so simple that they did not reveal reasoners' strategies or differences among them. A recent discovery, however, bears out the model theory's assumption: Different individuals do develop different strategies (Van der Henst et al., 2002). In an initial study, the participants were given a series of problems, such as the following one about the contents of a box:

There is a blue pill or else a brown pill, but not both.
There is a brown pill or else a white pill, but not both.
There is white pill if and only if there is a red pill.
Does it follow that if there is a blue pill then there is a red pill?

The problems were easy, and the participants made no errors in evaluating the conclusions, though they were not always right for the right reasons. They were given pencil and paper, and asked to think aloud while they tackled the problems. Their protocols revealed a variety of strategies. Such data are controversial, because the need to think aloud, and the use of paper and pencil, may change the nature of reasoning. But, Bell (1999) has compared patterns of inferential results using this procedure with those that occur when individuals think to themselves in the usual way, and she showed comparable patterns of latencies in both conditions. But, even if the observed strategies occur only when participants think aloud – an unlikely event, psychologists still need to account for them.

The most frequent strategy (used on about a third of the trials in an initial study) is to construct an *incremental diagram* of the possibilities. The participants draw lines, horizontally or vertically, on the page, and use them to keep track of the different possibilities. With the blue, brown, white, and red problem, for instance, a participant drew a horizontal line across the page, and, working through the premises, built up the following diagram of the two possibilities:

blue   white   red
_____

brown

When people are taught to use this strategy in a systematic way – a procedure that takes about two minutes to teach, their reasoning is both faster and much more accurate (Bell, 1999).

A second strategy depends on a sequence of inferential *steps*, starting with a categorical assertion in the premises, or with a *supposition*, that is, an assumption for the sake of argument (Byrne & Handley, 1997). Reasoners then follow up the consequences of this single model step-by-step. A typical protocol is as follows (for the problem above): "Suppose there is a blue pill. It follows from the first premise that that there isn't a brown pill. It then follows from the second premise that there is a white pill. The third premise then implies there is a red pill. So, yes, the conclusion does follow."

A third strategy is similar. Reasoners transform each premise, if necessary, into a conditional in order to construct a *chain* of conditionals leading from one clause in the conclusion to the other clause. The conclusion may be one that reasoners construct for themselves or a given conclusion that they have to evaluate. For the problem above, a typical protocol is:

If there is a blue pill then there isn't a brown pill.
If there isn't a brown pill then there is a white pill.
If there is a white pill then there is a red pill.

The chain of conditionals is now complete. It leads from the first clause of the conclusion to its second clause, and so the participant simply said: "Yes."

A fourth strategy is to draw a *compound* conclusion, that is, one containing a connective, directly from a pair of compound premises, and then to draw another from this conclusion and another premise, and so on until the reasoner reaches the putative conclusion or a proposition inconsistent with it. Typical protocols illustrating compound inferences are:

There is a pink pill or else a brown pill.
There is a pink and a white pill.
So, if there is a brown pill then there isn't a white one.

and:

There is a red pill or else a blue one.
There's a blue pill or else a gray one.
So, possibly there is a grey and a red pill.

The fifth strategy occurs only when participants have to construct a conclusion of their own rather than to evaluate a given one. They *concatenate* clauses in the premises to construct a compound conclusion. For example, one participant argued from premises of the form:

There is a red pill and a blue one.
There is a blue pill if and only if there is a green pill.
There is a green pill if and only if there is a brown pill.

to the concatenation:

Red and (blue if and only if green if and only if brown).

Although it is not obvious, this strategy depends on the meaning of assertions. There are many possible concatenations of premises, but reasoners prefer those that follow the mental models of the premises (Van der Henst et al., 2002).

The manipulation of models can account for the inferential steps in all five strategies. And the model theory predicts that the nature of the problems should influence the particular strategies that reasoners develop. As the number of possibilities that have to be kept in mind increases, so reasoners should be more likely to rely on incremental diagrams because, unlike the other diagrams, they keep track of all the possibilities. Likewise, disjunctive premises, which yield multiple possibilities, should foster incremental diagrams, whereas conditional premises should foster strategies tailor made for them, such as the step strategy or the strategy of constructing chains of conditionals. Experiments have borne out both these predictions (Van der Henst et al., 2002).

Bucciarelli and Johnson-Laird (1999) have investigated the strategies that naive reasoners use in reasoning with so-called *syllogisms*, such as the following valid example:

Some of the chefs are musicians.
All the musicians are painters.
Therefore, some of the chefs are painters.

The participants were videotaped as they used cut-out shapes to evaluate valid and invalid syllogisms. The most striking phenomenon was the diversity in the participants' strategies. They sometimes began by constructing an external model of the first premise to which they added the information from the second premise; they sometimes proceeded in the opposite order. They sometimes built an initial model that satisfied the conclusion and modified it to refute the conclusion; they sometimes built an initial model that immediately refuted the conclusion.

What strategies do reasoners use to refute invalid conclusions? One possible strategy is to search for a counterexample (see "Mental Models and Deduction" in this chapter). Given the following problem:

More than half of the people in the room speak French.
More than half of the people in the room speak English.
Does it follow that more than half of the people in the room speak both
    French and English?

reasoners spontaneously drew diagrams of counterexamples (Neth & Johnson-Laird, 1999). Figure 7.1 shows a typical example. A recent study

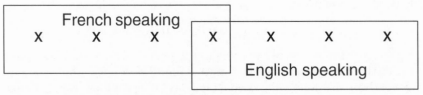

FIGURE 7.1. A typical diagram drawn by a participant to represent a counterexample. From Neth and Johnson-Laird, 1999.

of numerical versions of the same problems used functional magnetic resonance imaging (fMRI) to examine which parts of the brain were active during reasoning and during mental arithmetic from the same premises (Kroger, Cohen, & Johnson-Laird, 2002). The results showed more activity in the right frontal lobes of the brain during reasoning than during mental arithmetic. These regions are likely to mediate the representation of spatial and abstract relations, and so the model theory had predicted this result (Johnson-Laird, 1995). A striking phenomenon was that only those reasoning problems that elicit counterexamples activated the region known as the *right frontal pole*. This region is active during the processing of conflicts, and a counterexample yields a conflict: It is compatible with the premises, but incompatible with the conclusion.

Recent unpublished studies by Uri Hasson and the author suggest that a search for counterexamples is just one strategy that reasoners use to refute invalid conclusions (see also, Handley, Denis, Evans, & Capon, 2000). Other strategies are to establish that there is no relation between the premises and the conclusion, that a premise is missing from a valid argument, and that the conclusion is inconsistent with the premises – a strategy that cannot work with conclusions that are consistent with the premises but that do not follow from them. Our results, however, showed that the use of counterexamples is a frequent strategy: It was used on one or more occasions by every participant.

In summary, reasoners spontaneously develop a variety of strategies. Although some of the strategies are surprising, they all appear to rely on meaning and models. But, it is feasible that sophisticated reasoners could begin to formulate rules of inference like those of formal logic to help them to reason, just as those who have learned logic might use strategies based on such rules. The flexibility of the human strategic system has one drawback for psychologists. It makes the task of testing reasoning theories harder. The number of models called for by inferences, for example, yields only coarse predictions about their difficulty (Rijmen & de Boeck, 2001).

KNOWLEDGE AND BELIEFS MODULATE REASONING

How do people understand sentences in their natural language? The model theory holds to the long-standing view that they combine the meanings of words and phrases according to the syntactic relations among them (Johnson-Laird, 1983). But, the model theory also postulates a principle of modulation (Johnson-Laird & Byrne, 2002): *The meanings of clauses, links between them, and knowledge can modulate the interpretation of connectives, such as "or" and "if."* The modulation can add information to models, and it can also block the construction of otherwise feasible models. As an example of how modulation can occur as a result of general knowledge, consider the problem that readers were invited to solve in the Introduction to this chapter:

Omar is in Kandahar or at least he's in Afghanistan.
Omar is *not* in Afghanistan.
What follows?

The rule for disjunction in logic is as follows:

A or B. Not-B. Therefore A.

So, if you followed this rule, then you would have drawn the conclusion: Omar *is* in Kandahar. Few people draw this conclusion, however, unless they have been trained in logic. Most people draw the opposite conclusion: Omar is *not* in Kandahar, which contradicts the rule (Ormerod & Johnson-Laird, 2002). But this conclusion is sensible, because people know that Kandahar is in Afghanistan, and so they interpret the disjunction as compatible with only the following two possibilities:

(Omar (Kandahar) Afghanistan)
([Omar Kandahar] Afghanistan)

that is, Omar is not in Kandahar but is in Afghanistan in the first model, and Omar is in Kandahar and in Afghanistan in the second model. The categorical premise that Omar is not in Afghanistan eliminates both these possibilities. The two premises contradict one another, and in logic any conclusion whatsoever follows from a contradiction (Jeffrey, 1981). But, naive individuals do not follow logic on this point. They draw the conclusion sanctioned by their knowledge: If Omar is not in Afghanistan, then, they conclude, he is not in Kandahar. Modulation has a similar effect on conditionals, influencing both their interpretation and the ease of making inferences from them. For example, modus tollens is easier when general knowledge supports the appropriate conclusion, for example:

If Bill is in Rio de Janeiro then he is in Brazil.
Bill is not in Brazil.
Therefore, Bill is not in Rio de Janeiro.

Reasoners know that Rio de Janeiro is in Brazil, and so if Bill is not in Brazil then he cannot be in Rio (Johnson-Laird & Byrne, 2002).

The author has written a computer program to implement the model theory's account of how knowledge modulates the interpretation of assertions. It represents knowledge as explicit models. As an illustration of how it works, consider the following sort of inference, much studied by philosophers:

If sugar is in the tea then it tastes sweet.
Sugar is in the tea and ammonia is in the tea.
What follows?

The conclusion that follows logically is that the tea tastes sweet; the conclusion that people are likely to draw is that it tastes horribly bitter. The program has sets of models representing its knowledge. One such set represents the fact that if ammonia is in a liquid then the liquid tastes bitter (the opposite of sweet). This knowledge takes precedence over the models of the conditional above to yield a conclusion about the facts of the matter:

Sugar is in the tea and ammonia is in the tea but the tea is not sweet.

The same set of models in the program's knowledge is used to draw a further conclusion about a counterfactual state of affairs:

If it had not been the case that ammonia is in the tea and given that sugar is in the tea then it would have been the case that the tea is sweet.

Knowledge and beliefs not only modulate the interpretation of assertions, they also affect the *process* of reasoning. If individuals draw a conclusion that is compatible with what they know or believe, then tend to accept it. But if they reach a conclusion that seems preposterous in the light of their knowledge, then they search harder for a counterexample (see e.g., Oakhill, Garnham, & Johnson-Laird, 1990). This account is compatible with a robust finding: Knowledge and beliefs have a bigger effect on invalid inferences than on valid inferences (e.g., Cherubini, Oakhill, & Garnham, 1999; Evans, 1989). Logical deductions hinge solely on the meaning of logical terms, that is, connectives such as "if" and "or," and quantifiers such as "all" and "none." But deductions in daily life, as we have seen, go beyond the scope of logic. They also depend on the meanings of words and on general knowledge. These effects muddy the distinction between deduction and induction, because induction, to which we now turn, is dependent on knowledge.

INDUCTION

Text books often define induction as "arguing from the particular to the general," whereas deduction is "arguing from the general to the particular." These are examples of the two sorts of reasoning, but as definitions they are far too narrow. Deductions can also be from the particular to the particular, and from the general to the general. And so can inductions. What distinguishes the two is that deductions, if they are valid, do not go beyond the given information, whereas inductions do go beyond the given information. Hence, it is always possible that inductive conclusions are false even if their premises are true. No normative theory of induction exists, and so some philosophers of science eschew induction altogether on the grounds that it has no justification. But this step is like giving up sexual intercourse on the grounds that it does not always lead to pregnancy. In fact, many inferences in daily life are inductive, and they are based on knowledge. As two pioneers, Danny Kahneman and the late Amos Tversky have shown, a number of heuristics constrain the inductive use of knowledge. One heuristic is that inductions are shaped by the relative *availability* of pertinent knowledge (Tversky & Kahneman, 1973); and another is that they are based on the *representativeness* of evidence (Kahneman & Frederick, 2002). This second half of the present chapter takes for granted such heuristics. Its aim is to show the role of mental models in induction.

Inductive inferences can be rapid, involuntary, and outside awareness, but they can also be slow, voluntary, and at the forefront of awareness. This distinction between *implicit* and *explicit* inferences goes back at least to Pascal (1670/1966), and it was revived by Johnson-Laird and Wason (1977, p. 341 et seq.). Other psychologists have drawn similar distinctions (Evans & Over, 1996; Kahneman & Frederick, 2002; Sloman, 1996; and Stanovich, 1999). But, what is the mechanism underlying implicit inferences? The model theory postulates that implicit inferences are based on the construction of a *single* mental model, and that the implicit system does not attempt to search for alternative models unless it encounters evidence for them (Johnson-Laird, 1983, p. 127). The process is accordingly rapid, and it is as automatic as any other cognitive skill that calls for no more than a single mental representation at a time. Consider, for instance, the following passage:

The pilot put the plane into a stall just before landing on the strip. He just got it out of it in time, but it was a fluke.

Readers have no difficulty in understanding the passage, but every noun and verb in the first sentence is ambiguous. The search for the appropriate referents for the three occurrences of the pronoun "it" defeats even the most advanced computer programs for interpreting natural language. Humans have no difficulty with the passage because they can use general knowledge to construct a single model. This model is incompatible with other interpretations of the passage – albeit they are most improbable – and so the model could be wrong. One such alternative, for example, is that that the pilot is a ship's pilot who put a carpenter's tool into a compartment for an animal before the ship landed on a narrow stretch of land. Hence, implicit inferences lack the guarantee of validity. They are inductions rather than deductions. But the implicit system is not isolated from the mechanisms of deduction. Normally, the two systems work together in tandem.

The model theory postulates that *explicit* induction consists in the addition of information to models, sometimes with the consequence of eliminating a model of a possibility. The process is another instance of modulation by knowledge. To return to a problem in the Introduction of this chapter, you park a car in London, and when you return you discover a clamp on one of its wheels, and a note on the windshield telling you where to pay the fine to get the wheel released. Why should your wheel have been clamped? You know that such a punishment is contingent on your having broken a law. But, what law? *You have either parked illegally or committed some other offense, or both.* You then spot two yellow lines running along the side of the road. You infer that they probably indicate a "no parking" zone, and that you are guilty of illegal parking. Your disjunctive premise is consistent with three possibilities:

Illegal parking

　　　　　　　　　Driving offense

Illegal parking　　Driving offense

Your inference that you are guilty of illegal parking corresponds to the first of them. But, the third possibility shows that you could also be guilty of a driving offense. Hence, your conclusion goes beyond your premises. Yet, it is highly plausible. You may have based it on an unstated assumption that the chances are remote of your being guilty of two offenses. This assumption leads you to discount a possibility, and so your conclusion may be false.

EXPLANATION, ABDUCTION, AND REASONING TO CONSISTENCY

In logic, when a conclusion follows validly from premises, no subsequent information can invalidate it. Logic is said to be *monotonic* because when new premises are added to old, they lead merely to additional conclusions, and never to the withdrawal of an earlier conclusion. Logic means never having to be sorry about a valid conclusion. Life is not like logic, alas. You often withdraw valid conclusions when they conflict with subsequent evidence. Sometimes, you do so because a conclusion was based on an assumption that you made by default – an assumption warranted only if no evidence exists to the contrary. If I tell you about my terrier "Dusk," then you may infer by default that Dusk has four legs, a tail, and barks. But, when you learn that Dusk lost a leg in an accident, is tailless, and mute, you withdraw these conclusions. The model theory allows for the withdrawal of such default assumptions, and indeed the theory is unworkable without this assumption (Johnson-Laird & Byrne, 1991, Chap. 9). The notion of hierarchies of concepts, such as *animal-mammal-dog-terrier*, with default values for the values of their variables goes back to Minsky (1975), and it is built into so-called "object-oriented" programming languages. They allow, for example, that the concept of *dog* can be specified as having by default the value of *four* for its *number of legs*, and each sort of dog, including *terrier*, inherits this value. But, it can be overruled, as in the case of Dusk, by knowledge to the contrary.

Computer scientists who work in the area of artificial intelligence have developed many systems of *nonmonotonic* reasoning that allow valid conclusions to be withdrawn in certain circumstances. Not all such cases arise from violations of default values (see, e.g., Harman, 1986; Oaksford & Chater, 1991). Consider, for example, the first problem in this chapter:

The stabbing occurred on an Amtrak train to Washington. The suspect was in a cinema at the time of the stabbing. What follows?

Nearly everyone draws the conclusion: The suspect is innocent. It is a plausible induction. But, if you tell them that this conclusion is wrong, then they retract it, and they are able to generate various alternative possibilities. They tend to start with spatial manipulations of the situation, for example, the cinema was on the train. If you go on telling them that their conclusions are wrong, then they may consider action at a distance, for example, the suspect used an accomplice, or a spring-loaded knife in the seat. In general, the orders in which different people generate explanations for such a scenario are correlated. But, few individuals create the most ingenious explanations, such as the use of a radio-controlled robot to do the stabbing or of a posthypnotic suggestion for the victim to stab himself. These scenarios are most unlikely to be waiting in memory to be retrieved. The generation of alternatives depends on an active process of constructing models. It is a creative process rather than a rote operation. As Kahneman and Tversky (1982) observed, imagination is cognitively constrained rather than an idiosyncratic construction of possible scenarios.

Many inferences in daily life lead to conflicts with reality. Suppose you know, for example: If I turn on the ignition then the engine will start. You turn on the ignition. It follows validly from your beliefs that the engine will start. Unfortunately, nothing happens. There is a conflict, and something has to give. At the very least, you have to withdraw your conclusion. And, as with the murder in the cinema, you may try to generate an explanation that resolves the inconsistency. *Nonmonotonic* systems of reasoning try to deal with cases in which conclusions have to be withdrawn (see Brewka, Dix, & Konolige 1997; Gabbay, Hogger, & Robinson, 1994). But, no one knows what mental processes underlie human reasoning in such cases in which individuals try to reason their way back from an inconsistency to consistency. Such *reasoning to consistency* appears to call for three main steps: (1) the detection of an inconsistency, (2) the consequent revision of beliefs, and (3) the generation of a diagnostic explanation – a mental model – that resolves the inconsistency, for example, you explain why the engine did not start. The following sections examine each of these processes in turn.

The Detection of Inconsistency

The first step in reasoning to consistency is to detect an inconsistency. At first sight, the process seems straightforward. When there is a direct inconsistency between two simple assertions, its detection is trivial. I assert: Vivien is a woman. You assert: Vivien is not a woman. Plainly, our assertions are inconsistent. Not all inconsistencies are so simple. A *set* of assertions can be inconsistent, but with the interesting property that if any assertion is dropped from the set, the remaining assertions are consistent, for example:

> Ann is taller than Beth.
> Beth is taller than Chris.
> Chris is taller than Dave.
> Dave is taller than Ann.

These assertions cannot all be true, but drop any one of them, and the remaining assertions can all be true. Of course, inconsistent sets can contain many more assertions, and the task of evaluating consistency is computationally intractable (see – "Mental Models and Deduction"). You cope with it by keeping your beliefs in segregated sets (cf. Klein, 1998). You know, or you think you know, that *this* belief has no bearing on *that* belief. Your belief, say, that George Bush won the 2000 presidential election is, you suppose, independent of your belief that water contains oxygen.

The model theory makes the following assumption: *Individuals check the consistency of a set of assertions by searching for a single model (of a possibility) in which all the assertions are true.* My colleagues and I have tested this assumption, and it appears to be true (Johnson-Laird, Legrenzi, Girotto, & Legrenzi, 2000). The best evidence come from the litmus test of illusory inferences. In a recent study, the participants were told to write down the description of objects that satisfied descriptions or else, if they thought that nothing could satisfy a description, to say so (Legrenzi, Girotto, & Johnson-Laird, 2002a). Consider the following example:

> Only one of the following assertions is true:
> The tray is heavy or elegant, or both.
> The tray is elegant and portable.
> The following assertion is definitely true:
> The tray is elegant and portable.

Nearly all the participants wrote down that the tray is elegant and portable, and many added that it was light (not heavy). In fact, this response is an illusion. Nothing can satisfy the description of the tray, because it is inconsistent. If the tray were truly elegant and portable, then both of the alternative initial assertions would be true too, contrary to the rubric that only one of them is true.

The Revision of Beliefs and the Mismatch of Models

If there is an inconsistency between a valid consequence of your beliefs and the way the world is, then you need to revise your beliefs. You should abandon any dubious, improbable, or default belief. But, suppose that none of your relevant beliefs are of this sort, and that none of them is in a direct conflict with the facts, what then? Logic is no guide: It cannot tell you which belief to abandon. But, suppose there is one proposition that has a mental model conflicting with the evidence. It will appear to be inconsistent with the evidence, and so individuals are likely to reject it. In fact, there may be no inconsistency, but the compatibility of the evidence and the proposition depends on possibilities that are not represented in the proposition's mental models. These possibilities become apparent only in the *fully explicit* models of the proposition. But, according to the principle of truth (see "The Theory of Mental Models"), individuals normally overlook these models. What happens if there are no propositions with mental models conflicting with the evidence? If there is one proposition that fails to represent the evidence, that is, it has no mental models in which the evidence is represented, then individuals are likely to reject it. Given that this proposition is unique, the other propositions in the set match the evidence, that is, they have mental models that represent it, and so they are compatible with it. And if there is no unique proposition that fails to represent the evidence, then there are no grounds for giving up one proposition rather than another. These principles are summarized in the following *mismatch* assumption: *When an inconsistency occurs between incontrovertible evidence and a set of propositions, people reject whichever proposition has only mental models conflicting with the evidence, or else failing to represent the evidence* (Legrenzi, Girotto, & Johnson-Laird, 2002b). The mismatch principle is illustrated in the following two examples:

> VIVIEN SAYS: If the plane is on course, then the radar should show only water.
> EVELYN SAYS: The plane is on course.
> But, you know for sure that the radar does *not* show only water.

There is an inconsistency with the obvious modus ponens inference, but whose assertion should be rejected? The incontrovertible evidence clashes with the only mental model of the conditional that has any content, and so the mismatch principle predicts that in such cases reasoners should tend to reject the conditional. Now, consider a similar problem based on a modus tollens inference:

> VIVIEN SAYS: If the plane is on course, then the radar should show only water.
> EVELYN SAYS: The radar does not show only water.
> You know for sure that the plane is on course.

In this case, the incontrovertible evidence matches the explicit mental model of the conditional premise, but it is not represented in the model of the categorical premise. Hence, according to the mismatch principle, reasoners should tend to reject the categorical premise. Elio and Pelletier's (1997) pioneering study of nonmonotonic reasoning corroborated these two predictions.

If reasoners envisage fully explicit models of the conditional, then the prediction for the first of these examples is different. A biconditional, such as:

If, and only if, the plane is on course, then the radar should show only water

is consistent with only two possibilities, and so it is likely to yield fully explicit models:

plane-on-course	radar-shows-water
¬ plane-on-course	¬ radar-shows-water

The incontrovertible evidence that the radar does not show only water matches the second of these models, and so the mismatch principle now predicts that reasoners will reject the categorical premise that the plane is on course. Its model fails to represent the evidence. There is therefore an interaction between the mismatch principle and the extent to which reasoners flesh out their models explicitly. We return to this point later.

Legrenzi et al. (2002b) corroborated the predictions of the mismatch principle for a variety of problems. Consider, for example, the following problem:

> Paolo says: If the President owns a Rolls and a yacht then he owns either a plane or otherwise a castle, but not both.
> Vittorio says: The President owns a Rolls and a yacht.
> But, you know for sure that the President owns both a plane and a castle.
> According to you, who asserted a false proposition:
> Paolo. Vittorio. Neither of them. Both of them.

The definite evidence conflicts with the models of Paolo's remark, and so the mismatch principle predicts that reasoners should tend to reject his assertion rather than Vittorio's assertion. The majority of participants who rejected one of the beliefs indeed rejected Paolo's assertion. Now, consider the following contrasting example (based on the same content):

> Paolo says: The President owns a Rolls and a yacht, or otherwise if he owns a plane then he owns a castle.
> Vittorio says: The President owns a Rolls and a yacht.
> But, you know for sure that the President owns both a plane and a castle.
> According to you, who asserted a false proposition:
> Paolo. Vittorio. Neither of them. Both of them.

The definitive evidence matches a model of Paolo's assertion, and so the mismatch principle predicts that reasoners should reject Vittorio's assertion, because its models fail to represent the the evidence. Nearly all the participants rejected this assertion.

In sum, reasoners detect inconsistencies between their mental models of the incontrovertible evidence and of the assertions. They reject whatever mismatches the evidence. That is, direct clashes and dubious propositions aside, they reject whichever proposition has only mental models conflicting with the evidence or else failing to represent the evidence. Such models *appear* to be inconsistent with the evidence, even though they may not be.

Explanations and Models of Knowledge

There is more to coping with inconsistency than the revision of beliefs. You need to make sense of the inconsistency and to diagnose what may have gone wrong. This sort of reasoning yields explanations of an inductive sort, and the human propensity to generate explanations is extraordinarily powerful. To bring out its special nature, Peirce (1903) referred to it as *abduction*. It is a sort of induction because its results may be false even if its premises are true, but it goes beyond mere generalization into the domain of causality. As an example, consider the following case:

If the pilot fell from a plane without a parachute, the pilot died. This pilot did not die, however. Why not?

Most people give causal explanations, for example, the plane was on the ground, the pilot was already dead, the pilot fell into a deep snowdrift. Only a few give a "logical" response, explaining the anomaly by pointing out that a premise is missing: The pilot did not fall from a plane without a parachute. In a study of such problems, people created reliably more causal explanations than logical explanations. If knowledge normally takes precedence over contradictory assertions, then the explanatory mechanism should indeed dominate the ability to make deductions.

The abduction of explanations may seem unremarkable, but no existing computer program comes close to human ability. A study carried out in collaboration with Tony Anderson (of the University of Strathclyde) demonstrated the power of the explanatory mechanism by, in effect, asking participants to explain the inexplicable. They created a series of "inexplicable" situations by combining descriptions of totally unrelated events. They selected a sentence at random from one story and another sentence at random from another story, where both stories themselves had been selected a random from a set of stories. The result was an unrelated pair of sentences, such as:

Kenneth made his way to a shop that sold TV sets. Celia had recently had her ears pierced.

The participants had 10 seconds to devise an explanation of what was going on. They also used slightly edited pairs of sentences that had a referent in common, for example:

Celia made her way to a shop that sold TV sets. She had recently had her ears pierced.

The most striking feature of the results was the ability of the participants to create plausible scenarios for unrelated events. They went beyond the given information to account for what was happening. And they did so on 71% of trials with the unrelated sentences and on 86% of trials with the coreferential sentences (no participant ran counter to this trend). Given the preceding example, they proposed that Celia was getting reception in her earrings and wanted the TV shop to investigate, that she was wearing new earrings and wanted to see herself on closed circuit TV, that she had won a bet by having her ears pierced and was going to spend the money on a TV set, and so on. Some pairs of sentences suggested two distinct settings, for example:

After a few minutes, Andrew noticed a small pool of milk underneath his trolley. He walked into the lecture theatre.

Such a clash made it harder for the participants to create a scenario that integrated the two sentences. Nevertheless, they were only occasionally stumped for an explanation. They were also able to remember pairs of sentences much better after they had explained them than after they had tried to memorize them.

The abduction of explanations depends on background knowledge, particularly of causal relations. The model theory postulates that the meaning of causal relations depends on what is possible and what is impossible in the cooccurrence of various states of affairs (Goldvarg & Johnson-Laird, 2001). This account, unlike others, distinguishes between the meaning of causes and the meaning of enabling conditions, which make events possible without causing them. Experimental evidence confirms this distinction. The theory assumes that an assertion such as: *Vitamin B deficiency causes illness*, has as its most salient model the possibility in which the vitamin B deficiency and illness both occur, but that the assertion is compatible with three fully explicit possibilities:

Vitamin B deficiency	Illness
¬ Vitamin B deficiency	Illness
¬ Vitamin B deficiency	¬ Illness

with the temporal constraint that the illness cannot precede the vitamin deficiency. Causes therefore suffice to bring about their effects, but they are not necessary for those effects: Illness has causes other than vitamin deficiency. In contrast, an assertion of an enabling condition, *Vitamin B deficiency allows illness to occur*, is compatible with these fully explicit possibilities:

Vitamin B deficiency	Illness
Vitamin B deficiency	¬ Illness
¬ Vitamin B deficiency	¬ Illness

Enabling conditions are necessary for an effect to occur, but they do not suffice to bring it about: Even with a vitamin B deficiency illness may not occur.

In reasoning to consistency, causal knowledge is used to construct a chain from *cause* to *effect*, where the effect resolves the inconsistency. It at least makes possible the facts of the matter, and the proposition that knowledge overrules is taken to represent a counterfactual possibility (cf., the account in "Knowledge and Beliefs Modulate Reasoning" in this chapter). The chain thus provides an explanatory diagnosis that resolves the inconsistency. A computer program illustrates how abduction works. Consider, for example, the following case:

If one has a blow on the head, then one forgets some past events.
The woman had a blow on the head.
But, she did not forget any past events. Why not?

The mismatch principle predicts that individuals will cease to believe the conditional. It expresses a useful idealization, however, and so the program treats it as describing a counterfactual set of possibilities. The knowledge that the program has includes the following information: If a blow to the brain is cushioned, then one is able to avoid amnesia. The program does not reject the second premise, and the program uses it to model the facts of the matter:

The woman had a blow on the head.

This model triggers knowledge that serves as an explanation of the inconsistency:

The brain was cushioned. The person did not forget.

But, this model in turn can elicit its own causal explanation from available knowledge:

Why is the following the case: cushioned brain?
Answer: strong skull.

In other words, the program constructs two principal models, one of the facts and the other of the counterfactual possibilities corresponding to the conditional premise, but both are modulated by knowledge. The first model resolves the inconsistency:

The woman received a blow on the head but did not forget because her strong skull cushioned the blow.

The second model yields the counterfactual possibility:

If the woman had not had a strong skull, then she might have forgotten some past events.

Different explanations are possible, and even the present explanation might occur as a result of a different sequence of mental processes. Indeed, the generation of an explanatory diagnosis may lead to an implicit rejection of beliefs without any separate process depending on the mismatch principle. In any case, the original conditional premise is no longer strictly true: It has been modulated by the facts of the matter and available knowledge.

An important consequence of the model theory of causal relations is that it should be easier to infer an effect from a cause than to infer a cause from an effect. A cause is sufficient to yield, and so to infer, its effect. But, since an effect may have several causes, it is harder to infer its actual cause. There are exceptions (Cummins, Lubart, Alksnis, & Rist, 1991; Markovits, 1984), but the principle holds in general. The bias in inferrability, as well as the temporal constraint that causes precede their effects, may explain why inferences from causes to effects seem more plausible than inferences from effects to causes. As Tversky and Kahneman(1982) showed, conditional assertions in which the "if" clause is the cause of an effect stated in the other clause, such as: A girl has blue eyes if her mother has blue eyes, are judged as more probable than conditional assertions in which the "if" clause is evidence for the cause stated in the other clause: The mother has blue eyes if her daughter has blue eyes. These authors also demonstrated that the fluency of causal thinking inhibits individuals from revising their beliefs. For instance, given a description suggesting that a person is an engineer or computer scientist, individuals were reluctant to revise their impression of his character when they were told that he intended to work with disabled children. Instead, they created a causal explanation of why such an individual might nonetheless seek this career.

The author and his colleagues have shown that the mismatch principle and causal knowledge work together in individuals' preferred explanations to resolve inconsistencies (Girotto, Johnson-Laird, Legrenzi, & Sonino, 2000). Causal knowledge predicts that an assertion of a cause and an effect, in which the effect accounts for the inconsistency, should tend to be evaluated as more probable an explanation than one that consists of the cause alone. Consider the following inconsistency as an example:

If a person pulls the trigger then the pistol will fire. Someone has pulled the trigger, but the pistol did not fire. Why not?

In an initial study, the participants generated their own explanations for 20 different inconsistencies of this sort from a variety of domains. The explanations corroborated the mismatch principle: They ruled out the conditional premise on 90% of trials and the categorical premise on the remaining 10% of trials. These explanations provided the raw materials for two main studies.

The following explanation for the preceding problem describes a cause and its effect, and the effect explains why the pistol did not fire:

1. A prudent person had unloaded the pistol and there were no bullets in the chamber. (cause-and-effect)
   Individuals know that: If a person has unloaded the pistol, then there are no bullets in the chamber. Hence, an explanation that states only the cause:
2. A prudent person had unloaded the pistol. (cause)
   should enable reasoners to infer the consequent, and so this explanation should be judged as only slightly less probable than the explanation stating both cause and effect. A statement of the effect alone:
3. There were no bullets in the chamber. (effect)
   lacks an explanation of its cause. It should be judged as less probable than an explanation based on the cause alone. This pattern of judgments is an instance of the "conjunction" fallacy, in which a conjunction is judged to be more probable than its constituents (Tversky & Kahneman, 1983). These three causal explanations (cause-and-effect, cause alone, effect alone) are incompatible with the truth of the conditional assertion in the original problem: They fit the mismatch principle, which predicts that individuals should reject the conditional. The following explanation rejects the categorical assertion in the original problem:
4. The person did not really pull the trigger. (rejection of the categorical)
   The mismatch principle predicts that it should be ranked as less probable than the three explanations ruling out the conditional assertion. The experiment also contained one putative explanation that was a noncausal conjunction and two filler items. The participants' task was to rank order the probability of the resulting seven putative explanations for each of 20 different scenarios. Their rank orders in two experiments confirmed the prediction.

As we saw earlier, the mismatch principle predicts that a rejection of the categorical assertion should seem more probable if the participants construct explicit models of a biconditional, for example, they represent the following possibilities:

pulled-trigger   pistol-fired
¬ pulled-trigger   ¬ pistol-fired

In this case, the incontrovertible evidence that the pistol did not fire matches a model of the biconditional, and so reasoners should now be more likely to reject the categorical assertion. We tested this prediction in two further experiments. In the first experiment, the participants rank-ordered two versions of each scenario, with a three-hour interval between the two sets of problems. In one version, each scenario was based on an indicative conditional. In the other version, each scenario was based on a counterfactual biconditional, for example:

If, and only if, a person had pulled the trigger then the gun would have fired.

This assertion should tend to elicit the following models (see Byrne, 1997):

Fact: ¬ pulled-trigger   ¬ pistol-fired
Counterfactual possibility: pulled-trigger   pistol-fired

The results confirmed the prediction. The participants ranked the explanation ruling out the categorical assertion with a higher probability in the scenarios based on counterfactual biconditionals (an overall rank of 2.1 out of 7) than in the scenarios based on indicative conditionals (an overall rank of 4.2). The second study compared indicative conditionals with indicative biconditionals:

If, and only if, a person pulls the trigger then the pistol will fire.

The results again corroborated the mismatch principle. The participants ranked the explanation ruling out the categorical assertion as having a higher probability in the scenarios based on the biconditionals (an overall rank of 2.7) than in the scenarios based on the conditionals (an overall rank of 4.1).

In sum, reasoners detect inconsistencies in their mental models of incontrovertible evidence and their beliefs. They reject whatever mismatches the evidence. Direct clashes and dubious propositions aside, they reject whichever proposition has only mental models conflicting with the evidence or failing to represent the evidence. They use their available knowledge – in the form of explicit models – to try to create a causal scenario that makes sense of the facts of the matter. Their reasoning may resolve the inconsistency. It may yield an erroneous model. It may yield no model at all.

CONCLUSIONS

Reasoning matters. People who are good reasoners are likely to make progress in life. Those who are bad reasoners are likely to make a hash of things. The theory described in this chapter – the theory of mental models – makes sense of reasoning. It is based on a few simple principles:

1. *Each mental model represents a possibility.* Hence, a conclusion is necessary if it holds in all the models of the premises, probable if it holds in most of the equipossible models, and possible if it holds in at least one model. The theory, therefore, may provide a viable integration of deductive and probabilistic reasoning, at least when the probability of an event is *extensional*, that is, it equals the sum of the probabilities of the different ways in which the event can occur (Johnson-Laird et al., 1999).

2. *Insofar as possible, mental models are iconic.* Hence, reasoners can use a model to draw a conclusion that does not correspond to any of the assertions used to construct the model.

3. *Mental models represent what is true, but by default not what is false.* This principle reduces the processing load on working memory, but leads to systematic inferential illusions.

4. *Reasoners develop different strategies using inferential tactics based on mental models.* They may even develop strategies based on formal rules of inference, but the moral is: models first, rules after.

5. *The meanings of clauses, coreferential links between them, and knowledge of their context, modulate interpretation.* It can block models of possibilities that would otherwise be feasible.

6. *Individuals check the consistency of a set of assertions by searching for a single model in which all the assertions are true.* When an initial model turns out to be inconsistent with an assumption, reasoners have to search again and so the task is harder.

7. *When an inconsistency occurs between incontrovertible evidence and a set of propositions, people revise their beliefs according to a mismatch principle.* They tend to reject the proposition that has only mental models conflicting with the evidence, or failing to represent it.

The model theory does not have a monopoly: There are other theories of reasoning, most notably the view that it depends on rules of inference, either formal rules like those of logic (Braine & O'Brien, 1998; Rips, 1994) or rules with a content concerning causation or possibilities (Cheng & Holyoak, 1985; Kelley, 1973). The phenomena described in this chapter, however, are difficult for such theories to explain. They cannot account for the effect of number of models, erroneous conclusions arising from the neglect of models of the premises, illusory inferences, the development of different strategies of reasoning, and the use of counterexamples to refute invalid conclusions. The model theory, however, contains many gaps. It offers only relatively coarse predictions about the difficulties of different sorts of inference. Nevertheless, experimental results have corroborated each of the seven preceding principles. The author knows of no robust results contrary to them. One day, however, the theory may be overturned by the discovery of, say, sets of inferences in which multiple-model problems are easier than one-model problems, or of problems in which the main erroneous conclusions do not correspond to a subset of mental models, or of contraventions of the principle of truth in which predicted illusions fail to occur. The model theory could be refuted by its own principle that systematic counterexamples undo arguments.

References

Barsalou, L. W. (1999). Perceptual symbol systems. *Behavioral and Brain Sciences, 22,* 577–660.

Barrouillet, P., & Lecas, J-F. (1999). Mental models in conditional reasoning and working memory. *Thinking and Reasoning, 5,* 289–302.

Bauer, M. I., & Johnson-Laird, P. N. (1993). How diagrams can improve reasoning. *Psychological Science, 4,* 372–378.

Bell, V. (1999), *The model method*. Unpublished doctoral dissertation, Department of Psychology, Princeton University, NJ.

Bouquet, P., & Warglien, M. (1999). Mental models and local models semantics: The problem of information integration. *Proceedings of the European Conference on Cognitive Science (ECCS'99)*, (pp. 169–178). Siena: University of Siene.

Braine, M. D. S., & O'Brien, D. P. (Eds.) (1998). *Mental logic*. Mahwah, NJ: Erlbaum.

Brewka, G., Dix, J., & Konolige, K. (1997). *Nonmonotonic reasoning: An overview*. Stanford, CA: CLSI Publications, Stanford University.

Bucciarelli, M., & Johnson-Laird, P. N. (1999). Strategies in syllogistic reasoning. *Cognitive Science, 23,* 247–303.

Bucciarelli, M., & Johnson-Laird, P. N. (2001). *Deontic meaning and reasoning*. Manuscript submitted for publication.

Byrne, R. M. J. (1997). Cognitive processes in counterfactual thinking about what might have been. In Medin, D. K. (Ed.) *The psychology of learning and motivation, advances in research and theory: Vol. 37* (pp. 105–54). San Diego, CA: Academic Press.

Byrne, R. M. J., & Handley, S. J. (1997). Reasoning strategies for suppositional deductions. *Cognition, 62,* 1–49.

Byrne, R. M. J., & Johnson-Laird, P. N. (1989). Spatial reasoning. *Journal of Memory and Language, 28,* 564–575.

Byrne, R. M. J., & Tasso, A. (1999). Deductive reasoning with factual, possible, and counterfactual conditionals. *Memory & Cognition, 27,* 726–740.

Cheng, P. N., & Holyoak, K. J. (1985). Pragmatic reasoning schemas. *Cognitive Psychology, 17,* 391–416.

Cherubini, P., Oakhill, J., & Garnham, A. (1999). Can any ostrich fly? Some new data on belief bias in syllogistic reasoning. *Cognition, 69,* 179–218.

Craik, K. (1943). *The nature of explanation*. Cambridge: Cambridge University Press.

Cummins, D. D., Lubart, T., Alksnis, O., & Rist, R. (1991). Conditional reasoning and causation. *Memory and Cognition, 19,* 274–282.

Elio, R., & Pelletier, F. J. (1997). Belief change as propositional update. *Cognitive Science, 21,* 419–460.

Evans, J. St. B. T. (1977). Linguistic factors in reasoning. *Quarterly Journal of Experimental Psychology, 29*, 297–306.

Evans, J. St. B. T. (1989). *Bias in human reasoning: Causes and consequences.* Hillsdale, NJ: Erlbaum.

Evans, J. St. B. T. (1993). The mental model theory of conditional reasoning: Critical appraisal and revision. *Cognition, 48*, 1–20.

Evans, J. St. B. T., & Beck, M. A. (1981). Directionality and temporal factors in conditional reasoning. *Current Psychological Research, 1*, 111–120.

Evans, J. St. B. T., Newstead, S. E., & Byrne, R. M. J. (1993). *Human reasoning: The Psychology of Deduction.* Mahwah, NJ: Erlbaum.

Evans, J. St. B. T., & Over, D. E. (1996). *Rationality and reasoning.* Hove, UK: Psychology Press.

Gabbay, D. M., Hogger, C. J., & Robinson, J. A. (1994). *Handbook of logic in artificial intelligence and logic programming: Vol. 3. Nonmonotonic reasoning and uncertain reasoning.* (Vol. co-ordin.: D. Nute). Oxford: Clarendon Press.

García-Madruga, J. A., Moreno, S., Carriedo, N., Gutiérrez, F., & Johnson-Laird, P. N. (2001). Are conjunctive inferences easier than disjunctive inferences? A comparison of rules and models. *Quarterly Journal of Experimental Psychology, 54A*, 613–632.

Garnham, A., & Oakhill, J. V. (1994). *Thinking and reasoning.* Oxford: Basil Blackwell.

Girotto, V., Johnson-Laird, P. N., Legrenzi, P., & Sonino, M. (2000). Reasoning to consistency: How people resolve logical inconsistencies. In J. A. García-Madruga, N. Carriedo, and M. González-Labra (Eds.) *Mental Models in Reasoning* (pp. 83–97). Madrid: Universidad Naciónal de Educacion a Distanzia.

Girotto, V., Mazzocco, A., & Tasso. A. (1997). The effect of premise order in conditional reasoning: a test of the mental model theory. *Cognition, 63*, 1–28.

Goldvarg, Y., & Johnson-Laird, P. N. (2000). Illusions in modal reasoning. *Memory & Cognition, 28*, 282–294.

Goldvarg, Y., & Johnson-Laird, P. N. (2001). Naive causality: A mental model theory of causal meaning and reasoning. *Cognitive Science, 25*, 565–610.

Handley, S. J., Denis, I., Evans, J. St. B. T., & Capon, A. (2000). Individual differences and the search for counterexamples in syllogistic reasoning. In W. S. Schaeken, G. De Vooght, and G. d'Ydewalle (Eds.) *Deductive reasoning and strategies* (pp. 241–265). Mawah, NJ: Erlbaum.

Harman, G. (1986) *Change in view: Principles of reasoning.* Cambridge, MA: MIT Press, Bradford Book.

Hopcroft, J. E., & Ullman, J. D. (1979). *Formal languages and their relation to automata.* Reading, MA: Addison-Wesley.

Jeffrey, R. C. (1981) *Formal logic, its scope and limits* (2nd ed.). New York: McGraw-Hill.

Johnson-Laird, P. N. (1983). *Mental models: Towards a cognitive science of language, inference and consciousness.* Cambridge: Cambridge University Press; Cambridge, MA: Harvard University Press.

Johnson-Laird, P. N. (1995). Models in deductive thinking. In M. S. Gazzaniga (Ed.) *The cognitive neurosciences* (pp. 999–1008). Cambridge, MA: MIT Press.

Johnson-Laird, P. N. (1999). Reasoning: formal rules vs. mental models. In R. J. Sternberg (Ed.), *Conceptual issues in psychology.* Cambridge, MA: MIT Press.

Johnson-Laird, P. N., & Byrne, R. M. J. (1991). *Deduction*. Hillsdale, NJ: Erlbaum.

Johnson-Laird, P. N., & Byrne, R. M. J. (2002). Conditionals: A theory of meaning, pragmatics, and inference. *Psychological Review, 109*, 646–678.

Johnson-Laird, P. N., Byrne, R. M. J., & Schaeken, W. S. (1992). Propositional reasoning by model. *Psychological Review, 99*, 418–439.

Johnson-Laird, P. N., Legrenzi, P., Girotto, P., & Legrenzi, M. S. (2000). Illusions in reasoning about consistency. *Science, 288*, 531–532.

Johnson-Laird, P. N., Legrenzi, P., Girotto, V., Legrenzi, M., & Caverni, J-P. (1999). Naive probability: A mental model theory of extensional reasoning. *Psychological Review, 106*, 62–88.

Johnson-Laird, P. N., & Savary, F. (1999). Illusory inferences: A novel class of erroneous deductions. *Cognition, 71*, 191–229.

Johnson-Laird, P. N., & Wason, P. C. (Eds.). (1977). *Thinking*. Cambridge: Cambridge University Press.

Kahneman, D., & Frederick, S. (in press). Representativeness revisited: Attribute substitution in intuitive judgment. In T. Gilovich, D. Griffin, and D. Kahneman (Eds.), *Heuristics of intuitive judgment: extensions and applications*. New York: Cambridge University Press.

Kahneman, D., & Tversky, A. (1982) The simulation heuristic. In D. Kahneman, P. Slovic, and A. Tversky (Eds.), *Judgment under uncertainty: Heuristics and biases* (pp. 201–208). Cambridge: Cambridge University Press.

Kelley, H. H. (1973). The processes of causal attribution. *American Psychologist, 28*, 107–128.

Klein, G. (1998). *Sources of power: How people make decisions*. Cambridge, MA: MIT Press.

Kroger, J. K., Cohen, J. D., & Johnson-Laird, P. N. (2002). A double dissociation between logic and mathematics. Under submission.

Legrenzi, P., Girotto, V., & Johnson-Laird, P. N. (2002a). *Models of consistency*. Manuscript submitted for publication.

Legrenzi, P., Girotto, V., & Johnson-Laird, P. N. (2002b). *Models and the revision of beliefs*. Manuscript submitted for publication.

Markman, A. B., & Dietrich, E. (2000). Extending the classical view of representation. *Trends in Cognitive Science, 4*, 470–475.

Markovits, H. (1984). Awareness of the "possible" as a mediator of formal thinking in conditional reasoning problems. *British Journal of Psychology, 75*, 367–376.

Marr, D. (1982). *Vision*. San Francisco: Freeman.

Minsky, M. (1975). A framework for representing knowledge. In P. Winston (Ed.) *The psychology of computer vision* (pp. 211–277). New York: McGraw-Hill.

Neth, H., & Johnson-Laird, P. N. (1999). The search for counterexamples in human reasoning. *Proceedings of the Twenty First Annual Conference of the Cognitive Science Society* (p. 806). Mahwah, NJ: Erlbaum.

Oakhill, J., Garnham, A., & Johnson-Laird, P. N. (1990). Belief bias effects in syllogistic reasoning. In K. Gilhooly, M. T. G. Keane, R. H. Logie, and G. Erdos (Eds.), *Lines of thinking* (Vol 1, pp. 125–138). London: Wiley.

Oaksford, M., & Chater, N. (1991). Against logicist cognitive science, *Mind & Language, 6*, 1–38.

Ormerod, T. C., & Johnson-Laird, P. N. (2002). *How pragmatics modulates the meaning of sentential connectives*. Manuscript under submission.

Ormrod, J. E. (1979). Cognitive processes in the solution of three-term series problems. *American Journal of Psychology, 92,* 235–255.

Pascal, B. (1966). *Pensées.* Harmondsworth, UK: Penguin. (Original work published in 1670)

Peirce, C. S. (1903). Abduction and induction. In J. Buchler (Ed.), *Philosophical writings of Peirce.* New York: Dover, 1955.

Polk, T. A., & Newell, A. (1995). Deduction as verbal reasoning. *Psychological Review, 102,* 533–566.

Quinton, G., & Fellows, B. J. (1975). "Percepual" strategies in the solving of three-term series problems. *British Journal of Psychology, 66,* 69–78.

Richardson, J., & Ormerod, T. C. (1997). Rephrasing between disjunctives and conditionals: Mental models and the effects of thematic content. *Quarterly Journal of Experimental Psychology, 50A,* 358–385.

Rijmen, F., & de Boeck, P. (2001). Propositional reasoning: The differential contribution of "rules" to the difficulty of complex reasoning problems. *Memory & Cognition, 29,* 165–175.

Rips, L. J. (1994). *The psychology of proof.* Cambridge, MA: MIT Press.

Schaeken, W. S., Johnson-Laird, P. N., & d'Ydewalle, G. (1996). Mental models and temporal reasoning. *Cognition, 60,* 205–234.

Sloman, S. A. (1996). The empirical case for two systems of reasoning. *Psychological Bulletin, 119,* 3–22.

Stanovich, K. E. (1999). *Who is rational? Studies of individual differences in reasoning.* Mahwah, NJ: Erlbaum.

Thompson, V. A., & Byrne, R. M. J. (2000). *Reasoning counterfactually: Making inferences about things that didn't happen.* Manuscript is under submission.

Tversky, A., & Kahneman, D. (1973). Availability: A heuristic for judging frequency and probability. *Cognitive Psychology, 5,* 207–232.

Tversky, A., & Kahneman, D. (1982). Causal schemas in judgements under uncertainty. In D. Kahneman, P. Slovic, and A. Tversky (Eds.), *Judgement under uncertainty: Heuristics and biases* (pp. 117–128). Cambridge, Cambridge University Press.

Tversky, A., & Kahneman, D. (1983). Extensional versus intuitive reasoning: The conjunction fallacy in probability judgment. *Psychological Review, 90,* 292–315.

Van der Henst, J-B., Yang, Y., & Johnson-Laird, P. N. (2002). Strategies in sentential reasoning. Manuscript is under submission.

Vandierendonck, A., & De Vooght, G. (1997). Working memory constraints on linear reasoning with spatial and temporal contents. *Quarterly Journal of Experimental Psychology, 50A,* 803–820.

Wood, D. J., Shotter, J. D., & Godden, D. (1974). An investigation of the relationships between problem-solving strategies, representation and memory. *Quarterly Journal of Experimental Psychology, 26,* 252–257.

Yang, Y., & Johnson-Laird, P. N. (2000). How to eliminate illusions in quantified reasoning. *Memory & Cognition, 28,* 1050–1059.

8

Mental-Logic Theory

What It Proposes, and Reasons to Take This Proposal Seriously

David P. O'Brien

This chapter begins by addressing why one should expect a mental logic: In order to represent propositional information in declarative memory, the mind needs some logical predicate/argument structure. The chapter then turns to a vigorous debate that has taken place in the cognitive-psychology literature concerning whether there is a mental logic and addresses the principal argument against the idea made by some prominent cognitive researchers: Participants in laboratory experiments often make judgments that are at odds with a standard logic of the sort found in a typical logic text book. I argue that we have no reason to expect that mental logic should correspond consistently to logic as developed by professional logicians and, therefore, findings that judgments sometimes differ from standard logic need not be interpreted as evidence against a mental logic. The chapter then describes the mental-logic theory developed by Braine and O'Brien and evidence that supports it (see Braine & O'Brien, 1998, for the most detailed description of the theory and evidence for it). The theory has predicted, successfully, which logical-reasoning judgments people make easily and which they find difficult, which inferences are made effortlessly during text comprehension, and which judgments differ from what should be expected if people were using standard logic instead of mental logic. Finally, the chapter addresses whether an adequate account can be given of human reasoning processes without the inclusion of a mental logic, and argues that an adequate account of human reasoning requires inclusion of a mental logic. An adequate account requires more than the content-dependent processes described by some theories, such as pragmatic-schemas theory (e.g., Cheng & Holyoak, 1985) and social-contract theory (e.g., Cosmides, 1989) and it requires a logical representational structure that is lacking in mental-models theory (e.g., Johnson-Laird & Byrne, 1991).

WHY ONE SHOULD EXPECT THE EXISTENCE OF A MENTAL LOGIC

The expectation that there is a mental logic stems from the fact that there is a declarative memory; that is, humans have knowledge that is expressible in the form of linguistic propositions. The mental-logic approach shares with Fodor (1975) and Macnamara (1986) an epistemological assumption that in order for a declarative memory to exist, there must be a format for the storage of propositional information (Braine & O'Brien, 1998). Put simply: If there is no format for storing propositional information, then there is no propositional information. This format must be capable of representing properties and the entities that have those properties, to distinguish between the entities and the properties, and to keep track of which entities have which properties and of which properties go with which entities. For example, to understand that *the boy is wearing a red shirt*, one needs to know that the entity *boy* has the property of *wearing a red shirt* and that *shirt* is an entity that has the property of *redness*. In other words, the mind must have some basic logical predicate/argument structure. Further, the mind should have some ways of representing alternatives among the properties and among the entities that have those properties, as well as conjunctions, suppositions, and negations both of properties and of entities – the sorts of things that are done, for example, with English-language words, such as, *or*, *and*, *if*, and *not*, respectively.

Given the assumption that there is a logical representational format, one also would expect there to be some logical inferential processes: In order for a species to be intelligent, members of that species must make inferences that go beyond the presented information, and there ought to be some ways to ascertain which of these inferences are coherent. The central concern of logic is to be certain that false propositions are not drawn from true premises, that is, to ensure the soundness of arguments, and one thus would expect an intelligent species to have some inferential abilities that maintain inferential soundness. From the perspective of our assumptions, the central psychological issue thus concerns not whether there is a mental logic, but what it is like and how it works.

MENTAL LOGIC IS NOT EQUIVALENT TO STANDARD LOGIC

The question of whether – or to what extent – there is a mental logic has been debated vigorously over the past two decades. Several leading researchers have come to generally negative conclusions about the possibility of a mental logic. Cosmides (1989), for example, wrote that people rarely reason "according to the canons of logic" (p. 191), Cheng, Holyoak, Nisbett, and Oliver (1986) wrote of their generally negative conclusions about the use of any content-general logical inference procedures, and from the perspective of their mental-models theory, Johnson-Laird and his associates have consistently argued against any use of a mental logic (Johnson-Laird, 1983; Johnson-Laird & Byrne, 1991, 1993; Johnson-Laird, Byrne, & Schaeken, 1992). Much of this debate, however, has not addressed what would constitute an adequate or appropriate theory for a mental logic, and claims against the existence of a mental logic typically consist merely of showings that judgments of research participants have failed to correspond to some feature or another of a standard logic of the sort typically found in an introductory-logic textbook. Yet, we have no more reason to assume that a mental logic should be identical to a standard logic of the sort found in a typical textbook than we have reason to assume that basic human intuitions about quantities should correspond to some particular formal mathematical calculus, or than we have reason to think that basic linguistic intuitions should correspond to the proscriptions presented in some editor's style guide. Just as Monsieur Jourdan in Moliere's *Le Bourgeoise Gentilhomme* expressed surprise at the discovery that he had spoken prose for decades, some readers of this chapter may be surprised when they discover that they have been organizing their thoughts and reasoning with a mental logic.

Many of the representational formats, as well as their corresponding inferential procedures, that one typically finds in a contemporary standard logic textbook are not necessary features of a logic, much less of a mental logic, but are ways in which logic came to be represented by professional logicians. Reading a good history of logic, such as Kneale and Kneale (1962), reveals that some common representational formats that are found in a contemporary standard logic textbook appeared quite peculiar to many earlier logicians when they were proposed. Consider, for example, the standard truth table for conditionals, which interprets *if p then q* in terms of the $\supset$ of material implication, which assigns values for truth and falsity exhaustively to the constituent propositions p and for q and then defines which combinations result in a true or a false conditional:

1.

p	q	$p \supset q$
true	true	true
false	true	true
true	false	false
false	false	true

Note that from this truth-tabular perspective, which equates *if p then q* with $p \supset q$, *if p then q* is true so long as p is false. As Kneale and Kneale noted, the idea that conditional propositions should be understood in this way was not greeted enthusiastically by other logicians of ancient Greece when the proposal originally was made by Philo of Megara. Indeed, the suggestion that *if p then q* is true whenever p is false seemed entirely counterintuitive to Philo's contemporaries, and this idea that an *if*-statement is true so long as its antecedent is false (i.e., $\sim p \supset [p \supset q]$) continues to be referred to by modern logicians as a paradox of material implication. Yet, because defining the operators of logic in terms of truth tables has proved convenient to professional logicians when they work out the sorts of things that are important to them, such as constructing metalogical proofs of the soundness or the completeness of formal systems, logic textbooks typically introduce *if* with the truth table of material implication in spite of the fact that ordinary intuitions about conditionals view this definition as paradoxical. Simply because logic textbooks typically introduce *if* with the standard truth table for material implication, however, provides no reason for us to assume that ordinary logical intuitions should correspond to the truth table for material implication, or that the truth table should provide a standard against which to evaluate human performance. Further, findings that ordinary intuitions about conditionals do not correspond to the truth table should not surprise us and need not lead us to conclude that human intuitions are lacking in logic. In particular, such facts provide no basis for rejecting the idea that there are ordinary logical intuitions about the meanings of terms like *if, and, not, or, some,* and *all* and about the inferences that can be drawn using such terms.

WHAT PROPERTIES SHOULD ONE EXPECT IN A MENTAL LOGIC?

Given that a mental logic need not correspond exactly to what one finds in a logic textbook, how closely should one expect mental logic to correspond to a standard logic, and in what ways should mental logic be expected to differ from the sort of logic found in a typical logic textbook? Let me suggest that responses to these questions can be given focus by comparing the motivations for the development of formal logic to the motivations for the bio-evolutionary origins that I assume led to a mental logic. As noted above, logicians have a professional interest in constructing meta-logical proofs about the properties of logic systems, for example, discovering whether all possible valid inferences can be drawn from all possible premise sets by some particular set of inferential procedures, or ascertaining whether all inferences that could be drawn from all possible premise sets would in principle be sound, or ascertaining whether certain large sets of propositions are consistent, such as the set of all possible propositions that can be inferred from some particular set of axiomatically true premises. The procedures developed to construct such metalogical proofs tend to be extremely complex, such as the proof procedures of mathematical induction, and I know of no reason to expect that ordinary untutored people should be accomplished at performing such tasks. Indeed, ordinary reasoning would seem to have little interest in assessing the consistency either of large premise sets or of large sets of potential theorems, and people often believe in contradictory propositions simultaneously without realizing that they are doing so. Truth tables of the sort described earlier have been seductive to professional logicians because they allow many sorts of meta-logical analyses of logical-semantic questions to be reduced to a single sort of tabular notation, but there are logical inferences that would be judged as valid when viewed from the perspective of truth tables that are counterintuitive when viewed from the perspective of ordinary intuitions, and I know of no a priori reason to expect that they should provide a plausible psychological model. Thus, there are ample reasons to think that most of the complex proof procedures of standard logic differ from what would be found in a mental logic, and that the sorts of tabular representations provided by truth tables will not correspond to the sorts of representational formats found in a mental logic.

Mental-logic theory developed from the assumption that the mental logic has a bio-evolutionary history, and that the environmental pressures faced by our hunter/gatherer ancestors would have led not to the development of complex reasoning processes designed for construction of metalogical proofs, but rather to simple procedures that are appropriate for making short, direct, and immediate inferences. For example, it would be advantageous, knowing that Arakan went either fishing or hunting, and then discovering that Arakan did not go hunting, to infer that he went fishing. Or, suppose that one knows that if Arakan finished building his canoe then he went down river to visit his brother, and one then discovers that Arakan did finish building his canoe; it would be useful to be able to infer that he must have gone down river to visit his brother. Mental-logic theory thus was developed from the expectation that there are inference-making procedures that draw such short, immediate, and direct inferences, rather than procedures for constructing complex arguments. Construction of complex sorts of logical arguments probably became of interest with the advent of intellectual classes that arose only recently in civilized history, including legal scholars, mathematicians, theologians, cognitive scientists, and the like. The expectation thus is that a mental logic should consist of simple procedures that draw immediate and direct inferences from propositions that are assumed to be true, that is, it should be based on some simple schemas for drawing inferences directly from known propositions. The procedures would not include mechanisms for constructing sets of possible truth assignments, and would not attempt to keep track of which possible propositions are consistent with one another.

The assumption that the basic inference-making procedures of mental logic have a bio-evolutionary origin, and thus that they were motivated to address practical problems of the sort that would have been encountered by our hunter/gatherer ancestors, leads to the further assumption that the logical inference-making procedures are embedded in a profoundly pragmatic architecture (Braine & O'Brien, 1991). Inferences made on purely logical grounds would feed into inferences that are made on pragmatic grounds, and vice versa, and although cognitive scientists are interested in knowing which inferences are made with which type of process, we have no reason to expect that ordinary reasoners would monitor the sorts of processes they use to obtain any particular inference; that is, ordinarily people are not aware of whether an inference stemmed from logical, pragmatic, or any other sort of inference-making process, including from general epistemic knowledge, but would know at most that some proposition has been inferred.

THE REPRESENTATIONAL FORMAT AND THE INFERENCES SCHEMAS

Propositional representations can be found both at the level of a sentential logic and at the level of a predicate logic. Constructing a mental-logic theory at the sentential level is an easier task, because a theoretical proposal at the predicate-logic level requires that additional decisions be made about the internal structure of propositions. The difference between the two levels can be illustrated by considering how alternatives (i.e., disjunctions) and the sorts of inferences drawn from them can be represented. Consider Schema 3 in Table 8.1, which can be represented at the sentential level as:

2.   *p or q; not p;* therefore *q*

where individual propositions are separated by semicolons. For example, in reference to an imaginary blackboard with letters written on it (a sort of content used in studies by Braine, O'Brien, Noveck, Samuels, Lea, Fisch, & Yang, 1995; Braine, Reiser, & Rumain, 1984; O'Brien, Braine, & Yang, 1994), *there is either an X or a T on the blackboard; there is not an X on the blackboard;* therefore, *there is a T.* This sentential-level inference can be drawn entirely on the basis of the lexical meanings of the sentential operators *or* and *not,* and does not require any further analyses of the internal structure of the constituent propositions and their relations.

Now consider two universally quantified predicate-level versions of the same schema, which include representations of predicate/argument structures and ways of keeping track of which predicates go with which arguments and vice versa (i.e., of which properties go with which entities and vice versa), and includes representation of quantification and of quantificational scope. The first is typical of the sorts of representational formats found in a standard logic textbook:

3. $(\forall x)(S_1 x \text{ or } S_2 x);\ \sim(S_1\alpha);\ \therefore\ S_2\alpha,$

that is, for all x, x satisfies S_1 or satisfies S_2; α does not satisfy S_1; therefore α satisfies S2. The second is a predicate-logic version that is included in

TABLE 8.1. *Inference Schemas for the Mental Sentential Logic*

Core Schemas:

1. $\sim\sim p \equiv p$
   E.g., It is false that there is no cat in the hat
   $\therefore$ There is a cat in the hat

2. IF p_1 OR ... OR p_n THEN q; p_i
   $\therefore$ q
   E.g., If there is either a cat or a hamster then there is a quail; There is a cat
   $\therefore$ There is a quail

3. p_1 OR ... OR p_n; $\sim p_i$
   $\therefore p_1$ OR ... OR p_{i-1} OR p_{i+1} OR ... OR p_n
   E.g., There is a dog or a tiger; There is not a dog
   $\therefore$ There is a tiger

4. $\sim(p_1 \& ... \& p_n)$; p_i
   $\therefore \sim(p_1 \& ... \& pi - 1 \& pi + 1 \& ... \& pn)$
   E.g., It is false that there is both a giraffe and an iguana; There is a giraffe
   $\therefore$ There is not an iguana

5. p_1 OR ... OR p_n; IF p_1 THEN q; ... ; IF p_n THEN q
   $\therefore$ q
   E.g., There is a piranha or a raccoon; If there is a piranha then there is a lion;
   If there is a raccoon then there is a lion
   $\therefore$ There is a lion

6. p_1 OR ... OR p_n; IF p_1 THEN q_1; ... ; IF p_n THEN q_n
   $\therefore q_1$ OR ... OR q_n
   E.g., There is an kayak or a canoe; If there is an kayak then there is a walrus;
   If there is a canoe then there is a piranha
   $\therefore$ There is a walrus or a piranha

7. IF p THEN q; p
   $\therefore$ q
   E.g., If there is a tiger then there is a lion; There is a tiger
   $\therefore$ There is an lion

Principal Feeder Schemas:

8. p_1; p_2; ... p_n
   $\therefore p_1$ AND p_2 AND ... AND p_n
   E.g., There is a giraffe; There is a gorilla
   $\therefore$ There is a giraffe and a gorilla

9. $p_1 \& ... \& p_i \& ... \& p_n$
   $\therefore p_i$
   E.g., There is an ostrich and a zebra
   $\therefore$ There is an ostrich

Incompatibility Schemas:

10. p; $\sim p$
    $\therefore$ INCOMPATIBLE
    E.g., There is a monkey; There is not a monkey
    $\therefore$ INCOMPATIBLE

(continued)

TABLE 8.1 *(continued)*

11. p_1 OR ... OR p_n; $\sim p_1$ AND ... AND $\sim p_n$
     ∴ INCOMPATIBLE
     E.g., There is a cobra or a crocodile; There is not a cobra and there is not a
       crocodile
     ∴ INCOMPATIBLE

Supposition Schemas:
12. Given a chain of reasoning of the form
     Suppose p
     ∴ q
     One can conclude: IF p THEN q
13. Given a chain of reasoning of the form
     Suppose p
     - - - -
     ∴ INCOMPATIBLE
     One can conclude: $\sim$p

Note: Where there are subscripts, i indicates any one of the subscripted propositions. "$\sim$"
is negation and can be expressed as "It is false (not the case) that. . . ." Schema 12 states
that when q can be derived with the aid of the supposition p, one can conclude IF p
THEN q. Schema 13 says when a supposition leads to an incompatibility, the supposition is
false.

mental-logic theory (see Schema 1a in Table 8.2):

  4. S_1[All X] OR S_2[PRO-All X]; NEG $S_2[\alpha]$; $[\alpha] \subseteq$ [X]; ∴ $S_1[\alpha]$,

that is, all of the X's satisfy S_1 or they satisfy S_2; α does not satisfy S_2; α is
included among the X's; therefore α satisfies S_1. Both (3) and (4) would be
used to translate English-language sentences such as:

  The cars in the parking lot are Toyotas or they are Fords. Bill's car is not a
  Toyota; Bill's car is in the parking lot. Therefore, Bill's car is a Ford.

  This difference between the mental-logic notation in (4) and the notation
of a typical standard logic system in (3) illustrates the sorts of decisions
that are required in constructing a theory of mental logic about how to
represent the internal structure of propositions when one moves beyond
the sentential level. Standard logic represents quantification with outside
scope and with content-domain generality – in (3) the universal quantification is marked outside the expression being quantified and the quantifier
has scope over all instances of the bound variables within the parentheses
regardless of the content predicates to which the variables are attached. The
mental predicate logic, however, proposes inside quantificational scope
that is specific to a content domain – the universal quantification in the
major premise in (4) is placed inside the proposition and the quantification
is attached directly to the entities and content predicates so marked. The

TABLE 8.2. *Some Examples of Schemas for a Mental Predicate Logic*

1a. S1[All X] OR S2[PRO-All X]; NEG S2[α]; [α] $\subseteq$ [X] $\therefore$ S1[α]

E.g., The boys either went fishing or they went to a festival;
Fernando and Henrique did not go fishing
$\therefore$ Fernando and Henrique went to a festival

1b. S1[All X] OR S2[PRO-All X] $\therefore$ S2[All X: NEG S1[PRO]]

Note: Requires E[Some X: NEG S1[PRO]]
E.g., The boys either went fishing or they went to a festival
$\therefore$ The boys who did not go fishing went to a festival

2a. NEG E[~Some X: S1[PRO] &S2[PRO]~]; S2[α]; [α] $\subseteq$ [X] $\therefore$ NEG S1[α]

E.g., There are no package tours that stop both in Salvador and Maceió;
The package tour that leaves at 3 PM stops in Salvador
$\therefore$ The package tour that leaves at 3 PM does not stop in Maceió

2b. NEG (S1[All X] & S2[PRO-All X]) $\therefore$ NEG S2[All X: S1[PRO]]

(Note: This schema requires that there is some X that satisfies S)
E.g., The boys did not visit Manaus and travel by bus
$\therefore$ The boys who visited Manaus did not travel by bus

3a. S[X]; [α] $\subseteq$ [X] $\therefore$ S[α]

E.g., The third grade children went to the museum
$\therefore$ The third grade children from Porto Velho went to the museum

3b. NEG S[~Some X~]; [α] $\subseteq$ [X] $\therefore$ NEG S[α]

E.g., None of the boys wore silly hats
$\therefore$ Fernando and Henrique did not wear silly hats

---

decision to place quantificational scope inside the proposition, rather than outside, as is done in standard logic, was made principally because natural languages typically mark quantification in this way. Ioup (1975), for example, surveyed 14 languages and found no tendency for quantifiers to have outside scope, and found that quantifiers tended instead to be lexicalized inside noun phrases.

In moving from the outside domain-general scope of quantifiers typically found in standard logic to the inside domain-specific scope proposed by mental-logic theory, the mental predicate logic has borrowed a representational mechanism for keeping track of which objects and properties correspond to one another that is found in natural languages: pronominalization. The pronominal device is illustrated with the "PRO" notation in (4), which could be expressed in English as "All of the Xs satisfy S_1 or *they* satisfy S_2," where *they* is an anaphoric reflex of *the Xs*, and with both clauses marked for universality. Again, this strikes us as being a linguistically more natural way for keeping track of quantifier scope than is the outside quantificational scope typically found in standard logic, and in both clauses of the expression the quantification is linked to the content expressed by the predicate, which again strikes us as more natural than what is found typically in standard-logic systems. The difference in naturalness between (3) and (4) that stems from the use of inside quantification and pronominalization in (4) can be illustrated by casting (3) directly into English, "For all X, X satisfies S_1 or X satisfies S_2," which seems less natural than what is expressed in (4).

The need to coordinate negation with predicate/argument structure and quantification requires additional decisions about representational format, which can be illustrated with Schema 3b in Table 8.2, as follows:

5.   NEG S[~Some X~]; $[\alpha] \subseteq [X]$; ∴ NEG S[α]

This major premise in (5) can be paraphrased as "It is not true that some X satisfies S" or as "No X satisfies S." When one then discovers that α is included among the Xs, as the minor premise states, one can conclude that α does not satisfy S.[1] The presence of the tildes around "Some X" indicates that "Some X" is within the scope of the negation, that is, that one can infer that instantiations of the Xs will inherit the negation. For example, knowing that "Mrs. Hogan's son is in the third grade" and discovering that "none of the third graders went to the zoo," allows one to conclude that Mrs. Hogan's son did not go to the zoo. Note that some devise that indicates the scope of negation is required in order to differentiate such expressions for which the possible instances fall within the scope of the negation from those expressions for which its possible instances do not. For example, when one knows that "some of the Xs do not satisfy S," one cannot infer, upon discovery that β is included among the Xs, that β does not satisfy S – knowing that "some of the students in Miss Jones's class did not pass the exam" and that "Sam is one of the students in Miss Jones's class," one cannot infer whether Sam passed the exam or not.

HOW TO DECIDE WHICH SCHEMAS BELONG IN A THEORY OF MENTAL LOGIC

A major part of what a mental-logic theory needs to accomplish is to discover which schemas to include, that is, which forms of short and direct inferences belong in the proposed mental logic. There are both theoretical and empirical reasons on which to base such decisions. Given, for example, the theoretical assumption that the inferential steps of a mental logic have resulted from bio-evolutionary processes, and, thus, they should apply to make immediate and direct inferences rather than to make complex judgments, one would expect that each schema defines a single step in reasoning, rather than a complex chain of inferences. One also would expect that each basic inference step would be made essentially without error on maximally simple problems that could be solved using it. The schemas also should be available early in development, and should be available in all cultures and languages. Finally, one would expect that the schemas should relate inferences that are essential to the meanings of the logic particles; for example, *if, and, not, or*, typically used in their representations. That is, the meanings of the logic particles should be revealed in the inferences that are sanctioned by the particles. Thus, although a variety of inferences might follow from a set of premises both on standard logic and on some more sophisticated reasoning strategies, only those inferences that are central to the meaning of a logic particle should be expected to be included among the basic schemas. Consider, for example, the typical particle for conditionals – *if*. If the truth table for the material conditional that was described earlier conveyed the essential meaning of *if*, for example, then the truth table would provide a plausible candidate for the mental logic of *if*. The fact that material implication sanctions inferences that are paradoxical, however, is sufficient for us to judge that it does not provide a plausible candidate as a part of a mental-logic theory.

Consideration of these criteria has led to the inclusion of the sentential-logic schemas that are shown in Table 8.1. Table 8.2 illustrates some of the predicate-logic schemas that have been included. (See Table 11.3 in Braine & O'Brien, 1998, for a complete list of the predicate-logic schemas that have been included in the proposal.) Inspection of the sentential-level schemas in Table 8.1 reveals that the theory has divided schemas into different types. Schemas 1 through 7 are referred to as "core" schemas,[2] Schemas 8 and 9 are referred to as "feeder" schemas; Schemas 10 and 11 are "incompatibility" schemas; and Schemas 12 and 13 are referred to as "supposition" schemas. (All the predicate-level schemas that are shown in Table 8.2 are core schemas. See Table 11.3 in Braine & O'Brien, 1998, for other sorts of predicate-level schemas.) These designations concern differences in the ways the schemas are applied by a reasoning program, to which we turn now.

THE REASONING PROGRAM

A reasoner could not construct a line of reasoning from the schemas alone, but would need a set of instructions about when to apply the schemas. The reasoning program proposed by mental-logic theory contains both a direct-reasoning routine (the DRR) and some additional reasoning strategies that allow for construction of more sophisticated lines of reasoning. The theory claims that the DRR is universally available and is the first process involved in reasoning and in text comprehension, whereas the reasoning strategies are thought to be available only in varying degrees and applicable only in various situations. The most basic prediction of the theory, therefore, is that those inferences available on the DRR alone should be made routinely in situations that are maximally simple, whereas inferences that require resources that go beyond the DRR should be made systematically less often.

The most basic schemas are the core schemas, and these are applied most freely by the reasoning program. The DRR applies the core schemas so long as the propositions required for their application are conjointly considered in working memory. For example, Schema 7 of Table 8.1 will be applied to infer q whenever propositions of the form *if p then q* and p are held conjointly in working memory. The theory includes the sentential-level Schemas 1–7 of Table 8.1 and all of the predicate-logic schemas of Table 8.2 as core schemas, but the application of the core predicate-logic schemas is governed not only by the presence in working memory of the requisite propositions for their application, but also by the presence of a "topic set," and the DRR applies any predicate-logic core schema that applies to the topic set, given that the propositions are conjointly held in working memory.[3] For example, consider a problem presented in a study by O'Brien, Grgas, Roazzi, Dias, and Brooks (2002) which asked participants to figure out what they could about the topic set of "the fat children" from the following premises:

6. There are no children eating hamburger on the beach.
   Every child is either at the park or on the beach.
   The children at the park are playing football.
   The fat children are eating hamburgers.

The presence of the topic set leads to the application of Schema 2a to the last premise in the set together with the first premise to infer that the fat children are not on the beach. This then triggers Schema 1a when the second premise in encountered to infer that the fat children are in the park, which triggers in turn Schema 3a when the third premise in encountered to infer that they are playing fooball. (For a discussion of topic sets in the functioning of the DRR with the predicate-logic schemas, see Braine, 1998).

The feeder schemas are not applied as freely as are the core schemas, but are restricted so that they are applied only when their output provides for the application of a core schema. For example, suppose that propositions of the following forms are held conjointly in working memory: p, q, and *if p and q then r*. The application of Schema 8 of Table 8.1, which is a feeder schema, can lead from the separate propositions p and q to the inference of p *and* q, which then could activate the core Schema 7 of Table 8.1 to infer r. In this circumstance, the feeder Schema 8 will be applied because it provides the condition for the application of the core Schema 7. Otherwise, Schema 8 is unlikely to be applied.

There are both empirical and theoretical reasons to differentiate between core and feeder schemas. The empirical reason is straightforward: When participants in experiments have been asked to write down everything they could infer from sets of premises, they almost always wrote down the output of the core schemas, but they wrote down the output of the feeder schemas only occasionally, and then usually when they lead to the application of a core schema (Braine et al., 1995; O'Brien et al., 1994; O'Brien et al., 2002). This finding is consistent with a theoretical reason to consider Schemas 8 and 9 as feeder, rather than core schemas: Freely applying these schemas could lead to construction of infinite loops, for example, with the two propositions *p* and *q* leading to *p and q*, and then to *p and p and q*, and then to *p and p and q and p and q*, and so forth, and there is no evidence that people construct such lines of reasoning (see discussions in Lea, O'Brien, Fisch, Noveck, & Braine, 1990; O'Brien, 1993).

Sometimes people are required to evaluate a tentative conclusion from a set of premise propositions. When such a conclusion is held in working memory as having been inferred from the schemas, it is straightforward to judge that it follows from the premises, that is, that it is true given the truth of the premises from which it was inferred. Schemas 10 and 11, the incompatibility schemas, are used by the DRR to make judgments that a conclusion that has been presented for evaluation is false given the truth of the premises. Indeed, without some sort of procedure for detecting an incompatibility, a logic system would not be able to make a "false" judgment.[4] Note that the two incompatibility schemas are fairly rudimentary, and thus many lines of reasoning that could lead to "false" judgments would not be predicted from the proposed reasoning repertory.

Schema 12, referred to as the schema for conditional proof, is applied by the DRR when there is a conditional conclusion to be evaluated from a set of premise assumptions. In such a case, the DRR adds the antecedent of the conditional, *p*, to the premise set as an additional suppositional premise, and then seeks to evaluate the conclusion of the conditional, *q*, as the conclusion to be tested. When *q* can be inferred from the premise propositions together with the suppositional premise, the conclusion, *if p then q*, is judged to follow from the premises; when *q* is judged false, however, through the application of either of the two incompatibility schemas, the conditional conclusion is judged false.

Schema 13 also concerns supposition, and provides another way to draw an inference following a suppositional line of reasoning. When a line of reasoning under a supposition leads to a contradiction (as identified by either Schema 10 or 11), a reasoner can infer that the proposition that has been supposed must be false.

The reasoning program of the DRR is relatively impoverished in the ways that it provides for something to be supposed. Indeed, it is only when there is a tentative conditional conclusion to be evaluated that the DRR provides a way to make a supposition. Setting up a supposition in the service of an argument is not a basic part of the reasoning repertory, but something that requires additional reasoning sophistication. Indeed, the sorts of reasoning that dazzle readers of Sherlock Holmes stories, for example, tend to be cases in which a supposition leads to an unexpected conclusion – the dog that would have barked, *if* the murderer had been a stranger, did not bark, thus showing that the murderer was not a stranger is an application of Schema 13 after Holmes cleverly set up the supposition in the service of seeking a contradiction.

Not all suppositions are made in the service of sophisticated reasoning strategies, however, and sometimes suppositions are made simply out of curiosity or for pragmatic reasons. In such cases, Schemas 10–13 are available to make sense out of what follows under the supposition. Bowerman (1986) provided several examples of two-year-olds making spontaneous assertions that demonstrate the use of these suppositional schemas, for example, "If we go out there we haf' wear hats," "If I get my graham cracker in the water, it'll get all soapy," and "Don't kiss me 'cause it will fall off if you do that." These examples show that suppositions are made early in development and the utterances associated with them correspond to what is described in Schemas 10–13. The latter example is especially interesting because it demonstrates the use of Schema 13; in spite of the imperative nature of the utterance, the child is demonstrating an understanding that the supposition of being kissed will lead to a paper crown falling into the water, which contradicts what the child supposed, which then is expressed in a negative form. Thus, even when a supposition presumably has not been set up in the service of a sophisticated reasoning strategy, the schemas that make such a strategy comprehensible are available even to preschool children.

SOME INDIRECT REASONING STRATEGIES

Several reasoning strategies that involve setting up suppositions in ways that go beyond what is provided by the DRR have been found to be available to many college students at least some of the time. One of these is a supposition-of-alternatives strategy. This strategy can be applied when a set of premise propositions includes a set of alternatives. One can then suppose each of the alternatives one at a time and try to derive a conditional with it as antecedent, using Schema 12. When some common proposition can be inferred as the outcome of each of the suppositional lines of reasoning, one can infer this proposition on the set of premise propositions alone. For example, one knows that either *p or q*, and ascertains that *if p then r* and that *if q then r*; one can then conclude *r*. Note that Schema 5 allows the inference of *r* when *p or q*, *if p then r* and *if q then r* are presented as premises; what the supposition-of-alternatives strategy adds is the supposition of each of the two alternatives as a strategy to find a common inference under each suppositional line of reasoning.

A similar reasoning strategy is the enumeration of alternatives a priori. In this case, when a set of premise propositions contains conditionals of the forms *if p then* ... and *if not p then* ..., one can add the disjunction of the antecedents to the premise set (*p or not p*). For example, a problem presented by Braine et al. (1984) presented the two premises: *If there is an M then there is a Y* and *If there's not an M then there is a Y* together. The conclusion to be evaluated is *There is a Y*. The enumeration of alternatives *a priori* strategy also feeds Schema 5 of Table 8.1. A third strategy is known as the *reductio ad absurdum*. On this strategy, to test the falsity of a proposition, one adds that proposition to the premise set and tries to derive an incompatibility. The strategy leads to the application of Schema 13 of Table 8.1, and on finding an incompatibility, one can infer that the supposition is false. An alternative use of this strategy is to suppose the negation of a proposition in order to derive an incompatibility. Then, using a combination of Schemas 1 and 13, one can assert the un-negated complement of the supposition. It is important to note that it is the strategic use of suppositions, rather than the resulting use of Schemas 5 or 13, that leads to the increased reasoning difficulties involved in the solution of the problems described here. As the data reported by Bowerman (1986) described above revealed, even two-year-olds can appreciate the outcome of such arguments, although the ability to set up such suppositions in the service of constructing these sorts of arguments is far from universal even among university students.

INDIVIDUAL DIFFERENCES

As a general proposition, those inferences that can be made using the DRR alone should be available universally, whereas individual differences are apt to be found on those inferences that require reasoning resources that go beyond what the DRR provides. In practical terms, individual differences concerning the inferences predicted by the DRR should be minimal; as long as the premise propositions that lead to an inference on the DRR are held conjointly in working memory, such inferences should be forthcoming. For example, when propositions of the form *p or q* and *not p* are considered conjointly, the inference *q* will be forthcoming. This does not ensure, of course, that in laboratory situations 100% of judgments on problems presenting such premises will correspond to the prediction. Lapses in attention or failures of motivation can block someone from making even the most straightforward inference at times, and participants in laboratory studies are not always completely motivated to provide their complete attention. Nonetheless, the basic expectation is that inferences available on the DRR will be made routinely and without significant individual differences.

People make a large variety of inferences that go beyond those that follow from the procedures of the DRR. However individual differences are expected for such inferences. Included are inferences that rely on the more sophisticated reasoning strategies described earlier, inferences that follow from story grammars, scripts, and other sorts of world knowledge, as well as inferences that are based on a variety of pragmatically based processes. Further, some judgments might follow from one's imagining the possibility of a situation that provides a counterexample to a tentative inference made on nonlogical grounds. This sort of judgment is tantamount to using a mental model (see the discussion of mental-models theory later). On all of these various sorts of inferences that go beyond those provided by the DRR, we expect to find both inter- and intra-individual differences, whereas we do not expect to find individual differences for inferences made on the DRR alone.

SOME EVIDENCE FOR MENTAL-LOGIC THEORY

Mental-logic theory has predicted successfully which reasoning problems people solve, the perceived relative difficulties of those problems, the order in which intermediate inferences are made in lines of reasoning, and which logical inferences are made routinely and effortlessly in text comprehension, and has established that those inference are made online during text comprehension as the information enters working memory. Further, the theory has established that when the predictions of mental-logic theory differ from what one would expect if people were reasoning according to the sort of standard logic one finds in a typical logic text book, the data correspond to the predictions of mental-logic theory.

Findings in Braine et al. (1984/1998) clearly supported the most basic prediction of the theory – that those inferences that follow from application of the DRR will be made routinely, whereas those inferences requiring strategies that go beyond the DRR will be made far less often. Participants were presented two types of sentential-level problems: Fifty-four problems were solvable by application of the schemas of Table 8.1 and the DRR, and another 19 problems required reasoning strategies that went beyond the DRR. Each problem presented a set of premises together with a conclusion to be evaluated as true or false. To minimize possible effects of problem content, the problems referred to letters written on an imaginary blackboard (e.g., "If there is an L on the blackboard, there is a Z"). Almost no errors were made on the direct-reasoning problems, but, as was expected, on the problems that required more sophisticated reasoning strategies errors were made much more often. Thus, one could predict whether a problem could be solved by knowing whether the problem would be solved by the DRR alone or required other more sophisticated reasoning strategies.

Braine et al. (1984/1998) and Yang, Braine, and O'Brien (1998) provided an additional sort of evidence to support the claim that not only were the direct-reasoning problems being solved, but that they were being solved in the way described by the DRR. On sentential-level problems (Braine et al., 1984), and on predicate-level problems (Yang et al., 1998), participants were directed to rate the perceived relative difficulty of each problem on a Lichert-type scale, and regression models were constructed from the perceived-difficulty rating data that assigned a weight to each schema. This enabled prediction of the difficulty of each problem (as being equal to the sum of the weights of each schema required for problem solution in the lines of reasoning as predicted by the DRR). For example, a sentential-level problem with premises of the form *p or q, if q then r, not both r and s,* and *not p,* and requiring evaluation of *not s* would lead first to the application of Schema 1 of Table 8.1 to the first and last of the premises, which yields *q,* then to application of Schema 2, which yields *r,* and finally to application of Schema 3, which yields *not s;* the predicted difficulty of this problem is the sum of the difficulty weights for Schemas 1, 2, and 3. On sentential-level problems, correlations between predicted and observed difficulties accounted for 66% of the variance (53% with problem length partialed out), even when the weights were obtained with one set of problems and the observed ratings were obtained with another set of problems and different participants. On predicate-level problems, the ratings predicted by the schema weights again were correlated highly with the observed rating (69% of the variance; 56% when problem length was partialed out), even when observed ratings came from new problems and different participants than those used to generate the schema weights.[5]

Lea (1995) and Lea et al. (1990) provided evidence for the use of the schemas of Table 8.1 in text processing, as did Soskova and O'Brien (2002) for the schemas of Table 8.2. Both sets of studies reported that the core inferences are made routinely when their premises are embedded within short story vignettes. Further, these inferences are made so easily that people usually do not realize that any inferences are being made at all.

Further, the mental-logic inferences are unlike other sorts of inferences made while reading. Whereas other sorts of inferences, such as inferences from story grammars, scripts, etc., are made only when they are bridging inferences (i.e., required to maintain textual coherence), the mental-logic inferences are made so long as their requisite premises are held conjointly in working memory. Included among the text-comprehension studies were online measures of reaction times investigating sentential-level schemas (Lea, 1995) and predicate-level schemas (Soskova & O'Brien, 2002). For example, in one story version presented by Lea (1995) the reader was told that Mary will wear her black dress if a party is a Halloween party, and Mary discovers that it is a Halloween party. In a control version Mary does not discover whether or not it is a Halloween party. When subjects subsequently were presented a naming task on which they were to say the word "black" when it was presented on a computer screen, they responded faster following the former story than the latter, showing that inferences can be measured online.

The sorts of evidence described above are supportive of the mental-logic account, but only indirectly address whether participants were constructing the predicted lines of reasoning when asked to solve problems that require constructions of lines of reasoning with multiple inferences. A direct sort of evidence was reported by O'Brien et al. (1994) and by Braine et al. (1995) to support the claim that sentential-level problems were being solved by the application of the sentential-level schemas. In these studies, participants were presented premise sets and were asked to write everything down in the order that they figured things out. Some problems presented conclusions to be evaluated and asked participants to write down everything they figured out on the way to their final judgment; other problems presented only premises, and on these problems participants were asked to write down everything they could figure out from the premises in the order that they figured things out. In some experiments the orders in which the premise sets were presented were varied, testing the prediction that the order in which participants would write down their reasoning steps would correspond to the order in which the schemas became available, and thus the order in which inferences were written down would not differ when the order in which the premises were presented differed.[6]

As an example, two parallel problems were presented in O'Brien et al. (1994), with premises of the forms that referred to letters written on an imaginary blackboard:

Problem 1	Problem 2
(a) N or P	(a) Not both Z and S
(b) Not N	(b) If H then Z
(c) If P then H	(c) If P then H
(d) If H then Z	(d) Not N
(e) Not both Z and S.	(e) N or P

On Problem 1 the DRR applies Schema 1 of Table 8.1 to the first two premises, deriving P. Schema 2 of Table 8.1 then is applied when premise (c) is read, deriving H, which allows Schema 2 to be applied again when premise (d) is read, deriving Z, which allows Schema 3 to be applied when premise (e) is read, deriving *not S*. Problem 2 presented the same premises in the reverse order. When the premises are read in this order, the DRR is unable to apply any of the core schemas until all of the premises have been read, but then it applies Schema 1 to premise (e), *N or P*, and premise (d), *Not N* (now the last two premises encountered), to infer P, which then allows Schema 2 to be applied (to the output of Schema 1 together with premise (c) *if P then H*) to infer H, which then leads to application of Schema 2 again to derive Z when premise (b) *if H then Z* is considered, and then finally to application of Schema 1 when premise (a), *not both Z and S*, is considered to derive *not S*. The DRR thus predicts that the same inferences will be made in the same order on the two problems, even though the premises of the two problems are presented in opposite orders, because the order of the predicted inferences is determined by the order in which the core schemas become available and not by the order in which the premises are presented. O'Brien et al. found that the order in which participants wrote down inferences on both problems corresponded to those predicted by the DRR.

Similar results were obtained by O'Brien et al. (2002) with predicate-logic problems that referred to bags containing beads of various colors, sizes, shapes, and materials, such as the following problem and another that presented the same premises except in a scrambled order:

7. None of the red beads are square.
8. All of the beads are triangular or square.
9. The triangular beads are striped.
10. None of the striped beads are wooden.

Participants in the experiment were asked to write down everything they could figure out about the red beads. In the problem as it is presented above, Schema 1 of Table 8.2 can be applied to the premises (7) and (8) as they are encountered to infer that the red beads are triangular, Schema 2 then can be applied to the output of Schema 1 as premise (9) is read to infer that the red beads are striped, and then Schema 3 can be applied as premise (10) is read to infer that none of the red beads are wooden. When the premises were presented in another problem in a scrambled order (premise [8] first, followed by premise [9] second, and then by premise [7] third, and then by premise [10] fourth), participants wrote down the same inferences in the same order. Thus, both for the sentential-logic problems presented by O'Brien et al. (1994) and Braine et al. (1995) and the predicate-logic problems presented by O'Brien et al. (2002), the order of output was determined not by the order of input of premises, but by the order in which the schemas became available as the premises were entered into working memory (as assisted by the ability to reread the premises as needed).

At times the predictions of mental-logic theory differ from what would be predicted from the sorts of procedures typically found in a standard-logic textbook. For example, the procedures of mental-logic theory lead to different expectations about the judgments that should be made when a conditional proposition is to be evaluated as a conclusion. Following the DRR, when presented with a conditional conclusion to judge against a set of premise assumptions, a reasoner would add the antecedent of the conditional conclusion to the premise set as an additional suppositional premise and then seek to evaluate the consequent of the conditional conclusion. When the consequent can be deduced, the conditional is judged as true on the premises alone, but when the negation of the consequent can be deduced, the conditional is judged as false. This latter evaluation would not be made following the logic found in a typical standard-logic textbook, where such a judgment would be withheld because of the possibility that the antecedent of the conditional might be false. For example, from the premise *p or q*, the mental-logic procedure leads to the conclusion *if not p then q* (because the supposition of *not p* leads to the conclusion of *q* on Schema 3 of Table 8.1). This conclusion would not be valid in standard logic with its truth table for material implication, however, because *not p* might not be true.

This difference in predictions between mental logic and standard logic was tested with adults by Braine et al. (1984) and with school-age children by O'Brien, Dias, Roazzi, and Braine (1998). Problems with forms like the following were presented:

11. There is either a cat or a hat in the box; therefore if there is not a hat there is a cat.
12. There is either a cat or a hat in the box; therefore if there is not a hat there is not a cat.
13. There is not both a cat and a hat in the box; therefore if there is a cat there is not a hat.
14. There is not both a cat and a hat in the box; therefore if there is a cat there is a hat.

The procedures of the DRR would evaluate the conclusions in (11) and (13) as true, and the conclusions in (12) and (14) as false. Someone following standard logic, however, would not make these judgments on (12) and (14), however, because of the possibility that the antecedent of the conditionals might be false. Braine et al. (1984) and O'Brien et al. (1998) found that both adults and children consistently made the judgments predicted by mental-logic theory.

ON THE CLAIMS OF MENTAL-MODELS ADVOCATES THAT NO LOGIC IS NEEDED

We turn now to claims by advocates of a mental-models theory that a psychological account of deductive reasoning does not require a mental logic – in particular, that valid inferences can be drawn without a logic. Johnson-Laird and Byrne (1991) and Johnson-Laird et al. (1992) described how models theory proposes to account for a valid deduction without a mental logic, using an argument form parallel to Schema 7 of Table 8.1 as an example, that is, with premises *if p then q* and *p*. From their perspective, these two premises lead to the following initial representations:

15. [*p*]   *q*; *p*; *p   q*
    . . .

where the model sets for each of the premises and then their combination are separated by semicolons. The first premise is represented by the two models in the left-hand column. One includes both p and q; the square brackets around the token for p in this model indicate that p is exhausted in relation to q, that is, that tokens for p cannot occur in other models without tokens for q (Johnson-Laird & Byrne, 1991, p. 119). The second model of the first set is an ellipsis that functions as a reminder that the ellipsis could be "fleshed out" to include alternative models in which p is false.[7] When the categorical model that represents the second premise is combined with the two models that represent the first premise, the elliptical model is lost, leaving a single final model that is equivalent to the conclusion p *and* q. However, argue Johnson-Laird and his colleagues (e.g., Johnson-Laird & Byrne, 1991; Johnson-Laird et al., 1992), p is not included in the response that is stated by participants because of a pragmatic constraint not to restate the obvious, so subjects state only q as a conclusion. Thus, the valid deduction that corresponds to the output of the mental-logic Schema 7 of Table 8.1 need not rely on a mental-logic schema, say these advocates of the mental-models theory, but requires only construction and combination of models.

The models used to represent predicate-level propositions are similar to those used for simple unquantified propositions; the similarity follows in part because the elements of models never include variables, but refer only to individual exemplars (Johnson-Laird & Byrne, 1991, p. 212). Representations of quantified propositions at the predicate-logic level thus appear much like those at the sentential level. The universally quantified sentence form that is parallel to the conditional, *if p then q*, is *all p are q*, which has the following fully fleshed-out model (i.e., the ellipsis included in the representation provided above for the sentential-level representation has been fleshed out for the following representation of the universally quantified proposition):

16. $[p]$ $[q]$
    $[p]$ $[q]$
    $[\sim p]$ $[q]$
    $[\sim p]$ $[\sim q]$

The expression *all customs inspectors are bridge players*, for example, leads to a model containing a couple of tokens for people who are both customs inspectors and bridge players, another for a person who is a not a customs inspector and a bridge player, and another for someone who is neither a customs inspector nor a bridge player. When a minor premise states that John is a customs inspector, one can conclude that John is a bridge player, because the information from the minor premise eliminates the third and fourth models, and the remaining models include tokens only for a person who is both a customs inspector and a bridge player. Thus, as was the case for the sentential argument that corresponds to Schema 7 of Table 8.1, the models theorists claim that no logic is required to support the predicate-logic inference that corresponds to the output of Schema 3a of Table 8.2, because the reasoning relied only on representation and manipulation of models.

This claim that such inferences are made without anything logical, including the use of any variables, however, turns out to be problematically deceptive. Johnson-Laird and Byrne (1993, p. 376) wrote that although the models do not contain variables, variables do occur "in the initial semantic representations" from which models are constructed. Let us consider Johnson-Laird and Byrne's description of how this works. Quantifiers provide "the raw material for a recursive loop that is used in building or manipulating a model. Thus, the universal quantifier 'all' elicits a recursion that deals with a set exhaustively, whereas the existential quantifier 'some' elicits a recursion that does not" (Johnson-Laird & Byrne, 1991, p. 178). They provide the following example: *all x's are equal to the sum of some y and some z*, which first is parsed to yield:

17. $(All \ x)(Some \ y)(Some \ z)(x = y + z)$

A model is then constructed by giving some arbitrary value to the first variable term in the equation (x), some arbitrary value to the second variable term (y), and, because the degrees of freedom have been exhausted, a constrained value is assigned to the third variable term in the equation (z). This procedure loops over the equation several times, recording the output on each pass, resulting in a model such as:

18. $[8 \ 6] \ (1 \ 6 \ 4 \ 2) \ (7 \ 7 \ 2 \ 2 \ 4 \ 4)$

in which both of the numbers in the first set are equal to some number in the second set plus some number in the third set.[8]

As Johnson-Laird and Byrne (1991, p. 180) wrote, "the procedure is analogous to the standard interpretation of quantifiers in the predicate calculus, except that it constructs a model of the assertion." They are correct that the representation in (17) and the procedure that generates (18) – with its arbitrary instantiations – include quantifiers and variables. The model in (18) that results from the procedure, however, does not convey the meaning of the expression from which it was generated. Note that the expression in (17) could not be retrieved from the model in (18). The model merely provides a couple of numbers, each of which is the sum of two other numbers from the adjacent sets, but in no way does the model in (18) capture the meaning of universality of the expression in (17), nor the relations among x, y, and z in (17). The square brackets around [8 6] do not indicate universality; they merely indicate that "once the set is complete no further items can be added to it" (Johnson-Laird & Byrne, 1991, p. 180), and thus the square brackets do not convey the meaning of *All x's* bearing a particular arithmetic relation to some y's and z's. Nor is there any indication in the model that infinitely many other models could be constructed. A model for such an expression is merely a set of instantiations that are consistent with that expression, and does not itself have any logical structure with which one can know which information can be integrated, and how, or which, inferences can be drawn. Put simply: The semantic meaning from which the model is constructed is not contained in the model that finally is constructed. If reasoning really takes place at the level of such models, then it must be taking place devoid of crucial information that had been contained at the input level of premodels representations.

To understand how different a model of this sort is from the proposition from which it is generated, consider whether the universally quantified proposition that *all natural numbers that end in zero are divisible by five* is true. According to models theory, this judgment can be made only in relation to a model, and models include neither variables nor quantifiers. To assess the truth of the proposition, one would generate a model in which there are tokens of the following sort: (a) natural numbers that end in zero and are divisible by five, (b) a natural number that does not end in zero and is divisible by five, or (c) a natural number that does not end in zero and is not divisible by five, leading to a model set that includes, for example, 50, 990, 15, and 19. Note, however, that nothing in such a model would convey the universal scope of the proposition – that for *any* natural number, if *it* ends in zero then *it* is divisible by five[9]; and nothing about the model is of obvious use in determining whether the proposition is true[10] – unless a mistake has been made, the model must be consistent with the expression. Clearly, the cognitive representation that allows one to understand both the proposition, and to judge that it is true, must keep track of the entities and their properties, and to keep track of which goes with which, and the models per se are not up to this task.

Johnson-Laird and his colleagues have consistently contended that reasoning does not include any use of a logic. Surely they would have difficulty in denying the presence of logic in models were the models to contain some predicate/argument structure, so one thus can understand their motivation for excluding both variables and quantifiers from the models they propose. Clearly, however, both quantifiers and variables exist in the initial premodels representations from which, and the procedures by which, models are constructed, so it is misleading to say that reasoning in their system is taking place without the use of any logic for variables or quantifiers. A predicate/argument structure in actuality is proposed by models theory, although this structure exists only in the premodels representations from which models are constructed and this logical structure is lost by the time one moves from the premodels representations to the models themselves, a fact that I find quite peculiar, given that in the removal of such structure the models themselves have lost a significant portion of the meaning of the propositions they are supposed to represent. Indeed, if one has only the model, and not the history from which the model was constructed, including the premodels representations, it often is impossible to ascertain what is being represented by a model with its missing logical structure.

Mental-logic theory does not claim that people never use models in reasoning. The ability to imagine a model that provides a counterexample to a supposition or to a possible inference made on extralogical grounds, for example, would be a valuable addition to one's reasoning skills. So also would be a strategy for proving the undecidability of a conclusion, which seeks two plausible alternatives that both are consistent with the premises, but with one being consistent with the conclusion and the other not. However, the mental-models theory described by Johnson-Laird and his associates is inadequate precisely because it excludes the representational structure provided by a mental logic. Indeed, without a logical structure it often is impossible to know what a model is representing. This observation is consistent with the base assumption of mental-logic theory: Without a propositional format to record propositional information, there can be no propositional information, and with models alone it often is impossible to ascertain the propositional information.

ON CLAIMS THAT MENTAL-LOGIC THEORY FAILS TO APPRECIATE MEANING IN REASONING

Some researchers have claimed that because the basic inferential processes described by mental-logic theory refer to the forms of propositions, for example, as disjunctions, conjunctions, negations, conditionals, etcetera, the theory fails to acknowledge, much less account for, the role of meaning in reasoning. Some have argued, for example, that reasoning is governed primarily – if not exclusively – by content-specific processes, rather than by any content-general processes, such as those proposed by mental logicians (e.g., Cheng & Holyoak, 1985; Cosmides, 1989; Fiddick, Cosmides, & Tooby, 2000), and critics sympathetic to the mental-logic approach have argued that whereas mental-models theory accounts for reasoning in terms of the meanings of logical terms such as *if*, *and*, *not*, *or*, etcetera, the syntactical rules described by mental-logic theory do not provide a logical semantics (e.g., Evans & Over, 1997a, 1997b; Johnson-Laird, 1983; Johnson-Laird & Byrne, 1991, 1993). The problem, say such critics, is that mental-logic theory does not say anything about the conditions in which a logical proposition is true or false, whereas models theory states explicitly with which models a proposition is true. Thus, they imply, models theory provides a logical semantics – that is, an account of the meaning of a logical proposition – whereas mental-logic theory does not.

There are, however, both empirical and conceptual reasons to question claims of these types. First, there is a straightforward empirical reason to doubt any claim that an adequate account of reasoning can be provided without processes that are content-general: There is a growing set of reasoning problems without content of any sort that seems likely to provide a basis for solution, yet people consistently provide responses on these problems that demonstrate an appreciation of which inferences are sound and which are not. Some such problems have been described in this chapter, using content such as arbitrary numbers and letters written on an imaginary blackboard, or arbitrary toy animals and fruits in boxes, or beads of arbitrary shapes, colors, and sizes. Such materials seemingly preclude the use of possible knowledge about problem content as a source for judgments of soundness, and the data thus are impossible to explain without the use of content-general reasoning processes.

Further, without the inclusion of some content-general processes, it would be impossible to understand why content of widely varied sorts is conveyed with the same linguistic/logical forms, for example, as alternatives, as conditionals, as universally or existentially quantified, and so forth. Consider the two content-specific reasoning theories that have been presented most completely: the pragmatic-reasoning-schemas theory introduced by Cheng and Holyoak (1985) and the social-contract theory of Cosmides (1989). Both of these theories have been presented within the extremely limited empirical scope of performance on a single sort of reasoning task – Wason's selection task – and for extremely limited sorts of content – either social permissions and obligations or social contracts regulating costs and benefits, and with only a single sort of sentence form – conditionals. Neither theory provides any account of reasoning about alternatives, conjunctions, negations, or suppositions. Neither provides any account of the sorts of predicate-argument structures that would be needed to keep track of which properties and which entities go together, and neither provides an account of the enormous variety of inferences people make that go beyond those narrowly accounted for by the specific content domains they address. Pragmatic-reasoning-schemas theory, because it is based on general principles of inductive learning, at least has the potential of accounting eventually for an increasingly wide set of sorts of content, as well as of sentence forms and of inference-making tasks. Note, however, the enormity of the promissory note that thus must eventually become due if that theory is to become more than an account of an extremely limited set of reasoning circumstances.

Mental-logic theory does not argue against the influences of problem content on reasoning, any more than advocates of theories of syntax in linguistics argue against the existence of a lexicon that provides meanings to words beyond the knowledge that they are verbs, nouns, modifiers, and so forth. Note, however, that if a researcher were to propose – given the fact that people include the meaning of sentence content in their interpretations of sentences – that the field of linguistics does not need to include a theory of syntax, we would reject that proposal as clearly missing the point. Just as the field of linguistics needs more than just an account of the lexicon, but also needs a content-general theory of grammar, the field of reasoning research needs to include more than an account of the influences of problem content, but also needs a content-general theory of inferences based on logical forms, that is, of predicate/argument structure, of quantifiers and of quantificational scope, of supposition, negation, disjunction and conjunction, and of the inferences that are drawn with these logical structures.

Finally, let us turn to the question of how mental-logic theory provides a logical semantics, that is, with how mental-logic theory deals with the meanings of logical terms. A notion that is basic to the mental-logic approach is that the essential meaning of a logical term is found in the inferences that it sanctions, and we have referred to this approach as a procedural semantics (e.g., O'Brien & Bonatti, 1999). Indeed, if someone did not understand what is represented in Schema 3a of Table 8.2, S[X]; [α] ⊆ [X] ∴ S[α], for example, *all Joe's brothers won medals, Sam is one of Joe's brothers*, thus *Sam won a medal*, that person could be said not to understand the meaning of "all." Similarly, someone who fails to infer that *Sam won an archery medal* from the knowledge that *Either Jim or Sam won the medal in archery* and that *Jim did not win the archery medal*, that is, the sort of inference defined by Schema 3 of Table 8.1, could not be said to understand the meaning of "or."

The debate about the procedural semantics of mental-logic theory has concerned primarily the inference procedures for *if*. From the perspective of mental-logic theory, the schema for conditional proof reveals the basic meaning of *if* is to suppose something. Braine and O'Brien (1991) argued that a line of reasoning that is developed under a supposition must be consistent with that supposition. In other words, once one has supposed something to be true, one cannot then introduce into a line of reasoning under that supposition something that would not be true, given the supposition. This constraint is, from the perspective of mental-logic theory, consistent with the meaning of supposition. Mental-logic theory thus provides a logical semantics that is based on the procedures of the inference schemas as they are applied by the reasoning routine. The inference procedures specify the conditions under which a logical proposition is judged as true or as false. It is true, of course, that the application of these procedures at times requires resources that go beyond what is described explicitly by the mental logic alone. Decisions about what would, or would not, still be true, given some supposition, often rely on social or political considerations, for example, and often are the grist for debate among interlocutors. But this problem exists as well for any other approach, including the mental-models approach. Note that mental-models theory has provided nothing to account for how decisions are made about which models to include or to exclude as model sets are fleshed out, except to note in passing that such decisions in principle should be influenced by general world knowledge.

Thus the sorts of problems faced by a mental-models theory in dealing with meaning are the same sorts of problems faced by mental-logic theory, and neither approach seems to have an a priori advantage in dealing with how knowledge outside of logical operators is integrated into decisions that influence decisions about when particular proposition are true.

Note that the basic assumption of mental-logic theory – that the meaning of a logic term is provided by its inference procedures – puts us at odds with a mental-models theory of the sort that has been proposed by Johnson-Laird and his associates (Johnson-Laird & Byrne, 1991; Johnson-Laird et al., 1992), where the meaning of a logic term is defined by mental models that essentially are truncated truth-table entries. If, on the one hand, one thinks that the meaning of *if* is provided by the truth table for material implication that was introduced in the beginning of this chapter, then defining its meaning using the sorts of mental models described by Johnson-Laird and his associates could be appealing. If, on the other hand, one thinks that the basic meaning of *if* is provided by reasoning procedures that are consistent with the meaning of supposition, the procedural semantics of mental-logic theory should be more appealing. The difference between the two sorts of theories lies not in whether one theory provides an account in terms of meanings and the other theory in terms of form, but, rather, the difference concerns the ways the two sorts of theories account for the meanings of the terms. Mental-models theory provides an account of the meanings of logic particles in terms of which models they sanction; mental-logic theory provides an account of the meanings of logic particles in terms of which inferences they sanction. The reader is invited to consider and evaluate which way of dealing with meaning is the more psychologically plausible.

Notes

1. Where α can be either a proper or improper subset of the Xs, and could be an individual entity.
2. Schema 1 is a core schema in the left-to-right direction; in the right-to-left direction it is a feeder schema.
3. A topic set can be provided by an experimenter's instructions or by pragmatic or other interests on the part of a reasoner.
4. Rips (1994) has proposed an alternative mental-logic theory that does not contain any incompatibility schemas; clearly it would benefit from inclusion of something like schemas 10 and 11 of Table 8.1.
5. Johnson-Laird et al. (1992) claimed that their models theory also could account for the perceived difficulty ratings of the sentential-level problems. O'Brien et al. (1994) showed why the models theory is unable to provide as good a fit for the data as does the mental-logic theory. The arguments are too detailed to present here.
6. The problems were designed so that varying premise orders would not change the order in which the schemas became available. Other problems could be

constructed so that alteration of the orders of the premises would alter the order in which schemas become available.

7. Although Evans (1993) referred to models for conditionals with an exhausted token for *p* as indicating that *all the ps are qs*, this description cannot be taken literally given that the models are for an unquantified proposition.

8. I assume that one also should construct models that correspond to *not p and q* and to *not p and not q* that correspond to the standard truth table entries in which *p* is false to get the completely fleshed out model sets, although this remains elliptical in the presentation by Johnson-Laird and Byrne (1991).

9. Compare the models, which cannot include either variables nor quantifiers, to the linguistic representation that includes a quantifier (any) and a pronoun to keep track of the quantification (it).

10. A moment's reflection should convince the reader that this proposition is true.

References

Bowerman, M. (1986). First steps in acquiring conditionals. In E. Traugott, A. Meulen, J. S. Reilly, & C. A. Ferguson (Eds.), *On conditionals*. Cambridge, UK: Cambridge University Press.

Braine, M. D. S. (1998). Steps towards a mental-predicate logic. In M. D. S. Braine & D. P. O'Brien (Eds.), *Mental logic*. Mahwah, NJ: Erlbaum.

Braine, M. D. S., & O' Brien, D. P. (1991). A theory of *if*: A lexical entry, reasoning program, and pragmatic principles. *Psychological Review, 98*, 182–203. (Reprinted in *Mental logic* by M. D. S. Braine & D. P. O'Brien, Eds., 1998. Mahwah, NJ: Erlbaum.)

Braine, M. D. S., & O'Brien, D. P. (Eds.) (1998). *Mental logic*. Mahwah, NJ: Erlbaum.

Braine, M. D. S., O'Brien, D. P., Noveck, I. A., Samuels, M., Lea, R. B., Fisch, S. M., & Yang, Y. (1995). Predicting intermediate and multiple conclusion is propositional logic inference problems: Further evidence for a mental logic. *Journal of Experimental Psychology: General, 124*, 263–292. (Reprinted in *Mental logic* by M. D. S. Braine & D. P. O'Brien, Eds., 1998. Mahwah, NJ: Erlbaum.)

Braine, M. D. S., Reiser, B. J., & Rumain, B. (1984). Some empirical justification for a theory of natural propositional logic. In G. Bower (Ed.), *The psychology of learning and motivation: Advances in research and theory. Vol. 18*. New York: Academic Press. (Reprinted in *Mental logic* by M. D. S. Braine & D. P. O'Brien Eds., 1998, Mahwah, NJ: Erlbaum).

Cheng, P., & Holyoak, K. J. (1985). Pragmatic reasoning schemas. *Cognitive Psychology, 17*, 391–416.

Cheng, P., Holyoak, K. J., Nisbett, R. E., & Oliver, L. M. (1986). Pragmatic vs. syntactic approaches to training deductive reasoning. *Cognitive Psychology, 18*, 293–328.

Cosmides, L. (1989). The logic of social exchange: Has natural selection shaped how humans reason? Studies with the Wason selection task. *Cognition, 31*, 187–276.

Evans, J. St. B. T. (1993). The mental model theory of conditional reasoning: Critical appraisal and revision. *Cognition, 48*, 1–20.

Evans, J. St. B. T., & Over, D. E. (1997a). Rationality in reasoning: The problem of deductive competence. *Cahiers de Psychologie Cognitive, 16*, 3–38.

Evans, J. St. B. T., & Over, D. E. (1997b). Reply to Barrouillet and Howson. *Cahiers de Psychologie Cognitive, 16*, 399–405.

Fiddick, Cosmides, L., & Tooby, J. (2000). No interpretation without representation: The role of domain-specific representations and the inferences in Wason's selection task. *Cognition, 77*, 1–79.

Fodor, J. (1975). *The language of thought.* Cambridge, MA: Harvard University Press.

Ioup, G. (1975). Some universals for quantifier type. In J. Kimball (Ed.), *Syntax & semantics: Vol. 4.* New York: Academic Press.

Johnson-Laird, P. N. (1983). *Mental models.* Cambridge, MA: Harvard University Press.

Johnson-Laird, P. N., & Byrne, R. M. J. (1991). *Deduction.* Mahwah, NJ: Erlbaum.

Johnson-Laird, P. N., & Byrne, R. M. J. (1993). Mental models or formal rules? *Behavioral and Brain Sciences, 16*, 368–380.

Johnson-Laird, P. N., Byrne, R. M. J., & Schaeken, W. (1992). Propositional reasoning by models. *Psychological Review, 101*, 734–739.

Kneale, W., & Kneale, M. (1962). *The development of logic.* Oxford, UK: Clarendon Press.

Lea, R. B. (1995). Online evidence for elaborative logical inference in text. *Journal of Experimental Psychology: Learning, Memory, and Cognition, 21*, 1469–1482.

Lea, R. B., O'Brien, D. P., Fisch, S. M., Noveck. I. A., & Braine, M. D. S. (1990). Predicting propositional logic inferences in text processing. *Journal of Memory and Language, 29*, 361–387.

Macnamara, J. (1986). *A border dispute: The place of logic in psychology.* Cambridge, MA: MIT Press.

O'Brien, D. P. (1993). Mental logic and irrationality: We can put a man on the moon, so why can't we solve those logical reasoning problems? In K. I. Manktelow & D. E. Over (Eds.), *Rationality: Psychological and philosophical perspectives.* London: Routledge. (Reprinted in *Mental logic* by M. D. S. Braine & D. P. O'Brien, Eds., 1998. Mahwah, NJ: Erlbaum.)

O' Brien, D. P., & Bonatti, L. L. (1999). The semantics of logical connectives and mental logic. *Cahiers de Psychologie Cognitive (Current Psychology of Cognition), 18*, 87–97.

O'Brien, D. P., Braine, M. D. S., & Yang, Y. (1994). Propositional reasoning by model: Simple to refute in principle and in practice. *Psychological Review, 101*, 711–724.

O'Brien, D. P., Dias, M. G., Roazzi, A., & Braine, M. D. S. (1998). Conditional reasoning: The logic of supposition and children's understanding of pretense. In M. D. S. Braine & D. P. O'Brien (Eds.), *Mental logic.* Mahwah, NJ: Erlbaum.

O'Brien, D. P., Grgas, J., Roazzi, A., Dias, M. G., & Brooks, P. J. (2002). *Predicting the orders in which multiple inferences are made on predicate-logic reasoning problems: Direct evidence in support of a theory of mental predicate logic.* Unpublished manuscript.

Rips, L. (1994). *The psychology of proof: Deductive reasoning in human thinking.* Cambridge, MA: MIT Press.

Soskova, J., & O'Brien, D. P. (2002). *The role of predicate-logic inferences in text comprehension.* Unpublished manuscript.

Yang, Y., Braine, M. D. S., & O'Brien, D. P. (1998). Some empirical justification of the mental-predicate-logic model. In M. D. S. Braine & D. P. O'Brien (Eds.), *Mental logic.* Mahwah, NJ: Erlbaum.

9

Heuristics and Reasoning I
Making Deduction Simple

Maxwell J. Roberts

The term *heuristic* appears many times in the literatures on reasoning and decision making. For example, we have the heuristic-analytic theory (Evans, 1989), the probability heuristics model (Chater & Oaksford, 1999), judgment heuristics (Kahneman, Slovic, & Tversky, 1982) and simple heuristics that make us smart (Gigerenzer & Todd, 1999). What these theories have in common is that they suggest that people make inferences by using processes that are relatively simple to apply. Hence, people are able to make reasonably speedy and accurate decisions without recourse to lengthy and possibly computationally intractable procedures. Thus, they can avoid the need to form comprehensive and detailed representations of the world and/or consider many alternative possibilities. However, implicit in the use of the word *heuristic* is that it is possible to identify processes that are *not* heuristics, and that these have actually been proposed as models of human reasoning. However, in this chapter, I will argue that a distinction between heuristic versus nonheuristic processes is not necessarily psychologically appropriate, as the term heuristic implies an inherent degree of inaccuracy, thus ruling out similarly simple procedures that also save time and effort, but instead lead to accurate answers. Heuristics will therefore be considered as part of a wider category of short-cut procedures. Their purpose is to reduce processing load, and their use and development will be considered with respect to deductive reasoning.

HEURISTICS VERSUS ALGORITHMS

A distinction is often made between *algorithms* and heuristics. Briefly, an algorithm is a procedure that is guaranteed to give the correct answer – assuming that it is executed correctly. For example, suppose that you wish to visit three towns by using the shortest possible route: In which order should the towns be visited?[1] An algorithm for solving this problem would be to calculate distances for every possible permutation of visits: Town A first, then Town B, then Town C; Town A first, then Town C, then Town B, and so on. With three towns, there are six possible routes (ABC, ACB, BCA, BAC, CBA, CAB), and identifying the shortest is easy. The problem with this algorithm is the *combinatorial explosion*: Assuming that one permutation could be calculated every second, just 11 towns would require over a year to calculate the shortest route, and this would leave no time for eating or sleeping. Using a fast computer only postpones the problem: It would take over 10 years to calculate the shortest route for 17 towns in this way even if 1,000,000 routes per second were evaluated.

Many algorithms are impossible to apply, and therefore are of theoretical interest only. As another example, in theory a computer could calculate every possible game of chess, thus ensuring victory over any opponent without this capability. In practice, this may never be possible no matter how fast computers become. For humans this difficulty is even more acute. For example, *which occur more often in the English language: words beginning with K, or words with K as the third letter?* With an appropriately setup computer database, it would be easy to identify all relevant items and give the correct answer. The way in which words are organized in human memory means that such a search is simply not possible. It would be scarcely feasible for a person to write out every single word that he or she knows, so the only alternative is to attempt to think of examples. Words beginning with *K* are somewhat easier to bring to mind than words with K as the third letter, hence the former are more *available* (Tversky & Kahneman, 1973). This appears to be the basis on which people make their decision, preferring to respond to the question *words beginning with K*, when in fact this is the wrong answer. Hence, this is an example of the use of the availability heuristic: *Easy to recall events occur more frequently than hard to recall events.*

In fact, compared with computers, human working memory constraints are very severe indeed. Even a relatively straightforward task such as identifying the correct conclusion to the following *categorical premise pair* can cause great difficulty:[2]

Some of the artists are not beekeepers.
Some of the chefs are beekeepers.

Therefore:

a. All of the chefs are artists.
b. None of the chefs are artists.
c. Some of the chefs are artists.
d. Some of the chefs are not artists.
e. No valid conclusion linking chefs in terms of artists.

We could imagine the problem premises represented above as possible situations on Venn diagrams (the numerous possibilities are given in

FIGURE 9.1. The 72 Venn diagrams compatible with the premises *some of the artists are not beekeepers, some of the chefs are beekeepers*. *A* stands for people who are artists, *B* for beekeepers, and *C* for chefs. Shaded regions indicate the existence of individuals. It is assumed that instances of artists, beekeepers, and chefs all exist.

Figure 9.1). One algorithm for obtaining the correct answer would be to generate every possible Venn diagram, and identify a conclusion that is compatible with all of them. However, the premise pairs for the above item yield 72 different Venn diagram permutations (80 is the greatest number for any premise pair). Even if we ignore the beekeepers, there are still five different ways in which artists and chefs can be linked, as shown in Figure 9.2. Generating just these five states of affairs and then identifying the conclusion common to all must be extremely difficult: Dickstein (1978) found that almost two thirds of people gave an incorrect answer to the example problem, preferring to choose *some of the chefs are not artists* over *no valid conclusion*.

There are many theories of how people identify conclusions for categorical premise pairs. These theories need to explain why some items are much easier than others. However, irrespective of which theory best accounts for performance, one thing is certain: *People either do not apply, or have great difficulty applying the algorithms described so far. If this were not the case, performance at identifying conclusions to categorical premise pairs would be at ceiling level.*

FIGURE 9.2. The five possible relationships between artists and chefs compatible with the premises *some of the artists are not beekeepers, some of the chefs are beekeepers.* Shaded regions indicate the existence of individuals. It is assumed that instances of artists and chefs exist.

People generally perform poorly when identifying conclusions from categorical premise pairs, but not because they guess the answers – performance averaged over all 64 possible premise pairs tends to range from one third to one half of items correct, which is well above chance level (Roberts, Newstead, & Griggs, 2001). How might people be solving them? One possibility derives from the principle of *bounded rationality* (e.g., Simon, 1983), in other words people are competent in theory but fallible in practice. Hence, while people may intend to consider as many possibilities as possible, working memory constraints halt the process before it can be completed, meaning that people are only able to consider a very small number. This is the principle underlying *mental-models* theory (Johnson Laird & Byrne, 1991; see also Johnson-Laird, this volume), although one recent suggestion is that people's limitations are so severe that they only consider one single represented possibility (or mental model) (e.g., Evans, Handley, Harper, & Johnson-Laird, 1999).

In the remainder of this chapter, any algorithmic procedure in which every one of multiple possibilities needs to be considered in order to guarantee the correct answer for each of a set of similar problems will be described as an *exhaustive search strategy.* An alternative to people applying such a strategy is that, rather than apply algorithms to the best of their ability – which will usually be incompletely – people apply various shortcuts in order to identify plausible answers. When identifying conclusions from categorical premise pairs, an example of this is the *atmosphere strategy* (e.g., Wetherick & Gilhooly, 1995). Effectively, this entails identifying a conclusion from two rules of thumb: (1) if either premise contains *some* then the conclusion will contain *some*; and (2) if either premise contains a negation, then the conclusion will contain a negation. Applying these would give the conclusion *some of the chefs are not artists* for the earlier example. In fact, this strategy is not particularly effective, giving the correct answer just 23% of the time when applied to all 64 possible premise pair combinations.[3]

However, this is still slightly better than chance, where 20% correct would be expected on average for a five-option multiple choice. Hence, the atmosphere strategy qualifies (just!) as a heuristic. (See Chater & Oaksford, 1999, for an updated version of this strategy, which it is claimed mimics human responses better, and improves overall expected performance across all 64 premise pairs to 67% correct.)

Heuristic is a term that is difficult to define precisely, but its essentials can easily be captured. Briefly, a heuristic can be thought of as a rule of thumb that will provide a reasonable answer. Returning to the traveling salesman problem, a reasonable heuristic would be to visit the nearest town, then the nearest town to that, then the nearest unvisited town to that, and so on. This is very unlikely to give the shortest route, but without too much effort will provide a reasonable route. Heuristics and algorithms are easy to contrast: An algorithm is guaranteed to give the correct answer, while a heuristic will merely give an acceptable answer (or an acceptable *set* of answers) albeit with much less time and effort. Hence, the atmosphere strategy will give a reasonable set of answers, with far less effort than an exhaustive search strategy. Here, the definition of reasonable or acceptable is merely *better than chance*. Obviously, in life or death situations, people at the receiving end of a decision would prefer somewhat improved odds. Nonetheless, if an algorithm is too time consuming, or costly, to apply, a barely acceptable heuristic will have to suffice.

In broader terms, one of the recurring themes when considering human behavior is that people have limited processing capacity and the world is a complicated, computationally intractable place (e.g., Oaksford & Chater, 1995). This has been recognized for at least 100 years, ever since William James coined the phrase "blooming, buzzing confusion" to describe the way in which the senses of a baby are assailed (1890, p. 488). What are the difficulties facing a person or machine making inferences in such an environment? The *combinatorial explosion* has already been described. Hence, we have the option of either performing algorithms incompletely, or applying heuristics instead. In addition, there is also the *inferential explosion*: Faced with input from the world, there is an enormous number of inferences that we can make, most of which are of little use. Making endless trivial inferences will overwhelm any system, but sorting out the wheat from the chaff is not an easy problem. The success with which humans overcome both difficulties can only really be appreciated by taking a close look at work by artificial intelligence researchers. Their attempts to program computers to behave intelligently have been fraught with problems for decades (Copeland, 1993; Dreyfus, 1993). Hence, although computers are now better than humans at playing chess, this is primarily due to their superior speed and short-term memory rather than their possession of clever heuristics.

Thus far, I have contrasted heuristics and algorithms, and while these are easy to distinguish in the formal sense, it is worth considering whether this is a useful distinction in the *psychological sense*. In other words, is the most interesting distinction between (1) correct versus (2) incorrect but useful procedures, or might some other categorization be preferable?

The first point to consider is that shortcuts need not yield incorrect answers. Returning to categorical premise pairs, there are two rules of thumb that are guaranteed to give the correct answer: (1) the twosomes rule (if both premises contain the quantifier *some* then there is no valid conclusion); and (2) the two negations rule (if both premises contain *negations* then there is no valid conclusion) – Galotti, Baron, and Sabini (1986). When applied to categorical premise pairs – guessing where the rule is not applicable – this will on average give 55% correct responses for a five-item multiple choice format, a considerable improvement over the atmosphere strategy, and possibly better than using an exhaustive search strategy. Technically, these two simple rules are algorithms. However, do these really have more in common with an exhaustive search strategy than with the atmosphere strategy?

We should then consider whether people who curtail the use of algorithms, due to capacity constraints, are really using algorithms at all. Recall the recent suggestion that people routinely consider one and only one possibility (or mental model) when identifying conclusions for categorical premise pairs (Evans, Handley, Harper, & Johnson-Laird, 1999). This must call into question the status of their procedure. Are people really applying an algorithm that constantly grinds to a premature halt, or are they applying the heuristic: *More often than not, the first possibility considered will enable a good approximation to the correct answer, and so no other possibilities ever need to be considered.*

The algorithm versus heuristic divide becomes even more complicated when considering the issue from the point of view of the subject. This can be illustrated with the *compass point directions task*. Where would a person end up, relative to the starting point, after taking one step north, one step east, one step north, one step east, one step south, one step west, one step west, one step west? The most common strategy is to attempt to trace the path, mentally if no external means of representation are available (the *spatial strategy*). A generally faster, more accurate, and less stressful approach is to use *cancellation*: Opposite directions cancel, and those that remain constitute the correct answer (see Newton & Roberts, 2000; Roberts, Gilmore, & Wood, 1997; Wood, 1978). Here, cancellation can be regarded as a shortcut strategy that bypasses the need to construct an accurate spatial representation. The interesting detail here is that a sizable number of subjects identify cancellation as a plausible alternative, but reject the strategy because they believe that it will not provide sufficiently correct answers. Hence, they reject the shortcut as invalid, whereas in reality its adoption would have improved their performance (Roberts & Newton, 2003). From the point of view of strict definitions, both cancellation and the spatial strategies are algorithms. However, from the point of view of certain subjects, the spatial strategy is an algorithm, while cancellation is an unacceptable heuristic.

We have seen that some procedures are cumbersome and time consuming, and hence are liable to be error prone when people apply them. Various means can be utilized to circumvent this problem. Cumbersome procedures may be curtailed, or even replaced by entirely different procedures that offer valuable shortcuts. These will vary in their inherent accuracy, and the extent to which they offer an improvement over and above the more cumbersome alternatives. Shortcut methods may be useful even if they only yield performance that is slightly better than guessing, or they may yield far better accuracy than if so called algorithms had been applied. Rather than making a rigid distinction between heuristics and algorithms, a close consideration of this categorisation yields a number of related questions:

What procedures do people use in order to make inferences and draw conclusions?
What steps do people take in order to reduce processing demands?
How should the different procedures be categorized?
How do people determine which procedures to use?

Fundamentally, the issue of interest in this chapter is: *How do people reduce the demands entailed by making inferences and drawing conclusions*? More specifically, what measures can be taken in order to reduce the extent to which information must be exhaustively and accurately represented, and also reduce the number of processing steps necessary in order to make an inference, in order to perform acceptably well?

GENERAL VERSUS SHORTCUT REASONING PROCESSES

Having identified *shortcut* reasoning processes, it is now necessary to be more specific as to the nature of the lengthy reasoning procedures that they circumvent. In other chapters in this book, you will have read about a variety of theories of reasoning. For example, people may make inferences by constructing mental models of states of affairs and identifying conclusions from them (e.g., Johnson Laird & Byrne, 1991, see also Johnson-Laird, this volume). Alternatively, people may apply inference rules to abstract logical propositions derived from reality (e.g., Braine & O'Brien, 1998; Rips, 1994; see also O'Brien, this volume). Although the precise means of representation and inference differ, both of these theories have much in common.

1. The theories explain performance on the basis of capacity limitations. For the mental models theory, the number of models necessary in

order to make a correct inference often overwhelms working memory capacity, leading to the construction of either incorrect models, or an incomplete set of models. Similarly, the more inference rules necessary to make an inference, the more likely that there will be at least one incorrect outcome. In other words, both types of theory posit algorithms for producing correct conclusions. These may often be lengthy and difficult to apply, leading to errors. It is precisely where the use of such processes become cumbersome in this way that various shortcut procedures become advantageous.

2. The theories posit *general* reasoning processes. Both inference rule and mental-model theories are general in the sense that they each offer a tool kit that can be applied to a variety of reasoning tasks. Hence, although the algorithms may be difficult to apply, they may at least be applied widely. Historically, researchers in both camps have advocated their theories as *universal reasoning theories*: An attempt is made to explain all occurrences of reasoning by one theory utilizing one type of process. Hence it is necessary for the relevant procedures to be applicable to a wide variety of types of reasoning – categorical, conditional, disjunctive, and relational reasoning (to name but a few) in the case of mental models theory.

3. The theories advocate *domain-free* procedures. Processes that are domain-free operate in the same way regardless of content and context. This means that once the essentials of a task have been identified and represented, the processes that operate on the represented information, and their outputs should be the same irrespective of the topic. For example, assuming that a person applies logically equivalent interpretations to *if there is a dax then a med will be present* and *if there is a blacksmith then an anvil will be present*, then on being further informed that *a med is present* or that *an anvil is present* there should be equivalent conclusions. For both general theories, any content or context effects that can be identified therefore must impinge either on the processes of constructing the representation (so that different content/context puts different emphasis on what must be represented) or on the control processes (so that depending on the content/context, reasoning procedures may be applied fully or curtailed).

4. The theories are the outcomes of optimistic attempts to identify a fundamental reasoning mechanism. One assumption often made by inference rule and mental model researchers is that a *fundamental reasoning mechanism* exists and that they are identifying the processes supported by this. In the weaker sense, this merely means identifying a set of reasoning procedures that all people apply to all tasks. In the stronger sense, this means that there exists a reasoning module, which automatically makes deductions when appropriate

input is presented. The difficulty in identifying the processes of the fundamental reasoning mechanism have been discussed elsewhere (Roberts, 1993, 1997, 2000a). The key issue here is how a researcher can know whether a set of observed reasoning processes are genuinely fundamental: Identifying how people reason for a particular task cannot answer this question unless it turns out that everyone reasons in the same way for all tasks, and there are no individual differences. I therefore have argued that it only makes sense to discuss reasoning in terms of strategies that people apply, where a strategy is *a coherent set of goal-directed procedures whose application is not compulsory* (see also Siegler, 1996; Siegler & Jenkins, 1989). Hence, people may reason by the use of variants of inference rule or mental-model strategies, or they may use less demanding alternatives.

Defining strategy in this way my cause some confusion due to the fact that two categories of definition may be identified in the literature. *Broad definitions* assert that any self-contained set of goal-directed procedures constitutes a strategy, as long as these are optional, so that their utilisation by any given person is not guaranteed. *Narrow definitions* add optional extras to this, such as the requirement that a strategy must be a nonfundamental process (Bjorklund, Muir-Broaddus, & Schneider, 1990) and must be consciously applied (Evans, 2000). However, Roberts and Newton (2003) argue that narrow definitions deflect debate away from the more interesting questions (how and why do people differ in their reasoning procedures) and toward a futile debate concerning whether or not a given set of procedures genuinely constitute a strategy.

What are the qualities of shortcut reasoning procedures? Their primary and defining characteristic is that they simplify the process of making inferences by reducing the need for lengthy reasoning procedures. Many of the examples that we will consider achieve this by reducing the amount of information that needs to be considered. With less information to consider, less needs to be represented, and so fewer demands are made on limited resources. Hence, both the atmosphere strategy and the two "somes"/two negations rules focus merely on the presence or absence of key words, so that the actual relationships between the entities they describe do not matter. Similarly, the cancellation strategy removes the need to construct an accurate representation of the path taken by a person, replacing this with the need merely to keep a running total of the outcome of cancelling opposite directions. Other shortcuts operate by providing rules of thumb for when to terminate reasoning procedures and when to continue. Other than this, shortcuts can be hard to define other than on a "you know one when you see one" basis. This must engender a certain sense of caution when identifying this as a coherent category of strategies, and only time will tell whether this is appropriate.

Shortcut reasoning procedures also tend to be *narrow* in their applicability: Usually, they can only be applied to particular types of task, sometimes to a particular task only if it is presented in a particular format. For example, cancellation is difficult to apply when each of a set of directions of a trial is presented individually, and then removed before the next is shown, as opposed to all together. Also, cancellation is extremely difficult to identify if directions for two people are given, and the final compass point of one relative to the other is required. Hence, a person equipped only with the generally applicable procedures of, say, mental models theory and nothing else, will still in theory be able to make inferences and draw conclusions in a variety of situations. This will be the case not just in the laboratory with artificial tasks, but also in the real world, for example when reading a piece of text. In comparison, a person equipped only with the two *somes* rule and nothing else will be in far more difficulty. Other than when receiving premise pairs in which each premise contains the word *some*, no reasoning will be possible, and even in the unlikely event that an appropriate pair of premises presents itself, all that can be concluded is that there is no valid conclusion. Of course, if people possess sufficient numbers of shortcuts, then they may be able to function adequately well. Even so, it is not clear that more general procedures could be completely dispensed with, particularly as it will be suggested later that shortcuts often develop from them.

All of the shortcut procedures described so far, like the general procedures, are domain free. For example, the two *somes* rule may be applied to any categorical syllogism irrespective of content. However, this is not a defining feature, and *knowledge* may also provide the basis for valuable shortcuts when reasoning, particularly in the everyday world. Hence, if we know that the car will not start, and its headlamps are dim, then it is likely that the battery is flat. This knowledge enables us to make a diagnosis infinitely more rapidly than from first principles. Also, suppose that we know that the car will not start and that the headlights are bright, but inferences are required in order to identify the fault. In this circumstance, knowledge enables us to regard with suspicion a conclusion that the battery is flat. Many demonstrations of the use of heuristics depend upon giving people difficult-to-answer questions that evoke knowledge and beliefs. Under certain circumstances, this can lead to incorrect answers. For example: *Estimate the probability of a massive flood somewhere in North America in 1983, in which more than 1,000 people drown.* On average, people tended to assign a *lower* probability to this than other people given the following more explicit question: *Estimate the probability of an earthquake in California sometime in 1983, causing a flood in which more than 1,000 people drown* (Tversky & Kahneman, 1983). It is the *former* probability that *must* be higher: Other events apart from earthquakes can also cause floods, and they can happen anywhere in North America, not just California. The key here is that California is more famous for earthquakes than North America is for floods, and people's knowledge of this causes them to inflate their estimates (this is an example of the action of the *representativeness* heuristic: *Events that conform to stereotypes are more likely to happen than events that do not*). As a final example: *Which town has a team in the Premier Football League of England and Wales: Nottingham or Ipswich?* For people who do not know the answer, Nottingham is the better choice because the city is the more famous by far (and is also the most populous). This *take-the-best* heuristic is a good rule of thumb (Gigerenzer & Todd, 1999) but at the time of writing gives an incorrect answer to this question.

Finally, for shortcut procedures, their developmental status, and their relationship to the notional fundamental reasoning mechanism, are far from clear. Some recent work on strategy selection and discovery will be described, but in the main, the origin of many reasoning processes is uncertain (see also Markovits, this volume). The main problems are that it is extremely difficult to evaluate the reasoning capabilities of very young children in isolation of their ability to follow instructions and make responses, and just because all people possess a particular reasoning procedure, or acquire a particular set of procedures in a set order, this does not enlighten us regarding whether the acquisition of such procedures has any modular, innate or programmed basis. Individual differences in the use of reasoning procedures is widespread (e.g., Bucciarelli & Johnson-Laird, 1999; Johnson-Laird, Savary, & Bucciarelli, 2000; Roberts, 2000a; Roberts & Newton, 2003), and even where we can identify shortcuts that are apparently universal, this can merely indicate that they are relatively easily learnt and advantageous to apply. Hence, given the preference for a broad definition of strategy, the shortcuts to be discussed will be considered to be a subcategory within the umbrella term of strategies: part of a wide-ranging cognitive tool kit, but differing in important ways from more general procedures such as mental models and deduction rules strategies.

REASONING VERSUS DECISION-MAKING TASKS

Thus far, I have considered numerous examples derived from many different tasks. In psychology, there has been a tendency for researchers into higher cognitive processes to specialize in particular domains, and with time this has resulted in different emphasis, different theories, and different vocabularies. For example, researchers into deductive reasoning have traditionally been interested in people's ability to make logically valid inferences – that is, inferences that must be true provided that the information given is true – how they achieve this, and why they often fail. Researchers into judgment and decision making tend to focus on the inferences that people make when where is insufficient information to draw a conclusion that is guaranteed to be correct. In such circumstances, people must determine the likelihood that a particular event will take place, or which is the most likely scenario when there are several to choose from. Here, the impact of people's knowledge and beliefs plays a far more central role, although believability effects have also been investigated by deductive reasoning researchers. Findings in the two domains are generally compatible: *Inference processes tend to cease once people identify an answer that is plausible and does not conflict with their beliefs.*

In the remainder of this chapter, I will focus on the shortcuts that people apply in order to solve deductive reasoning problems (a discussion of judgment and decision-making problems will be given by Gigerenzer and colleagues in this volume). Here, problems have definite answers, and the use of knowledge and beliefs is not needed, and indeed may be inadvisable. Hence, I will mainly focus on reasoning by the use of domain-free shortcut strategies, rather than by the use of domain-specific knowledge and procedures that only operate on relevant content placed in appropriate context. However, although for deduction tasks people are requested to identify conclusions that necessarily follow, the shortcuts that they apply will often result in conclusions that are only possibly true given the information. If this phenomenon is widespread, then the implications for everyday reasoning are somewhat disturbing. There is a need for deductively correct conclusions in many walks of life. For example, untrained jurors are expected only to pass a verdict of *guilty* if this is beyond reasonable doubt. In other words, a person should only be declared guilty if this is necessarily true, not merely possibly true.

DOMAIN-FREE SHORTCUTS APPLIED TO REASONING TASKS

In the previous sections, I have tried to give an idea as to the types of reasoning processes that qualify as shortcuts. These are relatively easily applied procedures that circumvent the inherent limitations of general reasoning strategies. They enable us to attain reasonable (or even correct) answers with a fraction of the time and effort that may otherwise be necessary. In the remainder of this chapter, I will outline examples of processes identified in the deduction literature that can be placed in this category. The intention is not to give a comprehensive overview of all relevant research, instead it is to give an idea of the range of shortcuts that have been identified. As we will see, these may be applied to just about every component of the reasoning process.

Reducing Cognitive Load by Restricting What is Attended To

The most well-known example of a theory in which attentional processes constrain what is reasoned about is the heuristic-analytic account developed by Evans and colleagues (e.g., Evans, 1989, 1998b; Evans & Over,

1996). This is effectively a two-stage theory of reasoning in which initial heuristic processes focus attention on relevant aspects of the environment, and analytic processes are subsequently focused only on these. The logic underlying this theory is that in the real world, there is too much that is potentially of interest, and it is, therefore, essential for procedures to be in place that can constrain on what information inference processes are focused. As we will see, this is primarily a theory of attention direction: The processes are applied to focus attention before inference procedures commence. The attention directing procedures are termed *heuristics* because they provide a useful, but not infallible, means of identifying important information, and hence reduce the cognitive load. They are said to be unconsciously applied (i.e., they are automatic, or implicit). The nature of the actual analytic processes are not specified in the basic heuristic-analytic theory, although in later work, Evans (e.g., Evans & Over, 1996) suggests that mental models theory provides the best candidate in this respect.

The heuristic-analytic theory was derived as a result of people's behavior on a reasoning task that has bemused both experimenters and subjects for over 30 years: The *Wason 4-Card Selection Task*. In its simplest form, the standard (or abstract) version of the task consists of (1) a brief explanatory paragraph, (2) a rule of the form *if p then q* – a conditional rule – in which *p* and *q* stand for arbitrary symbols, and (3) pictures of four cards showing the logical values *p*, *not-p*, *q*, and *not-q*. Subjects are told that each card has two mutually exclusive symbols, one on each side, such as letters and numbers. Their task is to decide which of the cards should be turned over in order to determine whether the rule is true or false. An example is given in Figure 9.3. For this, the logically correct response is to select the *A* and 7 cards: If the 7 card had an *A* on the back, then there would be a card with an *A* on one side that is without a 4 on the other side, and so the rule would be false. Typically, fewer than 10% of people make this response. Instead, *A* and 4 would be the most popular 2-card selection for the example.

One insight into why this task is so difficult comes when the *full-negations* paradigm is used. For this, four separate trials are given, and negations are included in three of the rules, for example: *If a card has an E on one side, then it does not have a 2 on the other side; if a card does not have an I on one side, then it has a 6 on the other side; and if a card does not have a U on one side, then it does not have an 8 on the other side.* Surprisingly, although the negations should change people's selections, there is still a strong tendency to select the items explicitly named in the rule, a phenomenon known as *matching bias* (Evans, 1998b; Evans & Lynch, 1973). Cards with values named in the rule tend to be chosen more often than cards with values not named in the rule, irrespective of whether the cards should or should not be chosen.

This is where the heuristic-analytic theory comes in. Evans and colleagues suggest that a matching heuristic determines that the entities named in the rule, that is ignoring negations, are relevant for further

The squares below represent four cards. Each card has a capital letter on one side and a single figure number on the other. The following rule applies to these four cards and may be true or false:

IF A CARD HAS AN *A* ON ONE SIDE THEN IT HAS A *4* ON THE OTHER SIDE

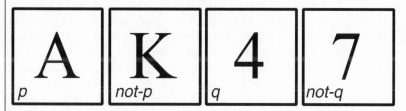

Which card(s) should be turned over in order to discover whether or not the rule is true?

(Note, the *p* and *q* values on the cards denote their logical status and would not be present for the actual task.)

FIGURE 9.3. An example of an abstract selection task problem.

consideration. The rationale behind this, as stated by Evans and Over (1996), is that: "The linguistic function of 'not' is to direct attention to (i.e., heighten the relevance of) the proposition that it denies" and that "if we say 'We are going to choir practice tonight' or 'We are not going to choir practice tonight,' the topic of discourse is the same in either case" (p. 57). Hence, the number of possibilities that we might have to think about are reduced by the following unconsciously applied linguistic heuristic: *When someone talks about a negated concept, it is very unlikely that we need to think about everything except the concept, instead it is better to focus on the concept itself.* This can also be illustrated with the following: Do not think of green elephants. Most of the time, the heuristic will be useful, but the special case of the selection task defeats it.

Matching behavior has been identified in other reasoning tasks, such as truth table tasks, in which subjects have either to identify or construct instances that verify, falsify, or are irrelevant to a conditional rule. For both tasks, another interesting finding occurs when instances are presented as *explicit negations*: In the example in Figure 9.3, the "K" and "7" values are examples of cards that implicitly negate the rule. In contrast, explicit negations directly deny the values stated in the rule: For example, for the selection task, a rule, such as, *if there is not an A then there is not a 3* may be presented with four cards showing *there is an A*, *there is not an A*, *there is a 3*, and *there is not a 3*. With explicit negations on the cards, matching bias is reduced: Now, all elements match the components of the rule, and so the matching heuristic is unable to focus attention on any cards at the expense of others. Matching bias has also been identified when using other logical rules with the selection task (e.g., *p only if q, q if p* – Evans, Clibbens, & Rood, 1996; *p only if q, there is not both p and q* – Evans, Legrenzi, & Girotto, 1999). However, puzzlingly, matching bias has proved to be harder to identify with disjunctive rules (*either there is a p or a q* – Roberts, 2002).

It is undoubtedly the case that matching bias occurs, but is this *explained* by the action of a matching heuristic? The problem is that by itself, this explanation of matching behavior is tautologous: Why do people match? Because of the action of the matching heuristic. How do we know that a matching heuristic is applied? Because people show matching behavior. It is therefore important to identify converging evidence for the action of the heuristic, and recently this has focused directly on the attentional nature of the theory. One key suggestion by Evans (1996) is that an attentional bias should manifest itself in terms of the amount of time devoted to considering each card: People should spend more time inspecting relevant cards – cards which are subsequently accepted – than nonrelevant cards – cards that are subsequently rejected. This was confirmed in a recent study by Roberts and Newton (2001) in which the selection task was converted into a *change task*: Subjects solved computer-presented versions of the task in which some cards were presented as already selected and others as not selected. They were asked to change the statuses of the cards where necessary, so that only the cards that a subject wished to select were displayed as selected on the computer. Subjects were also asked to use a mouse pointer to point to a card when it was under consideration. This slightly unusual method made it possible to identify cumulative inspection times for each card, and also analyze the inspection times for changed versus nonchanged cards separately from selected versus nonselected cards, thus removing some potential artefacts from the study (see Evans, 1996, 1998a; Roberts, 1998a, 1998b). The overall outcome confirmed the original prediction: Inspection times for selected cards were slightly greater than inspection times for nonselected cards, although the difference was relatively small, in the order of 0.3 seconds. This is very similar to the size of the difference identified when using gaze-tracking studies (see Ball, Lucas, Miles, & Gale, 2000).

Overall, the imbalance in inspection times does seem to imply an attentional imbalance when viewing information for the inspection task, and, therefore, does offer corroboration for the heuristic-analytic theory. Alternative explanations for the imbalance are hard to identify. Despite this, the imbalance is smaller by an order of magnitude than was originally claimed by Evans (1996), and Roberts and Newton (2001) query whether a small difference represents the action of heuristic processes that irrevocably determine behavior, or merely cause some bias in the event of uncertainty. However, the power of attention directing heuristics is separate to the issue of whether they exist, and any shortcuts that bias our attention toward more important aspects of the environment at the expense of less important aspects must be of some importance in reducing the cognitive load entailed when making inferences.

Reducing Cognitive Load by Restricting What is Represented

Once information worthy of further consideration is attended to, the key aspects of this must be extracted so that inferences can be made. This is an important feature of inference rule theories of reasoning: The abstract essentials of a situation are identified and represented, and these are passed on to be processed by inference rules. However, depending on what is deemed to be a key aspect, an inference may be trivially easy or extremely difficult to make. Consider the following well-known conundrum:

Consider a chessboard and a set of dominoes. Each domino is large enough to cover exactly two squares on the chessboard. With 32 dominoes, it is possible to cover the entire chessboard with no overhang and no overlap. Question: Suppose that two diagonally opposite corner squares are removed from the chessboard. Is it still possible to cover the entire chessboard with no overhang and no overlap? If not, why not?

The reason why this problem can be difficult to answer is that many people neglect to consider that each and every domino on this chess board *must* cover exactly one white and one black square, and that if two diagonally opposite corner squares are removed, they will both be the same color. Hence, this will leave a chess board with (say) 30 black squares and 32 white squares. Once this essential feature of the problem is identified, it becomes far easier to solve (see Figure 9.4).

Many different shortcuts operate by applying processes only to key aspects of a problem. Often, they capitalize on the fact that applying general strategies can entail many redundancies: steps that did not need to be applied. Hence, if regularities can be identified, redundant steps can be

 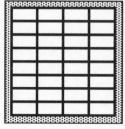 

FIGURE 9.4. A standard chessboard, a standard chess board completely covered with dominoes, and a chessboard with two diagonally opposite squares removed.

dispensed with. For example, when identifying conclusions from categorical premise pairs, the atmosphere strategy has at its basis a prediction concerning recurring features in a problem: The presence of certain properties in the premises will result in the presence of these properties in the conclusion. In reality, the correlation is low, and the prediction yields an almost false rule of thumb. In contrast, the two *somes* and two *negations* rules exploit a genuinely recurring problem feature. Thus, in applicable cases, representing the possibilities implied by the premises is a redundant procedure. The cancellation strategy for the compass point directions task is similar in this respect. At its basis is an appreciation that if (say) steps east, north, and west are taken, the final outcome is merely one step north. Ultimately, it must be appreciated that any two opposing steps can be canceled no matter how many others intervene, and that the entire process of constructing the spatial representation is also redundant. In other words, the exact route taken is an irrelevance – and possibly a distraction if people are so intent on constructing an accurate path that they miss the possibility of cancellation. Interestingly, very occasionally, subjects have reported a *last-two* strategy for this task, in which the last two steps on a set of compass point directions is given as the answer, ignoring all previous steps. On the surface, this strategy appears to be *pathological*. In other words, even worse than guessing (see Roberts & Newton, 2003). However, much to my surprise, on analyzing the items used for previous compass point directions task studies (for which the chance score is approximately 3%) the last-two strategy was found to offer a benefit over guessing: typically 10% to 15% correct depending on the nature of the trials (see Roberts & Newton, 2003). Hence, this is another task where, similarly to identifying conclusions to categorical premise pairs, subjects have been known to devise a strategy that is poor at giving correct responses, but nonetheless is able to yield performance that is better than chance.

As a final example, consider the following extended linear reasoning problem:

Who is taller, John or Ian,
if . . . John is taller than Paul.
Dave is taller than Paul.
Tom is taller than Dave.
Ian is taller than Tom.
Dave is taller than John.

Although it is possible to solve this problem by constructing an ordered representation encompassing the relative heights of all components, this problem can also be solved by scanning the two sides of the display. John and Ian both appear on the left, but only John appears on the right, and so Ian must be the taller (see Wood, 1978). Again, regularity in the problem renders redundant the need to construct a full representation. However, it is easy to devise linear reasoning problems that cannot be solved by this scanning strategy, for example by using *shorter than* as well as *taller than* to link the people, and to present each line of the problem one at a time, that is individually, so as to prevent scanning.

Unlike the attention-directing heuristics discussed in the previous section, most of the shortcuts identified here appear to be applied with some degree of conscious awareness and control. For example, it is relatively easy to instruct people to use the cancellation strategy, and their performance very closely resembles people who report adopting the strategy spontaneously (Roberts & Newton, in press). Another distinction is that for the shortcuts described in the current section, there are substantial individual differences in their adoption. For example, Gilhooly, Logie, Wetherick, and Wynn (1993) identified approximately 20% of subjects as atmosphere strategy users. Users of the two *somes* and two *negations* rules are, if anything, even more rare (Galotti et al., 1986). The numbers of cancellation strategy users vary, but in various studies conducted by Roberts and colleagues, these users have never exceeded half of the subjects (Roberts & Newton, in press).

Much of the evidence obtained so far suggests that shortcuts are discovered online by certain subjects during problem solving, and the mechanisms of discovery are discussed in a later section. For now, it should be noted that many recurring patterns and redundancies in deduction tasks can be, and are identified by subjects, and exploiting them can vastly improve performance by reducing the burden of representing states of affairs and/or performing lengthy procedures on the representations. However, while some shortcuts correctly exploit redundancies, other shortcuts may only offer partial success, but nonetheless offer advantages over guessing. One of the major challenges for researchers therefore is to identify and explain which people discover which shortcuts.

Reducing Cognitive Load by Misinterpreting Logical Meanings

In earlier sections, I have mentioned various shortcut strategies that people may apply when identifying conclusions to categorical premise pairs. These are based upon simple rules of thumb that vastly reduce the burden of representing information. If a person does not apply these shortcuts, then there will be a need to consider the various possibilities that are compatible with premises. This can generate large numbers of states of affairs to consider. However, even here there are other means by which people appear to reduce the cognitive load. Recall that the quantifiers that may be used in categorical premises are *all, no, some,* and *some . . . not*. The possible meanings of these are shown in Table 9.1, where it can be seen that whereas *none of the chefs are artists* is straightforward, with just one possible relationship between the two terms, the rest are ambiguous.

TABLE 9.1. *Examples of the Meanings of the Categorical Quantifiers in terms of Euler Circles*

Quantifier	Example	Meaning
		Logical Quantifier Interpretations
all	all of the chefs are artists	(A C) (A Ⓒ)
no	none of the chefs are artists	ⒶⒸ
some	some of the chefs are artists	(A C) Ⓐ)C (AⒸ) ⒶⒸ
some … not	some of the chefs are not artists	Ⓐ)Ⓒ (Ⓐ)C ⒶⒸ
		Reversible Quantifier Interpretations
all	all of the chefs are artists	(A C)
no	none of the chefs are artists	Ⓐ)Ⓒ
some	some of the chefs are artists	(A C) Ⓐ)C (AⒸ) ⒶⒸ
some … not	some of the chefs are not artists	Ⓐ)Ⓒ ⒶⒸ
		Gricean Quantifier Interpretations
all	all of the chefs are artists	(A C) (A Ⓒ)
no	none of the chefs are artists	Ⓐ)Ⓒ
some	some of the chefs are artists	(Ⓐ)C ⒶⒸ
some … not	some of the chefs are not artists	(Ⓐ)C ⒶⒸ

There is good evidence that errors in identifying conclusions may be due to the misinterpretations that people make when reading quantifiers. However, much of the evidence is indirect, based upon simple premise interpretation tasks. For example, Newstead and Griggs (1983) administered immediate inference tasks, in which single premises were presented, and subjects were requested to decide which other quantifiers must follow. For example (N.B. letters rather than words were used in the original study):

If all of the artists are chefs,
then which (if any) of the following also must be true?

a. all of the chefs are artists
b. none of the chefs are artists   c. none of the artists are chefs
d. some of the chefs are artists   e. some of the artists are chefs
f. some of the chefs are not   g. some of the artists are not
   artists   chefs

Many subjects incorrectly made *reversible* interpretations for *all* and *some . . . not*: Approximately one third incorrectly believed that *all of the chefs are artists* necessarily implied that *all of the artists are chefs*, while approximately two thirds incorrectly believed that *some of the chefs are not artists* necessarily implied that *some of the artists are not chefs*. However, Newstead (1989) found that subjects were more successful when asked to identify which Euler Circle relationships matched various premises, implying that misinterpretations are rarer if this task is taken as the benchmark. By comparison, *Gricean*, or *conversational* errors are somewhat more common in simple quantifier interpretation tasks (Newstead, 1995): In logical terms, *some of the chefs are artists* indicates that *at least one chef is an artist, and possibly all of the chefs are artists*. However, in conversation, if a person knows that *all of the chefs are artists*, then he or she is expected to say so. If *some of the chefs are artists* is stated despite this, then there is a violation of the Gricean conversational principle that in normal circumstances people will be maximally informative and will not withhold information. The logical meaning for *some . . . not* also violates this principle.

Which ever way premises are misinterpreted, this will simplify the process of making inferences: All of the misinterpretations give fewer possibilities to consider for at least some of the quantifiers. With fewer possibilities to consider for individual premises, this will often result in fewer outcomes to consider when the states of affairs of each of a pair of premises are combined (see Table 9.2). The difficulty is that for simple quantifier interpretation tasks, Gricean interpretations are much more frequent than reversible interpretations. In contrast, when people identify conclusions from categorical premise pairs, there is little evidence solely for Gricean interpretations by themselves (Newstead, 1995), instead, reversible interpretations dominate, possibly with Gricean interpretations

TABLE 9.2. *Relationship Among Quantifier Interpretation, Meanings, and Conclusion Generated*

Quantifier Interpretation	Meanings	Conclusion (chefs – artists direction)
	all of the beekeepers are artists some of the chefs are not beekeepers	
logical	(A C) (A)(C) (A)(C) (A)(C) (A)(C)	no valid conclusion
reversible	(A)(C) (A)(C)	some of the chefs are not artists
Gricean	(A C) (A)(C) (A)(C) (A)(C)	some of the chefs are artists
	all of the beekeepers are artists some of the beekeepers are chefs	
logical	(A C) (A)(C) (A)(C) (A)(C)	some of the chefs are artists
reversible	(A C) (A)(C) (A)(C) (A)(C)	some of the chefs are artists
Gricean	(A)(C) (A)(C)	some of the chefs are artists
	some of the beekeepers are artists some of the beekeepers are not chefs	
logical	(A C) (A)(C) (A)(C) (A)(C) (A)(C)	no valid conclusion
reversible	(A C) (A)(C) (A)(C) (A)(C) (A)(C)	no valid conclusion
Gricean	(A C) (A)(C) (A)(C) (A)(C) (A)(C)	no valid conclusion

These are examples of how misinterpreted quantifiers reduce the numbers of possibilities that need be considered when identifying conclusions to categorical premise pairs. Although quantifier misinterpretation will often lead to incorrect answers, this will not always be the case.

additionally applied (Roberts et al., 2001). For the task of identifying conclusions from categorical premise pairs, this pattern of findings suggests that the relevant quantifier misinterpretations constitute a shortcut in reasoning: People's misinterpretations when problem solving do not match their interpretations in relatively simple comprehension tasks. Hence, the misinterpretations constitute an attempt to simplify reasoning procedures rather than being a mere consequence of natural language understanding. The misinterpretations also appear to be highly systematic, suggesting that there is some underlying principle that drives the process of simplification, rather than this representing the outcome of an arbitrary curtailment of problem representation once working memory capacity limits are reached.

Thus far, it has been suggested that when performing the demanding task of identifying conclusions from categorical premise pairs, the meanings considered for quantifiers are curtailed in a systematic way that is similar from problem to problem. The goal of Roberts et al. (2001) was to identify the most plausible misinterpretations given that this was the case. Misinterpreting quantifiers has the automatic outcome of reducing the numbers of possibilities that will be considered in many cases: Certain possible outcomes are blocked, and examples are shown in Table 9.2. Thus, the cognitive load of identifying conclusions is reduced. Because these possibilities have been blocked due to misinterpreted quantifiers, no amount of encouragement to consider all possibilities will result in their consideration, unless this results in correct quantifier meanings being utilized instead. However, an alternative point of view, to be considered in the next section, is that meanings of logical terms are interpreted correctly, but that the consideration of different possibilities is nonetheless curtailed, so that failure to consider all possibilities is a working memory capacity phenomenon rather than an interpretation phenomenon.

Reducing Cognitive Load by Curtailing the Search for Alternative Possibilities

One of the key aspects of mental models theory is the search for counterexamples: Once an initial mental model is constructed, and a putative conclusion identified, the next stage is to attempt to construct further models in order to see whether any contradict this conclusion, and if so, to identify a conclusion common to all models. Assuming that people at least sometimes reason using this strategy, this could lead to the construction of very many mental models indeed. One possible way of reducing cognitive load is that people stop constructing further mental models once working memory capacity is reached. However, there have been several recent suggestions that there are more systematic means for determining the extent to which the search process takes place.

The most straightforward curtailment method of all has been suggested by Evans, Handley, Harper, and Johnson-Laird (1999). Their suggestion is simply that in normal circumstances, people attempt to represent just one possibility compatible with the premises, and identify a suitable conclusion. End of reasoning process. The main difficulty with this account is that it is necessary for people to consider at least two possibilities in order to respond *no valid conclusion*, and this is typically the most popular response when identifying conclusions from categorical premise pairs. Any theory that makes this conclusion difficult to draw must therefore be problematic. Contrast this with Roberts, et al. (2001), where quantifier misinterpretations will prevent more than one possibility being considered for some premise pairs, but nonetheless still permit the consideration of multiple possibilities for others, with the result that no valid conclusion can still be a response in some circumstances (see Table 9.2).

The issue of whether people consider multiple possibilities when reasoning is currently under considerable debate (Bucciarelli & Johnson-Laird, 1999; Evans, Handley, Harper, & Johnson-Laird, 1999; Newstead, Handley, & Buck, 1999; Polk & Newell, 1995; Roberts, 2000b) and the extent to which this occurs appears to depend upon the working memory load of a task, along with a person's understanding of what is required (Roberts, in press). However, we are looking for more systematic means by which a person may decide whether to search for alternatives, or terminate a search, and one source of information appears to be whether or not a conclusion is unbelievable.

Where people's beliefs influence the conclusions that they endorse or produce, this is known as belief bias. For example, consider the following categorical syllogism:

No addictive things are inexpensive.
Some cigarettes are inexpensive.
Therefore, some addictive things are not cigarettes.

Although believable, the conclusion is not valid because it is not compatible with every state of affairs implied by the premises. Because it is compatible with some but not all states of affairs, the conclusion is *possible*, but does not *necessarily* follow. Hence, it is *indeterminately invalid*. This type of conclusion is usually accepted almost as frequently as believable valid conclusions. Believability effects are therefore much stronger for invalid syllogisms, so that the belief bias effect is primarily due to the acceptance of too many believable invalid conclusions, while unbelievable invalid conclusions are correctly rejected (see Figure 9.5). Such effects have been found not just where categorical conclusions are believable or unbelievable (e.g., Evans, Barston, & Pollard, 1983) but also with temporal conclusions (Roberts &

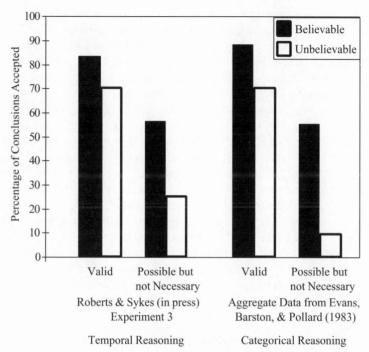

FIGURE 9.5. Believability x validity interaction for a temporal conclusion evaluation task, compared with an equivalent categorical syllogism conclusion evaluation task.

Sykes, in press). For example:

Churchill was Prime Minister before Thatcher.
Blair was Prime Minister before Thatcher.
Nelson Mandela was released while Blair was prime minister.
Prince Charles was born while Churchill was prime minister.
Therefore, Prince Charles was born before Nelson Mandela was released.

Conclusions can also be *determinately invalid*: impossible given the premises, that is incompatible with every possible state of affairs, as in the following example. For these, belief bias effects tend to be small, if present at all (e.g., Newstead, Pollard, Evans, & Allen, 1992):

All fish are phylones.
No phylones are trout.
Therefore, all trout are fish.

Overall, large belief bias effects are primarily due to subjects' inability to respond appropriately to conclusions that are believable and possible, but not do not necessary follow.

Why are people particularly likely to accept conclusions that are believable and compatible with some (but not all) of the possibilities implied by the premises? One possibility is suggested by Oakhill and Johnson-Laird (1985). If we again assume that people attempt to solve such problems by the use of mental models, then one possibility is that identifying an unbelievable conclusion particularly motivates people to search for further possibilities, while believable conclusions offer no such encouragement, so that searching for alternatives is more likely to cease in such circumstances. In other words, *assume that what you believe to be true about the world is a reasonably accurate source of information. Conclusions compatible with beliefs are likely to be equally accurate and therefore can be accepted. Conclusions incompatible with beliefs are unlikely to be accurate, and therefore should be submitted to close scrutiny.* Although this rule of thumb may lead to errors, the assumption that a person's beliefs match reality means that the strategy of only challenging unbelievable conclusions is far more economical than exhaustively searching through every possibility whenever a conclusion is to be produced. (For some more recent accounts of belief bias that attempt to present a slightly different picture, see Evans, Handley, and Harper, 2001; and Klauer, Musch, and Naumer, 2000.)

Reducing Cognitive Load by Restricting the Ways in which Conclusions Are Updated

A final example of a means by which cognitive load can be reduced also involves using a mental-models strategy in order to identify conclusions to categorical premise pairs. Suppose that a mental model is constructed from a premise pair and a conclusion is identified. Next, suppose that a further model can be constructed that falsifies the conclusion. Now, a new conclusion must be sought (in a five-option multiple choice, there would be four remaining to choose from) and this must be compatible with both mental models. How could the demands of this process be reduced. More specifically, what steps can be taken to simplify updating a conclusion in the light of new information?

In order to answer this question, a recent study by Roberts and Sykes (2001) is relevant. For this study, rather than ask people to identify conclusions from premise pairs, people were asked to identify conclusions from diagrams. These diagrams showed possible relationships between two categories of people, and the task was to find a conclusion compatible with each and every one of a set of diagrams. Examples of sets of diagrams are shown in Figures 9.6 and 9.7. For each individual diagram, pairs of words on the same line indicate that people exist who are simultaneously in two categories, whereas unpaired words indicate that people exist who are in one category but not the other. Effectively, this can be treated as a premise pair evaluation task in which the initial procedures of interpreting and

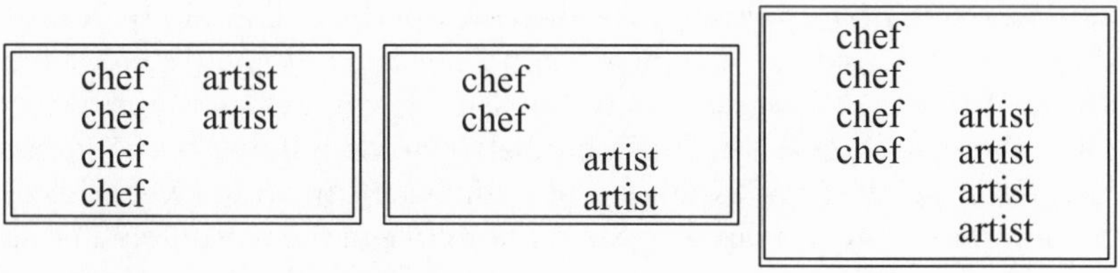

chef	artist
chef	artist
chef	
chef	

chef	
chef	
	artist
	artist

chef	
chef	
chef	artist
chef	artist
	artist
	artist

a)   all of the chefs are artists

b)   none of the chefs are artists

c)   some of the chefs are artists

d)   some of the chefs are not artists

e)   no valid conclusion linking chefs in terms of artists

FIGURE 9.6. A three-diagram conclusion identification problem. *Some of the chefs are not artists* is the only conclusion that is compatible with every diagram.

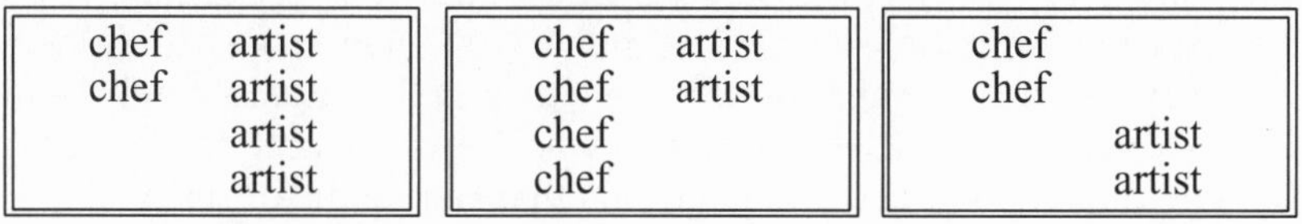

chef	artist
chef	artist
	artist
	artist

chef	artist
chef	artist
chef	
chef	

chef	
chef	
	artist
	artist

a)   all of the chefs are artists

b)   none of the chefs are artists

c)   some of the chefs are artists

d)   some of the chefs are not artists

e)   no valid conclusion linking chefs in terms of artists

FIGURE 9.7. A three-diagram conclusion identification problem. There is no conclusion describing chefs in terms of artists that is compatible with every diagram.

representing premises have been removed, and representations are presented directly to subjects. How might people solve such problems? As an analogue to the mental-models strategy, they might focus on one diagram, identify a putative conclusion, then focus on another diagram. If the putative conclusion is incompatible with the second diagram, a new conclusion must be identified compatible with all diagrams considered so far. This will be named *the full-diagram conclusion updating strategy.*

Roberts and Sykes (2001) identified two findings that are relevant for the current discussion. First, there was no *number-of-diagrams effect*. In other words, for sets of diagrams with the same quantifier as the correct answer, there was never a relationship between the number of diagrams to be considered and the likelihood of giving the correct answer. This surprising finding goes against a general principle in the reasoning literature that the more information that must be considered, the less likely that the correct answer will be identified. The second relevant finding was that there was never an effect of presentation. Answers were indistinguishable irrespective of whether the diagrams of a set were displayed simultaneously or individual members of a set were presented one at a time and permanently removed after viewing. This finding is also surprising if we assume that people are reasoning by using the full-diagram conclusion updating strategy described previously. Presenting diagrams individually and then removing them permanently should cause some measurable difficulties if people need to refer back to them in order to update their conclusions.

Roberts and Sykes (2001) explained these findings by proposing a modification to the full-diagram conclusion updating strategy. When a new diagram means that a conclusion must be modified, instead of identifying a conclusion compatible with all diagrams considered so far, people merely modify their current conclusion bearing in mind that there are only certain legal sequences of conclusions that may be drawn. Hence, the conclusions drawn so far constrain the conclusions that can be drawn in the light of new information. For example, suppose a person correctly concludes *all of the chefs are artists* for a first diagram, but finds that this conclusion is incompatible with a second diagram. Irrespective of the precise nature of the second diagram, it is never possible to transform *all of the chefs are artists* to *none of the chefs are artists* or *some of the chefs are not artists*, as this will always be incompatible with the first diagram. Concluding *all of the chefs are artists* to a first diagram therefore confines subsequent modifications either to *some of the chefs are artists*, or to *no valid conclusion*. For example, looking at Figure 9.6, and considering diagrams from left to right, *some of the chefs are artists* should be drawn as the first putative conclusion. However, this is incompatible with the middle diagram, but knowing that *some of the chefs are artists* was the conclusion for the initial diagram means that *some of the chefs are not artists* is the only possible putative conclusion on reaching the middle diagram. It is never possible to transform *some of the chefs are artists* into *all of the chefs are artists*, or into *none of the chefs are artists*. *There is therefore no need to refer back to the first diagram in order to make the transformation*. The putative conclusion derived from the middle diagram is also compatible with the third diagram and so stands as the final answer. Looking at Figure 9.7, and again considering diagrams from left to right, *all of the chefs are artists* should be drawn as the first putative conclusion. However, this is incompatible with the middle diagram, but knowing that *all of the chefs are artists* was the conclusion for the initial diagram means that either *some of the chefs are artists* or *no valid conclusion* are the only possible alternatives for the middle diagram. However, having correctly concluded that *some of the chefs are artists*, on reaching the second diagram, this conclusion is incompatible with the final diagram, and now *no valid conclusion* is the only viable alternative.

Having identified a plausible model for reasoning from diagrams, why should this be considered a candidate model for the very different and more difficult task of reasoning from premise pairs? The key point here is that for the diagrams task, people were making categorical judgments under ideal conditions. Even in circumstances where they were supplied with all necessary representations permanently in view, their data nonetheless indicated that they were transforming conclusions rather than referring back to previous representations. The strategy of referring back to previous representations is undoubtedly the more demanding option. *If people prefer to use a less demanding strategy even for a task that is relatively undemanding in terms of cognitive load, then it is even more likely that they will prefer a less demanding strategy when presented with a more demanding task.*

Overall, when modifying conclusions in the light of new information, there appears to be good circumstantial evidence to support the notion that people are able to simplify the task by using the fact that the type of conclusion currently drawn will constrain how this can be modified in the future. Hence, there is no need exhaustively to ensure that a new putative conclusion is compatible with not just the currently considered state of affairs, but also every previous one considered. In effect, this particular shortcut simplifies the task of *nonmonotonic reasoning*, that is reasoning in which there is provision for new knowledge to require the updating of previous conclusions. Implementing procedures with this capability has proved to be extremely difficult for researchers attempting to program computers with intelligence.

WIDER ISSUES

Having surveyed a range of shortcuts used in order to simplify the process of making deductions, I will consider two other issues related to the use of shortcuts in reasoning. First, how are these discovered, and second, what are the implications of individual differences in the use of shortcuts for the question of whether a fundamental reasoning mechanism, or a reasoning module, is likely to exist.

The Development of Shortcuts

What is the origin of shortcuts? This is a difficult question to answer because of the wide variety that can be identified. In some instances, researchers have proposed possible mechanisms for the discovery of new shortcut procedures. This is particularly the case where these enable general strategies to be dispensed with, such as the cancellation strategy and the two somes rule. For these shortcuts, people often do not possess them on commencement of a task, but discover them while solving a series of trials. This means that the relationship between item type and strategy discovery can be investigated, and attempts can be made to identify which people are most likely to make such discoveries. Considerable research into the topic of strategy discovery has also taken place in the domain of mathematics (e.g., Siegler, 1996; Siegler & Jenkins, 1989) and many of the findings are relevant when considering deduction.

Ultimately, the study of strategy discovery is the study of what a person can learn about a task while performing it. This detail is crucial, because it immediately becomes apparent that if people are approaching tasks in different ways, or even if they are all performing tasks in the same way, but with different levels of skill, then different people will learn different things. An obvious shortcut to one person may not even have occurred to another. The key factor in this respect appears to be *success*. For example, Galotti et al. (1986) found that people who were good at identifying conclusions to categorical premise pairs were more likely to discover the two somes and two negations rules than bad reasoners. The reason for this is simple: If a person is consistently failing to identify correct conclusions, then the pattern that certain quantifiers are associated with certain conclusions will be less likely to manifest itself. Similarly, the origin of the rules of conclusion transformation proposed by Roberts and Sykes (2001) could also be explained by an identification of repeating patterns. Hence, as a result of experience at updating conclusions with reference to all current and previously represented possibilities, it is learnt that only certain transformations are possible, and there is no need to refer back to previous possibilities.

Success is also implicated in the discovery of the cancellation strategy. Roberts et al. (1997) found that people with high spatial ability were more likely to use the cancellation strategy for the compass-point directions task and were also better able to reason by the use of a spatial strategy when given problems that inhibited the use of cancellation. Initially, this is counterintuitive: Why should the more spatial people be less likely to reason spatially? Again, the answer is straightforward: If a person consistently finds that taking one step east, one step north, and one step west always results in a heading of due north, it is straightforward to identify the repeating pattern that opposite steps may be canceled no matter how many others intervene. Compare this with a person whose answers range from northeast to northwest for the same steps: there is no repeating pattern to identify. Also, in the domain of deductive reasoning, Wood (1978) found that the people who discovered shortcut scanning strategies for extended linear reasoning problems were those who were initially best at solving them by using general strategies. Finally, Siegler (1996) has found that in general, successful execution of arithmetic strategies is more likely to lead to the recall of answers on subsequent presentations of the same problems: A child who finds that 9 + 7 always gives the answer 16 will be far more likely to memorize this solution, so that counting procedures become redundant, especially compared with a child who finds that the same item gives answers that range from 14 to 18.

The recurring theme in explaining the above findings appears to be that the more successful problem solver is better able to represent information accurately and stably. More fundamentally, successful performance equals consistent performance. Hence, the successful performer is better able to detect regularities, remove redundant solution steps, and create less cumbersome, more elegant strategies. Simultaneously, the effectiveness of new shortcuts can also be more easily evaluated by the best performers. The most effective strategies are those that give consistent, precise answers with the minimum of effort. Conversely, unsuccessful performance will also prevent the discovery of shortcuts: The noisy representations that lead to poor performance mean that regularities are less detectable. All of these findings indicate that the best performers are also the more likely to improve their performance still further by discovering more effective strategies. The worst performers at a task are hence doubly penalized, these people would benefit the most from implementing more effective strategies, yet they are least likely to discover them. (For other accounts of success-based strategy discovery, see Crowley, Shrager, and Siegler, 1997; Karmiloff-Smith, 1992; and Wood, 1978.)

Accounting for the use of other shortcuts is harder, not least because many inevitably lead to incorrect answers. Clearly, where a shortcut involves curtailing the use of a general strategy, for example by failing to consider all possibilities, it is easy to propose a mechanism based upon the taxation of cognitive resources. To a certain extent, people will have little choice in the matter. Reasoning must cease once there are no remaining resources, and clearly a conclusion reached by a limited amount of reasoning is more likely to be accurate than a conclusion reached by no reasoning at all. Other shortcuts present more of a puzzle. For example, when identifying conclusions to categorical premise pairs, why do people tend to misinterpret the meanings of quantifiers in systematic ways which do not necessarily correspond to everyday interpretations? The use of the atmosphere strategy also presents a puzzle. Chater and Oaksford's (1999) update of this, the probability heuristics model has at its basis the principle that people determine that some quantifiers are more informative than others in terms of how much information they convey (*all* is the most informative, followed by *some*, *no*, and *some . . . not*). Following from this, uninformative premises yield uninformative conclusions, so that *all* in one premise and *some* in the other will tend to yield *some* in the conclusion. The question, therefore, is *how do people know that this principle should be applied?* If identifying conclusions from categorical premises is too difficult using general strategies, how can it be known whether some flawed but useful rules offer a useful approximation? Why not use a different principle instead: Informative premises yield informative conclusions, so that *all* in one premise and *some* in the other will tend to yield *all* in the conclusion?

Fundamentally, the difficulty in explaining the origin of many shortcuts is that it is hard to see how this process is constrained. If a person has difficulty in solving or understanding a problem, it is hard to see what criteria have been used in order to generate a useful shortcut. Why not a useless one instead that results in worse than chance solution rates? For example, although the last-two strategy is very occasionally reported for the compass-point directions task and has been shown to be better than chance for the materials employed, no subject has ever reported the use of a first-two strategy, or a first-and-last strategy. Clearly, such strategies are not plucked out of thin air, but the factors that constrain their derivation will inevitably be harder to identify compared with algorithmic shortcuts. Overall, the area of strategy discover in general is one in which more research is urgently required.

Fundamental Procedures

People are able to draw upon a wide variety of strategies in order to reduce the burden of having to reason exhaustively. Not only this, but there is considerable evidence that people differ in the extent to which shortcuts are applied. Although it is sometimes possible to identify tasks in which the majority of people use similar strategies, these probably form the minority (Roberts, 2000a; Roberts & Newton, 2003). In reality, few, if any, of the shortcuts outlined earlier are applied by all people all of the time. Hence, we must ask: What are the implications of the existence of shortcuts and individual differences in the use of shortcuts, for the existence of a fundamental reasoning mechanism? Together, these make the identification of a core set of fundamental processes common to all people very difficult indeed. Practically any component of the reasoning procedure can be curtailed, modified, or dispensed with altogether, in different ways by different people. Only the heuristic attention-direction processes proposed by Evans and colleagues (Evans & Over, 1996) appear to be outside the realm of optional processes, although the extent to which these determine (as opposed to influence) the conclusions that people draw is open to debate.

Whereas ten years ago, deterministic, irrevocable, mechanistic procedures might have been proposed to account exclusively for all people's inferences, researchers today seem to place more emphasis on the variety of strategies that people apply (Bucciarelli & Johnson-Laird, 1999;

Johnson-Laird, et al., 2000; Roberts & Newton, 2003). Where does this leave us? The view taken in this chapter is that people possess a tool kit of useful strategies for making inferences. Different people may possess different tools, may use them with different levels of proficiency, and may use different tools to achieve the same task. However, for the types of task that most people may encounter, certain tools are particularly important and will be used time and time again for many different tasks. Nonetheless, just because a screwdriver is a versatile and almost universal component of any tool box, that does not make it anything special in any deeper sense. It is just another tool after all.

SUMMARY AND CONCLUSIONS

What have we learned about shortcuts? Although I have attempted to place these in a single category, this clearly encompasses a very wide range of procedures indeed, and the various properties are summarized in Table 9.3. Sometimes shortcuts appear to be unconscious implicit procedures, at other times they appear to be deliberately applied. Their use has been identified at just about every point of the reasoning process. The common feature is, of course, that they all are means of reducing processing demands. Sometimes shortcuts circumvent general procedures by enabling simple rules to replace detailed representations and lengthy search procedures, at other times general procedures are retained, but are curtailed or refined. This might be expected to lead to improved performance due to a lower likelihood of overwhelmed resources. However, although some shortcuts offer improved algorithms that will yield the correct answer with a fraction of the work that would normally be entailed, other shortcuts are almost guaranteed to lead to errors.

While it is clear that shortcuts may either be algorithms or heuristics, it is far from clear whether this distinction represents an important categorization from a psychologist's point of view, although Roberts and Newton (2003) suggest that there are likely to be important differences in general ability level between people who tend to identify and use heuristic shortcuts (low in general ability) versus people who tend to identify and use algorithmic shortcuts (high in general ability). However, one important point of discussion is whether the use of heuristic shortcuts is generally advisable. They are only useful if we make at least two assumptions:

1. *Reasoning without the use of heuristic shortcuts would be even more error prone, or might even be impossible.* If we accept that human capacity places restrictions on what we can do, then the issue becomes one of making appropriate tradeoffs. If applying general strategies is so demanding that errors are inevitable, then bad shortcuts may be better than no shortcuts at all. The more extreme position, that reasoning without shortcuts

TABLE 9.3. *List of Shortcuts and Associated Features of Application*

Short-Cut	Section	Task	Consciously Applied?	Heuristic/ Algorithm	General Strategy Procedures
Matching Heuristic	5.1	Selection Task	No	Heuristic	Reduced
Atmosphere	5.2	Categorical Syllogisms	???	Heuristic	Replaced
Two "Somes"	5.2	Categorical Syllogisms	Yes	Algorithm	Replaced
Two Negations	5.2	Categorical Syllogisms	Yes	Algorithm	Replaced
Cancellation	5.2	Directions Task	Yes	Algorithm	Replaced
Last Two	5.2	Directions Task	Yes	Heuristic	Replaced
Scanning	5.2	Linear Syllogisms	Yes	Algorithm	Replaced
Quantifier Misinterpretation	5.3	Categorical Syllogisms	???	Heuristic	Reduced
Curtailed search with believable conclusions	5.4	Categorical Syllogisms	???	Heuristic	Reduced
Restricted conclusion updating	5.5	Diagram Evaluation	???	Algorithm	Reduced

Summary of the shortcuts described in this chapter, showing the task used when the shortcut was identified, whether a conscious decision is made to apply the shortcut, whether the shortcut is a heuristic or an algorithm, and how a general strategy is modified in order to create the shortcut.

may be impossible, is given credence by observing the success of artificial intelligence research, or rather, its lack of success. Programming computers so that they are capable of the rudiments of intelligent behavior has proved to be profoundly difficult (Copeland, 1993; Dreyfus, 1993). Despite the efforts of many researchers, computers are still barely capable of communicating using natural language or of displaying common-sense understanding. This is despite the fact that computers can be given working memory capabilities that far exceed any human. Part of the problem is undoubtedly that we live in a computationally intractable world, and the appropriate application of shortcuts is the only means by which we can hope to make sense of the world and interact with it appropriately.

2. *Heuristic shortcuts do not always offer correct answers, but they will usually give satisfactory answers.* The principle of giving a useful answer rapidly rather than the correct answer slowly (if at all) is known as *satisficing* (Simon, 1959; Slote, 1989). Clearly, this is something that humans have to be good at, and it cannot be denied that we are currently a successful species. Unfortunately, it is very difficult to know whether the answers that we obtain by satisficing really are good enough for the challenges that currently face humanity as a whole. Most decisions that we make are relatively inconsequential and can be corrected if necessary. However, we live in a very different world today than even 200 years ago, even more so than the one that we evolved to fit. Only time will tell whether our potentially flawed shortcuts really are good enough. Once the nuclear button is pressed, it will be particularly difficult to unpress.

Identifying the ways in which shortcuts are applied in order to make reasoning tractable is undoubtedly an interesting exercise, and the variety of shortcuts that can be applied is undoubtedly impressive. Unfortunately, the sheer diversity means that unifying themes and conclusions are difficult to identify, and it is quite possible that general strategies versus shortcuts will ultimately prove not to be the most appropriate means of categorization. Despite this, some sort of attempt at unifying what is currently a particularly diverse collection of phenomena scattered amongst domains of deductive reasoning should prove helpful in the long run. This will be the case if only because proposing a bad taxonomy will spur other researchers into proposing better taxonomies.

One recurring point that the reader may have noticed is that the majority of shortcuts identified have mental models theory as their basis. This should not be taken to reflect a bias on the part of the author. Instead this is because the way in which the theory is phrased means that it lends itself to shortcuts. An incomplete sequence of steps can still yield a useful conclusion, and hence there is scope for an investigation of the factors that may lead to curtailment. In comparison, for inference rule theories, it is far less clear that an incomplete sequence of steps can yield a useful solution.

Hence, the shortcuts that may apply to inference rule processes will be more along the lines of constraining the input, or the identification of rules which circumvent a more lengthy sequence of inference rules.

So where does this chapter leave a person who wishes to improve his or her ability to make inferences and identify conclusions. There are four pieces of advice resulting from the arguments so far:

1. *Prioritize and plan.* Ultimately, most decisions that we make are of little consequence. A good-enough answer will suffice, whether arrived at by an incompletely executed general strategy or a reasonable heuristic. Situations which demand the most certainty in the validity of a conclusion are obvious. Also of interest are situations where the same or similar tasks will be repeated several times. In both cases 2 to 4 below, should be considered.

2. *Put the greatest possible effort into representing the possible states of affairs.* Garbage in, garbage out: If you are not sure what you are thinking about, not only are you less likely to identify the correct answer, but you will be less able to generate, let alone recognize effort-saving algorithmic shortcuts.

3. *Do not curtail procedures unless absolutely necessary.* Although it is tempting to curtail the search for a conclusion without considering all possibilities, particularly when a plausible conclusion is identified, this should be avoided. It is very likely that a valid conclusion has not been identified. Where similar tasks are to be repeated, curtailing search will lead to many incorrect answers, which may prevent the identification of repeating patterns, which in turn will prevent the discovery of effort-saving algorithmic shortcuts.

4. *Look for repeating patterns.* Always be aware that shortcuts may be possible. Look for repeating patterns in the information that is given, it may be linked to repeating patterns in the answers. If you do identify a potential shortcut, evaluate it carefully. Test its accuracy with a range of problems for which you possess the correct answer. However, be aware that it is possible to identify false patterns, so be cautious about generalizing a shortcut beyond the domain in which it seems to work.

Notes

1. This is known as the "traveling salesman problem" and has occupied mathematicians and computer scientists for decades. More details can be found in Lawler, Lenstra, Rinnooy-Kan, and Shmoys (1985).
2. A categorical syllogism consists of two premise pairs and a conclusion. These link three entities, A, B, and C. The first premise links the A and B terms (in either order), the second premise links the B and C terms (in either order), and the conclusion links the A and C terms (traditionally expressing C in terms of A). Each component contains one of four possible quantifiers (*all, no, some,* and *some . . . not*). Overall, with four different quantifiers for each premise, and two possible term orders within each, there are 64 premise pair combinations.

3. It should be noted that in every case, the atmosphere strategy produces a conclusion that is compatible with the premises, that is, one that is *possible*, but does not *necessarily* follow. In many everyday circumstances, it is sufficient to identify a solution that is possibly correct.

References

Ball, L. J., Lucas, E. J., Miles, J. M. V., & Gale, A. G. (2000). *Inspection times and the selection task: What do eye movements reveal about relevance effects.* Unpublished manuscript.

Bjorklund, D. F., Muir-Broaddus, J. E., & Schneider, W. (1990). The role of knowledge in the development of strategies. In D. F. Bjorklund (Ed.), *Children's strategies* (pp. 93–128). Hillsdale, NJ: Erlbaum.

Braine, M. D. S., & O'Brien, D. P. (1998) *Mental logic.* Mahwah, NJ: Erlbaum.

Bucciarelli, M., & Johnson-Laird, P. N. (1999). Strategies in syllogistic reasoning. *Cognitive Science, 23,* 247–303

Chater, N., & Oaksford, M. (1999). The probability heuristics model of syllogistic reasoning. *Cognitive Psychology, 38,* 191–258.

Copeland, B. J. (1993). *Artificial intelligence: A philosophical introduction.* Oxford: UK, Blackwell.

Crowley, K., Shrager, J., & Siegler, R. S. (1997). Strategy discovery as a competitive negotiation between metacognitive and associative mechanisms. *Developmental Review, 17,* 462–489.

Dickstein, L. (1978). The effect of figure on syllogistic reasoning. *Memory and Cognition, 6,* 76–83.

Dreyfus, H. L. (1993). *What computers still can't do.* Cambridge, MA: MIT Press.

Evans, J. St. B. T. (1989). *Bias in human reasoning: Causes and consequences.* Hove, UK: Psychology Press.

Evans, J. St. B. T. (1996). Deciding before you think: Relevance and reasoning in the selection task. *British Journal of Psychology, 87,* 223–240.

Evans, J. St. B. T. (1998a). Inspection times, relevance and reasoning: A reply to Roberts. *Quarterly Journal of Experimental Psychology, 51A,* 811–814.

Evans, J. St. B. T. (1998b). Matching bias in conditional reasoning: Do we understand it after 25 years? *Thinking and Reasoning, 4,* 45–82.

Evans, J. St. B. T. (2000). What could and could not be a strategy in reasoning? In W. Schaeken, G. De Vooght, A. Vandierendonck, & G. d'Ydewalle (Eds.), *Deductive reasoning and strategies* (pp. 1–22). Mahwah, NJ: Erlbaum.

Evans, J. St. B. T., Barston, J. L., & Pollard, P. (1983). On the conflict between logic and belief in syllogistic reasoning. *Memory and Cognition, 11,* 295–306.

Evans, J. St. B. T., Clibbens, J., & Rood, B. (1996). The role of implicit and explicit negation in conditional reasoning bias. *Journal of Memory and Language, 35,* 392–409.

Evans, J. St. B. T., Handley, S. J., Harper, C. N. J. (2001). Necessity, possibility, and belief: A study of syllogistic reasoning. *Quarterly Journal of Experimental Psychology, 54A,* 935–958.

Evans, J. St. B. T., Handley, S. J., Harper, C. N. J., & Johnson-Laird, P. N. (1999). Reasoning about necessity and possibility: A test of the mental model theory of deduction. *Journal of Experimental Psychology: Learning, Memory and Cognition, 25,* 1495–1513.

Evans, J. St. B. T., Legrenzi, P., & Girotto, V. (1999). The influence of linguistic form on reasoning: The case of matching bias. *Quarterly Journal of Experimental Psychology, 52A,* 185–216.

Evans, J. St. B. T., & Lynch, J. S. (1973). Matching bias in the selection task. *British Journal of Psychology, 64,* 391–397.

Evans, J. St. B. T., & Over, D. E. (1996). *Rationality and reasoning.* Hove, UK: Psychology Press.

Galotti, K. M., Baron, J., & Sabini, J. P. (1986). Individual differences in syllogistic reasoning: Deduction rules or mental models? *Journal of Experimental Psychology: General, 115,* 16–25.

Gigerenzer, G., & Todd, P. M. (1999). *Simple heuristics that make us smart.* New York: Oxford University Press.

Gilhooly, K. J., Logie, R. H., Wetherick, N. E., & Wynn, V. (1993). Working memory and strategies in syllogistic-reasoning tasks. *Memory and Cognition, 21,* 115–124.

James, W. (1890). *The principles of psychology: Vol. 1.* New York: Henry Holt.

Johnson-Laird, P. N., & Byrne, R. M. J. (1991). *Deduction.* Hove, UK: Psychology Press.

Johnson-Laird, P. N., Savary, F., & Bucciarelli, M. (2000). Strategies and tactics in reasoning. In W. Schaeken, G. De Vooght, A. Vandierendonck, & G. d'Ydewalle (Eds.), *Deductive reasoning and strategies* (pp. 209–240). Mahwah, NJ: Erlbaum.

Kahneman, D., Slovic, P., & Tversky, A. (1982). *Judgment under uncertainty: Heuristics and biases.* Cambridge: Cambridge University Press.

Karmiloff-Smith, A. (1992). *Beyond modularity: A developmental perspective on cognitive science.* Cambridge, MA: MIT Press.

Klauer, K. C., Musch, J., & Naumer, B. (2000). On belief bias in syllogistic reasoning. *Psychological Review, 107,* 852–884.

Lawler, E. L., Lenstra, J. K., Rinnooy-Kan, A. H. G., & Shmoys, D. B. (Eds.) (1985). *The traveling salesman problem: A guided tour of combinatorial optimization.* New York: John Wiley.

Newstead, S. E. (1989). Interpretational errors in syllogistic reasoning. *Journal of Memory and Language, 28,* 78–91.

Newstead, S. E. (1995). Gricean implicatures and syllogistic reasoning. *Journal of Memory and Language, 34,* 644–664.

Newstead, S. E., & Griggs, R. A. (1983). Drawing inferences from quantified statements: A study of the square of opposition. *Journal of Verbal Learning and Verbal Behavior, 22,* 535–546.

Newstead, S. E., Handley, S. J., & Buck, E. (1999). Falsifying mental models: Testing the predictions of theories of syllogistic reasoning. *Memory and Cognition, 27,* 344–354.

Newstead, S. E., Pollard, P., Evans, J. St. B. T., & Allen, J. L. (1992). The source of belief bias in syllogistic reasoning. *Cognition, 45,* 257–284.

Newton, E. J., & Roberts, M. J. (2000). An experimental study of strategy development. *Memory and Cognition, 28,* 565–573.

Oakhill, J., & Johnson-Laird, P. N. (1985). The effect of belief on the spontaneous production of syllogistic conclusions. *Quarterly Journal of Experimental Psychology, 37A,* 553–570.

Oaksford, M., & Chater, N. (1995). Theories of reasoning and the computational explanation of everyday inference. *Thinking and Reasoning, 1,* 121–152.

Polk, T. A., & Newell, A. (1995). Deduction as verbal reasoning. *Psychological Review, 102,* 533–566.

Rips, L. J. (1994). *The psychology of proof.* Cambridge, MA: MIT Press.

Roberts, M. J. (1993). Human reasoning: deduction rules or mental models, or both? *Quarterly Journal of Experimental Psychology, 46A,* 569–589.

Roberts, M. J. (1997). On dichotomies and deductive reasoning research. *Cahiers de Psychologie Cognitive (Current Psychology of Cognition), 16,* 196–204.

Roberts, M. J. (1998a). How should relevance be defined? What does inspection time measure? *Quarterly Journal of Experimental Psychology, 51A,* 815–817.

Roberts, M. J. (1998b). Inspection times and the selection task: Are they relevant? *Quarterly Journal of Experimental Psychology, 51A,* 781–810.

Roberts, M. J. (2000a). Individual differences in reasoning strategies: A problem to solve or an opportunity to seize? In W. Schaeken, G. De Vooght, A. Vandierendonck, & G. d'Ydewalle (Eds.), *Deductive reasoning and strategies* (pp. 23–48). Mahwah, NJ: Erlbaum.

Roberts, M. J. (2000b). Strategies in relational inference. *Thinking and Reasoning, 6,* 1–26.

Roberts, M. J. (2002). The elusive matching bias effect in the disjunctive selection task. *Experimental Psychology, 49,* 89–97.

Roberts, M. J. (in press). Falsification and mental models: It depends on the task. In W. Schaeken, A. Vandierendonck, W. Schroyens, & G. d'Ydewalle (Eds.), *The Mental Models Theory of Reasoning: Refinements and Extensions.* Mahwah, NJ: Erlbaum.

Roberts, M. J., Gilmore, D. J., & Wood, D. J. (1997). Individual differences and strategy selection in reasoning. *British Journal of Psychology, 88,* 473–492.

Roberts, M. J., Newstead, S. E., & Griggs, R. A. (2001). Quantifier interpretation and syllogistic reasoning. *Thinking and Reasoning, 7,* 173–204.

Roberts, M. J., & Newton, E. J. (2001). Inspection times, the "change" task and the "rapid-response" selection task. *Quarterly Journal of Experimental Psychology, 54A,* 1031–1048.

Roberts, M. J., & Newton, E. J. (2003). Individual differences in the development of reasoning strategies. In D. Hardman & L. Macci (Eds.), *The international handbook of reasoning and decision making.* Chichester: John Wiley.

Roberts, M. J., & Newton, E. J. (in press). Strategy usage for the compass point directions task: Overview and implications. In M. J. Roberts & E. J. Newton (Eds.), *Methods of thought: Individual differences in reasoning strategies.* Hove, UK: Psychology Press.

Roberts, M. J., & Sykes, E. D. A. (in press). Belief bias in relational inference. *Quarterly Journal of Experimental Psychology.*

Roberts, M. J., & Sykes, E. D. A. (2001). *Categorical reasoning from multiple diagrams.* Unpublished manuscript.

Siegler, R. S. (1996). *Emerging minds: The process of change in children's thinking.* New York: Oxford University Press.

Siegler, R. S., & Jenkins, E. A. (1989). *How children discover new strategies.* Hillsdale, NJ: Erlbaum.

Simon, H. A. (1959). Theories of decision making in economics and behaviorial science. *American Economic Review, 49,* 252–283.

Simon, H. A. (1983). *Reason in human affairs.* Stanford: Stanford University Press.

Slote, M. (1989). *Beyond optimizing.* Cambridge, MA: Harvard University Press.

Tversky, A., & Kahneman, D. (1973). Availability: A heuristic for judging frequency and probability. *Cognitive Psychology, 5,* 207–232.

Tversky, A., & Kahneman, D. (1983). Extensional versus intuitive reasoning: The conjunction fallacy in probability judgment. *Psychological Review, 90,* 293–315.

Wetherick, N. E., & Gilhooly, K. J. (1995). "Atmosphere," matching, and logic in syllogistic reasoning. *Current Psychology, 14,* 169–178.

Wood, D. J. (1978). Problem solving – the nature and development of strategies. In G. Underwood (Ed.), *Strategies in information processing* (pp. 329–356). London: Academic Press.

10

Cognitive Heuristics

Reasoning the Fast and Frugal Way

Barnaby Marsh, Peter M. Todd, and Gerd Gigerenzer

It is commonly assumed that more information can lead to more precision and better decisions. Consider for instance, the task of catching a baseball. In order to catch the ball, the ballplayer must be at the appropriate spot on the field, where the incoming ball lands. How could this spot be determined? One way to arrive at a precise prediction of the landing point would be to find the ball's launch angle and initial velocity. However, this would lead to an incorrect prediction unless other considerations, such as wind speed, humidity, and the spin of the ball were taken into account. Additional considerations such as differences in wind speed at different parts of the ball's flight could be used to further refine the estimate. Of course, any of these considerations might not be easily or perfectly knowable, and there is a chance that an important consideration would be overlooked. Given that there are typically only a few seconds to gather information and take action, it is likely that by the time that all necessary calculations have been made, the ball would have already landed.

What is the player to do? One way to solve the problem effectively is to forget all the calculations and use the *gaze heuristic*. Following this heuristic, the player fixates visually on the ball and starts running in the general direction where the ball is likely to land, adjusting running speed so that the angle of gaze to the ball remains constant (see McLeod & Dienes, 1996). If the player can run fast enough to maintain the specific angle of gaze, the player will be in the right place to catch the ball as it nears the ground. As this example illustrates, finding a workable solution to a problem does not need to depend on taking all causally relevant information into account (in fact, for many tasks in everyday life, this is not feasible anyway). In contrast, a simple rule, or heuristic can be used. Heuristics have specific qualities that are often absent in other solutions: First, they are *fast*, meaning that they can be used in cases when time constraints would greatly restrict the use of other methods. Second, they are *frugal*, meaning that they make use of only a few pieces of information, rather than taking all available information into account. Surprisingly, heuristics can often compete successfully against standard problem-solving methods that use more information and which require greater computational power. Additionally, the decisions that heuristics produce can be more accurate and robust across different problem situations than those made by comparative formal methods.

In the past few years, a new research approach has emerged on how and when specific heuristics can work, when people use them, and how they compare with more complex decision mechanisms (Gigerenzer, Todd, & the ABC group, 1999; Todd & Gigerenzer, 2000; Gigerenzer & Selten, 2001). This chapter gives an overview of some of the specific heuristics that have been investigated within this research program, showing how heuristics can be used in a variety of decision problems involving choice, categorization, estimation, elimination, and other tasks faced by real decision makers. However, before discussing specific examples, we will first briefly outline the conceptual background that has motivated and guided our search for fast and frugal heuristics.

The term *heuristic* has acquired a range of meanings since its introduction to English in the early 1800s. For instance, in his 1905 paper in quantum physics entitled, "On a Heuristic Point of View Concerning the Generation and Transformation of Light," Einstein used the term *heuristic* to indicate a view that was incomplete and unconfirmed, but nonetheless useful. In early psychological contexts, *heuristics* have come to refer to useful mental shortcuts, approximations, or rules of thumb used for guiding search and making decisions (Duncker, 1945; Polya, 1954). Since the 1970s, much attention has focused on ways that heuristics can lead to errors or bias in human judgment (Camerer, 1995; Kahneman, Slovic, & Tversky, 1982; Kahneman & Tversky, 2000; Nisbett & Ross, 1980). Our use of the term heuristic stands in contrast to this more recent fashion and is more closely related to earlier psychology traditions in that we place our emphasis on heuristics as adaptive tools for making decisions, given real constraints. Specifically, we are interested in the relationship between heuristics and the structure of the environment, and how heuristics might be able to provide tenable solutions to commonly faced problems.

BENCHMARKS FOR HEURISTIC TOOLS

A starting point in the study of heuristics from an adaptive point of view rests in selecting the proper standard by which they can be evaluated. For instance, many behavioral regularities uncovered by research on heuristics and biases have been found to violate standard models of rational choice. However, this does not mean that such behaviors are "irrational" in wider contexts, because standard rational choice models typically do not allow for natural constraints that affect real decision makers, such as limitations in time, knowledge, and computational capacity. As such, these methods cannot be confidently used to assess the true goodness of observed decision strategies.

Rather, the ultimate test of the "rationality" of a heuristic can be found in its fitness consequences relative to real constraints and real environmental structures. To illustrate, findings such as a systematic avoidance of variability (risk aversion) may seem puzzling from a normative profit-maximizing perspective, but may make more sense when viewed in terms of the costs of extra time generally needed to learn about the nature of variance in real environments and nonlinearity in payoff value (such as diminishing marginal utility for larger amounts; see Bernoulli, 1738/1954). In this light, the observation of aversion to variance may not seem so irrational after all – it can in fact be ecologically rational in the right circumstances. Similar analyses can be applied to other biases (Gigerenzer, 1991).

The study of ecological rationality involves analyzing the structure of commonly encountered environments, the structure of specific cognitive heuristics, and the fit between the two. Incorporating a perspective of ecological rationality into the study of behavior enables a clearer understanding of why humans and animals solve problems as they do when faced by different conditions. Our approach in exploring heuristics assumes that organisms make inferences on the basis of stable but possibly uncertain or noisy cues. Furthermore, various stable patterns of environmental features have existed over long periods of time, allowing selective pressures to operate on the design of decision-making processes matched to those environmental structures. In particular, we expect cognitive mechanisms to have been selected to be both quick, by needing to gather little information, and effective, by using the most appropriate cues (Todd, 2001). Our working hypothesis is that people use a range of heuristics depending on the particular details of the environmental context. In this sense, the evolved mind functions as an adaptive tool box, providing specific heuristic tools to solve particular types of problems that are commonly faced in real environments.

UNPACKING THE TOOL BOX: FAST AND FRUGAL HEURISTICS

Just like tools from any tool box, heuristic tools can range from the quite specific to the more general. It is also often the case that solving a problem may require several tools to be used, rather than just one. We have investigated a range of heuristics that can all be defined in precise computational terms, allowing us to evaluate and analyze them rigorously. Most of the heuristics can be broken down into a set of simple building blocks, that control their search for information, how the search is stopped, and what is done with the results of the search. By developing a better understanding of the psychological building blocks from which heuristics can be composed, we can get a bottom-up handle on what tools fill the mind's adaptive tool box.

In general, then, our approach to studying heuristic tools involves (a) using knowledge of behavior and psychologically plausible building blocks to design computational models of candidate heuristics, (b) analyzing the environmental structures in which these heuristics are expected to perform well, (c) testing their performance in real-world environments, and (d) determining whether and when people (and other animals) really use these heuristics. The results of the investigatory stages (b), (c), and (d) can be used to revise the next round of theorizing in stage (a). We now turn to several specific fast and frugal heuristics that we have identified and tested. These heuristics fall into four distinct classes, depending on the structure of the problem situation that is being addressed.

Ignorance-Based Decision Making

One of the most common and fundamental problems that decision makers face is to infer which of two options scores higher on some criterion or more generally to choose one option from two possibilities. Sometimes, the only information available is whether or not the option has ever been encountered before. If one option is recognized and the other is not, then the decision maker can use recognition as a cue in making the decision. This is known as the recognition heuristic (Goldstein & Gigerenzer, 1999, 2002). In computational terms, the recognition heuristic can be formulated as follows (for simplicity, we assume here that there is a positive relation between recognition and the choice criterion):

The Recognition Heuristic
Given: Two options that may or may not have been encountered before.
Find: Which of the two options has the higher value on some criterion. If one option is recognized and the other is not, *then* select the recognized object, otherwise choose at random.
To illustrate: Imagine that you are traveling in an exotic country, and you are offered ham and eggs. Suppose, further, that you are offered the choice between eggs that have either green or yellow yolks. Using the recognition heuristic, you would select the yellow-yoked eggs because they are recognized.

The recognition heuristic has been investigated in a range of different contexts. Test results indicate both that the recognition heuristic is often used, and that it is efficacious in many environments (Goldstein & Gigerenzer, 1999, 2002). For instance, common wisdom has it that people should invest in companies that they know. One can test whether using the recognition heuristic in the construction of investment portfolios is actually a good idea – that is, whether or not it will make money in the complex environment of the stock market. In a series of experiments, we addressed this question by forming real investment portfolios based on firms most recognized by German and American pedestrians. Surprisingly, we found that by forming portfolios by recognition alone, it was possible to match and often beat experienced investment professionals, despite the fact that this latter group has extensive information and a formidable range of tools at its disposal (see Borges, Goldstein, Ortmann, & Gigerenzer, 1999 for details).

A counterintuitive consequence of the use of the recognition heuristic is what we have called the *less-is-more effect*, in which an intermediate amount of (recognition) knowledge about a set of objects can yield the highest proportion of correct answers. Knowing (i.e., recognizing) more than this will actually *decrease* the decision-making performance (Goldstein & Gigerenzer, 1999, 2002). Thus, for instance, performance on a multiple-question exam about relative sizes of cities or heights of mountains or wealth of people can go down if the exam is given repeatedly over a number of weeks, because any difference in recognition knowledge that exam takers could bring to bear the first time they saw the questions (and hence use via the recognition heuristic) is erased by the repeated exposure to exam items, rendering everything recognized.

One-Reason Decision Making

For most of the decisions we make, however, we have more information than just recognition to go on. In these cases, other heuristics can be employed. When multiple cues are available for guiding decisions, what methods might be used to make a choice? The most frugal approach is to use one-reason decision making (Gigerenzer & Goldstein, 1996, 1999), choosing between options based on the first cue found that favors one over the others:

One-Reason Decision-Making Heuristics
Given: Two objects and their corresponding values on cue dimensions that can be used to infer their relative value on some criterion.
Find: The object with a higher value on the decision criterion.
a. Select any cue dimension.
b. Look for the corresponding cue value for each object.
c. If they differ, then stop and choose the object with the cue indicating a greater criterion value.
d. If they do not differ, then return to the beginning of this loop (a) to look for another cue dimension.
To illustrate: Suppose that you are shopping for fresh pasta and the two products available differ in terms of, color, moistness, and smell. Using one-reason decision making, if your criterion was freshness, you would select any one cue (for instance, color), and compare the two options on this single cue. You would then select the product having the most appealing color. If there is a tie, then you would select another cue (such as moistness), and make your decision on the basis of that cue, and so on.

The four-step loop incorporates two of the important building blocks of simple heuristics: a stopping rule (here, stopping after a single cue is found that enables a choice between the two options) and a decision rule (here, deciding on the option to which the one cue points). This class of heuristics does not need to compute an optimal cost-benefit tradeoff, as in optimization under constraints. In fact, it need not compute any costs or benefits at all. Specific one-reason decision heuristics can be created by using particular search rules that dictate how the appropriate cue dimensions are selected (step a); we have explored three such heuristics that differ only in their search rule (see Gigerenzer & Goldstein, 1996). The *take the best heuristic* searches for cues in the order of their validity – that is, how often each cue has indicated the correct versus incorrect option (when it discriminated between them). The *take the last heuristic* looks for cues in the order determined by their past success in stopping search, so that the cue that was used for the most recent previous decision (whether or not it was correct) is checked first when making the next decision. Finally, the *minimalist* heuristic selects cues in a random order. These three heuristics can be understood conceptually as follows:

The Take The Best Heuristic
Given: A pair of objects to choose between according to some criterion, each with associated binary cue values (some of which may be unknown) where value 1 is associated with higher criterion values.
Find: The object with the higher value on the criterion.
a. If applicable, use the recognition heuristic (see above): If one object is recognized, predict that object as having a higher value on the criterion; if neither is recognized, simply guess randomly; if both are recognized:
Then
b. Ordered search: Choose the cue with the highest validity that has not yet been tried in the current decision. Look up the values of the two objects.
c. If one object has a cue value $= 1$ and the other does not (i.e., value $= 0$ or unknown) then stop search and go to step "d." Otherwise, go back to step "b" and search for another cue. If no further cue is found, then guess.
d. Predict that the object with the cue value $= 1$ has the higher value on the criterion.
To illustrate: Suppose that you are choosing between two holiday packages – one to Bali, the other to Tahiti, and that your most important vacation criterion is the potential for active outdoor leisure time. Since you recognize both destinations, you look to the cue that you feel is most important – whether it is likely to be sunny at the time of year when you are wanting to travel. You find that both destinations have acceptable weather during the month of anticipated travel (e.g., the options are tied on this cue), and so you then turn to the next most important cue – whether or not the hotel happens to be on the beach. Upon looking up this cue, you discover that both hotels are on beachfronts, and so you look to the next most important cue– whether boat rental is available. You find that boats are easily available in Tahiti but not near the hotel in Bali. On the basis of this cue, you select Tahiti as your holiday destination for this year.

The Take The Last Heuristic

a. If applicable, use the recognition heuristic (see above): If one object is recognized, predict that object as having a higher value on the criterion; if neither is recognized, simply guess randomly; if both are recognized:

Then

b. Memory search: if there is a record of which cues stopped search during previous decisions, choose the cue that stopped search on the most recent decision but which has not yet been tried on the current one. Look up the cue values of the two objects. If there is no record, try a random cue.

c. If one object has a cue value = 1 and the other does not (i.e., value = 0 or unknown) then stop search and go to step "d." Otherwise, go back to step "b" and search for another cue. If no further cue is found, then guess.

d. Predict that the object with the cue value = 1 has the higher value on the criterion.

To illustrate: Suppose that that you are once again looking for a beach vacation package. This year you are choosing between the Bahamas or Jamaica – both destinations that you recognize. You then perform a memory search and recall that last year whether or not the hotel had easy access to boat rental was the decisive inference cue. You then use this cue in current inference. You discover that only the hotel in the Bahamas has easy access to boat rental; on the basis of this cue, you decide on the package to the Bahamas.

The Minimalist Heuristic

a. If applicable, use the recognition heuristic (see above), if one object is recognized, predict that object as having a higher value on the criterion; if neither is recognized, simply guess randomly; if both are recognized:

Then

b. Random search: Draw a cue randomly (without replacement) and look up the cue value of the two objects.

c. If one object has a cue value = 1 and the other does not (i.e., value = 0 or unknown) then stop search and go to step "d." Otherwise, go back to step "b" and search for another cue. If no further cue is found, then guess.

d. Predict that the object with the cue value = 1 has the higher value on the criterion.

To illustrate: Suppose once again that you are faced with a choice between two vacation packages-one to the Bahamas and the other to Jamaica. Your primary criterion is to be someplace that permits ample outdoor leisure time. Since you recognize both, you next select any cue at random that may relate to your criterion. For instance, you look at whether the hotel has a pool. Since the hotel in Jamaica has a pool but the hotel in the Bahamas does not, you select the package to Jamaica.

What we found when we tested the performance of these one-reason decision-making heuristics was surprising. Despite their simplicity, they still made very accurate choices. When we compared these heuristics against a range of more traditional information-combining methods such as multiple regression, we found that the simple heuristics always came close to, and in the case of take the best even often exceeded, the efficacy of

TABLE 10.1. *Performance of Different Decision Strategies Across 20 Data Sets*

Strategy	Frugality	Accuracy (% correct)	
		Fitting	Generalization
Minimalist	2.2	69	65
Take the Best	2.4	75	71
Dawes's Rule	7.7	73	69
Multiple regression	7.7	77	68

Note: The performance of two fast and frugal heuristics (Minimalist, Take the Best) and two linear strategies (Dawes's Rule, Multiple Regression) is shown for a range of data sets. The mean number of predictors available in the 20 data sets was 7.7. "Frugality" indicates the mean number of cues actually used by each strategy. Fitting Accuracy indicates the percentage of correct answers achieved by the strategy when fitting data (test set = training set). Generalization Accuracy indicates the percentage of correct answers achieved by the strategy when generalizing to new data (cross validation, i.e., test set $\neq$ training set).

the traditional methods (see Czerlinski, Gigerenzer, & Goldstein, 1999; see Table 10.1). Thus, making good decisions need not rely on the standard approach of collecting all available information and combining it according to the relative importance of each cue; simply betting on one good reason can be sufficient.

Those who are used to working with formal models might be suspicious of the prospect of using only a few cues instead of many. How can we expect simple domain-specific heuristics to be as accurate as complex general strategies that work with many free parameters? Perhaps the key answer lies in their robustness in providing accurate answers across a range of environments. More complex general strategies that work by making use of a large number of free parameters, such as multiple linear regression, can suffer from trying to make sense of every piece of information they encounter. This failure of generalization, known as *overfitting* (Geman, Bienenstock, & Doursat, 1992; Massaro, 1988), stems from assuming that every detail is of relevance. Fast and frugal heuristics can reduce overfitting by ignoring the noise inherent in many cues and looking instead for the most important cues. Thus, simply using only one or a few of the most useful cues can automatically yield robustness.

In the scenarios above, we assume that different options can be selected or rejected on the basis of differences in the presence or absence of specific cues. What would happen if there are more than two options to choose from, but all share the same set of cues? As a test of this question, we investigated the performance of one-reason decision making in the domain of parental investment (Davis & Todd 1999; see also Rieskamp & Hoffrage,

1999, for a different test of this sort). Specifically, we modeled the food provisioning task faced by parent birds: after arriving at the nest with a recently caught insect, the parent must decide which nestling to feed. Cues that may be considered include the size of each chick, variations in vocal begging intensity between different chicks (e.g., hunger), and the position of each chick in the nest. Several cues can be used, or just one. It was found that one-cue feeding rules can perform significantly better (in terms of total chick growth) than traditional rules that combine information from multiple cues.

Elimination Heuristics for Multiple-Option Choices

In situations where there are more available options than values in each available cue dimension, one-reason decision making will usually not suffice because a single cue will be unable to distinguish between all of the alternatives. One way to select a single option from among multiple alternatives is to follow the simple principle of elimination. Successive cues are used to eliminate alternatives until a single option can be selected (see Tversky, 1972). Such rules can be more effective when they rely on some knowledge of the validities of different cues.

One fast and frugal heuristic that works this way is the *QuickEst heuristic* (Hertwig, Hoffrage, and Martignon, 1999), which can be applied to estimation tasks. The QuickEst heuristic can exploit aspects of the commonly encountered J-shaped distribution of features and objects in the environment in order to make quick and useful estimates. J-shaped distributions reflect the tendency in many domains for objects to be unevenly distributed, and highly clustered at one end of a given criterion range. For example, if we ask 1,000 random people to name characters in a Shakespeare play, there will be many more people who are able to name a small number of characters than there are who come up with a long list. If we plot these responses by the number of characters identified, then the resulting plot is likely to look like a "J" tipped on its side, with many people who can name 0–10 characters, and only few in the range of naming 40–50. Similarly, if we plot the number of a nation's cities in different size ranges, there is expected to be a much greater number of cities with populations between 10,000–100,000 than there are with populations between 1,000,000 and 1,090,000. To exploit the common J-shaped environmental structure, QuickEst works in the following way:

The QuickEst Heuristic

Given: An object and a set of corresponding cue values.
Find: An estimate of the object's value on some criterion.
a. Identify a cue that is expected to separate the most common objects from all of the others.

b. Look at the next cue that is expected to separate the remaining common objects from the rest of the distribution tail. Continue looking for cues in this way until a cue is found that no longer places the object with the most common objects.

Then

c. Assign a value to the object based on the value expected based on the attributes of the cue it stopped with.

To illustrate: Imagine that you manage a company and need to estimate the size of a competitor's advertising budget. Since the size of the budget is likely to be related to advertising channels, you look to find a channel that the competitor uses that separates it from most others. For instance, many firms may use local newspapers, but relatively few advertise in larger city or regional papers. You find that your competitor advertises in these larger papers, so you then turn to the next cue: whether the competitor uses spots on national radio. Again, you find that your competitor uses this medium in advertising, so you next check television. Here, you find that your competitor does not use television, and so you stop your search. You then make your estimate on the basis of the expected budget size of a firm that uses newspaper and radio, but not television.

Note that when using QuickEst, no cue combination is necessary at any point. This eliminates complexity problems associated with the integration of a potentially large number of different cue values as found in information-and-computation-intensive methods such as multiple regression and estimation trees. Yet, in a test of this heuristic against these methods, QuickEst consistently matches or outperforms them (Hertwig et al., 1999).

Another elimination-based heuristic is *categorization by elimination* (Berretty, Todd, & Blythe, 1997). This heuristic can be used when the task is to select a single category from several possible categories that a given object might best fall into. The heuristic can be understood as follows:

The Categorization by Elimination Heuristic

Given: An object to be categorized, a set of cue values for the object, a set of possible categories, and which cue values are associated with what categories.

Find: The category to which the object belongs, using as few cues as possible.

a. Rank the cues in terms of their validity (i.e., how often each cue alone indicates the correct category across all objects).

b. Select the highest-validity unchecked cue dimension and check the object's value for that cue.

c. Eliminate from further consideration all categories that do not encompass the current cue value.

d. If only one category remains, it is the final choice; otherwise, if cue dimensions remain, return to "step b", and if there are no more cues to check, pick a category randomly from those left.

To illustrate: Suppose that you need to describe a bottle of an alcoholic beverage. Your basic categories are beer (amber brown, beer bottle), red wine (red, wine bottle), white wine (white, wine bottle), rose (pink, wine bottle), sauterne (yellow, wine bottle) or champagne (white, champagne bottle). Cues thus include bottle shape and color. Since in this case color is the higher validity cue (since color alone will correctly identify the type of beverage in four cases, while bottle shape alone will suffice in only two cases), you first look at the color. Since the color is red, you can eliminate all categories except red wine. If needed, one would next consider the cue validity with the next-highest validity, though in the present case this is not necessary – only one candidate happened to be red.

Categorization by elimination thus uses successive cues to reduce the set of possible categories until only a single possible category remains. Its performance comes within a few percentage points of the accuracy of complex categorization algorithms such as exemplar and neural network models, and yet it uses only about a quarter of the information needed by these other models. Thus, it is a robust candidate for categorization particularly in situations where information about objects is costly or difficult to obtain.

Satisficing Heuristics

All of the heuristics that we have discussed so far are for choosing a single option from multiple alternatives, assuming that all alternatives are presently available. But different heuristics are needed when alternatives (as opposed to cue values) appear sequentially over an extended period or spatial region. In this type of choice task, the stopping rule must specify which object stops search, just as in the previously described heuristics the stopping rule specified which cue stops search. An instance of this type of problem is found in the context of individuals who are searching for a mate from a stream of potential candidates that are seen one at a time – when should the searcher stop and stay with the current candidate?

To address such sequential search problems, agents can satisfice (Simon 1955, 1990). Satisficing works by setting an aspiration level and searching until a candidate is found that exceeds that aspiration. Satisficing eliminates the need to compare a large number of possible outcomes with one another, thus saving time and the need to acquire large amounts of information. The question is how to set the aspiration level in the first place. One way is to examine a certain number of alternatives and use the best criterion value seen in that sample as the aspiration level for further search. Consider the problem of finding the single best alternative from a sequence of fixed length drawn from an unknown distribution – an extreme form of sequential search. In this scenario, using an initial sample of 37% of all available alternatives for setting the aspiration level provides the highest likelihood of picking the best (the optimal solution to the so-called secretary or dowry problem – see Ferguson, 1989). However, much less search (e.g., setting an aspiration using 10% of the available alternatives) is required for attaining other more realistic goals such as maximizing the mean criterion value found across multiple searches (Todd & Miller, 1999). Other search rules have also been explored, such as stopping search after encountering a long gap between attractive candidates (Seale & Rapoport, 1997). In a mutual search setting, for instance where both males and females are searching for a suitable mate, heuristics that learn an aspiration level based on the rejections and offers one receives can lead to successful matching of the two populations of searchers, again with relatively little information (Todd & Miller, 1999).

GOING TO WORK: FUTURE TESTS OF HEURISTIC TOOLS

In this chapter, we have introduced several candidate heuristics and heuristic building blocks that can provide good solutions for various kinds of common decision problems without using too much computation, time, or information. We have also shown how to formalize some of these heuristic solutions in terms of their computational building blocks, and how to test them across different environmental structures where they might be used. Overall, we have found evidence that simple heuristics can work remarkably well for many kinds of problems. Heuristics tend to work well for several reasons. First, they benefit explicitly from not taking all information into account, but only the information that is likely to be important in solving the problem at hand. This particularly has advantages in new or changing environments where more complete detailed knowledge might not be helpful but might actually lead the decision maker astray. Furthermore, they are able to provide relatively quick solutions using specialized decision processes that are suited to the specific nature of the problem domain. This stands in contrast to more complex methods that might need to be fine tuned to give optimal solutions for each and every type of decision process. Finally, by using a set of relatively simple processes, heuristics can offer competitive advantages in terms of computation time, which is often an important consideration in many real-life decisions

However, much work remains. Some of the problems to be explored include (see Todd, Gigerenzer, & the ABC Research Group, 2000, for a full development): further examination of where heuristics come from – how they are learned, or socially constructed, or evolved, or culturally transmitted; how heuristics are selected from the adaptive tool box, including the role of the environment in triggering the use of particular heuristics; how environment structure can be characterized in terms of patterns of cues, social relationships, J-shaped distributions of alternatives, and so on; development of methodology for studying which heuristics people use, when, and how effectively; and specification of criteria that can be used to evaluate the performance of heuristics including Bayesian and other benchmarks. We must also develop studies outside the laboratory to explore how people use heuristics to solve problems when time pressure, competition, and emotions are at play (e.g., Klein, 1998). We also can look at the conditions under which the heuristics that we have studied begin to break down. For instance, we know that the recognition heuristic becomes less effective as the number of recognized options increases. If all options are recognized, then this heuristic is no longer able to provide an advantage. We would like to look at how the use of heuristics might be expected to change as the structure of the environment changes.

Despite these multiple challenges, the study of heuristic strategies nonetheless promises to change the way that decision behavior is understood. In the past, cognitive scientists, economists, and biologists have often addressed issues of how people make choices by building elaborate models and endowing organisms with unlimited abilities to know, memorize, and compute. In other cases, when rational models could not account for real human behavior, researchers often resorted to mere descriptions of decisions made. Work on understanding behavior in the context of ecologically rational heuristics provides a third way forward. We can put aside unattainable hyperrational models and mere collections of facts to construct and test models of the psychological mechanisms used to solve the real problems faced by real decision makers.

References

Bernoulli, D. (1738). *Specimen theoriae novae de mensura sortis* [*Exposition of a new theory on the measurement of risk*]. Translated by L. Sommer, *Econometrica* (1954), 22, 23–36.

Berretty, P. M., Todd, P. M., & Blythe, P. W. (1997). Categorization by elimination: A fast and frugal approach to categorization. In M. G. Shafto & P. Langley (Eds.), *Proceedings of the Nineteenth Annual Conference of the Cognitive Science Society* (pp. 43–48). Mahwah, NJ: Erlbaum.

Borges, B., Goldstein, D. G., Ortmann, A., & Gigerenzer, G. (1999). Can ignorance beat the stock market? Name recognition as a heuristic for investing. In G. Gigerenzer, P. M. Todd, & the ABC Research Group. *Simple heuristics that make us smart*. New York: Oxford University Press.

Camerer, C. (1995) Individual decision making. In J. H. Kagel & A. E. Roth (Eds.), *The handbook of experimental economics*. Princeton, NJ: Princeton University Press.

Czerlinski, J., Gigerenzer, G., & Goldstein, D. G. (1999). Accuracy and frugality in a tour of environments. In G. Gigerenzer, P. M. Todd, & the ABC Research Group. *Simple heuristics that make us smart*. New York: Oxford University Press.

Davis, J. N. & Todd, P. M. (1999). Simple decision rules for parental investment. In G. Gigerenzer, P. M. Todd, & the ABC Research Group. *Simple heuristics that make us smart*. New York: Oxford University Press.

Duncker, K. (1945). On problem solving (L. S. Lees, Trans.). *Psychological Monographs, 58* (5 Whole no. 270). (Original work published 1935.)

Ferguson, T. S. (1989). Who solved the secretary problem? *Statistical Science, 4*, 282–296.

Geman, S.,Bienenstock, E., & Doursat E., 1992. Neural networks and the bias/variance dilemma. *Neural Computation, 4*, 1–58.

Gigerenzer, G. (1991). How to make cognitive illusions disappear. Beyond heuristics and biases. In W. Stroebe & M. Hewstone (Eds.), *European review of social psychology* (vol. 2, pp. 83–115). Chichester, UK: Wiley.

Gigerenzer, G., & Goldstein, D. G., (1996). Reasoning the fast and frugal way: Models of bounded rationality. *Psychological Review, 103*, 650–669.

Gigerenzer, G., & Goldstein, D.G. (1999). Betting on one good reason: Take the best and its relatives. In G. Gigerenzer, P. M. Todd, & the ABC Research Group (1999). *Simple heuristics that make us smart*. New York: Oxford University Press.

Gigerenzer, G., & Selten, R. (Eds.) (2001). *Bounded rationality: The adaptive toolbox* (Dahlem Workshop Report). Cambridge, MA: MIT Press.

Gigerenzer, G., Todd, P. M., & the ABC Research Group (1999). *Simple heuristics that make us smart*. New York: Oxford University Press.

Goldstein, D. G., & Gigerenzer, G. (1999). The recognition heuristic: How ignorance makes us smart. In G. Gigerenzer, P. M. Todd, & the ABC Research Group. *Simple heuristics that make us smart*. New York: Oxford University Press.

Goldstein, D. G., & Gigerenzer, G. (2002). Models of ecological rationality: The recognition heuristic. *Psychological Review, 109*, 75–90.

Hertwig, R., Hoffrage, U., & Martignon, L. (1999). Quick estimation: Letting the environment do some of the work. In G. Gigerenzer, P. M. Todd, & the ABC Research Group. *Simple heuristics that make us smart*. New York: Oxford University Press.

Kahneman, D., Slovic, P., & Tversky, A. (1982). *Judgement under uncertainty: Heuristics and biases*. Cambridge: Cambridge University Press.

Kahneman, D., & Tversky, A. (Eds.). (2000). *Choices, values, and frames*. Cambridge: Cambridge University Press

Klein, G. (1998). *Sources of power: How people make decisions*. Cambridge, MA: MIT Press.

Massaro, D. W. (1988). Some criticisms of connectionist models of human performance. *Journal of Memory and Language, 27*, 213–234.

McLeod, P., & Dienes, Z. (1996). Do fielders know where to go to catch the ball or only how to get there? *Journal of Experimental Psychology: Human perception and performance, 22*, 531–543.

Nisbett, R. E., & Ross, L. (1980). *Human inference: Strategies and shortcomings of social judgement*. Englewood Cliffs, NJ: Prentice-Hall.

Polya, G. (1954). *Mathematics and plausible reasoning: Vol. 1. Induction and analogy in mathematics*. Princeton, NJ: Princeton University Press.

Rieskamp, J., & Hoffrage, U. (1999). When do people use simple heuristics and how can we tell? In G. Gigerenzer, P. M. Todd, & the ABC Research Group. *Simple heuristics that make us smart*. New York: Oxford University Press.

Seale, D. A., & Rapoport, A. (1997). Sequential decision making with relative ranks: An experimental investigation of the "secretary problem." *Organizational Behavior and Human Decision Processes, 69*(3), 221–236.

Simon, H. A. (1955). A behavioral model of rational choice. *Quarterly Journal of Economics, 69*, 99–118.

Simon, H. A. (1990). Invariants of human behavior. *Annual Review of Psychology, 41*, 1–19.

Todd, P. M. (2001). Fast and frugal heuristics for environmentally bounded minds. In G. Gigerenzer & R. Selten (Eds.), *Bounded rationality: The adaptive toolbox (Dahlem Workshop Report)* (pp. 51–70). Cambridge, MA: MIT Press.

Todd, P. M., & Gigerenzer, G. (2000). Simple heuristics that make us smart. *Behavioral and Brain Sciences, 23*(5), 727–741.

Todd, P. M., Gigerenzer, G., & the ABC Research Group (2000). How can we open up the adaptive toolbox? (Reply to commentaries.) *Behavioral and Brain Sciences, 23*(5), 767–780.

Todd, P., & Miller, G. (1999) From pride and prejudice to persuasion: Satisficing in mate search. In G. Gigerenzer, P. M. Todd, & the ABC Research Group. *Simple heuristics that make us smart.* New York: Oxford University Press.

Tversky A. (1972). Elimination by Aspects: A theory of choice. *Psychological Review, 79*, 281–299.

PART THREE

THE BASES OF REASONING

11

The Assessment of Logical Reasoning

Jacqueline P. Leighton

Suppose a colleague tells you that another colleague, Sally, has submitted a paper to a conference in Rio de Janeiro and that she will be away for week. Further imagine that you know Sally better than the colleague who delivered the news. Knowing Sally well, you are fairly confident that if she were to go to Rio, she would stay longer than a week. You have inside knowledge about Sally that others do not have. Now suppose the colleague said the following to you:

"If Sally goes to Rio, then she will be away for a week."

And at a later date, you learn the following:

Sally goes to Rio.

What do you conclude about her length of stay? According to your colleague and *his knowledge* about Sally, he thinks you will conclude, as he has, that Sally will be away for a week. However, according to your knowledge about Sally, you have to conclude that she will stay in Rio longer than a week because you know from conversations with her that she has always wanted to visit Rio and travel around the country of Brazil, and a week will certainly be too short of a stay for her to see it all. Hence, you conclude that she will be away longer than a week. Who is right? According to rules of formal logic (i.e., material implication), your colleague is right because given a conditional *if p → q*, and *p*, then *q* follows. However, according to your inside knowledge about Sally, then *if p → q* only holds if *p* represents a city other than Rio de Janeiro.

If deducing Sally's length of stay in Rio had been set up as a task to assess your logical reasoning skill, and your background knowledge about Sally were neglected, then your conclusion would have been evaluated

The author wishes to thank Stephen P. Norris and Mark J. Gierl for their insightful feedback and comments on earlier versions of this manuscript.

as incorrect and, perhaps, your reasoning skill as faulty. This assessment of your conclusion would misrepresent your reasoning skill by failing to consider the relevant knowledge from which you were reasoning. This simple scenario about Sally is used to illustrate the relevance of people's background knowledge in psychological assessments of logical reasoning.

Most, if not all, studies of logical reasoning do not take into account the background knowledge participants use to solve reasoning tasks (Leighton & Sternberg, in press). If the participants who took part in these studies were also trained in formal logic then disregarding their background knowledge would seem reasonable at one level – all participants would have the same knowledge level so, as a constant, it could be factored out. However, given that the participants who take part in these studies are not trained in formal logic, then the question of what knowledge participants bring to bear to these studies and use to solve the tasks presented to them seems imperative to evaluating the adequacy of their reasoning (Leighton & Sternberg, in press).

By neglecting the background knowledge that untrained participants use to solve logical reasoning tasks, we risk violating basic standards in the assessment of performance skills (Standards, 1999), and compromising the empirical basis on which theories of human reasoning rest. Nevertheless, the effects of background knowledge have not been integrated in the psychological assessment of logical reasoning (Evans & Over, 1996; Leighton & Sternberg, in press).

In the present chapter, we examine how psychologists have defined and assessed logical reasoning in participants who *lack* training and background knowledge in formal logic. We then discuss the role of everyday background knowledge in interpreting logical tasks, including how background knowledge might influence the interpretation of rules and statements, and in drawing inferences. Finally, we conclude by discussing the theoretical and applied consequences of evaluating logical reasoning without taking into account background knowledge. Although our discussion will borrow primarily from studies of deductive reasoning and hypothesis testing, the conclusions we draw in the end can be applied to any study of reasoning – inductive, probabilistic, analogical – that fails to take into account the raw material with which reasoners approach cognitive tasks – background knowledge. But first, we discuss why knowledge should even be considered in the assessment of reasoning.

BACKGROUND KNOWLEDGE AND THE INTERPRETATION OF LOGICAL REASONING TASKS

Although some forms of reasoning, and by extension some reasoning tasks, might be seen as impermeable to background knowledge (e.g., deductive reasoning because the conclusions derived from deductive tasks follow necessarily or do not follow at all from the structure of the premises, irrespective of the content of the premises), they turn out to be more permeable than we might think. Reasoning is permeable to background knowledge insofar as reasoners must interpret or make sense of the information presented in reasoning tasks (Fillenbaum, 1993; see Henle, 1962). The act of making sense of a task or the information presented therein involves reconciling the requirements of the task with what one knows.

To say that reasoners interpret or make sense of a task is deliberate and needs to be distinguished from the idea that reasoners comprehend the task. Norris and Phillips (1994) explain this distinction in the context of reading. When a person reads a text and, following reading, assigns a meaning to the text, the meaning assigned may or may not coincide with the meaning intended by the author or the meaning agreed upon by others (e.g., a community of scholars). If the reader's assigned meaning coincides with the meaning intended by the author or agreed upon by others, then the reader is typically said to have comprehended the text (Norris & Phillips, 1994). In contrast, if the reader's assigned meaning does not coincide with the meaning intended by the author or the canonical meaning others have imposed on the text, then the reader is typically said to have interpreted the text. Although in both of these cases – comprehending and interpreting – the reader must make sense of the text, the distinction between comprehending and interpreting serves to underscore the importance of background knowledge. In order to comprehend a text, the reader is likely to have specific knowledge about the author's intentions or motives at the time of writing the text, including possibly the historical and sociological events of the time. In contrast, to interpret a text, the reader need not have specific knowledge about the author's intentions; to interpret a text, the reader must simply bring to bear some knowledge (whatever that might be) that he or she deems relevant to making sense of the text.

In the course of our discussion, we will use the term *interpretation* instead of comprehension to refer to how reasoners, who are naive about formal, propositional logic, make sense of reasoning tasks. It would not be sensible to assume otherwise; that is, to assume that reasoners who lack training in formal logic might comprehend a logical reasoning task in a way similar to the way a logician might make sense of it. A basic difference between a logician and a novice is the training a logician receives so as to comprehend material in his or her domain of expertise. Of course, if the reasoner has any training in formal logic, then it is much more likely that the reasoner will comprehend the task as a logical task and assign a meaning to the task that coincides with the meaning endorsed by logicians. In such a case, assessing the reasoner's skill would become an exercise in determining whether he or she has applied properly the procedures of formal logic. However, if the reasoner has no training in formal logic, then it is an open question as to how he or she has interpreted the task, and the evaluation of his or her reasoning depends on the specific knowledge the reasoner has deemed relevant for making sense of the task. It is at this point that the untrained reasoner's background knowledge becomes necessary to evaluating the adequacy of his or her reasoning skill; the conclusion or product of reasoning must be judged in relation to the knowledge made relevant by the reasoner for the purpose of solving a task in a specific context (Norris, 1988; Norris & Phillips, 1994).

From another perspective, considering reasoners' background knowledge in the assessment of reasoning is strongly recommended by the Standards for Educational and Psychological Testing (1999). These standards suggest that drawing judgments about students' performance without collecting evidence of the thoughts and strategies (background knowledge) students employ when solving the task can compromise the veracity of the judgments made about their performance. In addition, assessing skills generally without giving students the opportunity to learn the skills being tested is considered an unfair testing practice.

The Standards for Educational and Psychological Testing (1999) were created in part to provide criteria "for the evaluation of tests, testing practices, and the effects of test use" (p.2). Although the findings from psychological investigations of reasoning are not used to make life-changing decisions about participants (e.g., to decide whether participants will gain entrance into educational or professional programs), the results from basic psychological research are used to build theories of reasoning. If the theories fail to include important background variables, these omissions can have serious consequences, especially if nonpsychologists choose to use these theories for applied purposes. For instance, there is a strong movement in the educational measurement community to use psychological theories to inform the development of standardized test items that measure higher-level thinking skills (e.g., Pellegrino, Baxter, & Glaser, 1999). Results from standardized tests, including "high stakes" tests such as the Scholastic Assessment Test (SAT), are often used to make life-changing decisions about students' educational opportunities (Phelps, 1998). If psychological theories represent an incomplete description of human reasoning, the consequences of this description might lead to the inadequate development, evaluation, and use of educational tests.

In a field of study that parallels closely the psychological assessment of reasoning – the educational measurement of critical thinking (Ennis, 1993; Ennis & Norris, 1991; Norris, 1988) – the importance of background knowledge has been recognized for some time. For instance, Ennis and Norris (1990) write:

Knowledge of a topic is at least very helpful, often necessary, for thinking about the topic. This feature seems quite acceptable and implies that students who are unfamiliar with a topic, whether it be a school subject or not, will have difficulty in a test that calls for thinking about the topic. (p. 20)

Although general principles and strategies are also recognized elements of critical thinking (Ennis & Norris, 1991; Nickerson, 1988; Sternberg, 1987), background knowledge is considered essential in coordinating the application of principles and strategies (Norris, 1988; Sternberg, 1987).

In fact, some multiple-choice tests of critical thinking (e.g., Cornell Critical Thinking Test, Level 10) have been criticized for not requiring students to state the background assumptions behind their judgments (Ennis & Norris, 1991). Norris (1988) maintains that if a student activates specific background assumptions (that are distinct from the ones made by the test developers) to draw a conclusion to an item, it is plausible for the student to generate a correct answer from the assumptions considered, but an incorrect answer with respect to the "keyed" answer. The student's answer is marked incorrect despite the correctness of his or her reasoning skill because the background assumptions he or she considered in answering the item are different from the ones considered by the test developers when creating the item (Ennis & Norris, 1991; Norris, 1988). Hence, in order to assess reasoning skills accurately, the background assumptions students consider when responding to test items need to be taken into account. Despite the recognition of background knowledge in critical thinking, it is often disregarded in psychological investigations of logical reasoning. Even definitions of logical reasoning fail to mention the importance of background knowledge.

DEFINING LOGICAL REASONING

In their book entitled *Deductive Reasoning and Strategies*, Schaeken, Vooght, Vandierendonck, and d'Ydewalle (2000) define deductive reasoning as goal-directed reasoning that begins with a definite starting point (the premises), and leads to conclusions that follow necessarily from the premises (based on the principles of formal logic). Successful deductive reasoning is also associated with specific processes such as searching for multiple mental models of counterexamples to a set of premises (Johnson-Laird, 1999) or applying mental rules to a set of premises (Rips, 1994). Background knowledge is normally not included in these descriptions of "successful reasoning."

Johnson-Laird and Byrne (1991), in their influential book *Deduction*, stated "A world without deduction would be a world without science, technology, laws, social conventions, and culture " (p. 5). This is indeed true, but reasoning deductively (and successfully) about science, technology, laws, and social conventions, and culture would be truly challenging in the absence of background knowledge about these specific domains. At the minimum, background knowledge is needed to select relevant information; that is, to select the relevant set of premises from which one should start reasoning. Scientists, engineers, and other professionals are identified not only according to the skills they manifest within their domain of expertise but also according to the background knowledge they have accumulated within that domain (Charness & Schultetus, 1999).

To be sure, some investigators have recognized the interplay of knowledge, context, and performance and have proposed domain-specific reasoning algorithms (Cheng & Holyoak, 1985, 1989; Cosmides, 1989; Cosmides & Tooby, 1996; Gigerenzer & Hug, 1992; Koslowski, 1996). These algorithms, learned inductively from contact with the social environment, are invoked to facilitate logical reasoning in specific domains (Cheng & Holyoak, 1985; Cosmides, 1989; Cosmides & Tooby, 1996). Domain-specific algorithms (e.g., permission schema and social contract algorithms) are invoked in contexts where committing reasoning errors is costly such as in contexts where permissions and obligation are specified (e.g., Cheng & Holyoak, 1985) or in contexts where contracts are negotiated and hence a mistake could be costly to the reasoner (e.g., Cosmides, 1989). In addition, some studies have examined how general beliefs influence the evaluation of conclusions (e.g., Evans & Manktelow, 1993).

Notwithstanding studies of domain-specific algorithms, there are almost no psychological studies that focus specifically on the role that background knowledge plays in how premises, conclusions, and logical tasks are interpreted (Liberman & Klar, 1996). Many investigators have suggested that background knowledge is extraneous to the study of logical reasoning because logical/deductive skills apply to the form of premises and not to their content (Braine, 1978; O'Brien, 1993; Rips, 1994, 1995). Even theories that focus on the meaning that assertions have for individuals advance reasoning algorithms that are applied independently of knowledge (e.g., Johnson-Laird, 1999; Johnson-Laird & Byrne, 1991). In short, reasoning in psychology is largely associated with the process of drawing conclusions from evidence and it is largely assumed to operate independently of knowledge. Such a delimited definition is reflected in the psychological assessment of logical reasoning.

THE TASK OF ASSESSING LOGICAL REASONING

The assessment of logical reasoning mirrors the way in which it has been defined. Psychologists have generally used reasoning tasks that are simple to administer but lack considerable context for participants. Thereby complicating and even obscuring the decision of what background knowledge to use to solve the task. Given that studies of deductive reasoning, for example, are assumed to provide a window to how untrained participants might reason in daily life (Galotti, 1989), the failure to use meaningful tasks that exploit reasoners' background knowledge is a noteworthy omission and calls into the question the ecological validity of the findings. Participants must nevertheless interpret these contextually sparse tasks using their background knowledge, but it is unclear how they interpret them (see Chapter 5 of this book for a more detailed discussion of the ways in which reasoners might interpret logical tasks).

Three well-known logic tasks used in psychological studies include categorical syllogisms, conditional syllogisms, and Wason's selection task (Wason, 1966). It is possible that because these tasks are easily available to psychologists and are easily used within experimental laboratory settings, they have supported and even bred a highly circumscribed definition of logical reasoning that excludes background knowledge. The relationship between how a phenomenon is defined and measured is probably one of mutual influence. In what follows, each task is described.

Categorical Syllogisms

One of the three standard tasks used to assess logical reasoning includes *categorical syllogisms* (Evans et al., 1993; Sternberg & Ben-Zeev, 2001). Categorical syllogisms consist of two quantified premises and a quantified conclusion. The premises reflect an implicit relation between a subject (S) and a predicate (P) via a middle term (M), while the conclusion reflects the relation between the *subject* and *predicate* explicitly as follows:

All M are P.
All S are M.

Therefore, All S are P.

Both the premises and the conclusion are normally structured in one of four *moods*. The moods are identified with the letters A (i.e., all A are B), I (i.e., some A are B), E (i.e., No A are B), and O (i.e., some A are not B).

Another feature of the categorical syllogism is that its premises and conclusion must be organized in one of four figures. A figure characterizes the location of the subject, predicate, and middle term. Figure 11.1 shows the four traditional figures of a syllogism. Given that a categorical syllogism must be in one of four figures and that its premises and conclusion must each be in one of four moods, 256 different syllogisms can be created (i.e., $4 \times 4 \times 4 \times 4 = 256$). Of these 256 syllogisms, only 24 are considered logically valid. The logical validity of these 24 syllogisms may be proven

(1)	(2)	(3)	(4)
M-P	P-M	M-P	P-M
S-M	S-M	M-S	M-S
S-P	S-P	S-P	S-P

FIGURE 11.1. The Four Traditional Figures of the Categorical Syllogism.

using either proof-theoretic methods or, more commonly, a model-theoretic method, in which a valid syllogism is one whose premises cannot be true without its conclusion also being true (Garnham & Oakhill, 1994). Reasoning studies employing categorical syllogisms normally use either abstract or thematic syllogisms. In abstract syllogisms, letters are used to represent the subject, predicate, and middle terms (e.g., all A are B), whereas in thematic categorical syllogisms, nouns or other ostensibly meaningful terms (e.g., all cooks are painters) are used. When categorical syllogisms are used to assess reasoning, participants are required to generate a conclusion to a set of premises, judge whether a presented conclusion follows from a set of premises, or choose the conclusion that best follows from a set of premises from a list of alternatives.

Although participants are able to endorse or draw correct conclusions in response to some categorical syllogisms under some conditions (Ceraso & Provitera, 1971; Johnson-Laird & Bara, 1984), they still commit systematic errors. Despite the errors, many investigators reject the idea that human reasoning is inherently faulty (Evans et al., 1993; Henle, 1962). Instead, many investigators speculate that participants can reason logically if they interpret the premises logically without allowing everyday knowledge to obstruct their interpretations (Begg & Harris, 1982; Ceraso & Provitera, 1971; Henle, 1962; Johnson-Laird & Byrne, 1991; Revlin & Leirer, 1978; and Revlin, Leirer, Yopp, & Yopp, 1980; Rips, 1994, 1995).

The errors participants commit when reasoning about abstract and thematic categorical syllogisms are systematic and suggest the existence of fairly stable background assumptions that are continually brought to bear to the task (Begg & Denny, 1969; Ceraso & Provitera, 1971; see Evans et al., 1993 for a review; Johnson-Laird, 1999; Johnson-Laird & Bara, 1984; Johnson-Laird & Byrne, 1991; Sternberg & Ben-Zeev, 2001). For example, participants typically endorse or draw conclusions that match the atmosphere of the syllogism's premises (i.e., draw conclusions that match the surface features of the premises), irrespective of whether the conclusion necessarily follows (Begg & Denny, 1969; Woodworth & Sells, 1935). Studies have also shown that participants are more likely to respond in accord with the atmosphere of the premises when this response follows necessarily from the premises (e.g., Ceraso & Provitera, 1971), and when participants are asked to draw conclusions that fit the syntax of the categorical syllogism. Interestingly, when participants are asked to state the conclusion that follows from a pair of premises in their own words, they frequently respond that nothing follows (Johnson-Laird & Bara, 1984). To state that nothing follows is the proper conclusion to draw to logically invalid syllogisms. However, when this conclusion is drawn in response to valid syllogisms, it suggests that participants are not interpreting the quantifiers normatively (i.e., they are not comprehending the task).

That participants are not interpreting the quantifiers normatively is not surprising given that they lack training in formal logic (Evans et al., 1993). Investigations of how participants interpret quantifiers suggest that they interpret logical quantifiers according to everyday linguistic principles (see Chapter 9 of this volume for a detailed description of participants' interpretation of quantifiers). Participants divide quantifiers typically into three distinct categories: none, some but not all, and all (Begg & Harris, 1982). According to Begg and Harris (1982), participants interpret the quantifier "no" as complete exclusion, the quantifiers "some" and "some not" as some but not all, and the quantifier "all" as complete distribution (see also Newstead, 1989).

In addition, Greene (1992) makes the point that participants may fail to generate proper conclusions to valid syllogisms because the quantifiers reflected in these conclusions represent unconventional linguistic constructions in everyday speech. For example, Greene (1992) suggests that the conclusion to the following valid syllogism (taken from Johnson-Laird, Byrne, & Tabossi, 1989) is uncommon is everyday speech and, hence, difficult for participants to generate:

None of the X are related to any of the Y.
All of the Y are related to some of the Z.

Therefore, *none* of the X are related to *some* of the Z.

In a study to determine whether participants were less likely to generate "none-some" sentences compared to "non-any" sentences, Greene (1992) showed 40 participants a series of diagrams illustrating relations between sets of objects. Below each diagram were a series of quantified sentences describing the relation shown in the diagram. Participants were asked to select from the sentences below each diagram, all those that could be used to describe the diagram. Although the construction "none-some" was consistent with four times as many diagrams as the construction "none-any," only 17 participants selected the "none-some" construction for any of the diagrams, with many more participants selecting the "none-any" construction.

One interpretation of these studies (e.g., Begg & Harris, 1982; Greene, 1992) is that everyday knowledge obstructs logical or deductive reasoning because everyday linguistic principles lead participants to misunderstand logical statements (e.g., Braine, 1978; Braine & O'Brien, 1991; see also Henle, 1962; Newstead, 1989). But if participants do not have knowledge of formal logic, what other knowledge will they use to solve deductive tasks except their everyday knowledge? It would not be sensible to say that background knowledge obstructs logical reasoning when untrained reasoners have only their everyday background knowledge to use when faced with solving an unfamiliar deductive task. Hence, untrained participants have little choice but to use their everyday background knowledge to solve categorical syllogisms. Therefore, an assessment of their logical reasoning on categorical syllogisms should take into account the everyday background assumptions they have selected as relevant to respond to the task.

Findings of *belief-bias* provide an interesting illustration of the pragmatic value of background knowledge in reasoning (see Evan and Feeney's Chapter 4 in this volume for a complete account of belief bias). Belief-bias is the tendency for participants to reject unbelievable conclusions to categorical syllogisms and to accept believable conclusions, irrespective of whether the conclusions follow necessarily from the premises (Evans, Barston, & Pollard, 1983; Janis & Frick, 1943; Lefford, 1946; Newstead, Pollard, Evans, & Allen, 1993; Oakhill & Garnham, 1993; Oakhill & Johnson-Laird, 1985; Oakhill, Johnson-Laird, & Garnham, 1993). Findings of belief-bias are robust. For example, across three experiments conducted by Evans et al. (1983), an average of 10% of participants accepted invalid conclusions to unbelievable syllogisms but an average of 71% of participants accepted invalid conclusions to believable syllogisms. An example of a believable but invalid categorical syllogism is shown below (taken from Newstead et al., 1992):

All police dogs are vicious dogs.
No vicious dogs are highly trained.

Therefore, All police dogs are highly trained.

Although the conclusion to the premises is believable, it does not follow necessarily from the premises. Some investigators have suggested that participants who exhibit belief-bias ignore the instructions of the task by basing their responses on belief rather than logical necessity (e.g., Evans, Barston, & Pollard, 1983). Alternatively, the believability of the conclusion is assumed to foreclose a participant's "reasoning space," leading him or her to accept the conclusion without an exhaustive search for alternative conclusions (Newstead et al., 1992; see Ormerod, 2000).

Using prior beliefs to solve categorical syllogisms is considered undesirable because, in principle, syllogisms must be solved using only the information provided in the premises – background knowledge is not needed. Background knowledge is thought to obstruct the inferential process by altering the way the premises are interpreted, that is, by making logically unnecessary conclusions appear necessary. However, if untrained participants do not use their everyday beliefs to reason about categorical syllogisms, what beliefs are they to use if they lack training in formal logic?

Belief-bias may not be a bias after all (Evans, 2000; Evan & Manktelow, 1993). Invoking prior beliefs, which are well established and have some empirical support (e.g., police dogs are indeed highly trained dogs), is essential when reasoning in everyday situations. In support, Evans (2000) suggests that pragmatic or *adaptive rationality* for reasoning in informal and everyday domains needs to be distinguished from *normative rationality* for reasoning in formal (i.e., logical and mathematical) domains (see also Anderson, 1990). He suggests that "normative theories such as logic and decision theory may not provide appropriate criteria for rational action in a complex world of poorly defined information. . . ." (p. 3). Although using prior beliefs to reason about logical/deductive problems may lead to reasoning errors and biases according to normative criteria, Evans and Over (1996) suggest that it is adaptive to reason from all relevant belief in everyday situations. Consequently, the rationality of untrained participants who use their everyday background knowledge to solve formal logic tasks needs to be evaluated according to adaptive criteria; that is, the adequacy of participants' conclusions must be evaluated in relation to the background assumptions they have invoked to solve the task, and not normative criteria.

Conditional Syllogisms

Abstract and thematic conditional syllogisms have also been used to assess logical reasoning (Evans et al., 1993; Sternberg & Ben-Zeev, 2001). A conditional syllogism consists of two premises and a conclusion. The first premise involves a conditional rule of the form *if p → q*, where *p*, the antecedent, and *q*, the consequent, represent propositions. The second premise conveys information about one of the propositions (or its negation) represented in the conditional rule as follows:

if P → Q (e.g., if Mary goes to the market, then it is Friday)

P (e.g., Mary goes to the market)

The conclusion that is inferred from the conditional syllogism involves the proposition not mentioned in the second premise as follows:

Q (e.g., then it is Friday).

The conclusion of this conditional syllogism (then it is Friday) represents the logically valid inference known as modus ponens (MP). If the second premise in our example had been "It is not Friday" or *not-q* then another logically valid inference labeled modus tollens (MT) could have been drawn. The MT inference would lead us to conclude that "Mary does not go to the market" or *not-p*. Two additional, but fallacious, inferences are normally associated with the conditional syllogism: denial of the antecedent (DA) and affirmation of the consequent (AC). These inferences take the following form:

Denial of the Antecedent:	Affirming the Consequent:
if $p \rightarrow q$; *not-p*	*if* $p \rightarrow q$; q
$\therefore$ not-Q	$\therefore$ P

When conditional syllogisms are used to assess reasoning, participants are presented with a series of partially complete syllogisms and asked to either generate a conclusion to each syllogism or choose from a list of alternatives the necessary conclusion to each syllogism. Alternatively, participants are presented with a set of complete syllogisms and asked to indicate whether they accept or reject the conclusion to each syllogism.

What have psychologists inferred about human logical reasoning from participants' responses to conditional syllogisms? In the absence of any thematic context, investigators have found that participants normally draw the fallacious inferences, DA and AC (Braine, 1978; Braine & O'Brien, 1991; Johnson-Laird & Byrne, 1991; Taplin, 1971). A common explanation for these errors is that participants interpret the conditional rule, mistakenly, as a biconditional rule. Conditional rules are easily "misinterpreted" as biconditionals (Fillenbaum, 1975) because conditional constructions in everyday speech often evoke biconditional interpretations (Fillenbaum, 1975; Grice 1975). Consider an everyday promise, "If the lawn is mowed, then you will receive ten dollars." In everyday speech, the converse of the rule is likely to be assumed (i.e., if the lawn is not mowed, then you will not receive ten dollars), thus lending itself to a biconditional interpretation (see Grice, 1975 for a detailed discussion of conversational maxims). When the conditional rule is interpreted as a biconditional rule, the inferences DA and AC are no longer fallacious (Legrenzi, 1969; Taplin & Staudenmayer, 1973).

Although participants endorse fallacious inferences in response to conditional syllogisms, they also endorse the logically valid inferences, MP, and to a lesser extent MT (Braine, 1978; Rips, 1994). The ease with which MP inferences are made has led some investigators to propose that human beings possess logical reasoning rules (e.g., Braine, 1978, Rips, 1994). However, if human beings do possess logical reasoning rules, the application of these rules can be easily blocked. In the presence of thematic context, participants can be induced to withhold drawing logically valid inferences (Byrne, 1989; Cummins et al., 1991; Cummins, 1995; Staudenmayer, 1975). For example, Cummins et al. (1991) demonstrated that participants endorsed few MP and MT inferences when they were presented with causal conditional rules that suggested the antecedent was unnecessary for bringing about the consequent (e.g., if I eat candy often, then I get cavities) (Cummins et al., 1991). In contrast, participants endorsed many MP and MT inferences when they were presented with causal conditional rules that suggested the antecedent was necessary for the occurrence of the consequent (e.g., If my finger is cut, then it bleeds) (Cummins et al., 1991). Depending on the specific context employed, logically valid and invalid inferences could be induced or suppressed (see also Byrne, 1989, 1991).

The findings obtained by Cummins et al. (1991) and Byrne (1989, 1991) suggest that participants are highly sensitive to the contextual circumstances of conditional syllogisms and less sensitive to their strict "logical" requirements (whether an inference is logically admissible or not). Given participants' lack of training in logic, it stands to reason that if they are sensitive to any variable in the task, they will be most sensitive to the thematic context of the syllogism – the only task variable that they can exploit for clues about the relevant background knowledge to use in reasoning about the syllogism. Although the inferences participants draw on thematic conditional syllogisms can be logically valid, this occurrence is likely to be observed when the inference also "makes sense" within the specific thematic context of the task. Hence, the conclusions participant draw to conditional syllogisms must be evaluated by considering the background assumptions *they have selected as relevant* to solving the syllogisms. Although evaluating conclusions in this way might not correspond to normative criteria, the rationality or sensibility of the conclusion can nonetheless be evaluated for its cohesiveness with the background assumptions invoked to solve the task (Thagard, 1989).

Wason's Selection Task

The finding that participants make inferences more in line with what "makes sense" in a given context and less in line with what is strictly logical is confirmed in studies of Wason's selection task (Wason, 1966). This task has been intensively studied in the psychological literature partly for its simplicity and partly because it elicits consistently poor performance from participants (Evans et al., 1993). In its standard abstract form, the task consists of presenting a participant with an abstract conditional rule; *If there is a vowel on one side of the card, then there is an even number on the other side*, and four cards displaying instances of a *vowel* (i.e., *p*), a *consonant* (i.e, *not-p*), an *even number* (i.e., *q*), and an *odd number* (i.e., *not-q*). Figure 11.2 illustrates how the four cards may be positioned in front of participants. Although participants see only one side of each card, they are told that the flip side of each card contains information about another category. For example, a 4 or 7 might be found on the flip side of the A card, and an A or K might be found on the flip side of the 4 card. Participants are then instructed to test the truth or falsity of the rule by selecting the fewest possible cards from the set of four.

According to formal logic proofs, only a pairing of the antecedent (i.e., the "A" in this case) with a negation of the consequent (i.e., the "7" in this

Conditional Rule: If there is a vowel on one side of the card, then there is an even number on the other side of the card.

FIGURE 11.2. Example of the Wason Selection Task.

case) can falsify and, therefore, test the truth or falsity of the conditional rule (Garnham & Oakhill, 1994). As a result, the A card should be turned over in case there is a 7 on its flip side, as well as the 7 card in case there is an A on its flip side; neither the K nor the 4 needs to be selected because they cannot falsify the rule. For example, even if card 4 were paired with a K, it does not falsify the rule because the conditional rule does not exclude the possibility of an even number following a consonant.

Wason's task appears to be a simple problem, but this simplicity is deceptive. Participants invariably and overwhelmingly get it wrong (for a review see Evans et al., 1993). For instance, an average of only 10% of participants select the correct cards. In contrast, an average of 90% of participants make either incomplete selections by choosing only the A card or incorrect selections by choosing the A card along with the 4 card. Again, the participants who are tested on this task do not have training in logic or in formal methods of hypothesis testing. Nonetheless, their performance is judged against a normative standard that assumes a strictly logical or formal interpretation of the conditional rule, the evidence (cards), and the task as a whole. Given that the majority of participants who are tested on this task make logically incorrect selections, it does not appear that they are *interpreting* the task normatively (Liberman & Klar, 1996).

Given their lack of training in formal logic, it is not surprising that participants do not assign a formal interpretation to the task. In fact, Leighton (1999) found that participants tended to assume the truth of the conditional rule before they even began to select evidence to test the rule. In addition, participants assumed that the rule could be tested conclusively with positive instances. For instance, many participants commented that the p card could be used to test the rule (because *not-q* might be found on the other side) and that the q card could also be used to test the rule (because *not-p* might be found on the other side).

Peter Wason (1966, 1983) accounted for the tendency to test the rule with positive instance or as he termed it, "verification bias," by concluding people possessed faulty reasoning processes. In Wason's opinion, little else could justify participants' overwhelming bias to test a conditional rule with confirming evidence instead of falsifying evidence. Other investigators (e.g., Cox & Griggs, 1983; Evans, 1989; Evans & Lynch, 1973; Manktelow & Evans, 1979) did not necessarily agree with Wason's (1983) assessment and proposed other accounts of participants' performance. These investigators suggested that instead of confirming the rule with their selection of cards, participants were attempting to *match* their card selections to the propositions reflected in the rule. These investigators argued that if participants were operating under a verification or confirmation bias, then given a conditional such as "*if p → not-q*," participants should test the rule by selecting the cards "*p*" and "*not-q*."

In studies where the conditional rule was manipulated to include all possible valence combinations (i.e., *if p → q, if not-p → q, if p → not-q*, and if *not-p → not-q*), Manktelow and Evans (1979) found that participants displayed a significant tendency to match their card selections to the topics or propositions of the rule (regardless of a negation) and not to verify the propositions in the rule. For instance, given the rule "*if p → not-q*," participants tested this rule by selecting the cards *p* and *q* suggesting a tendency to match their card selections to the topic of the rule rather than to verify the rule (which would have led to the selection of *p* and *not-q* cards) (Evans et al., 1993).

In contrast to abstract versions of the task, thematic versions of the task commonly elicit from participants what appears to be normatively correct performance. For example, given a thematic version of the rule, *if drinking beer → over 21 years of age*, along with the instructions to select those cards that violate the rule, participants are much more inclined to respond to the task by selecting the cards *drinking beer* (i.e., *p*) and *under 21 years of age* (i.e., *not-q*) (Evans et al., 1993). Indeed, depending on the specific thematic context used, some investigators report that up to 78% of participants select the logically correct cards in response to the task (e.g., Cosmides, 1989). Wason (1983) and other investigators (Griggs, 1983; O'Brien, 1993) have argued, however, that most thematic versions of the task do not measure logical reasoning but instead measure something else, perhaps memory of a situation similar to that described in the task.

Findings do seem to support Wason (1983) and his supporters on this point. Research results indicate that participants are more inclined to test thematic conditional rules with evidence that makes sense given the context of the rule than with evidence that is normatively correct but makes little sense given the context (Gigerenzer & Hug, 1992; Manktelow, Fairley, Kilpatrick, & Over, 2000; Maktelow & Over, 1991). If participants' card selections change as a result of contextual changes to the thematic rule, then it supports the notion that thematic tasks are not necessarily eliciting formal logical reasoning. For example, Manktelow and Over (1991) examined how an individual's perspective influenced reasoning on the selection task. These investigators gave participants the following conditional rule:

If you tidy your room, then you may go out to play.

The above rule, which was presented as coming from a mother to her son, was shown to participants along with four cards. Each card had a record on one side of whether the boy had tidied his room and, on the other, whether the boy had gone out to play, as follows: room tidied (p), room not tidied (*not-p*), went out to play (q), or did not go out to play (*not-q*). Participants were then asked to detect possible violations of the rule from either the mother's perspective or from the son's perspective. Participants who were asked to assume the son's perspective selected the "room tidied" (p) and "did not go out to play" (*not-q*) cards most frequently as instances of possible violations of the rule. These instances correspond to the normative solution. Participants who were asked to assume the mother's perspective, however, selected the "room not tidied" (*not-p*) and "went out to play" (q) cards most frequently as instances of possible violations – the mirror image of the normative solution. From these responses, participants appeared to be more sensitive to the evidence that made sense given the context (their assumed perspective) of the task and less by the evidence that satisfied a logically correct response (e.g., Gigerenzer & Hug, 1992; Light, Girotto, & Legrenzi, 1990).

I have presented three tasks that are commonly used to assess logical reasoning in psychology. The tasks share two main characteristics: First, the tasks are structurally simple insofar as they do not require a significant amount of reading or writing. Second, the tasks are laboratory tasks that are not highly representative of everyday tasks. Nevertheless, these tasks appeal to investigators because they are self-contained – they supposedly contain all the necessary information required for participants to generate a solution. Participants are not expected to search their background knowledge for a solution and, hence, investigators are not expected to control for differences in participants' prior knowledge because it is not expected to influence task performance. The use of these laboratory tasks is assumed to allow investigators to exercise control over background knowledge, thereby making inferences about human reasoning abilities easier to draw but perhaps less ecologically valid.

Critics have charged that using categorical and conditional syllogisms, in addition to Wason's task, to assess logical reasoning underestimates and grossly simplifies human reasoning (Galotti, 1989; Sternberg, 1985). One critique is that these tasks measure the reasoning process as if the process could be isolated from variables such as background knowledge, motivation, and emotion that are known to influence thinking (Cosmides

& Tooby, 1996; Evans & Manktelow, 1993; Harman, 1986). However, instead of focusing on the tasks themselves, we might redirect our attention to how logical reasoning is defined. When logical reasoning is defined as the process of drawing conclusions from principles and from evidence (Wason & Johnson-Laird, 1972) without mention of background knowledge, such a circumscribed definition serves and is served by a highly controlled assessment of reasoning; an assessment that focuses strictly on participants' ability to draw inferences from available evidence on laboratory tasks that are unrepresentative of everyday tasks and problems. If the participants tested on these tasks had training in formal logic, then perhaps the use of these tasks and their criteria for correct performance would be less controversial. But the participants tested on these tasks are not trained in formal logic, so these tasks and the findings associated with them are contentious.

CONCLUSION AND DISCUSSION

In the Standards for Educational and Psychological Testing (Standards, 1999), standard 1.8 reads as follows:

> If the rationale for a test use or score interpretation depends on premises about the psychological processes or cognitive operations used by examinees, then theoretical or empirical evidence in support of those premises should be provided. (p. 19)

This standard suggests that before we draw judgments about task performance, we need to collect evidence of the thoughts and strategies participants employ when solving the task – in order to verify that what we think participants are doing is in fact what they are doing. This standard would suggest that before concluding that participants have reasoned incorrectly on a task, the background knowledge they used to solve the task should be taken into consideration. If the background knowledge a participant uses on a reasoning task supports the conclusion he or she has generated, then the soundness of his or her reasoning process should be reevaluated and recognized (Norris, 1988), even if it does not correspond to the background knowledge the investigator expected the participant to use.

In the Standards for Educational and Psychological Testing (Standards, 1999), it is also suggested that individuals who are given a test should have had the opportunity to learn the subject matter of the test. This standard has implications for the assessment of reasoning in psychology. When untrained participants are tested on formal logic tasks, it might be unrealistic to judge their performance against normative criteria. Untrained participants will likely not use normative knowledge (or models) to reason because they have not had the opportunity to learn this knowledge; participants will reason about these tasks using everyday assumptions and beliefs.

Thinking critically about how reasoning is assessed in psychological experiments is imperative, but not because it is high stakes testing. The participants who are tested in psychological reasoning experiments are not depending on the results from these experiments to win admittance to prestigious programs or schools (as is the case with some high-stakes educational tests such as the SAT and GRE). Students will not be denied entrance to a professional program because they failed to make the correct selections to Wason's selection task. Nevertheless, establishing the correctness or appropriateness of psychological procedures and tasks used to assess reasoning is imperative because the findings from psychological studies are used to develop theories of human reasoning. These theories form a body of knowledge within a discipline that can be taken as truth and used inappropriately by nonpsychologists – for example, by test developers to create new educational tests. The application of psychological findings to build (and scrutinize) educational tests that measure higher-level reasoning and problem solving is becoming more customary among educational researchers (e.g., Embretson, 1999; Katz, Bennet, & Berger, 2000; Mislevy, 1996). Psychological theories are taken as "truth" and applied for practical purposes. Rom Harre (1986) has suggested that "a scientific observation statement is to be thought of as prefaced by 'Trust me', or 'You can take my word for it' " (p. 165). Psychologists must be very careful in how they test and develop their theories because psychological theories, as scientific statements, can have immense power on how lay individuals come to think of social and cognitive phenomena. Consequently, questioning the appropriateness of the methods (i.e., reasoning tasks, procedures, and participants) used to develop psychological theories of reasoning is imperative to building more accurate theories of how human beings reason.

In the book, *The Right to Be Intelligent*, Machado (1980) writes, "Every man is born with a live computer of limitless possibilities, but without the instruction manual. The most important job of science today is to draw up that manual." It seems that in writing the manual of how we think, background knowledge must be one of the chapters. Recognizing the role of background knowledge may lead to messier experimental designs and less control by investigators but will ultimately lead to more accurate and possibly more useful theories of human reasoning than if it is neglected or not fully incorporated.

References

American Educational Research Association (AERA), American Psychological Association (APA), & National Council on Measurement in Education (NCME). (1999). *Standards for educational and psychological testing*. Washington, DC: Author.

Anderson, J. R. (1990). *The adaptive character of thought*. Hillsdale, NJ: Erlbaum.

Begg, I., & Denny, P. (1969). Empirical reconciliation of atmosphere and conversion interpretations of syllogistic reasoning errors. *Journal of Experimental Psychology, 81*, 351–354.

Begg, I., & Harris, G. (1982). On the interpretation of syllogisms. *Journal of Verbal Learning and Verbal Behavior, 21*, 595–620.

Braine, M. D. S. (1978). On the relation between the natural logic of reasoning and standard logic. *Psychological Review, 85*, 1–21.

Braine, M. D. S., & O'Brien, D. P. (1991). A theory of *if*: A lexical entry, reasoning program, and pragmatic principles. *Psychological Review, 98*, 182–203.

Braine, M. D. S., & O'Brien, D. P. (1998). The theory of mental-propositional logic: Description and illustration. In M. D. S. Braine & D. P. O'Brien (Eds.), *Mental logic* (pp. 79–89). Mahwah, NJ: Erlbaum.

Byrne, R. M. J. (1989). Suppressing valid inferences with conditionals. *Cognition, 31*, 61–83.

Ceraso, J., & Provitera, A. (1971). Sources of error in syllogistic reasoning. *Cognitive Psychology, 2*, 400–410.

Charness, N., & Schultetus, R. S. (1999). Knowledge and expertise. In F. T. Durso, R. S. Nickerson, R. W. Schvaneveldt, S. T. Dumais, D. S. Lindsay, & M. Chi (Eds.), *Handbook of applied cognition* (pp. 57–81). New York: Wiley.

Cheng, P. W., & Holyoak, K. J. (1985). Pragmatic reasoning schemas. *Cognitive Psychology, 17*, 391–416.

Cheng, P. W., & Holyoak, K. J. (1989). On the natural selection of reasoning theories. *Cognition, 33*, 285–313.

Cosmides, L. (1989). The logic of social exchange: Has natural selection shaped how human reason? Studies with the Wason selection task. *Cognition, 31*, 187–276.

Cosmides, L., & Tooby, J. (1996). Are humans good intuitive statisticians after all? Rethinking some conclusions from the literature on judgement under uncertainty. *Cognition, 58*, 1–73.

Costa, A. L. (1984). Thinking: How do we know students are getting better at it? *Roeper Review, 6*, 197–199.

Cummins, D. D. (1995). Naïve theories and causal deduction. *Memory & Cognition, 23*, 646–658.

Cummins, D. D., Lubart, T., Alksnis, O., & Rist, R. (1991). Conditional reasoning and causation. *Memory & Cognition, 19*, 274–282.

Ennis, R. H. (1993). *Critical thinking assessment. Theory Into Practice, 32*, 179–186.

Ennis, R. H., & Norris, S. P. (1990). Critical thinking assessment, status, issues, needs. In S. Legg & J. Algina (Eds.), *Cognitive assessment of language and math outcomes: Vol. 36. Advances in Discourse Processes* (R. O. Freedle, Ed.). Norwood, NJ: Ablex.

Evans, J. St. B. T. (2000). What could and could not be a strategy in reasoning. In W. Schaeken, G. de Vooght, A. Vandierendonck, A. & G. d'Ydewalle, (Eds.). *Deductive reasoning and strategies*. Mahwah, NJ: Erlbaum.

Evans, J. St. B. T., Barston, J. L., & Pollard, P. (1983). On the conflict between logic and belief in syllogistic reasoning. *Memory & Cognition, 11*, 295–306.

Evans, J. St. B. T., & Lynch, J. S. (1973). Matching bias in the selection task. *British Journal of Psychology, 64*, 391–397.

Evans, St. B. T. J., Newstead, S. E., & Byrne, R. M. (1993). *Human reasoning: The psychology of deduction*. Hillsdale, NJ: Erlbaum.

Evans, J. St. B. T., & Over, D. E. (1996). *Rationality and reasoning*. Hove, UK: Psychology Press.

Evans, J. St. B. T., Over, D. E., & Manktelow, K. I. (1993). Reasoning, decision making, and rationality. *Cognition, 49*, 165–187.

Fillenbaum, S. (1975). If: Some uses. *Psychological Research, 37*, 245–260.

Galotti, K. M. (1989). Approaches to studying formal and everyday reasoning. *Psychological Bulletin, 105*, 331–351.

Garnham, A., & Oakhill, J. (1994). *Thinking and reasoning*. Cambridge, MA: Blackwell.

Gigerenzer, G., & Hug, K. (1992). Domain-specific reasoning: Social contracts, cheating, and perspective change. *Cognition, 43*, 127–171.

Greene, S. B. (1992). Multiple explanations for multiply quantified sentences: Are multiple models necessary? *Psychological Review, 99*, 184–187.

Grice, H. P. (1975). Logic and conversation. In P. Cole and J. L. Morgan (Eds.), *Syntax and semantics Vol. 3. Speech Acts* (pp. 41–58). London: Academic Press.

Griggs, R. A. (1983). The role of problem content in the selection task. In J. St. B. T. Evans (Ed.), *Thinking and reasoning: Psychological approaches* (pp. 16–43). London: Routledge and Kegan Paul.

Henle, M. (1962). On the relation between logic and thinking. *Psychological Review, 69*, 366–378.

Holland, J. H., Holyoak, K. J., Nisbett, R. E., & Thagard, P. R. (1986). A framework for induction. *Induction: Processes of inferences, learning, and discovery* (pp. 1–28). Cambridge, MA: MIT Press.

Janis, I. L., and Frick, F. (1943). The relationship between attitudes toward conclusions and errors in judging logical validity of syllogisms. *Journal of Experimental Psychology, 33*, 73–77.

Johnson-Laird, P. N. (1999). Deductive reasoning. *Annual Review of Psychology, 50*, 109–135.

Johnson-Laird, P. N., & Bara, B. G. (1984). Syllogistic inference. *Cognition, 16*, 1–61.

Johnson-Laird, P. N., & Byrne, R. M. J. (1991). *Deduction*. Hillsdale, NJ: Erlbaum.

Johnson-Laird, P. N., Byrne, R. M. J., & Schaeken, W. (1992). Propositional reasoning by model. *Psychological Review, 99*, 418–439.

Johnson-Laird, P. N., Byrne, R. M. J., & Tabossi, P. (1989). Reasoning by model: The case of multiple quantification. *Psychological Review, 96*, 658–673.

Koslowski, B. (1996). *Theory and evidence: The development of scientific reasoning*. Cambridge, MA: The MIT Press.

Lefford, A. (1946). The influence of emotional subject matter on logical reasoning. *The Journal of General Psychology, 34*, 127–151.

Legrenzi, P. (1969). Relations between language and reasoning about deductive rules. In G. B. Flores d'Arcais and W. J. M. Levelt (Eds.), *Advances in psycholinguistics*. London: North Holland.

Leighton, J. P. (2001, April). *An analysis of students' hypothesis testing skills*. Paper presented at the Annual meeting of the American Educational Research Association, Seattle, WA.

Leighton, J. P., & Sternberg, R. J. (in press). Reasoning and problem-solving. In A. F. Healy and R. W. Proctor (Eds.), *Experimental psychology: Handbook of psychology*. NY: Wiley.

Liberman, N., & Klar, Y. (1996). Hypothesis testing in Wason's selection task: Social exchange, cheating detection, or task understanding. *Cognition, 58*, 127–156.

Light, P., Girotto, V., & Legrenzi, P. (1990). Children's reasoning on conditional promises and permissions. *Cognitive Development, 5*, 369–383.

Manktelow, K. I., & Evans, J. St. B. T. (1979). Facilitation of reasoning by realism: Effect or non-effect? *British Journal of Psychology, 70*, 477–488.

Manktelow, K. I., Fairley, N. Kilparick, S. G., & Over, D. E. (2000). Pragmatics and strategies for practical reasoning. In W. Schaeken, G. De Vooght, & G. d'Ydewalle (Eds.), *Deductive reasoning and strategies* (pp. 23–48). Mahwah, NJ: Erlbaum.

Manktelow, K. I., & Over, D. E. (1991). Social roles and utilities in reasoning with deontic conditionals. *Cognition, 39*, 85–105.

Newstead, S. E. (1989). Interpretational errors in syllogistic reasoning. *Journal of Memory and Language, 28*, 78–91.

Newstead, S. E., Pollard, P., Evans, J. St. B. T., & Allen, J. L. (1992). The source of belief bias effects in syllogistic reasoning. *Cognition, 45*, 257–284.

Norris, S. P. (1988). Controlling for background beliefs when developing multiple-choice critical thinking tests. *Educational Measurement: Issues and Practice, Fall*, 5–11.

Norris, S. P., & Phillips, L. M. (1994). The relevance of a reader's knowledge within a perspectival view of reading. *Journal of Reading Behavior, 26*, 391–412.

Oakhill, J., & Garnham, A. (1992). On theories of belief bias in syllogistic reasoning. *Cognition, 46*, 87–92.

Oakhill, J., Johnson-Laird, P. N., & Garnham, A. (1989). Believability and syllogistic reasoning. *Cognition, 31*, 117–140.

O'Brien, D. P. (1993). Mental logic and human irrationality: We can put a man on the moon, so why can't we solve those logical-reasoning problems? In K. I. Manktelow and D. E. Over (Eds.), *Rationality: Psychological and philosophical perspectives* (pp. 110–135) London: Routledge.

O'Brien, D. P., & Bonatti, L. L. (1999) The semantics of logical connectives and mental logic. *Cahiers de Psychologie Cognitive, 18*, 87–97.

Ormerod, T. C. (2000). Mechanisms and strategies for rephrasing. In W. Schaeken, G. de Vooght, A. Vandierendonck, A., & G. d'Ydewalle, (Eds.). *Deductive reasoning and strategies*. Mahwah, NJ: Erlbaum.

Over, D. E., & Evans, J. St. B. T. (1999). The meaning of mental logic. *Cahiers de Psychologie, 18*, 99–104.

Phelps, R. P. (1998). The demand for standardized student testing. *Educational Measurement: Issues and Practice, 17*, 5–23.

Politzer, G., & Braine, M. D. S. (1991). Responses to inconsistent premises cannot count as suppression of valid inferences. *Cognition, 38*, 103–108.

Revlin, R., & Leirer, V. O. (1978). The effects of personal biases on syllogistic reasoning: Rational decisions from personalized representations. In R. Revlin & R. E. Mayer (Eds.), *Human reasoning*. Washington DC: Wiley.

Revlin, R., Leirer, V., Yopp, H., Yopp, R. (1980). The belief bias effect in formal reasoning: The influence of knowledge on logic. *Memory & Cognition, 8*, 584–592.

Rips, L. J. (1994). *The psychology of proof.* Cambridge, MA: MIT Press.

Rips, L. J. (1995). Deduction and cognition. In E. E. Smith and D. N. Osherson (Eds.), *Thinking: Vol. 3. An invitation to cognitive science* (2nd ed., pp. 297–343). Cambridge, MA: MIT Press.

Schaeken, W., de Vooght, G., Vandierendonck, A. & d'Ydewalle, G. (Eds.). (2000). *Deductive reasoning and strategies.* Mahwah, NJ: Erlbaum.

Staudenmayer, H. (1975). Understanding conditional reasoning with meaningful propositions. In R. J. Falmagne (Ed.), *Reasoning: Representation and process in children and adults.* Hillsdale, NJ: Erlbaum.

Sternberg, R. J. (1987). Teaching critical thinking: Eight easy ways to fail before you begin. *Phi Delta Kappan, 68,* 456–459.

Sternberg, R. J. (1999). *Cognitive psychology* (2nd ed.). Ft. Worth, Texas: Harcourt Brace College Publishers.

Sternberg, R. J., & Ben Zeev, T. (2001). *Complex cognition: The psychology of human thought.* NY: Oxford University Press.

Taplin, J. E., (1971). Reasoning with conditional sentences. *Journal of Verbal Learning and Verbal Behavior, 10,* 219–225.

Taplin, J. E., & Staudenmayer, H. (1973). Interpretation of abstract conditional sentences in deductive reasoning. *Journal of Verbal Learning and Verbal Behavior, 12,* 530–542.

Thagard, P. (1989). Explanatory coherence. *Behavioral and Brain Sciences, 12,* 435–502.

Wason, P. C. (1966). Reasoning. In B. M. Foss (Ed.), *New Horizons in Psychology.* New York: Penguin.

Wason, P. C. (1983). Realism and rationality in the selection task. In J. St. B. T. Evans (Ed.), *Thinking and reasoning: Psychological approaches.* London: Routledge and Kegan Paul.

Wason, P. C., & Johnson-Laird, P. N. (1972). *Psychology of reasoning: Structure and content.* Cambridge, MA: Harvard University Press.

Woodwort, R. S., & Sells, S. B. (1935). An atmosphere effect in formal syllogistic reasoning. *Journal of Experimental Psychology, 18,* 451–460.

12

The Development of Deductive Reasoning

Henry Markovits

The ability to make deductive inferences is one of the defining characteristics of advanced human thinking. Being able to take some given premises as a base and then to explore the kinds of necessary deductions that can be made from them is a critical component of mathematics and science. More broadly, making inferences underlies much of our day-to-day thinking in varied contexts (e.g., Lea, O'Brien, Fisch, Noveck, & Braine, 1990). Understanding how this ability develops is a correspondingly important question, both for theoretical and practical reasons. However, the study of the development of deductive reasoning presents some major problems. As we shall see, there is not much consensus about just what children and adults can actually do, or about what, if anything, develops in deductive reasoning.

Underlying at least some of the problems that are present in this domain is an important question concerning the status of logic in the study of reasoning. There is a clear distinction to be made between deductive reasoning and logical reasoning (Overton, 1990). Deduction refers to the process of reaching a conclusion on the basis of some given premises. Logic is a formal domain that attempts to characterize specific forms of argument as being valid or invalid. In other words, logic provides textbook norms for correct deductions, norms that are often explicitly used in academic contexts to evaluate the adequacy of deductive reasoning. The importance of logical norms to describe arguments is so intuitively clear that the expression "not being logical" is a commonly used way of describing a person whose arguments are considered to be bad. Whether logic is considered to

Preparation of this manuscript was supported by grants from the National Sciences and Engineering Council of Canada (NSERC) and from the Fonds pour la Formation de Chercheurs et l'Aide a la Recherche (FCAR).
I would like to particularly thank Pierre Barrouillet for his most useful and stimulating comments.

be a model for the human mind, as did Boole (1854), one of the founders of modern logic, or whether it is simply used to provide cues as to what constitutes a correct response to a deductive problem, the presence of logic as a normative system has had an important effect on both theoretical and empirical explorations of reasoning.

This has specifically affected developmental studies of reasoning in several ways. The most important of these is the fact that many, if not all, developmental studies have taken logical reasoning as the baseline for evaluating reasoning performance. The results of most developmental studies can be synthesized by one or the other of the following two descriptions: Children are logical or adolescents are more logical than children. Logical reasoning is thus, at least implicitly, seen as either the starting point or the end point of development. It is telling in this respect to compare developmental studies to those that look specifically at reasoning in adults. The results of a large majority of studies of adult reasoning can be synthesized by the description: "Adults are not logical." This has, in turn, prompted many researchers to raise the question of whether or not people are indeed able to make normative inferences, or in other words, whether people are, or even can be, rational (Manktelow & Over, 1993). It is clear that developmental researchers and those examining reasoning in adults have generally come to very different conclusions about the relationship between logic and reasoning. I will not make any specific suggestions at this point, but it is worth remarking that developmental and adult studies do not examine different species, and that interpretations of the outcomes of these studies must, in the end, be mutually compatible.

As I have previously suggested, data on how children and adults perform on deductive reasoning problems have been interpreted in very different ways. On the one hand, empirical work has shown that educated adults have great difficulty in making logical inferences on some basic forms of reasoning (Evans, 1982). Conversely, other studies appear to show that very young children can make logical inferences on these same basic forms of reasoning (Ennis, 1976; Hawkins, Pea, Glick, & Scribner, 1984). As Moshman (1990) has so aptly remarked, this pattern of results suggests that reasoning competence peaks in early childhood and rapidly declines afterward (which anyone who has tried to raise young children may not find surprising). One of the challenges of any developmental theory is to explain this apparent contradiction. This chapter will start with an overview of some of the major theories that have attempted to explain the nature and development of logical reasoning (some of these theories will necessarily overlap with content from other chapters). Subsequently, certain key results of empirical studies that have looked at reasoning in a developmental context will be examined. Finally, I will present a recent approach based on mental-model theory (Johnson-Laird, 1983) that attempts to account for both early competence and later incompetence within a specific procedural model.

LOGICAL REASONING IN PIAGET'S THEORY

Inhelder and Piaget (1958) were among the first researchers to systematically examine the development of deductive reasoning. The capacity to make logical deductions was seen as one of the defining characteristics of formal thinking, which was considered to be the final stage of cognitive development. As such, a formal operational thinker was considered to have the basic competence to reason in a way that was consistent with basic propositional logic. This did not imply that inferential reasoning was beyond the ability of younger, more concrete thinkers. In fact, Piaget (Piaget, Grize, Szeminska, & Bang, 1977) considered that making inferences is a fundamental part of cognition at all levels. For example, a child who claims that if liquid in a container is emptied into another container of different form, then the height of liquid in the two containers will be identical is making an inference. What distinguishes these, more primitive forms of inference from formal deductive inferences is a major part of Inhelder and Piaget's qualitative description of formal thinking. Since this description has rarely been exploited in subsequent research, it is worth giving it some degree of attention.

One of the key notions used to characterize formal thinking is the idea that formal inferences are not made in isolation, but can be combined in an inferential structure, where each inference has an impact on other components. Thus, a formal reasoner has the capacity to perform the kind of complex reasoning that would allow a given conclusion to impact on previously accumulated information (e.g., I can conclude that P must be true from these premises, but observation X suggests that P is false, etc.). In contrast, more concrete modes of reasoning act in a sequential manner, such that the conclusion of one inference remains unrelated to the conclusion made from a previous inference. Younger reasoners can be easily lead to making what appear be to internally contradictory conclusions (see also Piaget, 1974). A second important characteristic of formal thought (which is related to the previous point) is the nature of the relationship between a deductive inference and empirical observation. Concrete reasoning is essentially led by observation, both because observation is important in order to specify the nature of the concepts that are used in reasoning and, more importantly, because any conflict between inference and observation will tend strongly to be resolved in favor of observation. Formal reasoning is characterized by an inversion of this relationship. When a formal reasoner is faced with a conflict between a deductive inference and observation, he or she will tend to put relatively more weight on inference than on observation. This is because a formal inference can be seen as being part of a larger structure that considers multiple interrelations between observation and conclusions. Thus, when a formal inference is (correctly) made, it must not only be locally consistent with the immediate premises, but also globally consistent with previous conclusions and observations. For example, when a logical conclusion is reached that "P must be true," this conclusion has implications for a variety of other components that include other observations. Thus, if an observation is made that suggests that "P is false," this observation might put into doubt, not only the immediate conclusion, but also other empirical observations. In this case, the formal reasoner might well be prepared to question the observation more readily than the logical conclusion. A final point is the relation between necessity and what is referred to as possibility. A logical conclusion is generally defined as a necessary one. Simply put, P is a necessary conclusion from A if, given premises A, it is not possible that P is false. What Inhelder and Piaget (1958) claimed was that the underlying necessity of logical inferences was a function of the ability of a reasoner to conceive of a more or less greater range of possibilities (see also Piaget, 1987a, 1987b). The degree of necessity of a given conclusion depends on how many of the potential alternatives are accounted for in the course of making a given inference; a conclusion is truly necessary when it takes into account all possible alternatives. Thus, they considered that one of the chief underlying abilities for formal thought was the ability to systematically (and combinatorially) generate all possible states in any given situation. Since younger, more concrete, thinkers are generally not able to generate all possibilities, their inferences show what might be called local necessity, since the same inference might be judged to be not necessary if different possibilities are considered by the same reasoner.

Inhelder and Piaget (1958) also attempted to provide a characterization of what a formal reasoner was ideally able to do, that is, a description of the basic competencies underlying formal thinking. Generally, they claimed that standard propositional logic was an appropriate competence model for formal reasoners. Specifically, they stated that a formal reasoner should be able to correctly use the 16 binary operations composed of all possible combinations of (p.q, p.not-q, not-p.q, not-p.not-q). For example, the conditional *if p then q* can be defined by a truth table for which p.q, not-p.q, not-p.not-q are true and p.not-q is false. The most straightforward interpretation of this claim is that formal reasoners have inferential rules that correspond to all of these combinations (e.g., rules for making conditional inferences). (It should be noted that a fair interpretation could less stringently claim that formal reasoners have unspecified cognitive processes that allow them to make systematically correct inferences to these logical forms in ideal conditions). Concrete reasoners, in contrast, can occasionally make some of these inferences correctly, but not systematically, and only if aided by some kind of concrete support.

Now, the most direct claim that can be made on the basis of this analysis is that only adolescents and adults should be able to reliably make correct inferences to verbally presented inferential problems. Another related claim is that most adolescents and adults should be able to do this, although this latter is less compelling. Following Inhelder and Piaget's (1958) analysis of formal thinking, there was a concerted effort to examine these claims, mostly using logical inferences related to conditional (if-then) reasoning. Early results were somewhat inconsistent with these two predictions. For example, studies did show that before adolescence, the proportion of reasoners who could give correct responses to the four logical forms that characterize conditional reasoning was very small (Wildman & Fletcher, 1977). However, children as young as six or seven years of age could make correct inferences to verbal problems on certain of the logical forms (Ennis, 1976). In addition, many studies showed that even adults had great difficulties in making logically correct inferences (e.g., Markovits, 1985). One of the more striking of these was a seminal study by Wason (1968), who presented a group of highly educated students with a task based on conditional logic, referred to as the selection task. The proportion of these reasoners who gave the correct response was remarkably low and led Wason to conclude that Piaget's analysis of reasoning was incorrect. Whatever the interpretation of these results is, it is clear that there is a great deal of variability in inferential performance at all ages. It is this fact that underlies Overton's competence-performance model.

OVERTON'S COMPETENCE-PERFORMANCE MODEL

The first studies that examined the more strict interpretations of Piaget's model suggested that these could not really be sustained in their initial form. Overton (Overton, 1985, 1990; Overton & Newman, 1982) subsequently presented a model of reasoning that relies on the distinction between competence and performance factors in order to explain this initial pattern of results. Specifically, this model claims that Piaget's basic analysis was correct, that is that younger children do not have the basic competence to make logically correct inferences, while adolescents and adults do. However, the inconsistency in performance that is often observed with older reasoners can be accounted for by performance factors of various kinds that do not allow the full expression of this competence. Simply put, this model claims that adolescents and adults generally possess cognitive processes that, when properly deployed, allow them to make consistently logical inferences to deductive reasoning problems. However, various factors that are unrelated to these basic processes result in their being used in a suboptimal way, or not being used at all. Among such factors are classical ones such as fatigue and memory load and others that are more fundamental, such as familiarity (see also Piaget,

1972, for a more general analysis of how familiarity might affect formal reasoning).

This model allows for two related predictions. The first relies on the claim that poor inferential performance in children and in older reasoners does not have the same source. Younger reasoners do not possess the basic competence (i.e., the requisite cognitive processes) required to make logically correct inferences. Older reasoners do possess these cognitive processes, but may not show their competence because of various performance factors. What would then happen if younger and older reasoners who are equally hapless in initial inferential performance were helped out in some way that should cue improved performance. Helping younger reasoners should be relatively futile, since they do not have the requisite competence to profit from any intervention. However, this same intervention should be quite profitable in the case of older reasoners. This particular prediction was indeed confirmed in a set of studies (O'Brien & Overton, 1980, 1982; Overton, Byrnes & O'Brien, 1985) that used a procedure by which reasoners were given information designed to contradict a faulty interpretation of a conditional rule. Generally, this intervention was effective in improving performance among reasoners at grade 12 and older, but ineffective before this age. Another, related, prediction that Overton's model allows concerns the effects of variables such as familiarity and the related concept of relevance (Ward & Overton, 1990). Generally, within the competence-performance model, familiar and/or relevant material is considered to facilitate reasoning, since it provides cues that activate appropriate cognitive procedures, when these are available. In the case of younger reasoners who do not possess this basic competence level, familiarity would not do this, since these procedures are not available. Once again, in a series of studies that examined performance on a modified version of the selection task, this prediction was confirmed (Mueller, Overton, & Reene, 2001; Overton, Ward, Black, Noveck, & O'Brien, 1987; Ward & Overton, 1990). In this case, familiarity resulted in improved performance only among older reasoners, although at an earlier age than was observed with the previous studies.

This model provides a useful counterpoint to the Piagetian model that serves as its base. It makes quite explicit the idea that inferential performance is highly variable, even among educated adults who are, at least theoretically, at a high level of formal competence. It presents the important idea that this variability can be understood in an interactive way as a function of a reasoner's initial level of competence.

Overton's model specifically addresses the question of the status of *logically incorrect* responses produced by reasoners who are expected to be at a high level of competence. In addition, there is another class of problematic responses that also raises questions for the Piagetian model. These are cases in which quite young reasoners can consistently give the logically correct response to at least some deductive reasoning problems (Ennis,

1976; Hawkins et al., 1984; Kuhn, 1977). Results of this kind have been interpreted in differing ways. Piagetian theorists claim (Byrnes & Overton, 1986; Knifong, 1974; Overton, 1990) that a major criterion for formal reasoning involves the general structure of the inferences that are made. This position supposes that processes that are not truly formal could lead to logically correct responding to one or two isolated logical forms. For example, it has been claimed that young children can use various surface-level strategies that lead to logically correct responses to simple inferences (Knifong, 1974; Markovits, Schleifer, & Fortier, 1989). It is the ability to respond logically to a wide range of inferential problems that truly corresponds to formal reasoning.

However, there are alternative approaches to reasoning that consider that the capacity to give the logically correct answer to a limited subset of inferential problems should, in fact, be considered as an indication of some basic competence. The best known of these is Braine's theory of natural logic (Braine, 1978; Braine, 1990; Braine & O'Brien, 1991; Braine & O'Brien, 1998).

BRAINE'S THEORY OF NATURAL LOGIC

Braine's theory of natural logic makes two major claims. The first part of Braine's theory is the claim that reasoning involves the use of specific inferential schemas. In this respect, this theory resembles Piagetian theory (at least on a strict interpretation of the latter). However, Braine did not, as Piaget did, use standard propositional logic as a model for human reasoning. Natural or mental logic is seen as incorporating a subset of basic rules that are used to make real-life inferences. While most of these correspond to standard logical norms, a few do not. Thus, the mental logic model, while in most ways consistent with standard logic, does allow for some incorporation of reasoners' unschooled intuitions.

Braine's analysis of the developmental trajectory of reasoning competence is quite different from the Piagetian analysis. There are some important reasons for this difference. In Braine's theory, there are no interconnections between different inference schemas. More importantly, Braine (1990) makes the strong claim that some of the inferential rules that appear to be available to young children (which he refers to as primary reasoning skills) are biologically based. The specific argument is that certain inferences are so critical to behavior, particularly with respect to language comprehension and the integration of information derived from diverse sources, that the selection pressure to incorporate them into the basic architecture of the human mind would have been very strong (see also Cohen, 1981; MacNamara, 1986). These inferential procedures involve direct inferences that are controlled by a simple program. One important example is the modus ponens inference, which is considered to be one of the key rules, since it allows the kind of elementary inference that would be critical to basic communication (e.g., "If a lion, then danger. There's a lion. There must be danger"). Other primary schemas include those for negation, and basic connectives such as *and* and *or* (see Braine & O'Brien, 1998, p. 80–81 for a complete list). More complex inference schemas are referred to as indirect reasoning strategies or secondary skills. These generally involve some form of recursive reasoning. The classic *reductio ad absurdum* argument (this is an argument form that requires assuming the falseness of the proposed conclusion in addition to the premises and then proving that this combination leads to a false conclusion) is an example of one of these schemas. Indirect schemas are acquired with training and experience, particularly experience with language and in academic contexts.

This theory thus supposes that some of the basic inferential rules required for making deductive inferences are a part of a biologically determined cognitive architecture. Inferential schemas of the kind that are postulated here have a form that relies on the basic syntax of the particular deduction that is required. Thus, the rule for modus ponens looks like:

if p then q; p
q

Theoretically, the conclusion to any inference that shares this basic structure will be formally identical, since all such inferences will be mapped onto the same rule. Does this mean that these basic inferences will always be correctly made? Not necessarily. The natural logic model explicitly recognizes the fact that untrained reasoners usually receive inferential problems that are phrased in ordinary language. The model contains an initial, interpretative stage that allows for a semantic analysis of premises. This initial evaluation invokes various pragmatic principles that can in fact alter the way that a real-life inferential problem is actually solved. There are, at least, two levels to this evaluation. The first level concerns the global form of processing that is to be used by the reasoner. Following previous work by Luria (1971) and Scribner (1977), Braine (1990) distinguishes between natural reasoning and analytic reasoning. Natural reasoning is reasoning that invokes the full range of the reasoner's knowledge about whatever phenomena are referred to in a given inference, in order to derive and evaluate a conclusion. Analytic reasoning is reasoning that only uses the specific syntactic information given in an inferential problem to arrive at a conclusion. Natural reasoning is thus reasoning for which the logical status of a possible conclusion is not the only important element in evaluating the conclusion. For example, if a logical conclusion violates strongly held beliefs, then these beliefs may well (and reasonably) take precedence over logical validity. In contrast, analytic reasoning looks only at the syntax of a given problem and suppresses use of beliefs. Thus, one level of interpretation that is involved in analyzing an inferential problem is determining the overall goal of the problem, specifically, whether the reasoner should take an analytic or a natural stance when making a conclusion

There is a second level of interpretation that is also invoked. This concerns the possible use of pragmatic or conversational principles (Grice, 1975) that may modify the interpretation of a given logical form. One classical example is the use of if-then in the context of promises and threats. Statements such as "If you eat your supper, you'll have dessert" are commonly used in ordinary conversation. Although such statements contain an if-then surface appearance, they are in fact usually intended to be effective biconditionals (if and only if) (Fillenbaum, 1975, 1976). In the previous example, the intention of the speaker is clearly to imply that "If you don't eat your supper, you won't have dessert." A strict conditional interpretation of this utterance would allow for the possibility of not eating supper and still having dessert, something that would certainly reduce the effectiveness of the underlying threat implied by the initial statement. Thus, it is clear that in many circumstances, reasoners make implicit inferences on the basis of pragmatic principles that may alter the underlying logical structure of a given statement. Thus, one goal of any interpretative module is to establish which specific inferential rule is intended in a given utterance. One key developmental trend that has been analyzed in this way is the strong tendency of younger children to respond to conditional statements as if these were biconditionals (Wildman & Fletcher, 1977). Braine's model suggests that any tendency to misinterpret conditional statements should be due to children's generating inappropriate implicit inferences. Rumain, Connell, and Braine (1983) hypothesized that if young children were given supplementary cues that contradicted any implicit biconditional inference, then they should be able to respond correctly to the two uncertain logical forms of the conditional. They did indeed find this to be the case, and accordingly claimed that the general developmental improvement in performance on these forms is due to the increased facility with which older reasoners can set aside such implicit inferences. Interestingly, a differing developmental prediction based on the same notion of pragmatic inferences was made by Cahan and Artman (1997). Their basic argument was that since the effects of pragmatic inferences depend mainly on experience, there should actually be a developmental increase in the tendency of reasoners to respond biconditionally. They used an ingenious technique to attempt to dissociate large-scale developmental trends (which could be due either to learning and/or to developmental processes) from the more local effects of increased experience with pragmatic inferences, and did indeed find evidence for a developmental tendency to increased biconditional responding.

Overall, Braine's theory considers that evidence of early competence reflects the precocious existence of certain basic deductive schemas that

are, on the whole, logical. Development follows basically through training and experience and consists of subsequent acquisition of more complex schemas and the increasing ability to play the logical game. One key
component of development is the acquisition of an analytic stance, that is
the ability to reason strictly on the basis of given premises without using
available real-world knowledge (although see Leevers & Harris, 1999 for
an alternate view on this issue). Another component would involve learning of the more complex indirect schemas. This could be tied to specific
training, or, as suggested by Falmagne (1980, 1990), to experience with language. A final component would be the ability to increasingly discount
various pragmatic influences on reasoning, which would allow reasoners
to behave increasingly logically, at least when the appropriate inference
schemas were part of their cognitive repertoire.

METACOGNITIVE DEVELOPMENT

Another response to the question of what characterizes development, if
young children are indeed assumed to have a basic ability to make logically appropriate inferences, has been given by Moshman (1990, 1995,
1998). His analysis of the empirical results that have been briefly cited
makes two points. First, he accepts that young children do have the competence to make simple logical inferences. He also notes that much of
the adult literature requires reasoners to make more complex inferences
under sometimes difficult circumstances. Moshman makes a distinction
between logic, which is seen as the capacity to make simple inferences,
and metalogic, which involves a more explicit metacognitive awareness
of a reasoner's own logical reasoning processes. He accepts Braine's argument that some basic inferential schemas are available to very young
children, and then claims that further development is characterized by
the increasing ability to reflect upon one's own reasoning, that is, that the
major advances in reasoning ability beyond early childhood are mediated
by greater metalogical abilities. Moshman (1990) also makes the strong
claim that metalogical development progresses toward greater rationality.
He distinguishes four major stages of metalogical development. The first
stage is characterized by the ability to make implicit inferences. The second is characterized by the use of explicit inferential procedures and by
an implicit understanding of logical distinctions. This kind of reasoning
appears at about age six and develops throughout elementary school. The
third stage consists of the ability to make explicit logical distinctions, something that appears at around 11 years of age. Explicit understanding of a
variety of concepts, including the distinction between logical validity and
empirical truth (Moshman & Franks, 1986), and the nature of tautologies
(Osherson & Markman, 1975), are not explicitly understood before 11 years
of age (but see Morris, 2000), but appear to develop in older reasoners. The

fourth stage represents the basic culmination of metalogical development (although further analyses have led to the idea that there might be more than four stages) and is characterized by the ability to reflect upon logic as a formal system.

WHAT DO EMPIRICAL STUDIES SHOW ABOUT THE DEVELOPMENT OF REASONING ABILITIES?

Despite their common evocation of logic as a competence model for reasoning, these theories make quite divergent predictions about the way that children and adults can be expected to reason. To what extent do empirical studies that have examined deductive reasoning in children and adults support these various conceptions of development? Each of the presented theories uses a selected subset of the many studies that have examined reasoning in order to support its particular predictions, while often either ignoring other studies or claiming that their results are inconclusive for various reasons. Given this, it seems particularly useful to present a resume of some of the principle findings of studies that have looked at performance on two key deductive reasoning problems, with a particular emphasis on the contradictory interpretations that these studies might allow.

Is There Evidence that Young Children Can Reason "Logically"?

One of the key claims of Braine's theory is that there are some inferential rules that are so basic that they will, at the very least, develop quite early. The most studied of these is probably the modus ponens inference. This involves starting from the premises "if p then q, p is true" and concluding that "q is true." Some of the cited studies use syllogisms of the form "all X are Y, A is X, thus A is Y." Since both propositional and syllogistic forms appear to lead to quite similar response patterns (Markovits, Venet, Janveau-Brennan, Malfait, Pion, & Vadeboncoeur, 1996; Roberge & Paulus, 1971) no distinction will be made between them. Now, several studies have indeed shown that children as young as five years old correctly make the modus ponens inference either when familiar content is used in the premises (Ennis, 1976) or when abstract content is used (Hawkins et al., 1984). Young children do have problems making this inference when contrary-to-fact premises are used (Dias & Harris, 1988, 1990; Hawkins et al., 1984; Markovits & Vachon, 1989). For example, if given premises such as "if it is raining, then the grass is dry," young children show a strong tendency to conclude that "it is raining" implies that "the grass is wet." However, when these children are given some external support, either by embedding the premises into a fantasy context (Dias & Harris, 1988, 1990; Markovits & Vachon, 1989) or by giving instructions to focus on the premises (Leevers & Harris, 1999), they consistently make the logical modus ponens inference, even with contrary-to-fact premises. These results show that when given appropriate instructions to "suppose that the premises are true" and some, fairly simple additional support, children as young as five years old can make the modus ponens inference quite consistently with a variety of familiar, abstract or contrary-to-fact premises.

The above results are certainly consistent with the idea that quite young children do have the logical competence required to make the modus ponens inference. Now, if very young children possess the competence to reason logically on modus ponens, then one would certainly expect that older children and adults would become increasingly expert in this form of reasoning, and that there should be a generalized increase in logically correct responding to the modus ponens inference. Evidence that this was not the case would be disconcerting, at the least. To put this into a different perspective, the hypothesis that young children can acquire the rule that $1 + 1 = 2$ and use it in many circumstances would reasonably lead to the assumption that this judgment would be made with increasing frequency in older children. The (probably false!) observation that many adults think that $1 + 1 = 3$ would certainly make the description of what young children are really doing when they respond that $1 + 1 = 2$ more problematic.

There are, in fact, a number of studies that suggest that modus ponens reasoning does not show the kind of generalized consistency that one would expect from the existence of early competence. Some studies have shown a developmental decrease in logically correct responding to modus ponens (Janveau-Brennan & Markovits, 1999; Markovits, 2002; Markovits, Fleury, Quinn, & Venet, 1998) when reasoning with causal conditionals ("if cause p then effect q"). Adolescents will deny the modus ponens inference when the logical conclusion is unbelievable (Markovits & Bouffard-Bouchard, 1992). Many studies have also shown that even educated adults have problems making this inference when presented with premises that are not believable (George, 1995, 1997), when responding to premises for which there are many possible ways that the antecedent might be true with the consequent being false (Cummins, 1995; Cummins, Lubart, Alksnin, & Rist, 1991; Thompson, 1994), when given additional premises with the same consequent (Byrne, 1989; Chan & Chua, 1994) or when they are simply asked to produce an alternative antecedent (Markovits & Potvin, 2001).

The studies that have examined reasoning on modus ponens thus present a varied profile. Some of the results are consistent with the conclusion that "young children are logical" and others, with the conclusion that "adolescents and adults are not logical." At this point, I will simply note that the available empirical evidence is globally inconsistent, and that reconciling the large variation in performance observed in adolescents and adults with the hypothesis that young children possess some basic logical competence appears difficult at best.

Is There Evidence that Only Older Adolescents Can Reason "Logically"?

The Piagetian or neo-Piagetian approach would in contrast, claim that the basic competence required for formal reasoning is the result of a developmental process and only appears during later adolescence. Studies starting from this perspective have typically examined more complex forms of reasoning than that involved in modus ponens (MP). The most frequently studied forms are the two invalid inferences of conditional logic (which are often grouped together since they present a similar developmental pattern). The first of these inferences is affirmation of the consequent (AC). This corresponds to the following premises: "if *p* then *q*, *q* is true." The second such inference is denial of the antecedent (DA). This corresponds to the following premises: "if *p* then *q*, *p* is false." Neither of these logical forms leads to a single, necessary conclusion. The most frequent logically incorrect response in both cases is to make a biconditional inference, that is, to respond to these forms as if they used if-and-only-if as a connective. Specifically, for the AC form, the most frequent nonlogical response is to conclude, "*p* is true." For the DA form, the most frequent nonlogical response is to conclude, "*q* is false." Several studies have in fact shown clear developmental trends in reasoning with the two invalid forms, affirmation of the consequent and denial of the antecedent. Many studies have shown that children younger than 12 years of age produce a very high proportion of logically incorrect conclusions to both of these forms, and that there is a general increase in the proportion of logically correct responses with age (Klaczynski & Narasimham, 1998; Markovits & Vachon, 1990; O'Brien & Overton, 1980, 1982; Taplin, Staudenmayer, & Taddonio, 1974; Wildman & Fletcher, 1977). These results certainly appear to be consistent with the idea that logical competence is not accessible before adolescence and that it is the product of a developmental process.

However, there are two sets of results that raise some problems with this initial interpretation. On the one hand, some studies have shown that children as young as six or seven years old, can, in some cases, reliably make logical inferences to both affirmation of the consequent and denial of the antecedent with purely verbal premises (Markovits, 2000; Markovits et al., 1998; Markovits et al., 1996). Other studies have shown that children as young as seven years of age can give the logically correct response to these logical forms, when these are supported by concrete materials (Kuhn, 1977) or when they are supplied with additional information contradicting a biconditional interpretation and with training on producing uncertainty responses (Rumain et al., 1983). On the other hand, the idea that logical competence is acquired during adolescence implies that use of this competence should increase with age and experience. However, Klaczynski and Narasimham (1998) have observed a developmental decrease in logically correct responding to certain kinds of causal conditionals. In addition, several studies have shown that educated adults often produce incorrect biconditional responses to both affirmation of the consequent and denial of the antecedent (Cummins, 1995; Cummins et al., 1991; Markovits, 1985; Staudenmeyer & Bourne, 1977; Thompson, 1994). There are also many studies that have shown very large content-related effects in the way that both children and adolescents (Janveau-Brennan & Markovits, 1999; Klaczynski & Narasimham, 1998; Markovits, 2000; Markovits et al., 1998; Markovits & Vachon, 1990; Venet & Markovits, 2001) and adults (Cummins, 1995; Cummins et al., 1991; Quinn & Markovits, 1998; Thompson, 1994) reason with these forms. Thus, once again, there is a great deal of variability in the results of studies that have examined these more complex forms of reasoning. Although I have concentrated on the two invalid forms of conditional reasoning, it should be noted that similar degrees of variability are indeed observed across several kinds of reasoning tasks. For example, studies examining performance on the selection task have found very early abilities to produce logical responses on modified versions of this task (Cummins, 1996; Girotto & Light, 1993; Harris & Nùñez, 1996), others have observed a developmental increase in logical performance (Overton et al., 1987; Ward & Overton, 1990), while still others have observed very poor logical performance in educated adults (Evans, Newstead, & Byrne, 1993; Wason, 1968). This variability is found even for the metacognitive processes involved in the understanding of logical validity (Morris, 2000; Moshman & Franks, 1986) and the understanding of logical necessity (Miller, Custer, & Nassau, 2000; Shapiro & O'Brien, 1971).

Clearly, the inferential performance of both children and adults is strongly affected by both the content and the context of reasoning. There is strong evidence for both logical competence and logical incompetence in both children and adults on all of these forms of reasoning. Specifically, subsets of these results have been cited to support the following set of claims: (1) that very young children are logical in their responses, (2) that young children are not logical, but that reasoning ability develops in a way that leads to more logical performance, and (3) that both children and adults often do not reason logically.

These kinds of results pose clear problems for most of the developmental theories that have been described earlier. Almost all of these theories consider some level of logical competence to exist when reasoners can begin to respond normatively to some given set of inferential problems. While the notion of competence in developmental theories is complex, the simplest interpretation of this claim is that at some point in time, children or adolescents possess cognitive procedures that, when properly implemented, allow them to consistently respond logically to some set of inferences. A certain amount of variation in performance is not in itself a real problem, since the notion of competence does not imply total consistency. However, one would expect that at some point, the procedures that determine competence would be well established enough to allow a reasonable level of consistency. There is no real evidence that this is the case.

In fact, competence theories often attempt to minimize one or another of these claims. For example, neo-Piagetian theories such as Overton's generally suppose that young children's logical responses are the result of some, unspecified, nonformal procedure or heuristic. Early competence theories, such as that of Braine (1990), suppose that variation in performance is not related to logical competence, but only to peripheral, pragmatic factors. However, none of these attempts to reduce the scope of the extensive variations in performance are really satisfactory, particularly since these explanations rely, at least for the moment, on relatively unspecified mechanisms. And none of these theories can really explain how basic competence could be as fragile as the empirical results show them to be.

This basic problem is a direct consequence of the supposition that reasoning depends on the use of cognitive procedures that will invariably produce responses that are logical if correctly applied. If, in contrast, this assumption is not made, then what appears to be contradictory evidence can be reinterpreted very differently. Specifically, if it is supposed that the cognitive procedures that are used to make inferences in both children and adults have no necessary relation to logic, then the three conclusions stated previously can be rephrased in the following way: (1) the procedures used by young children to make inferences lead to responses that are, in some cases, the same as logical norms, (2) the procedures used by young children develop in such a way that the rate of responses that correspond to logical norms increases with age for at least some subset of inferential problems, and (3) the procedures used by both children and adults can lead to inconsistent responding on formally similar problems with variable content.

A DEVELOPMENTAL ADAPTATION OF JOHNSON-LAIRD'S MENTAL-MODEL THEORY

This suggests that one way to resolve the apparent contradiction in the empirical results would be to specify a procedural model that does not assume logic as a norm. Johnson-Laird's mental model theory (Johnson-Laird, 1983; Johnson-Laird & Byrne, 1991), which has been very successful in describing adult inferential performance, does just that. Briefly, this theory (see Johnson-Laird, Chapter 7 this book) supposes that reasoning requires the construction of a mental representation of the possible states of affairs described by the premises. Mental tokens are used to represent these states, and a process that requires both combining tokens and an active search for counterexamples is used for making inferences. Connectives are initially represented in a way that minimizes the cognitive load (the initial model) and if necessary are represented in a more complete way by a process that is referred to as fleshing out, which is the result of a semantic interpretation of the premises. The major constraint in reasoning concerns the necessity to retain several models in a limited working memory.

However, while mental-model theory has proven quite successful in describing the way that fairly complex reasoning is done by educated adults, the theory's developmental component is not clearly specified (Markovits & Barrouillet, in press). In fact, the adult version of this theory presupposes the existence of quite advanced cognitive processes that might not reasonably be available to children. The representations and procedures used in the theory correspond to what might well be considered to be quite high levels of symbolic processing; for example, the procedure hypothesized for generating complete sets of alternative models and the symbolic term used to indicate negation. Implicit to the theory is the hypothesis that all reasoners have access to the same basic procedures and symbolic representations irrespective of their level of expertise, and that imperfect reasoning is due to basically peripheral factors such as limitations in working-memory capacity.

Indeed, it could be claimed that mental-model theory appears to have logic as an implicit competence model, since the processes described by the theory will always lead to a logical conclusion if performed adequately. This is due, at least partly, to some basic characteristics of the theory; the relatively abstract form of the tokens that are used in models, the presence of an interpretative component (fleshing out) that often assigns a standard meaning to logical connectives in an unexplained manner, and the presence of an algorithm for searching for alternative models. For example, the theory assumes that tokens are basically abstract representations of premises. However, it is not clear that young children are capable of either generating or manipulating such kinds of symbols (see Sigel, 1999, for recent discussions of representational development). Similarly, the ability to search for alternative models requires a version of the kind of combinatorial ability that Piaget identified with formal thought. Research on the ability of children to systematically generate alternatives has shown that this can be very difficult even for adolescents (Roberge & Flexer, 1979). Markovits and Barrouillet (in press) have suggested a model in order to account for these developmental problems in a way that is both consistent with empirical data and that retains the adult version of mental-model theory as a developmental end point. In the following, I will present a brief version of some of the key points of this approach.

Firstly, mental tokens used by young children are assumed to refer to specific concrete elements (Barrouillet & Lecas, 1998; Markovits et al., 1996), that progress through a developmental sequence from referring to a specific element, to referring to classes of elements, and ultimately to more abstract elements (Venet & Markovits, 2001) via a redescriptive process such as that suggested by Karmilov-Smith (1992). Use of tokens that refer directly to specific elements (or classes of elements) in semantic memory provides for the concurrent activation of associated elements (Anderson, 1993). Markovits and Barrouillet (in press) have suggested that for most children and adolescents, models of premises are automatically fleshed out by a process of activation of information in long-term memory. The nature of the information that is activated depends on the specific connectives used, on the way that information has been encoded in memory, on task instructions, and on working-memory limitations.

The first major implication of these modifications is that when a child is in the process of attempting to make a conclusion on the basis of some major and minor premises, they have immediate access to whatever models have been generated by the activation process. This has implications for one of the key procedures postulated by mental-model theory; specifically, that putative conclusions for a given major and minor premise are evaluated by a two-pronged process, consisting of (1) generating additional models by an active search for alternatives and then (2) searching for models in which the minor premise is true. If there are any such models in which the putative conclusion is false and others in which this conclusion is true, then the reasoner will conclude that there is no certainty to this specific conclusion. Without the requirement to actively generate alternative models, only the second part of this process is necessary. This basically requires that children be able to detect uncertainty by searching for the presence of models with contradictory conclusions. This is well within children's competence. There have been many studies that have examined children's abilities to detect uncertainty. These have shown that young children can do so when the informational load of a given problem is relatively low and that there is a clear developmental increase in the ability of children to detect uncertainty in more complex situations (Fabricius, Sophian, & Wellman, 1987; Horobin & Acredolo, 1989; Sophian & Somerville, 1988; Wollman, Bat-Sheva, & Lawson, 1979).

A second important point is that fleshing out becomes a process that is constrained by two basic limitations. First, the nature of the information that is integrated into the fleshed-out models is determined by the nature and the structure of information that is stored in a reasoner's long-term memory. This translates the reasoner's experience with the connective and reflects the sum of the influences, both semantic and pragmatic, that are associated with use of the connective. Second, the specific content of fleshed-out models when making a specific inference is limited both by limited working memory and the efficiency of online information retrieval. And, as we shall see, these basic information processing constraints imply that inference making by younger reasoners will exhibit a form of the kind of local necessity which is implied by the Piagetian analysis of reasoning.

At this point, it is useful to use a specific example to understand how this model might function. I will use the same two logical forms, modus ponens and affirmation of the consequent, that were examined previously. Both of these problems require conditional (if-then) reasoning. The first question that must be answered to see how this model might work concerns the semantic space that is determined by a reasoner's understanding of a conditional (if p then q) relation. Since even very young children have extensive experience with conditional statements of many forms (Scholnick, 1990), it can be assumed that this experience results in the generation of a semantic space that allows them to translate some of the basic structural characteristics of conditional relations. One key structural aspect, that reflects the way that conditionals are generally used, implies that the p term is generally understood as one possible object/event among many, while the q term produces a dichotomization of potential objects/events into q and *not-q*. For example, a reasoner who is given a premise such as "if it rains, then the street will be wet," will consider "it rains" as one event among many possible ones ("the sun shines," "it is cloudy," "a cleaner has passed," etc.). However, the consequent term allows for two basic possibilities, "the street is wet" or "the street is not wet." This basic decomposition of possible objects/events that are associated with the original premise is accompanied by the partitioning of the conceptual space of objects/events relevant to the conditional into three classes. The first concerns cases in which the objects or events concerned are complementary to those specified in the original conditional, that is, cases where objects or events that are different from p are related to *not-q* (we will refer to this as the complementary class). In the example we are using, this class would be composed of related events such as "if it is sunny, then the street will not be wet," or "if it is only cloudy, then the street will not be wet," etc.). The second class concerns possible objects/events that share the same relation to q as p does, that is, cases of *not-p* implies q (we will refer to this as the alternatives class). For example, "if the street cleaner passes, then the street will be wet" is one such example. Finally, the third class concerns what Cummins (1995) has called "disabling conditions," that is, conditions that allow the relationship between p and q to be violated (we will refer to this as the disabling class). For example, "if it rains, but the street is covered, then the street will not be wet" is one such example.

Now, what happens when a reasoner makes an inference that corresponds to the modus ponens form? Specifically, suppose that someone is given a problem of the form: Suppose that it is true that "if a rock is thrown at a window, the window will break. A rock is thrown at a window." The models that will be constructed by the reasoner will contain the model that is consistent with the major premise, which is the following:

Rock thrown at window – window broken

Additional models will reflect the nature of information that is activated in memory, using the minor premise as an additional memory cue. In other words, the three classes of information that are cued by the child's basic semantic understanding of the if-then relation (complementary, alternatives, disabling) will be differentially activated by information contained in the minor premise. In this case, "a rock is thrown at a window" will most strongly cue for potential disabling conditions. If a disabling condition (e.g., the window is made of Plexiglas) is strongly activated, then a second model will be added to the initial one:

Rock thrown at Plexiglas window – window not broken

If only the initial model is generated, then the immediate conclusion that "*q* is true" will be drawn by the reasoner. If the two models are generated, then there is no conclusion to be drawn. Now, if it is reasonably assumed that young children have both less knowledge and more difficulty in accessing this knowledge (Kail, 1992), then a first consequence of this analysis is that young children would be expected to very often give what is in this case the logical response, that "*q* is true." Given that development is characterized by an increase in knowledge, and in particular an increase in knowledge of potential disabling conditions, and by an increase in facility in accessing this knowledge, then older reasoners would be expected to produce the two models more frequently, and thus to produce the nonlogical response that there is no certain conclusion more frequently than younger reasoners. In addition, specific content would be expected to have a strong effect on the kinds of inferences made to the modus ponens form, since it is relatively difficult to think of disabling conditions for a premise such as "all dogs have feet" than for a premise such as "if a stone is thrown at a window, the window will break." While a full explanation of the model would have to include the use of instructions to inhibit activation of potential disabling conditions (Markovits & Potvin, 2001; Vadeboncoeur & Markovits, 1999), this basic explanation clearly allows for both a high probability of very young children producing the logical response to many MP inferences, and for adults to have problems doing the same thing. It also clearly accounts for content variation, since the number of available disabling conditions is highly variable across contents (Cummins, 1995; Thompson, 1994).

A second example that can be used to illustrate the general developmental thrust of the model more completely is that of reasoning involving the affirmation of the consequent (AC) inference. Once again, I give a simplified version of the complete analysis. Making an AC inference requires reasoning with a "*p* implies *q*" major premise and a "*q* is true" minor premise. In this case, the minor premise will cue for both the complementary class and the alternatives class. If only information corresponding to the complementary class is highly activated, then the reasoner will produce the two following models:

    Rock thrown at window   –   window broken
    Rock not thrown at window –   window not broken

In this case, the conclusion "that a rock was thrown at the window" follows from the minor premise "the window is broken." However, suppose that at least one example of the alternatives class is also highly activated, then the following three models will be produced:

    Rock thrown at window   –   window broken
    Rock not thrown at window –   window not broken
    Chair thrown at window   –   window broken

In this case, the reasoner will be able to conclude that there is no certain conclusion that follows from the minor premise "the window is broken." There are several interesting consequences of this explanation. Activation of relevant information is done online during the reasoning process, that is, when the reasoner is actively attempting to derive a conclusion. Thus, there is a concurrent cognitive load that corresponds to the effort required to keep all premises in working memory, to attention to instructions, etcetera, that limits the amount of resources available for searching through memory. This, in addition to the inherently probabilistic functioning of memory search implies that a reasoner will not consistently succeed in activating alternatives when reasoning with differing contents. In other words, if a reasoner is given a sequence of identical inferential problems, which vary only in the specific content of the premises, they will arrive at different conclusions, which has indeed been found to be true (Markovits, 1985). Another consequence of this is that content should affect the probability of activating a potential alternative in a way that is consistent with many observed results (Cummins, 1995; Markovits & Vachon, 1990; Thompson, 1994). More specifically, reasoning should reflect the way that information about alternatives is structured in long-term memory, something that has indeed been found to be true (Markovits et al., 1998; Quinn & Markovits, 1998). Finally, there are a number of interesting developmental consequences. When reasoning from concrete premises, younger children differ from older reasoners chiefly because they have a more limited working memory and relatively inefficient retrieval processes. When a young child constructs models of the premises, these are based on a relatively smaller search of their actual knowledge base than would be the case with older reasoners. A conclusion that is arrived at by a younger reasoner has a much higher probability of actually being an inaccurate reflection of the reasoner's own knowledge. Younger reasoners would thus be expected to produce conclusions that are only very locally valid, that is they are valid within only a small subset of available knowledge. For example, a young child has a fairly high probability of concluding that "if a window is broken, then a stone has been thrown at it" in the above example, despite their clear knowledge that things like chairs can also break windows (Markovits et al., 1998). This conclusion is considered valid at the moment of reasoning only because it is too difficult for the child to access all of his or her relevant knowledge during reasoning. At the moment that inference is made, the conclusion would be considered valid, although at another time, the same child might well activate a given alternative highly enough to generate a different conclusion to the same premises. Older reasoners would be able to access a greater portion of their knowledge, and their conclusions would thus be based on a much larger portion of their relevant knowledge. The chances of reaching a conclusion that was contradictory to stored knowledge would be less than for younger reasoners. Thus, in a very basic way, our mental-model analysis corresponds quite well to the Piagetian analysis of the relation between possibility and necessity which underlies the basic notion of formal thinking.

One other important developmental difference concerns the form of the models produced by reasoners. One of the key developmental processes that is postulated by Markovits and Barrouillet (in press) concerns the re-description of concrete elements into more abstract forms (Karmilov-Smith, 1992). Thus, younger children will use mostly specific concrete representations in their models of premises, but that older children will be able to represent classes (e.g., "things that can break window") and eventually, be able to use abstract representations as tokens (Markovits, Doyon, & Simoneau, in press; Venet & Markovits, 2001). Another possible difference might allow for a transition between an automatic activation process to a more combinatorial form of searching for alternative models that would, once again, provide a process that is consistent with the current formulation of the theory. These kinds of developmental changes would allow reasoning to more closely approximate what is considered to be logical, at least in circumstances where the reasoner adopted a more abstract form of reasoning.

I have only sketched an outline of what a fully developmental version of mental-model theory might look like. This description shows how this theory could account for observations (1) that young children can, in some cases, make inferences that correspond to logical norms, (2) that there is a developmental trend toward increased normative responding when more abstract modes of reasoning are employed, and an opposite trend in some cases when increased use of knowledge might lead to nonnormative responding, and (3) that there is a great deal of variability in reasoning at all developmental levels. While the details of this theory might well be put into doubt, it does seem to strongly suggest that the study of the development of reasoning might well profit from less attention to logical norms toward the more basic question of trying to understand the processes that underlie reasoning, logical or otherwise.

References

Anderson, J. R. (1993). *Rules of the mind.* Hillsdale, NJ: Erlbaum.

Barrouillet, P., & Lecas, J. F. (1998). How can mental models account for content effects in conditional reasoning: A developmental perspective. *Cognition, 67*, 209–253.

Boole, G. (1854). *An investigation of the laws of thought.* London: Walton & Maberly.

Braine, M. D. S. (1978). On the relation between the natural logic of reasoning and standard logic. *Psychological Review, 85*, 1–21.

Braine, M. D. S. (1990). The "natural logic" approach to reasoning. In W. F. Overton (Ed.). *Reasoning, necessity, and logic: Developmental perspectives.* Hillsdale, NJ: Erlbaum.

Braine, M. D. S., & O'Brien, D. P. (1991). A theory of *if*: A lexical entry, reasoning program, and pragmatic principles. *Psychological Review, 98*, 182–203.

Braine, M. D. S., & O'Brien, D. P. (1998). *Mental logic.* Mahwah, NJ: Erlbaum.

Byrne, R. M. J. (1989). Suppressing valid inferences with conditionals. *Cognition, 30*, 61–83.

Byrnes, J. P., & Overton, W. F. (1986). Reasoning about certainty and uncertainty in concrete, causal, and propositional contexts. *Developmental Psychology, 22*, 793–799.

Cahan, S., & Artman, L. (1997). Is everyday experience dysfunctional for the development of conditional reasoning. *Cognitive Development, 12*(2), 261–279.

Chan, D., & Chua, F. (1994). Suppression of valid inferences: syntactic views, mental models, and relative salience. *Cognition, 53*, 217–238.

Cohen, L. J. (1981). Can human irrationality be experimentally demonstrated. *Behavioral and Brain Sciences, 4*, 317–370.

Cummins, D. D. (1995). Naive theories and causal deduction. *Memory & Cognition, 23*, 646–658.

Cummins, D. D., (1996). Evidence of deontic reasoning in 3- and 4-year-old children. *Memory and Cognition, 24*(6), 823–829.

Cummins, D. D., Lubart, T., Alksnis, O., & Rist, R. (1991). Conditional reasoning and causation. *Memory & Cognition, 19*, 274–282.

Dias, M. G., & Harris, P. L. (1988). The effect of make-believe play on deductive reasoning. *British Journal of Developmental Psychology, 6*, 207–221.

Dias, M. G., & Harris, P. L. (1990). The influence of the imagination on reasoning. *British Journal of Developmental Psychology, 8*, 305–318.

Ennis, R. H. (1976). An alternative to Piaget's conceptualization of logical competence. *Child Development, 47*(4), 903–919.

Evans, J. St. B. T. (1982). *The psychology of deductive reasoning.* London, UK: Erlbaum.

Evans, J. St. B. T., Newstead, S. E., & Byrne, R. M. J. (1993). *Human reasoning.* Hillsdale, NJ: Erlbaum.

Fabricius, W. V., Sophian, C., & Wellman, H. M. (1987). Young children's sensitivity to logical necessity in their inferential search behavior. *Child Development, 58*, 409–423.

Falmagne, R. J. (1990). Language and the acquisition of logical knowledge. In W. F. Overton (Ed.), *Reasoning, necessity, and logic : Developmental perspectives* (pp. 111–131). Hillsdale, NJ: Erlbaum.

Falmagne, R. J. (1980). The development of logical competence : A psycholinguistic perspective. In R. Kluwe & H. Spada (Eds.), *Developmental models of thinking* (pp. 171–197). New York: Academic Press.

Fillenbaum, S. (1975). *If*: Some uses. *Psychological Research, 37*, 245–260.

Fillenbaum, S. (1976). Inducements: On the phrasing and logic of conditional promises, threats and warnings. *Psychological Research, 38*, 231–250.

George, C. (1995). The endorsement of the premises: Assumption-based or belief-based reasoning. *British Journal of Psychology, 86*, 93–111.

George, C. (1997). Reasoning from uncertain premises. *Thinking & Reasoning, 3*, 161–189.

Girotto, V., & Light, P. (1993). The pragmatic bases of children's reasoning. In P. Light and G. Butterworth (Eds.), *Context and cognition* (pp. 134–156). Hillsdale, NJ: Erlbaum.

Grice, H. P. (1975). Logic and conversation. In P. Cole & J. L. Morgan (Eds.), *Syntax and semantics III: Speech acts* (pp. 41–58). New York: Academic Press.

Harris, P. L., & Núñez, M. (1996). Understanding of permission rules by preschool children. *Child Development, 67*, 1572–1591.

Hawkins, J., Pea, R. D., Glick, J., & Scribner, S. (1984). "Merds that laugh don't like mushrooms": Evidence for deductive reasoning by preschoolers. *Developmental Psychology, 20*(4), 584–594.

Horobin, K., & Acredolo, C. (1989). The impact of probability judgements on reasoning about multiple possibilities. *Child Development, 60*, 183–200.

Inhelder, B., & Piaget, J. (1958). *The growth of logical thinking from childhood to adolescence*. New York: Basic Books.

Janveau-Brennan, G., & Markovits, H. (1999). Reasoning with causal conditionals: Developmental and individual differences. *Developmental Psychology, 35*(4), 904–911.

Johnson-Laird, P. N. (1983). *Mental Models*. Cambridge: Harvard University Press.

Johnson-Laird, P. N., & Byrne, R. M. J. (1991). *Deduction*. Hillsdale, NJ: Erlbaum.

Kail, R. (1992). Processing speed, speech rate, and memory. *Developmental Psychology, 28*, 899–904.

Karmiloff-Smith, A. (1992). *Beyond modularity: A developmental perspective on cognitive science*. Cambridge, MA: Bradford Books, MIT Press.

Klaczynski, P. A., & Narasimham, G. (1998). Representations as mediators of adolescent deductive reasoning. *Developmental Psychology, 5*, 865–881.

Knifong, J. D. (1974). Logical abilities of young children: Two styles of approach. *Child Development, 45*, 78–83.

Kuhn, D. (1977). Conditional reasoning in children. *Developmental Psychology, 13*, 342–353.

Lea, R. B., O'Brien, D. P., Fisch, S. M., Noveck, I. A., & Braine, M. D. S. (1990). Predicting propositional logic inferences in text comprehension. *Journal of Memory and Language, 29*, 361–387.

Leevers, H., & Harris, P. (1999). Transient and persisting effects of instruction on young children's syllogistic reasoning with incongruent and abstract premises. *Thinking and Reasoning, 5*(2), 145–174.

Luria, A. (1971). Towards the problem of the historical nature of psychological processes. *International Journal of Psychology, 6*, 259–272.

Macnamara, J. (1986). *A border dispute: The place of logic in psychology*. Cambridge, MA: MIT Press.

Manktelow, K. I., & Over, D. E. (Eds.) (1993). *Rationality: Psychological and philosophical perspectives*. London: Routledge.

Markovits, H. (1985). Incorrect conditional reasoning among adults: Competence or performance? *British Journal of Psychology, 76*, 241–247.

Markovits, H. (2000). A mental model analysis of young children's conditional reasoning with meaningful premises. *Thinking and Reasoning, 6*(4), 335–348.

Markovits, H. (2002). *Are older adolescents less "logical" than younger ones?: The interaction between knowledge and reasoning when accepting the premises in conditional reasoning*. Manuscript submitted for publication.

Markovits, H., & Barrouillet, P. (in press). The development of conditional reasoning: A mental model account. *Developmental Review*.

Markovits, H., & Bouffard-Bouchard, T. (1992). The belief-bias effect: Competence and performance in the development of logical reasoning. *British Journal of Developmental Psychology, 10*, 269–284.

Markovits, H., Doyon, C., & Simoneau, M. (in press). Individual differences in working memory and conditional reasoning with concrete and abstract content. *Thinking and Reasoning*.

Markovits, H., Fleury, M.-L., Quinn, S., & Venet, M. (1998). Conditional reasoning and the structure of semantic memory. *Child Development, 64*(3), 742–755.

Markovits, H., & Potvin, F. (2001). Suppression of valid inferences and knowledge structures: The curious effect of producing alternative antecedents on reasoning with causal conditionals. *Memory and Cognition, 29*(5), 736–744.

Markovits, H., Schleifer, M., & Fortier, L. (1989). The development of elementary deductive reasoning in young children. *Developmental Psychology, 25*(5), 787–793.

Markovits, H., & Vachon, R. (1989). Reasoning with contrary-to-fact propositions. *Journal of Experimental Child Psychology, 47*, 398–412.

Markovits, H., & Vachon, R. (1990). Conditional reasoning, representation and level of abstraction. *Developmental Psychology, 26*, 942–951.

Markovits, H., Venet, M., Janveau-Brennan, G., Malfait, N., Pion, N., & Vadeboncoeur, I. (1996). Reasoning in young children: Fantasy and information retrieval. *Child Development, 67*, 2857–2872.

Miller, S. A., Custer, W. L., & Nassau, G. (2000). Children's understanding of the necessity of logically necessary truths. *Cognitive Development, 15*(3), 383–403.

Morris, A. K. (2000). Development of logical reasoning: Children's ability to verbally express the nature of the distinction between logical and nonlogical forms of argument, *Developmental Psychology, 36*(6), 741–758.

Moshman, D. (1990). The development of metalogical understanding. In W. F. Overton (Ed.) *Reasoning, necessity, and logic: Developmental perspectives* (pp. 205–225), Hillsdale, NJ: Erlbaum.

Moshman, D. (1995). Reasoning as self-constrained thinking. *Human Development, 38*(1), 53–64.

Moshman, D. (1998). Cognitive development beyond childhood. In W. Damon (Series Ed.) and D. Kuhn & R. Siegler (Vol. Eds.) (1998), *Handbook of child psychology: Vol. 2. Cognition, perception and language* (5th ed., pp. 947–978). New York: Wiley.

Moshman, D., & Franks, B. A. (1986). Development of the concept of inferential validity. *Child Development, 57*(1), 153–165.

Mueller, U., Overton, W. F., & Reene, K. (2001). Development of conditional reasoning: A longitudinal study, *Journal of Cognition and Development*, 2(1), 27–49.

O'Brien, D. P., Costa, G., & Overton, W. F. (1986). Evaluations of causal and conditional hypotheses. *Quarterly Journal of Experimental Psychology*, *38A*, 493–512.

O'Brien, D. P., & Overton, W. F. (1980). Conditional reasoning following contradictory evidence: A developmental analysis. *Journal of Experimental Child Psychology*, *30*, 44–61.

O'Brien, D. P., & Overton, W. F. (1982). Conditional reasoning and the competence-performance issue: A developmental analysis of a training task. *Journal of Experimental Child Psychology*, *34*, 274–290.

Osherson, D. N., & Markman, E. (1975). Language and the ability to evaluate contradictions and tautologies. *Cognition*, *21*, 213–226.

Overton, W. F. (1985). Scientific methodologies and the competence-moderator-performance issue. In E. Neimark, R. DeLisi, and J. Newman (Eds.), *Moderators of competence* (pp. 15–41). Hillsdale, NJ: Erlbaum.

Overton, W. F. (1990). Competence and procedures: Constraints on the development of logical reasoning. In W. F. Overton (Ed.) *Reasoning, necessity, and logic: Developmental perspectives* (pp. 1–34), Hillsdale, NJ: Erlbaum.

Overton, W. F., Byrnes, J. P., & O'Brien, D. P. (1985). Developmental and individual differences in conditional reasoning: The role of contradiction training and cognitive style. *Developmental Psychology*, *21*, 692–701.

Overton, W. F., & Newman, J. L. (1982). Cognitive development: A competence-activation/utilization approach. In T. M. Field, A. Huston, H. C. Quay, L. Troll, & G. E. Finley (Eds.), *Review of human development*. New York: Wiley.

Overton, W. F., Ward, S. L., Black, J., Noveck, I. A., & O'Brien, D. P. (1987). Form and content in the development of deductive reasoning. *Developmental Psychology*, *23*(1), 22–30.

Piaget, J. (1972). Intellectual development from adolescence to adulthood. *Human Development*, *15* (1), 1–12.

Piaget, J. (1974). *Recherches sur la contradiction: 1. Les différentes formes de la contradiction* [Studies on contradiction : 1. The different forms of contradiction] Paris: Presses Universitaires de France.

Piaget, J. (1987a). *Possibility and necessity. Vol. 1: The role of possibility in cognitive development* (H. Feider, Trans.). Minneapolis: University of Minnesota Press. Original work published in 1981.

Piaget, J. (1987b). *Possibility and necessity: Vol. 2. The role of necessity in cognitive development* (H. Feider, Trans.). Minneapolis: University of Minnesota Press. (Original work published in 1983)

Piaget, J., Grize, J.-B., Szeminska, A., Bang, V. (1977). *Epistemology and psychology of functions* (J. Castellanos & V. Anderson, Trans.). Dordrecht, Netherlands: D. Reidel. (Original work published in 1967)

Quinn, S., & Markovits, H. (1998). Conditional reasoning, causality, and the structure of semantic memory: Strength of association as a predictive factor for content effects. *Cognition*, *68*, B93–B101.

Roberge, J. J., & Flexer, B. K. (1979). Further examinations of formal operational reasoning abilities. *Child Development*, *50*(2), 478–484.

Roberge, J. J., & Paulus, D. H. (1971). Developmental patterns for children's class and conditional reasoning abilities. *Developmental Psychology*, *4*, 191–200.

Rumain, B., Connell, J., & Braine, M. D. S. (1983). Conversational comprehension processes are responsible for reasoning fallacies in children as well as adults: If is not a biconditional. *Developmental Psychology*, *19*, 471–481.

Scholnick, E. K. (1990). The three faces of *if*. In W. F. Overton (Ed.). *Reasoning, necessity and logic: Developmental perspectives*. Hillsdale, NJ: Erlbaum.

Scribner, S. (1977). Modes of thinking and ways of speaking: Culture and logic reconsidered. In P. N. Johnson-Laird and P. C. Wason (Eds.), *Thinking: Readings in cognitive science* (pp. 483–500). New York: Cambridge University Press.

Shapiro, B. J., & O'Brien, T. C. (1971). Logical thinking in children ages six through thirteen. *Child Development*, *41*(3), 823–829.

Sigel, I. E. (Ed.) (1999). *Development of mental representation: Theories and applications*. Mawah, NJ: Erlbaum.

Sophian, C., & Somerville, S. C. (1988). Early developments in logical reasoning: considering alternatives possibilities. *Cognitive Development*, *3*, 183–222.

Staudenmeyer, H., & Bourne, L. E. (1977). Learning to interpret conditional sentences: A developmental study, *Developmental Psychology*, *13*(6), 616–623.

Taplin, J. E., Staudenmayer, H., & Taddonio, J. L. (1974). Developmental changes in conditional reasoning: Linguistic or logical? *Journal of Experimental Child Psychology*, *17*, 360–373.

Thompson, V. A. (1994). Interpretational factors in conditional reasoning. *Memory & Cognition*, *22*, 742–758.

Vadeboncoeur, I., & Markovits, H. (1999). The effect of instructions and information retrieval on accepting the premises in a conditional reasoning task. *Thinking and Reasoning*, *5*(2), 97–113.

Venet, M., & Markovits, H. (2001). Understanding uncertainty with abstract conditional premises. *Merrill-Palmer Quarterly*, *47*(1), 74–99.

Ward, S. L., & Overton, W. F. (1990). Semantic familiarity, relevance, and the development of deductive reasoning. *Developmental Psychology*, *26*, 488–493.

Wason, P. C. (1968). Reasoning about a rule. *Quarterly Journal of Experimental Psychology*, *20*, 272–281.

Wildman, T. M., & Fletcher, H. J. (1977). Developmental increases and decreases in solutions of conditional syllogism problems. *Developmental Psychology*, *13*, 630–636.

Wollman, W., Bat-Sheva, E., & Lawson, A. E. (1979). Acceptance of lack of closure: Is it an index of advanced reasoning? *Child Development*, *50*, 656–665.

13

The Evolution of Reasoning

Denise Dellarosa Cummins

Cognition is a biological function, not a cultural invention. Our nervous systems detect, encode, and process information, not because someone invented these capacities in antiquity, but because evolutionary forces shaped the organs that instantiate these biological functions. Cognition is the function that ensures a nonarbitrary relation between perception and action. Historically, psychologists have tended to overlook or downplay the role of biology and evolution when developing theories of cognitive functions, with the inevitable result that our theories have often provided inadequate predictions and explanations of cognitive phenomena, from basic inductive processes to higher cognition.

EVOLUTION AND BASIC INDUCTIVE PROCESSES

Consider first investigations of spatial learning in the rat. In one standard paradigm, a rat is placed on a central platform with alleys radiating out from the platform like spokes in a wheel. A cache of food is placed at the end of one of the alleys. The maze is constructed such that the rat cannot see the ends of the alleys, and air flow is directed such that no olfactory cues are present to guide the rat to the food. The rat is allowed to explore the maze. After it has found and consumed the food, the rat is removed and placed again on the platform, and the same alley rebaited. What will the rat do now?

Reinforcement theory predicts that the rat will return to the alley where it previously found food because that choice was reinforced (see Hilgard & Bower, 1975, pp. 206–251). But in fact, the rat avoids that alley, exploring virtually every other one before returning to that one (Gaffan, Hansel, & Smith, 1983; Olton, 1978, 1979; Olton & Samuelson, 1976). Only by painstaking repeated trials will the rat eventually behave in accordance with reinforcement theory, returning to the alley that is always baited with food.

After observing this behavior, we may be tempted to conclude that rats are indeed very stupid creatures, failing to notice a very salient contingency between location and food, or that they have very poor spatial memory. But subsequent research suggested otherwise. Suppose on the second trial, another alley is baited, and the rat, during its wanderings discovers the food and consumes it. When given another chance to explore the maze, the rat will now avoid both alleys where it previously encountered food. This effect has been demonstrated in up to eight alleys, with rats studiously avoiding the eight locations where they previously encountered food. This pattern of behavior suggests that rats in fact have excellent spatial memory, but they capitalize on it in order to avoid previous food caches. This seemingly paradoxical result becomes entirely comprehensible if one considers the type of species one is examining – a forager. When foraging in a natural environment, food intake is maximized if locations that have already been stripped of food are avoided. So perhaps the rats' choices are indeed rational, having been shaped by a very long evolutionary history in which the effectiveness of an individual's foraging strategies played a large role in its survival and reproductive success. We cannot explain this behavior in terms of learning because the rats used in these studies were naive laboratory-raised creatures with no foraging experience. The biases they demonstrated were clearly not a result of learning. Their inductive performance gave researchers a pristine view of how evolution had shaped the mind of this foraging species. This is not to say that rats cannot learn to return always to a particular location. Indeed, they can. But it takes a large number of learning trials to overcome this innate foraging bias.

The second example that amply demonstrates the impact of evolutionary constraints on basic inductive processes is the Garcia effect, an effect that has been replicated numerous times in dozens of species (Garcia, Brett, & Rusiniak, 1989; Garcia & Koelling, 1966). In the standard paradigm, animals are allowed to drink bitter-tasting quinine-adulterated water in a room with flashing lights. Half receive a brief electric shock and the remaining half are irradiated to produce nausea. The question is what the animal learns from these experiences. Early learning theories rested on the assumption that an association could be made between any two stimuli through repeated pairings, as in the simple association Pavlov's dogs made between food and ringing bells (see Hilgard & Bower, 1975, pp. 62–89). In the Garcia paradigm, however, the painful shock is paired with flashing lights and bitter-tasting water, so according to simple learning induction principles, the animal should form a negative association equally to both. But that is not what happens. Instead, those shocked avoid drinking while the lights are flashing but are indifferent to bitter-tasting water. Conversely, those who experienced nausea will avoid bitter-tasting water but are indifferent as to whether lights are flashing while they drink.

This effect has been replicated in a number of species, including naive laboratory-raised rats who could not possibly rely on previous experience with lightning or other worldly phenomena to guide their inductive processes. As this oft replicated effect shows, some associations are more readily induced than others. This is equally true of humans: People who happen to become ill (e.g., with the flu) after eating an unusual food typically develop long-lasting aversions to the food, even if a day or two intervenes between ingestion and nausea (Bernstein & Borson, 1986; Logue, 1988). Phobias also show this preparedness to induce; people (and naive laboratory-raised monkeys) are far more likely to develop fear responses to spiders, snakes, or other creatures that proved dangerous during their species' evolutionary histories than to benign creatures or artifacts, such as rabbits, flowers, or spatulas (Cook & Mineka, 1989; Seligman, 1971). In contrast, other types of associations (such as blinking in response to a light that is paired with a jarring puff of air to the eye) take numerous, carefully paced trials to acquire. Clearly, not all associations are equal in the mind's eye, and our theories must accommodate these evolutionarily based biases if they are to remain true to our data.

In each of these cases, researchers risked misconstruing the cognitive capacities of the species under consideration and the nature of their inductive learning because they failed to consider evolutionary constraints on otherwise domain-general inductive processes. When taken into account, a very different picture of the cognitive phenomena emerged.

EVOLUTION AND HIGHER COGNITION

Cognitive psychologists who fail to take evolutionary history into account when investigating higher cognition risk making the same type of mistake. In his book on visual cognition, David Marr (1982) argued that psychological research and theory ought to be guided by consideration of the types of problems the system was designed (by evolution) to solve. Although Marr's interest was visual cognition, this exhortation applies equally to all aspects of cognition. Generally speaking, psychologists consider evolutionary constraints only when faced with mounting disconfirming data or seemingly paradoxical, irrational behavior. In the case of higher cognition, the resistance toward considering evolutionary constraints has been strong enough that many have entirely capitulated to the view that human reasoning is error-prone, faulty, biased, and frequently irrational (e.g., Evans, 1989; Piatelli-Palmarini, 1994). Given the considerable scientific, technological, and artistic accomplishments that are the intellectual offspring of human reasoning, this constitutes a paradox indeed. How could a species whose reasoning is as deficient and error-prone as some accounts would have us believe possibly have produced rocket science, sophisticated market-based economies, and the great symphonic works of the nineteenth century? I offer here four examples of how seemingly faulty or irrational human reasoning performance takes on a very different appearance when viewed as psychological adaptations to frequently occurring problems in our species' evolution.

Psychological Adaptations for Reciprocity as an Explanation for Cooperation

Individual self-interest is a fundamental assumption of economics, yet there is ample evidence of cooperative behavior that is inconsistent with this assumption (Camerer & Thaler, 1995; Dawes & Thaler, 1988; Thaler, 1988). Among the most striking demonstrations are results from experimental economics games that involve interactions between anonymous strangers. In the *dictator* game, for example, two subjects are assigned a provisional $10. One subject, the dictator, then decides how the money is to be split between the two. While some dictators will give themselves the whole $10, as standard self-interested economic analyses would suggest, a significant number of dictators – and in many cases the majority – will give the other person a nontrivial amount of the money (Forsythe, Howowitz, Savin, & Sefton, 1994; Hoffman, McCabe, Shachat, & Smith, 1994; Hoffman, McCabe, & Smith, 1996; Johannesson & Persson, 2000). In another version of this task, called the *ultimatum game*, the second player, the responder, has the opportunity to either accept the proposed split or turn it down causing both subjects to walk away with nothing. Significantly more proposers offer the responder a nontrivial amount of the money with the modal offer usually being a 50:50 split. Yet, according to standard game-theoretic analyses, the addition of this second phase of play should make little difference to the proposed divisions. By backward induction, responders should favor any amount of money over nothing, and the proposers, knowing this, should offer the responders the smallest amount possible. Other studies show that when the subject's task is to decide whether to betray a collaborator and win a fixed amount of money, or trust them and possibly win more or less than the fixed amount (prisoner's dilemma game), subjects typically show a greater willingness to trust and a greater unwillingness to forgive betrayals of trust than is predicted by standard game theoretic analyses (Weg & Smith, 1993). Again, our data violate our theories – in this case, normative standards of rationality – and they again do so by showing us characteristic performance patterns that are stable and repeatable.

We can shore up our theories by pointing out that game-theoretic analyses of repeated games show that cooperation in the form of reciprocity – returning kindness for kindness and nastiness for nastiness – is indeed an equilibrium outcome of rationally self-interested play. These analyses, however, leave much unexplained. Reciprocity is just one of many equilibrium outcomes, yet it seems to be the most frequent one observed in experimental settings. Further, the dictator and ultimatum games are not repeated games, so the participants have no prior experience with their partners upon which to base their decisions. Instead, participants seem to enter these games with a definite bias toward cooperation, and violations of cooperation are responded to quite vehemently. This bias is quite specific and robust. The question is whether it is the result of prior experience with similar situations in the course of everyday life, or whether (like the Garcia effect and foraging biases) it constitutes something more fundamental in the nature of human cognition.

In his seminal essay on reciprocal altruism (cooperative effort for mutual benefit), Trivers (1971) hypothesized that due to ancestral humans' long lifespans, low dispersal rates, and mutual dependence, there would have been many repeated opportunities for mutually cooperative interactions, and hence the evolution of reciprocity. Subsequent evolutionary analyses of reciprocity repeatedly showed that reciprocity cannot evolve as an evolutionarily stable strategy unless cheaters can be recognized and excluded from future transactions (e.g., Axelrod, 1984; Axelrod & Hamilton, 1981). Using this evolutionary foundation, Cosmides and Tooby (1989, 1992; Cosmides, 1989) proposed an adaptationist account of social exchange (social contract theory) in which they hypothesized that humans evolved psychological adaptations for engaging in mutually beneficial, reciprocal exchanges. Essentially, this is a commitment to the claim that humans are biologically predisposed to detect, engage in, and reason effectively about social exchange. A social exchange is defined in terms of mutual benefits, and can be expressed propositionally as: *if benefit [to party X from party Y] then benefit [to party Y from party X]*. When such a situation is encountered, algorithms for reasoning about social exchange are activated. One key algorithm (as predicted by evolutionary analyses of reciprocity) is cheater detection. Cooperators should be particularly keen on monitoring the behavior of their partners to ensure that cheating has not occurred, that is, that the partner has not reneged on reciprocation of benefits after having accepted the benefit offered.

When viewed from this evolutionary perspective, the bias for reciprocity that subjects show in experimental economics studies no longer seems surprising or paradoxical. If humans evolved predispositions for engaging in social exchange, these tendencies are likely to be invoked in modern experimental economics games where there is the potential for cooperative interaction. Even though experimental settings often are contrived to be one-shot games, the psychological mechanisms that are invoked evolved in repeated game situations. Consistent with this interpretation is the observation that the ability to detect and punish cheaters has a large influence in producing cooperative outcomes that deviate from standard game-theoretic predictions (Fehr & Gächter, 2000; Fehr, Gächter, & Kirchsteiger, 1997).

An alternative explanation for subjects' predispositions for reciprocity is simply that these experimental economics games, as contrived as they appear to be, are sufficiently similar to other situations that humans are likely to encounter frequently during everyday life (Camerer & Thaler, 1995). Other converging evidence from the developmental and comparative literatures, however, speaks against this interpretation. Within the first year of life, infants engage in reciprocal turn-taking behavior with caregivers (Vandell & Wilson, 1987), and by at least the third year of life, children are selective in their distribution of altruistic acts, preferring to aid those who have aided them in the past (Smith, 1988). Children as young as four years of age reason effectively about reciprocal exchange, correctly identifying instances of compliance as well as instances of cheating (Harris, in press). Their performance on this type of social reasoning task contrasts sharply with typical performance on other types of reasoning tasks, such as transitive reasoning or syllogistic reasoning, which do not reliably emerge until considerably later in childhood (Bryant & Trabasso, 1971; Overton, Ward, Noveck, Black, & O'Brien, 1987).

Reciprocity also has been observed in the interactions of nonhuman animals, which is why evolutionary biologists took an interest in it in the first place. The most celebrated example is the reciprocity of vampire bats, which feed on the blood of other species (Wilkinson, 1984). Bats who have not been successful in their nightly foraging for blood will beg for some regurgitated blood from roostmates. They are most likely to receive aid from bats with whom they have shared blood in the past. Similarly, vervet monkeys are more likely to respond to calls for help from nonkin in agonistic encounters if the caller has groomed them recently, and they also form the strongest alliances with individuals who groom them most often (Seyfarth, 1976; Seyfarth & Cheney, 1984). Chimpanzees retaliate against individuals who show a low rate of food distribution relative to others, either by directly aggressing against them when they themselves request food (de Waal, 1989) or by misinforming or failing to inform them about the location of food (Woodruff & Premack, 1979). Chimpanzees also show reciprocity of supportive and retaliative interventions in that the rate of intervention by individual A *on behalf* of B correlates with the rate by B on behalf of A, and the rate of intervention *against* A by B correlates with the rate of intervention against B by A (de Waal, 1992).

Reciprocity also appears to be the cement that binds alliances together, and the strength of one's alliances determines one's rank within the social group. Among male chimpanzees, rank is acquired and maintained through dyadic aggression, and alliances determine the fate of outranked individuals, including alpha males whose rank is usurped (Chapais, 1988, 1992; Datta, 1983a, 1983b; Riss & Goodall, 1977; Uehara, Hiraiwa-Hasegawa, Hosaka, & Hamai, 1994). Alpha males who form or already possess strong alliances with other males maintain a relatively high, stable position within the group, while those who have no alliances or weak alliances are ostracized, maintaining a solitary existence outside the group. This is a particularly important finding because rank correlates with reproductive success (Altmann, et al., 1996), and reproductive success is the engine that drives the evolution of species. Essentially this means that reproductive success depends on alliance formation, and alliance formation in turn depends on forming and monitoring relationships based on reciprocity. With such evolutionary pressure surrounding this capacity, it should come as no surprise that reciprocity emerges very early in human development.

So perhaps, like rats in star mazes, human subjects in experimental economics studies are behaving quite rationally, and their performance patterns are providing a pristine view of how evolution shaped the nature of human cognition. The bias toward reciprocity is perhaps like the Garcia effect and the foraging behavior of rats – more biological bias than experientially induced. The early emergence of reciprocity in human development, its prominent role in evolutionary theory, its substantial contribution to reproductive success in other species, and the ubiquity with which it appears as a bias in experimental economics studies collectively substantiate this claim.

Reasoning about Behavior versus Reasoning about Truth: Psychological Adaptations for Deontic Reasoning

Imagine someone tells you something odd about a mutual friend of yours, namely:

If John stays overnight at his cabin, then he always comes home with a sack of garbage. (If p, then q)

As proof, your friend has kept tabs on John, writing down where he went and what he brought home with him every day for the past three months. He stored the daily information on file cards. On one side of each card, he wrote down where John went and on the back he wrote down whether or not John returned with a sack of garbage. Here are four of these cards. Two are shown face side-up and two are back side-up.

April 3	April 15	April 20	April 25
John stayed overnight at his cabin.	John stayed overnight elsewhere.	John returned home with a sack of garbage.	John returned home without a sack of garbage.

Suppose you wanted to prove your friend was wrong. Which card or cards would you turn over?

This is a truth-testing problem; your job is to find out whether the statement is true or false. This type of reasoning is sometimes called theoretical or discursive reasoning. When asked to test the truth of statements like this, people typically choose to inspect instances of *p* and *q* (e.g., to inspect the cards labeled John stayed overnight at his cabin [*p*] and John returned home with a sack of garbage [*q*]).

Now imagine that John's cabin is in a wildlife preserve, and it is required that all overnight visitors take their garbage out with them in order to protect the environment and discourage scavenging. Suppose your job is to make sure John is not breaking the rule. Which card or cards would you turn over?

In this case, we are not concerned with the truth of the rule. We assume the rule is true. Instead, we are interested in rule compliance because this rule is prescriptive. If John stays at his cabin, he is obligated to carry his garbage out. Reasoning about obligations, permissions, and prohibitions is called deontic (or practical) reasoning. We engage in deontic reasoning whenever we are concerned with determining what one may, must, or must not do. The typical answer on deontic problems like this is *p* and *not-q* (e.g., to inspect the cards labeled John stayed overnight at his cabin and John returned without a sack of garbage).

These typical answers may seem so obvious that one may wonder why I am discussing them at all. But consider this: In the truth-testing case, had we inspected the occasions in which John came home without a sack of garbage (*not-q* card) and discovered that he had been to his cabin, this would have provided incontrovertible proof that the statement was false. Instead, we tend to choose the *q* card. Suppose we inspect the *q* card and find that John had been somewhere else when he returned with a sack of garbage. Does that mean the statement is false? No. The statement does not say that he returns with garbage only when he has been to the cabin. Suppose we inspect the same card and discover that he had been to the cabin. Can we safely conclude that the statement is true? No. That card only shows that he returned with garbage on that occasion. It provides supporting but not conclusive evidence. In fact, suppose instead of one card, the display above represents entire stacks of cards, all of them oriented the way the top card is displayed. Now suppose we inspected every single *q* card and found that everytime he returned with garbage, he had been to his cabin. Can we conclude the statement is true? No. That stack does not contain all the occasions when he visited the cabin. The *p* stack contains all of those. Inspecting the *q* card (or stack) is pretty uninformative either way you look at it, while inspecting the *not-q* card (or stack) is potentially more informative. So we should choose to inspect *p* and *not-q* in both versions of the task. Yet it does not occur to us to look for potential violations of the statement in the truth-testing case. The need only seems apparent in the deontic case.

If this apparent deficiency in our truth-testing reasoning seems more like a curiosity than something researchers should be getting exercised about, consider that this type of reasoning constitutes the foundation of scientific endeavors, jurisprudence, and investigative reporting. In each of these disciplines, decisions must be made about which evidence to seek, how evidence is to be evaluated, and what constitutes sufficient proof upon which to base a conclusion. In each, we are concerned with discovering the truth, often by testing assertions or hypotheses. Resoundingly poor performance on truth-testing tasks in psychological investigations therefore should give us considerable pause. We appear to perform better when evaluating compliance than when evaluating truth, and this deontic effect has been replicated in dozens of experiments using a variety of experimental tasks over the course of 30 years (see Cummins, 1996b for a review of this literature). The question is why.

A number of explanations for the deontic effect have been offered, none without controversy. Peter Wason first reported the confirmation-bias response pattern on the truth-testing version of this task in 1968 using an abstract problem involving cards and letters. The conditional used in the task was, If a card has a vowel on one side, then it has an even number on the other side. Subsequent studies reported better performance on conditionals with more thematic content, and the poor performance observed on the original Wason task was attributed to the abstractness of the original materials (Johnson-Laird, Legrenzi, & Legrenzi, 1972). Subsequent research falsified this interpretation because not all familiar content produced a shift in response bias (Griggs & Cox, 1982; Reich & Ruth, 1982). It was not so much rule-familiarity that was found to produce the shift in performance but a difference in the type of reasoning that was evoked by the task. Truth testing typically evokes a rule-confirming strategy while compliance-testing typically evokes a violation-detection strategy. Cheng and Holyoak (1985) argued that this shift in reasoning reflected the evocation of class-specific schemas, schemas that were induced through experience with frequently occurring, highly important classes of situations (such as permissions). This explanation, however, is insufficient because it either rests on an implicit assumption that people have more experience with cheating than with mistakes or lying (which pushes the envelope of credibility) or implies that we induce the correct strategy from our experiences with cheating but the wrong strategy from our experiences with testing truth.

A number of researchers have appealed to the notion of expected utility in explaining the deontic effect. For example, Oaksford and Chater (1994) have argued that the shift in selection patterns on the truth-testing and deontic versions of the Wason task indicates that people view these tasks in terms of optimal data selection, and shift their strategies from maximizing expected information gain on the truth-testing version to maximizing

expected utility on the deontic version. Further, they argue that both strategies are rational and perfectly adapted to the structure of the tasks. The key
to this rationality lies in the assumptions one makes about the distribution
of p and q cases in the population. When p and q are rare, q cases yield
higher potential information gain than *not-q* cases, so selecting q cases on
the truth-testing task optimizes expected information gain. Going back to
our earlier example, suppose John rarely stays overnight at his cabin (p),
but, given that he travels frequently, he often stays overnight at other places
(*not-p*). Suppose also that he rarely brings home garbage (q) but frequently
brings home other things (*not-q*) due to his frequent travels. Given that
information, one would assume that the p and q stacks would be pretty
small, but the *not-p* and *not-q* stacks would be quite large. If you had better
things to do with your time other than search through these stacks, it would
make more sense to sample the q stack than the *not-q* stack. It is smaller in
number and the incidence of p cases is small as well, so the likelihood of
getting useful information on any given draw from the q deck is greater
than from the *not-q* deck. You would not get the definitive proof that you
needed about the truth of the statement, but you are more likely to at least
accumulate useful information (i.e., p & q cases) in a shorter period of time.
To get definitive proof, you would need to search the *not-q* deck, but, again,
if the number of cards in that deck is very large and the incidence of p cases
is very small, the likelihood of finding the information you need (a p case
in the *not-q* deck) is very small. (If p were abundant, then selecting *not-q*
would be more informative.) There is one exception to the need to examine
not-q cases: If you knew that John had gone to the cabin exactly, say, five
times, you could also get definitive proof if you just checked q cases. If
you found only four cases of John stayed overnight at his cabin (p) in the
q deck, you would know the missing p case would have to be in the *not-q*
deck, so the statement is false. If you found all five in the q deck, you would
know the statement is true. In actual cases of hypothesis testing, however,
we rarely have the means to examine every case in an entire population.
Typically, we must sample the population and draw inferences on the basis
of the distribution characteristics of that sample.

This entire explanation, however, depends on the rarity assumption and
it is not clear how often or under what circumstances people make such
an assumption. Consider again our example of John and his garbage. No
mention was made about the frequency with which John either visits his
cabin or lugs home garbage. While one could possibly argue that people
assume lugging home garbage is pretty rare, it seems a stretch to argue
that they also assume John visits his cabin infrequently. In fact, the preferred p and q selection response has been demonstrated repeatedly with
conditionals that do not seem to invite this assumption, such as "when I
go to work, I hurry," (Reich & Ruth, 1982) or "if a person is over 19, then
the person must be drinking beer" (Cox & Griggs, 1982).

Oaksford and Chater (1994, 1996) explain the shift in response pattern on the deontic version of the task by arguing that people shift away from rule-testing to rule use. They argue that under these conditions people seek to maximize expected subjective utility. In so doing, they attempt to avoid the criticism of invoking without explaining the deontic concepts of obligation and entitlement that appear to be pivotal in people's reasoning (Manktelow & Over, 1991), an approach taken by others as well (Kirby, 1994; Manktelow & Over, 1990, 1991, 1995). The rarity assumption is relaxed because the authors believe it is not reasonable to prejudge rarity on this task. Instead, it is assumed that people assign utilities to cards based on their goals, which are defined in terms of identifying rule violations or discovering instances of unfairness. The basic idea is that people look to satisfy their interests by obtaining benefits and minimizing costs. Subjective utility is assigned in advance to the cards, but the basis upon which those assignments are made is not addressed other than to say that those are the cards that would be of use given the nature of deontic structures such as obligations and permissions. For example, they argue that an enforcer's goal is to discover instances of rule violation, which consist of cases where the person being monitored performs an action without first satisfying its precondition, and these are the only instances that are assigned positive utility.

Manktelow and Over (1990, 1991, 1995) also explain performance on the deontic version of the selection task by modeling it as a process in which subjects seek to maximize subjective expected utility. Reasoners construct a model of the conditional statement along with possible outcomes, and evaluate these outcomes in terms of costs (negative utility) and benefits (positive utility). To explain the selection pattern on the truth-testing version of the task, Evans and Over (1996) invoke the concept of subjective epistemic utility rather than Oaksford and Chater's expected information gain. Subjective epistemic utility is defined as the usefulness of data in determining the truth status of an hypothesis relative to a rival hypothesis. Reasoners try to maximize expected epistemic utility by choosing evidence that will reduce their uncertainty about a particular claim relative to another. A card's informativeness depends on the magnitude of the difference between the certainty of one's belief in the statement before and after turning the card. If one revises the certainty of one's belief after turning the card, then the card has been informative. Consider again the tendency to choose the q card on the truth-testing version of the task. If one's degree of uncertainty in the truth of the statement decreases as a result of turning this card, then the card has positive epistemic utility.

What should be apparent in this discussion is the stark asymmetry in the need for explanation between the two versions of the task. Virtually all researchers agree that people are concerned with subjective utility when testing compliance with prescriptive rules, but substantial disagreement exists concerning what counts as an efficacious and rational strategy when testing a statement's truth. Oaksford and Chater's (1994, 1996) analysis of truth testing, for example, has drawn fire from a number of fronts (see Oaksford & Chater, 1996 for summaries and replies to these objections). One might ask, "Why?" Why is the deontic version of the task so much clearer and easier for humans to reason about while the truth-testing version is not – even though they often require identical responses? Why, in fact, do people perform well on the deontic version of the task regardless of general intellectual ability or level of education while performance on the truth-testing version correlates positively with intelligence (Stanovich & West, 1998)? Is it something about the nature of the tasks or something about the nature of human cognition?

Perhaps what tilts the balance of evidence in favor of the latter is the early emergence of the deontic effect in human development. Unlike other reasoning skills that show pronounced performance improvements during development, children as young as three years of age show the same deontic effect that is apparent in adult reasoners: When presented with social rules, they spontaneously adopt a violation detection strategy (Cummins, 1996a), readily distinguish rule-violating behavior from compliant behavior (Harris & Nunez, 1996), and can give cogent explanations as to why noncompliance constitutes violations of social rules (Harris & Nuñez, 1996). Like adults, they also adopt a confirmation-seeking strategy when testing the truth of utterances (Cummins, 1996a). They also have difficulty distinguishing truth-violating from truth-preserving instances (Harris & Nunez, 1996), and cannot give coherent explanations as to why a truth-violating instance is inconsistent with the rule (Harris & Nunez, 1996). From very early in childhood, we seem perfectly capable of inducing the rules that constrain behavior in our social groups, monitoring the behavior of others with respect to them, and detecting noncompliance. Evaluating truth, in contrast, proves decidedly more difficult.

As should be expected from our previous discussion of other cognitive phenomena, some researchers returned to the basic question of how evolution shaped cognition in order to explain this paradoxical cognitive phenomenon, which emerges early in life and remains constant throughout the lifespan. The first to offer an evolution-based explanation was Leda Cosmides (1989), who explained the shift in performance on the two versions of the Wason task in terms of social contract theory. She argued that the shift in response bias occurs only when subjects interpret the materials as social contracts with reciprocal benefit structures. An offer to engage in social exchange can be expressed by a rule of the form: *If benefit [to party X, from party Y] then benefit [to party Y, from party X]*. Subjects encountering such a rule should perceive that individuals who have accepted a benefit without returning a benefit are cheating. From party X's perspective, the rule has the cost/benefit structure of a social contract: *If benefit accepted then cost paid*. The four cards would now represent the contingencies: *benefit accepted (p), benefit not-accepted (not-p), cost paid (q)*, and *cost not-paid (not-q)*. Social contract theory predicts that subjects looking to see if party X cheated will select the *benefit accepted (p)* and *cost not-paid (not-q)* cards because those are the cases that constitute potential instances of cheating. Using the example above, it seems apparent to us that we need to check the *p* and *not-q* cards because that is how John could cheat – by going to the cabin (*p*) without carrying out his garbage (*not-q*).

According to social contract theory, then, the deontic effect is simply cheater detection, a phenomenon that biologists have shown to be necessary for the evolution of reciprocity. To support this interpretation, Cosmides (1989) and, subsequently, Gigerenzer and Hug (1992) showed that selection patterns switch to other cards when the reasoner's perspective switches. For example, consider the rule: If a customer spends $100 or more on a purchase (*p*), the customer should be given a $20 discount voucher (*q*). The store could cheat the customer by not giving the discount voucher even though a purchase for $100 or more was made. So from a customer's perspective, it's important to check instances where $100 was spent on a purchase (*p*) to make sure the $20 discount voucher was given, and instances where a $20 discount was not given (*not-q*) to make sure the purchase was for less than $100. But the store can be cheated if the $20 discount was given even though the customer did not spend $100 or more. So from a store manager's perspective, it's important to check instances where less than $100 was spent (*not-p*) to make sure no discount voucher was given, and instances where the $20 discount voucher was given (*q*) to make sure the purchase was for $100 or more. And that is in fact what happens: People switch their response bias depending on which perspective they adopt. When they adopt the customer's perspective, they tend to select *p* and *not-q*, but when they adopt the store manager's perspective, they tend to select *not-p* and *q* (Cosmides, 1989; Gigerenzer & Hug, 1992; Manktelow & Over, 1990; Politzer & Nguyen-Xuan, 1992). These shifts in response patterns are entirely rational because they indicate that people are protecting their interests by ensuring that they have not been cheated.

The social contract interpretation of the deontic effect has not been without its critics. Researchers have argued that evolution need not be invoked to explain perspective effects because they can be explained through reference to learned schemas (e.g., Holyoak & Cheng, 1995; Politzer & Nguyen-Xuan, 1992) or expected subjective utility (Kirby, 1994; Manktelow & Over, 1995; Oaksford & Chater, 1994). One could argue, however, that Cosmides provided an explanation of how and why subjective utility matters by rooting these notions in terms of costs and benefits that impacted our ancestors' survival. Perhaps the most problematic aspect of the theory is that the rules employed in many of the studies evidencing the deontic effect do not appear to fit the definition of cooperative effort for mutual benefit. Instead, they appear to better fit the definition of social regulations or social norms.

Social norms are constraints on behavior that are imposed either through convention or by authority. The distinction between a social contract (as defined in social contract theory) and a social norm is analogous to the distinction between a contract and a law. Contracts are typically mutually agreed-upon obligations between two or more individuals. Laws are rules that govern all members of a social group and membership in the group either requires or implies adhering to the rules. Social contract theory is particularly restrictive because it applies only to contracts based on reciprocal obligations for mutual benefit; this is because its theoretical machinery draws directly from evolutionary analyses of reciprocity and the key role played by cheater detection in those analyses. That leaves unexplained why the deontic effect has been observed for rules such as:

Drinking law: If a person is drinking beer, then the person must be over 19. (Griggs & Cox, 1982)
Postal regulation: If an envelope is sealed, then it must have a 20-cent stamp. (Cheng & Holyoak, 1985)
Tribal law: If a man eats cassava root, then he must have a tattoo on his face. (Cosmides, 1989)

It is a stretch to make these rules fit the definition of a contract between two or more individuals for mutual benefit. They better fit the definition of a social regulation or social norm. The last of these is of particular interest because it was one of the rules used by Cosmides as evidence in support of social contract theory. The rule was instituted by tribal elders to restrict the use of cassava root (which was an aphrodisiac) to married men (married men sported tattoos in this mythical tribe).

For this reason, I (Cummins, 1996a, 1996b, 1996c, 1997, 1998, 1999, 2000, 2002) have argued that the deontic effect applies more broadly to any rules that constrain social behavior – not just contracts imposing reciprocal obligations for mutual benefit, and that its robustness can be accounted for by our evolutionary heritage as a social species. According to standard evolutionary analyses, the fundamental problem that an organism must solve is maximizing reproductive success. That is how natural selection works: Individuals differ, some of these differences provide competitive advantage, allowing them to survive better or longer and therefore leave more offspring who live to reproduce themselves (which is called fitness). Maximizing reproductive success in turn reduces to solving problems of acquiring mates, accessing sufficient food, and avoiding or reducing the risk of death due to predation. One common solution to these problems found in nature is sociality – living in social groups. Despite the clear benefits that derive from sociality, living in social groups also imposes costs in terms constraints on the behavior of individuals. These constraints are termed *social norms*. Social norms appear not just in the societies of humans but in the societies of nonhuman animals as well, where they constrain virtually every activity, including who is allowed to sit next to, play with, share food with, groom, and mate with whom (Aruguete, 1994; Hall, 1964). In order to avoid agonistic encounters and ostracism, members of a social group must learn which behaviors are permitted, prohibited, and obligated under which conditions. Flouting these norms carries great risk. In fact, perceived violations of the social code has been designated as the single most common cause of aggression in primate groups (Hall, 1964). Cheater detection, therefore, applies to the breaking of social norms as much as it does to violations of reciprocity.

Explaining the deontic effect in this way accounts for more of the published data than does explaining it in terms of social contract theory. Numerous studies have demonstrated the deontic effect using rules that better fit the definition of social norm than social contract (see Cummins, 1996b for a review of this literature). It also provides an evolutionary foundation upon which this type of cognition could plausibly emerge. Our deontic intuitions concerning obligations, permissions, and prohibitions are rooted in the evolution of social cognition, that is, the cognition that subserves extracting the regularities of the social environment (social norms), and monitoring the behavior of oneself and others with respect to them. Deontic concepts and reasoning strategies emerge early in cognitive development because they are crucial to survival.

The analysis of the social environment and its impact on cognition would not be complete, however, without addressing one final and crucially important aspect: social dominance. I call the complete analysis dominance theory. In addition to increasing opportunities for cooperation, sociality results in increased competition for resources. In most mammalian and avian species, this competition produces a complex social structure called a *dominance hierarchy*. In functional terms, a dominance hierarchy is simply the observation that particular individuals in social groups have regular priority of access to resources in competitive situations (Clutton-Brock & Harvey, 1976). A fundamental tenet of dominance theory is that, from a cognitive standpoint, a social dominance hierarchy constitutes a set of implicit social norms that reflect which behaviors are permitted, prohibited, or obligated given one's rank. In most species, there is a direct relationship between dominance rank and survival, with higher ranking members being less likely to die of predation or starvation (Cheney & Seyfarth, 1990, pp. 33–34), and more likely to leave living offspring (e.g., Clutton-Brock, 1988; Dewsbury, 1982; Ellis, 1995; Fedigan, 1983; Hausfater, 1975; Tutin, 1979; Watts & Stokes, 1971). Among primate species in which dominance rank is unstable, the level of reproductive success achieved by any individual is directly related to the length of time during which the individual is high ranking (Altmann et al., 1996). Maximizing reproductive success, therefore, is intimately connected to maximizing one's rank.

Low-ranking individuals attempt to improve their access to resources through cheating and deception. For example, they maintain possession of desirable objects or engage in forbidden behaviors by hiding them from view, acting quietly so as not to attract attention, avoiding looking at a desirable object themselves, or distracting attention away from the desired object or forbidden behaviors (Byrne, 1995; Mitchell, 1986; Whiten & Byrne, 1988). They also move forbidden trysts out of line of sight of dominant individuals and suppress copulation cries to avoid detection (Kummer, 1988; de Waal, 1988).

As is apparent, most of these acts of cheating and deception allow lower-ranking individuals to violate social norms without getting caught. This can have enormous beneficial consequences for the cheater or deceiver. The costs associated with cheating, however, can be quite high because dominant individuals maintain priority of access to resources by detecting and punishing cheaters, that is, individuals who attempt to access resources to which they are not entitled. (Interestingly, Cosmides and Tooby, 1997, p. 147, have recently redefined cheating as taking a benefit that one is not entitled to.) For example, high-ranking individuals often punish acts of cheating as benign as grooming or sharing food with forbidden individuals (de Waal, 1992, pp. 246–249) as well as more serious transgressions such as attempting to mate with estrus females (de Waal, 1992).

Cheater detection is therefore crucial not just to reciprocity and preserving social norms, but to preserving the status quo. The benefits that accrue to individuals for compliance are continued acceptance within the social group (i.e., avoiding ostracism) and avoidance of agonistic encounters with dominants who preserve the status quo. The costs that accrue for compliance include lost opportunities to form alliances or garner a larger share of resources. High-status individuals preserve the status quo by punishing individuals who violate social norms, access resources to which they are not entitled, or engage in disputes with other subordinates.

Dominance theory is based on an analysis of sociality in various species of nonhuman animals, particularly primates. Can this analysis be extended to humans? On the face of it, it would seem odd if it could not. This type of social organization and the cognition that subserves it were present and thriving prior to the emergence of protohumans, and natural selection operates on traits that are already present. Further, humans were (and still are) subject to the same pressures from the social environment that other social species are – inducing the norms that constraint behavior in one's social group. It has been argued, however, that despite humans sharing over 97% of our DNA with our closest biological cousin (the common chimpanzee), it is that last 3% that produces the enormous cognitive differences between them and us. So perhaps this is an adequate analysis of struggles in the wild, but it has little to do with modern Homo sapiens. Testing dominance theory therefore is in order, and can be done in a number of ways. I will discuss just two avenues of evidence here: If dominance theory applies to humans, one would expect to find status hierarchies in human social groups, and to find that consideration of status impacts expectations regarding acceptable behavior. There is evidence to support both of these assertions.

With respect to the first assertion, status hierarchies emerge early in human development, having been observed in the playgroups of children as young as two years of age (Frankel & Arbel, 1980), and is the earliest and most enduring dimension of peer group social organization (Hold-Cavell & Borsutsky, 1986; La Freniere & Charlesworth, 1983; Lemerise, Harper, & Howes, 1998; Strayer & Trudel, 1984). By four years of age, children can reliably report the structure of these hierarchies indicating conscious awareness of status differences (Smith, 1988). In human socioeconomic and sociopolitical systems, instances of dominance hierarchies include monopolies, monarchies, social stratification, caste and class systems, sexism, and racism. In each case, social, political, and economic power falls disproportionately into the hands of some members of a society at the expense of others. I think I need not point out that inequitable distribution of resources leads inevitably to social strife and disharmony, and that various attempts have been made throughout history to redistribute wealth and power (e.g., the Bolshevik Revolution, the Magna Carta, legal codes, graduated tax laws, and even affirmative action) with varying degrees of success. It is probably safe to say that the bulk of human political history is a chronicle of struggles for and against dominance (privileged access to resources).

Dominance also influences sociopolitical decision making (Pratto, Tatar, Conway-Lanz, 1999). People who score high on measures of social dominance tend to prefer hierarchical relationships in society, distribution of resources based on merit, conservative ideology, military programs, and punitive justice policies. These are all consistent with maintaining priority of access to resources. Those scoring low on social dominance measures tend to favor social equality, distribution of resources based on need, and social programs. In fact, social dominance measures have been found to account for much of the sex-linked variability in American political attitudes (Pratto, Stallworth, & Sidanius, 1997).

The latter assertion – that consideration of status impacts expectations concerning acceptable behavior – is a prediction that has been tested and supported experimentally. Cummins (1999) found higher levels of cheater detection when reasoners believed themselves to be of higher status than the individuals whose compliance they were monitoring with respect to a social norm. The Wason (1968) task was embedded in a scenario that encouraged the reasoner to adopt the perspective of either a student or a dormitory resident assistant. The rule employed was that *if someone is assigned to tutor a study session, that person is required to tape record the session*. The people whose behavior was being monitored were either students or resident assistants, so reasoners who adopted the perspective of a resident assistant believed themselves to be checking on others who were either lower status (students) or equally high status (resident assistants) while reasoners who adopted the perspective of a student believed themselves to be checking on others who were either higher status (resident assistants) or equally low status (students). The proportion of cheater detection responses (p and $not\text{-}q$) was significantly higher when reasoners adopted the perspective of a resident assistant checking on students than in any other condition. In contrast, status perspective had no impact on the truth-testing version of the task. In this version, reasoners were told they overhead someone saying, "If I'm assigned to tutor a session, I always tape record the session." Their job was to select the cards that would allow them to discover whether or not the person told the truth. The modal response in this version of the task was p and q, regardless of status perspective. These results were replicated in a second experiment that employed a within-subject design. In related work using a face recognition paradigm, Mealey and colleagues found that people were more likely to remember low-status cheaters than high-status cheaters or noncheaters of either status (Mealey, Daood, & Krage, 1996). Social contract theory, as it is currently stated, cannot readily accommodate these findings, in part because it is based on an implicit assumption of contracts between individuals of equal exogenous status. Dominance theory better accounts for these results because (a) it casts cheating as a violation of social norms, not just a violation of reciprocity and (b) the consequences of cheating depend on the individual's status.

The early emergence of the deontic effect in development, its endurance and robustness in adult reasoning, and the central role played by implicit permissions, obligations, and prohibitions in the social interactions of other social mammals are all consistent with an evolutionary interpretation. We are social beings from the moment of birth, and a crucial part of sociality is inducing the rules that constrain behavior and knowing when those rules are being violated. The paradox of selection patterns on the Wason task is no paradox: Of the two version of this task, only one has deep evolutionary roots. This seems to be the most parsimonious explanation of the deontic effect.

Reasoning about Frequencies and Covariation

Consider the following medical reasoning problem discussed by Gigerenzer (1998):

The probability that a person has colon cancer is 0.3%.
If a person has colon cancer, the probability that the test is positive is 50%.
If the person does *not* have colon cancer, the probability that the test is positive is 3%.
What is the probability that person who tests positive actually has colon cancer?

The inference from an observation (a positive test) to an hypothesis (diagnosis) is referred to as Bayesian inference because it can be modeled by Bayes Theorem. Applying Bayes rule to these data yields a probability of 4.7%. Twenty-four physicians were given this problem and asked to answer the final question. Only one physician came up with the Bayesian answer; the median estimate for the rest was 47% – an order of magnitude higher. Contrast this dismal result with physicians' performance on the following problem:

Thirty out of every 10,000 people have colon cancer.
Of these 30 people with colon cancer, 15 will test positive.
Of the remaining 9,970 people *without* colon cancer, 300 will still test positive.

Imagine a group of people who test positive. How many of these will actually have colon cancer? Using this natural frequency format, 67% of the physicians came up with the correct Bayesian answer. (Similar results were reported in a study involving 100 physicians.) In another study, college students worked 30 problems in which natural frequency and probability formats alternated from problem to problem (Gigerenzer & Hoffrage, 1995). These students performed consistently well on the natural frequency format problems and consistently poorly on the probability format problems. The benefits of natural frequency formats on reasoning performance have been replicated numerous times with a variety of populations (see Chapter 5 of this volume for a complete discussion of this phenomenon).

Paradoxical results like these led many researchers to conclude that human reasoning is hopelessly biased, irrational, error prone, and dependent on misleading heuristics. Considering that our medical, legal, technological, and social institutions are all creations of human reasoning, this is a discomfiting conclusion. But, again, these paradoxical results appear far less paradoxical from an evolutionary viewpoint. Cognition is a biological adaptation for processing information from the physical and social environments. That information does not present itself in terms of single event probabilities and odds/ratios. It comes to us in the form of frequencies of entities and events. Probabilities and percentages are, evolutionarily speaking, quite recent forms of quantitative representations, emerging in the mid-seventeenth century (Hacking, 1975). Percentages did not become common notation until the nineteenth century, and even then were used for interest and taxes rather than as expressions of uncertainty (Gigerenzer, Swijtink, Porter, Daston, Beatty, & Krüger, 1989). It was not until the second half of the twentieth century that the terms probability and percentage became part of common parlance. It took millennia of literacy and numeracy to develop these notions culturally, and now takes years of schooling for individuals to develop them as everyday reasoning tools.

In contrast, the ability to automatically monitor absolute and relative frequencies appears to be a fundamental cognitive capacity. Numerous studies using a variety of stimuli have reported that people can track frequencies virtually effortlessly and flawlessly (see Hasher & Zacks, 1979), and are remarkably sensitive to covariations among events (Mandel & Lehman, 1998; Spellman, 1996; Waldmann, 2000). Infants as young as six months of age can enumerate objects and sequential actions (Starkey, Spelke, & Gelman, 1983, 1990; Wynn, 1996, 1998). Further, this capacity is not particular to humans. A large body of evidence indicates that a wide variety of vertebrate species are capable of monitoring absolute and relative frequencies as well as covariations. Rats can be trained to press a lever a specific number of times before pressing a second lever a single time to obtain a reward (Platt & Johnson, 1971). Rats, birds, and raccoons are capable of selecting objects based on their ordinal position in an array and learning to turn down the third, fourth, or fifth tunnel in a maze (Davis, 1984; Davis & Bradford, 1986; Pastore, 1961), and chimpanzees can be trained to select the Arabic numeral that correctly corresponds to the numerosity of display items (Matsuzawa, 1985). The results reported in these studies obtained even though potential non-numerical cues were controlled, such as size of the display, stimulus density, odor, location of targets, and elapsed time. And literally hundreds of experiments on conditioning have repeatedly shown that a variety of species (including humans) are sensitive to contingencies among stimuli. If event Y follows event X with sufficient regularity, animals (including humans) will show responses to event X that indicate they anticipate the occurrence of event Y (see Hilgard & Bower, 1975, chap. 3), and humans will also verbally express the contingency (Waldmann, 2000).

Frequency monitoring and covariation detection are apparently unlearned biological functions that allow entities and events in the environment to be tracked. They contrast sharply with symbolic mathematical systems, which are cultural inventions that must be painstakingly taught. It took the genius of a Newton and a Leibniz to discover the connection between derivatives and integrals, thereby providing the foundation of the symbolic system known as the calculus. Unlike frequency monitoring and covariation detection, symbolic mathematical systems like the calculus must be taught through explicit education. The former capacities are biological capacities shaped by evolutionary forces, the latter are cultural inventions.

Evolution and Physical Reasoning

Early theories of cognitive development rested on the assumption that infants were little more than sensory-motor systems, and that complex concepts were constructed from these simple building blocks through experience with the environment (Piaget, 1952). But this tabula rasa view of the human mind has given way under the weight of two decades of research on infant cognition. Some types of domain-specific knowledge appear to emerge quite early in infancy, before infants have had sufficient time to induce that knowledge through experience. Rather than Piagetian sensory-motor systems, infants appear to be cognitively predisposed to interpret the world in terms of agents and objects whose behaviors are constrained by different sets of principles (Leslie, 1994; Shultz, 1982; Spelke, 1991, 1994).

Infants as young as two and a half months of age evidence particular expectations concerning objects and their behavior, a sort of naive physics. They appreciate that objects are solid, rigid, and permanent entities that travel in continuous paths, cannot pass through each other, and can causally influence one another only by making direct contact (Leslie, 1994; Leslie & Keeble, 1987; Spelke, 1994; Spelke, Phillips, & Woodward, 1996). Our inferences about their cognition is based on repeated observations of their looking preferences. Infants spend less time looking at displays of objects whose behavior is consistent with these principles than at displays of objects whose behavior appears to violate them. But their impressive performance on these physical reasoning tasks breaks down when the tasks require an appreciation of gravity and inertia. For example, if a ball is dropped behind a screen, and the screen is lifted to reveal the ball hovering in midair above a table, very young infants do not find this any more surprising than if the ball is revealed to have landed on the table. It is not until the end of the first year of life that they begin to look longer at the hovering ball, suggesting a budding appreciation of the effects of gravity. Like gravity, appreciation of inertia seems slow to emerge during infanthood. Until about nine months of age, infants do not find it surprising when a ball rolled with great force seems to stop suddenly or change direction of its own accord.

The intriguing thing about this pattern of results is that the physical knowledge that emerges first in infancy appears to constitute a core group of concepts that influence our reasoning even as adults (Spelke, 1991, 1994). In contrast, the knowledge that emerges later remains foreign to our world view and is difficult to learn and understand. For example, in studies of naive physics, adults who had not studied physics were asked about the behavior of physical objects (McCloskey & Kohl, 1983). Rarely did they make mistakes regarding continuity, solidity, rigidity, or direct causation. These things seem perceptually obvious to them. Errors frequently occurred, however, on judgments concerning inertia and gravity. For example, approximately 50% of volunteers in these studies believed bombs would drop straight down out of airplanes, instead of obeying the law of inertia and continuing to travel forward until gravity acted on them. They also believed that a ball emerging from a spiral casing would continue on a spiral path, again, instead of obeying the law of inertia and continuing to travel in the same direction it was traveling when it left the casing. College sophomores are not alone in these erroneous beliefs. So believed nearly every ancient and medieval scholar (see Cummins, 1995, pp. 170–174). For centuries, it was believed that setting an object in motion impressed in the object a force, or impetus, that served to keep it in motion. When released, it continued to trace the same trajectory until the force dissipated, even if that trajectory was a spiral. It was not until the 16th century A.D. that we as a species began to appreciate and understand the true physical laws of inertia and gravity, and it took the genius of Galileo and Newton to discover and explicate them. In fact, we owe nearly all of modern technology to the genius of just a handful of gifted people who were able to go beyond the cognitive biases shaped by evolution in order to discover and elucidate the true laws of the physical world.

CONTROVERSIES SURROUNDING THE USE OF EVOLUTIONARY THEORY TO EXPLAIN AND PREDICT COGNITIVE PHENOMENA

I began this chapter by pointing out that cognition is what the brain does, and the brain is a product of evolutionary forces. It therefore follows that the mind – the collection of cognition capacities that make up the mind – is also a product of evolutionary forces. There are few cognitive and behavioral researchers who would object to this argument. Considerable controversy exists, however, over how evolutionary theory should be used to inform the study of cognition, and what it implies about the nature and structure of mind.

A viable evolutionary cognitive psychology requires that specific cognitive capacities be (a) heritable and (b) quasi-independent (Lewontin, 1978). They must be heritable, because there can be no evolutionary response to selection for traits that are not. They must also be quasi-independent because adaptive variations in a specific cognitive capacity could have no distinctive consequences for fitness if effecting those variations required widespread changes in other traits and capacities as well. The dominant paradigm in evolutionary cognitive psychology attempts to satisfy these constraints by proposing that the mind can be characterized as a collection of innate cognitive modules (Cosmides & Tooby, 1992; Tooby & Cosmides, 1995). These modules constitute solutions to frequently occurring problems that our hunter-gatherer ancestors faced during the Pleistocene, which, after Bowlby (1969) is referred to as the environment of evolutionary adaptiveness, or EEA (Symons, 1987, 1989). This position is succinctly captured by the following quote:

Our cognitive architecture resembles a confederation of hundreds or thousands of functionally dedicated computers (often called modules) designed to solve adaptive problems endemic to our hunter-gatherer ancestors. Each of these devices has its own agenda and imposes its own exotic organization on different fragments of the world. There are specialized systems for grammar induction, for face recognition, for dead reckoning, for construing objects and for recognizing emotions from the face. There are mechanisms to detect animacy, eye direction, and cheating. There is a "theory of mind" module . . . a variety of social inference modules . . . and a multitude of other elegant machines. (Tooby & Cosmides, 1995, pp. xiii–xiv)

Since what is innate is heritable, the requirements of heritability and quasi-independence would be satisfied by innate cognitive modules on the plausible assumption that modules are relatively decoupled from each other and from other traits. By "innate," proponents of the dominant paradigm do not mean "present at birth," but rather, encoded in the genome. For example, secondary sex characteristics are innate in that their development is encoded in the human genome, but they are not present at birth. The relevant notion of a cognitive module derives from Fodor (1983). But, whereas Fodor held that modules were largely peripheral mechanisms, the modules proposed by these researchers know no such boundaries. Nor are all of Fodor's characteristics always, or even typically, assumed. Rather, the key features are (1) domain specificity, (2) universality – that is, present in every normal mind in the species (assuming it has gone to fixation), and (3) relative encapsulation – insensitivity to collateral information.

This paradigm is dominant because advocates and critics alike take this view to be the main theoretical contender defining the field. This is unfortunate because this view has been heavily criticized for its logical and theoretical incoherence, as well as its incompatibility with what is known about developmental neurobiology. Because of these objections, many researchers have concluded that an evolutionary cognitive psychology is not possible. I will briefly summarize the major objections leveled against this view.

Criticisms of Innate Modules

Innate cognitive modules require innate knowledge of some sort, either in the form of explicitly represented knowledge or in the form of knowledge implicit in the logic and structure of special purpose processors. Either way, direct genetic specification of an innate module would presumably require specifying synaptic connections in the cortex. If cognitive capacities are specified in the genome, the genome must encode for specific patterns of synaptic connections.

The problem is that the human genome does not appear to have the resources to directly specify a significant amount of cortical connectivity. It is now known that human genotypes contain many fewer genes than previously thought (around 30,000 to 40,000 instead of a 100,000). Among these, it is estimated that from 20%–30% (Wills, 1991) to perhaps as many as half (Thompson, 1993) may be implicated in brain development. However, our brains literally contain trillions of synaptic connections and 5,000 to

15,000 genes are clearly insufficient to directly encode all of these (Buller & Hardcastle, 2000; Churchland, 1995). Moreover, it seems that very few of the genes involved in brain development are concerned with cortical development. Most of the genes involved in brain development are dedicated to making sure our sensory transducers are properly hooked up. These observations appear to be inconsistent with the notion of innate modules that are present at birth or whose development is prespecified by the genome.

Evolutionary scientists have also pointed out that the notion of innate modules is inconsistent with certain aspects of evolutionary theory (Smith, Borgerhoff Mulder, & Hill, 2000, 2001). First, the existence of multiple distinct modules is at odds with the accepted view of how evolutionary processes operate, namely by modifying existing evolved traits in ways that co-opt them to solve novel adaptive problems. Second, there is the problem of adaptive trade-off, which Smith et al. (2001) elegantly summarize as follows:

Although physiological and behavioral phenotypes are indeed specialized to perform specific functions, evolutionary logic suggests that they face significant design constraints reflecting the multiple goals of living organisms. If the heart were designed to be simply an effective blood pump, we would expect it to be larger and beat at a relatively constant speed; however, it is constrained in size and performance because the goal of optimal blood flow is traded-off against other fitness-related goals and other uses of energy. Given these constraints, natural selection has designed the heart to be a "fitness-maximizing pump" rather than simply a blood pump. This is a crucial distinction that many proponents of domain-specific adaptation fail to grasp. (p. 132)

This same argument can be made with respect to other adaptations. For example, the larynx serves not just as a means of vocal communication but also as a valve for regulating entry to and exit from the trachea. The impact of fitness trade-offs is apparent from its lowered position in adult humans, which, relative to a high-larynx position, simultaneously increases the range of sounds we are capable of making but also increases the likelihood of choking. Given that most of our organs show evidence of this type of trade-off in fitness effects, why would we expect cognitive design to be any different?

Criticisms of Appealing to an EEA

Central to evolutionary explanations of phenotypic variation is the notion of inclusive fitness, that is, the contribution an individual makes to its own reproductive success and that of its relatives. Adaptive traits are those that maximize inclusive fitness within a particular environmental niche. According to the dominant paradigm in evolutionary psychology, this environmental niche was the Pleistocene. The idea here is that the hominid brain underwent substantial expansion during this period, hence, cognitive algorithms constitute adaptations to the ancestral environment. As Symons (1989, pp. 138–139) put it "a well-formed description of an adaptation must consist *solely* of words for things, events, relations, and so forth, that existed in the EEA, which, in the case of human beings, means the Pleistocene world of nomadic foragers."

There are two implications of this view. The first is that, to the extent that there exists a mismatch between the EEA and modern environments, the effectiveness of our cognitive adaptations will suffer. We will have "Stone age minds and bodies" trying to survive in "unnatural" modern environments. The second implication is that measures of current inclusive fitness are irrelevant to determining the adaptive significance of contemporary human behavior.

While it is undoubtedly true that the current design of our brains is a product of a very long evolutionary history, there are at least three major problems with the dominant paradigm's reliance on appeal to a Pleistocene EEA in constructing evolution-based explanations of cognitive phenomena. First, paleoanthropologists and other evolutionary scientists point out that the Pleistocene encompassed a highly variable set of physical environments and hominid social systems (Foley, 1996). Because of this, explaining a cognitive trait as an adaptation that maximized fitness in an unobserved and highly variable EEA renders the explanation not only untestable, but dangerously close to a "just so" story. Second, focusing on the Pleistocene and hominid brain expansion implies that no cognitive functions (or none of interest to evolutionary cognitive psychologists) existed on the planet prior to the hominid brain expansion. To put it differently, evolution of brain design in other species is irrelevant to understanding the human brain and hence the human mind. Yet cognitive psychologists are heavily invested in studying the design of cognitive functions (and their underlying neurophysiology) in a number of different species. We study cognitive functions such as face recognition, spatial and event memory, and the neurological circuitry involved in the experience of emotion in rats, cats, monkeys, and other species precisely because we have rightly assumed that these functions will have been duplicated (through either homological or analogical processes) in the human brain. Why assume that other adaptations of interest to evolutionary psychologists, such as the mechanisms underlying mate selection or reciprocity, would be specific to the evolution of the hominid mind in the relatively recent Pleistocene? Finally, focusing on hominid brain expansion during the Pleistocene as the origins of cognitive adaptations casts evolution as something that happened in the distant past rather than as an ongoing dynamic process. This assumption contrasts sharply with that of other evolutionary scientists, such as human behavioral ecologists who apply theoretical perspectives of animal behavioral ecology to human populations in order to examine the degree to which behavior is adaptively adjusted to environmental conditions (see Smith et al., 2000, 2001, for a review of this branch of evolutionary science). The goal of these researchers is to identify conditional strategies that maximize current fitness among living organisms.

Alternative Approaches to the Dominant Paradigm

A viable evolutionary psychology does not require the existence of modules in order to satisfy the innate and quasi-independence constraints. These requirements could also be satisfied by heritable learning biases, perhaps in the form of architectural or chronotopic constraints, that operate to increase the *canalization* of specific cognitive capacities (Cummins & Cummins, 1999). Chronotropic constraints are constraints on the time course of development (Elman et al., 1996). Canalization is a biological term used to refer to the combination of genetic and environmental factors that cause development to follow a particular pathway (Ariew, 1996; Baillargeon, Kotovsky, & Needham, 1996; Lewontin, 1974; McKenzie & O'Farrell, 1993; Waddington, 1975). Once begun, development is more or less likely to achieve a particular end state depending on the type and amount of environmental stimulation the organism receives. Thinking of development in terms of chronotopic constraints, learning biases, and canalization is more consistent with what we know about the developing brain. The environment has profound effects on the developing brain during sensitive periods (Banich, 1997, p. 508). The nervous system is tremendously plastic during development, changing the type and location of cells and how they are interconnected with one another (Gazzaniga, Ivry, & Mangun, 1998, p. 484). Thus, there are neurological biases present at birth, but it is not clear that they fit the notion of a Fodorian module.

For example, binocular columns (used in depth perception) are not present at birth, but appear in the visual cortex during a critical period after the infant has received visual input (Banich, 1997, p. 472). If the brain does not receive the critical input (as in the case of strabismus or exotropy), these columns may not develop at all. Other visual cortical cells show diffuse line orientation preferences at birth, firing maximally to lines of a particular orientation (e.g., vertical), but responding to lines of other orientations as well, albeit to a lesser degree (Hubel, 1988). After receiving visual input, however, these cell preferences are sharpened so that they respond maximally only to lines of a particular orientation (Blakemore, 1974). Further, if visual input is restricted to only a single orientation (e.g., the animal is exposed only to lines of vertical orientation), the majority of cells will shift their preferences to match their visual experiences, responding maximally to lines of vertical orientation even if their initial preferences were for lines of other orientations (Blakemore & Cooper, 1970; Hirsh & Spinelli, 1970). The animal, in short, is blind to all line orientations except that to which it was exposed during this critical period. These effects are not seen in adult animals. They can be demonstrated only in the developing brain.

Development of visual cognitive functions therefore depends on tightly coupled transactions between neurological predispositions and environmental inputs. Under normal circumstances, binocular columns will form in a particular area of visual cortex, and initial diffuse biases in visual cortical cells will sharpen into definite response preferences as a result of environmental stimulation during a critical period of development. The neurological predispositions are there at birth, but require an environmental coauthor to fully develop into functions that subserve visual cognition.

With respect to higher cognition, high canalization can be the consequence of biasing learning/acquisition processes in ways that favor the development of concepts and cognitive functions that proved adaptive to an organism's ancestors. The end result of these biases is an adult organism that exhibits a number of highly specialized cognitive abilities that have many of the characteristics associated with modules: functional specialization, reliable emergence in spite of considerable environmental variability, and some degree of informational encapsulation. Perhaps the best example of this is language acquisition. Like vision, language development also shows a complex pattern of interplay between innate biases and environmental input. Deaf babies will begin to babble vocally just as hearing babies do, but their babbling declines and eventually ceases, presumably because they do not receive the auditory feedback hearing babies do (Oller & Eilers, 1988). In other words, babbling deaf babies are practicing sounds that they have never heard. Infants are also born with the capacity to hear all phonetic contrasts that occur in human communicative systems, yet within the first year of life they lose the capacity to distinguish among phonemes that are not marked in their language community (Eimas, 1975; Kuhl, 1987). Thus, they initially exhibit an auditory bias in processing speech sounds that treats the phonemes of human language as signal and everything else as noise, and subsequent language inputs modify this bias to include as signal only the phonemes of the child's native tongue. There also appears to be a critical period for language acquisition that ends approximately at puberty. Children who do not acquire their first language during this critical period fail to acquire the rules governing the use of grammatical morphemes and the syntactic constraints necessary for forming grammatical sentences (Curtiss, 1977; Pinker, 1994). Further, the ability to extract the grammatical rules of a natural language is selectively impaired in certain genetic disorders (Gopnik, 1990a, 1990b). Language development therefore is highly canalized, though not so highly as limb development. Though highly canalized, it is still learned. Biology puts strong constraints on what properties a language must have to be learnable (as a first language), and it virtually guarantees that language will be learned in a huge variety of environments. This is what is meant by the claim that language acquisition is highly canalized.

This framework can be readily extended to other cognitive capacities. Consider, for example, the deontic effect. As was discussed earlier, this effect emerges early in human development, having been observed in children as young as three years of age. But expectations concerning agents generally emerge much earlier. Newborns (no more than a few minutes old) show a distinct bias for looking at faces as compared to other equally complex stimuli (Goren, Sarty, & Wu, 1975). They will become distressed if an agent stands silently before their cribs, but are indifferent if a similarly sized stationary object is placed in the same location (Tronick, Als, Adamson, Wise, & Brazelton, 1978). They also show distinct preferences for interacting with agents, and a keen knowledge concerning their emotional states. Ten-week-old infants distinguish among emotional facial expressions (Haviland & Lelwica, 1987) that other studies have shown to be universally recognized, such as anger, disgust, and happiness (Ekman, 1973). Within the first year of life, infants also engage in social referencing, looking at their caregivers' reactions to novel stimuli (Stenberg & Hagekull, 1997). By 18 months of age, they can succeed at tasks that require them to grasp another's goals, desires, or preferences (Bartsch & Wellman, 1989; Meltzoff, 1995). And by at least 24 months of age, reference to deontic concepts appear in their justifications of behavior (Dunn, 1988).

Infants' preference for attending to social stimuli, their precocity at interpreting emotional facial expressions and their proclivities for engaging in social referencing, constitute developmental biases that can fast track the induction of social norms and the development of compliance-monitoring strategies. Their proclivity for engaging in reciprocal play can also fast track the development of strategies for engaging in and monitoring reciprocity.

In short, highly specialized functions need not be present at birth. Instead, the balance of comparative, developmental, and neuroscientific evidence weighs in on the side of fast-track learning through biological biases or predispositions that entrain the focus of our attention on the environmental stimuli and contingencies that really mattered – and continue to matter – to the survival and reproductive success of our ancestors. Our biological predispositions impose the framework that is necessary to learn the things most vital for survival in a complex social environment, while neurological plasticity allows our actual environmental experiences the final say in whether and how those predispositions are expressed.

References

Altmann, J., Alberts, S. C., Haines, S. A., Dubach, J., Muruth, P., Coote, T., Geffen, E., Cheesman, D. J., Mututua, R. A., Saiyalel, S. N., Wayne, R. K., Lacy, R. C., & Bruford, M. W. (1996). Behavior predicts genetic structure in a wild primate group. *Proceedings of the National Academy of Sciences, 93*, 5795–5801.

Ariew, A. (1996). Innateness and canalization. *Philosophy of Science, 63,* S19–S27.

Aruguete, M. (1994). Cognition, tradition, and the explanation of social behavior in non-human primates. Review of Social processes and mental abilities in non-human primates. *American Journal of Primatology, 33,* 71–74.

Axelrod, R. (1984). *The evolution of cooperation.* New York, NY: Basic Books.

Axelrod, R., & Hamilton, W. D. (1981). The evolution of cooperation. *Science, 211,* 1390–1396.

Banich, M. T. (1997). *Neuropsychology: The neural bases of mental function.* Boston: Houghton-Mifflin.

Baillargeon, R., Kotovsky, L., & Needham, A. (1996) The acquisition of physical knowledge in infancy. In D. Sperber, D. Premack, & A. James Premack (Eds.), *Causal cognition: A multidisciplinary debate* (pp. 79–116). Oxford: Clarendon Press.

Bartsch, K., & Wellman, H. M. (1989) Young children's attribution of action to beliefs and desires. *Child Development, 60,* 946–964.

Bernstein, I. L., & Borson, S. (1986) Learned food aversion: A component of anorexia syndromes. *Psychological Review, 93,* 462–472.

Blakemore, C. (1974). Developmental factors in the formation of feature extracting neurons. In F. G. Worden and F. O. Smith, (Eds.), *The neurosciences, 3rd study program.* Cambridge, MA: MIT Press.

Blakemore, C., & Cooper, G. F. (1970). Development of the brain depends on visual environment. *Nature, 228,* 477–478.

Bowlby, J. (1969) *Attachment.* New York: Basic Books.

Bryant, P. E., & Trabasso, T. (1971). Transitive inference and memory in young children. *Nature, 240,* 456–458.

Byrne, R. (1995). *The thinking ape: Evolutionary origins of intelligence.* Oxford: Oxford University Press.

Buller, D. J., & Hardcastle, V. G. (2000). Evolutionary psychology, meet developmental neurobiology: Against promiscuous modularity. *Brain and Mind, 1,* 307–325.

Camerer, C., & Thaler, R. (1995). Anomalies: Ultimatums, dictators and manners. *Journal of Economic Perspectives, 9,* 209–219.

Chapais, B. (1988). Rank maintenance in female Japanese macaques: Experimental evidence for social dependency. *Behavior, 104,* 41–59.

Chapais, B. (1992). Role of alliances in the social inheritance of rank among female primates. In A. Harcourt and F. B. M. De Waal (Eds.), *Cooperation in contests in animals and humans* (pp. 29–60). Oxford: Oxford University Press.

Cheney, D. L., & Seyfarth, R. M. (1990). *How monkeys see the world.* Chicago: University of Chicago Press.

Cheng, P. W., & Holyoak, K. J. (1985). Pragmatic reasoning schemas. *Cognitive Psychology, 17,* 391–416.

Churchland, P. M. (1995). *The engine of reason, the seat of the soul: A philosophical journey into the brain.* Cambridge, MA: MIT Press.

Clutton-Brock, T. H. (1988). Reproductive success. In T. H. Clutton-Brock (ed.), *Reproductive success.* Chicago: University of Chicago Press.

Clutton-Brock, T. H., & Harvey, P. H. (1976). Evolutionary rules and primate societies. In P. P. G. Bateson & R. A. Hinde (eds.), *Growing points in ethology,* Cambridge: Cambridge University Press.

Cook, L. M., & Mineka, S. (1989). Observational conditioning of fear to fear-relevant versus fear-irrelevant stimuli in rhesus monkeys. *Journal of Abnormal Psychology*, *98*, 448–459.

Cosmides, L. (1989) The logic of social exchange: Has natural selection shaped how humans reason? Studies with the Wason Selection Task. *Cognition*, *31*, 187–276.

Cosmides, L., & Tooby, J. (1989). Evolutionary psychology and the generation of culture, part II. Case study: A computational theory of social exchange. *Ethology and Sociobiology*, *10*, 51–97.

Cosmides, L., & Tooby, J. (1992). Cognitive adaptations for social exchange. In J. Barkow, L. Cosmides, & J. Tooby (Eds.), *The adapted mind* (pp. 163–228). New York, NY: Oxford University Press.

Cosmides, L., & Tooby, J. (1997). Dissecting the computational architecture of social inference mechanisms. In *Characterizing human psychological adaptations* (pp. 132–161). Ciba Foundation Symposium 208. Chichester, UK: Wiley.

Cox, J. R., & Griggs, R. A. (1982). The effects of experience on performance in Wason's selection tasks. *Memory & Cognition*, *10*, 496–502.

Cummins, D. D. (1995). *The other side of psychology: How experimental psychologists find about the way we think and act*. New York: St. Martin's Press.

Cummins, D. D. (1996a). Evidence of deontic reasoning in 3- and 4-year-olds. *Memory & Cognition*, *24*, 823–829.

Cummins, D. D. (1996b). Evidence for the innateness of deontic reasoning. *Mind & Language*, *11*, 160–190.

Cummins, D. D. (1996c). Dominance hierarchies and the evolution of human reasoning. *Minds & Machines*, *6*, 463–480.

Cummins, D. D. (1997). Rationality: Biological, psychological, and normative theories. *Current Psychology of Cognition*, *16*, 78–87.

Cummins, D. D. (1998). Social norms and other minds: The evolutionary roots of higher cognition. In D. D. Cummins & C. Allen (Eds.), *The evolution of mind* (pp. 30–50). New York: Oxford University Press.

Cummins, D. D. (1999). Cheater detection is modified by social rank. *Evolution & Human Behavior*, *20*, 229–248.

Cummins, D. D. (2000). How the social environment shaped the evolution of mind. *Synthese*, *122*, 3–28.

Cummins, D. D. (2002). Adaptive cognitive mechanisms: reasoning about social norms and other minds. In R. Elio (Ed.), *Common Sense, Reasoning and Rationality: Vancouver Studies in Cognitive Science* (pp. 132–147). Oxford: Oxford University Press.

Cummins, D. D., & Cummins, R. C. (1999). Biological preparedness and evolutionary explanation. *Cognition*, *73*, B37–B53.

Curtiss, S. (1977). *Genie: A psycholinguistic study of a modern day wild child*. New York: Academic Press.

Davis, H. (1984). Discrimination of the number three by a raccoon (*Procyon lotor*). *Animal Learning and Behavior*, *12*, 409–413.

Davis, H., & Bradford, S. A. (1986) Counting behavior by rats in a simulated natural environment. *Ethology*, *73*, 265–280.

Datta, S. B. (1983a). Relative power and the acquisition of rank. In R. A. Hinde (Ed.), *Primate social relationships* (pp. 93–102). Oxford: Blackwell.

Datta, S. B. (1983b). Relative power and the maintenance of rank. In R. A. Hinde (Ed.), *Primate social relationships* (pp. 103–111). Oxford: Blackwell.

Dawes, R., & Thaler, R. (1988). Anomalies: Cooperation. *Journal of Economic Perspectives, 2*, 187–197.

Dewsbury, D. A. (1982). Dominance rank, copulatory behavior and differential reproduction. *Quarterly Review of Biology, 57*, 135–159.

Dunn, J. (1988). *The beginnings of social understanding*. Oxford: Basil Blackwell.

Eimas, P. D. (1975). Speech perception in early infancy. In L. B. Cohen and P. Salapafek (Eds.), *Infant perception*. New York: Academic Press.

Ekman, P. (1973). Cross-cultural studies of facial expressions. In P. Ekman (Ed.), *Darwin and facial expression*. New York: Academic Press.

Ellis, L. (1995). Dominance and reproductive success among nonhuman animals: A cross-species comparison. *Ethology & Sociobiology, 16*, 257–333.

Elman, J. L., Bates, E. A., Johnson, M. H., Karmiloff-Smith, A., Parisi, D., & Plunkett, K. (1996). *Rethinking innateness: A connectionist perspective on development*. Cambridge, MA: Bradford.

Evans, J. St. B. (1989). *Bias in human reasoning*. Englewood Cliffs: Erlbaum.

Evans, J. St. B., & Over, D. (1996). Rationality in the selection task: Epistemic utility versus uncertainty reduction. *Psychological Review, 103*, 356–363.

Fehr, E., & Gächter, S. (2000). Cooperation and punishment in public goods experiments. *American Economic Review, 90*, 980–994.

Fehr, E., Gächter, S., & Kirchsteiger, G. (1997). Reciprocity as a contract enforcement device: Experimental evidence. *Econometrica, 65*, 833–860.

Fedigan, L. (1983). Dominance and reproductive success in primates. *Yearbook of Physical Anthropology, 26*, 91–129.

Fodor, J. A. (1983). *The modularity of mind: An essay on faculty psychology*. Cambridge, MA: Bradford/MIT Books.

Foley, R. A. (1996). The adaptive legacy of human evolution: A search for the environment of evolutionary adaptiveness. *Evolutionary Anthropology, 4*, 194–203.

Forsythe, R., Howowitz, J., Savin, N., & Sefton, M. (1994). Fairness in simple bargaining experiments. *Games & Economic Behavior, 6*, 347–369.

Frankel, D. G., & Arbel, T. (1980). Group formation by two-year-olds. *International Journal of Behavioral Development, 3*, 287–298.

Gaffan, E. A., Hansel, M. C., & Smith, L. E. (1983). Does reward depletion influence spatial memory performance? *Learning and Memory, 14*, 58–74.

Garcia, J., & Koelling, R. A. (1966). The relation of cue to consequence in avoidance learning. *Psychonomic Science, 4*, 123–124.

Garcia, J., Brett, L. P., & Rusiniak, K. W. (1989). Limits of Darwinian conditioning. In S. B. Klein and R. R. Mowrer (Eds.), *Contemporary learning theories: Instrumental conditioning theory and the impact of biological constraints on learning*. Hillsdale, NJ: Erlbaum.

Gazzaniga, M. S., Ivry, R. B., & Mangun, G. R. (1998). *Cognitive neuroscience: The biology of the mind*. New York: W. W. Norton.

Gigerenzer, G. (1998.) Ecological intelligence: An adaptation for frequencies. In D. D. Cummins and C. Allen (Eds.), *The evolution of mind* (pp. 9–29). New York: Oxford University Press.

Gigerenzer, G., & Hoffrage, U. (1995) How to improve Bayesian reasoning without instruction: Frequency formats. *Psychological Review, 102*, 684–704.

Gigerenzer, G., & Hug, K. (1992). Domain specific reasoning: Social contracts, cheating, and perspective change. *Cognition, 43*, 127–171.

Gigerenzer, G., Swijtink, Z., Porter, T., Daston, L., Beatty, J., & Krüger, L. (1989). *The empire of chance: How probability changed science and everyday life.* Cambridge: Cambridge University Press.

Gopnik, M. (1990a). Feature blindness: A case study. *Language Acquisition: A Journal of Developmental Linguistics, 1*, 139–164.

Gopnik, M. (1990b). Feature blind grammar and dysphasia. *Nature, 344*, 715.

Goren, C. C., Sarty, M., & Wu, P. Y. K. (1975). Visual following and pattern discrimination of face-like stimuli by newborn infants. *Pediatrics, 59*, 544–549.

Griggs, R., & Cox, J. (1982). The elusive thematic-materials effect in Wason's selection task. *British Journal of Psychology, 73*, 407–420.

Hacking, I. (1975). *The emergence of probability.* Cambridge: Cambridge University Press.

Hall, K. R. L. (1964). Aggression in monkey and ape societies. In J. Carthy & F. Ebling, (Eds.), *The natural history of aggression* (pp. 51–64). London: Academic Press.

Harris, P. L. (in press). Let's swap: Children's understanding of social exchange. *Memory & Cognition.*

Harris, P. L., & Nuñez, M. (1996), Understanding of permission rules by preschool children. *Child Development, 67*, 1572–1591.

Hasher, L., & Zacks, R. T. (1979) Automatic and effortful processes in memory. *Journal of Experimental Psychology: General, 108*, 356–388.

Hausfater, G. (1975). Dominance and reproduction in baboons (*Papio Cynocephalus*): A Quantitative Analysis. *Contributions in Primatology, 7*, 1–150.

Haviland, J. M., & Lelwica, M. (1987). The induced affect response: 10-weeks-old infants' responses to three emotion expressions. *Developmental Psychology, 23*, 97–104.

Hilgard, E. R., & Bower, G. H. (1975). *Theories of learning.* Englewood Cliffs, NJ: Prentice-Hall.

Hirsh, H. V. B., & Spinelli, D. N. (1970). Visual experience modifies distribution of horizontally and vertically oriented receptive fields in cats. *Science, 168*, 869–871.

Hold-Cavell, B. C., & Borsutzky, D. (1986). Longitudinal study of a group of preschool children. *Ethology & Sociobiology, 7*, 39–56.

Hoffman, E., McCabe, K., Shachat, K., & Smith, V. (1994). Preferences, property rights, and anonymity in bargaining games. *Games & Economic Behavior, 7*, 346–380.

Hoffman, E., McCabe, K., & Smith, V. (1996). Social distance and other-regarding behavior in dictator games. *American Economic Review, 86*, 653–660.

Holyoak, K. J., & Cheng, P. (1995). Pragmatic reasoning with a point of view. *Thinking and Reasoning, 1*, 289–313.

Hubel, D. H. (1988). *Eye, brain, and vision.* New York: W. H. Freeman.

Johannesson, M., & Persson, B. (2000). Non-reciprocal altruism in dictator games. *Economics Letters, 69*, 137–142.

Johnson-Laird, P. N., Legrenzi, P., & Legrenzi, M. S. (1972). Reasoning and a sense of reality. *British Journal of Psychology 63*, 395–400.

Kirby, K. (1994). Probabilities and utilities of fictional outcomes in Wason's four-card selection task. *Cognition, 51*, 1–28.

Kuhl, P. K. (1987). Perception of speech and sound in early infancy. In L. B. Cohen and P. Salapafek (Eds.), *Infant perception*. New York: Academic Press.

Kummer, H. (1988). Tripartite Relations in Hamadryas Baboons. In R. W. Byrne & A. Whiten (Eds.), *Machiavellian intelligence* (pp. 113–121). Oxford: Oxford University Press.

La Freniere, P., & Charlesworth, W. R. (1983). Dominance, attention, and affiliation in a preschool group: A nine-month longitudinal study. *Ethology & Sociobiology* 4, 55–67.

Lemerise, E. A., Harper, B. D., & Howes, H. M. (1998). The transition from kindergarten to ungraded primary: Longitudinal predictors of popularity and social reputation. *Early Education & Development*, 9, 187–210.

Leslie, A. M. (1994). ToMM, ToBY, and agency: Core architecture and domain specificity. In L. A. Hirshfeld & S. A. Gelman (Eds.) *Mapping the mind: Domain specificity in cognition and culture* (pp. 119–148). Cambridge: Cambridge University Press.

Leslie, A. M., & Keeble, S. (1987). Do six-month-old infants perceive causality? *Cognition*, 25, 265–288.

Lewontin, R. C. (1974). The analysis of variance and the analysis of causes. *American Journal of Human Genetics*, 26, 400–411.

Lewontin, R. C. (1978, Sept.) Adaptation. *Scientific American*, 239, 157–169.

Logue, A. W. (1988). A comparison of taste aversion learning in humans and other vertebrates: evolutionary pressures in common. In R. C. Bolles and M. D. Beecher (Eds.), *Evolution and learning*, Hillsdale, NJ: Erlbaum.

Mandel, D. R., & Lehman, D. R. (1998). Integration of contingency information in judgments of cause, covariation, and probability. *Journal of Experimental Psychology: General*, 127, 269–285.

Manktelow, K., & Over, D. (1990). Deontic thought and the selection task. In K. Gilhooly, M. Keane, R. Logie, & G. Erdos (Eds.), *Lines of thought: Reflections of the psychology of thinking* (pp. 153–164). London: Wiley.

Manktelow, K. I., & Over, D. E. (1991). Social roles and utilities in reasoning with deontic conditionals. *Cognition* 39, 85–105.

Manktelow, K. I., & Over, D. E. (1995). Deontic reasoning. In S. E. Newstead & J. St. B. Evans, (Eds.), *Perspectives on thinking and reasoning*. Englewood Cliffs, NJ: Erlbaum.

Marr, D. (1982). *Vision: A computational investigation into the human respresentation and processing of visual information*. San Francisco: Freeman.

Matsuzawa, T. (1985). Use of numbers by a chimpanzee. *Nature*, 315, 57–59.

McCloskey, M., & Kohl, D. (1983). Naive physics: the curvilinear impetus principle and its role in interactions with moving objects. *Journal of Experimental Psychology: Learning, Memory, & Cognition*, 9, 146–156.

McKenzie, J. A., & O'Farrell, K. (1993). Modification of Developmental Instability and Fitness: Malathion-Resistance in the Australian Sheep Blowfly. *Genetica*, 89, 67–76.

Mealey, L., Daood, C., & Krage, M. (1996). Enhanced memory for faces of cheaters. *Ethology and Sociobiology*, 17, 119–128.

Meltzoff, A. N. (1995). Understanding the intentions of others: Re-enactment of intended acts by 18-month-old children. *Developmental Psychology*, 31, 838–850.

Mitchell, R. W. (1986). A framework for discussing deception. In R. W. Mitchell and N. S. Thompson (Eds.), *Deception: Perspectives on human and non-human deceit* (pp. 3–40). New York: SUNY Press.

Oaksford, M., & Chater, N. (1994). A rational analysis of the selection task as optimal data selection. *Psychological Review, 101*, 608–631.

Oaksford, M., & Chater, N. (1996). Rational explanation of the selection task. *Psychological Review, 103*, 381–391.

Oller, D. K., & Eilers, R. E. (1988). The role of audition in infant babbling. *Child Development, 59*, 441–449.

Olton, D. S. (1978). Characteristics of spatial memory. In S. H. Hulse, H. Fowler, & W. K. Honig (Eds.), *Cognitive proceses in animal behavior* (pp. 341–373). Hillsdale, NJ: Erlbaum.

Olton, D. S. (1979). Mazes, maps, and memory. *American Psychologist, 34*, 583–596.

Olton, D. S., & Samuelson, R. J. (1976). Remembrance of places passed: Spatial memory in rats. *Journal of Experimental Psychology: Animal Behavior Processes, 2*, 97–116.

Overton, W., Ward, S., Noveck, I., Black, J., & O'Brien, D. (1987). Form and content in the development of deductive reasoning. *Developmental Psychology, 23*, 22–30.

Pastore, N. (1961). Number sense and "counting" ability in the canary. *Zeitschrift für Tierpsychologie, 18*, 561–573.

Piaget, J. (1952). *The origins of intelligence in children*. New York: International University Press.

Piattelli-Palmarini, M. (1994). *Inevitable illusions: How mistakes of reason rule our minds*. New York: Wiley.

Pinker, S. (1994). *The language instinct*. New York: W. Morrow.

Platt, J. R., & Johnson, D. M. (1971). Localization of position within a homogeneous behavior chain: Effects of error contingencies. *Learning and Motivation, 2*, 386–414.

Politzer, G., & Nguyen-Xuan, A. (1992). Reasoning about conditional promises and warnings: Darwinian algorithms, mental models, relevance judgments or pragmatic schemas? *Quarterly Journal of Experimental Psychology, 44A*, 401–421.

Pratto, F., Tatar, D. G., Conway-Lanz, S. (1999). Who gets what and why: Determinants of social allocations. *Political Psychology, 1*, 127–150.

Pratto, F., Stallworth, L. M., & Sidanius, J. (1997). The gender gap: Differences in political attitudes and social dominance relations. *British Journal of Social Psychology, 36*, 49–68.

Reich, S. S., & Ruth, R. (1982). Wason's selection task: Verification, falsification, and matching. *British Journal of Psychology, 73*, 395–405.

Riss, D. C., & Goodall, J. (1977). The recent rise to the alpha-rank in a population of free-living chimpanzees. *Folia Primatologica, 27*, 134–151.

Seligman, M. E. P. (1971). Phobias and preparedness. *Behavior Therapy, 2*, 307–320.

Seyfarth, R. M. (1976). Social relationships among adult female monkeys. *Animal Behavior, 24*, 917–938.

Seyfarth, R. M., & Cheney, D. L. (1984). Grooming, alliances, and reciprocal altruism in vervet monkeys. *Nature, 308*, 541–543.

Shultz, T. R. (1982). Causal reasoning in the social and nonsocial realms. *Canadian Journal of Behavioral Science, 14*, 307–322.

Smith, E. A., Borgerhoff Mulder, M., & Hill, K. (2000) Evolutionary analyses of human behavior: A commentary on Daly & Wilson. *Animal Behavior, 60,* F21–F26.

Smith, E. A., Borgerhoff Mulder, M., & Hill, K. (2001) Controversies in the evolutionary social sciences: A guide for the perplexed. *Trends in Ecology and Evolution, 16,* 128–135.

Smith, P. K. (1988). The cognitive demands of children's social interactions with peers. In R. W. Byrne & A. White (Eds.), *Machiavellian intelligence: Social expertise and the evolution of intellect in monkeys, apes, and humans.* Oxford: Oxford University Press.

Spelke, E. S. (1991). Physical knowledge in infancy: Reflections on Piaget's theory. In S. Carey & R. Gelman (Eds.). *The epigenesis of mind* (pp. 133–169). Hillsdale, NJ: Erlbaum.

Spelke, E. (1994). Initial knowledge: Six suggestions. *Cognition, 50,* 431–445.

Spelke, E., Phillips, A., & Woodward, A. L. (1996). Infants' knowledge of object motion and human action. In D. Sperber, D. Premack, & A. James Premack (Eds.), *Causal cognition: A multidisciplinary debate* (pp. 44–78). Oxford: Clarendon Press.

Spellman, B. A. (1996). Acting as intuitive scientists: Contingency judgments are made while controlling for alternative potential causes. *Psychological Science, 7,* 337–342.

Stanovich, K. E., & West, R. F. (1998). Cognitive ability and variation in selection task performance. *Thinking & Reasoning, 4,* 193–230.

Starkey, P., Spelke, E. S., & Gelman, R. (1983). Detection of intermodal numerical correspondences by human infants. *Science, 222,* 179–181.

Starkey, P., Spelke, E. S., & Gelman, R. (1990). Numerical abstraction by human infants. *Cognition, 36,* 97–127.

Stenberg, G., & Hagekull, B. (1997). Social referencing and mood modification in 1-year-olds. *Infant Behavior & Development, 20,* 209–217.

Strayer, F. F., & Trudel, M. (1984). Developmental changes in the nature and function of social dominance among young children. *Ethology and Sociobiology, 5,* 279–295.

Symons, D. (1987) If we're all Darwinians, what's all the fuss about? In C. Crawford, M. Smith, & D. Krebs (Eds.), *Sociobiology and psychology: Ideas, issues, and applications* (pp. 121–146). Hillsdale, NJ: Erlbaum.

Symons, D. (1989) A critique of Darwinian anthropology. *Ethology and Sociobiology, 10,* 131–144.

Thaler, R. (1988). Anomalies: The ultimatum game. *Journal of Economic Perspectives, 2,* 195–206.

Thompson, R. F. (1993). *The brain: A neuroscience primer.* New York: W. H. Freeman.

Tooby, J., & Cosmides, L. (1995). Foreword. In S. Baron-Cohen, *Mindblindness* (pp. xi–xviii). Cambridge, MA: Bradford.

Trivers, R. (1971). The evolution of reciprocal altruism. *Quarterly Review of Biology, 46,* 35–57.

Tronick, E. Z., Als, H., Adamson, L., Wise, S., & Brazelton, T. B. (1978). The infant's response to entrapment between contradictory messages in face-to-face interaction. *Journal of the American Academy of Child Psychiatry, 17,* 1–13.

Tutin, C. E. G. (1979). Mating patterns and reproductive strategies in a community of wild chimpanzees (*Pan Troglodytes Schweinfurtii*). *Behavioral Ecology and Sociobiology, 6,* 29–38.

Uehara, S., Hiraiwa-Hasegawa, M., Hosaka, K., & Hamai, M. (1994). The fate of defeated alpha male chimpanzees in relation to their social networks. *Primates, 35,* 49–55.

Vandell, L., & Wilson, K. S. (1987). Infant's interactions with mother, sibling, and peer: Contrasts and relations between interaction systems. *Child Development, 58,* 176–186.

de Waal, F. (1988). Chimpanzee Politics. In R. W. Byrne, & A. Whiten (Eds.), *Machiavellian intelligence (*pp. 122–131*).* Oxford: Oxford University Press.

de Waal, F. (1989). Food sharing and reciprocal obligations among chimpanzees. *Journal of Human Evolution, 18,* 433–459.

de Waal, F. (1992). Coalitions as part of reciprocal relations in the Arnhem chimpanzee colony. In A. H. Harcourt and F. De Waal (Eds.), *Coalitions and alliances in humans and other animals* (pp. 233–258). Oxford: Oxford University.

Waddington, C. H. (1975). *The evolution of an evolutionist.* Ithaca, NY: Cornell University Press.

Waldmann, M. R. (2000). Competition among causes but not effects in predictive and diagnostic learning. *Journal of Experimental Psychology: Learning, Memory, & Cognition, 26,* 53–76.

Wason, P. (1968). Reasoning about a rule. *Quarterly Journal of Experimental Psychology, 20,* 273–281.

Watts, C. R., & Stokes, A. W. (1971). The social order of turkeys. *Scientific American, 224,* 112–118.

Weg, E., & Smith, V. (1993). On the failure to induce meager offers in ultimatum games. *Journal of Economic Psychology, 14,* 17–32.

Whiten, A., & Byrne, R. W. (1988). The manipulation of attention in primate tactical deception. In R. W. Byrne & A. Whiten (Eds.), *Machiavellian intelligence.* Oxford: Oxford University Press.

Wilkinson, G. S. (1984). Reciprocal food sharing in the vampire bat. *Nature, 308,* 181–184.

Wills, C. (1991). *Exons, introns, and talking genes: The science behind the human genome project.* New York: Basic Books.

Woodruff, G., & Premack, D. (1979). Intentional communication in the chimpanzee: The development of deception. *Cognition, 7,* 333–362.

Wynn, K. (1996) Infants' individuation and enumeration of sequential actions. *Psychological Science, 7,* 164–169.

Wynn, K. (1998) An evolved capacity for number. In D. D. Cummins and C. Allen (Eds.), *The evolution of mind* (pp. 107–126). New York: Oxford University Press.

14

Individual Differences in Thinking, Reasoning, and Decision Making

Keith E. Stanovich, Walter C. Sá, and Richard F. West

The literature on individual differences in thinking and reasoning is quite scattered and does not form a coherent research paradigm. Instead, it rides parasitically alongside other research programs and other theoretical controversies such as the mental models versus mental-logic debate. Despite its nonprogrammatic nature, work on individual differences in reasoning has begun to provide some insights that would not have been available had the field ignored this important conceptual and methodological tool. In this chapter, we wish to highlight some examples of how work on individual differences serves to clarify issues in the cognitive psychology of reasoning. We will begin by discussing some examples that arise from within some of the well-developed areas in the reasoning literature including: mental logic, mental models, componential analysis, and crosscultural studies in reasoning. We will then discuss three programmatic themes from our own research studies on individual differences to show how we have attempted to demonstrate how individual differences research can lead to cumulative progress on theoretical issues of general importance.

MENTAL LOGIC AND INDIVIDUAL DIFFERENCES

Perhaps the most notable investigation of individual differences carried out within the mental logic (Braine & O'Brien, 1998; Rips, 1994), or mental rules, framework is that of Rips and Conrad (1983). They examined individual differences in reasoning with the propositional connectives *if*, *and*, *or*, and *neither*. Their work introduced the useful strategy of distinguishing individual differences in reasoning that result from random noise (e.g., temporary distractions and attentional lapses), from those differences deriving from differences in real deductive reasoning competence (see

Preparation of this chapter was supported by a grant from the Social Sciences and Humanities Research Council of Canada to Keith E. Stanovich.

Stanovich, 1999, and Stein, 1996, for discussions of the use of the competence/performance distinction in reasoning). Rips and Conrad (1983) argued that reasoning performance differences that result from the latter (but not the former) should demonstrate an appreciable degree of stability. This stability in performance was observed in the Rips and Conrad study. Participants' performance patterns demonstrated stability across various reasoning tasks, and across a six-week period of time – precisely the pattern expected of individual differences grounded in deductive reasoning competence.

Having demonstrated that individual differences in deductive paradigms were not merely due to idiosyncratic factors, Rips and Conrad next explored the factors that led to systematic variation in performance. Specifically, they examined argument-by-subject interactions – whether arguments sharing a particular logical property were consistently judged to be valid by one group of subjects and consistently judged as invalid by yet another group of subjects. For example, relatively consistently one group of subjects handled disjunctive introduction in the exclusive sense (p or q is true in the case where exactly one of the disjuncts is true), whereas another group of subjects consistently handled disjunctive introduction in the inclusive sense (p or q is true in the case where either one or both of the disjuncts is true).

From their investigation, Rips and Conrad (1983) concluded that a view of mental logic as a universal set of rules is inaccurate. Although some universal rules may exist, other rules may not be universal features of human cognitive architecture. In addition, Rips and Conrad argued that deficiencies in mental logic may be amendable through education. They found that subjects who had had training in logic were more likely to treat several important logical properties (including disjunctive introduction) in a manner congruent with the propositional calculus. As mental-logic theorists however, Rips and Conrad (1983) do maintain that despite the individual differences obtained in the instantiation of various logical rules all subjects carry out the processes involved in deduction by using some form of mental logic (i.e., rules).

MENTAL MODELS AND INDIVIDUAL DIFFERENCES

Mental-model accounts of reasoning (Johnson-Laird, 1999; Johnson-Laird & Byrne, 1991, 1993) offer yet a different mechanism underlying the processes involved in deductive reasoning. The mental-rules account views mental processes as operating directly on the form of the premises. Mental-models accounts, in contrast, emphasize the construction of intermediate representations between the given premises and a formulation of a conclusion. Under the mental-models view, an individual transforms the premises of an argument into a representation of individual tokens or a set of relationships that is consistent with those premises – that is, a mental model. This first representation is used in formulating a tentative conclusion. Additional mental models that are consistent with the premises may or may not be formed subsequent to this initial model. The construction of additional models (where possible) is desirable however because they will often demonstrate that the tentative conclusion is in fact invalid.

Early on in the development of this account, proponents of mental models acknowledged the existence of individual differences in reasoning (Johnson-Laird, 1983, Johnson-Laird & Bara, 1984). Writing in reference to syllogistic reasoning, Johnson-Laird and Bara (1984) noted that "there are undoubtedly differences from one individual to another in the way in which [their participants made] syllogistic inferences.... Certainly, the cause of individual differences is a major problem that remains to be solved" (p. 50). One source of individual differences often implicated within the mental-model account is variation in working memory capacity. For example, Johnson-Laird and Byrne (1992) have pointed out that the model theory can "account for these individual differences in terms of such factors as the processing capacity of working memory" (p. 62). As Johnson-Laird and colleagues (Johnson-Laird, 1983, 1999; Johnson-Laird & Bara, 1984; Johnson-Laird & Byrne, 1991, 1993; see also Evans, Newstead, & Byrne, 1993) have emphasized, individual differences under the mental-models account may arise because some individuals more completely flesh out their models and because some individuals are able to keep multiple models in mind better than other individuals.

In short, because many problem-solving situations optimally can be evaluated by constructing all of the mental models that are consistent with the premises as presented, and because constructing all of the models might be limited by working memory constraints, one would expect the latter to predict performance on reasoning tasks. As expected under a mental-models account, performance on syllogistic reasoning tasks deteriorates in proportion to the number of alternative models that are required to solve the problem (Johnson-Laird & Steedman, 1978; see also Johnson-Laird, 1983). Furthermore, significant correlations have been obtained between measures of working memory capacity and performance in solving syllogisms (Johnson-Laird, 1983; Johnson-Laird & Bara, 1984; Bara, Bucciarelli, & Johnson-Laird, 1995; Bucciarelli & Johnson-Laird, 1999).

Bara et al. (1995) studied syllogistic inference in children, adolescents, and adults and identified five basic cognitive factors that affect performance: the interpretation of quantifiers; the referential integration of assertions across the premises; the search for counterexamples; the ability to notice identities between constructed models; and the processing capacity of working memory. Each of these cognitive factors was separately operationalized by performance on a task designed to tap that particular component. For example, an operationalization of the fifth factor (i.e., the processing capacity of working memory) was attained by using the common methodology of having participants recall a series of spoken digits – both forward and backward trials were used. The criterion variable in the Bara et al. (1995) investigation was measured by having participants generate conclusions for several syllogisms. A series of regression analyses revealed the ability to notice identities between constructed models and the processing capacity of working memory accounted for significant variation in syllogistic inference. While working memory capacity and the perception of identities account for a substantial portion of the variance in syllogistic reasoning performance (39% in the Bara et al., 1995, study), Bucciarelli and Johnson-Laird (1999) caution that "we are far from answering this important question" (p. 300).

QUALITATIVE INDIVIDUAL DIFFERENCES IN STRATEGIES: MENTAL MODELS VERSUS MENTAL RULES

A common research strategy used by both advocates of mental models and advocates of mental-logic approaches is to pit the predictions of these two opposing views against one another. Advocates of each have sought a universal reasoning mechanism for deductive reasoning. The fact that both accounts have received some support suggests that each view may be correct under certain types of conditions or for certain individuals. The reasoning of different individuals might be best characterized by a mental models or a mental-logic theory.

Such a conclusion is suggested by an important study conducted by Galotti, Baron, and Sabini (1986). In line with the popular strategy, Galotti et al. (1986) pitted the predictions of a mental-models account against those of a mental-rules account of syllogistic reasoning performance. Their first experiment examined whether the differences between poor and good reasoners occur early or late in their reasoning process. The two theoretical views hold different expectations in this regard. The mental-model account views individuals as constructing an initial mental model that is consistent with the premises. Errors in reasoning occur because individuals fail to construct the requisite number of additional premise-consistent models that are required to evaluate the validity of a conclusion. Thus poor and good reasoners can be seen as differing in the latter stages of the reasoning process. In contrast, the mental-logic account views reasoners as applying a fixed repertoire of rules directly to the premises. This scenario is consistent with the notion that errors occur early in the reasoning process.

Galotti et al. (1986) had their subjects provide "could be true" conclusions to syllogistic arguments on some trials and "must be true" conclusions on other trials. Since mental-model accounts view both good and poor reasoners as first engaging in the construction of a one premise-consistent model (i.e., a could be true conclusion), good and poor reasoners should not differ in their generation of a could be true conclusion that turns out to be an error under the instruction of detecting necessarily true conclusions. On the other hand, the mental-models account predicts that subjects will differ when asked to generate must be true conclusions. Good reasoners will distinguish this instruction from could be true and accordingly generate more premise-consistent models. The distinction becomes particularly pertinent for "nothing follows" (NF) syllogisms because they require the construction of two or more mental models. Thus, on the mental-models account, the errors and latencies of good reasoners should resemble poor reasoners in the could be true trials, and differ from poor reasoners in the must be true trials. Although rules accounts make no specific predictions about error or latencies, an observed lack of differences – clearly inconsistent with the mental-models account – can be viewed as consistent with the rules account.

The results of the Galotti et al. (1986) experiment revealed that good and poor reasoners did not actually differ in accuracy when generating the could be true conclusions. This finding is consistent with the mental-models account. More importantly, the good and poor reasoners did differ on the must be true conclusions that used NF syllogisms. This finding was also consistent with the mental-models account. Although the data pattern involving group accuracy was consistent with the mental-models account, the latency data were not completely consistent with its predictions, because the good reasoners took reliably more time than the poor reasoners only under some of the must be true conditions.

Other components of the Galotti et al. (1986) investigation showed that the thinking of at least some subjects was consistent with a mental-logic account. Galotti et al. (1986) recalled most of their subjects to another testing session where they were asked to think aloud as they worked through syllogisms. The protocols revealed that some subjects used deduction rules in solving the syllogisms – an observation obviously consistent with a mental-logic account. Good reasoners were found to be more likely to announce a rule than the poor reasoners. In addition, poor reasoners were more likely to misinterpret "some" to mean "not all." This latter finding is in line with Rips and Conrad's (1983) demonstration that stable individual differences can be found in how subjects interpret logical connectives. In Experiment 2 of their investigation, Galotti et al. (1986) added an expert group in addition to the groups of poor and good reasoners. The expert group consisted of graduate students in psychology and computer science who had had some experience studying logic. The performance of the experts was best accommodated by a mental-rules account.

Many aspects of the Galotti et al. (1986) investigation seem to suggest that neither a mental-rules account nor a mental-models account merits the status of being deemed the fundamental reasoning mechanism. Instead,

Galotti et al. (1986) conclude their paper by suggesting that more research needs to be done to determine what circumstances lead people to apply rules or construct mental models. Even more importantly, what their investigations suggest is that individual differences might arise from reasoning processes that are qualitatively different from each other. Individual differences might encompass more than just differing parameter settings but instead might reflect differences in the basic cognitive mechanisms applied to the problem.

INDIVIDUAL DIFFERENCES AND COMPONENTIAL ANALYSIS

A similar conclusion can be derived from the earlier work by Sternberg (1977, 1980; Schustack & Sternberg, 1981; Sternberg & Weil, 1980). In a componential analysis of analogical reasoning, Sternberg (1977) identified six separate cognitive sources of individual differences. The sixth category is particularly relevant here since it implicates differences in the mental representation on which components act – that is, it implicates qualitative differences. Sternberg found that some of his subjects represented information primarily in a linguistic mode, whereas others represented the same information primarily in a spatial mode. Similarly, in further investigations involving linear syllogisms, some subjects were found to operate on array-like representations (more like mental models), others seemed to be operating upon linguistic-like representations that were more like mental rules. Some used a mix of the two mechanisms.

Outcomes like those of Galotti et al. (1986) and Sternberg's work using componential analysis to identify individual differences in reasoning tasks provides the context for a critical review by Roberts (1993) of the search for basic reasoning mechanisms. In his analysis, Roberts (1993) highlights the importance of individual differences and the futility of searching for reasoning patterns that are universal. Disputes such as those between the mental models and mental rules view are unlikely to result in an unequivocal winner of the theoretical contest. Instead, an outcome like that of Sternberg's componential analyses seems more likely – subgroups of individuals will be identified that among themselves show some common reasoning strategies. In addition, the choice of strategy can be viewed as partially a function of the task selected by the experimenter. Thus for example, tasks that would exceed working-memory constraints under a mental-model strategy may be conducive to the application of rules. The facilitation of mental-models use in syllogistic reasoning can be achieved by presenting the premises one at a time; ideally in a verbal mode as opposed to visual presentation (see Roberts, 1993). Conversely, the presentation of the problem premises simultaneously in written form encourages deductive rule strategies.

INDIVIDUAL DIFFERENCES IN REASONING EXPLORED
FROM A CROSSCULTURAL PERSPECTIVE

The final tradition which provides a perspective for studies of individual differences in reasoning is one in which established reasoning tasks and paradigms are explored from a crosscultural perspective. The most notable recent programmatic exploration of individual differences has been conducted by Richard Nisbett and colleagues (e.g., Nisbett, Peng, Choi, & Norenzayan, 2001; Norenzayan & Nisbett, 2000; Peng & Nisbett, 1999). They have attempted to empirically demonstrate the existence of different reasoning styles in Eastern and Western cultures. Although controversial (Hong, Morris, Chiu, & Benet-Martinez, 2000), the work of Nisbett and colleagues seems to have at least suggested that individuals grounded in Western cultures seem to prefer analytic thinking styles. These styles are characterized by a focus on object attributes, categorization based on these attributes, the use of explicit rules and formal logic, and an intolerance for contradiction. In contrast, Nisbett's work has suggested that individuals grounded in Eastern cultures prefer holistic styles characterized by a focus on context. In short, Western cultures can be seen as emphasizing decontextualized modes (see Stanovich, 1999), whereas Eastern cultures place importance on contextualized modes.

Nisbett and colleagues have examined these trends using a variety of tasks, but their work on reasoning about contradiction will serve as an illustration. Peng and Nisbett (1999) found that a group of Chinese subjects preferred dialectical proverbs containing apparent contradictions (e.g., "too humble is half proud") more than their American counterparts. This finding was replicated in an additional experiment that used proverbs foreign to both the Chinese and Americans. Consistent differences between their Chinese and American subjects were also found in a third experiment on resolving social contradictions. Chinese and American subjects were provided with scenarios that outlined a conflict between two parties and were asked to resolve this conflict. Responses were classified as either dialectical or nondialectical strategies. Dialectical resolutions were those that addressed the issues from both sides of the dispute. Nondialectical resolutions typically assigned fault to one of the parties. The results showed the majority of their American subjects engaged in a nondialectical resolution, whereas Chinese subjects were more likely to assign some level of blame or fault to both parties and to resolve the conflict by some form of compromise.

Peng and Nisbett (1999) demonstrated differences in preferences for formal argumentation in a fourth experiment. Both logical arguments and dialectical arguments were presented to their subjects. The logical argument applied the rule of noncontradiction (no statement can be both true and false at the same time), whereas the dialectical argument applied the principle of holism (emphasis on the idea that nothing is isolated and in-dependent, instead, everything is connected). The American subjects were found to prefer arguments that contained the law of noncontradiction, whereas the Chinese subjects showed the opposite preference. Finally, in a fifth experiment, Peng and Nisbett (1999) demonstrated an analogous set of cultural differences when reasoning about scientific information and conclusions. In this and other studies (Nisbett et al., 2001; Norenzayan & Nisbett, 2000) cultural differences are associated with individual differ-ences in the reasoning strategies and styles used to engage with a variety of reasoning and problem-solving tasks.

SYSTEMATIC INVESTIGATION OF THREE ISSUES IN REASONING WITH AN INDIVIDUAL DIFFERENCES APPROACH

As the previous sampling of research indicates, the importance of individ-ual differences across a variety of reasoning paradigms has not gone un-noticed. However, with the exception of the research of the Nisbett group, work on individual differences in reasoning has lacked thematic focus. In the remainder of this chapter we will try to illustrate how such focus may be achieved by illustrating how we have used inferences from patterns of individual differences to address three conceptual issues in the psychology of reasoning and decision making.

The first issue we have addressed is the issue of whether, across the many tasks in the reasoning literature, there are commonalities in the per-formance patterns. That is, is there such a thing as a general tendency to reason optimally – or does the tendency toward normatively appropriate responding display extreme domain specificity (the reigning assumption in cognitive science and developmental psychology throughout the 1990s; see Ceci, 1996, Hirschfeld & Gelman, 1994; Samuels, 1998)? Secondly, what are the roles of cognitive ability and thinking dispositions in accounting for variance in reasoning ability? Finally, an innovative but controversial aspect of our research program is the attempt to use individual differences to adjudicate disputes about the appropriate normative models to apply to experimental tasks in the heuristics and biases literature.

ISSUE 1: IS THERE DOMAIN GENERALITY IN REASONING TENDENCIES ACROSS TASKS?

The starting point for our research on this question was the so-called heuris-tics and biases literature, now several decades in the making. Our point of demarcation was the fact that literally hundreds of empirical studies conducted over nearly three decades – have firmly established that peo-ple's responses often deviate from the performance considered normative on many reasoning tasks. For example, people display confirmation bias,

TABLE 14.1. *Intercorrelations among Several Reasoning Tasks*

Variable	1	2	3
1. Syllogisms			
2. Selection task	.363**		
3. Statistical reasoning	.334**	.258**	
4. Argument Evaluation	.340**	.310**	.117

** = p < .001, all two-tailed; Ns = 188 to 195.

they test hypotheses inefficiently, they do not properly calibrate degrees of belief, they overproject their own opinions onto others, they allow prior knowledge to become implicated in deductive reasoning, and they display numerous other information processing biases (for summaries of the large literature, see Baron, 1998, 2000; Dawes, 1998; Evans et al., 1993; Evans & Over, 1996; Hastie & Dawes, 2001; Johnson-Laird, 1999; Kahneman & Tversky, 2000; Manktelow, 1999; Medin & Bazerman, 1999; Nickerson, 1998; Shafir & Tversky, 1995; Stanovich, 1999). However, for a long time, one aspect of this empirical literature received little attention – that although the average person in these experiments might well display a reasoning error, some did not. We wondered whether, across various tasks, these might tend to be the same people, thus indicating some domain generality in thinking as operationalized by giving the standard normative response on reasoning tasks. It is precisely this question that we have addressed in a number of studies.

A typical set of results, taken from one of our studies (Stanovich & West, 1998c) is displayed in Table 14.1. The tasks investigated here included a syllogistic reasoning task in which the believability of the conclusion contradicted logical validity (Evans, Barston, & Pollard, 1983). Next were five selection tasks (Wason, 1966). All employed nondeontic content, were difficult to solve, and thus were the type of problem about which there has been considerable debate in the research literature (Manktelow, 1999; Newstead & Evans, 1995). The third task was derived from the literature on statistical reasoning, and was inspired by the work of Nisbett and Ross (1980). Their work suggests the tendency for human judgment to be overly influenced by vivid but unrepresentative personal and case evidence and to be underinfluenced by more representative and diagnostic, but pallid, statistical evidence. The fourth task was an argument evaluation task (Stanovich & West, 1997) that taps reasoning skills of the type studied in the informal reasoning literature (see Baron, 1995; Klaczynski, 2000; Klaczynski, Gordon, & Fauth, 1997; Kuhn, 2001; Perkins, 1989). Importantly, to do well on it, one has to adhere to the Bayesian-like stricture not to implicate prior belief in the evaluation of evidence.

As Table 14.1 indicates, five of the six correlations among tasks were significant at the .001 level. The syllogistic reasoning task displayed significant correlations with each of the other three tasks, as did the selection task. The only correlation that did not attain significance was that between performance on the argument evaluation task and statistical reasoning. Although the highest correlation obtained was that between syllogistic reasoning and selection task performance (.363), correlations almost as strong were obtained between tasks deriving from the deductive reasoning literature (syllogistic reasoning, selection task) and inductive reasoning literature (statistical reasoning). These systematic tendencies may be even greater than indicated here because of the modest reliability of most of the tasks. The positive manifold displayed by the tasks suggests that some domain generality is present and that it makes at least some sense to talk about a general tendency toward rational thought.

Similar relationships were obtained in a second study (see Stanovich & West, 1998c, Study 2) where we expanded the selection of tasks by adding further reasoning tasks to those used in the original study. Added to our multivariate battery was a covariation detection task modeled on the work of Wasserman, Dorner, and Kao (1990). Next was a hypothesis testing task modeled on Tschirgi (1980) in which the score on the task was the number of times subjects attempted to test a hypothesis in a manner that confounded variables. Outcome bias was measured using tasks introduced by Baron and Hershey (1988). This bias is demonstrated when subjects rate a decision with a positive outcome as superior to a decision with a negative outcome even when the information available to the decision maker was the same in both cases. Finally, if/only bias refers to the tendency for people to have differential responses to outcomes based on the differences in counterfactual alternative outcomes that might have occurred (Epstein, Lipson, Holstein, & Huh, 1992; Miller, Turnbull, & McFarland, 1990). The bias is demonstrated when subjects rate a decision leading to a negative outcome as worse than a control condition when the former makes it easier to imagine a positive outcome occurring.

Modest but significant correlations were found among these new measures and between them and several of the tasks displayed in Table 14.1. Other work by our research group (Sá & Stanovich, 2001; Sá, West, & Stanovich, 1999; Stanovich & West, 1998a, 1998b, 1998c, 1998d, 1999, 2000b) and others (Parker & Fischhoff, 2000; Slugoski & Wilson, 1998) has converged in indicating some domain generality to normative responding on reasoning and decision-making tasks. Certainly there is considerable domain specificity involved here as well, but this was to be expected given the current emphasis on the domain specificity of cognitive functioning in cognitive science (Cosmides & Tooby, 1994; Hirschfeld & Gelman, 1994; Samuels, 1998; Sperber, 1994, 2000). Thus, the critical issue here is whether any domain generality at all can be detected, and our investigations have indicated that across a wide domain of tasks it does make sense to speak about a generalized tendency toward normative responding on reasoning tasks.

ISSUE 2: COGNITIVE ABILITY AND THINKING DISPOSITIONS AS PREDICTORS OF INDIVIDUAL DIFFERENCES IN REASONING

What is the source of the common variance in performance on these tasks? One obvious source of common variance is general cognitive ability. That is, the common variance we observed might simply be due to general computational limitations that the tasks imposed on limited-capacity cognitive structures that vary among individuals. In our studies, we have operationalized general cognitive capacity in terms of well-known cognitive ability and aptitude tasks such as the Scholastic Assessment Test (SAT), Raven Matrices, and various vocabulary and reading comprehension tests. All are known to load highly on psychometric *g*. Most of the analyses throughout this chapter will focus on SAT Total scores.

It should be emphasized that other measures of cognitive ability not involving verbal problem solving (such as the Raven matrices and checklist vocabulary measures) produced largely redundant findings. The correlations observed are not due to verbal reasoning items on the SAT bearing similarities to items on the thinking and reasoning tasks – an issue that we dealt with at length in the responses to the commentators on our "Behavioral and Brain Sciences" article on the rationality debate (Stanovich & West, 2000b). The reasoning and heuristics and biases literature from which we have drawn our tasks encompasses vastly more than the syllogistic reasoning literature – where, granted, items may resemble verbal reasoning on aptitude tests (although even here, the latter never contain a belief-bias component). The entire set of tasks used were varied and extended well beyond syllogistic reasoning. The choice between a vivid case and a statistical fact on an inductive reasoning problem (Nisbett & Ross, 1980; Stanovich & West, 1998c) is nothing like an item on the SAT; neither is an informal reasoning item in which prior belief must be ignored (Stanovich & West, 1997); neither is the combining of a diagnostic indicator and base-rate information (Stanovich & West, 1998d); neither is covariation assessment in the face of belief bias (Levin, Wasserman, & Kao, 1993; Stanovich & West, 1998d); and so on down a long list of tasks. The correlations between general ability and performance on such measures are of genuine interest.

The top half of Table 14.2 indicates the magnitude of the correlation between SAT total scores and the four reasoning tasks from Study 1 of Stanovich and West (1998c). SAT scores were significantly correlated with performance on all four rational thinking tasks. The correlation with syllogistic reasoning was the highest (.470) and the other three correlations were

TABLE 14.2. *Correlations Between Performance on the Reasoning Tasks and SAT Total Score*

Data from Study 1 of Stanovich and West (1998c)	
Syllogisms	.470*
Selection task	.394*
Statistical reasoning	.347*
Argument Evaluation	.358*
Replication and Extension (Study 2 of Stanovich & West, 1998c)	
Syllogisms	.410*
Statistical reasoning	.376*
Argument evaluation task	.371*
Covariation detection	.239*
Hypothesis testing bias	−.223*
Outcome bias	−.172*
If/Only thinking	−.208*
Composite #1	.530*
Composite #2	.383*
Composite, All Tasks	.547*

Note: Composite #1 = standard score composite of performance on argument evaluation task, syllogisms, and statistical reasoning. Composite #2 = standard score composite of performance on covariation judgment, hypothesis testing task, if/only thinking, and outcome bias. Composite, All Tasks = rational thinking composite score of performance on all seven tasks in the replication and extension experiment.

* = p < .001, all two-tailed; Ns = 527 to 529 in the replication and extension.

roughly equal in magnitude (.347 to .394). All were statistically significant. The remaining correlations in the table are the results from a replication and extension experiment (Study 2 of Stanovich & West, 1998c). These correlations indicate that the correlations involving the syllogistic reasoning task, statistical reasoning task, and argument evaluation task were similar in magnitude to those obtained in Study 1. The correlations involving the four new tasks were also all statistically significant. The sign on the hypothesis testing, outcome bias, and if/only thinking tasks was negative because high scores on these tasks reflect susceptibility to non normative cognitive biases. The correlations on the four new tasks were generally lower (range .172 to .239) than the correlations involving the other tasks (.371 to .410). However, it must again be emphasized that the logistical constraints dictated that the scores on some of the new tasks were based on an extremely small sample of behavior. The outcome bias score was based on only a single comparison and the if/only thinking score was based on only two items.

The remaining correlations in Table 14.2 concern composite variables. The first composite involved the three tasks that were carried over from

TABLE 14.3. *Intercorrelations Among Several Reasoning Task*

Variable	1	2	3	4
1. Syllogisms		.237**	.222**	.213**
2. Selection task	.363***		.150	.215**
3. Statistical reasoning	.334***	.258***		−.014
4. Argument Evaluation	.340***	.310***	.117	

Source: Data from Study 1 of Stanovich & West, 1998c.
Note: Zero-order correlations are below the diagonal and correlations with SAT Total score partialed out are presented above the diagonal.
* = p < .05, ** = p < .01, *** = p < .001, all two-tailed; Ns = 188 to 195.

the previous experiment – the syllogistic reasoning, statistical reasoning, and argument evaluation tasks. The scores on each of these three tasks were standardized and summed to yield a composite score. The composite's correlation with SAT scores was .530. A second composite was formed by summing the standard scores of the remaining four tasks: covariation judgment, hypothesis testing, outcome bias, and if/only thinking (the latter three scores reflected so that higher scores represent more normatively correct reasoning). SAT Total scores displayed a correlation of .383 with this composite. Finally, both of the composites were combined into a composite variable reflecting performance on all seven tasks and this composite displayed a correlation of .547 with SAT scores.

So there is no question that cognitive ability is implicated in performance on many of these reasoning tasks and to some extent may be accounting for the domain generality of performance across the tasks. One further question that we have addressed is whether the residual variance (after cognitive ability is accounted for) is systematic or whether instead it appears to be error variance. Such a model – to be elaborated shortly – could preserve a Panglossian assumption of perfect human rationality[1] (see Stanovich, 1999; Stanovich & West, 2000b). Differences in algorithmic-level computational capacity would explain part of the discrepancy between normative and descriptive models of behavior, and any remaining deviations from the prescriptive could be attributed to performance errors. There would be no need to posit a systematically suboptimal cognitive functioning at the intentional level of analysis. In contrast, evidence that the residual variance (after partialing cognitive ability) was systematic would mean that not all of the normative/descriptive gap could be attributed to computational limitations and performance errors, and it would support the idea that the intentional-level model of behavior is characterized by systematic suboptimal functioning.[2]

The data in Table 14.3 are relevant to this issue. The correlations from the four tasks in Study 1 of Stanovich and West (1998c) are recapitulated below the diagonal. What is different in this table is that above the diagonal are presented the correlations among the tasks after differences in cognitive ability have been statistically removed. The results indicate that four of the six associations were still significant even after variance in SAT scores had been partialed out.

A similar analysis was carried out on the composite rational thinking variables from Study 2 of Stanovich and West (1998c) displayed at the bottom of Table 14.2 and described previously. The two composite scores – despite being composed of vastly different reasoning tasks – displayed a significant correlation of .395 (p < .001, n = 546) this is another way of capturing the domain generality in normative responding that we discussed earlier. However, both Composite #1 and Composite #2 displayed significant correlations with SAT scores (.530 and .383, respectively, both ps < .001). Thus again the possibility remains that the association between the two thinking indices derives from their common association with cognitive ability. However, the correlation between Composite #1 and Composite #2 when the variance due to SAT scores was partialed out remained significant (partial r = .242, F(1, 526) = 32.82, p < .001). In summary, the two separate multivariate studies presented here (as well as others that we have conducted) both produced evidence indicating that there is systematic variance in various reasoning tasks that is not explained by variation in cognitive ability.[3]

There are actually two different ways to examine whether computational limitations plus random performance errors explain all of the variance in performance on these tasks. The first is that which we have just applied – to determine the covariance among reasoning tasks after cognitive ability has been partialed out. The second is to examine whether there are personality variables – that is, thinking dispositions of the type that have been studied in the critical thinking literature – that can explain the variation in performance after cognitive ability has been accounted for. We have examined this question as well.

The latter analyses are framed by an assumption that often is unarticulated in the psychological literature: that cognitive abilities and thinking dispositions are constructs at different levels of analysis in a cognitive theory (Anderson, 1990; Dennett, 1987; Marr, 1982; Newell, 1982; Stanovich, 1999) and that they may do separate explanatory work in a descriptive theory of human reasoning performance. Specifically, each level of analysis in cognitive theory frames a somewhat different issue. At the biological level the paramount issue is whether the physical mechanism has the potential to instantiate certain complex algorithms. At the algorithmic level, the key issue is one of computational efficiency. In contrast, it is at the intentional level that issues of rationality arise. Omnibus measures of cognitive capacities, such as intelligence tests, index individual differences in the efficiency of processing at the algorithmic level. In contrast, thinking dispositions as traditionally studied in psychology (Cacioppo, Petty, Feinstein, &

TABLE 14.4. *Correlations between the Reasoning Tasks and
SAT Total Score and Thinking Dispositions Composite Score*

	SAT Total	TDC
Argument evaluation task	.371*	.296*
Syllogisms	.410*	.329*
Statistical reasoning	.376*	.263*
Covariation: Δp	.239*	.176*
Hypothesis testing bias	−.223*	−.167*
Outcome bias	−.172*	−.175*
If/Only thinking	−.208*	−.205*
RT1 Composite	.530*	.413*
RT2 Composite	.383*	.324*
RT Composite, All Tasks	.547*	.442*

Source: Data from Study 2 of Stanovich & West, 1998c.

Note: TDC = Thinking dispositions composite score: Composite #1 = standard score composite of performance on argument evaluation task, syllogisms, and statistical reasoning. Composite #2 = standard score composite of performance on covariation judgment, hypothesis testing task, if/only thinking, and outcome bias. Composite, All Tasks = rational thinking composite score of performance on all seven tasks.

* = p < .001, two-tailed.

Jarvis, 1996; Kardash & Scholes, 1996; Klaczynski et al., 1997; Kruglanski & Webster, 1996; Schommer, 1990, 1993, 1994; Stanovich & West, 1997; Sternberg, 1997) index individual differences at the intentional level of analysis. They are telling us about the individual's goals and epistemic values – and they are indexing broad tendencies of pragmatic and epistemic self-regulation. If thinking dispositions correlate with individual differences residualized on cognitive ability, then this will be an additional indication that variance in reasoning performance is caused by *actual* differences in intentional psychology.

The left column of figures in Table 14.4 recapitulates the results regarding cognitive ability from Study 2 of Stanovich and West (1998c) that were discussed previously. The second column of figures in this table includes the correlations with a composite measure of thinking dispositions that was employed in that study. This measure is the additive combination of several questionnaire subscales designed to tap epistemic self-regulation (Goldman, 1986; Harman, 1995; Nozick, 1993; Thagard, 1992). The subscales overrepresented dispositions with potential epistemic significance, for example: "the disposition to weigh new evidence against a favored belief heavily (or lightly), the disposition to spend a great deal of time (or very little) on a problem before giving up, or the disposition to weigh heavily the opinions of others in forming one's own" (Baron, 1985, p. 15).

Baron (1985, 1988) has called such tendencies dispositions toward actively open-minded thinking. Overall, the subscales in this thinking dispositions questionnaire measure the following dimensions: epistemological absolutism, willingness to perspective-switch, willingness to decontextualize, and the tendency to consider alternative opinions and evidence (see also Sá et al., 1999; Schommer & Walker, 1995; Stanovich & West, 1997; Webster & Kruglanski, 1994).

The second column of correlations in Table 14.4 indicates that the thinking dispositions composite score (TDC) displayed significant correlations with each of the tasks in the Stanovich and West (1998c) study. In each case, the direction of the relationship was the same as that observed for cognitive ability. In most cases, the correlations involving the TDC were lower than those involving the SAT, but in several cases (outcome bias, if/only thinking) the magnitude of the correlations was similar. The correlations between the TDC and the three composite indices of reasoning were moderate in size (.413, .324, and .442, respectively).

There appears to be no question that there are consistent and replicable relationships between intentional-level-thinking dispositions and performance on a variety of tasks from the reasoning and heuristics and biases literature. To find out whether the thinking dispositions explained unique variance after cognitive ability was controlled, a composite score was computed combining performance on all seven tasks. SAT total scores and the TDC attained a multiple R with this criterion variable of .627 ($F(2, 526) = 170.56, p < .001$). SAT total was a significant unique predictor (partial correlation = .496, unique variance explained = .198, $p < .001$) as was the TDC (partial correlation = .366, unique variance explained = .094, $p < .001$). Thus, there were consistent indications in the data of Stanovich and West (1998c) and in other studies (Sá et al., 1999; Stanovich & West, 1997) that thinking dispositions do in fact explain variance on a variety of reasoning and decision-making tasks after the variance in cognitive ability has been accounted for. The residual variance does appear to be systematic and predictable. These results refute the notion that all performance variability can be accounted for by algorithmic-level limitations and performance errors. Indicators of intentional-level epistemic attitudes are consistent unique predictors of normative response tendencies. And with this conclusion we have engaged our third issue.

ISSUE 3: INDIVIDUAL DIFFERENCES IN REASONING: IMPLICATIONS FOR THE RATIONALITY DEBATE?

The interpretation of the gap between descriptive models and normative models in the human reasoning and decision-making literature has been the subject of contentious debate for almost two decades now (see Baron, 1994; Cohen, 1981, 1983; Evans & Over, 1996; Gigerenzer, 1996; Kahneman,

1981; Kahneman & Tversky, 1983, 1996; Koehler, 1996; Samuels, Stich, & Tremoulet, 1999; Stein, 1996; Vranas, 2000). The debate has arisen because some investigators wished to interpret the gap as indicating that human cognition was characterized by systematic irrationalities. In our "Behavioral and Brain Sciences" target article on these debates (Stanovich & West, 2000b), these investigators were labeled the Meliorists, due to the emphasis that they place on reforming human cognition. Disputing the attribution of irrationality were numerous investigators (who were termed Panglossians in this discussion, see also Stanovich, 1999) who argued that there were other reasons why reasoning might not accord with normative theory (see Cohen, 1981 and Stein, 1996 for extensive discussions of the various possibilities) – reasons that prevent the ascription of irrationality to subjects.

Four alternative interpretations for the normative/descriptive gap were extensively discussed in Cohen's (1981) classic "Behavioral and Brain Sciences" article and in Stein's (1996) more recent book-length treatment of the rationality debate. First, reasoning might depart from normative standards due to performance errors – temporary lapses of attention, memory deactivation, and other sporadic information processing mishaps. Second, there may be stable and inherent computational limitations that prevent the normative response (Cherniak, 1986; Goldman, 1978; Harman, 1995; Oaksford & Chater, 1993, 1995, 1998; Stich, 1990). Third, in interpreting performance, we might be applying the wrong normative model to the task (Koehler, 1996; Vranas, 2000). Alternatively, we may be applying the correct normative model to the problem as set, but the subject might have construed the problem differently and be providing the normatively appropriate answer to a different problem (Adler, 1984, 1991; Berkeley & Humphreys, 1982; Broome, 1990; Hilton, 1995; Schwarz, 1996).

The data discussed in the earlier sections of this chapter relate to the first two of these alternative explanations. We have seen that several classic tasks from the reasoning and decision-making literature seem to have moderate computational limitations that might prevent some subjects from deriving the correct response – and, of course, performance errors are a factor in responding. However, Stanovich (1999; Stanovich & West, 2000b) defined a position – termed the Apologist position – which posited that the first two factors, performance errors and computational limitations, could explain all of the normative/descriptive gap. Such a view predicts that once capacity limitations have been controlled, the remaining variations from normative responding will be essentially unpredictable (all being due to performance errors). In contrast, we have just shown in the previous section that there is significant covariance among the residualized scores from a variety of tasks. The residual variance was also systematically associated with thinking dispositions that were conceptualized as characteristic intentional-level attitudes reflecting epistemic regulation. That cognitive/personality variables can explain normative/descriptive discrepancies that remain after computational limitations have been accounted for signals a systematically suboptimal intentional-level model of performance.

Thus, the Apologist's position does have a substantial grain of truth, but in the extreme cannot account for all the reliable individual differences. However, the Panglossian position does have two additional arguments to use in an attempt to completely close the normative/descriptive gap. First, the possibility of incorrect norm application arises because any particular laboratory problem must be matched to an appropriate normative model. Matching a problem to a normative model is rarely an automatic or clear cut procedure. The complexities involved in matching problems to norms make possible the argument that the gap between the descriptive and normative occurs because psychologists are applying the wrong normative model to the situation. It is a potent strategy for the Panglossian theorist to use against the advocate of Meliorism and such claims have become quite common in critiques of the heuristics and biases literature (see Cohen, 1981; Gigerenzer, 1996; Stanovich, 1999; Stein, 1996; Vranas, 2000).

A second possibility is the argument that although the experimenter may well be applying the correct normative model to the problem as set, the subject might be construing the problem differently and be providing the normatively appropriate answer to a different problem – in short, that subjects have a different interpretation of the task (see, for example, Adler, 1984, 1991; Broome, 1990; Henle, 1962; Hilton, 1995; Levinson, 1995; Margolis, 1987; Schick, 1987, 1997; Schwarz, 1996). As with incorrect norm application, the alternative construal argument locates the problem with the experimenter. However, it is different in that in the wrong norm explanation it is assumed that the subject is interpreting the task as the experimenter intended – but the experimenter is not using the right criteria to evaluate performance. In contrast, the alternative task construal argument allows that the experimenter may be applying the correct normative model to the problem the experimenter intends the subject to solve – but posits that the subject has construed the problem in some other way and is providing a normatively appropriate answer to a different problem.

How to decide whether experimenters are applying the appropriate normative model to a task and assuming the right task construal is a vexing problem. We have followed the lead of the Panglossian theorists here in consciously committing the naturalistic fallacy to get a foothold on this issue. What we are referring to is, to paraphrase Stein's (1996) terminology, the way the so-called "reject-the-experimenter" strategy is used by Panglossian theorists when the modal response on a task departs from the response deemed normative by the experimenter. It is noteworthy that this strategy is exclusively used to eliminate gaps between descriptive models of performance and normative models – although this connection is not a necessary one. When this type of critique is employed, the normative model or task construal that is suggested as a substitute for the one traditionally used is one that coincides perfectly with the descriptive model of the subjects' performance – thus preserving a view of human rationality as ideal. It is rarely noted that the strategy could be used in just the opposite way – to create gaps between the normative and descriptive. Situations where the modal response coincides with the standard normative model could be critiqued, and alternative models could be suggested that would result in a new normative/descriptive gap. But this is never done. The Panglossian camp, often highly critical of empirical psychologists, is never critical of psychologists who design reasoning tasks in instances where the modal subject gives the response the experimenters deem correct. Ironically, in these cases, according to the Panglossians, the same psychologists seem never to err in their task designs and interpretations.

There, perhaps, is some logic to this bias displayed by Panglossians. Might not the majority of subjects be telling us something – something that the experimenters missed? Hence our characterization of this attitude as a case of consciously committing the naturalistic fallacy – in our search for what is good reasoning, letting the subjects themselves tell us. What this means is that in an important sense the norms being endorsed by the Panglossian camp are conditioned by descriptive facts about human behavior. The rationality debate itself is, reflexively, evidence that the descriptive models of actual behavior condition expert notions of the normative. That is, there would have been no debate (or at least much less of one) had people behaved in accord with the then-accepted norms.

But if we are going to use descriptive facts about behavior to gives us clues as to what are the proper norms to apply and construals to consider reasonable, we must ask why the modal response is the only aspect of group performance that is relevant? Might the pattern of responses around the mode tell us anything? Or do the moments of the distribution contain no normative information? And finally, what about the the rich covariance patterns that would be present in any multivariate experiment? Are these totally superfluous – all norm-relevant behavioral information residing in the mode? We think not.

PUTTING INDIVIDUAL DIFFERENCES TO WORK IN THE
RATIONALITY DEBATE: THE UNDERSTANDING/
ACCEPTANCE PRINCIPLE

One goal of the present research program is to expand the scope of the descriptive information used to condition our views about appropriate norms and task construals by using Spearman's positive manifold as a diagnostic tool. Larrick, Nisbett, and Morgan (1993) made just such an argument in their analysis of what justified the cost-benefit reasoning of microeconomics. Their point was that: "Intelligent people would be more likely to use cost-benefit reasoning. Because intelligence is generally regarded as being the set of psychological properties that makes for effectiveness across environments . . . intelligent people should be more likely to use the most effective reasoning strategies than should less intelligent people" (p. 333). Larrick et al. (1993) are alluding to the fact that we may want to condition our inferences about appropriate norms based not only on what response the majority of people make but also on what response the most cognitively competent subjects make.

We traced this basic idea, which we termed the understanding/acceptance principle (see Stanovich, 1999; Stanovich & West, 1999, 2000b) to a 25-year-old paper by Slovic and Tversky (1974) in which in an imaginary dialog between Allais and Savage it was argued that it should be the case that "the deeper the understanding of the axiom, the greater the readiness to accept it" (pp. 372–373). Thus, a positive correlation between understanding and acceptance would suggest that the gap between the descriptive and normative was due to an initial failure to fully process and/or understand the task. The basic point is that a normative/descriptive gap that is disproportionately created by subjects with a superficial understanding of the problem provides no warrant for amending the models applied and task construals assumed by the designers of the problem.

There are two generic strategies for applying the understanding/acceptance principle based on the fact that variation in understanding can be created or it can be studied by examining naturally occurring individual differences. Slovic and Tversky (1974) employed the former strategy by providing subjects with explicated arguments supporting the Allais or Savage normative interpretation (see also Doherty, Schiavo, Tweney, & Mynatt, 1981; Stanovich & West, 1999). As an alternative to manipulating understanding, the understanding/acceptance principle can be transformed into an individual differences prediction. For example, the principle might be interpreted as indicating that more reflective, engaged, and intelligent reasoners are more likely to respond in accord with normative principles. Thus, it might be expected that those individuals with cognitive/personality characteristics more conducive to deeper understanding would be more accepting of the appropriate normative principles for a particular problem. This was the emphasis of Larrick et al. (1993) when they argued that more intelligent people should be more likely to use cost-benefit principles. Similarly, need for cognition – a dispositional variable reflecting the tendency toward thoughtful analysis and reflective thinking – has been associated with aspects of epistemic and practical rationality (Cacioppo, et al., 1996; Kardash & Scholes, 1996; Klaczynski et al., 1997; Smith & Levin, 1996; Stanovich & West, 1999; Verplanken, 1993).

In fact, it is probably helpful to articulate the understanding/acceptance principle somewhat more formally in terms of Spearman's positive manifold – the fact that different measures of cognitive ability almost always correlate with each other (see Carroll, 1993, 1997). The individual differences version of the understanding/acceptance principle puts positive manifold to use in areas of cognitive psychology where the nature of the appropriate normative model to apply is in dispute. The point is that scoring a vocabulary item on a cognitive ability test and scoring a probabilistic reasoning response on a task from the heuristics and biases literature are not the same. The correct response in the former task has a canonical interpretation agreed upon by all investigators; whereas the normative appropriateness of responses on tasks from the latter domain has been the subject of extremely contentious dispute (Cohen, 1981, 1982, 1986; Cosmides & Tooby, 1996; Einhorn & Hogarth, 1981; Gigerenzer, 1991, 1993, 1996; Kahneman & Tversky, 1996; Koehler, 1996; Stein, 1996). Positive manifold between the two classes of task would only be expected if the normative model being used for directional scoring of the tasks in the latter domain is correct.

Oaksford and Sellen (2000) have emphasized this point by arguing that "in studying reasoning it is important to bear in mind that unlike tasks in almost any other area of cognition, reasoning tasks do not come prestamped with the 'correct' answer. The correct answer has to be discovered because it depends on how people interpret the task (Oaksford & Chater, 1993, 1995, 1998). In this respect, paradoxical individual differences, where a dysfunctional trait correlates with some preconceived notion of the correct answer, are particularly compelling" (p. 692). Thus, an important part of our method was to use the very obviousness of positive manifold as a diagnostic tool. If positive manifold is indeed to be expected, then another observation of it (while unsurprising in and of itself) might then be viewed as converging evidence for the normative model applied and/or task construal assumed in the scoring of the problem. Conversely, violations of positive manifold might be thought to call into question the normative model and task construal used to score the problem.

It is important to emphasize that we are proposing here to use patterns of covariance to help to determine whether it is appropriate to apply a particular normative model to a specific problem rather than to justify particular normative models themselves. This is a distinction that we were forced to clarify in our reply to the *Behavioral and Brain Sciences* commentators (Stanovich & West, 2000b). We agreed with several commentators that such individual differences patterns do not bear on the validity of normative models themselves but instead relate to disputes about which normative model should be applied to a particular experimental situation. There are many cases of the latter situation that have heretofore resisted resolution by argument (the heuristics and biases literature is littered with examples; refer to the commentary on Cohen, 1981, and Kahneman & Tversky, 1996).

With this caveat in mind, it is thus interesting to note that the direction of all of the correlations displayed in Tables 14.1–4 is consistent with the standard normative models used by psychologists. The tasks – as traditionally scored – correlate among themselves and also with general intelligence. The directionality of the systematic correlations with intelligence is embarrassing for critics who question the appropriateness of the norms applied and construals assumed by the designers of these tasks. Surely we generally would want to avoid the conclusion that individuals with more computational power are systematically computing the nonnormative response. Such an outcome would be nearly unique in a psychometric field that is one hundred years and thousands of studies old (Brody, 1997; Carroll, 1993, 1997; Lubinski & Humphreys, 1997; Neisser et al., 1996; Sternberg & Kaufman, 1998). It would mean that Spearman's (1904, 1927) positive manifold for cognitive tasks – virtually unchallenged for 100 years (but see Sternberg et al., 2001) – had finally broken down. Obviously, parsimony dictates that positive manifold remains a fact of life for cognitive tasks and that the normative model originally assumed appropriate actually is.

However, an application of the understanding/acceptance principle does not always work out this way. We have occasionally observed negative correlations between cognitive ability and the traditional scoring of a task. Again, given that positive manifold is the norm for cognitive tasks, such negative correlations might be taken as signals that the wrong normative model is being applied or that there are alternative construals of the task that are more appropriate.

For example, in several experiments (Stanovich & West, 1998c, 1999), we have examined some of the noncausal base-rate problems (those involving base rates with no obvious causal relationship to the criterion behavior) that are notorious for provoking philosophical dispute. One was the infamous cab problem studied by Bar-Hillel (1980) and Tversky and Kahneman (1982). Using several versions of this problem (Stanovich & West, 1998c, 1999), we have never found a tendency for the Bayesian responders to have higher cognitive ability. In some experiments there have been no significant differences found, and in others we have even found that the Bayesian group actually had significantly lower SAT scores and/or scored significantly lower in need for cognition. So an application of the understanding/acceptance principle can support the Panglossian position by showing that more intelligent and reflective subjects sometimes differentially reject the task construals and normative models applied to tasks by the designers of the problems in the reasoning and decision-making literature.

Most important for present purposes, however, is not which tasks go in which direction, nor how many tasks do, but to simply illustrate how a particular use of individual differences may have implications for debates about theories of the gap between normative models and descriptive models of reasoning performance. In reply to Cohen's (1981) well-known critique of the assumptions in the reasoning literature – surely the most often cited of such critiques – Jepson, Krantz, and Nisbett (1983) argued that "Cohen postulates far too broad a communality in the reasoning processes of the 'untutored' adult" (p. 495). Jepson et al., we argue, were right on the mark, but their argument has been largely ignored in more recent debates. For example, philosopher Nicholas Rescher (1988) argues that "to construe the data of these interesting experimental studies . . . to mean that people are systematically programmed to fallacious processes of reasoning – rather than merely that they are inclined to a variety of (occasionally questionable) substantive suppositions – is a very questionable step" (p. 196). There are two parts to Rescher's (1988) point here: the "systematically programmed" part and the "inclination toward questionable suppositions" part. Rescher's (1988) focus, like that of many who have dealt with the philosophical implications of the idea of human irrationality (Cohen, 1981, 1982, 1986; Davidson, 1980; Dennett, 1987; Goldman, 1986; Harman, 1995; Kornblith, 1993; Stein, 1996; Stich, 1990), is on the issue of how humans are systematically programmed. "Inclinations toward questionable suppositions" are only of interest to those in the philosophical debates as mechanisms that allow one to drive a wedge between competence and performance (Cohen, 1981, 1982; Rescher, 1988) – thus maintaining a theory of near-optimal human rational competence in the face of a host of responses that seemingly defy explanation in terms of standard normative models.

Analogously to Rescher, Cohen (1982) argues that there really are only two factors affecting performance on rational thinking tasks: "normatively correct mechanisms on the one side, and adventitious causes of error on the other" (p. 252). Not surprisingly given such a conceptualization, the processes contributing to error ("adventitious causes") are of little interest to Cohen (1981, 1982). Human performance arises from an intrinsic human competence that is impeccably rational, but responses occasionally deviate from normative correctness due to inattention, memory lapses, lack of motivation, and other fluctuating but basically unimportant causes. There is nothing in such a view that would motivate any interest in patterns of errors or individual differences in such errors.

One of the purposes of the present research program is to reverse the figure and ground in the rationality debate, which has tended to be dominated by the particular way that philosophers frame the competence/performance distinction. From a psychological standpoint, there may be important implications in precisely the aspects of performance that have been backgrounded in this controversy ("adventitious causes," "peccadillos"). That is, whatever the outcome of the disputes about how humans are "systematically programmed" (Cosmides & Tooby, 1996; Johnson-Laird & Byrne, 1991, 1993; Johnson-Laird, Byrne, & Schaeken, 1994; Oaksford & Chater, 1994, 1996; O'Brien, Braine, & Yang, 1994; Rips, 1994), variation in the "inclination toward questionable suppositions" is of psychological interest as a topic of study in its own right. The experiments discussed in this chapter provide at least tentative indications that the "inclination toward questionable suppositions" has some degree of domain generality and that it is predicted by thinking dispositions that concern the epistemic and pragmatic goals of the individual and that are part of people's intentional-level psychology.

NEW DIRECTIONS FOR RESEARCH ON INDIVIDUAL DIFFERENCES IN REASONING: THE PRAGMATIC CALIBRATION OF KNOWLEDGE ACQUISITION

In the research program just described, we have applied our individual differences analyses to normative issues surrounding a variety of different *types* of rationality. That is, philosophers and decision scientists have distinguished many different concepts of rationality – and most have been addressed by at least one task included in our research program. Perhaps the clearest and most well-known distinction is that between rationality of belief and rationality of action (Audi, 1993a, 1993b; Harman, 1995; Nozick, 1993; Pollock, 1995; Sloman, 1999). The rationality of belief – how accurately a person's belief network represents the external world – has been variously termed theoretical rationality, evidential rationality, or epistemic rationality (Audi, 1993b; Foley, 1987; Harman, 1995). The rationality of action – how well a person's actions maximize the satisfaction of their desires, given their beliefs – has been variously termed practical, pragmatic, instrumental, or means/ends rationality (Audi, 1993b; Harman, 1995; Nathanson, 1994; Nozick, 1993).

Although the distinction between theoretical rationality and practical rationality is the most common distinction made in the philosophical literature, cognitive psychologists have discussed related distinctions and terms. For example, Kahneman (2000) has distinguished "the ability to reason correctly about immediately available information" (p. 682) from the "decision theory rationality [that] is defined by the coherence of beliefs and preferences" (p. 682). Alternatively, Evans and Over (1996) make the distinction between rationality$_1$ and rationality$_2$, the former defined as reasoning and acting "in a way that is generally reliable and efficient for achieving one's goals" (p. 8). Thus, rationality$_1$ sounds much like instrumental rationality, as traditionally defined. Rationality$_2$, in contrast, refers to reasoning and acting "when one has a reason for what one does sanctioned by a normative theory" (p. 8). The distinction drawn by Evans and Over (1996) brings to the fore the mechanism used to pursue personal goals (mechanisms of conscious, reason-based rule-following versus tacit heuristics).

We are currently examining individual differences in an aspect of rationality that is not captured by any of these previous distinctions. This is because this particular aspect of rationality is a peculiar amalgamation of epistemic and practical rationality as traditionally defined. In a nuanced discussion of the relation between epistemic and practical rationality, Foley (1991) discusses the arguments of the so-called "evidentialists" who argue that there cannot be good nonevidential reasons for belief. One argument of the evidentialists is that nonevidential reasons would be redundant because there is one overriding practical concern that directs epistemic cognitive operations, to "maintain a comprehensive stock of beliefs that contains few false beliefs" (p. 372). The reason for this is that we are constantly faced with a plethora of decision situations that cannot be anticipated in advance. Many of these require an online response under time constraints that do not allow for an additional period of information search and knowledge acquisition. Thus, without the time to collect more information, and not knowing what the decision will be in advance, an individual has to deal with the situation based on the stock of information already collected. The stock of beliefs that is most likely to foster good on-the-spot decision making is a stock of beliefs that is large and accurate. Thus, the argument goes that "you can usually ignore practical reasons in your deliberations about what to believe. You can do so because ordinarily these practical reasons simply instruct you to acquire beliefs for which you have good evidence" (p. 373).

But Pollock (1995) has argued that the interplay of epistemic and practical rationality plays out in ways that make the degree of rational justification for belief subject to normative evaluation based on practical concerns. He concocts the story of a ship's captain on a busman's holiday on a Caribbean cruise liner. The ship seems well equipped and the captain casually notes the lifeboats, wonders how many there are, and consults a cheap brochure given to all passengers. However, later on, an accident occurs, disabling the entire ship's crew and putting the ship in danger of sinking. The vacationing captain is now in charge of the cruise liner and immediately wants to know whether there are enough lifeboats on board. His belief based on the holiday brochure is no longer sufficient – he must have the lifeboats counted carefully and accurately. The changed decision pragmatics have implications for how we evaluate the proper justification for belief. The evaluation of whether the degree of justification was well calibrated depends on the importance of the situation. More generally, as Pollock (1995) notes, "the degree of interest in a question determines the degree of justification a rational agent must have for an answer" (p. 49).

We propose that this argument of Pollock's (1995) can be scaled up into a more general argument about knowledge acquisition. Consider a real-life case that is a problematic one to analyze using standard categories of types of rationality. Several years ago, in the mid-1990s, one of this chapter's authors heard a television report that the National Highway Safety Administration had determined that something like 40% (the actual percentage is immaterial to our example) of small children in America were still riding in automobiles without being secured with seatbelt restraints. How are we to interpret this appalling statistic from the standpoint of evaluating the rationality of the parents of those children? Starting with a Panglossian bias to preserve the rationality of the parents, we could call a certain percentage of these cases "performance errors" – some of these are children who are regularly belted but whose parents forgot on a certain occasion.

But highway safety commissions can assure us that this is not the entire story – some children are unbelted time after time. Their parents' behavior is not a performance error because it is systematic. How do we preserve the rationality of the parents in these cases? We are not prone to take one escape hatch that is available to the Panglossian – that perhaps the parents really do not value their children. What creates the paradox is that the parents' behavior (they are putting their children at great risk by not securing them with seatbelts) is at total odds with their desires and goals (they love their children and desire to protect them). One way out of the paradox is to deny the latter – like the Panglossian economist who replies to a person who claims to like widgets but does not purchase them that, in fact, they do not really like widgets. This assumption preserves the Panglossian default of perfect rationality but at the expense of a dim view of the characteristics of our fellow humans. Most prefer not to escape the paradox by going in this direction.

Instead, the more popular way to resolve the seeming paradox is to retreat to the extreme strictures of what Elster (1983) calls a thin theory of rationality – where beliefs are treated as fixed and not subject to evaluation and, likewise, the content of desires is not evaluated. That is, the individual's goals and beliefs are accepted as they are, and debate centers only on whether individuals are optimally satisfying desires given beliefs. The thin theory – plus a Panglossian default – then simply says that, in this case, given that the desire is fixed (these parents love their children) and the behavior is fixed (they did not, in fact, secure the children with seatbelts), then it must follow that the belief behind the action must have been incorrect. The parents must not have known that unbelted children in automobile collisions – the leading cause of childhood death (National Highway Traffic Safety Administration, 1999) – are in unusual danger.

But is this really a satisfactory solution? Are we really assuaged that there is nothing wrong here? We submit that there are still grounds for worry. If we merely slip the Panglossian blinders, we will see that this example points to an entire domain of rationality that is open to assessment – the calibration of knowledge acquisition according to practical goals. We submit that the seatbelt example does reveal a failure of rational thinking that is related to notions of epistemic responsibility that philosophers have discussed (e.g., Code, 1987). Specifically, it is fine to say, as the thin theory does, that the parents were not irrational because they did not know that unbelted children are in particular danger. But the issue we are raising here is that perhaps it is also appropriate to ask the question: Why didn't they know? The media has been saturated with seatbelt warnings for over two decades now. Educational efforts in schools and communities are directed toward it. Of course, it is a key component of all driver training courses. Information about the importance of seatbelts for children is not hard to acquire.

Just as in the Pollock (1995) ship captain example, there seems to be a requirement of calibration here. It was important for the ship's captain to calibrate his knowledge of the lifeboats to his situation (was he a mere passenger or was he in charge of the boat). Similarly, over a person's lifetime, it is critical to acquire knowledge in domains that are most relevant to fulfilling one's most important goals. This is what we are calling the *pragmatic calibration of knowledge acquisition*. The knowledge that an individual acquires is unevenly distributed, as is the importance of all possible activities in the person's life. As Foley (1991) notes, true beliefs in a given domain are most likely to foster goal achievement in that domain. But our goals are not evenly spread over domains. The distribution of true beliefs should thus be in line with the distribution of importance across the various domains of life.

Knowledge acquisition is effortful and the cognitive resources for it are limited. There is a limited amount of time and effort to spend in epistemic activities, and it is important that that effort be calibrated so that it is directed at knowledge domains that are connected to goals we deem important. If we say that something is of paramount importance to us (our children's safety, for example), then it is incumbent on us to know something about these things we deem of such importance. The parents of the unbelted children are irrational on this view – not from the peculiar slice-in-time perspective of the thin theory (with its emphasis on a particular instance where they did not belt their children because they "didn't know" they should) – but from a long-term perspective. They have instead poorly calibrated their knowledge acquisition over a long time period of their lives – they have a systemic problem in the domain of rational thought and cognitive activity. Individual differences in this new type of rationality are currently under investigation in our laboratory.

Notes

1. The Panglossian position is represented by philosophers and cognitive scientists who see no gaps between the descriptive and normative models of performance. The Panglossian feels that people reason as well as anyone could possibly reason. Observed discrepancies are attributed to transitory performance errors, the wrong norm being applied by the experimenter, or an alternative

construal of the task on the part of the subject (see Stanovich, 1999, pp. 4–9, for a discussion).

2. Following Dennett (1987) and the taxonomy of Anderson (1990), we distinguish the algorithmic/design level from the rational/intentional level of analysis in cognitive science. The latter provides a specification of the *goals* of the system's computations (*what* the system is attempting to compute and *why*). At this level, we are concerned with the goals of the system, beliefs relevant to those goals, and the choice of action that is rational given the system's goals and beliefs (see Stanovich, 1999, pp. 9–12, for a discussion).

3. Although we operationalized cognitive ability here using SAT total scores, separating out the verbal and mathematical scores on the SAT reveals essentially identical trends. Additionally, in many of our studies we have employed converging measures of cognitive ability – an additional test of crystallized intelligence such as a vocabulary measure; a measure of fluid intelligence such as Raven matrices, or a working memory task. The correlations obtained with these measures generally converge with those obtained with the SAT. Finally, there are good reasons to view such cognitive ability tests as crude indicators of the overall level of current computational efficiency (see Stanovich & West, 2000a, pp. 704–705, for a discussion).

References

Adler, J. E. (1984). Abstraction is uncooperative. *Journal for the Theory of Social Behaviour, 14*, 165–181.

Adler, J. E. (1991). An optimist's pessimism: Conversation and conjunctions. In E. Eells & T. Maruszewski (Eds.), *Probability and rationality: Studies on L. Jonathan Cohen's philosophy of science* (pp. 251–282). Amsterdam: Editions Rodopi.

Anderson, J. R. (1990). *The adaptive character of thought*. Hillsdale, NJ: Erlbaum.

Audi, R. (1993a). *Action, intention, and reason*. Ithaca, NY: Cornell University Press.

Audi, R. (1993b). *The structure of justification*. Cambridge: Cambridge University Press.

Bar-Hillel, M. (1980). The base-rate fallacy in probability judgments. *Acta Psychologica, 44*, 211–233.

Bara, B. G., Bucciarelli, M., & Johnson-Laird, P. N. (1995). Development of syllogistic reasoning. *American Journal of Psychology, 108*, 157–193.

Baron, J. (1985). *Rationality and intelligence*. Cambridge: Cambridge University Press.

Baron, J. (1988). *Thinking and deciding*. Cambridge, England: Cambridge University Press.

Baron, J. (1994). Nonconsequentialist decisions. *Behavioral and Brain Sciences, 17*, 1–42.

Baron, J. (1995). Myside bias in thinking about abortion. *Thinking and Reasoning, 1*, 221–235.

Baron, J. (1998). *Judgment misguided: Intuition and error in public decision making*. New York: Oxford University Press.

Baron, J. (2000). *Thinking and deciding* (3rd Ed.). Cambridge, MA: Cambridge University Press.

Baron, J., & Hershey, J. C. (1988). Outcome bias in decision evaluation. *Journal of Personality and Social Psychology, 54,* 569–579.

Berkeley, D., & Humphreys, P. (1982). Structuring decision problems and the "bias heuristic." *Acta Psychologica, 50,* 201–252.

Braine, M. D. S., & O'Brien, D. P. (Eds.). (1998). *Mental logic.* Mahwah, NJ: Erlbaum.

Brody, N. (1997). Intelligence, schooling, and society. *American Psychologist, 52,* 1046–1050.

Broome, J. (1990). Should a rational agent maximize expected utility? In K. S. Cook & M. Levi (Eds.), *The limits of rationality* (pp. 132–145). Chicago: University of Chicago Press.

Bucciarelli, M., & Johnson-Laird, P. N. (1999). Strategies in syllogistic reasoning. *Cognitive Science, 23,* 247–303.

Cacioppo, J. T., Petty, R. E., Feinstein, J., & Jarvis, W. (1996). Dispositional differences in cognitive motivation: The life and times of individuals varying in need for cognition. *Psychological Bulletin, 119,* 197–253.

Carroll, J. B. (1993). *Human cognitive abilities: A survey of factor-analytic studies.* Cambridge: Cambridge University Press.

Carroll, J. B. (1997). Psychometrics, intelligence, and public perception. *Intelligence, 24,* 25–52.

Ceci, S. J. (1996). *On intelligence : A bioecological treatise on intellectual development (Expanded Ed.).* Cambridge, MA: Harvard University Press.

Cherniak, C. (1986). *Minimal rationality.* Cambridge, MA: MIT Press.

Code, L. (1987). *Epistemic responsibility.* Hanover, NH: University Press of New England.

Cohen, L. J. (1981). Can human irrationality be experimentally demonstrated? *Behavioral and Brain Sciences, 4,* 317–370.

Cohen, L. J. (1982). Are people programmed to commit fallacies? Further thoughts about the interpretation of experimental data on probability judgment. *Journal for the Theory of Social Behavior, 12,* 251–274.

Cohen, L. J. (1983). The controversy about irrationality. *Behavioral and Brain Sciences, 6,* 510–517.

Cohen, L. J. (1986). *The dialogue of reason.* Oxford: Oxford University Press.

Cosmides, L., & Tooby, J. (1994). Beyond intuition and instinct blindness: Toward an evolutionarily rigorous cognitive science. *Cognition, 50,* 41–77.

Cosmides, L., & Tooby, J. (1996). Are humans good intuitive statisticians after all? Rethinking some conclusions from the literature on judgment under uncertainty. *Cognition, 58,* 1–73.

Davidson, D. (1980). *Essays on actions & events.* Oxford: Oxford University Press.

Dawes, R. M. (1998). Behavioral decision making and judgment. In D. T. Gilbert, S. T. Fiske, & G. Lindzey (Eds.), *The handbook of social psychology* (vol. 1, pp. 497–548). Boston: McGraw-Hill.

Dennett, D. C. (1987). *The intentional stance.* Cambridge, MA: MIT Press.

Doherty, M. E., Schiavo, M., Tweney, R., & Mynatt, C. (1981). The influence of feedback and diagnostic data on pseudodiagnosticity. *Bulletin of the Psychonomic Society, 18,* 191–194.

Einhorn, H. J., & Hogarth, R. M. (1981). Behavioral decision theory: Processes of judgment and choice. *Annual Review of Psychology, 32,* 53–88.

Elster, J. (1983). *Sour grapes: Studies in the subversion of rationality*. Cambridge, England: Cambridge University Press.

Epstein, S., Lipson, A., Holstein, C., & Huh, E. (1992). Irrational reactions to negative outcomes: Evidence for two conceptual systems. *Journal of Personality and Social Psychology, 62*, 328–339.

Evans, J. St. B. T., Barston, J., & Pollard, P. (1983). On the conflict between logic and belief in syllogistic reasoning. *Memory & Cognition, 11*, 295–306.

Evans, J. St. B. T., & Over, D. E. (1996). *Rationality and reasoning*. Hove, UK: Psychology Press.

Evans, J. St. B. T., Newstead, S. E., & Byrne, R. M. J. (1993). *Human reasoning: The psychology of deduction*. Hove, UK: Erlbaum.

Foley, R. (1987). *The theory of epistemic rationality*. Cambridge, MA: Harvard University Press.

Foley, R. (1991). Rationality, belief, and commitment. *Synthese, 89*, 365–392.

Galotti, K. M., Baron, J., & Sabini, J. P. (1986). Individual differences in syllogistic reasoning: Deduction rules or mental models? *Journal of Experimental Psychology: General, 115*, 16–25.

Gigerenzer, G. (1991). How to make cognitive illusions disappear: Beyond "heuristics and biases." *European Review of Social Psychology, 2*, 83–115.

Gigerenzer, G. (1993). The bounded rationality of probabilistic mental models. In K. Manktelow & D. Over (Eds.), *Rationality: Psychological and philosophical perspectives* (pp. 284–313). London: Routledge.

Gigerenzer, G. (1996). On narrow norms and vague heuristics: A reply to Kahneman and Tversky (1996). *Psychological Review, 103*, 592–596.

Goldman, A. I. (1978). Epistemics: The regulative theory of cognition. *Journal of Philosophy, 55*, 509–523.

Goldman, A. I. (1986). *Epistemology and cognition*. Cambridge, MA: Harvard University Press.

Harman, G. (1995). Rationality. In E. E. Smith & D. N. Osherson (Eds.), *Thinking* (vol. 3, pp. 175–211). Cambridge, MA: The MIT Press.

Hastie, R., & Dawes, R. M. (2001). *Rational choice in an uncertain world*. Thousand Oaks, CA: Sage.

Henle, M. (1962). On the relation between logic and thinking. *Psychological Review, 69*, 366–378.

Hilton, D. J. (1995). The social context of reasoning: Conversational inference and rational judgment. *Psychological Bulletin, 118*, 248–271.

Hirschfeld, L. A., & Gelman, S. A. (Eds.). (1994). *Mapping the mind: Domain specificity in cognition and culture*. Cambridge: Cambridge University Press.

Hong, Y., Morris, M. W., Chiu, C., & Benet-Martinez, V. (2000). Multi-cultural minds: A dynamic constructivist approach to culture and cognition. *American Psychologist, 55*, 709–720.

Jepson, C., Krantz, D., & Nisbett, R. (1983). Inductive reasoning: Competence or skill? *Behavioral and Brain Sciences, 6*, 494–501.

Johnson-Laird, P. N. (1983). *Mental models*. Cambridge, MA: Harvard University Press.

Johnson-Laird, P. N. (1999). Deductive reasoning. *Annual Review of Psychology, 50*, 109–135.

Johnson-Laird, P. N., & Bara, B. G. (1984). Syllogistic inference. *Cognition, 16*, 1–61.

Johnson-Laird, P. N., & Byrne, R. M. J. (1991). *Deduction*. Hillsdale, NJ: Erlbaum.

Johnson-Laird, P. N., & Byrne, R. M. J. (1992). Domain-specific reasoning: Social contracts, cheating, and perspective change. *Cognition, 43*, 173–182.

Johnson-Laird, P. N., & Byrne, R. M. J. (1993). Precis of "deduction." *Behavioral and Brain Sciences, 16*, 323–333.

Johnson-Laird, P. N., Byrne, R. M. J., & Schaeken, W. (1994). Why models rather than rules give a better account of propositional reasoning. *Psychological Review, 101*, 734–739.

Johnson-Laird, P. N., & Steedman, M. J. (1978). The psychology of syllogisms. *Cognitive Psychology, 10*, 64–99.

Kahneman, D. (1981). Who shall be the arbiter of our intuitions? *Behavioral and Brain Sciences, 4*, 339–340.

Kahneman, D. (2000). A psychological point of view: Violations of rational rules as a diagnostic of mental processes. *Behavioral and Brain Sciences, 23*, 681–683.

Kahneman, D., & Tversky, A. (1983). Can irrationality be intelligently discussed? *Behavioral and Brain Sciences, 6*, 509–510.

Kahneman, D., & Tversky, A. (1996). On the reality of cognitive illusions. *Psychological Review, 103*, 582–591.

Kahneman, D., & Tversky, A. (Eds.). (2000). *Choices, values, and frames*. Cambridge: Cambridge University Press.

Kardash, C. M., & Scholes, R. J. (1996). Effects of pre-existing beliefs, epistemological beliefs, and need for cognition on interpretation of controversial issues. *Journal of Educational Psychology, 88*, 260–271.

Klaczynski, P. A. (2000). Motivated scientific reasoning biases, epistemological beliefs, and theory polarization: A two-process approach to adolescent cognition. *Child Development, 71*, 1347–1366.

Klaczynski, P. A., Gordon, D. H., & Fauth, J. (1997). Goal-oriented critical reasoning and individual differences in critical reasoning biases. *Journal of Educational Psychology, 89*, 470–485.

Koehler, J. J. (1996). The base rate fallacy reconsidered: Descriptive, normative and methodological challenges. *Behavioral and Brain Sciences, 19*, 1–53.

Kornblith, H. (1993). *Inductive inference and its natural ground*. Cambridge, MA: MIT University Press.

Kruglanski, A. W., & Webster, D. M. (1996). Motivated closing the mind: "Seizing" and "freezing." *Psychological Review, 103*, 263–283.

Kuhn, D. (2001). How do people know? *Psychological Science, 12*, 1–8.

Larrick, R. P., Nisbett, R. E., & Morgan, J. N. (1993). Who uses the cost-benefit rules of choice? Implications for the normative status of microeconomic theory. *Organizational Behavior and Human Decision Processes, 56*, 331–347.

Levin, I. P., Wasserman, E. A., & Kao, S. F. (1993). Multiple methods of examining biased information use in contingency judgments. *Organizational Behavior and Human Decision Processes, 55*, 228–250.

Levinson, S. C. (1995). Interactional biases in human thinking. In E. Goody (Eds.), *Social intelligence and interaction* (pp. 221–260). Cambridge: Cambridge University Press.

Lubinski, D., & Humphreys, L. G. (1997). Incorporating general intelligence into epidemiology and the social sciences. *Intelligence, 24*, 159–201.

Manktelow, K. I. (1999). *Reasoning & Thinking*. Hove, UK: Psychology Press.

Margolis, H. (1987). *Patterns, thinking, and cognition*. Chicago: University of Chicago Press.

Marr, D. (1982). *Vision*. San Francisco: W. H. Freeman.

Medin, D. L., & Bazerman, M. H. (1999). Broadening behavioral decision research: Multiple levels of cognitive processing. *Psychonomic Bulletin & Review, 6*, 533–546.

Miller, D. T., Turnbull, W., & McFarland, C. (1990). Counterfactual thinking and social perception: Thinking about what might have been. In M. P. Zanna (Ed.), *Advances in Experimental Social Psychology* (pp. 305–331). San Diego: Academic Press.

Nathanson, S. (1994). *The ideal of rationality*. Chicago: Open Court.

National Highway Traffic Safety Administration. (1999). *Traffic safety facts 1999: Children*. [Fact sheet: DOT HS 809 087]. Washington, DC: Author. Retrieved November 24, 2000, from http://www.nhtsa.dot.gov/people/ncsa/pdf/child99.pdf

Neisser, U., Boodoo, G., Bouchard, T., Boykin, A. W., Brody, N., Ceci, S. J., Halpern, D. F., Loehlin, J. C., Perloff, R., Sternberg, R. J., & Urbina, S. (1996). Intelligence: Knowns and unknowns. *American Psychologist, 51*, 77–101.

Newell, A. (1982). The knowledge level. *Artificial Intelligence, 18*, 87–127.

Newstead, S. E., & Evans, J. St. B. T. (Eds.) (1995). *Perspectives on thinking and reasoning*. Hove, UK: Erlbaum.

Nickerson, R. S. (1998). Confirmation bias: A ubiquitous phenomenon in many guises. *Review of General Psychology, 2*, 175–220.

Nisbett, R. E., Peng, K., Choi, I., & Norenzayan, A. (2001). Culture and systems of thought: Holistic versus analytic cognition. *Psychological Review, 108*, 291–310.

Nisbett, R. E., & Ross, L. (1980). *Human inference: Strategies and shortcomings of social judgment*. Englewood Cliffs, NJ: Prentice-Hall.

Norenzayan, A., & Nisbett, R. E. (2000). Culture and causal cognition. *Current Directions in Psychological Science, 9*, 132–135.

Nozick, R. (1993). *The nature of rationality*. Princeton, NJ: Princeton University Press.

Oaksford, M., & Chater, N. (1993). Reasoning theories and bounded rationality. In K. Manktelow & D. Over (Eds.), *Rationality: Psychological and philosophical perspectives* (pp. 31–60). London: Routledge.

Oaksford, M., & Chater, N. (1994). A rational analysis of the selection task as optimal data selection. *Psychological Review, 101*, 608–631.

Oaksford, M., & Chater, N. (1995). Theories of reasoning and the computational explanation of everyday inference. *Thinking and Reasoning, 1*, 121–152.

Oaksford, M., & Chater, N. (1996). Rational explanation of the selection task. *Psychological Review, 103*, 381–391.

Oaksford, M., & Chater, N. (1998). *Rationality in an uncertain world*. Hove, UK: Psychology Press.

Oaksford, M., & Sellen, J. (2000). Paradoxical individual differences in conditional inference. *Behavioral and Brain Sciences, 23*, 691–692.

O'Brien, D. P., Braine, M., & Yang, Y. (1994). Propositional reasoning by mental models? Simple to refute in principle and in practice. *Psychological Review, 101*, 711–724.

Parker, A. M., & Fischhoff, B. (2000, July). *An individual differences measure of decision-making competence*. Unpublished manuscript.

Peng, K., & Nisbett, R. E. (1999). Culture, dialectics, and reasoning about contradiction. *American Psychologist, 54*, 741–754.

Perkins, D. N. (1989). Reasoning as it is and could be: An empirical perspective. In D. Topping, D. Crowell, & V. Kabayashi (Eds.), *Thinking across cultures*, (pp. 175–194). Hillsdale, NJ: Erlbaum.

Pollock, J. L. (1995). *Cognitive carpentry: A blueprint for how to build a person.* Cambridge, MA: MIT Press.

Rescher, N. (1988). *Rationality: A philosophical inquiry into the nature and rationale of reason.* Oxford: Oxford University Press.

Rips, L. J. (1994). *The psychology of proof.* Cambridge, MA: MIT Press.

Rips, L. J., & Conrad, F. G. (1983). Individual differences in deduction. *Cognition and Brain Theory, 6,* 259–285.

Roberts, M. J. (1993). Human reasoning: Deduction rules or mental models, or both? *Quarterly Journal of Experimental Psychology, 46A,* 569–589.

Sá, W., & Stanovich, K. E. (2001). The domain specificity and generality of mental contamination: Accuracy and projection in mental content judgments. *British Journal of Psychology, 92,* 281–302.

Sá, W., West, R. F., & Stanovich, K. E. (1999). The domain specificity and generality of belief bias: Searching for a generalizable critical thinking skill. *Journal of Educational Psychology, 91,* 497–510.

Samuels, R. (1998). Evolutionary psychology and the massive modularity hypothesis. *British Journal for the Philosophy of Science, 49,* 575–602.

Samuels, R., Stich, S. P., & Tremoulet, P. D. (1999). Rethinking rationality: From bleak implications to Darwinian modules. In E. Lepore & Z. Pylyshyn (Eds.), *What is cognitive science?* (pp. 74–120). Oxford: Blackwell.

Schick, F. (1997). *Making choices: A recasting of decision theory.* Cambridge, Cambridge University Press.

Schick, F. (1987). Rationality: A third dimension. *Economics and Philosophy, 3,* 49–66.

Schommer, M. (1990). Effects of beliefs about the nature of knowledge on comprehension. *Journal of Educational Psychology, 82,* 498–504.

Schommer, M. (1993). Epistemological development and academic performance among secondary students. *Journal of Educational Psychology, 85,* 406–411.

Schommer, M. (1994). Synthesizing epistemological belief research: Tentative understandings and provocative confusions. *Educational Psychology Review, 6,* 293–319.

Schommer, M., & Walker, K. (1995). Are epistemological beliefs similar across domains? *Journal of Educational Psychology, 87,* 424–432.

Schustack, M. W., & Sternberg, R. J. (1981). Evaluation of evidence in causal inference. *Journal of Experimental Psychology: General, 110,* 101–120.

Schwarz, N. (1996). *Cognition and communication: Judgmental biases, research methods, and the logic of conversation.* Mahwah, NJ: Erlbaum.

Shafir, E., & Tversky, A. (1995). Decision making. In E. E. Smith & D. N. Osherson (Eds.), *Thinking* (vol. 3, pp. 77–100). Cambridge, MA: The MIT Press.

Sloman, S. A. (1999). Rational versus arational models of thought. In R. J. Sternberg (Ed.), *The nature of cognition* (pp. 557–585). Cambridge, MA: MIT Press.

Slovic, P., & Tversky, A. (1974). Who accepts Savage's axiom? *Behavioral Science, 19,* 368–373.

Slugoski, B. R., & Wilson, A. E. (1998). Contribution of conversation skills to the production of judgmental errors. *European Journal of Social Psychology, 28,* 575–601.

Smith, S. M., & Levin, I. P. (1996). Need for cognition and choice framing effects. *Journal of Behavioral Decision Making, 9,* 283–290.

Spearman, C. (1904). General intelligence, objectively determined and measured. *American Journal of Psychology, 15,* 201–293.

Spearman, C. (1927). *The abilities of man.* London: Macmillan.

Sperber, D. (1994). The modularity of thought and the epidemiology of representations. In L. A. Hirschfeld & S. A. Gelman (Eds.), *Mapping the mind: Domain specificity in cognition and culture* (pp. 39–67). Cambridge: Cambridge University Press.

Sperber, D. (2000). Metarepresentations in evolutionary perspective. In D. Sperber (Eds.), *Metarepresentations: A Multidisciplinary Perspective* (pp. 117–137). Oxford: Oxford University Press.

Stanovich, K. E. (1999). *Who is rational? Studies of individual differences in reasoning.* Mahwah, NJ: Erlbaum.

Stanovich, K. E., & West, R. F. (1997). Reasoning independently of prior belief and individual differences in actively open-minded thinking. *Journal of Educational Psychology, 89,* 342–357.

Stanovich, K. E., & West, R. F. (1998a). Cognitive ability and variation in selection task performance. *Thinking and Reasoning, 4,* 193–230.

Stanovich, K. E., & West, R. F. (1998b). Individual differences in framing and conjunction effects. *Thinking and Reasoning, 4,* 289–317.

Stanovich, K. E., & West, R. F. (1998c). Individual differences in rational thought. *Journal of Experimental Psychology: General, 127,* 161–188.

Stanovich, K. E., & West, R. F. (1998d). Who uses base rates and P(D/~H)? An analysis of individual differences. *Memory & Cognition, 28,* 161–179.

Stanovich, K. E., & West, R. F. (1999). Discrepancies between normative and descriptive models of decision making and the understanding/acceptance principle. *Cognitive Psychology, 38,* 349–385.

Stanovich, K. E., & West, R. F. (2000a). Advancing the rationality debate. *Behavior and Brain Sciences, 23* (5), 701–726.

Stanovich, K. E., & West, R. F. (2000b). Individual differences in reasoning: Implications for the rationality debate? *Behavioral and Brain Sciences, 23,* 645–726.

Stein, E. (1996). *Without good reason: The rationality debate in philosophy and cognitive science.* Oxford: Oxford University Press.

Sternberg, R. J. (1977). Component processes in analogical reasoning. *Psychological Review, 84,* 353–378.

Sternberg, R. J. (1980). Representation and process in linear syllogistic reasoning. *Journal of Experimental Psychology: General, 109,* 119–159.

Sternberg, R. J. (1997). *Thinking styles.* Cambridge: Cambridge University Press.

Sternberg, R. J., & Kaufman, J. C. (1998). Human abilities. *Annual Review of Psychology, 49,* 479–502.

Sternberg, R. J., Nokes, C., Geissler, P. W., Prince, R., Okatcha, F., Bundy, D. A, & Grigorenko, E. L. (2001). The relationship between academic and practical intelligence: A case study in Kenya. *Intelligence, 29,* 401–418.

Sternberg, R. J., & Weil, E. M. (1980). An aptitude *x* strategy interaction in linear syllogistic reasoning. *Journal of Educational Psychology, 72,* 226–239.

Stich, S. P. (1990). *The fragmentation of reason.* Cambridge: MIT Press.

Thagard, P. (1992). *Conceptual revolutions.* Princeton, NJ: Princeton Uiversity Press.

Tschirgi, J. E. (1980). Sensible reasoning: A hypothesis about hypotheses. *Child Development*, *51*, 1–10.

Tversky, A., & Kahneman, D. (1982). Evidential impact of base rates. In D. Kahneman, P. Slovic, & A. Tversky (Eds.), *Judgment under uncertainty: Heuristics and biases* (pp. 153–160). Cambridge: Cambridge University Press.

Verplanken, B. (1993). Need for cognition and external information search: Responses to time pressure during decision-making. *Journal of Research in Personality*, *27*, 238–252.

Vranas, P. B. M. (2000). Gigerenzer's normative critique of Kahneman and Tversky. *Cognition*, *76*, 179–193.

Wason, P. C. (1966). Reasoning. In B. Foss (Eds.), *New horizons in psychology* (pp. 135–151). Harmonsworth, UK: Penguin:

Wasserman, E. A., Dorner, W. W., & Kao, S. F. (1990). Contributions of specific cell information to judgments of interevent contingency. *Journal of Experimental Psychology: Learning, Memory, and Cognition*, *16*, 509–521.

Webster, D. M., & Kruglanski, A. W. (1994). Individual differences in need for cognitive closure. *Journal of Personality and Social Psychology*, *67*, 1049–1062.

15

Teaching Reasoning

Raymond S. Nickerson

As used in the psychological literature, *reasoning* has a variety of connotations that differ in their inclusiveness. At one extreme, the term is used to connote what once was called ratiocination, the process of deductive inferencing. At the other, it encompasses many aspects of thinking, in addition to deduction, that are involved in drawing conclusions, making choices, solving problems, and trying to figure out what to believe. Researchers and educators who have written about the teaching of reasoning have, I believe, had relatively inclusive connotations of reasoning in mind when doing so, and it is reasoning in a broad sense that is of interest here.

SOME DISTINCTIONS

Among many distinctions that have been made regarding reasoning by philosophers and psychologists, perhaps none is more basic than the distinction between deduction and induction. Deduction involves making explicit in conclusions what is contained by implication in the premises of an argument; induction, in contrast, involves going beyond what is implicitly contained in the evidence from which conclusions are drawn. Polya (1954a, 1954b), whose distinction between demonstrative and plausible reasoning is essentially the same as the distinction between deduction and induction, characterizes the distinction as the difference between reasoning that is "safe, beyond controversy, and final" and that that is "hazardous, controversial, and provisional."

Deduction is readily formalized; induction is not. Widely accepted standards are available for evaluating the quality of deductive reasoning; how to evaluate inductive reasoning is a matter of considerable debate. Whitehead's (1956) reference to the theory of induction as "the despair of philosophy" (p. 405) reflects the frustration that scholars have experienced in trying to codify inductive reasoning; but recognition of the importance of this type of reasoning is seen in Polya's (1954a) observation that "in dealing with problems of any kind, we need inductive reasoning of some kind" (p. 76).

The ability to reason deductively is challenged by various types of "brain teasers" that one sometimes finds in introductory logic books and in Sunday newspaper supplements. "A certain village is populated by two types of people, truth tellers who always tell the truth and liars who never do so. . . . " A characteristic of many of these puzzles is that all the information that is needed to solve them is provided; the solution is implicit in the problem statement and all one needs to do to find it is to make a series of deductions. But the series of deductions that is required can vary greatly in complexity. The following puzzle was given to me by my granddaughter, who had it as a seventh-grade homework assignment. (She solved it without my help; I elected to work on it in the privacy of my study.)

There are five houses, each of a different color and inhabited by men of different nationalities with different pets, drinks, and cars. The Englishman lives in the red house. The Spaniard owns the dog. Coffee is drunk in the green house. The Ukranian drinks tea. The green house is immediately to the right (your right) of the ivory house. The Ford driver owns snails. A Toyota driver lives in the yellow house. Milk is drunk in the middle house. The Norwegian lives in the first house on the left (your left). The man who drives a Chevy lives in the house next to the man with the fox. A Toyota is parked by the house next to the house where the horse is kept. The Dodge owner drinks orange juice. The Japanese man owns a Porsche. The Norwegian lives next to the blue house. Who owns the zebra, and who drinks the water?

Problems that, like this one, are solvable strictly by deduction are interesting and, at least for some people, fun. Can people's ability to solve them be improved by training? If so, does enhancement of performance on such problems improve people's ability to deal with problems requiring deduction in practical contexts?

One might argue that problems of this sort are really toy problems and bear little resemblance to the kinds of challenges to reasoning that one is likely to encounter in life outside the classroom. On the other hand, explicating and integrating the implications of a variety of pieces of information are important aspects of many real-world reasoning tasks, such as the trouble shooting of equipment malfunctions, the debugging of computer programs, the diagnosis of medical illnesses, and the evaluation of circumstantial evidence in criminal investigations. Whether training in the solution of toy problems is likely to help people be more proficient at solving real-life deduction problems is another matter, but there can be no doubt that people do encounter problems outside the classroom that require deduction.

However, most of the challenges to reasoning that life presents are not solvable simply by a series of deductions from the information given. Most real-life problems do not come with all the information that is essential to their solution; typically one must do some searching for information to fill in what is missing, or to resolve ambiguities, just to make a decent start. Even when one has obtained all the information that can reasonably be obtained, it is likely to be impossible to organize the situation so that the solution will be the final conclusion of a neat deductive chain. There is likely to be a need to make some assumptions, to engage in probabilistic thinking, and to settle for conclusions that are less than certain. This is what it means to reason inductively.

There are other distinctions besides that between deduction and induction that are important to an understanding of reasoning. The distinction between inferencing that is done automatically, effortlessly and, for the most part, unconsciously and that that is done deliberately, effortfully and with awareness is a case in point (Nickerson, 1986). The first type of inferencing is important in language comprehension; upon reading that Sarah is the valedictorian of her class, for example, one is very likely to infer that Sarah is probably very smart and industrious. The second type is illustrated by what one does when one tries to solve a problem – trouble shoot a malfunctioning appliance – by making sense of a variety of clues regarding what might be wrong.

I want to make a distinction that is related to that between deductive and inductive reasoning, but is not the same. This is the distinction between reasoning as a process of coming to conclusions and reasoning as justification of conclusions. Both involve deduction and induction. The first tends to be informal and to include conjectures, false starts and often much "churning." The second tends to be more formal and terse, and expressed as carefully developed argumentation. The first is what one does when trying to decide what to believe on some subject. The second is what one does when one explains, as clearly and concisely as one can, why one has come to a particular conclusion on the matter: "I have concluded X and here is my reasoning."

The distinction is similar to the distinction between informal and formal reasoning, but I hesitate to use these terms here because they have a variety of connotations in the literature. For present purposes, I prefer the terms *exploratory* reasoning and *justificatory* reasoning to connote the distinction I have in mind. Exploratory reasoning is reasoning that goes into the development and refinement of an argument; justificatory reasoning is the argument in its final form.

This distinction is illustrated by the difference, in mathematics, between the process of proof development and the resulting proofs. A proof of a theorem is generally presented in a textbook as a carefully structured argument, beginning with certain givens or assumptions and proceeding through a series of deductions to the desired conclusion. Typically the argument presented is as lean as possible; nothing unessential is included.

The statement of the proof reveals all the reasoning that is necessary to establish the conclusion, but it does not reveal the reasoning process that went into the proof's construction.

Mathematicians, as a group, have not been much inclined to reveal the exploratory reasoning they have done in the process of developing proofs, but have generally preferred to publish only the finished products. This preference is illustrated in the attitude of the great mathematician, Carl Friedrich Gauss, about publishing, which is described by Bell (1937/1956) this way: "Contemplating as a youth the close, unbreakable chains of synthetic proofs in which Archimedes and Newton had tamed their inspirations, Gauss resolved to follow their great example and leave after him only finished works of art, severely perfect, to which nothing could be added and from which nothing could be taken away without disfiguring the whole. The work itself must stand forth, complete, simple, and convincing, with no trace remaining of the labor by which it had been achieved" (p. 305). Gauss defended this attitude with the observation that "when one has constructed a fine building, a scaffolding should no longer be visible" (quoted in Stewart, 1987, p. 142). The reluctance of mathematicians to document the reasoning that typically goes into proof making is unfortunate from a psychological point of view; investigators of reasoning owe a debt of gratitude to the few mathematicians, like Polya (1954a, 1954b) and Lakatos (1976), who have taken close looks at the process and written about it.

The distinction between reasoning to arrive at a conclusion and reasoning to justify a conclusion is well illustrated in mathematics, but it applies more generally. We may distinguish between an argument that is presented to a judge or jury in support of a desired outcome of a legal proceeding and the reasoning that went into the argument's development. The logic of the design of a scientific experiment typically is the result of reasoning that may have included the consideration and rejection of other possible designs; presentation of the rationale for the final design usually does not include a recounting of the process that led to it. In explaining a diagnosis, a physician may lay out a logical rationale for believing a patient is suffering from a particular illness, without necessarily providing the details of the surmising, weighing of evidence, and vacillating that occurred on the way to the final opinion. Just as it is easier to judge the validity of mathematical proofs than to judge the quality of the reasoning that went into their construction, because there are widely accepted criteria for doing the former but not for doing the latter, so it is easier to judge the quality of reasoning as the explication of reasons for believing a conclusion to be true than to judge the quality of the reasoning that went into the arrival at the conclusion initially.

For purposes of this chapter, reasoning is taken to include both deduction and induction and both exploratory and justificatory reasoning, as

distinguished above. It involves the making of inferences or the drawing
of conclusions, as well as such closely related cognitive activities as
searching for and weighing evidence, analyzing implications, constructing and evaluating arguments and counterarguments, identifying missing
assumptions, judging plausibility, establishing and evaluating beliefs, and
diagnosing situations. It is implicated in problem solving, decision making, goal evaluation, and other cognitively demanding activities that are
critically important to intelligent behavior.

WHAT IS GOOD REASONING AND WHAT FACILITATES IT?

Experts do not agree on what should be considered normative standards of
reasoning in specific instances. The reader who doubts this is encouraged
to read Cohen (1981) and commentaries and Stanovich and West (2000) and
commentaries. What I mean by good reasoning in this chapter is reasoning
that leads to the drawing of justified conclusions and their explication; poor
reasoning, in contrast, is reasoning that leads to the drawing of conclusions
that are not justified. This conceptualization begs the question of what it
means for a conclusion to be justified – justified in the eyes of whom?
Equating justification with being well supported by evidence does not help
a lot, because evidence also is a matter of interpretation to some degree.
But discussion of such difficulties is beyond the scope of this chapter. I shall
assume a sufficient consensus regarding the difference between justified
and unjustified conclusions for present purposes.

A question of some importance to the teaching of reasoning is that of
the degree to which the characteristics of good reasoning are the same independently of the domain with respect to which the reasoning is done, or
of the person who does it. Is good reasoning the same for mathematicians,
biologists, homemakers, historians, physicists, carpenters, lawyers, auto
mechanics, and physicians? Does good reasoning in science differ from
good reasoning in the humanities, or history, or law, or theology? Does the
diagnosis of an illness require a qualitatively different type of reasoning
than the diagnosis of an automotive problem?

I want to argue that there are many qualities, abilities, and propensities
that are supportive of good reasoning independently of who does it or the
subject on which it is focused. They do not guarantee that one will reason
well, but they increase the likelihood. With no claim to exhaustiveness, I
offer the list in Table 15.1 as some of the abilities, qualities and propensities
that good reasoners are likely to possess.

Just as there are many aspects of good reasoning, there are many ways
in which reasoning can be impaired. Lack of any of the qualities, abilities,
or propensities mentioned in Table 15.1 would be expected to diminish the
quality of reasoning to some degree. Lack of several of them could ensure
that reasoning would be poor indeed.

TABLE 15.1. *Abilities, Qualities and Propensities that Good Reasoners are Likely to Possess*

- Intelligence
- Domain-specific knowledge
- General knowledge about human cognition
- Knowledge of common limitations, foibles, pitfalls
- Self knowledge
- Knowledge of tools of thought
- Ability to analyze and evaluate arguments
- Good judgment
- Ability to estimate
- Sensitivity to missing information
- Ability to deal effectively with uncertainty
- Ability to take alternative perspectives
- Ability to reason counterfactually
- Ability to manage own reasoning
- Reflectiveness
- Curiosity, inquisitiveness
- Strong desire to hold true beliefs
- Willingness to work at reasoning

The results of a considerable body of research suggest that there are certain ways in which reasoning commonly goes astray. Given the lack of general agreement among experts regarding what should be considered normative standards of reasoning in all cases, any list of common reasoning faults is likely to be controversial. Nevertheless, I would expect a considerable degree of consensus on the claim that good reasoning can be impeded by such factors as confusion between reasoning and rationalization, confusion between reasoning and case-building, the operation of confirmation and my-side biases, resort to overly simple causal explanations, the making of unwarranted generalizations, rushing to conclusions, wishful thinking, and emotional influences.

REASONABLE OBJECTIVES FOR INSTRUCTION IN LIGHT OF CURRENT IDEAS

What should the specific objectives of efforts to teach reasoning be? The obvious answer is to help students develop the abilities, qualities and propensities that we associate with good reasoning and avoid or compensate for impediments to the same. Some of these things are undoubtedly easier to develop than others, and there are likely to be differences among students with respect to their potential to acquire them. How much emphasis is merited by each of the abilities, qualities, and propensities mentioned probably depends on the existing characteristics of the students and teachers involved and on a number of situational variables, but all of them deserve consideration, and improvement with respect to any of them should translate into better reasoning.

Numerous attempts have been made to develop practical approaches to the teaching of reasoning and other aspects of thinking. Reviews of different subsets of these efforts are readily available, including those of Beyth-Marom, Fischhoff, Quadrel, and Furby (1991); Bransford, Sherwood, Vye and Rieser (1986); Chance (1986); Halpern (1989); Nickerson (1988/1989, 1994); Nickerson, Perkins and Smith (1985); Perkins (1995); Presseisen (1986); and Resnick (1987). I will not again review individual programs here, but will note what appear to me to be reasonable foci for the teaching of reasoning in light of the list in Table 15.1 and current knowledge and theory about the nature of reasoning.

Intelligence

There can be little doubt that intelligence, as measured by conventional IQ tests, is a reasonably good predictor of success both in academic performance and in the world of work. Other things equal, high intelligence is an asset for good reasoning (Stanovich, 1999). For people interested in the possibility of improving reasoning ability, the question naturally arises as to whether intelligence can be increased by training. This is an old question, and one that is still being debated. The debate is clouded, however, by issues of definition. To the extent that intelligence is equated with Spearman's g, the prevailing opinion appears to be that training is unlikely to increase it very much (Jensen, 1998). Although there are reasons to believe that at least modest gains are possible (Herrnstein, Nickerson, Sanchez & Swets, 1986; Neisser, 1997; Whimbey, 1975). If one takes a broad view of what constitutes intelligence, as several theorists do (Gardner, 1985; Perkins, 1995; Sternberg & Wagner, 1986), the possibility of increasing it substantially in one or more respects is generally seen to be feasible (Gardner, Krechevsky, Sternberg, & Okagaki, 1994; Sternberg, 1986; Swartz, 1991).

Perkins (1995), who distinguishes three dimensions of intelligence – neural, experiential, and reflective – argues that both experiential intelligence ("the contribution of a storehouse of personal experience in diverse situations to intelligent behavior" [p. 14]) and reflective intelligence ("the contribution of knowledge, understanding, and attitudes about how to use our minds to intelligent behavior" [p. 14]) are learnable, and only neural intelligence is not. "Without question, two of the three dimensions of intelligence can be advanced by learning – experiential intelligence through in-depth experiences and reflective intelligence through the cultivation of strategies, attitudes, and metacognition" (p. 115). Perkins sees a focus on reflective intelligence – "the control system for experiential and neural intelligence" – as providing the best opportunity for improving people's reasoning.

The distinction between experiential intelligence and reflective intelligence is similar to distinctions that others have made between two types of intelligence (Horn, 1989; Sternberg & Wagner, 1986). Stanovich and West (2000) briefly review 12 dual-process theories of intelligence and note their commonalties in identifying two systems of reasoning, one of which is more associative, holistic, and automatic, and the other more rule-based, analytic, and controlled.

For purposes of this chapter, it suffices to note that many researchers believe that some aspects of intelligence can be improved by training, or at least that the likelihood that people will engage in what passes for intelligent behavior can be increased (Nickerson, 2000). People who hold this view tend to conceive of intelligence as involving much more than Spearman's *g* and would look for indications of improvement elsewhere than in conventional tests of IQ.

A caveat: Although high intelligence is an asset for good reasoning, it is not a guarantee of it. It does not, for example, ensure that those who have it will be immune to the foibles, such as a my-side bias in argument production that afflict less gifted mortals (Perkins, Farady, & Bushey, 1991). More generally, high intelligence does not ensure that those who have it will hold only well-justified beliefs (Sokal & Bricmont, 1998). The debate regarding the teachability of intelligence is likely to continue. However that debate progresses, if intelligence, however defined, is teachable, teaching it is a commendable goal, but not enough by itself to ensure better reasoning broadly conceived.

Knowledge

Researchers have emphasized the role of knowledge of several types in good reasoning. Not all agree regarding the relative importance of the different types, but few, if any, would question the assertion that all of the types mentioned in what follows play some nontrivial role.

Domain Specific Knowledge. Some researchers believe that reasoning ability is relatively domain specific; others believe that good reasoning is the same independently of the domain in which it occurs. One question regarding the possibility of improving reasoning through training that has evoked much discussion is that of whether it is better to try to teach principles and strategies of reasoning in a domain-independent way, with the expectation that what is learned will be applicable across domains, or to teach reasoning within domains – how to reason about mathematics, how to reason about history, law, automotive mechanics, and so on. Regardless of what one considers the answer to this question to be, it is obvious that one cannot reason very deeply about a subject unless one has some knowledge of that subject, and no one, so far as I know, contends otherwise. So, if one wishes to reason well about a particular subject, one needs to learn what one can about that subject.

Researchers have presented evidence of the importance of domain-specific knowledge as a major determinant of performance in specific contexts, such as playing chess (de Groot, 1965), solving problems in physics (Larkin, McDermott, Simon, & Simon, 1980b), and performing effectively in a variety of job situations (Hunter, 1986). This is not to deny that general intelligence also contributes to performance in these contexts – perhaps by way of facilitating the acquisition of the domain-specific knowledge required.

The importance of domain knowledge for reasoning has been stressed by many researchers for some time. The reciprocal relationship – the importance of reasoning, or thinking more generally, to knowledge acquisition – has also received some attention. Recent conceptualizations of learning – at least of good learning – give thinking a central role. The learning even of the basics, reading, writing, mathematics, is seen as problem solving (Resnick & Klopfer, 1989). The problem to be solved in reading is that of constructing meaning from text, in writing the problem to be solved is that of expressing and conveying meaning with text, and in mathematics it is that of making sense of numerical and quantitative relationships. In all cases, the most effective learning is an active, constructive, thoughtful process in which the learner consciously works toward specific goals with a view not to rote memorization of facts and operations but to understanding of principles and relationships. Good learning is seen as strategic learning and the model learner as one who consciously uses strategies to plan, monitor, and control his or her own learning activities (Jones, Palincsar, Ogle & Carr, 1987; Paris, Lipson, & Wixson, 1983).

General Knowledge about Human Cognition. The literature on human knowledge is very large. While it is not reasonable to expect everyone to be fully aware of what this literature contains, the following distinctions and ideas seem fundamental to good reasoning.

• The difference between reasoning and case building. One is reasoning when one impartially considers evidence and attempts to determine what conclusion(s) it justifies. One is case building when one attempts to marshal evidence to support a conclusion while ignoring or discounting evidence that tells against it. Case building is what one does when one engages in a debate with the goal of winning, whether or not one believes the proposition one is committed to defend. This distinction is different from the one made earlier between exploratory and justificatory reasoning. In justificatory reasoning, as conceptualized above, the intention is to make clear why, when all pertinent evidence is considered, a particular conclusion should be believed to be true; no effort is made to ignore evidence that would tell against that conclusion, which is always subject to reevaluation, especially in the light of new information. In case building, the intention is to support a desired conclusion by presenting the strongest evidence one can in its favor, while deliberately failing to acknowledge evidence that might show it to be false. There are many illustrations of the distinction between reasoning and case building in the research literature, but I can think of no more revealing illustrations of case building than the exchanges one sees on television between spokespersons for opposing political persuasions explaining the implications of politically controversial newsworthy events.

• The difference between reasoning and rationalizing. There is a great difference between impartially looking for evidence to determine what one should believe or do and attempting to put an existing belief or something one has done in the best possible light. We appear to be quite good at coming up with reasons for decisions we have made, after having made them, but it is often doubtful that those reasons were instrumental in the actual decision process (Soelberg, 1967). The tendency to rationalize is easy to understand; no one wants to admit that one holds beliefs that are unfounded or makes decisions that do not have a rational basis. But unawareness of the difference between reasoning and rationalizing, and of the propensity we all have to rationalize, can only compound the problem.

• Overly simple causal explanations. It appears that our minds, as Gabor (1972) has argued, cannot tolerate a vacuum; they find an explanation for everything. Moreover, the tendency is to account for events in terms of simple, often single-factor, causes. What caused the American Revolution? Taxation without representation. Why is Mr. X so stingy? Because he grew up during the Great Depression. Such explanations rest on the assumption that events typically have simple, single-factor causes. Reflection makes it clear that this assumption must be wrong and that what are, at best, contributing factors are often mistaken for sufficient causes.

• Emotional factors. Can anyone doubt that emotions affect reasoning? Heated disputes are seldom won by reason. Typically when two people are engaged in one, each is motivated to marshal as much support as possible for the position he or she is defending, and to give as little credence as possible to anything said or unsaid that weighs against it. The more emotional the confrontation, the less motivated the parties are likely to be to treat evidence objectively.

Knowledge of Common Reasoning Limitations, Foibles, and Pitfalls. Research has revealed a variety of limitations of human reasoning and many ways in which it often goes wrong. Some knowledge of common

difficulties, biases, and foibles should be useful in helping one both to recognize them when one encounters them and, perhaps, to avoid displaying
them oneself. People should know about such documented human tendencies as those of giving more credence to claims that one likes than to
those one dislikes (Gilovich, 1991; Lefford, 1946; McGuire, 1960), of seeking evidence to confirm favored hypotheses while ignoring or discounting
evidence that would tell against them (Nickerson, 1998), of finding it easier to believe what one prefers to believe (Lefford, 1946; McGuire, 1960),
of generally being overconfident of the accuracy of one's own judgments
(Keren, 1991; Lichtenstein, Fischhoff, & Phillips, 1982; O'Connor, 1989), of
misjudging the extent to which one could anticipate events before they
occurred (hindsight bias) (Christensen-Szalanski & Fobian Willham, 1991;
Fischhoff, 1975; Hawkins & Hastie, 1990), of overestimating the size of
one's own contribution to a group effort relative to the contributions of
other members of the group (Dawes, Orbell, Simmons, & van de Kragt,
1986; Johnston, 1967; Ross & Sicoly, 1979), of overestimating the degree
to which other people's knowledge, beliefs, and behavior are similar to
one's own (Granberg & King, 1980; Marks & Miller, 1982; Nickerson, 1999,
2001).

Self-Knowledge. In addition to knowing about cognition in general, an
individual should benefit from knowing something of his or her own particular strengths and limitations that relate to reasoning. The realization
that one has a tendency to jump to conclusions without giving adequate
attention to available evidence, or that one characteristically fails to consider arguments that could be brought against positions one holds, or that
one typically accepts claims that one reads without making an attempt
to assess their plausibility, could be a point of departure for an effort to
improve one's reasoning in specific respects.

Tools of Thought. By tools of thought I mean to include both formal systems (logic and mathematics) that have been developed to facilitate deductive reasoning and informal strategies or heuristics (rules-of-thumb) that
have been claimed to benefit problem solving in a wide range of contexts.

• Logic. One can find a variety of views in the literature regarding the
relationship between logic and thought. Some writers have argued that
people naturally reason logically, at least in their more rational moments
(Boole, 1854; Piaget, 1928), or that their logical intuitions are sound (Cohen,
1982; Henle, 1962; Lycan, 1988; Rips, 1983; Stevenson, 1993; Wetherick,
1993). Others have taken the position that logic, at least formal logic, has
little to do with the way people actually reason (Cheng & Holyoak, 1985;
Evans, 1982, 1989; Harman, 1986; Johnson-Laird & Byrne, 1991; Oaksford
& Chater, 1995; Toulmin, 1958).

Whether or not people do naturally think logically, the teaching of logic has been a staple of higher education for a very long time. One of the reasons, though not the only one, for offering courses in logic has been the assumption that in learning the rules of logic one would improve one's ability to reason well. The importance that was attached by some to training in logic is seen in the following quote from John Stuart Mill (1867/1984), who considered such training necessary to avoid the numerous errors of deductive inference that we have a natural tendency to make:

Of Logic I venture to say, even if limited to that of mere ratiocination, the theory of names, propositions, and the syllogism, that there is no part of intellectual education which is of greater value, or whose place can so ill be supplied by anything else. Its uses, it is true, are chiefly negative; its function is, not so much to teach us to go right, as to keep us from going wrong. But in the operations of the intellect it is so much easier to go wrong than right; it is so utterly impossible for even the most vigorous mind to keep itself in the path but by maintaining a vigilant watch against all deviations, and noting all the byways by which it is possible to go astray – that the chief difference between one reasoner and another consists in their less or greater liability to be misled. (p. 238)

It is worth noting that Mill's assessment of the need for training in inductive reasoning is no less imperative:

There is nothing in which an untrained mind shows itself more hopelessly incapable, than in drawing the proper general conclusions from its own experience. And even trained minds, when all their training is on a special subject, and does not extend to the general principles of induction, are only kept right when there are ready opportunities of verifying their inferences by facts. Able scientific men, when they venture upon subjects in which they have no facts to check them, are often found drawing conclusions or making generalizations from their experimental knowledge, such as any sound theory of induction would show to be utterly unwarranted. (p. 240)

Logic can certainly be taught. People can and do learn logic (at least some people can and some of those who can do). Whether knowledge of logic improves everyday reasoning is less clear. The prevailing opinion among many psychologists who study reasoning is that training in formal logic is not enormously helpful in dealing with the kinds of reasoning problems that people typically encounter in daily life. Some have contended that a more promising approach to the improvement of reasoning would be to focus training on certain pragmatic rule systems, that can be built on pre-existing knowledge structures that many people appear to have, such as permission and obligation schemas (Cheng & Holyoak, 1985; Cheng, Holyoak, Nisbett, & Oliver, 1986).

I believe that knowledge of logic can be an aid to reasoning, especially to what I am calling justificatory reasoning. The sine qua non of a compelling argument, whether in the form of a mathematical proof, a legal summation, a theoretical interpretation of a scientific finding, or a justification of a personal belief, is logical consistency. It is through the teaching of logic that such essential concepts as entailment and validity can be made clear (Hatcher, 1985).

• Mathematics As Problem Solving. Although the idea that learning geometry is good because in doing so one acquires skill in rigorous deductive reasoning that will find expression in other contexts does not have much credence among today's psychologists, it is hard to deny that knowledge of mathematics is immensely useful for reasoning about quantitative matters. Increasingly researchers and educators are calling for the teaching of mathematics as problem solving (Kaplan, Yamamoto, & Ginsburg, 1989; Romberg, 1984; Schoenfeld, 1979, 1985); when this is done, what is learned should more readily transfer to nonmathematical problem contexts as well. Evidence that problem-solving approaches learned in one context do sometimes transfer readily to other contexts has been presented by some investigators (Schoenfeld, 1985; Silver, 1987).

For the teaching of mathematics as problem solving to be effective, however, students must learn something about problem solving as a process. Apparently many students learn how to solve problems in mathematics classes without understanding what they are doing at a more than superficial level; if a problem is formulated for them, they are able to solve it in the sense of computing the correct answer, but this does not mean that they understand in any very substantive sense why they perform the steps that they have learned by rote to perform and this level of learning is unlikely to transfer (Rosnick & Clement, 1980).

• Heuristics. Several investigators of problem solving, beginning perhaps with Polya (1957), have argued that there are certain techniques that can be used to good effect on problems independently of their domains (Bransford & Stein, 1984; Hayes, 1989; Whimbey & Lochhead, 1982; Wickelgren, 1974). Among the techniques, sometimes called heuristics, strategies, or rules-of-thumb, that have been proposed are the following.

—Strive to understand the problem. Problems are sometimes expressed very informally or even vaguely. It is important in such instances to gain a clear understanding of exactly what the nature of the problem is. Restating (paraphrasing) it in one's own terms can help.

—Analyze ends and means. An attempt to articulate explicitly the problem's ends, or goals, and to identify various possible means of making progress toward them can also help clarify the problem situation and make a start toward solution.

—Make assumptions explicit. Often problems are stated incompletely or ambiguously. When this is the case, it is important to identify the essential information that is missing and fill it in with the required assumption(s). When assumptions are necessary, it is also important to be explicit about the assumptions one is making, because they may differ from the tacit or stated assumptions of others, including those of whoever originated the problem statement.

—Make a representation of the problem (e.g., a table, a figure), and of partial solutions. Nearly everyone who writes about problem solving agrees that it is a good idea to represent a problem in a suitable way. The reader who tries to solve the deduction problem given at the beginning of this chapter will discover quickly that a systematic method of representing the inferences that are made is a great help in dealing with it. People can learn about the usefulness of specific representations in specific contexts, but there is little guidance in the literature regarding how to produce a representation for types of problems one has not seen before. How to improve people's ability to invent effective representations for novel problems is a challenge for research.

—Break the problem down into manageable subproblems. Complex problems usually can be decomposed into subproblems each of which is less daunting than the parent problem. In solving any of the subproblems one contributes to the solution of the parent problem, and sometimes such partial solutions can provide insights that will permit reorganizing the parent problem in a helpful way.

—Work backward. Some problems have the characteristic that the desired end state is known (e.g., the classic river-crossing puzzles in which the goal is to get all the wolves and sheep safely across the river) and the problem is to devise a method for achieving that state. In such cases, it can sometimes be advantageous to work from the goal backward, as well as from the initial state forward.

—Simplify. Problem solvers often tackle a complex problem by first considering a simplified version of it that preserves certain characteristics of the complex one. The trick is illustrated in the context of economics by the following quotes from Rogers (1991): "Suppose a community consists of two individuals, Mr. A and Ms. B; that the total output of the economy can be divided between them; and that both are affected by whatever public goods or environmental conditions result from the operation of the economy" (p. 128). Again, "consider an economy that produces just two commodities: rice grown under irrigation and water-based recreation" (p. 130). Communities of only two people, or economies with only two commodities, are of little interest to economists; but by considering such simplified fictions, economists can sometimes get insights about relationships among variables that can then be applied in more complex contexts of practical interest. The simplification strategy is equally applicable to contexts other than economics.

—Consider extreme cases. Sometimes it helps one get a grasp of a problem to modify it by greatly reducing the number of entities involved or by greatly multiplying it. The preceding example illustrates the approach of reducing the number of entities. The opposite strategy of multiplying entities is seen in one of the arguments that has been made to resolve a puzzle that is sometimes called "Monty's dilemma," after Monty Hall, the long-time host of "Let's Make a Deal." As stated by Vos Savant (1991) the problem is as follows: "Suppose you're on a game show, and you're given a choice of three doors. Behind one door is a car; behind the others, goats. You pick a door – say, No. 1 – and the host, who knows what's behind the doors, opens another door – say, No. 3 – which has a goat. He then says to you, 'Do you want to pick door No. 2?' Is it to your advantage to switch your choice?" (p. 12). Given certain assumptions, which seem reasonable to make, the answer is that it is to your advantage to switch (Nickerson, 1996). To convince skeptical readers of her column that this is the correct answer, Vos Savant suggested that one imagine being given the chance to select one from among 1,000 doors (behind 999 of which is a goat) and then, after the host has revealed a goat behind 998 of the 999 doors that one did not select, being given the chance to swap one's original choice for the other remaining unopened door.

—Find an analogous or more familiar problem. This approach is illustrated by Euler's solution of the famous puzzle of the bridges of Königsberg. (The puzzle requires determining whether it is possible to plan a walk in such a way as to cross each of seven bridges connecting a specified configuration of four land areas once and only once.) Euler found a way to transform the original bridge-crossing problem into one of finding a letter sequence with specified properties, and in solving the letter-sequence problem, which he presumably found to be easier than the original bridge problem, he solved the latter as well. A detailed discussion of Euler's approach to the Königsberg bridges problem can be found in Newman (1953). The point to made here is that finding an analogous and easier problem is often an effective approach to problem solving.

There are other strategies that can be taught to facilitate reasoning about problems of various types. Not all such strategies will be effective, or even appropriate, for all problems. What will be useful is likely to depend on the specifics of the situation as well as on the knowledge and skill of the user. However, there can be little doubt that such strategies can be taught and that they can be useful aids to reasoning, especially of the exploratory kind.

The Need for Both Tools of Thought and Domain Knowledge. When computer technologists first started trying to give computers the ability to do some of the things that people do – recognize patterns, play chess, understand natural language – they took the approach of trying to give the machines general-purpose problem-solving heuristics and the ability to learn from interacting with their environments (Newell & Simon, 1963). The basic assumption was that, equipped with a few powerful general-purpose techniques and the ability to adapt in response to feedback regarding success or failure in specific situations, a machine would be able to acquire the ability to behave intelligently in a variety contexts.

When only limited success was realized with this approach, researchers began to provide "expert systems" that were intended to be able to deal effectively with specific types of problems – medical diagnosis, computer system configuration, electronic trouble-shooting – with much knowledge about the specific domains of application (Feigenbaum, 1983). The latter approach was successful in leading to the implementation of expert systems that proved to be useful in limited applications, but such systems tend to be narrowly focused and not able to adapt to areas other than those for which they were designed. It seems clear that systems that are to have the capability to function effectively in a broad range of domains will need to have not only domain-specific knowledge in one or a few domains to get started, but also some domain-independent capabilities that will allow them to acquire competence in areas other than those for which they were initially programmed.

This story has a parallel in the recent history of attempts to improve thinking ability through instruction. Some researchers have advocated the teaching of domain-independent thinking skills or processes (Ehrenberg & Ehrenberg, 1982; Feuerstein, Rand, Hoffman, & Miller, 1980; Klausmeier, 1980; Marzano, Brandt, Hughes, Jones, Presseisen, Rankin, & Suhor, 1988) or general-purpose heuristics (Bransford & Stein, 1984; Hayes, 1989; Polya, 1957; Rubenstein, 1975; Schoenfeld, 1979, 1980, 1985). Others have stressed the importance of domain-specific knowledge as a sine qua non of competent performance in specific domains (Ericsson & Charness, 1994; Gagne, 1980; Glaser, 1984; Larkin, McDermott, Simon, & Simon, 1980a; McPeck, 1990).

In their review of programs to teach thinking, Sternberg and Ben-Zeev (2001) partition programs into two groups, which they characterize as those that teach thinking from the general to the specific and those that teach thinking from the specific to the general. They associate programs in the first group with the cognitivist view (which focuses on the individual's cognitive strengths and weaknesses) and those in the second with the situative view (which emphasizes the importance of the context in which thinking occurs). Advocates of general-to-specific approaches tend to favor the teaching of general reasoning and problem-solving skills and strategies in courses separate from conventional courses and assume that what is learned will be applied appropriately in specific domains. Advocates of specific-to-general approaches tend to favor the teaching of thinking in the context of specific domains, so that students learn how to think in the process of acquiring traditional subject matter knowledge. Proponents of both views have an interest in transfer. Advocates of the first view want what is learned in a relatively domain-independent way to transfer to any domain in which one has occasion to work. Advocates of the second view want what is learned in the context of one specific domain to transfer to performance in other, especially closely related, domains.

Much of the discussion of the roles of domain-independent capabilities and domain-specific knowledge as determinants of effective reasoning, problem solving, and decision making has taken the form of polarized debate, promoting the importance of one type of ability at the expense of that of the other. There is also the view, however, that both domain-specific knowledge and domain-independent capabilities are likely to be involved in truly competent performance wherever it is found. The latter view is the more convincing one to this writer.

Specific Abilities

There are many specific abilities that are important to good reasoning. Here I shall mention a few, but the list could easily be extended.

The Ability to Analyze and Evaluate Arguments. Given the important roles that arguments (both formal and informal) play in our lives – in the formation, modification, and defense of beliefs – an inability to analyze and evaluate arguments is a serious impediment to good reasoning. I have already mentioned some knowledge of logic as an important aid to good reasoning. Such knowledge is essential to an ability to distinguish between valid and invalid formal arguments. There is a great deal of evidence in the literature that many people have difficulty in this respect. Of special relevance to the possibility of improving reasoning through instruction is the finding of a considerable degree of consistency in the types of errors that people make in syllogistic reasoning tasks. Certain logical forms are much more problematic than others for many people and tend to evoke consistent error patterns (Dickstein, 1978a, 1978b; Erickson, 1978; Roberge, 1970). Evidence also suggests that the conclusions that people draw are sometimes influenced by information that is irrelevant to those conclusions (Gaeth & Shanteau, 1981, 1984) and that information that is relevant and at hand is sometimes ignored (Beyth-Marom & Fischhoff, 1983). To the extent that people can be taught to deal more competently with commonly problematic forms their reasoning should be improved.

But as already noted, most arguments encountered in daily life are not entirely deductive and even those that are are seldom expressed syllogistically. Typically they are discursive in form and contain assertions that are something other than ostensible statements of fact. This being so, competence with formal logic, while helpful, does not suffice to ensure good reasoning in everyday contexts. One needs also to be able to extract the essence of an argument from unessential verbiage in which it may be embedded, to detect ambiguities, to notice critical information that may be missing or assumptions that must be made, and so on.

Although there is no generally agreed-upon procedure for evaluating inductive or informal arguments, I think it is possible to identify some general principles that apply. A few that I have suggested elsewhere (Nickerson, 1986) can be summarized as follows:

Understand the argument. Identify the key assertion that is made and the assertions that are offered in its support. Consider whether the supporting assertions are true and, if they are, whether they really make the key assertion more believable. Consider what true assertions can be made that tend to make the key assertion less believable. Decide whether the weight of the evidence favors the key assertion or its denial. (p. 368)

Such a procedure does not guarantee that only arguments supporting true conclusions will be accepted, of course, but it does ensure that some notice is given to the possibility of evidence that runs counter to a conclusion; and the results of research indicate that this possibility is often overlooked or, worse, intentionally ignored.

Good Judgment. The ability to judge the plausibility of claims that come to all of us every day from the media, from employers or employees, from teachers, from friends and acquaintances is essential to good reasoning. Some of these claims are essential components of arguments. In order to evaluate such arguments, to know whether to accept their conclusions, one must be able not only to judge the validity of the logic but also the tenability of the claims that serve as the premises. The question of how people judge the plausibility of assertions that comprise informal arguments has not received a lot of attention from researchers. Empirical studies of argument evaluation typically have taken the factuality of the assertions comprising an argument as given, and attention has been focused on the question of the legitimacy of the reasoning process that gets one to the conclusion from those assertions. This is unfortunate, because generally in real-life situations, one wants to know whether to accept an argument's conclusion, and this requires not only evaluating the argument's validity, but also judging the plausibility of the assertions that comprise it.

Ability to Estimate. The ability to estimate (quantities, magnitudes, durations, distances, frequencies, probabilities) is closely associated with – perhaps a component of – the quality of good judgment and extraordinarily useful in many contexts. It can help one check whether the results of calculations are in "the right ball park." The student who has it will know, for example, that the product of 674 (which is close to 700) and 521 (which is close to 500) must be on the order of 350,000 and that a computation that has produced a number greatly different from this must be wrong. The problem of estimating how long it will take to do something is a commonly encountered one in both inconsequential and consequential situations.

Research findings suggest that some of the estimates people make tend to be biased in certain ways. For example, people generally underestimate how long it will take them to perform a specific task (Buehler, Griffin, & Ross, 1994; Hayes-Roth & Hayes-Roth, 1979; Kidd, 1970). They also typically overestimate the probability of conjunctions of independent events and underestimate the probability of disjunctions (Bar-Hillel, 1973; Cohen, Chesnick, & Haran, 1971).

Despite the usefulness of estimation, it has not received a lot of emphasis in traditional mathematics education or in any other educational domain. However, perhaps as a consequence of the increasing interest in the teaching of higher-order cognitive skills in general, and of mathematical problem solving in particular, the subject has received some attention from The National Council of Teachers of Mathematics. One of six major recommendations of the council's 1980 agenda-setting report directly addressed the importance of estimation: "Teachers should incorporate estimation activities into all areas of the program on a regular and sustaining basis, in particular encouraging the use of estimating skills to pose and select alternatives and to assess what a reasonable answer might be" (p. 7). The importance of estimation skills has also been stressed by the Curriculum Framework Task Force of the Mathematical Sciences Education Board (1988).

Sensitivity to Missing Information. People are likely to accept without complaint the set of options provided on multiple-choice questions, even when the best options are not in that set (Schuman & Scott, 1987). They are likely, too, to overestimate the completeness of the set of possibilities they consider when trying to think of all the possible causes of specified events. In using fault trees in diagnosis, for example, they tend to overestimate the probability of any possibility that is listed in a tree, to be relatively insensitive to possibilities that are not shown explicitly, and not to compensate adequately (by increasing the probability of a catch-all branch sufficiently) for items that have been pruned from the tree (Dube-Rioux, & Russo, 1988; Fischhoff, Slovic, & Lichtenstein, 1978).

Being alert to the tendency to overestimate the completeness of information provided, or recalled, that is germane to a problem one is trying to solve or a decision one must make should motivate search for missing information and perhaps result in more effective performance of problem solving and decision-making tasks. Similarly, inasmuch as most arguments are expressed incompletely, recognition of this fact should produce a greater sensitivity to the need for assumptions to make such arguments complete as an important aspect of careful reasoning.

Ability to Deal Effectively with Uncertainty. Uncertainty is among the more common features of the problems with which people have to deal in daily life. The same point holds with respect to the problems faced by organizations, communities, and nations. Seldom is all the information that is relevant to a problem that must be dealt with, or a decision that must be made, available to the problem solver or decision maker. To be an effective reasoner one must be able to take the fact of incomplete information into account. This means that gaps must be plugged with assumptions, estimations, actuarial data, or subjective probabilities. Moreover, good reasoning requires that one be aware of when and how one is resolving uncertainty and plugging information holes. Tacitly making assumptions without being aware of doing so can be problematic.

Given the uncertainty that characterizes many of the challenges to reasoning that we encounter, some familiarity with probability theory – the major tool for dealing with uncertainty in a quantitative way – should be an asset in coping with them. It should be especially helpful in analyzing and evaluating arguments that are composed of premises that are less than certain and that vary in their degree of credibility. I do not mean to suggest that the full-blown theory of probability should be taught to grade school children. It does seem to me useful, however, to introduce the concept of chance and some of its implications at a relatively early age, and I want to argue that a rudimentary knowledge of probability theory is at least as important to everyday reasoning as are the areas of mathematics that are traditionally far more likely to be covered in high school mathematics courses. Evidence suggests that training in probability and statistics improves reasoning in situations where probabilistic or statistical thinking is required (Fong, Krantz, & Nisbett, 1986; Kosonen & Winne, 1995; Lehman, Lempert, & Nisbett, 1988; Nisbett, Fong, Lehman, & Cheng, 1987).

Ability to Take Alternative Perspectives and to Engage in Counterfactual Thinking. The ability to see things from perspectives other than one's own is normally in evidence in children by about the age of four or five years (Gopnik, 1993; Mossler, Marvin, & Greenberg, 1976; Perner, 1991). The ability to look at a situation from a variety of perspectives – especially from the point of view of others who are likely to have values and frames of reference that differ from one's own – and the inclination to exercise it, undoubtedly differ considerably among older children and adults. Good reasoning, especially reasoning about other people, their beliefs, feelings, and actions, requires this ability and the exercise of it. Closely related, and also important, is the ability to think counterfactually, to engage in "what if" thinking, to explore in one's imagination probable or plausible consequences of behavior or possible courses of action.

Ability to Manage Own Reasoning. Several investigators have stressed the importance of being able to manage (plan, monitor, and assess) one's own reasoning performance (Brown, 1978; Flavell, 1981, 1987; Weinert, 1987). Palincsar and Brown (1989), among others, argue that self-management, self-monitoring, and self-evaluation are important to effective learning in general. They also note that self-regulated learners are motivated to use their metacognitive knowledge and to take responsibility for their own learning. Being a good manager of one's own cognitive resources means being able to stay focused on a task, to maintain attention against distractions. It also means being able to gauge accurately one's knowledge, degree of understanding, level of expertise, limitations, and need for help. Experts are considerably more likely to make use of such metacognitive skills in the performance of cognitively demanding tasks than are novices (Schoenfeld, 1985, 1989).

DISPOSITIONS, INCLINATIONS, PROPENSITIES, VALUES

The importance of dispositions to good thinking has been emphasized by several writers (Ennis, 1986; Facione & Facione, 1992; Halpern, 1998; Norris & Ennis, 1989; Perkins, 1995; Perkins, Jay, & Tishman, 1993; Tishman, Jay, & Perkins, 1993). Knowing how to reason well does not guarantee that one will reason well in any particular situation that calls for doing so. Resnick and Klopfer (1989) suggest that good thinkers and problem solvers differ from poorer ones less in the particular skills they possess than in their tendency to use those skills.

The Disposition of Reflectiveness or Thoughtfulness. Reflectiveness is treated by some writers as a disposition, attitude, or even character trait, and as one that is especially important to good reasoning (Ennis, 1985, 1987; Newmann, 1991; Resnick, 1987). As a character trait, reflectiveness means being habitually in a reflective frame of mine – being reflective with respect to material that one is attempting to understand, with respect to relationships, meanings, implications, and one's own understanding or level of comprehension of a situation. It means looking for relationships, connections, and analogies.

Impulsiveness, the antithesis of reflectiveness, has been identified as a significant impediment to good reasoning, and to the development of effective cognitive skills more generally (Ault, 1973; Kagan, 1966; Kurtz & Borkowski, 1987). The idea that impulsiveness is a major problem finds support in the argument, advanced by several researchers, that people often draw conclusions on the basis of consideration of only a small fraction of the relevant evidence. Having considered enough information to provide the basis for a conclusion with which they are comfortable, they stop looking for additional information that could conceivably invalidate the conclusion they have drawn (Kruglanski, & Klar, 1987; Kruglanski & Webster, 1996). Baron (1985, 1994) argues that insufficient search is the cause of many reasoning difficulties.

This problem may stem in part from failure to see the necessity to seek more information once a conclusion has been drawn, however tentative that conclusion ought to be, but it is undoubtedly also partly a problem of motivation, an unwillingness to put more effort into searching for information than we typically do. This view is consistent with the idea that people tend to be willing to spend only a relatively small amount of cognitive effort on problems; that we tend to be, in the unflattering words of some investigators, cognitive misers (Fiske & Taylor, 1991; Taylor, 1981) or intellectually lazy organisms (McGuire, 1960). Perkins and his colleagues (Perkins, Allen, & Hafner, 1983; Perkins, Farady, & Bushey, 1991) have shown that people's failure to consider evidence that might tell against a conclusion they have drawn is not necessarily due to an inability to find such evidence or to bring it to mind; when explicitly asked to think of counterarguments to something they have concluded people often are able to do so. Students need to know of the tendency of people to draw conclusions too hastily, and of the importance of testing the tenability of an initial conclusion by seeking information that might tell against it.

Curiosity, Inquisitiveness. A good reasoner is a seeker of information. Many people believe that most children are inquisitive by nature. There are reasons to suspect, however, that schooling sometimes inhibits children's natural curiosity by discouraging the asking of questions. Children are unlikely to ask questions if they fear that doing so will expose their ignorance or make them appear unintelligent in the eyes of their classmates or teachers (Patterson, 1978). That students do not, as a rule, ask many questions in class has been noted by several investigators (Gall, 1970; Good, Slavings, Hobson-Harel, & Emerson, 1987; Johns, 1968).

This suggests that a reasonable goal for teaching is the provision of an atmosphere in which questioning is not only tolerated, but encouraged, and where curiosity is rewarded. There are few things a teacher can do for a child that are more valuable for his or her life-long education than to cultivate his or her natural curiosity, without which there is little joy in learning. Millar (1992, 2000) argues that questioning needs to be cultivated in the classroom and offers suggestions regarding how this might be done. Dillon (1988) has also made some suggestions regarding how teachers can encourage effective questioning by students.

Strong Desire to Hold True Beliefs. Probably most people would claim that they want to have beliefs that are true. But presumably people vary with respect to the strength of this value. Some will try hard to bring beliefs into correspondence with evidence of which they are aware and will modify beliefs when newly acquired information indicates the need to do so; others will form beliefs on the basis of scanty evidence and will protect them from additional information that could threaten their tenability. Ideally, one not only should want to hold beliefs that are consistent with evidence at hand, but also should maintain a proactive attitude toward seeking evidence and a willingness to change one's mind – to revise conclusions one has drawn – in response to evidence that indicates the need for a change.

Strongly desiring to hold true beliefs means being willing to trace out the implications of beliefs. "If I accept X as true, this means that I must accept whatever X implies as true also. So what does X imply?" This may involve the ability to concretize, to imagine specific instances of general statements, to engage in "for instance" thinking. Strongly desiring to hold true beliefs means also having a propensity to look for counterexamples to hypotheses one is considering or, more generally, to seek information that would show an initial conclusion that has been drawn to be unwarranted. These are things that most of us tend not to do spontaneously (Nickerson, 1998; Oakhill & Johnson-Laird, 1985), hence the need for training with respect to their importance.

Willingness to Work at Reasoning. Searching for evidence, fairly evaluating what is found, judging the plausibility of claims, and other aspects of good reasoning can be hard work. It is much easier to come to conclusions quickly, without worrying much about whether the conclusions drawn would be justified if more evidence were found and considered. Not everyone is willing to expend the mental energy required to reason well. How to instill this willingness where it does not exist is a major challenge to teaching; at the very least, students need to be made aware that good reasoning is not something that one learns how to do easily and quickly and that practicing it requires commitment and effort.

The foregoing comments have emphasized things that might be done in the interest of improving the quality of reasoning of students. We should not overlook the possibility that it might also be beneficial to discontinue doing some of the things that are currently being done. It is at least a plausible conjecture that some impediments to good reasoning may actually result from, or be reinforced by, teaching practices. The tendency to generate overly simple explanations, for example, may be encouraged by the practice of giving students tests that promote the idea that most questions of fact have single, simply expressed, unchallengeable answers. My-side bias may be reinforced by having students give reasons for beliefs they hold or opinions they have formed, without trying to think also of reasons that might tell against them. Students may be encouraged to jump to conclusions by a general equating of indecisiveness with weakness that can be conveyed inside the classroom and outside by direct or subtle means.

TEACHING FOR TRANSFER

Much of the debate about the teaching of thinking centers on the question of the degree to which learning is situation or context specific, or that of the extent to which what is learned in one situation or context will transfer to different situations or contexts. Investigators appear to be in agreement that transfer often does not occur spontaneously, that principles or procedures that are learned in one context often are not used spontaneously in different contexts for which they would be appropriate. This does not settle the debate on the relative merits of teaching principles or procedures in a relatively context-free way as opposed to teaching them only as they apply to specific problem areas, because investigators who advocate the former approach argue that transfer can be effected if the teaching is done in such a way as to promote it (Anderson, Simon, & Reder, 1997; Gick & Holyoak, 1983; Perkins & Salomon, 1989).

One answer to the objection that what is learned in classes intended to teach general-purpose heuristics for problem solving typically does not transfer readily to problems or problem types other than that with which the learning occurred has been the recommendation to teach for transfer intentionally (Adey & Shayer, 1994; Perkins & Salomon, 1989). Perkins and Salomon distinguish "low road" and "high road" transfer, the former of which occurs spontaneously, as when experience in driving a car provides know-how that transfers to the task of driving a truck, and the latter of which occurs as a result of intentional abstracting of principles learned in one context that may be applied to good effect in another. "High road" transfer, Perkins and Salomon argue, typically does not occur spontaneously but can be facilitated by instruction, and attention to it should be a feature of any effort to teach generally useful thinking skills and strategies.

Helping students become more effective reasoners would surely be acknowledged by most educators, past and present, as a primary goal of education. Few would be prepared to argue, I suspect, that the goal has been realized to anything close to a satisfactory degree. Why this is so is a question for continuing research; needs undoubtedly include both a better understanding of how to teach reasoning effectively and institute changes that will facilitate application of what is learned in this regard. As I hope the forgoing discussion has shown, research that has already been done provides a rationale for a variety of specific objectives that can be targeted in an effort to improve reasoning with a reasonable expectation of success.

References

Adey, P. S., & Shayer, M. (1994). *Really raising standards: Cognitive intervention and academic achievement*. New York: Routledge.

Anderson, J. R., Simon, H. A., & Reder, L. M. (1997). Situative versus cognitive perspectives. *Educational Researcher, 26*, 18–21.

Ault, R. L. (1973). Problem-solving strategies of reflective, impulsive, fast-accurate, and slow-inaccurate children. *Developmental Psychology, 1*, 717–725.

Bar-Hillel, M. A. (1973). On the subjective probability of compound events. *Organizational Behavior and Human Performance, 9*, 396–406.

Baron, J. (1985). *Rationality and intelligence*. New York: Cambridge University Press.

Baron, J. (1994). *Thinking and deciding* (2nd ed.). New York: Cambridge University Press.

Bell, E. T. (1956). The prince of mathematicians. In J. R. Newman (Ed.) *The world of Mathematics* (pp. 295–339). New York: Simon and Schuster. Original published in 1937.

Beyth-Marom, R., & Fischhoff, B. (1983). Diagnosticity and pseudodiagnosticity. *Journal of Personality and Social Psychology, 45*, 1185–1195.

Beyth-Marom, R., Fischhoff, B., Quadrel, M. J., & Furby, L. (1991). In J. Baron & R. V. Brown (Eds.), *Teaching decision making to adolescents* (pp. 19–59). Hillsdale, NJ: Erlbaum.

Boole, G. (1854). *An investigation of the laws of thought on which are founded the mathematical theories of logic and probabilities*. London: Walton G. Maberly.

Bransford, J. D., Sherwood, R., Vye, N., & Rieser, J. (1986). Teaching thinking and problem solving. *American Psychologist, 41*, 1078–1089.

Bransford, J. D., & Stein, B. S. (1984). *The ideal problem solver: A guide for improving thinking, learning, and creativity*. New York: Freeman.

Brown, A. L. (1978). Knowing when, where, and how to remember: A problem of metacognition. In R. Glaser (Ed.), *Advances in instructional psychology* (vol. 1, pp. 77–165). Hillsdale, NJ: Erlbaum.

Buehler, R., Griffin, D., & Ross, M. (1994). Exploring the "planning fallacy": Why people underestimate their task completion times. *Journal of Personality and Social Psychology, 67*, 366–381.

Chance, P. (1986). *Thinking in the classroom*. New York: Teachers College Press.

Cheng, P. W., & Holyoak, K. J. (1985). Pragmatic reasoning schemas. *Cognitive Psychology, 17*, 391–416.

Cheng, P. W., Holyoak, K. J., Nisbett, R. E., & Oliver, L. M. (1986). Pragmatic versus syntactic approaches to training deductive reasoning. *Cognitive Psychology, 18*, 293–328.

Christensen-Szalanski, J. J., & Fobian Willham, C. (1991). The hindsight bias: A meta-analysis. *Organizational Behavior and Human Decision Processes, 48*, 147–168.

Cohen, L. J. (1981). Can human irrationality be experimentally demonstrated? *Behavioral and Brain Sciences, 4*, 317–331.

Cohen, L. J. (1982). Are people programmed to commit fallacies? Further thoughts about the interpretation of data on judgment. *Journal of the Theory of Social Behavior, 12*, 251–274.

Cohen, L. J., Chesnick, E. I., & Haran, D. (1971). Evaluation of compound probabilities in sequential choice. *Nature, 232*, 214–216.

Dawes, R. M., Orbell, J. M., Simmons, R. T., & van de Kragt, A. J. C. (1986). Organizing groups for collective action. *American Political Science Review, 80,* 1171–1185.

de Groot, A. D. (1965). *Thought and choice in chess.* The Hague: Mouton.

Dickstein, L. S. (1978a). The effect of figure on syllogistic reasoning. *Memory and Cognition, 6,* 76–83.

Dickstein, L. S. (1978b). Error processes in syllogistic reasoning. *Memory and Cognition, 6,* 537–543.

Dillon, J. T. (1988). The remedial status of student questioning. *The Journal of Curriculum Studies, 20,* 197–210.

Dube-Rioux, L., & Russo, J. E. (1988). An availability bias in professional judgment. *Journal of Behavioral Decision Making, 1,* 223–237.

Ehrenberg, S. D., & Ehrenberg, L. M. (1982). *BASICS: Building and applying strategies for intellectual competencies in students.* Coshocton, OH: Institute for Curriculum and Instruction. New York: David McKay Company.

Ennis, R. H. (1985). Critical thinking and the curriculum. *National Forum, 65,* 28–31.

Ennis, R. H. (1986). A taxonomy of critical thinking dispositions and abilities. In J. B. Baron & R. S. Sternberg (Eds.), *Teaching thinking skills: Theory and practice* (pp. 9–26). New York: Freeman.

Ennis, R. H. (1987). A taxonomy of critical thinking dispositions and abilities. In J. B. Baron & R. J. Sternberg (Eds.), *Teaching thinking skills: Theory and practice* (pp. 9–26). New York: Freeman.

Ericsson, K. A., & Charness, N. (1994). Expert performance: Its structure and acquisition. *American Psychologist, 49,* 725–747.

Erickson, J. R. (1978). Research on syllogistic reasoning. In R. Revlin and R. E. Mayer (Eds.), *Human Reasoning.* New York: Holt, Rinehart and Winston.

Evans, J. St. B. T. (1982). *The psychology of deductive reasoning.* London: Routledge & Kegan Paul Ltd.

Evans, J. St. B. T. (1989). *Bias in human reasoning: Causes and consequences.* Hillsdale, NJ: Erlbaum.

Facione, P. A., & Facione, N. C. (1992). *The California critical thinking dispositions inventory.* Millgrae, CA: The California Academic Press.

Feigenbaum, E. A. (1983). Knowledge engineering: The applied side. In J. E. Hayes & D. Michie (Eds.), *Intelligent systems: The unprecedented opportunity.* New York: Halstead Press.

Feuerstein, R., Rand, Y., Hoffman, M. B., & Miller, R. (1980). *Instrumental enrichment: An intervention programme for cognitive modifiability.* Baltimore, MD: University Park Press.

Fischhoff, B. (1975). Hindsight is not equal to foresight: The effect of outcome knowledge on judgment under uncertainty. *Journal of Experimental Psychology: Human Perception and Performance, 1,* 288–299.

Fischhoff, B., Slovic, P., & Lichtenstein, S. (1978) Fault trees: Sensitivity of estimated failure probabilities to problem representations. *Journal of Experimental Psychology: Human Perception and Performance, 4,* 330–344.

Fiske, S. T., & Taylor, S. E. (1991). *Social cognition* (2nd ed.). New York: McGraw-Hill.

Flavell, J. H. (1981). Cognitive monitoring. In W. P. Dickson (Ed.), *Children's oral communication skills* (pp. 35–60). New York: Academic Press.

Flavell, J. H. (1987). Speculations about the nature and development of metacognition. In F. Weinert & R. Kluwe (Eds.), *Metacognition, motivation, and understanding* (pp. 21–30). Hillsdale, NJ: Erlbaum.

Fong, G. T., Krantz, D. H., & Nisbett, R. E. (1986). The effects of statistical training on thinking about everyday problems. *Cognitive Psychology, 18,* 235–292.

Gabor, D. (1972). *The mature society.* New York: Praeger.

Gaeth, G. J., & Shanteau, J. (1981). *A bibliography of research on the effects of irrelevance in psychology* (Applied Psychology Rep. No. 81-13). Manhattan: Kansas State University, Department of Psychology.

Gaeth, G. J., & Shanteau, J. (1984). Reducing the influence of irrelevant information on experienced decision makers. *Organizational Behavior and Human Performance, 33,* 263–282.

Gagne, R. (1980). Learnable aspects of problem solving. *Educational Psychologist, 15,* 84–92.

Gall, M. D. (1970). The use of questioning in teaching. *Review of Educational Research, 40,* 707–721.

Gardner, H. (1985). *Frames of mind: The theory of multiple intelligences.* New York: Basic Books.

Gardner, H., Krechevsky, M., Sternberg, R. J., & Okagaki, L. (1994). Intelligence in context: Enhancing students' practical intelligence for school. In K. McGilly (Ed.), *Classroom lessons: Integrating cognitive theory and classroom practice* (pp. 105–127). Cambridge, MA: MIT.

Gick, M. L., & Holyoak, K. J. (1983). Schema induction and analogical transfer. *Cognitive Psychology, 15,* 1–38.

Gilovich, T. (1991). *How we know what isn't so: The fallibility of human reason in everyday life.* New York: The Free Press.

Glaser, R. (1984). Education and thinking: The role of knowledge. *American Psychologist, 39,* 93–104.

Gopnik, A. (1993). How we know our minds: The illusion of first-person knowledge of intentionality. *Behavioral and Brain Sciences, 16,* 1–14.

Good, T., Slavings, R., Hobson-Harel, K., & Emerson, H. (1987). Student passivity: A study of question asking in K-12 classrooms. *Sociology of Education, 60,* 181–199.

Granberg, D., & King, M. (1980). Cross-lagged panel analysis of the relation between attraction and perceived similarity. *Journal of Experimental Social Psychology, 16,* 573–581.

Halpern, D. F. (1998). Teaching critical thinking for transfer across domains: Dispositions, skills, structure training, and metacognitive monitoring. *American Psychologist, 53,* 449–455.

Halpern, D. F. (1989). *Thought and knowledge: An introduction to critical thinking* (2nd ed.). Hillsdale, NJ: Erlbaum.

Harman, G. (1986). *Change in view: Principles of reasoning.* Cambridge, MA: MIT Press.

Hatcher, D. (1985). A critique of critical thinking. *Teaching Thinking and Problem Solving, 7*(10), 1,2,5.

Hawkins, S. A., & Hastie, R. (1990). Hindsight: Biased judgments of past events after the outcomes are known. *Psychological Bulletin, 107,* 311–327.

Hayes, J. R. (1989). *The complete problem solver.* (2nd ed.). Hillsdale, NJ: Erlbaum.

Hayes-Roth, B., & Hayes-Roth, F. (1979). A cognitive model of planning. *Cognitive Science, 3,* 275–310.

Henle, M. (1962). On the relation between logic and thinking. *Psychological Review, 69,* 366–378.

Herrnstein, R. J., Nickerson, R. S., Sanchez, M, & Swets, J. A. (1986). Teaching thinking skills. *American Psychologist, 41,* 1279–1289.

Horn, J. (1989). Models of intelligence. In R. Linn (Ed.), *Intelligence: Measurement, theory, and public policy* (pp. 29–73). Chicago: University of Illinois Press.

Hunter, J. E. (1986). Cognitive ability, cognitive aptitudes, job knowledge, and job performance. *Journal of Vocational Behavior, 29,* 340–362.

Jensen, A. R. (1998). The *g* factor and the design of education. In R. J. Sternberg & W. M. Williams (Eds.), *Intelligence, instruction, and assessment* (pp. 111–131). Mahwah, NJ: Erlbaum.

Johns, J. P. (1968). The relationship between teacher behaviors and the incidence of thought-provoking questions by students in secondary schools. *Journal of Educational Research, 62,* 117–122.

Johnson-Laird, P. N., & Byrne, R. M. J. (1991). *Deduction.* Hillside, NJ: Erlbaum.

Johnston, W. A. (1967). An individual performance and self-evaluation in a simulated team. *Organizational Behavior and Human Performance, 2,* 309–328.

Jones, B. F., Palincsar, A. S., Ogle, D. S., & Carr, E. G. (1987). Learning and thinking. In B. F. Jones, A. S. Palincsar, D. S. Ogle, & E. G. Carr (Eds.), *Strategic teaching and learning: Cognitive instruction in the content areas* (pp. 3–32). Alexandria, VA: Association for Supervision and Curriculum Development.

Kagan, J. (1966). Reflection-impulsivity: The generality and dynamics of conceptual tempo. *Journal of Abnormal Psychology, 71,* 17–24.

Kaplan, R. G., Yamamoto, T., & Ginsburg, H. P. (1989). Teaching mathematics concepts. In L. B. Resnick & L. E. Klopfer (Eds.), *Toward the thinking curriculum: Current cognitive research. 1989 ASCD Yearbook* (pp. 59–82). Alexandria, VA: Association for Supervision and Curriculum Development.

Keren, G. B. (1991). Calibration and probability judgments: Conceptual and methodological issues. *Acta Psychologica, 77,* 217–273.

Kidd, J. B. (1970). The utilization of subjective probabilities in production planning. *Acta Psychologica, 34,* 338–347.

Klausmeier, H. J., with the assistance of Sipple, T. S. (1980). *Learning and teaching concepts – a strategy for testing applications of theory.* New York: Academic Press.

Kosonen, P., & Winne, P. H. (1995). Effects of teaching statistical laws on reasoning about everyday problems. *Journal of Educational Psychology, 87,* 33–46.

Kruglanski, A. W., & Klar, Y. (1987). A view from the bridge: Synthesizing the consistency and attribution paradigms for a lay epistemic perspective. *European Journal of Social Psychology, 17,* 211–241.

Kruglanski, A. W., & Webster, D. (1996). Motivated closing of the mind: "Seizing" and "freezing." *Psychological Review, 103,* 263–283.

Kurtz, B. E., & Borkowski, J. G. (1987). Development of strategic skill in impulsive and reflective children: A longitudinal study of metacognition. *Journal of Experimental Child Psychology, 43,* 129–148.

Lakatos, L. (1976). *Proofs and refutations: The logic of mathematical discovery.* J. Worrall & E. Zahar (Eds.). NY: Cambridge University Press.

Larkin, J. H., McDermott, J., Simon, D. P., & Simon, H. A. (1980a). Expert and novice performance in solving physics problems. *Science, 208,* 1335–1342.

Larkin, J. H., McDermott, J., Simon, D. P., & Simon, H. A. (1980b). Modes of competence in solving physics problems. *Cognitive Science, 4,* 317–345.

Lefford, A. (1946). The influence of emotional subject matter on logical reasoning. *Journal of General Psychology, 34,* 127–151.

Lehman, D. R., Lempert, R. O., & Nisbett, R. E. (1988). The effects of graduate training on reasoning: Formal discipline and thinking about everyday events. *American Psychologist, 43,* 431–443.

Lichtenstein, S., Fischhoff, B., & Phillips, L. D. (1982). Calibration of probabilities: The state of the art to 1980. In D. Kahneman, P. Slovic, & A. Tversky (Eds.), *Judgment under uncertainty: Heuristics and biases* (pp. 306–334). Cambridge, UK: Cambridge University Press.

Lycan, W. C. (1988). *Judgment and justification.* New York: Cambridge University Press.

Marks, G., & Miller, N. (1982). Target attractiveness as a mediator of assumed attitude similarity. *Personality and Social Psychology Bulletin, 8,* 728–735.

Marzano, R. J., Brandt, R. S., Hughes, C. S., Jones, B. F., Presseisen, B. Z., Rankin, S. C., & Suhor, C. (1988). *Dimensions of thinking: A framework for curriculum and instruction.* Alexandria, VA: Association for Supervision and Curriculum Development.

Mathematical Sciences Education Board (1988). *A framework for the revision of K-12 mathematical curricula.* Final report to the Mathematical Sciences Education Board from its Curriculum Frameworks Task Force.

McGuire, W. J. (1960). A syllogistic analysis of cognitive relationships. In M. J. Rosenberg, C. I. Hovland, W. J. McGuire, R. P. Abelson, & J. W. Brehm (Eds.), *Attitude organization and change* (pp. 65–110). New Haven, CT: Yale University Press.

McPeck, J. E. (1990). Critical thinking and subject specificity: A reply to Ennis. *Educational Researcher, 19*(4), 10–12.

Mill, J. S. (1984). Inaugural address delivered to the University of Saint Andrews. In J. M. Robson (Ed.) *Essays on equality, law, and education* (pp. 217–257): Vol 21. J. M. Robson (Gen. Ed.) *Collected works of John Stuart Mill.* London: Routledge & Kegan Paul. Originally published in 1867.

Millar, G. (1992). *Developing student questioning skills – A handbook of tips and strategies for teachers.* Bensenville, IL: Scholastic Testing Service.

Millar, G. (2000). Questioning. In E. P. Torrance (Ed.). *On the edge and keeping on the edge* (pp. 101–122). Westport, CN: Ablex.

Mossler, D. G., Marvin, R. S., & Greenberg, M. T. (1976). Conceptual perspective taking in 2- to 6-year old children. *Developmental Psychology, 12,* 85–86.

National Council of Teachers of Mathematics (1980). *Agenda for action: Recommendations for school mathematics of the 1980s.* Reston, VA: Author.

Neisser, U. (1997). Rising scores on intelligence tests. *American Scientist, 85,* 440–447.

Newell, A., & Simon, H. A., (1963). GPS, a program that simulates human thought. In E. A. Feigenbaum & J. Feldman (Eds.), *Computers and thought.* New York: McGraw-Hill.

Newman, J. R. (1953). Leonhard Euler and the Koenigsberg bridges. *Scientific American*, 189(1), 66–70.

Newmann, F. M. (1991). Higher order thinking in the teaching of social studies: Connections between theory and practice. In J. F. Voss, D. N. Perkins, & J. W. Segal (Eds.), *Informal reasoning and education* (pp. 381–400). Hillsdale, NJ: Erlbaum.

Nickerson, R. S. (1986). Reasoning. In R. F. Dillon & R. J. Sternberg (Eds.), *Cognition and instruction* (pp. 343–373).

Nickerson, R. S., (1988/1989). On improving thinking through instruction. In E. Z. Rothkopf (Ed.), *Review of research in education* (vol. 15, pp. 3–58). Washington, DC: American Educational Research Association.

Nickerson, R. S. (1994). The teaching of thinking and problem solving. In R. J. Sternberg (Ed.), *Thinking and problem solving: Vol. 12*. E. C. Carterette & M. Friedman (Eds.), *Handbook of perception and cognition* (pp. 409–449). San Diego, CA: Academic Press.

Nickerson, R. S. (1996). Ambiguities and unstated assumptions in probabilistic reasoning. *Psychological Bulletin, 120*, 410–433.

Nickerson, R. S. (1998). Confirmation bias: A ubiquitous phenomenon in many guises. *Review of General Psychology, 2*, 175–220.

Nickerson, R. S. (1999). How we know – and sometimes misjudge – what others know: Imputing one's own knowledge to others. *Psychological Bulletin, 125*, 737–759.

Nickerson, R. S. (2000). Teaching intelligence. In A. E. Kazdin (Ed.), *Encyclopedia of psychology* (vol. 2, pp. 498–501). New York: Oxford University Press.

Nickerson, R. S. (2001). The projective way of knowing: A useful heuristic that sometimes misleads. *Current Directions in Psychological Research, 10*, 168–172.

Nickerson, R. S., Perkins, D. N., & Smith, E. E. (1985). *The teaching of thinking*. Hillsdale, NJ: Erlbaum.

Nisbett, R. E., Fong, G. T., Lehman, D. R., & Cheng, P. W. (1987). Teaching reasoning. *Science, 238*, 625–631.

Norris, S. P., & Ennis, R. H. (1989). *Evaluating critical thinking*. Pacific Grove, CA: Midwest Publications.

Oakhill, J. V., & Johnson-Laird, P. N. (1985). Rationality, memory and the search for counterexamples. *Cognition, 20*, 79–94.

Oaksford, M., & Chater, N. (1995). Theories of reasoning and the computational explanation of everyday inference. *Thinking and Cognition, 1*, 121– 152.

O'Connor, M. (1989). Models of human behavior and confidence in judgment: A review. *International Journal of Forecasting, 5*, 159–169.

Palincsar, A. S., & Brown, A. L. (1989). Instruction for self-regulated reading. In L. B. Resnick & L. E. Klopfer (Eds.), *Toward the thinking curriculum: Current cognitive research. 1989 ASCD Yearbook* (pp. 19–39). Alexandria, VA: Association for Supervision and Curriculum Development.

Paris, S. G., Lipson, M. Y., & Wixson, K. K. (1983). Becoming a strategic reader. *Contemporary Educational Psychology, 8*, 293–316.

Patterson, C. (1978, April/May). Teaching children to listen. *Today's Education*, 52–53.

Perkins, D. N. (1995). *Outsmarting IQ: The emerging science of learnable intelligence.* New York: The Free Press.

Perkins, D. N., Allan, R., & Hafner, J. (1983). Difficulties in everyday reasoning. In W. Maxwell (Ed.), *Thinking: The frontier expands.* Hillsdale, NJ: Erlbaum.

Perkins, D. N., Farady, M., & Bushey, B. (1991). Everyday reasoning and the roots of intelligence. In J. Voss, D. N. Perkins, & J. Segal, (Eds.), *Informal reasoning* (pp. 83–105). Hillsdale, NJ: Erlbaum.

Perkins, D. N., Jay, E., & Tishman, S. (1993). Beyond abilities: A dispositional theory of thinking. *The Merrill-Palmer Quarterly, 39,* 1–21.

Perkins, D. N., & Salomon, G. (1989). Are cognitive skills context-bound? *Educational Researcher, 18,* 16–25.

Perner, J. (1991). *Understanding the representational mind.* Cambridge, MA: MIT Press.

Piaget, J. (1928). *Judgment and reasoning in the child.* London: Routledge and Kegan Paul.

Polya, G. (1954a). *Mathematics and plausible reasoning: Vol. 1. Induction and analogy in mathematics.* Princeton, NJ: Princeton University Press.

Polya, G. (1954b). *Mathematics and plausible reasoning, Vol. 2. Patterns of plausible inference.* Princeton, NJ: Princeton University Press.

Polya, G. (1957). *How to solve it: A new aspect of mathematical method.* Garden City, NY: Doubleday. (Originally published in 1945.)

Presseisen, B. Z. (1986). *Critical thinking and thinking skills: State of the art definitions and practice in public schools.* Philadelphia, PA: Research for Better Schools.

Resnick, L. B. (1987). *Education and learning to think.* Washington, DC: National Academy Press.

Resnick, L. B., & Klopfer, L. E. (1989). Toward the thinking curriculum: An overview. In L. B. Resnick & L. E. Klopfer (Eds.), *Toward the thinking curriculum: Current cognitive research. 1989 ASCD Yearbook* (pp. 1–18). Alexandria, VA: Association for Supervision and Curriculum Development.

Rips, L. J. (1983). Cognitive processes in propositional reasoning. *Psychological Review, 90,* 38–71.

Roberge, J. J. (1970). A study of children's abilities to reason with basic principles of deductive reasoning. *American Educational Research Journal, 7,* 583–596.

Rogers, P. (1991). The economic model. In R. A. Chechile & S. Carlisle (Eds.), *Environmental decision making: A multidisciplinary perspective* (pp. 120–155). New York: Van Nostrand Reinhold.

Romberg, T. A. (1984). *School mathematics: Options for the 1990s: Chairman's report of a conference.* Washington, DC: U.S. Government Printing Office.

Rosnick, P., & Clement, J. (1980). Learning without understanding: The effect of tutoring strategies on algebra misconceptions. *Journal of Mathematical Behavior, 3,* 3–27.

Ross, M., & Sicoly, F. (1979). Egocentric biases in availability and attribution. *Journal of Personality and Social Psychology, 37,* 322–336.

Rubenstein, M. F. (1975). *Patterns of problem solving.* Englewood Cliffs, NJ: Prentice-Hall.

Schoenfeld, A. H. (1979). Explicit heuristic training as a variable in problem solving performance. *Journal for Research in Mathematics Education, 10,* 173–187.

Schoenfeld, A. H. (1980). Teaching problem-solving skills. *American Mathematical Monthly, 87*, 794–805.

Schoenfeld, A. H. (1985). *Mathematical problem solving.* New York: Academic Press.

Schoenfeld, A. H. (1989). Teaching mathematical thinking and problem solving. In L. B. Resnick & L. E. Klopfer (Eds.), *Toward the thinking curriculum: Current cognitive research. 1989 ASCD Yearbook* (pp. 83–103). Alexandria, VA: Association for Supervision and Curriculum Development.

Schuman, H., & Scott, J. (1987). Problems in the use of survey questions to measure public opinion. *Science, 236*, 957–959.

Silver, E. A. (1987). Foundations of cognitive theory and research for mathematics problem-solving instruction. In A. H. Schoenfeld (Ed.), *Cognitive science and mathematics education* (pp. 33–60). Hillsdale, NJ: Erlbaum.

Soelberg, P. O. (1967). Unprogrammed decision making. *Industrial Management Review, 8*, 19–29.

Sokal, A., & Bricmont, J. (1998). *Fashionable nonsense: Postmodern intellectuals' abuse of science.* New York: Picador USA.

Stanovich, K. E. (1999). *Who is rational? Studies of individual differences in reasoning.* Mahwah, NJ: Erlbaum.

Stanovich, K. E., & West, R. F. (2000). Individual differences in reasoning: Implications for the retionality debate? *Behavioral and Brain Sciences, 23*, 645–726.

Sternberg, R. J. (1986). *Intelligence applied: Understanding and increasing your intellectual skills.* San Diego, CA: Harcourt Brace Jovanovich.

Sternberg, R. J., & Ben-Zeev, T. (2001). *Complex cognition: The psychology of human thought.* New York: Oxford University Press.

Sternberg, R. J., & Wagner, R. K. (Eds.). (1986). *Practical intelligence.* New York: Cambridge University Press.

Stevenson, R. J. (1993). Rationality and reality. In K. I. Manktelow & D. E. Over (Eds.). *Rationality: Psychological and philosophical perspectives* (pp. 61–82). London: Routledge.

Stewart, I. (1987). *The problems of mathematics.* New York: Oxford University Press.

Swartz, R. J. (1991). Structured teaching for critical thinking and reasoning in standard subject area instruction. In J. F. Voss, D. N. Perkins, & J. W. Segal (Eds.), *Informal reasoning and education* (pp. 415–450). Hillsdale, NJ: Erlbaum.

Taylor, S. E. (1981). The interface of cognitive and social psychology. In J. H. Harvey, (Ed.), *Cognition, social behavior, and the environment.* Hillsdale, NJ: Erlbaum.

Tishman, S., Jay, E., & Perkins, D. N. (1993): Thinking dispositions: From transmission to enculturation. *Theory into Practice, 32*, 147–153.

Toulmin, S. E. (1958). *The uses of argument.* Cambridge University Press.

Vos Savant, M. (1991). Ask Marilyn. *Parade Magazine,* February 17, p. 12.

Weinert, F. E. (1987). Introduction and overview: Metacognition and motivation as determinants of effective learning and understanding. In F. Weinert & R. Kluwe (Eds.), *Metacognition, motivation, and understanding* (pp. 1–16). Hillsdale, NJ: Erlbaum.

Wetherick, N. E. (1993). Human rationality. In K. I. Manktelow & D. E. Over (Eds). *Rationality: Psychological and philosophical perspectives* (pp. 83–109). London: Routledge.

Whimbey, A. (1975). *Intelligence can be taught.* New York: E. P. Dutton.

Whimbey, A., & Lochhead, J. (1982). *Problem solving and comprehension* (3rd ed.). Philadelphia, PA: Franklin Institute Press.

Whitehead, A. N. (1956). Mathematics as an element in the history of thought. In J. R. Newman (Ed.) *The world of mathematics* (*vol. 1*, pp. 402–416). New York: Simon and Schuster.

Wickelgren, W. A. (1974). *How to solve problems*. San Francisco, CA: W. H. Freeman.

16

What do We Know about the Nature of Reasoning?

Robert J. Sternberg

When one reads a book on the current state of any field of psychology, whether reasoning or anything else, there can be a tendency to feel a sense of despair because it is so difficult to distinguish what psychologists *know* about the phenomena in the field, versus what individual psychologists or groups of psychologists *believe* about those phenomena. Because all psychologists, and especially experts writing about an area, have an opinion on contentious matters, they themselves may lose sight of the difference between what is known and what they believe. I have myself gotten involved in countless debates where scholars spoke as though what they believe is correct and where they view their job as convincing non experts in the field that they are correct and that their opponents are, at best, misled, and, at worst, foolish or even malevolent.

Such debates have a special significance in the study of reasoning, where one would think that reasoning could be used to resolve at least some of these debates. So far, it has not worked. As readers of these chapters can see, the field of reasoning is just as contentious as any other field in psychology. For example, the debate between theorists who prefer rule-based accounts of reasoning, such as O'Brien, and those who prefer mental-models accounts, such as Johnson-Laird, shows no sign of abating at any time in the near future.

Debates such as these can be frustrating to students and other novices in the field, because it is hard, at times, to figure out what, if anything, we really know. Yet such debates are a sign of vitality, not of sickness or

Preparation of this article was supported by Grant REC-9979843 from the National Science Foundation and by a government grant under the Javits Act Program (Grant No. R206R000001) as administered by the Office of Educational Research and Improvement, U.S. Department of Education. Grantees undertaking such projects are encouraged to express freely their professional judgment. This article, therefore, does not necessarily represent the positions or the policies of the U.S. government, and no official endorsement should be inferred.

stagnancy in a field. The fact that scientists are hotly debating what the facts are shows that the field is progressing and that it is in a period of growth rather than of quiescence or decline.

THINGS KNOWN ABOUT REASONING WITH SOME CONFIDENCE

Despite the disagreements, there are things about reasoning we know with some confidence. My goal in this chapter will be to discuss those things about reasoning that we know, if not for sure, at least, with very high confidence. In particular, I have attempted to extract from each chapter in this book at least one generalization about the field of reasoning that seems to be as close as we come in psychology to being "beyond debate."

However distinct or even balkanized reasoning may be as a field of psychological inquiry, there is no encapsulated "reasoning" module in the brain that is distinct from all other modules in the brain that are studied in other fields of cognitive science (Lawson; Stenning, & Monaghan).

Reasoning is a distinct field within psychology, in particular, and cognitive science, in general. It has its own nomenclature (e.g., "deductive reasoning," "categorical syllogism," "new riddle of induction," "Wason selection task"), its own distinctive set of problems (e.g., mental models versus rule-based reasoning, evolutionary versus permission-schema versus other interpretations of errors on the Wason selection task), it own journals (e.g., *Thinking and Reasoning*), and its own set of "star" investigators past and present (e.g., Martin Braine, Jonathan Evans, Phil Johnson-Laird, and Peter Wason). I believe that, in recent years, as the issues in the field of reasoning have become more technical, the study of reasoning, like the study of other psychological phenomena, has become more encapsulated. Part of the reason is simply the amount of time an investigator has to invest to learn about the key issues in the field and then to study them effectively. But however encapsulated the field may have become, we need to remember that reasoning is not encapsulated. It is part and parcel of a wide array of cognitive functions. As Lawson points out, many cognitive processes, including visual perception, contain elements of reasoning in them. Ultimately, therefore, it will not be just the study of reasoning that enlightens us about reasoning, but rather, the study of all cognitive processes.

Thus, the goal of studying reasoning and its relation to the brain should not be to reinvent the phrenological approach of Franz Gall, who would have sought a particular set of bumps on the head corresponding to the location where reasoning takes place. For example, it seems beyond dispute that prefrontal regions are involved in reasoning. But these regions are involved in other higher cognitive processes as well, at the same time that reasoning is not limited to these areas. It is quite likely, for example, that learning occurring in the hippocampus or emotional responses in the amygdala affect and are affected by the processing happening in the prefrontal lobes. Our goal, therefore, should not be to construct some sort of geographical atlas of the structure of reasoning, but rather to map the neural pathways involved in the functioning of reasoning.

Working memory plays a central role in deductive and inductive reasoning (Gilhooly).

In the past, reasoning seemed to be near the top of a kind of cognitive hierarchy that had physiological processing at the bottom, followed by sensation, then perception, then memory, and then reasoning, with perhaps only problem solving at a higher level. Although such single-hierarchy models are no longer popular in cognitive science, they are still very much alive in the field of education, where Bloom's (1976) taxonomy remains a popular conceptualization for teaching children subject matter.

This model is dead in the water as far as psychology is concerned. The work of Baddeley (starting with Baddeley & Hitch, 1974, and proceeding at least through Baddeley, 2000), his colleagues, and his successors has made clear that memory is not just a series of passive storage receptacles, but rather, a dynamic and interactive set of processes.

The working-memory model is neutral with respect to a number of different specific claims about how reasoning occurs. For example, if reasoning occurs through the use of rules, then one of the sources of difficulty in reasoning problems could be the number of rules and results of applications of rules that need to be held in working memory at one time. If reasoning occurs through the use of mental models, then a source of difficulty could be the number of models and intermediate results of the application of those models that needs to be held in working memory at one time.

Working memory is involved in both deductive reasoning and inductive reasoning. Gilhooly's chapter focuses primarily upon deductive tasks. But working memory also has been found to be central to performance on inductive tasks. Kyllonen and Christal (1990) found that performance on inductive-reasoning tasks could be accounted for largely in terms of working memory, and subsequent research has been largely consistent with that claim (Lohman, 2000). For example, what would make a number-series problem difficult would be, in part, the load on working memory of the results of multiple intermediate computations needed to arrive at an answer as to what number might come next. What would make a problem difficult on the Raven Progressive Matrices would be, in part, the number of attributes that are manipulated whose results need to be kept in working memory while a test taker decides which of several alternatives should fill in for the missing box.

In sum, reasoning does not appear to be a set of processes that is distinct from working memory, but rather, a complex interaction of working memory with other dynamic processes. Memory is not superimposed on reasoning: It is part of reasoning.

People have a tendency toward confirmation bias (Evans).

It has long been known that people show various content effects in their reasoning (e.g., Wason & Johnson-Laird, 1972). Relatively recent research has suggested that better thinkers are more resistant to content effects, and especially, to belief-bias effects, than are others (Stanovich & West, 1997). Yet, everyone is susceptible in greater or lesser degree. One of the simple effects to which people are susceptible is confirmation bias, the tendency to seek evidence that confirms what people already believe. Wason's 2, 4, 6 problem is often presented as strong evidence of this bias. Asked to provide examples to test a rule that generates this series, people typically generate exemplars that seek to confirm, rather than disconfirm, their hypothesis (which is usually "increasing even numbers").

Confirmation bias is, in a sense, one of the most powerful problems the world faces today. Terrorists seek evidence to justify their attacks; respondents to their attacks seek evidence for why their responses are appropriate to the nature and magnitude of the threat. At this moment, George W. Bush is intent on proving that he is justified in planning an attack on Iraq, while opponents to his plan (which includes most of the world besides the governments of the United States and possibly of Great Britain) are busily showing how foolish such an attack would be. At this same moment, the union in my university (Yale) is busily justifying why a strike makes good sense, while the administration of the university is equally convinced that a strike is unjustified. The problem is that it is often difficult to find any truth when people are so busy trying to prove what they believe rather than find the truth.

Frighteningly, perhaps, court proceedings work the same way, at least in the United States. A verdict in a criminal case often depends much more on which of two attorneys – a prosecutor and a defense lawyer – can provide a more convincing set of arguments, rather than on what actually happened that led to the case in the first place.

These examples show how important the study of reasoning is not just to cognitive science, but also, to the world. They also show that it is important that some cadre of reasoning researchers investigate reasoning as it applies in the everyday world. Experimental psychologists often feel most comfortable working with highly abstract materials in abstracted settings. Evans's chapter shows how important it is to understand how the content of what one thinks, and the setting in which one thinks about it, affect the reasoning one produces.

Heuristics are common in everyday reasoning, and they can greatly facilitate or seriously impede the quality of that reasoning (Girotto; Roberts; Marsh, Todd, & Gigerenzer).

Thinking about heuristics has undergone an evolutionary process over the years. Early research on reasoning suggested that they were mostly negative. For example, one of the classic articles in the field of reasoning suggested that people's errors in reasoning were largely due to an atmosphere effect whereby people tended to choose negative responses to syllogism problems with a negative in them, and particular responses to problems with particular quantifiers in them (Woodworth & Sells, 1935). Although Woodworth and Sells did not refer to the atmosphere effect as a heuristic, that is what it was. Chapman and Chapman (1959) continued in this tradition, suggesting that many errors in deductive reasoning were due to conversion, or reversal of the meanings of premises (i.e., reading "if A then B" as equivalent to "if B then A" or "all A are B" as equivalent to "all B are A"). But the scientists who really pushed the heuristics view the most undoubtedly were Tversky and Kahneman (1974), who showed that many errors in everyday reasoning could be attributed to heuristics such as availability (i.e., choosing as an answer to a problem a solution that readily comes to mind) and representativeness (i.e., choosing as an answer a solution that seems to represent what a solution should look like).

The early research was so strongly directed toward the negative effects of heuristics that it began to look as though shortcuts in reasoning were something like shortcuts in auditing – a recipe for disaster. Cohen (1981) showed that, in many respects, Tversky and Kahneman's view of heuristics was too negative – that heuristics could be viewed in a much more positive way than had been thought. More recently, Gigerenzer, Todd, and the ABC Research Group (1999) have shown that "fast and frugal" heuristics can have an enormously positive effect on reasoning. For example, the "take-the-best" heuristic, whereby one makes decisions on the basis of a single powerful criterion rather than an assortment of criteria of various degrees of power, often yields better decisions than do more complex decision rules.

Thus, we should not ourselves use the simple heuristic that leads us to view all use of heuristics as bad for reasoning. Whether they are bad depends on what they are and the circumstances under which they are used. Even Tversky and Kahneman's heuristics, which can lead to bad reasoning or decision making, also can lead to positive outcomes. As a simple example, if a government or other organization has committed egregious acts in the past (e.g., Nazi Germany, Iraq, Al Quaeda), and a new egregious act is committed, one cannot immediately assume that one of these organizations is the perpetrator. But using the availability heuristic to start with the initial hypothesis that such an organization is responsible for a new egregious act is generally a reasonable way to go. The heuristic is useful, however, only to the extent one does not fall prey to confirmation bias.

The question of representation and process is often one of what is used under what circumstances by whom rather than what is used (Johnson-Laird; O'Brien).

Johnson-Laird has presented impressive evidence over the years, dating back at least 20 years (Johnson-Laird, 1983), for the viability of mental models as an explanatory basis for deductive and possibly other forms of reasoning. At the same time, others, such as Rips (1994) and Braine and O'Brien (1998) have provided impressive evidence in favor of mental rules. The strength of the evidence on both sides almost leaves one at a loss as to how such compelling evidence could be obtained for both viewpoints, which seem, on their face, to be contradictory to each other.

Although there is no certain resolution, one view is that this is not a "winner-take-all" fight. There are many possibilities for why such strong evidence could accumulate on both sides. My goal here is not to resolve this debate, which has been going on for a long while and is unlikely to be resolved in any single essay, but rather to explore some of the possible reasons why two theories could seem to garner so much support.

One possibility is that reasoners use one form of representation/process pairing in earlier trials and then switch to another in later trials. A second possibility is that less expert individuals reason one way and more expert individuals in another way. A third possibility is that people with one pattern of abilities reason one way and that people with another pattern of abilities reason another way. A fourth possibility is that people use some kind of mixture of rules and mental models so that each is partially supported by the data. These are not idle speculations. The literature on linear-syllogistic reasoning seemed equally to support alternative linguistic and spatial models, until research was done suggesting that most people used some kind of mixture model combining linguistic and spatial modes of thinking, and that on top of that, there were individual differences in preferred models (Sternberg, 1980b; Sternberg & Weil, 1980). Moreover, how the problems were presented also had an effect upon the strategies used (Sternberg, 1980a).

Some people might take this counsel as the counsel of despair. After all, if psychologists cannot figure out something as basic as whether people use one form of process representation or another, then it would seem that there is little they can figure out. But there is no reason to despair. First, Anderson (1980) pointed out sometime ago that it is in fact extremely difficult to distinguish alternative models of mental representations or processes. Representation/process pairings can be distinguished, but even these only with great difficulty. Second, and perhaps more importantly, the main point is that the question of what people "really do" is probably the wrong one to ask. The question to ask is who does what under what circumstances?

One cannot assume that a task measures "logical reasoning" or anything else just because it appears to on its surface (Leighton; Markovits).

There was a time when people simply assumed that a task measures what it appears to measure. No longer. What the task measures is a property of the interaction of the examinee, the examiner, the task, and the situation, not just of the task. For example, the same apparent task may measure different things across different cultural or age groups. Consider some examples.

In a famous example, Cole, Gay, Glick, and Sharp (1971) asked adult members of the Kpelle tribe to sort names of various kinds of objects, such as names of fruits, names of vegetables, or names of vehicles of conveyance. They found that the adults sorted functionally rather than taxonomically. For example, they might sort "apple" with "eat" or "car" with "gas," rather than sorting various kinds of apples together, under the word "apple," and then "fruits," and perhaps then "foods." The Kpelle way of doing this task would be considered, in the West, cognitively immature. It is the way young children would complete the task. Indeed, virtually any theorist of cognitive development (e.g., Piaget, 1972) would view functional sorting as inferior; and on the vocabulary section of an intelligence test such as the Wechsler or the Stanford-Binet, a functional definition of, say, an automobile as using gas, would receive less credit than a taxonomic definition, say, of an automobile as a vehicle of conveyance. They tried without success to get the Kpelle to sort in an alternative way.

Finally, they gave up, and started packing up. As an afterthought, a researcher asked a member of the tribe how a stupid person would sort. The man had no trouble sorting the terms taxonomically. In other words, he considered stupid what a Western psychologist would consider smart. Why? Because in everyday life, for the most part, our thinking really is functional. For example, we think about eating an apple; we do not think about the apple as a fruit, which is a food, which is an organic substance.

Luria (1976) ran into similar issues in studies of peasants in one of the former Asian republics of the USSR. In one study, peasants were shown a hammer, a saw, a log, and a hatchet, and were asked which three items were similar. An illiterate central Asian peasant insisted that all four fit together, even when the interviewer suggested that the concept of "tool" could be used for the hammer, saw, and hatchet, but not for the log. The participant in this instance combined the features of the four items that were relevant in terms of his culture and arrived at a functional or situational concept (perhaps one of the "thing you need to build a hut").

In many of Luria's studies, the unschooled peasants have great difficulty in solving the problems given them. Often, they appear to be thrown off by an apparent discrepancy between the terms of the problem and what they know to be true. For example, take one of the math problems: "From Shakhimardan to Vuadil it is three hours on foot, while to Fergana it is six hours. How much time does it take to go on foot from Vuadil to Fergana?" The participant's response to this problem was, "No, it's six hours from Vuadil to Shakhimardan. You're wrong.... It's far and you wouldn't get there in three hours" (Luria, 1976, p. 129). Clearly, the peasant did not accept the task. What a task measures has to be determined through psychological analysis, not merely through logical analysis.

Reasoning skill correlates positive with various measures of intelligence (Stanovich; Cummins).

It is not totally surprising perhaps that reasoning skills should correlate with intelligence because many definitions of intelligence have had reasoning either at the core or as an important supporting part of intelligence. Probably the most well known study of experts' definitions of intelligence was one done by the editors of the *Journal of Educational Psychology* ("Intelligence and its measurement," 1921). Contributors to the symposium were asked to address two issues: (a) what they conceived intelligence to be and how it best could be measured by group tests, and (b) what the most crucial next steps would be in research. Fourteen experts gave their views on the nature of intelligence, with such definitions as the following:

1. The power of good responses from the point of view of truth or facts (E. L. Thorndike)
2. The ability to carry on abstract thinking (L. M. Terman)
3. Sensory capacity, capacity for perceptual recognition, quickness, range or flexibility of association, facility and imagination, span of attention, quickness or alertness in response (F. N. Freeman)
4. Having learned or ability to learn to adjust oneself to the environment (S. S. Colvin)
5. Ability to adapt oneself adequately to relatively new situations in life (R. Pintner)
6. The capacity for knowledge and knowledge possessed (B. A. C. Henmon)
7. A biological mechanism by which the effects of a complexity of stimuli are brought together and given a somewhat unified effect in behavior (J. Peterson)
8. The capacity to inhibit an instinctive adjustment, the capacity to redefine the inhibited instinctive adjustment in the light of imaginally experienced trial and error, and the capacity to realize the modified instinctive adjustment in overt behavior to the advantage of the individual as a social animal (L. L. Thurstone)
9. The capacity to acquire capacity (H. Woodrow)
10. The capacity to learn or to profit by experience (W. F. Dearborn)
11. Sensation, perception, association, memory, imagination, discrimination, judgment, and reasoning (N. E. Haggerty)

Others of the contributors to the symposium did not provide clear definitions of intelligence but rather concentrated on how to test it. B. Ruml refused to present a definition of intelligence, arguing that not enough was known about the concept. S. L. Pressey described himself as uninterested in the question, although he became well known for his tests of intelligence. But note that almost all of the definitions involved reasoning, whether directly or indirectly.

Sternberg and Detterman (1986) attempted a comparison of the views of the experts in 1986 (P. Baltes, J. Baron, J. Berry, A. Brown, E. Butterfield, J. Campione, J. Carroll, J. P. Das, D. Detterman, W. Estes, H. Eysenck, H. Gardner, R. Glaser, J. Goodnow, J. Horn, L. Humphreys, E. Hunt, A. Jensen, J. Pellegrino, R. Schank, R. Snow, R. Sternberg, E. Zigler) with those of the experts in 1921. These experts, too, heavily stressed reasoning.

In fact, reasoning has been at the core of how psychologists interpret intelligence even going back to Spearman, arguably the first great theorist of intelligence. Spearman (1923) proposed a theory of intelligence based on the processes used in analogical reasoning, namely, encoding of analogy terms (what he called "apprehension of experience"), inference of the relation between the first two analogy terms (what he called "education of relations"), and application of the inferred relation to the second two analogy terms (what he called "education of correlates"). Sternberg (1977) formulated this theory in modern information-processing terms.

Although Spearman's theory stressed inductive reasoning, deductive reasoning has also been seen as central to intelligence (see Sternberg, 1985). Thurstone (1938) originally had separate inductive and deductive reasoning factors in his theory, although he later removed the deductive factor, probably because it is highly correlated with spatial visualization. So the bottom line is this: To study reasoning is to study intelligence, and vice versa. One cannot study the one without studying the other.

Reasoning can be improved through systematic instruction (Nickerson).

Reasoning can be taught. Some of our own work over the years has been devoted to teaching students to become better reasoners.

Analytical reasoning skills can be taught. For example, in one study, Sternberg (1987) tested whether it is possible to teach people better to reason out the meanings of unknown words presented in context. In one study, Sternberg gave 81 participants in five conditions a pretest on their ability to induce word meanings. Then the participants were divided into five conditions, two of which were control conditions that lacked formal instruction. In one condition, participants were not given any instructional treatment. They were merely asked later to take a post-test. In a second condition, they were given practice as an instructional condition, but there was no formal instruction, per se. In a third condition, they were taught knowledge-acquisition component processes (how selectively to encode, compare, and combine information) that could be used to induce word meanings. In a fourth condition, they were taught to use context cues, such as antonyms or functional relations. In a fifth condition, they were taught to use mediating variables such as the position of the unknown word in a sentence. Participants in all three of the theory-based formal-instructional conditions outperformed participants in the two control conditions, whose performance did not differ. In other words, theory-based instruction was better than no instruction at all or just practice without formal instruction.

Creative-thinking skills also can be taught and a program has been devised for teaching them (Sternberg & Grigorenko, 2000). In some relevant work, the investigators divided 86 gifted and nongifted fourth-grade children into experimental and control groups. All children took pretests on insightful thinking. Then some of the children received their regular school instruction whereas others received instruction on insight skills. After the instruction of whichever kind, all children took a posttest on insight skills. The investigators found that children taught how to solve the insight problems using knowledge-acquisition components gained more from pretest to posttest than did students who were not so taught (Davidson & Sternberg, 1984).

Practical-reasoning skills also can be taught. Williams and her colleagues have developed a program for teaching practical thinking skills, aimed at middle-school students, that explicitly teaches students "practical intelligence for school" in the contexts of doing homework, taking tests, reading, and writing. Students taught via the program outperform students in control groups that did not receive the instruction (Williams et al., 2002).

A followup study (Sternberg, Torff, & Grigorenko, 1998) examined learning of and reasoning with social studies and science materials by third-graders and eighth-graders. The 225 third-graders were students in a very low-income neighborhood in Raleigh, North Carolina. The 142 eighth-graders were students who were largely middle to upper-middle class studying in Baltimore, Maryland, and Fresno, California. In this study, students were assigned to one of three instructional conditions. In the first condition, they were taught the course that basically they would have learned had there been no intervention. The emphasis in the course was on memory. In a second condition, students were taught in a way that emphasized critical (analytical) thinking. In the third condition, they were taught in a way that emphasized analytical, creative, and practical learning and reasoning. All students' performance was assessed for memory learning (through multiple-choice assessments) as well as for analytical, creative, and practical learning and reasoning (through performance assessments).

As expected, students in the successful-intelligence (analytical, creative, practical) condition outperformed the other students in terms of the performance assessments. One could argue that this result merely reflected the way they were taught. Nevertheless, the result suggested that teaching for these kinds of thinking succeeded. More important, however, was the result that children in the successful-intelligence condition outperformed the other children even on the multiple-choice memory tests. In other words, to the extent that one's goal is just to maximize children's memory for information, teaching for successful intelligence is still superior. It enables children to capitalize on their strengths and to correct or to compensate for their weaknesses, it allows children to encode material in a variety of interesting ways, and it allows them to think critically with the material so that they better understand it.

Grigorenko and her colleagues have now extended these results to reading curricula at the middle-school and the high-school level. In a study of 871 middle-school students and 432 high-school students, researchers taught reading either triarchically or through the regular curriculum. At the middle-school level, reading was taught explicitly. At the high-school level, reading was infused into instruction in mathematics, physical sciences, social sciences, English, history, foreign languages, and the arts. In all settings, students who were taught triarchially substantially outperformed students who were taught in standard ways with respect to comprehension and reasoning with text (Grigorenko, Jarvin, & Sternberg, 2002).

In sum, although many issues in the study of reasoning are contentious, not all are. The fact that many issues are contentious is not a bad sign but a good one. The field of reasoning is alive and vibrant and is moving forward at a rapid clip. The fact that at least some issues are resolved to most people's satisfaction is also a good sign. The field is solving puzzles as well as creating new ones.

References

Anderson, J. R. (1980). Concepts, propositions, and schemata: What are the cognitive units? *Nebraska Symposium on Motivation, 28,* 121–162.

Baddeley, A. D. (2000). The episodic buffer: a new component of working memory? *Trends in Cognitive Sciences, 4,* 417–423.

Baddeley, A. D., & Hitch, G. J. (1974). Working memory. In G. Bower (Ed.), *Advances in learning and motivation: Vol. VIII.* New York: Academic Press.

Bloom, B. S. (1976). *Human characteristics and school learning.* Chicago: University of Chicago Press.

Braine, M. D. S., & O'Brien, D. P. (Eds.) (1998). *Mental logic.* Mahwah, NJ: Erlbaum.

Chapman, L. J., & Chapman, A. P. (1959). Atmosphere effect re-examined. *Journal of Experimental Psychology, 58,* 220–226.

Cohen, L. J. (1981). Can human irrationality be experimentally demonstrated? *Behavior and Brain Sciences, 4,* 317–370.

Cole, M., Gay, J., Glick, J., & Sharp, D. W. (1971). *The cultural context of learning and thinking.* New York: Basic Books.

Davidson, J. E., & Sternberg, R. J. (1984). The role of insight in intellectual giftedness. *Gifted Child Quarterly, 28,* 58–64.

Gigerenzer, G., Todd, P. M., & the ABC Research Group (1999). *Simple heuristics that make us smart*. New York: Oxford University Press.

Grigorenko, E. L., Jarvin, L., & Sternberg, R. J. (2002). School-based tests of the triarchic theory of intelligence: Three settings, three samples, three syllabi. *Contemporary Educational Psychology*, 27, 167–208.

Intelligence and its measurement: A symposium (1921). *Journal of Educational Psychology*, 12, 123–147, 195–216, 271–275.

Johnson-Laird, P. N. (1983). *Mental models: Towards a cognitive science of language*. Cambridge, MA: Harvard University Press.

Kyllonen, P. C., & Christal, R. E. (1990). Reasoning ability is (little more than) working-memory capacity?! *Intelligence*, 14, 389–433.

Lohman, D. F. (2000). Complex information processing and intelligence. In R. J. Sternberg (Ed.), *Handbook of intelligence* (pp. 285–340). New York: Cambridge University Press.

Luria, A. R. (1976). *Basic problems of neurolinguistics*. The Hague, Netherlands: Mouton.

Piaget, J. (1972). *The psychology of intelligence*. Totowa, NJ: Littlefield Adams.

Rips, L. J. (1994). *The psychology of proof*. Cambridge, MA: MIT Press.

Spearman, C. (1923). *The nature of "intelligence" and the principles of cognition*. London: Macmillan.

Stanovich, K. E., & West, R. F. (1997). Reasoning independently of prior belief and individual differences in actively open-minded thinking. *Journal of Educational Psychology*, 89, 342–357.

Sternberg, R. J. (1977). *Intelligence, information processing, and analogical reasoning: The componential analysis of human abilities*. Hillsdale, NJ: Erlbaum.

Sternberg, R. J. (1980a). A proposed resolution of curious conflicts in the literature on linear syllogisms. In R. Nickerson (Ed.), *Attention and performance VIII* (pp. 719–744). Hillsdale, NJ: Erlbaum.

Sternberg, R. J. (1980b). Representation and process in linear syllogistic reasoning. *Journal of Experimental Psychology: General*, 109, 119–159.

Sternberg, R. J. (1985). *Beyond IQ: A triarchic theory of human intelligence*. New York: Cambridge University Press.

Sternberg, R. J. (1987). Most vocabulary is learned from context. In M. G. McKeown & M. E. Curtis (Eds.), *The nature of vocabulary acquisition* (pp. 89–105). Hillsdale, NJ: Erlbaum.

Sternberg, R. J., & Detterman, D. K. (1986). *What is intelligence: Contemporary viewpoints on its nature and definition*. Norwood, NJ: Ablex.

Sternberg, R. J., & Grigorenko, E. L. (2000). *Teaching for successful intelligence*. Arlington Heights, IL: Skylight.

Sternberg, R. J., Torff, B., & Grigorenko, E. L. (1998). Teaching triarchically improves school achievement. *Journal of Educational Psychology*, 90, 374–384.

Sternberg, R. J., & Weil, E. M. (1980). An aptitude-strategy interaction in linear syllogistic reasoning. *Journal of Educational Psychology*, 72, 226–234.

Thurstone, L. L. (1938). *Primary mental abilities*. Chicago: University of Chicago Press.

Tversky, A., & Kahneman, D. (1974). Judgment under uncertainty: Heuristics and biases. *Science*, 185, 1124–1131.

Wason, P. C., & Johnson-Laird, P. N. (1972). *Psychology of reasoning: Structure and content.* London: Batsford.

Williams, W. M., Blythe, T., White, N., Li, J., Gardner, H., & Sternberg, R. J. (2002). Practical intelligence for school: Developing metacognitive sources of achievement in adolescence. *Developmental Review, 22*(2), 162–210.

Woodworth, R. S., & Sells, S. B. (1935). An atmosphere effect in formal syllogistic reasoning. *Journal of Experimental Psychology, 18,* 451–460.

Index